MORALITY AND DEMOCRACY IN ATHENS

How were moral ideas and behaviour in ancient Athens formulated and made manifest? How did democratic Athens diffuse the inevitable tensions that surface in society? In this groundbreaking work, Professor Herman argues that rather than endorse the Mediterranean ethic of retaliation, democratic Athens looked to the courts to dispense justice. Drawing on a method of analysis taken from the behavioural sciences, he describes the exceptional strategy of inter-personal relationships that the Athenian democrats developed to resolve conflict, to increase co-operation and to achieve collective objectives. In a new departure, this work investigates moral ideas and behaviour alongside each other and expands the focus of the study to include all aspects of Athenian life, be it societal or economic. Highly illustrated throughout and interdisciplinary in approach, this work offers new light on society and behaviour in ancient Athens which might also serve as a model for similar ancient societies.

GABRIEL HERMAN is Professor of Ancient History at the Hebrew University in Jerusalem. He has held visiting fellowships at Churchill College, Cambridge, the Institute for Advanced Study, Princeton and the Institute for Research in the Humanities, Madison, Wisconsin. He is the author of *Ritualised Friendship and the Greek City* (1987) and numerous articles on Greek social history. This book was awarded the Polonsky Prize for Creativity and Originality in the Humanistic Disciplines by the Hebrew University of Jerusalem in 2005.

MORALITY AND BEHAVIOUR IN DEMOCRATIC ATHENS

A social history

GABRIEL HERMAN

CAMBRIDGE
UNIVERSITY PRESS

CAMBRIDGE UNIVERSITY PRESS
Cambridge, New York, Melbourne, Madrid, Cape Town, Singapore,
São Paulo, Delhi, Dubai, Tokyo

Cambridge University Press
The Edinburgh Building, Cambridge CB2 8RU, UK

Published in the United States of America by Cambridge University Press, New York

www.cambridge.org
Information on this title: www.cambridge.org/9780521125352

© Gabriel Herman 2006

This publication is in copyright. Subject to statutory exception
and to the provisions of relevant collective licensing agreements,
no reproduction of any part may take place without the written
permission of Cambridge University Press.

First published 2006
This digitally printed version 2009

A catalogue record for this publication is available from the British Library

ISBN 978-0-521-85021-6 Hardback
ISBN 978-0-521-12535-2 Paperback

Cambridge University Press has no responsibility for the persistence or accuracy of
URLs for external or third-party internet websites referred to in this publication, and
does not guarantee that any content on such websites is, or will remain, accurate or
appropriate.

TO THE MEMORY OF
M.I. FINLEY

. . . καὶ ἀστυνόμους ὀργὰς ἐδιδάξατο . . .
(. . . and [man] has taught himself a temper that enables him to live in communities . . .)

Sophocles, *Antigone* 355–6

Contents

Illustrations

Preface

The idea for this book came from five interrelated facts that began increasingly to intrigue me during the academic year 1990–91, which I spent on sabbatical in the stimulating atmosphere of Cambridge. Firstly, I observed that whereas many excellent works had been written on various sub-systems of Athenian society (politics, culture, economy, slavery, family, women and religion, for example), no attempt had been made to study them as parts of an integrated whole. In this book I shall try to examine the workings and interactions of these sub-systems in the context of the wider social system to which they and the individuals who participated in them belonged.

My second observation followed closely on the first. Since these sub-systems were all parts of a self-consistent social system, they must have been held together by some version of what is generally known as morality or a moral system. (Throughout this study I shall be using these terms in Hobbes' sense ('those qualities of humankind that concern their living together in peace and unity') rather than in the customary sense of rules concerning the suppression or regulation of vice, profane practice or debauchery.) Although many excellent books have been written about *Greek* morality, I do not believe that any work has yet been devoted exclusively to the study of *Athenian* morality. In this book I shall try to bring together and evaluate the evidence we currently have concerning the moral system that underpinned Athenian society throughout almost two hundred years of democratic rule.

The third observation was that most books on the subject of Greek morality had interpreted morality as a loosely defined assemblage of ideas that should be approached using conceptual tools derived from the history of ideas. No author had yet examined the Athenians' moral ideas *and* behaviour (or, more broadly, their moral *and* social systems) as interrelated entities. In this book I propose to reveal the characteristic features of the code of behaviour (or, in contemporary language, the 'unwritten laws') that the Athenians developed to make democracy practicable throughout the manifold and complex fields of activity that constituted their social life (politics, land tenure, the employment of slaves, interpersonal and class relations, conflict resolution, state power, the army, foreign relations, religion and the economy). This book is, in other words, also a social history of democratic Athens.

Fourthly, I observed a disparity between the conceptual tools with which classicists and ancient historians investigated the moral norms of ancient societies and those used in adjacent fields of research. The former group relied by and large on a personal and hence culturally determined concept of morality, often following K. J. Dover in believing that the researcher's own moral experience must be his or her best guide to unravelling that of the Greeks. This book will be taking a different approach to the Athenians' moral system, using analytical tools developed in psychology, the behavioural sciences, ethology and game theory. I believe that these tools are more impersonal and less likely to be compromised by cultural bias than any that rely upon the researcher's moral experience alone. Deriving from several disciplines, in which they have been greeted as considerable advances, they are brought together in my book to create a fully rounded analytical approach that is not merely appropriate to the study of ancient Athens, but may, with certain adjustments and refinements, be used to evaluate objectively the moral systems of many other small-scale societies, both past and present.

My fifth observation was that throughout the wider field of social studies the study of man's society and culture tended to be regarded as separate from the study of man as a biological organism. Dubious as to the legitimacy of the widespread practice of abstracting 'constitution' from 'society', 'society' from 'collective behaviour' and 'collective behaviour' from an individual's biologically and culturally conditioned sentiments, and inspired by Professor Burkert's call to apply 'biological methods' to the study of ancient societies (Burkert 1996), I shall be attempting in this book to reintroduce man's biological aspect into the study of Athenian society and mores. Though I am by training an ancient historian, my longstanding familiarity with the behavioural sciences has convinced me that their methods offer us a key to certain problems in ancient history that cannot satisfactorily be resolved using the ancient historian's analytical apparatus alone.

In the course of the thirteen-odd years that it has taken me to write this book, I have received endless help and advice from a long list of friends. I am more than grateful to Moshe Amit, Paul Cartledge, John Crook, Peter Garnsey, Manuela Giordano, Wilfried Nippel, Anthony Snodgrass and Nigel Spivey for many extremely helpful discussions. I have also profited by the comments and criticisms of the organisers of and participants in seminars and conferences in Bellagio, Cambridge, Chicago, Exeter, Jerusalem, Leicester, London, Naples, New York, Oxford, Princeton and Stanford. Special thanks are due to Paul Cartledge, Glen Bowersock, Christian Habicht, Nigel Spivey and Dick Whittaker for the practical help that made my extended visits to Cambridge and Princeton so pleasant. My greatest debt is to Avner Offer, Martin Ostwald, Brent Shaw, Frank Walbank, Alex Yakobson and the late John Graham, all of whom have shown the greatest patience in reading large sections of this book and helping me with their criticisms over long periods of time. The manuscript assumed its present form thanks to Rosamund Annetts' patient and extremely sensitive efforts. Last but not least, I would like to thank my wife Ora, my children Oriel, Jonathan and Ruth and my mother Clara for putting up with my systematic and all too authentic prioritisation of my commitments to Athenian society over my commitments to my family.

Finally, a few general remarks concerning the text that follows. All dates are BC unless otherwise indicated. All translations from the Greek are my own, except where otherwise indicated. I have used the term 'polis' (plural: poleis), without italics, to sidestep the ambiguities associated with 'state', 'city' and the cumbersome 'city-state'.

The fifty-five illustrations with which this book is punctuated are intended to give the text depth and dimension. The captions, many of which expand upon ideas that appear in the text only in outline, are an integral part of the book's argument.

CHAPTER I

Moral precepts and society

CATEGORIES OF MORAL INJUNCTION

The question of how one individual should behave to another within the framework of any more than fleeting relationship is one of the most intriguing dilemmas in the whole of social life. The reason for this is that people know at the back of their minds that certain types of social interaction affect not only themselves, the interacting parties, but also the communal system of which they are a part. Some moves made with respect to another person may indirectly and in the long run strengthen this system and promote the development of effective communal life; other moves can weaken it, setting in motion chain reactions that may surreptitiously undermine or forcibly overturn it. The cumulative, long term side effects of interpersonal interactions may thus devolve ultimately upon their initiators. As early as the eighth century the poet Hesiod spelt out this deeply felt but all too often suppressed association of ideas: 'He hurts himself who hurts another man | And evil planning harms the planner most.'[1]

Despite this instinctive understanding of the long term side effects of social interactions, human beings hold it to be self-evident that in interacting with another person some strategies are preferable to others. They are preferable for no other reason than that they pay off better. For instance, by using superior force one can change rules to fit one's own wishes, obtain control over others or remove obstacles that are preventing one from attaining desired goals, thus obtaining valued resources. The dilemma that presents itself is this: the types of behaviour that appear to the interacting individual to be the most immediately rewarding are precisely those that will in the long run harm the communal system most, while the types of behaviour that appear to the interacting individual to be less immediately rewarding are those that may in the long run benefit the communal system most.

---

[1] *Works and Days*, 265–6 (trans. D. Wender).

Legislators, religious teachers, rhetoricians, politicians, philosophers and social reformers down the ages have contemplated this dilemma without ever reaching any consensus as to which sort of behaviour should be regarded as in absolute terms preferable. At times they have privileged the individual interest over the communal; at times they have preferred the communal interest above the individual. As some of their pronouncements withstood the vicissitudes of time, the moral heritage of the western world filled up with a multiplicity of injunctions, proverbs, commandments, guides to behaviour and theoretical writings stemming from the manifold traditions of many ages.

The collection of moral precepts thus assembled looks perplexing at first. It seems to present us with a forest of pronouncements, a jumble of moral norms, so tangled and so intricate that it would be impossible to resolve it into any simple and consistent scheme whatsoever. I hope to show, however, that this impression is a false one. Irrespective of when, where or by whom they were proffered as answers to our central question, the injunctions, proverbs, commandments, guides to behaviour and theoretical writings that make up the moral tradition of the western world reveal an underlying order. Sharing, as they do, certain basic characteristics arising out of human nature in general, they can be reduced to three major categories. These categories cover, roughly speaking, the three main varieties of interpersonal interaction.

The *first* category contains those moral injunctions that license one to give free rein to one's own wishes or passions in flagrant disregard of the individual with whom one is interacting, of the communal system of which one is a part and perhaps even of one's own rational calculations of utility and self-interest. One symbolic representation of this precept, sometimes referred to as 'a head for an eye', appears in the book of Genesis. In a poem that expert opinion regards as one of the earliest parts of the Old Testament, Lamech, one of the antediluvian patriarchs, tells his two wives that he has killed a man and a youth who have done him injury. That Lamech is jubilant, that he means to strike a note of victory, comes clearly through the splendid parallel verses designed to reflect his mood: 'Adah and Zillah, hear my voice; ye wives of Lamech, hearken unto my speech; for I have slain a man for wounding me, and a young man for bruising me.' Lamech goes on to allude to the famous ancestor whose pattern of action inspired his own: 'If Cain shall be avenged sevenfold, truly Lamech seventy and sevenfold.'[2]

---

[2] Genesis 4.23–4, quoted from *The Holy Bible (Revised Version)*. For the question of who precisely was supposed to avenge Cain and for further examples of this sort of 'overkill', which is not typical of the

Lamech's response to his injuries puts in a nutshell a strategy of interaction to which mankind presumably resorted as a matter of course millennia before it emerged from the hunter-gatherer stage of its prehistory. According to this strategy, when one is offended or hurt one has the right to discard all considerations other than one's own craving for revenge; one is entitled to inflict injuries far more severe than those that one has sustained, since, according to the dictates of this age-old precept, extreme retaliation *is* justice.

There can be no doubt that in the past the emotions associated with this precept have been responsible for catastrophes that left in their wake the heaviest of casualties. When thousands of lives are lost and villages depopulated as a result of vendettas; when elderly people, women and children are massacred in the course of civil wars; when men go to war (and in particular when they wage the sort of war that is called 'holy' or 'total', the sort of war that can only end with the utter destruction of one party by the other), then we can be certain that we are watching Lamech's spirit of vengeance in action.[3]

Western tradition is also familiar with a more refined and certainly more civilised manifestation of this sort of egotistic self-assertion. This finds its supreme expression in the Machiavellian creed, whose well-known epitome, 'The end justifies the means', is often surreptitiously (but sometimes quite openly) invoked as justification for everyday actions. This precept differs from the last in that centre stage is taken by an active partner, rather than a passive one reacting to provocation. The two precepts overlap in that each answers the question of how one person should behave to another according solely and exclusively to what is likely to further his or her interests, without regard to those of others or of the community. The Machiavellian creed seeks to teach the individual that he or she *should not* allow any moral inhibitions to hinder his or her interactions with other people: that if one has set one's heart upon something it is acceptable to lie, to intrigue, to deceive and if necessary to use force to get whatever it is that one wants. The behaviour prescribed for princes dealing with civilian populations illustrates how this logic was meant to be carried into practice. Men, according to Machiavelli, must be either pampered or annihilated.

Old Testament, see Schapera 1955. For the attitude towards revenge that may be regarded as typical of the Old Testament, expressed in the passage 'Thou shalt not avenge, nor bear any grudge against the children of thy people, but thou shalt love thy neighbour as thyself' (Leviticus 19.18), see Lemaire 1984.

[3] The universality of the precept is illustrated by a German communiqué of 10 May 1940 that almost perfectly parallels the Biblical injunction: 'From now on, every enemy bombing of German civilians will be answered by five times as many German planes bombing English and French cities.' Cited in W. L. Shirer (1940) *Berlin Diary*. New York: Grosset and Dunlap: 268.

Annihilation is sometimes necessary because men take revenge for small injuries. If the injury is sufficiently great, however, they will not be able to. The implication is that any injury that a prince inflicts should be so crushing that he need have no fear of retributive vengeance.[4]

It is not always easy to pin down the manifold manifestations of these precepts in real life, variations on the Machiavellian creed often operating under the guise of efficiency. It is, however, worth pointing out that some of the more attenuated versions of these ways of thinking are even today quoted openly to justify everyday actions. For example, 'business is business', that supreme expression of cut-throat capitalism, recommends the cool-headed pursuit of gain above sympathetic consideration for others. Regularly put into practice, this principle has only occasionally come into conflict with a more humane conception of things mercantile. Writing in an age of nascent capitalism, the poet Heinrich Heine was among the very few to register a protest. In Heine's ballad *Das Sklavenschiff* the supercargo Mynheer van Koek, on being informed of the unusually high death rate among the blacks he is exporting to Brazil, supplicates the Almighty thus: 'Oh spare their lives, for Jesus' sake | Who died for our human salvation. | Unless there remain three hundred head | It spoils my calculation.'[5]

Within the domain of moral philosophy, advocates of egotistic self-assertion maintain that succeeding at the expense of others is a necessary condition of human existence. As early as the fifth century BC Pindar was claiming that the strong should rule and be free, while the weak should be their slaves.[6] In the generation that followed Pindar a group of Greek thinkers now usually known as 'the Sophists' elaborated upon this idea, anchoring it philosophically in the 'eternal unchanging laws of nature'.[7] One central tenet of their view was that justice naturally consisted of rule by the strongest, a doctrine that followed on from the dual vision of man inspired by the *physis* (nature) – *nomos* (convention) controversy that raged at the time. The conventional man, as Alasdair MacIntyre put it, lives in a particular polis and abides by her laws and conventions. The natural man lives in any polis or none and only pretends to abide by the rules and conventions of those around him: 'He has no moral standards of his

---

[4] N. Machiavelli (1961) *The Prince*. Harmondsworth: Penguin: 37–8 (Original edition, 1512); cf. Schellenberg 1982: ch. 9.

[5] Trans. Ernst Feise. The original reads: 'Verschone ihr Leben, um Christi will'n, | Der für uns alle gestorben! | Denn bleiben mir nicht dreihundert Stück, | So ist mein Geschäft verdorben.'

[6] Cf. Plato, *Laws* 4.714e: '. . . to quote Pindar – "the law marches with nature when it justifies the right of might"'.

[7] Popper 1966, vol. 1: 68.

own and is free from all constraints upon him by others. All men are by nature either wolves or sheep; they prey or are preyed upon.'[8] According to Thucydides the Athenians, presumably inspired by this way of thinking, claimed before they captured the tiny island of Melos and put to death all its men of military age (415 people) that the strongest reigned in accordance with a general and necessary rule of nature; anybody else possessed of the same sort of power would thus, of course, have acted in precisely the same way (5.105.2). Despite Plato's objections (*Republic* 1.339) this doctrine gained in strength amongst subsequent generations, providing the rulers of autocracies, slave systems and empires with a convenient justification for wielding their superior powers.[9]

Many people down the centuries seem to have been much taken with the idea that the strong could crush the weak without ever stepping outside the bounds of justice, with the result that it has kept reappearing throughout most phases of mankind's history. 'It is', writes Hartvig Frisch, in connection with Plato, 'not a problem that has arisen merely once and has then slipped back into oblivion and unawareness; but the question and the doubt that lurks behind it, have haunted mankind from one generation to another.'[10] More often than not the idea has been adopted all over again by new generations of thinkers and embellished and elaborated upon according to the trends of their age. In the seventeenth century Thomas Hobbes argued pessimistically that since people were animated by a desire to use others to their own profit or advantage a more or less permanent state of conflict was bound to exist. At the same time, however, he believed that the bleak conditions that he described could be mitigated, even in the absence of any concern for the community in the realm of ideas, by negotiating the terms of interpersonal interaction in the realm of social practices. If each individual relinquished part of his natural right to self-assertion in return for a similar concession on the part of the other, a self-interested balance of individual wills and rights would be established. This balance would create a social covenant that could in turn become the basis for the creation of a state. Hobbes warned, however, that even after the state had been created extreme measures would be necessary to prevent the disintegration of the social covenant. The best way to safeguard it was, in his opinion, irrevocably to confer sovereignty, not upon any parliament or other inefficient group of men, but upon an absolute monarch.[11]

---

[8] MacIntyre 1967: 16.
[9] For an analysis of the issue of power in the Melian dialogue, see Kallet 2001: 9–20; for the concept of 'might is right' in antiquity, see Frisch 1949.
[10] Frisch 1949: 12.   [11] R. Peters (1956) *Hobbes*. Harmondsworth: Penguin.

During the second half of the nineteenth century this idea took on a further twist when a series of writers applied Charles Darwin's discoveries in biology to the study of society and politics.[12] These 'social Darwinists', as they were called, espoused the idea, dismissed by Darwin as vulgar, that the theory of 'natural selection' that had been developed to account for animal evolution might also apply to human history.[13] Adopting the ancient position that might was right, Walter Bagehot went on to suggest that struggle was a necessary catalyst to most evolutionary change: 'In every particular state of the world, those nations which are strongest tend to prevail over the others; and in certain marked peculiarities the strongest tend to be the best.'[14] The triumph of a stronger over a weaker nation or tribe was, according to him, to be achieved by war, not by any more peaceful form of contest: 'The strongest nation has always been conquering the weaker; sometimes even subduing it, but always prevailing over it . . . Conquest improved mankind . . . But why is one nation stronger than another? In the answer to that, I believe, lies the key to the principal progress of early civilisation, and to some of the progress of all civilisation. The answer is that there are very many advantages – some small and some great – every one of which tends to make the nation which has it superior to the nation which has it not . . .'[15]

The advantages that Bagehot had in mind were subsumed under a term that he had already coined: 'the cake of custom'. Nations and tribes that developed good habits of discipline and conformity and had high standards of law, morality and religion would, he believed, triumph over groups whose 'cake of custom' was no good. The former would survive and flourish; the latter were doomed to extinction.

Bagehot was, however, no pitiless social Darwinist. According to his scheme, the very 'cake of custom' that promoted stability during the earlier stages of evolution became in its later stages an obstacle to progress. War had in the past, as he saw it, had beneficial consequences, but by the nineteenth century it had lost its original function. As a framework for regulating relationships between nations and individuals, he believed, it must eventually be superseded by constructive debate and rational decision-making.

[12] R. Hofstadter (1944) *Social Darwinism in American Thought*. Boston: The Beacon Press; Alexander 1979; G. Jones (1980) *Social Darwinism in English Thought*. Sussex/New Jersey: The Harvester Press/Humanities Press; Schellenberg 1982: ch. 3.

[13] In a letter to Sir Charles Lyell, Darwin wrote, 'I have received in a Manchester newspaper rather a good squib, showing that I have proved "might is right", and therefore that Napoleon is right, and every cheating tradesman is also right.'

[14] Bagehot 1872: 43.   [15] Bagehot 1872: 49–50.

In order for this to happen the old 'cake of custom' must be broken up, no matter how successful it might have been up to that point. When the cake was broken the 'little seed of adaptiveness' hidden in it would be released, allowing a new form of society to emerge. This society would be characterised by a decline in bigotry, by an openness to new ideas and by the creation of a new type of human being whose behaviour would be regulated not by 'the hereditary barbaric impulse' but by the freer operation of intelligence through discussion. The emergence of this creature of 'animated moderation' would, according to Bagehot, be a sign that humanity's advancement consisted in a progression from conflict to co-operation, from impulsiveness to rationality; that, as Peter Gay put it, 'aggression can be – and in civilised times ought to be – sublimated'.[16]

Bagehot's social Darwinism was unusual in that it contained a streak of liberalism. Other social Darwinists distanced themselves from any such idea, projecting Darwin's conception of nature onto society without qualification. Nature being an arena for pitiless struggle between selfish and individualistic animals, human society came to be seen as an arena for pitiless struggle between selfish and individualistic human beings. At times the very distinction between nature and society came to be blurred. Famously paraphrasing Hobbes (who had himself been inspired by Plato), T. H. Huxley called life 'a war of each against all' and, in an article published in an influential London periodical, a 'continuous free fight'. Competition between individuals of the same species was, as he saw it, not merely a law of nature, but the principal driving force in evolutionary change and progress. 'From the point of view of the moralist', he wrote in a famous passage, 'the animal world is about the same level as a gladiators' show. The creatures are fairly well treated and set to fight; whereby the strongest, the swiftest, and the cunningest live to fight another day. The spectator has no need to turn his thumbs down, as no quarter is given.'[17]

This was some sort of culmination of the ancient and widespread notion that man is naturally an aggressive animal and that aggression has supplied most of the fuel for historical action and change.[18] I shall not dwell on the tragic consequences of the real-life implementation of this mode of thought: the great cataclysms that befell Europe in the first half of the twentieth century, when 'might' suppressed 'right' in most international relationships and the idea of claiming 'a head for an eye' gained a foothold in

---

[16] Gay 1993: 55.
[17] T. H. Huxley (1888) 'The struggle for existence: a programme', *Nineteenth Century*, February. The idea of 'war of each against all' is foreshadowed in Plato, *Laws* 1.626a.
[18] Gay 1993: 3.

many forms of interpersonal relationship.[19] Nor do I wish to claim that this survey is exhaustive, or to suggest that all or even some European history is reducible to these simple principles. In moving on to the *second* category of moral injunctions, however, I shall attempt to show that the same principles have reappeared in different guises at all sorts of historical junctures, often transcending specific cultural, ethnic or national characteristics, so much so that it would be illogical not to assume that they spring directly from our common human nature.

The forms of behaviour that belong in this category appear to relate to what is perhaps the most ancient and universally venerated principle of primitive justice. The English 'tit for tat', the German 'Wie du mir, so ich dir' and the French 'Un prêté pour un rendu' are all versions of an age-old strategy of interpersonal interaction that turns up in world literature in a staggering number of variations and permutations. In Roman law it appears as the *lex talionis* (the law of like for like),[20] in later Judaism and early Christianity as 'the golden rule' ('Do as you would be done by' (Matthew 7.12)) and in the Old Testament and the Koran as 'an eye for an eye'. Here it will suffice to cite the Biblical version, by no means the earliest in humanity's long history: 'Eye for eye, tooth for tooth, hand for hand, foot for foot, burning for burning, wound for wound, stripe for stripe.'[21]

This system of commensurate action and reaction is neither so self-centred in outlook nor so unrestrained in spirit as Lamech's. Rather than seeing an interaction from the perspective of a single individual, it looks at it from the points of view of two; rather than licensing one individual to give free rein to his emotions, or ruthlessly to push his own interest at the expense of the other, it counsels both individuals to inflict equal harm – or, conversely, equal benefit – on each other. It should be noted, however, that the 'eye for eye' maxim in its original form merely prohibits retaliating by

---

[19] For the special form taken by social Darwinism in Germany, see Stein 1987.

[20] Some further examples: 'Ab alio exspectes alteri quod feceris', Publilius Syrus, *Sententiae* 2 (cited by Seneca, *Epistolae ad Lucilium* 94.43; '*Sua quisque exempla debet aequo animo pati*', Phaedrus, *Fabulae* 1.26.12 (following Aesop). For a general collection of passages on the theme of 'an eye for an eye' see Hobhouse 1915: 74–7; for a collection of passages on this theme from classical literature, see Hirzel 1907–10.

[21] Exodus 21.24–5. For alternative formulations of the same idea, see Leviticus 24.19–20, Deuteronomy 19.21 and Obadiah 15 ('as thou hast done, it shall be done unto thee; thy reward shall return upon thine own head'), to be read with Lemaire 1984. Judges 1.7, 1 Kings 20.39–42 and 2 Kings 10.24 give examples of 'an eye for an eye' in action; see also the Koran 5.45 (*The Table*). A still earlier variation occurs in the Code of Hammurabi: 'If a man has destroyed the eye of one of citizen status, they shall destroy his eye': W. Thomas (ed.) (1959) *Documents from Old Testament Times*. New York: Harper Collins: 33 (no. 196).

inflicting any injury that is greater than the one sustained; it does not rule out the option of violent response.

This exclusion appears only in a sub-category of the 'tit for tat' group: the doctrine of non-violent compensation (material or otherwise) deemed to be the economic equivalent of the harm done. In archaic Rome the Twelve Tables provided that anyone who killed without intent should hand over a ram to the victim's agnates,[22] while a law code from the fifth-century Greek city of Gortyn states that any person taken in adultery with a free woman in the house of her father, brother or husband shall be required to pay a certain sum of money.[23] Although both 'tit for tat' and commensurate compensation often coexisted with more aggressive strategies of interpersonal interaction, they clearly represent a more advanced stage of social evolution than the items included in the first category of moral injunctions.

The main reason for this is not merely that they reject the social-Darwinian view of society, but that in both its manifestations the idea of 'tit for tat' differs substantially from that of 'a head for an eye'. 'A head for an eye' does not depend upon a willing response for its success: the stronger party can injure or destroy the weaker to his or her own advantage regardless of what the weaker party does. Both commensurate compensation and a version of 'tit for tat' that I shall call 'positive' (people may, after all, exchange equivalent benefits as well as equivalent injuries) require willing responsiveness if they are to succeed. When people exchange benefits or provide compensation in return for injuries they introduce reciprocity into their relationships, and reciprocity is an indispensable prerequisite for co-operation.

This point can be seen better by considering one particular attempt to refute social Darwinism. In 1902 Peter Kropotkin, a Russian anarchist and revolutionary who renounced his aristocratic birthright, published a book entitled *Mutual Aid: A Factor in Evolution*. Basically this was a criticism of Huxley's picture of the natural world as a savage jungle, red in tooth and claw, that argued that Darwin's valuable theories had been distorted by his followers. While carrying out anthropological fieldwork in the exceedingly harsh conditions of eastern Siberia and northern Manchuria, Kropotkin came to the conclusion that although the Darwinian 'struggle for existence' was an important factor in promoting evolution and the progress of

---

[22] Twelve Tables 8.24a: '*si telum manu fugit magis quam iecit, aries subicitur*'.
[23] 'A hundred *staters*'; see R. F. Willets (1967) *The Law Code of Gortyn*. Berlin: Walter de Gruyter and Co.: 40 (Col. ii., 20–4).

species, it was not the only one. Co-operation and mutual support between members of the same species, he concluded, contributed far more to the survival of that species than did struggles between its members. Both the animal and the human groups that fared best were in his opinion the most co-operative ones. Morality, he argued, had evolved from the human impulse to sociability, from the unconscious recognition (or perhaps instinct, developed over the course of an extremely long evolution) 'of the close dependency of every one's happiness upon the happiness of all; and of the sense of justice, or equity, which brings the individual to consider the rights of every other individual as equal to his own'.[24]

However beneficial the 'tit for tat' strategy may prove, with or without ramifications in the communal interest, it is still a far cry from the strategy embodied in our *third* category of moral injunctions, which differs profoundly from the first two. The precepts in this group not only reject the idea of commensurate compensation, but enjoin under-reacting to injury, not reacting to it at all, or even repaying it with benefits. In its simplest version this doctrine is encapsulated in Christian precepts such as 'turning the other cheek' or 'not casting the first stone'. In its fully developed version it figures in the New Testament thus:

Never pay back evil for evil. Let your aims be such as all men count honourable. If possible, so far as it lies with you, live in peace with all men. My dear friends, do not seek revenge, but leave a place for divine retribution; for there is a text which reads, 'Justice is mine, says the Lord, I will repay' (*mihi vindicta, ego retribuam dicit Dominus*). But there is another text: 'If your enemy is hungry, feed him; if he is thirsty, give him a drink . . .'[25]

It cannot be claimed that this precept of self-restraint or under-reaction to violence has not at one time or another captured the imagination of past thinkers. Adam Smith, for instance, called it one of the 'great precepts of nature' and turned it into one of the central motifs of his *Theory of Moral Sentiments*:

And hence it is, that to feel much for others and little for ourselves, that to restrain our selfish, and to indulge our benevolent affections, constitutes the perfection of human nature; and can alone produce among mankind that harmony of sentiments and passions in which consists their whole grace and propriety. As to love our

---

[24] Kropotkin 1939: 16.
[25] Letter of Paul to the Romans 12.17–21, the New English Bible translation; cf. Nahum 1, 2–3. For the 'love of neighbour' motif in Greek, Roman, Christian and Jewish writings see Den Boer 1979: ch. 5.

neighbour as we love ourselves is the great law of Christianity, so it is the great precept of nature to love ourselves only as we love our neighbour, or what comes to the same thing, as our neighbour is capable of loving us.[26]

By the time he wrote his next book, *The Wealth of Nations*, however, Smith had had a change of heart, putting forward self-interest rather than benevolence as the main motivation for every human and hence every economic action.[27] In accordance with this he set out to demonstrate the social usefulness of free competition. The sum total of selfish actions was, according to him, guided by an 'invisible hand' that turned competition into a constructive social force and rendered benevolence redundant. He now deemed the influence of benevolence on trade to be in any case negligible, human beings in general preferring self-interest to benevolence and regarding themselves more highly than they did others.

Smith's suspicions appear to be confirmed by the very exceptions to this rule. At various times human beings have set great store by social types remarkable for their altruism. These types appear systematically and consistently to prefer benevolence to self-interest and to regard others more highly than themselves. When one sets out to evaluate their overall impact upon human affairs, however, one is bound to be disappointed. Saints, for example, are supposed to repay evil with good, thus apparently acting as exceptions to the rule that humans are largely motivated by self-interest. More often than not, however, the stories recording their actions turn out to be apocryphal. Heroes sacrifice themselves dramatically for communities, thinking of themselves *last*, just like William Tell. This sort of seemingly selfless devotion to an urgent communal cause (in which group pressure can, of course, play a part) is one thing, however, while more quietly forgiving a bad turn or doing a good one in expectation only of long-term communal benefit is quite another. Philanthropic rescuers may indeed put their own lives in jeopardy to help others, but within a wider perspective their actions appear as sporadic, atypical incidents in a sea of selfish performances. Freedom fighters sometimes begin by making non-violence their

[26] Adam Smith 1976: 25. Cf. 11.3, 34: 'The man of the most perfect virtue . . . is he who joins, to the most perfect command of his own original and selfish feelings, the most exquisite sensibility both to the original and sympathetic feelings of others.'
[27] Adam Smith 1970. Cf. Coase 1976. For the oft-debated question of the congruence of the *Moral Sentiments* with the *Wealth of Nations*, see G. Himmelfarb (1984) *The Idea of Poverty*. London and Boston: Faber and Faber: 47–8. In Himmelfarb's view, 'it is clear enough that Smith intended both as parts of his grand "design", that he had the *Wealth of Nations* in mind before he wrote *Moral Sentiments*, and that he remained committed to *Moral Sentiments*, reissuing and revising it long after the *Wealth of Nations* was published.'

shibboleth. Experience shows, however, that despite certain remarkable initial successes non-violence tends gradually to give way to an uncompromising form of the 'head for an eye' strategy as the group pursues its aims. Utopians regularly dream up societies ruled according to superhuman standards, reminiscent in some ways of those recommended in Romans. Unfortunately one is forced to conclude that their voices are going unheard: human affairs tend to be run by realists who dismiss people who think that bad turns should be forgiven, or even repaid with good deeds, as naïve at best and suckers at worst. All these examples taken together do not seem particularly to reinforce the contention that selfless devotion to others has been a major formative force in the history of past societies.[28]

Having examined the internal logic of moral precepts, we now turn to perhaps the most intriguing question ever to have engaged the attention of students of morality and behaviour. It is this: how do verbalised behavioural precepts actually manifest themselves in action, not in extreme cases of the sort discussed above, but in the routine, everyday life of people living in closely knit, stable communities?

Two diametrically opposed answers to this question have been proffered in recent times. During the first half of the twentieth century social scientists systematised the intuitive, common-sense idea that 'words are actions in miniature'. In practice, this ought to mean that questions and answers can be used to elicit reliable information about probable courses of action. Accordingly, social scientists claimed to be able to read the intentions and predict the actions of a large part of the western world's population in all sorts of fields such as politics, elections, consumption and work by 'measuring' their 'attitudes':[29] that is, by taking opinion polls about more general issues such as race, sex, war, religion and violence.

This apparently safe and unassailable method was, however, suddenly dealt a spectacular blow. In 1934 a Californian sociologist called Richard LaPierre published the results of an experiment whose consequence, the 'attitude/behaviour controversy', was to rage for years. LaPierre spent two years travelling from coast to coast with a young Chinese-born couple. He stopped at over 250 hotels, auto camps, cafés and restaurants, in all but one receiving normal or sometimes exemplary service. Six months after the trip he posted to each of these establishments a simple questionnaire that

---

[28] This point seems to be widely accepted in the social sciences. See (e.g.) Monroe 1996: 6.

[29] Attitude was defined by G. Allport as 'a mental and neural state of readiness, organized through experience, exerting a directive or dynamic influence upon the individual's response to all objects and situations with which it is related' (in C. Murchison (ed.) (1935) *A Handbook of Social Psychology*. Worcester, Mass.: Clark University Press: 810).

included the question, 'Will you accept members of the Chinese race in your establishment?' 92 per cent of the respondents replied 'No', in startling contradiction to the fact that they had served the Chinese couple not long before.[30]

LaPierre's experiment was not without its flaws. A whole series of new experiments conducted subsequently using more refined techniques did, however, support his findings. Words and actions appear indeed to be highly inconsistent with one another. People do not do what they say they are doing. They often act spectacularly differently from the way in which they would have predicted they would act if asked before the experiment. The professional literature of the late 1960s and 1970s is full of statements that it is impossible to infer behaviour from attitudes. Some scholars have even gone so far as to deny that what people think they will do has any relevance at all, and have branded verbal questions futile.

The pendulum has since swung back again. Distinctions (for instance, the distinction between a general attitude towards an object and a specific intention to act in a certain way towards that object at a certain time) have been refined and new techniques for asking questions and measuring results have been devised. At last the conclusion has emerged that in certain circumstances, which are extremely hard to define, verbalised precepts *are*, after all, relevant to actions.

For my purposes, however, this conclusion is beside the point. I have sketched this chapter in the history of the social sciences to counter the tendency, widespread among historians, to assume the existence of a simple, one-to-one relationship between verbal statements of principle and actions. By applying rigorous logic, we can use certain historical cases to make the same point. One of the most widely quoted precepts in the literature of the European Middle Ages is, in its various forms, the Christian doctrine of 'turning the other cheek': that prime example of the third category of moral injunctions, derived from the Letter of Paul to the Romans, that we discussed earlier. At the very time when the dicta inspired by Paul's letter were being so widely circulated, however, witches, heretics and criminals were being put to death at an appalling rate and violence in society was rampant, starkly denying the ideals of mercy, compassion, clemency and self-sacrifice championed by Paul's precept.[31]

---

[30] R. T. LaPierre (1934) 'Attitudes versus actions', *Social Forces* 13: 230–7.

[31] This point has been made more than once. For example, see Elias 1978b, esp. 234: 'There is abundant evidence that attitudes towards life and death among the secular upper classes of the Middle Ages by no means always accorded with those which prevail in books by the clerical classes and which are quite often considered typical of the period.'

Several factors may be considered to account for such discrepancies. By the nineteenth century psychologists were already suspecting that actions sprang mainly from subconscious physiological mechanisms in the brain and other organs and that the effect of culturally defined principles upon them was relatively small. These ideas were, however, by and large brushed aside during the first half of the twentieth century, when the view that human behaviour was overwhelmingly determined by culture (i.e. nurture) gained the upper hand in the great nature/nurture controversy.[32] Now that this position has been totally rejected the older paradigm has been revived and indeed reinstated, thanks in particular to a series of insights in biology. The work carried out by Hamilton and Williams in the 1960s and by Dawkins and Wilson in the 1970s has shown that individuals do not consistently do things that will benefit their groups, their relatives or even themselves; they consistently do things that will benefit their genes.[33] 'We are survival machines', wrote Dawkins, '– robot vehicles blindly programmed to preserve the selfish molecules known as genes.' If he is right, as mounting evidence suggests he is, then the dilemma described earlier in this chapter (the conflict between actions that benefit the individual and those that benefit the community) increases considerably in complexity. The possibility must be contemplated that at least some human actions are not intended to benefit either the mortal individual or the ephemeral community. It may instead be that, in ways that are still shrouded in uncertainty, they are intended to benefit the immortal genes.

Another problem surrounding the supposed correspondence between actions and moral precepts is that moral precepts are detached from society, their operation being conceived of, as it were, in a social vacuum. They thus fail to take into account a whole series of factors that intervene from day to day in almost every single instance of interpersonal interaction.[34] There are the reactions and interventions of 'third parties', either real (family, clan, state or fellow citizens) or imagined (a god or gods, demons, guardian angels; see **Figs. 9.7** and **9.9**). There are those subtle instructions as to what is 'proper', transmitted through public opinion, that individuals follow, at times without thinking, but most frequently out of a considered wish to conform. Finally, there are problems having to do with how people use moral precepts. Experience shows that they tend to invoke them haphazardly, often after performing the actions that they are used to justify. At

---

[32] Cf. Ridley 2003, who argues that genes are at the root of both nurture and nature, making culture possible.

[33] Hamilton 1964; G. C. Williams 1966; Dawkins 1989.

[34] The passage from Romans cited above is in this respect atypical, since it takes God into consideration.

times, moreover, actions are justified using not just one simple, unadulterated precept, but a mixture of ambiguous and even contradictory ones that are combinations of or variations upon the basic ideas being invoked.

All these considerations render the question of how people behave to each other within the framework of any more than fleeting relationship a much more complicated business than one might have envisaged.

A CODE OF BEHAVIOUR

What comes to our rescue is the concept of a 'code of behaviour', which may be defined, in conformity with established usage, as 'a set of moral principles accepted and used by society or a particular group of people.'[35] A code of behaviour, thus conceived of, differs markedly from two cognate fields of inquiry, 'ethics' and 'morality', even though it encompasses an almost identical range of phenomena. Ethics is a branch of philosophy. It requires self-conscious, ideally disinterested, reflection on the springs of moral action; on the question, as G. E. Moore put it, of 'what, in the conduct of us, human beings, is good, and what is bad, what is right and what is wrong'[36] – a search that is often inspired by a desire to improve man's lot on earth. Morality is, in John Dewey's words, 'largely concerned with controlling human nature'.[37] Seeking to regulate an only partly conscious set of dispositions, inclinations, attitudes and habits, it is the domain of teachers, politicians, moralists and anyone else who wants to induce people to behave in whatever ways he or she considers to be most appropriate. Gertrude Himmelfarb presumably had this homiletic sense of the word in mind when she described the Victorian morality as one that 'dignifies and civilises human beings, removing us from our natural brutish state and covering, as Burke said, our "naked shivering nature"'.[38]

A code of behaviour, by contrast, is analytical in intent. Its immediate purpose is neither to reflect on the springs of moral action nor to induce people to behave in certain ways. It is to lay bare the specific combination of rules in accordance with which the communal life of a particular group of people is administered. At its core lie three propositions that will gradually be clarified as the argument unfolds.

---

[35] *Cambridge International Dictionary of English*, 1995. Cambridge: Cambridge University Press.
[36] G. E. Moore (1959) *Principia Ethica*. Cambridge: Cambridge University Press. Original edition, 1903: 2. Moore later poses his questions more tersely: 'What is good, and What is bad?'
[37] J. Dewey (1922) *Human Nature and Conduct*. New York: Dover Publications: 1.
[38] G. Himmelfarb (1975) *Marriage and Morals among the Victorians*. New York: Faber and Faber: xiii.

The first is that moral principles and actual behaviour constitute a single inseparable whole, so much so that it is often more expedient to infer principles from behaviour than to do the opposite.[39] The second is that the sum total of individual behaviour (in particular behaviour that is repetitive, customary or habitual) is unique to each society. It is the product of a singular convergence of all the economic, social, demographic and cultural factors that act upon the individual, imprinting on society their distinctive marks.[40] The third is that it may be possible to evaluate the moral norms and the behaviour of each society not merely by reference to the subjective standards that the researcher brings to the process of value judgement, but also by reference to the more objective, independent standards derived within the behavioural sciences in pursuit of a better understanding of human behaviour.[41]

Since these propositions are not exactly taken for granted at the moment, I am not expecting anyone to accept them without further scrutiny and explanation. I shall, however, be doing my best to convince the reader that this approach to the study of ancient morality and behaviour is objectively preferable to the existing ones. As a beginning, I shall confront the concept of the code of behaviour advanced here with the body of thought that already exists on this subject. This will give a rough idea of how much this idea shares with the existing ones, how much of them it rejects and in what respects it diverges from them. Having gone through this material, the reader will be in a better position to judge whether the idea of a code of behaviour possesses any degree of analytical force or whether it is just one more futile concept introduced unnecessarily into the annals of the social sciences.

The idea that a life without rules would be chaotic, and its corollary, that orderly society is upheld by rules, is widespread and deeply seated. Writing at the beginning of the twentieth century, Hobhouse summarised centuries of thought on the subject. 'In no part of the world, and at no period of time', he wrote, 'do we find the behaviour of men left to unchartered freedom. Everywhere human life is in a measure organised and directed by customs, laws, beliefs, ideals which shape its end and guide its activities.'[42] A question that interested many concerned the precise nature of these restraining influences. Were they internalised or externalised? Were they inhibitions that repressed sentiments and emotions from deep within the psyche, or were

---

[39] This proposition is developed in pp. 101–7.
[40] This proposition is developed in pp. 30–8, 107–18 and 258–309.
[41] This proposition is developed at pp. 391–410.   [42] Hobhouse 1915: 1.

they boundaries, limitations and sanctions that circumscribed behaviour in concrete form from without?

The majority of Greek thinkers seem to have opted for an admixture of both. The poet Hesiod, writing at a time when the polis existed only in embryonic form, thought that internal restrictions were entirely insufficient to the task of curbing violent emotions or restraining savages; Silver Age people tended, so he tells us, to injure each other recklessly, leading brief, anguished lives (*Works and Days* 132–5). Demosthenes, active in the last decades of the independent polis, did not have much time for internalised restrictions either, instead expounding the humanising effect of statutory law: 'If laws were abolished and each individual were given licence to do what he liked, not only would our communal organisation vanish, but our very life would be in no way different from that of the beasts of the field' (25.20, *Against Aristogeiton*). In the heyday of the polis, Antiphon the Sophist taught that both legal and non-legal restraints were necessary if man was to lead an effective communal existence. Justice (*dike*) consisted, according to him, of not transgressing the observances of the polis of which one was a citizen. It is significant that the Greek word translated in his text as 'observances' (*ta nomima*) embraces laws as well as 'customs' (Frg. 44A Column 1).

The majority of the Greeks seem to have taken on board the point implicit in Antiphon's teaching: that statutory law alone could not cover all the complexities of social life. To achieve that end a broader framework of analysis was required, one that included certain restrictive influences that made no part of legislation. Greek authors have made some highly ingenious comments concerning these influences.

Protagoras, for instance (in Plato's dialogue of that name), identified them with what we would call dispositions and mutual attitudes. His account was couched in the form of a mythical simile. Men, after being created and provided with a 'divine portion', banded together to combat wild beasts. As soon as they had done so and founded poleis, however, 'they did wrong to one another through the lack of civic art (*politike techne*), and thus they began to be scattered again and to perish'. The attempt to set up poleis finally succeeded thanks to divine intervention. Zeus, fearing that man would be entirely destroyed, 'sent Hermes to bring shame (*aidos*)[43] and right (*dike*) among men, to the end that there should be regulation (*kosmoi*) of cities and friendly ties (*desmoi philias*) to draw them together' (*Protagoras* 322b–c).

---

[43] Also translatable as 'reverence', 'modesty' and 'respect'. Cf. Barker 1960: 71–2; Cairns 1993: 356–7.

The second-century Greek historian Polybius thought that the restrictive influences mentioned above were nothing but customs (*ethe*). Assuming a simplistic correlation between individual and communal behaviour,[44] he suggested that customs, in conjunction with the law, determined the true quality and form of every state: sound laws and customs rendered men's private lives righteous and well ordered and the general character of the state gentle and just, while unsound laws and customs had the opposite effect (6.47). Plato's late-Greek biographer Diogenes Laertius stated that in every city there was an 'unwritten law'[45] that differed from the written one in that it had arisen 'out of custom' (*kata ethe ginomenos*). He illustrated the workings of this law with a pedestrian example: most states had no statute (*nomos*) forbidding men to put in an appearance at the *agora* without any clothes on, or wearing women's clothes, but men abstained from this sort of conduct anyway because 'it is prohibited by an unwritten law' (3.86). Aristotle distinguished 'written' law, the particular (*idios*) law in accordance with which a state was administered, from the 'unwritten', general (*koinos*) law that appeared to be 'universally recognised'.[46] The Athenian speechwriter Andocides, finally, declared simply that 'unwritten' laws were any that were not inscribed upon the wall (1.84–7).

A number of Greek writers pondered the possibility that there was some sort of link between mundane restrictions and the supernatural. The pre-Socratic philosopher Heraclitus contended that all the laws of men were nourished by a single divine law.[47] The playwright Sophocles had one of his characters assert that the divine powers ruled the world by means of sacred, eternal and unwritten laws (*Antigone* 454–5) of which the laws of states were mere emanations.[48] Even Herodotus occasionally suspected that divine powers might be impinging upon human affairs. The Persian king, he states, took no revenge upon the Spartans for putting his heralds to death. Sixty years later, however, the sons of the Spartan heralds whose lives he had spared were put to death by the Athenians. This, according to Herodotus, was a clear indication' that in the end divine justice sees that everything is paid for (7.137).

'Customs', 'unwritten laws' and 'divine justice' were just some of the names given to these extra-legal restrictive influences. Others were *ethismata*, *ethe*, *synetheia*, *diaita*, *epitedeumata*, *nomima*, *nomizomena* and *nomoi*,

---

[44] For a similar idea see Plato, *Republic* 4.435e, in which Socrates says that there are in each of us the same principles (*eide*) and habits (*ethe*) as there are in the State.

[45] *Agraphos nomos*, elsewhere called *agraphon nomimon*.

[46] *Rhetoric* 1368b3. Cf. *Rhetoric* 1373b4, where a different typology is followed. See Ostwald 1973.

[47] Kirk, Raven and Schofield 1983: no. 250.   [48] Cf. Ehrenberg 1954.

words that have no precise modern equivalents but may loosely be rendered as 'customary law', 'habits', 'tradition', 'folk customs', 'ways of life', 'mores' or 'rules'. Whatever the correct term may be, it would seem that the Greeks may have caught a glimpse of an idea that was much later to become the cornerstone of social theory: that communal life is far more intricate than we tend to think and that its logic, which differs substantially from the logic that guides us as individuals, often escapes our perception.[49]

It is unnecessary here to produce a compendium of the Greeks' thoughts on the subject, or to iron out the frequent inconsistencies between them.[50] It will be far more helpful to extract from their remarks any features that may help us to turn our own concept of the code of behaviour into an effective analytical tool.

Greek ethical theorists seem to have agreed on one point: they believed that non-legal restrictive influences on behaviour were in a sense deeper and more fundamental than statutory laws. Plato, for instance, thought that they were the very foundations of the social order, the indispensable glue that held a community together. These were the ties (*desmoi*) that bound up the entire social framework (*politeia*), that linked all written and established laws with those yet to be passed; these bonds acted 'in the same way as ancestral customs (*patria . . . nomima*) dating from time immemorial, which by virtue of being soundly established and instinctively observed, shield and protect existing written law'. If unwritten laws are defective or go wrong, Plato continues, they can bring the entire edifice crashing down, laws along with institutions (*Laws* 7.793).

In the same vein, Thucydides rated respect for the unwritten laws as highly as obedience to the magistrates and to the laws themselves. In a famous passage in the Funeral Oration, he attributes these words to Pericles:

While in our private interactions we do our best to give no cause for offence, in public matters we restrain ourselves from illegal action out of reverence and fear; we subject ourselves to the magistrates in power and to the laws, especially those designed to protect the downtrodden and those that are held to convey disgrace upon anyone who breaks them, even though they do not exist in written form (*agraphoi nomoi*). (2.37.3)

Further on in his history, Thucydides gives a vivid example of what can happen when unwritten laws lose their grip on behaviour.[51] When the

---

[49] For Herodotus' contribution to the development of this point of view see J. Redfield 1985.

[50] For a summary of which see Hirzel 1900; for the notion of 'customary law' as opposed to law itself, see Ostwald 1986.

[51] Thucydides does not use the term 'unwritten law' here (2.52–3), but in my view the idea is implicit in his text.

plague broke out in Athens in 430, so he relates, a state of total lawlessness (*anomia*) descended on the city. Indirectly, this state was induced by the series of calamities that had struck the people of Athens: a high mortality rate, a sense of utter helplessness and sheer individual suffering. Its direct cause, however, was that amidst the general demoralisation people transgressed the elementary rules of social life. 'Brutalised by suffering', writes Thucydides, 'men had no idea where the next blow would fall and stopped caring about any law, sacred or profane' (2.52.3). The outward expression of this state of mind was ugly in the extreme. The bodies of the dying were piled up in heaps and half-dead sufferers could be seen wandering aimlessly about, or staggering round the fountains in search of water. The temples, in which some took refuge and then died, filled up with dead bodies. The practice of conducting funeral ceremonies with proper decorum fell apart altogether (see **Figs. 1.1** and **8.10**), some people tossing their dead onto funeral pyres built by others. People seemed to have lost all sense of shame, becoming insensitive to those expressions of approval or indignation that in normal times help to mould behaviour and preserve the social order. Acts of self-indulgence that would previously have been kept in the dark were now carried out openly. Money was spent like water on pleasure, since it now seemed as ephemeral as life itself. Whatever was regarded as constituting reputation or honour was no longer taken into account, 'so doubtful was it whether one would survive to enjoy the name for it' (2.53). Neither fear of the gods nor fear of man's laws exerted any restraining influence, the former because it clearly made no difference whether or not one worshipped the gods, the latter because no one who committed an offence expected to live long enough to be brought to trial.

The cumulative effect of passages such as these is clearly to reveal four properties attributed by these Greek writers to non-legal restraining

---

Figure 1.1 Communal graves from the Kerameikos underground station
Only on rare occasions can material remains be linked to the plague, which caused sufferings in Athens that were 'almost beyond the capacity of human nature to endure' (Thucydides 2.50). One such occasion was the discovery, during the recent construction of the Athenian Metro, of two communal graves (*polyandreia*) at Kerameikos. The dead interred here were buried hastily, as Thucydides describes: 'Brutalised by suffering, men . . . stopped caring about any law, sacred or profane. Since all the funeral customs that had previously been observed had now broken down, every man buried his dead however he could' (2.52.3–4). The civic authorities concerned with public health probably helped the people by preparing sites such as these for use as mass graves. The grave shown in the first photograph above contained at least 150 dead; the second contained 29 (Parlama and Stampolidis 2001: 271–3).

influences. The first was that these influences were more general in scope and fewer in number than the statutory laws, constituting a kind of sub-stratum of principles (reminiscent in some ways of the primordial matter of Greek physics) from which the whole of the orderly world was supposed to emanate.[52] The second was that they were implicit, consisting of clusters of ideas that were thought but not uttered, nebulous in their cloudy realm of sentiment and emotion (by contrast with laws, which were explicit and expressed with crystalline clarity in written form). The third property had to do with modes of enforcement: whereas written laws could be enforced by the agency of formal institutions, the sanction imposed by unwritten laws depended for its effect mainly upon that combination of looks, gestures and intonations that makes up the conglomeration of human behaviours otherwise known as social pressure. For the fourth property we shall return to Plato.

In the passage cited above, Plato states only that unwritten laws and ancestral customs are alike ('they act in the same way as *patria nomima*'), not that they are interchangeable. Certain striking differences stood out. Ancestral customs belonged to the realm of habit; unwritten laws existed in the realm of reflection. Ancestral customs involved an unconscious selection of standards of virtue and depravity; unwritten laws demanded a conscious selection. Ancestral customs relied upon an unquestioning acceptance of the premise 'It is customary, therefore it is right,' while unwritten laws treated that premise with appropriate scepticism: 'It is custom, but is it therefore necessarily right?' The unwritten laws, as conceived of by the Greek thinkers we are discussing, were, then, those implicit, mutually understood rules of behaviour that the people of the poleis taught each other as part of social-isation during the course of centuries of communal life: rules that could serve to guide behaviour not only during trivial, day-to-day interactions, but also at those critical moments of existence in which entire ways of life and indeed the very survival of communities were at stake.

These are the features that I propose to carry over into our own concept of a code of behaviour. *A code of behaviour is a complex of explicitly defined or implicitly recognised rules that a community of people accepts and makes pre-dominant, thus differentiating its moral profile from the total range of possible*

---

[52] Cf. Barker 1959: 34. It may not be without significance that de Tocqueville had similar ideas about the relationship between manners (which he defined as 'the various notions and opinions current among men, and to the mass of those ideas which constitute their character of mind') and the law: '. . . the physical circumstances [of a country] are less efficient [in maintaining democracy] than the laws, and the laws very subordinate to the manners of the people . . .' (A. de Tocqueville (1961) *Democracy in America*. New York: Schocken Books, vol. 1: 354 and 383, respectively).

human norms and types of behaviour. It is, in other words, a product of both nurture and nature.

IN CRISIS AND IN PEACE

The next stage in my campaign to convince my readers of the validity of this concept will consist of raising and answering objections. What we have said up to now implies that the rules that make up a code of behaviour, whether explicit or implicit, written or unwritten, externalised or inter-nalised, form some kind of permanent basis for morality. Against this it may be argued that behaviour in the wider communal sphere shows few signs of consistency. People, as we have seen, change their minds haphaz-ardly, often switching their principles in an effort to justify their actions. This is vividly illustrated by the decisions made by the citizens of Athens at their Assembly. In the course of nearly two hundred years of democratic rule they seem to have changed their minds a number of times, sometimes about matters of no trifling importance. In 431, for example, they decided to go to war with Sparta and to take Pericles' advice that they should evacuate Attica. Less than a year later, however, when their land had been devastated twice and their men were dying of the plague, 'they began to blame Pericles for having persuaded them to go to war and to hold him responsible for all the misfortunes that had overtaken them' (Thucydides 2.59).

It could be argued that in this case their change of mind resulted from a change in their circumstances. In 427, however, they are reported to have performed another *volte-face* even though their circumstances remained exactly the same. Only a day after they decided to put to death the entire male population of the city of Mytilene (a former member of the Delian league that had revolted against them), Thucydides tells us, 'there was a sudden change of feeling and people began to think how cruel and how unprecedented such a decision was – to destroy not only the guilty, but the entire population of a state'.[53]

Examples such as these would seem to confirm not only ancient assess-ments of crowds in general as volatile, erratic and unstable, but also certain views that have been adopted by historical scholarship, such as the idea, put forward by K. J. Dover, that popular morality is 'essentially unsys-tematic.'[54] The politicians who addressed the Assembly could, according

---

[53] Thucydides 2.36; see pp. 360–73. A similar *volte-face* in the year 406 is reported by Xenophon: not long after the Arginusae trial and the execution of the generals, 'the Athenians repented' (*metemele tois Athenaiois, Hellenica* 1.7.35).

[54] Dover 1974: xii.

to these views, tap into a whole range of alternative moral norms to sway the vote in whatever manner would best serve their purpose. Outward expressions of popular morality would, in other words, seem to belie its supposedly permanent basis, shifting public behaviour bespeaking shifting moral norms.

I shall argue, however, that neither the examples cited above nor those that Dover had in mind constitute moral norms: they are merely what we may call opinions. For an opinion to become a norm four conditions are necessary. Firstly, it must become the subject of so general a consensus and become so profoundly internalised as to make its agents more or less unaware of its existence. Secondly, it must extend in scope from the specific to the general, turning into a principle by reference to which other individual instances are judged. Thirdly, it must be consistent with widespread patterns of behaviour. Fourthly, and most importantly, it must have to do with types of behaviour that are repetitive, customary and habitual (as opposed to those that are unique, uncommon and infrequent). This point can best be illustrated by means of a modern analogy. In the USA the answer to the question of whether or not civilians should have unrestricted (or only slightly restricted) access to firearms is a matter of opinion. In the UK the belief that they should not is a moral norm; few people in the UK think that the average British person should have free access to firearms. This is a matter of principle from which all of the other measures designed by this society to curtail its members' opportunities to inflict violence flow. For example, in the UK policemen are in general only lightly armed or not armed at all, and the *widespread* pattern of behaviour is clearly not one in which thousands of people are shot every year on the streets and in schools, trains and underground railways.[55] The *isolated* instances of inconsistent behaviour that occur (armed robberies, for example) are insufficient to contradict the assumption of a permanent moral code and hence to blunt its force as an analytical tool. Provided the researcher knows where to look, moral systems may be found to reveal remarkable consistencies.

Problems remain, nonetheless. Not the least of these has to do with the frame of reference defined earlier. Brief consideration will suffice to show

[55] According to B. Jones (ed.) (1994) *Politics UK*. New York: Harvester Wheatsheaf, 2nd edn: 510–13, the percentages of American and British residents who reported suffering burglary or assault in 1988 were as follows: USA 3.8 per cent (burglary) and 3.0 per cent (assault); UK 0.7 per cent (burglary) and 0.6 per cent (assault). It is nonetheless widely believed that the UK has outstandingly high crime rates. They are in fact among the lowest in the western world. Cf. W. G. Runciman (1998) *The Social Animal*. London: Harper Collins: '. . . one of the most striking features of them [i.e. British murder statistics] is a big drop from something like the present-day American rate to something like the present-day British rate from the time at which men no longer carried swords' (at 105).

that this is far too wide. According to the principles outlined earlier, a code of behaviour would have to encompass the entire spectrum of behavioural patterns: all the movements and sensations through which people mediate their relationship with their external environment and all the ideas and moral precepts that circulate in their community. This is asking too much of a research strategy. It would be well-nigh impossible to produce an exhaustive inventory of Athenian society's mental baggage, taking into account the whole gamut of 'rights, duties, justice, amity, respect or wrong' that were presupposed as the 'basic moral axioms' of its social system.[56] What we need is some method of reducing this mass of complexity to its simpler components in such a way as to retain the data essential for our analysis while discarding everything superfluous.

I believe that such a method can be worked out. To demonstrate its feasibility, however, I shall have to introduce a new parameter into our discussion, one that bears on how communal norms operate in settled conditions and at times of crisis. It appears to me that a correct appreciation of the interdependence between the two will help us to cut our material down to size in an appropriate way.

There is a tradition in moral philosophy that assumes, as Alasdair MacIntyre has put it, that moral concepts are part of some kind of 'timeless, limited, unchanging, determinate species of concept, necessarily having the same features throughout their history, so that there is a part of language waiting to be philosophically investigated which deserves the title "*the* language of morals"'.[57] This tradition is now under attack, its increasing numbers of critics advancing the argument that moral concepts, rather than being fixed entities, are in fact historically conditioned variables. According to this view, they are embedded in and inseparable from the life of the community made up of the people who use them. If the lives of these people change the concepts change too. When conditions are stable the concepts can easily be recognised as involved in regulating behaviour and social life. When conditions are unsettled, however, moral concepts tend to undergo startling distortions. If, in particular, the rules that are supposed to control violence break down, the concepts lose touch with reality altogether.

Thucydides, whose work lies at the heart of our study, was perhaps the first known author to call attention to this dismal transformation. As soon as revolution broke out in Greece, so he relates, law and order broke down.

---

[56] M. Fortes (1949) *The Web of Kinship among the Tallensi*. Oxford: Oxford University Press: 346.
[57] MacIntyre 1967: 1 (his italics). This point is further developed at pp. 263–4.

As a result, people's conceptions of the most basic rules of social interaction changed considerably:

It was seen as far more impressive to have revenged oneself successfully than never to have been injured in the first place. Even if oaths of reconciliation were occasionally exchanged, they did not last long, since both parties saw them merely as stopgap measures in the absence of anything better. As soon as the opportunity offered, whichever of the two was the more daring would seize it at once, taking the other off guard and preening himself upon having succeeded by perfidy rather than by open attack, since this was not only a far safer approach, but showed everyone else how clever he was. (3.82.7)

This relapse into primeval violence was accompanied by a drastic transvaluation in the meanings of value terms:

Irrational daring came to be thought of as the courage proper to a member of one's clique; taking the time to consider matters sensibly was seen as specious cowardice, moderation (*to sophron*) as an attempt to hide lack of manliness and the ability to see all sides of a question as hopeless inability to act. Exploding at the slightest excuse was regarded as the mark of a real man, while rational consideration of one's actions revealed a cringing and probably perfidious disinclination for conflict. Irascible firebrands were invariably trustworthy, and disagreeing with them was highly suspicious behaviour. Anyone who succeeded in some piece of underhand chicanery was clearly clever; anyone who saw plots all around him must be cleverer still. A man who wanted absolutely nothing to do with any such behaviour was regarded as a seditious influence within the clique, easily cowed by any adversary. (3.82.4–5)

Social psychologists today would have no difficulty in recognising the state of collective mind that Thucydides is describing. It corresponds in every particular with what they would call 'de-individuation', a concept describing the submergence of the individual's identity in that of a group in such a way that the markers of his personality are reduced and his behaviour becomes uninhibited. In other words, modern research, drawing on independent observation and experiment, has reached conclusions about the disintegration of social norms that are very like those of Thucydides.

In order fully to grasp the implications of this correspondence, we should say a few words about the determinants of social behaviour. Drawing on a tradition that goes back to the distinction made by the Sophists between the aggressive and lustful 'natural man' and the 'conventional man' who adheres to constraining rules and regulations,[58] Kurt Lewin, the father of experimental social psychology, postulates that [S]ocial [B]ehaviour is a

---

[58] MacIntyre 1967: 16–17.

function of, or caused by, complex interactions between an individual's [P]ersonal qualities and the [S]ituational context in which he acts and is embedded: **SB = f(P, S)**.[59] In settled conditions the influence of each of these factors in directing behaviour is more or less equal. In extreme, unsettled conditions, however, the contextual forces can attain a magnitude capable of changing a person's state of consciousness completely. In such conditions personal dispositions lose altogether their power to determine social behaviour. Zimbardo, who conducted a pioneering experiment to test this idea, has described the ensuing state of de-individuation as one 'in which a series of antecedent social conditions lead to changes in the perception of self and others, and thereby to a lowered threshold of normally restrained behaviour. Under appropriate conditions what results is the "release" of behaviour in violation of norms of appropriateness. Such conditions permit overt expression of antisocial behaviour, characterised as selfish, greedy, power-seeking, hostile, lustful, and destructive.'[60]

Subsequent studies have confirmed Zimbardo's findings, while qualifying and refining his analysis. De-individuated people are released from the habitual inhibition of social and personal controls. Their behaviour becomes impulsive, irrational and regressive. Their awareness of themselves as individuals separate from the group is blocked. Their capacity to monitor their own behaviour is reduced.

The situational context that Thucydides believed to have brought about this condition was revolution (*stasis*). Modern social psychologists would identify simpler contexts, but most of these seem to be components of what Thucydides called *stasis*: anonymity, the opportunity to diffuse or share responsibility for one's actions, the opportunity to concentrate primarily on the present moment with past and future fading out of view, the occurrence of novel or unstructured situations (that is, situations so unusual that no appropriate behaviour has been prescribed for them) and the opportunity to rely on non-cognitive (i.e. physical) interactions and feedback. Social psychologists agree that although a state of de-individuation does not necessarily lead to aggression, it fosters antisocial behaviour.[61]

The correspondence between Thucydides' description of the people's state of mind following the outbreak of revolution and the modern concept of de-individuation is striking. This reveals Thucydides' excellent understanding of human nature. It also suggests that it is a general rule that whereas in settled conditions the behaviour of individuals differs markedly,

---

[59] K. Lewin (1951) *Field Theory in Social Science*. Westport, Conn.: Greenwood Press [repr. 1975].
[60] Zimbardo 1969: 251.   [61] Hogg and Vaughan 1995: 381.

in a state of de-individuation it assumes near-perfect uniformity (people in this sort of state, whether ancient or modern, have always behaved and continue to behave in remarkably similar ways). Above all, however, it shows that the mechanisms or forces that prevent the creation of situational contexts conducive to de-individuation when conditions are stable are the most significant components of the code of behaviour. If these mechanisms or forces lose their grip on behaviour, then the entire system of values collapses. By implication, then, for communal life to be effective these mechanisms and forces must be judged indispensable.

How, then, can we identify and capture these exceptionally important mechanisms or forces? Two complementary approaches would seem to be open to us. Firstly, we can look at society at the micro level and single out those instances of interpersonal behaviour that display the highest and the lowest levels of antagonism. In a settled community these will, of course, occur where members engage in either conflict or co-operation. These are the interactions in which the balance between actions that benefit the individual and those that benefit the community is most seriously put to the test. The manner in which members of a community interact when faced with choices in situations involving co-operation or conflict contains, in other words, the clue to unravelling that community's code of behaviour and indeed to evaluating its entire moral profile.[62]

The other approach that suggests itself concerns the macro level of society, or, more specifically, its mechanisms for controlling violence within the community. The paramount importance of these is apparent, since when they break down a lapse into a state of de-individuation inevitably occurs. It may therefore be argued, reversing the argument and slightly expanding it according to the suggestions of Norbert Elias, that it is inexpedient to assess a community's level of morality or civilisation without first forming an idea of the types of violence that its members regard as permissible, the mechanisms they deploy to control violence and the extent to which their collective consciousness is developed in this respect. It may without fear of overstatement be claimed that most of the norms, values, ideals and attitudes that are used under stable communal conditions to regulate behaviour that appears to have nothing to do with violence are ultimately all about controlling violence.[63]

---

[62] It is probably worth pointing out that while this book was in print, Robert Auman and Thomas Schelling were awarded the 2005 Nobel Prize in Economic Science 'for having enhanced our understanding of conflict and cooperation through game-theory analysis'.

[63] Elias 1978a, 1978b, 1986; Fontaine 1978.

Concentrating on these two aspects of a code of behaviour rather than on the entire spectrum of principles and behaviour used by a community of people will also help to effect the reduction whose necessity I pointed out earlier. I should point out that in adopting this line of inquiry I am not departing to any great extent from certain Greek or even from certain modern approaches. Regarding man as innately violent and conflict as inevitable, the Greeks sometimes conceived of the polis as an entity within which the human propensity to violence could be to some extent checked and regulated. A state is, as Aristotle put it, an arena for conflicting interests. Only in an impossible 'ideal' state could conflict be transcended entirely in the interest of achieving a good life for all.[64]

Similar conceptualisations of the problem appear in strands of thought that have recently been worked out, independently of each other, in a variety of academic disciplines. For instance, sociobiologists, who deal with the biological bases of social behaviour, have pointed to a correlation between degrees of genetic relatedness and degrees of conflict and co-operation. 'Societies that lack conflict and possess the highest degree of altruism and coordination', wrote Edward O. Wilson, 'are most likely to evolve where all the members are genetically identical.'[65] Among humans, the highest level of co-operation and the lowest level of conflict are found between identical twins. (Among other social animals, they are found between the members of ant colonies made up of clones.) The implication is that the more dissimilar people are, the more their genes will impel them to engage in conflict. Precisely this factor comes into play in the so-called complex societies, in which blood ties cease to act as a major organising principle. Members of such societies, being, as Aristotle remarked in connection with the polis, 'human beings differing in kind', or, as he said in connection with Athenian democracy, 'as much as possible intermingled with one another'[66] (that is, genetically dissimilar), will sooner or later cease to co-operate and engage in conflict unless measures are taken to counteract these genetic dispositions.

An insight derived from game theory and another borrowed from social anthropology may help to complete the picture. Game theorists contend that the essential feature of compact, stable and closely knit political systems

---

[64] Cf. Finley 1983: 2.   [65] E. O. Wilson 1980: 155.

[66] Aristotle, *Politics* 1261a22–4: 'And not only does a city consist of a multitude of human beings, it consists of human beings differing in kind (*ex edei diapheronton*)', and 1319b25–7: Cleisthenes attempts to strengthen Athens' democracy by, amongst other things, 'generally fixing things so that there is as much social intercourse as possible (*hopos an hoti malista anameichthosi pantes allelois*) and a breakdown of the former associations'.

is that conflicts do not assume the shape of a zero-sum game, in which one player's gain is another's loss, but rather that of a non-zero-sum game, in which the urge ruthlessly to press home any advantage is moderated by feelings of mutual dependence. The sense of belonging to the same social system somehow promotes accommodation and eventually collaboration, minimising the risk that conflict will erupt and checking the escalation of any conflict that does arise.[67] This conception is paralleled by the suggestion, progressively gaining ground in anthropological theory and in the behavioural sciences, that the principal driving force behind the evolution of cultures is not the social-Darwinian principle of 'war of each against all', but rather the impulse to attenuate conflict in everyday life by gradually subjecting it to the control of impartial institutions.[68]

In the light of theories such as these, my own suggestion that we should direct our attention to how members of a community interacted in situations involving co-operation and conflict should appear less radical and off-beat than might otherwise have been the case. I shall therefore make no apology either for adopting the line of inquiry outlined above or for consequently omitting from my analysis certain types of human activity that sometimes figure under the heading 'code of behaviour'. I should perhaps, however, warn the reader of one thing. This book will have much to say about how the people of Athens provided each other with moral support and practical assistance, how they reacted when cheated, offended, betrayed or assaulted by others and whether or not they involved their relatives, friends and gods in their quarrels and fights. It is, however, unlikely to say much about the sort of thing that the self-styled 'Member of the Aristocracy' who was the anonymous author of *Manners and Rules of Good Society* regarded as being of paramount importance, such as whether at a dinner party one should eat the oysters preceding the soup with a dinner-fork or a fish-fork.

CO-OPERATION, RECIPROCITY AND EXCHANGE

The concepts of co-operation and conflict have recently become prominent in the social sciences. These concepts are normally considered together with those of 'exchange' and 'reciprocity'. I should comment briefly on these concepts, although it is by no means my intention to give a full account of

---

[67] See, e.g., Rapoport 1974; Axelrod and Hamilton 1981; Axelrod 1984; Taylor 1987; Molm 1997; Wedekind and Milinski 2000. This proposition is developed in Chapter 10.

[68] See especially D. T. Campbell 1978; the articles collected in Hinde and Watson 1995; Hinde and Groebel 1991, incorporating earlier literature on the subject. This proposition is developed in Chapter 8.

the many theories that have been built around them, from Mauss through Malinowski and Polanyi to Sahlins and beyond. I intend rather to highlight those aspects of these concepts that bear most closely on the concept of the code of behaviour that I am advancing here.[69]

Exchange, in its most elementary form, is a co-operative activity designed to bridge the gap that separates production from consumption. Since human beings cannot usually achieve self-sufficiency by consuming exactly what they produce, exchange must be reckoned an indispensable building block of social life. Two people trade surpluses of different sorts, each exchanging something that he has in abundance for something that he lacks. The complexity of the transaction increases when the things that are being traded are qualitatively different: status and leadership, patronage and political support, loyalty and material benefits. When reciprocation thus comes in different currency, the definition of exchange must be extended to include actions and attitudes of a non-material nature. In exchange theory the total sum of 'things' of this sort flowing between the exchanging parties is subsumed under the title 'goods and services'. This term serves as a neutral cover-all for a great variety of objects, emotional states, actions and transactions that in different cultures become differentiated and acquire their own names and moral evaluations: gifts, payments, fees, loans, guarantees, bribes, prizes, rewards, goodwill, gratitude, sympathy and love.

Goods and services may flow from one party to another in diverse and manifold ways. A gift, for example, may be reciprocated with a gift or a service of inferior, equal or superior value, or may go entirely unreciprocated. A transaction may be a *prestation totale* (an exchange involving the whole of the parties' social personalities) or a narrow, specific bargain in which no personalities are involved. It may be a unique, one-off exchange or a lengthy, ongoing process. The initial transfer may, as Sahlins has observed, 'be voluntary, involuntary, prescribed, contracted; the return freely bestowed, exacted, or dunned, the exchange haggled or not, the subject of accounting or not.'[70] As time is another variable (returns may follow promptly upon the initial supply of goods or rendition of services, but may also be delayed for various lengths of time), variations in forms of exchange may be expected to increase at an exponential rate. Add to this the fact

---

[69] In addition to the works cited in the footnotes that follow, I have drawn in a more general way on Homans 1957–8; Mauss 1966; Finley 1978a; Gergen, Greenberg and Willis 1980; Donlan 1981–2, 1982, 1989, 1997a; I. Morris 1986a; Herman 1987; Gallant 1991: ch. 6; Offer 1997; Millett 1991; Davis 1992; J. Gould 1991; Ridley 1996; Mitchell 1997; Gill, Postlethwaite and Seaford 1998; van Wees 1998b; Konstan 1998.

[70] Sahlins 1974: 193.

that exchange occurs not just once, between two partners, but all the time, between all the members of a society, and we are confronted by a staggering multiplicity of exchanges, a number so large that it might be presumed to comprehend all the variant forms of exchange enumerated above.

It is important to realise that this is not so. Despite this multiplicity, not all societies practise the same range of exchange patterns. It is reasonable to assume that each society has a spectrum of its own, or rather a peculiar combination of exchanges whose details have been worked out and whose implicit rules have been passed on from one generation to another through a slow process of adjustment, trial and error. An example from anthropology may help to support this assumption. The social institutions that go by the household names of *kula*, *potlach* and *burita'ulo* can all be reduced to the parameters indicated above: reciprocity, delay, specificity and voluntariness. The argument that I would like to advance is that other exchange systems that are not identified by this sort of name also display these parameters.

This point may be reinforced using an example derived from empiricism. During the course of a lifetime every person takes part in a great many deals and social transactions (agreements, purchases, commitments, promises). These may or may not involve expressions of approval or indignation, or dispensations of love, liking, dislike or hatred. It is strikingly clear that these deals or transactions are neither haphazard nor erratic. They have certain regular features, expressed in specific forms that can only be recognised for what they are by reference to the group to which the parties belong. People all over the world contract marriage agreements and this in itself involves no rules or conventions. Contracting such an agreement in a particular way, however (by stipulating the payment of a bride-price or dowry, for example), does. People everywhere react badly to being slapped in the face and again the fact of that reaction involves no rules or conventions. The exact form that the reaction takes, however (whether the person who has been insulted returns the slap, kills his assailant, challenges him to a duel or takes him to court), does. The rules and conventions that determine specific forms of behaviour vary from one society to another, there being perhaps as many rules and conventions as there are societies. Every society, not just that of the Trobrianders, has, in other words, developed and made predominant a peculiar 'formula' (or a peculiar combination of formulae) for carrying out such transactions. It is my contention that, given adequate documentation, it is possible to uncover the particulars of this formula in any society, even if its members are unaware of them or incapable of expressing them in words.

I should perhaps add that I am not alone in this assumption. Seeking to define the essence of 'civilisation', Fernand Braudel came to a very similar conclusion by looking at the matter from a completely different angle. 'In every period', he wrote, 'a certain view of the world, a collective mentality, dominates the whole mass of society. Dictating a society's attitudes, guiding its choices, confirming its prejudices and directing its actions, this is very much a fact of civilization.'[71]

Let us now move on to the wider social phenomenon that is sometimes called 'positive reciprocity'. This kind of reciprocity takes place within the context of amicable (that is, non-hostile) relationships. By its operation, upon being given valuable goods or rendered useful services a person feels obliged to reciprocate, perhaps by returning even more valuable goods or rendering even more useful services. In 1859 Darwin referred to this as a 'lowly motive'. Subsequent research, however, revealed its force, observing that it served as a kind of peg on which throughout history numerous social institutions (friendship, patronage, feudalism and corruption, for example) had been hung. Social psychologists hold positive reciprocity to be an essential rule of behaviour (perhaps even a biological determinant) that has developed in humans in response to evolutionary pressures. 'A widely shared and strongly held feeling of future obligation', as Cialdini has put it, 'made an enormous difference in human social evolution because it meant that one person could give something (for example, food, energy, care) to another with confidence that it was not being lost.'[72] The recipient is left in a state of 'indebtedness', from which state he can redeem himself by returning goods or services whose value is equivalent to or greater than the original goods or services. It is not always realised how powerfully the sense of obligation to reciprocate is felt. A telling example of this can be seen in the free samples that are sometimes offered in modern supermarkets. Customers who taste a product tend to feel psychologically indebted and subconsciously bound to return the favour, unknowingly (and sometimes even unwillingly) purchasing considerably more of the product than those who resisted the temptation to taste it.[73]

'Returns' need not always be forthcoming immediately, nor need they be of the same order as the original gift or service. In the long run, however, and allowing for slight temporary imbalances, they must be equal to it in value and offer their recipient equal benefit. If this is achieved reciprocity is seen as well balanced, with neither party owing the other anything. If it is not,

---

[71] F. Braudel (1987) *A History of Civilisations*. Harmondsworth: Penguin: 22.
[72] Cialdini 1984: 30.   [73] Cialdini 2001: 62.

the non-reciprocating or under-reciprocating party is seen as being in the other's debt. People everywhere seem to have an intuitive understanding of the value of exchangeable items, integrating into their appraisals parameters such as norms, standards, ends, the status of each party in relation to the other, the history of the relationship and official hindrances. They may thus conceive of an exchange as 'fair' even if they rate it inequitable. Social scientists may be right in believing that this is the starting point of moral thinking and indeed one of the universals of social life.[74] A dread of unfair returns must have acted as a driving force behind the invention of coinage.

Early students of exchange focused their attention on the partners, on the items exchanged and on the ways in which reciprocity was structured, paying relatively little attention to the wider background against which such transactions were conducted; it seems to have been assumed that they were conducted, as it were, in a social vacuum. Only relatively lately has it become apparent that the operation of exchange relations should be examined within structures of mutual dependence, the partners being united by ties that should to a greater or lesser extent be regarded as enduring.[75] Within these structures three forms of exchange relation can be observed: direct, generalised and productive (see **Fig. 1.2**). In social life, of course, two or more of these types of exchange are generally combined; once again the nature of the combination may vary from one culture to another.

The mutual dependence between exchanging partners may also vary in degree. The rules of the game change substantially when the parties are tied by special bonds of intimacy that go beyond the general context of mutual dependence. Relations between kin, lovers and sometimes even friends are usually exempt from the scheme of commensurate returns. The parties in such relationships are generally supposed to provide goods and services altruistically, so that, as Marshall Sahlins has put it, 'the social side of the transaction repress[es] the material.'[76] Feeding one's children, for example, or helping one's aged parents, is not generally conditional upon reciprocation, nor is the widespread practice of helping one's relatives in an emergency.[77] (Modern studies show that the expectation that one

---

[74] Gouldner 1960; Greenberg 1980.

[75] I am indebted for what follows in the next paragraph to Molm 1997 and Thibaut and Kelley 1978. For the distinction between 'direct' and 'indirect' reciprocity, see Alexander 1979: 49–50; Wedekind and Milinski 2000.

[76] Cf. Sahlins 1974: 194.

[77] In the animal world, this principle could be expressed mathematically: individuals will be selected to perform altruistic acts for the benefit of relatives when $rb - c > 0$, c being the cost in fitness to the altruist, b the benefit in fitness to the beneficiary, and r their degree of genetic similarity (Hamilton 1964; cf. West, Pen and Griffin 2002).

Relations of **direct exchange** are characterised by the direct movement of goods and services from one partner to another, the outcome of each such movement depending on nothing but the other partner's behaviour.

a. Direct exchange

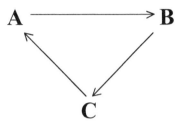 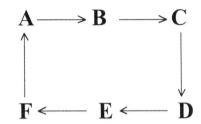

b.1 Generalised (indirect, simple) exchange

b.2 Generalised (indirect, compound) exchange

Relations of **generalised exchange** are marked by the indirect movement of goods and services from one partner to another with one or more further partners intervening in their flow. In the end the initiating partner may receive his or her return from somebody other than the first interacting partner. The larger such a system is, the more indirect, and therefore the more diffuse, the mutual benefits are perceived to be.

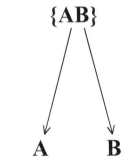

Relations of **productive exchange** are distinguished by the need for both partners to co-operate in order for either to obtain benefits: neither can obtain benefits for him/herself or for the other solely by means of his/her own actions (as when, for example, two partners co-author a book).

c. Productive exchange

Figure 1.2 Types of exchange (adapted from Molm 1997*)
The types of exchange that we are concerned with, rather than operating in a social vacuum, are normally contained within wider systems of mutual dependence. The partners' behaviour vis-à-vis each other is influenced by the fact that these systems are stable, enduring (in other words, having accomplished an exchange one cannot afford to forget about one's partner, but must take into account the possibility that one will have dealings with him/her in the future) and capable of exercising coercion (i.e., they may be used to force a defaulting partner to abide by his/her obligations). In the language of game theory, this principle may be expressed as follows: 'repetition and reciprocity combine to make mutual cooperation a viable strategy, because although a defector will receive an immediate reward, reciprocity means that he will suffer for this choice in the long run' (Stephens, McLinn and Stevens 2002).

*The distinction between simple and compound exchange is my own, not Molm's.

will help one's relatives in an emergency is deeply ingrained, perhaps even biologically conditioned: people tend to take the obligation for granted, extending help to their relatives, by blood or by marital ties, above friends or neighbours.)[78] The same holds good of relationships between lovers, which are renowned for the self-sacrifice that they entail. Friendship differs from both of these sets of relationships in that favours rendered within its context do generate a sense of obligation to reciprocate, often by returning a favour not merely equal to but more valuable than the favour received. The evaluation of fair requital is not, however, unconditional, but depends on the level of intimacy that exists between the partners. When this is low, a pedantic reckoning of outstanding debts is not out of the question. When it is high, this sort of reckoning is perceived as inappropriate. In particular, when friends are united by emotional rather than instrumental ties they tend to cherish, or at least feign, sentiments that impel altruistic actions. This principle has been formulated emblematically in a maxim incorporated into the *Problems* once attributed to Aristotle: 'Where a loan is involved, there is no friend; for if a man is a friend he does not lend but gives.'[79]

The rules change once again when exchanges take place within the context of a hostile relationship. Professional literature is full of suggestions as to how to conceptualise this kind of 'negative reciprocity'. Social psychologists who confront this problem in studying aggression, for example, distinguish between 'helping' and 'hurting' behaviour, breaking down the former into 'altruistic' and 'instrumental' behaviour and the latter into 'affective' and 'instrumental' behaviour. The legitimacy of some of these categories has on occasion been contested, but on the whole certain vague definitions such as those that follow tend to be accepted as valid. Altruistic help is defined as behaviour carried out to benefit another person without any anticipation of external reward (social recognition or gratitude, for example). Instrumental help, by contrast, is carried out in the anticipation of such reward. Affective hurt (or aggression) is behaviour designed to inflict injury or pain upon the victim or upon personal property in a way that will indirectly affect the victim's well-being. Instrumental hurt (or aggression) is behaviour that is intended to procure some personal or social good (such as money or excitement) or to fulfil some role expectation (as when a policeman injures a criminal), irrespective of the victim's well-being.[80]

---

[78] R. Firth, J. Hubert and A. Forge (1969) *Families and Their Relatives*. London: Routledge and Kegan Paul; A. M. Lang and E. M. Brody (1983) 'Characteristics of middle-aged daughters and help to their elderly mothers', *Journal of Marriage and the Family* 45: 193–202.

[79] [Aristotle], *Problems* 29.2.950a28.

[80] Hogg and Vaughan 1995: ch. 11; Geen 1990; Bandura 1973.

Sociology has evolved another way of looking at this problem. Sahlins, who defines negative reciprocity as 'the attempt to get something for nothing with impunity', has identified a whole range of variations within this context, including various forms of appropriation, haggling, barter, gambling, chicanery and theft. These are social situations in which the parties 'confront each other as opposed interests, each looking to maximize utility at the other's expense', the aim of both being 'unearned increment'. 'One of the most sociable forms, leaning toward balance', he writes, 'is haggling conducted in the spirit of "what the traffic will bear". From this, negative reciprocity ranges through various degrees of cunning, guile, stealth, and violence to the finesse of a well-conducted horse raid. The "reciprocity" is, of course, conditional again, a matter of defence of self-interest. So the flow may be one-way once more, reciprocation contingent upon mustering countervailing pressure or guile.'[81]

Having gone through this array of features, I should perhaps return to the concept of the code of behaviour and say a few words about how this is related to exchange theory. One difference in particular stands out. It concerns the distinctness or unity of the two major types of reciprocity, positive and negative. Exchange theory tends to view these categories as methodologically distinct, the implication being that they are conceived of as operating independently of each other: when concrete societies come under examination, attention is focused on either positive or negative reciprocity rather than on both simultaneously. Within the context of a code of behaviour, by contrast, every type of reciprocity, whether positive or negative, will be considered under the same heading. This will allow us to draw together into a single comprehensive whole the entire multiplicity of interactions in which an individual becomes involved, thus producing a much closer approximation to real-life patterns.

In this book I propose to examine how the various forms of reciprocity, exchange, co-operation and conflict were involved in structuring a single compact social system. Exchanges that took place between members of the community of ancient Athens will thus be examined in the light of the exchanges that took place between members of the community and the community itself, something that exchange theory has, to the best of my knowledge, never before attempted. To make myself clearer, I should perhaps present the problem in terms of the categories that we worked out earlier. What we have here is in fact an expanded version of the generalised type of exchange expounded in **Fig. 1.2**.

---

[81] Sahlins 1974: 195.

Anything done by an individual for the community of which he is a member may produce payoffs via two channels.[82] The directly personal channel (**P**) conveys specific payoffs through the medium of direct exchange (both positive and negative) with other members of the community. The impersonal channel (**C**) conveys more generalised payoffs via largely 'abstract' relationships with the community as a whole. The total reward (**R**) that converges upon the individual (which can be positive or negative) may be expressed by the simple equation $\mathbf{R} = \mathbf{P} + \mathbf{C}$. If **R** is negative, the willingness of the individual to act in the community's interest may be extinguished (unless he is a masochist); if **R** is positive, his devotion to the community will naturally be reinforced. If **P** is negative and **C** positive, then the absolute value of **P** must be less than that of **C** to produce a reinforcing reward.

The method of analysing interactions involving co-operation or conflict that I propose to use in this book will take into consideration both direct individual rewards (**P**) and rewards coming via the community (**C**). Individuals who know in their hearts that certain types of personal interaction will affect not only themselves but also the community of which they are a part will strive to strike a delicate balance such as to maximise the rewards accruing from both systems. Precisely how and why people achieved a certain kind of balance under the Athenian democracy is the principal question addressed in this book. The answer will reveal a code of behaviour highly unusual, if not unique, within the array of cultures that gave rise to western civilisation.

---

[82] This distinction, commonly made in the behavioural sciences (see Hardin 1978), is developed at pp. 391–402.

CHAPTER 2

Athenian society and government

PHYSICAL ENVIRONMENT AND POPULATION

Athens was one of the largest and perhaps one of the most atypical of about 1,500 small independent poleis that made up the Greek world. Before broaching the issue of co-operation and conflict within her wider communal system, we should remind ourselves of a little background information about her, which will be added to as the argument unfolds. This should help to make clearer the connections between Athens' values and behaviour and her large-scale systems.

To begin with, the Athenians did not merely live with their backs to the sea, as did many a Mediterranean seaboard community; they were seafarers *par excellence*. Early in the fifth century they had consciously decided to become maritime[1] and thenceforth they travelled, traded and fought by sea. They surrounded their city with a substantial wall that also incorporated the Peiraeus, turning its three landlocked harbours into a minor civic centre seething with people from all four corners of the Mediterranean; they built a fleet of more than 300 warships that virtually controlled the eastern Mediterranean and between 478 and 404 they ruled over a maritime empire that encompassed most of the coastal and island communities of the Aegean basin (see **Fig. 2.1**).

The Athenians were doing much more than adopting a way of life appropriate to their geographic situation. The 'wine-dark sea' that had once mesmerised Homer's audiences stirred their imagination too; it was often said to account for their restless and adventurous nature. The Athenians, complained the Corinthian delegates to Sparta on the eve of the Peloponnesian War, were always abroad, thinking that the farther they went the more they would get (Thucydides 1.70). The sea could take you away to unknown worlds, holding out the promise of adventure far beyond the

---

[1] Herodotus 1.144; *The Athenian Constitution* 22.7. For Themistocles' promotion of the decision, see Labarbe 1957. For the linking of the Peiraeus to the *asty*, see Amit 1961; 1965 and Garland 1987.

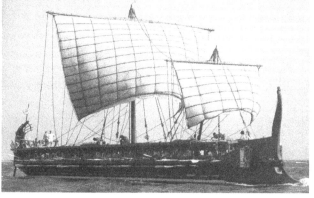

Figure 2.1 The Athenian warship

In the vase-painting shown in the upper photograph an Athenian warship (*trieres*), on the right, is ramming an enemy ship. The photograph below shows a modern reconstruction of a *trieres* (cf. Morrison, Coates and Rankov 2000). In the fifth and fourth centuries a warship of this type would have been c. 37m long and c. 6m wide. Propulsion was delivered by 170 oarsmen, arranged in groups of three and sitting one above another, supplemented by two sails. The crew also included sixteen ship's specialists (a steersman, a boatswain, a purser, a bow officer, a shipwright, a piper and ten sailors) and fourteen infantry soldiers (ten hoplites and four archers). The ship's principal weapon was a bronze ram fixed to the prow at the water-line. Eyes painted on the prow were intended magically to out-stare the enemy. Operating such a ship was a costly business that was undertaken by turns by the Athenian super-rich as one of their 'liturgies' (the services to the community upon which the wealthy were expected to spend part of their wealth and time). The ship, its basic equipment and its crew's wages were normally provided by the state, but its command and the costs of its maintenance for a year devolved upon the *trierarchos* (Gabrielsen 1994). On the eve of the Peloponnesian War, Pericles claimed that Athens numbered among her own citizens more and better steersmen and sailors than the rest of Hellas put together (Thucydides 1.143.1). A source of pride and strength, the warships anchored in the harbours could be seen from the Acropolis and the Pnyx. Meanwhile, seamen sailing in from Sounion would have seen the upper part of the colossal statue of the goddess Athena, dubbed 'Promachos' (Front-rank), rising above the Propylaea on the Acropolis (Pausanias 1.28.2).

reach of landlubbers. Sophocles sang the praises of man's daring and invention in contriving to subdue the sea's thunderous waves (*Antigone* 335–7) and another Athenian, Thucydides, contended that no mere farmer who knew nothing of the sea could hope to achieve anything of note (1.142.7). After the Sicilian debacle Thucydides looked back on the mood of 415 and opined that the Athenians had been carried away by their own fantasies. The men of military age, he said, had longed for distant sights and spectacles, quite confident that they would return home safely (6.24.3).

Not everybody judged the Athenians so indulgently. In a much-quoted passage Plato charmingly compared the entire Greek population to ants or frogs by a pond (*Phaedo* 109b). Elsewhere, probably with the ideal of the determinedly terrestrial Spartans in mind, he was less charitable, branding the sea a 'teacher of vice' (cf. Strabo 7.3.8), a source of corruption and moral degeneration that created 'a people of shopkeepers': 'for by filling the markets of the city with foreign merchandise and retail trading, and breeding in the men's souls knavish and tricky ways, it renders the city faithless and loveless, not to itself alone, but to the rest of the world as well'.[2] Aristotle was only slightly less scathing, believing that as far as commercial relations, intercourse with strangers and the increase of the maritime population were concerned the sea was indeed detrimental to the city's moral health and to good order. In economic and military terms, however, he deemed it indispensable.[3]

This disapproving belief that the sea had a pernicious effect upon human character was presumably fostered by a dislike of democracy. Athens' democracy was closely involved with the sea; much of her wealth and international status sprang from her mastery of the waves, a mastery achieved through the efforts of the lower classes. Writing during the second century of the Christian era, Plutarch echoed an entrenched enemy of democracy usually known as the Old Oligarch (1.2) when he remarked that after the completion of the long walls 'Themistocles did not only knead up, as Aristophanes says, the port and the city (polis) into one, but made the city absolutely the dependant and the adjunct of the port, and the land of the sea, which increased the power and confidence of the people (*demos*) against the nobility; the authority coming into the hands of sailors and boatswains and pilots' (*Themistocles* 19.4–5, trans. John Dryden, cf. Aristophanes, *Knights* 815).

---

[2] *Laws* 4.705a, trans. R. G. Bury. This was later echoed by Strabo: 'Plato thinks that those who want a well-governed city ought to shun the sea as a teacher of vice (*ponerodidaskalos*)' *Geography*, 7.3.8. On the 'corrupting sea' throughout the ages, see Horden and Purcell 2000.

[3] *Politics* 1321a13; cf. Amit 1965: 96.

The sea also helped to promote democracy in more subtle ways. It was a doorway to the rest of the world, subverting any tendency to introversion by conveying people, ideas and goods to and from Athens. (This may have been another reason for Plato's dislike of it; he admired the Spartans' seclusion.) Outside influences poured into Athens from every corner of the Mediterranean, diversifying the city's population and permanently enriching (or contaminating, this being a matter of opinion) its world view. Athens' language, its way of life and its modes of dress were all affected. The Athenians, writes the Old Oligarch clumsily, 'hear all dialects, and pick one thing from one, another from another; the other Greeks tend to adhere to their own dialect and way of life and dress, but the Athenians have mingled elements from all Greeks and foreigners' (*The Constitution of Athens* 2.8). Both necessities (especially wheat, without imports of which the city would have had difficulty in subsisting, iron, tin, copper and shipping timber, which was not sufficiently abundant locally) and luxuries (semi-precious stones, hides, leather and flax, to say nothing of the magnificent array of imports proudly listed by the contemporary comic playwright Hermippus: silphium stalks and ox-hides from Cyrene, mackerel and every variety of salt fish from the Hellespont, fine flour and ox ribs from Italy, pigs and cheese from Syracuse, rigged sails and papyrus from Egypt, frankincense from Syria, cypress for the gods from Crete, ivory from Libya, dried grapes and dried figs from Rhodes, pears and fat apples from Euboea, slaves from Phrygia, Paphlagonian chestnuts and shiny almonds, dates and fine flour from Phoenicia, rugs and multi-coloured head-cushions from Carthage)[4] flowed continually into the city under the aegis of the powerful Athenian navy.[5] Again the Old Oligarch had something to say about all this. The Athenians, he wrote censoriously (presumably he favoured traditional food), had discovered various 'gastronomic luxuries' by mingling with people from far-flung places: 'the specialities of Sicily, Italy, Cyprus, Egypt, Lydia, Pontus, the Peloponnese or any other area have all been brought back to Athens' (2.7). The Athenians in general seem to have taken great pride in their pan-Mediterranean status. 'Because of the greatness of our polis', boasts Pericles in the Funeral Oration, 'we import the fruits of the entire earth, and enjoy the goods of other countries quite as freely as our own' (Thucydides 2.38.2; cf. Isocrates 4.42, *Panegyricus*).

[4] Hermippus, Fragment 63, from the play known as *Phormophoroi*. Kassel and Austin, 1983–, vol. v: frg. 63, to be consulted with Gilula 2000. For the list of imports see Finley 1973: 133.
[5] For Athenian economic exchange, see pp. 374–91. For the Athenian navy, see B. Jordan 1975 and Gabrielsen 1994.

With her defeat by Sparta in 404 Athens lost her maritime empire, and with it the material benefits that poured into the city in general and into the pockets of the poorer classes in particular. For most of the fourth century, however, her democracy, her navy and her Mediterranean connections remained largely unaffected. Only with the destruction of the Athenian fleet by the Macedonians in 322 did democracy come to an end, and the end of Athens' democracy signalled the eclipse of her greatness.[6]

Despite her maritime preoccupations, Athens' main source of wealth was land. The thinness of the local soil notwithstanding,[7] Athens was an agricultural city-state. The townsmen who lived in Athens were sustained largely by the produce of the land they owned in the Attic countryside (see **Fig. 2.2a**). Here the countrymen, organised into thousands of independent households, lived on the land (see **Fig. 2.3**). In so generally arid a region (Attica gets less than 400 mm of rain a year) they had to exert themselves to make a decent living: to work and to husband the land, as Theophrastus put it.[8] Plots were usually small ('around 30 acres on average even for the wealthier citizens')[9] and belonged to one (or several) of the 139 village units (the so-called 'demes') that were spread all over the countryside. In both town and country the majority of citizens were moderately well-to-do. Poverty may have been the messmate of Hellas, as Herodotus reminds us (7.102.1), but as many as three-quarters of Athens' citizens owned some workable land and perhaps additional properties such as workshops, furnaces, ore-crushing mills or stone-working establishments.[10] Not even the poorest were impoverished in the proper sense of the term, or tormented by the traditional scourges of the peasantry: usurious debts, the accumulation of land in the hands of a few and extortionate dues exacted by a central government.[11] These 'primary producers', as a modern commentator has called them, owned the means of production, paying no regular taxes on

---

[6] Diodorus Siculus 18.15.9. For the brief revivals of democracy that took place during the Hellenistic Age (democracy in name alone, since subservience to external powers denied it the quintessential element of political independence) see Rhodes and Lewis 1997. For democracy in cities other than Athens in the Classical and Hellenistic periods, see Schuller 1979; O'Neil 1995; Robinson 1997. For the origin and 'prehistory' of the word democracy, see Sealey 1973; Hansen 1986; 1994; Asheri 2002.

[7] For physical background and landscape see Osborne 1987; Sallares 1991; Sauerwein 1998.

[8] For rainfall rates, see Osborne 1987: 33. For the life cycles of these ancient households and their strategies for responding to food shortages, see Gallant 1991. For a reconstruction of Attica's agricultural productivity in 329/8, based on epigraphical evidence (*IG* II² 1672), and for the evidential value of Theophrastus in this respect, see Garnsey 1992.

[9] Finley 1952: 58; cf. Burford 1977–8.

[10] On the proposal, made and rejected in 403, that political rights should be restricted to landholders, see p. 249.

[11] Cf. Millett 1991: 76, for the view that the poorer citizens of Athens were better off than many of their counterparts elsewhere in the Greek world.

(a)

Figure 2.2 Attica and Athens: city and country
Athens' territory of about 2,500 square kilometres (1,000 square miles) was no larger than
that of the duchy of Luxembourg. Unlike Luxembourg today, however, Athens was a
major power amidst hundreds of mostly much smaller Greek city-states (cf. Ehrenberg
1960: 26–7). Her society was run on a small scale by our standards and her political
institutions were organised in such a way as to make the physical presence of her citizens
indispensable (a citizen was not, for example, permitted to cast his vote on any general
civic issue from his deme). It has been calculated that more than a third of the rural
population lived more than 24km from the city (Osborne 1985a: 69). In order to attend an
Assembly meeting, these citizens would have had to spend at least one night in the city.
Many of those who did turn up probably owned houses in both the city and the country
(**Fig. 2.5**); others may have stayed with friends or relatives. The map (2.2a) shows a rough
outline of the territories of the Cleisthenic tribes, each including coastal, inland and city
trittyes. The plan (2.2b) shows the *agora* and the area surrounding it. For a plan of the
agora itself, see **Fig. 2.7**.

property or on income and enjoying self-sufficiency in basic foods (cereals,
vegetables, figs, olives and grapes). Except for the grain imports that were
needed in times of shortage, they were independent of the state for their
means of subsistence.[12]

---

[12] I. Morris 1991: 26; cf. Garnsey 1988; Ostwald 1995; Hanson 1998.

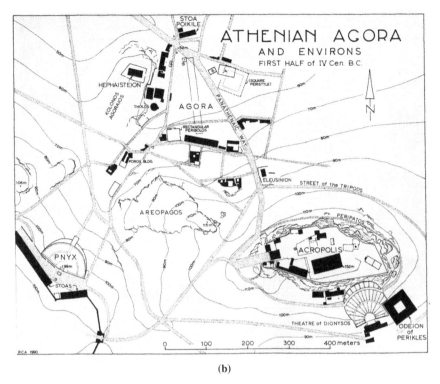

(b)

Figure 2.2 (*cont.*)

Town and country seem to have been remarkably well integrated. In Classical times the Athenians celebrated a festival called the *Synoecia* that commemorated the supposed joining together by the legendary king Theseus of many small rural communities into the single larger community of Athens. Whatever the historical truth behind this legend, the interplay between town and country in later times seems to have been marked by peaceful co-operation rather than by violent competition, conquest or exploitation.[13] Serious disagreements between central and local authorities (the demes had local councils modelled on the central civic institutions) were presumably avoided because the same people participated in both by turns. (The system of government worked out by Cleisthenes demanded a high degree of citizen participation by both town and country dwellers.) The remarkable absence of local faction, the uniformity of material culture

---

[13] For the Peiraeus, which may have been an exception in this respect, see Aristotle, *Politics* 1303b7, with von Reden 1995b.

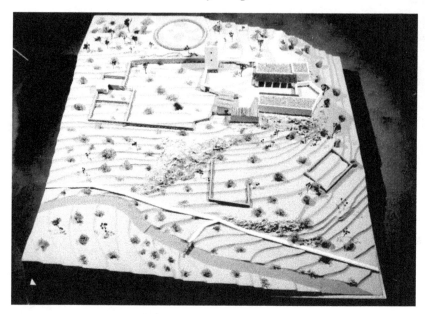

Figure 2.3 Model of a typical Attic farmstead
During the period we are discussing Attica was densely settled with farmsteads such as this
one, Palaia Kopraisia in Legraina (see **Fig. 2.2a**), reconstructed here by Hans Lohmann
(Lohmann 1992: 48). Although Classical farmsteads differed greatly in appearance, all
included living quarters (*oikia*), a courtyard (*aule*) and sometimes a tower (*pyrgos*). Some
also had threshing floors, oil mills and oil presses. A passage from Apollodorus' speech
Against Nicostratus gives a glimpse of the sort of agricultural resources that might have
been found on a farmstead: choice fruiting grafts and tree vines, nursery beds of olive trees
and rose beds ([Demosthenes] 53.15–16). Analysis of agricultural and settlement patterns
throughout Attica conveys a picture of prosperity in the fifth and fourth centuries
(Lohmann 1993; 1995). It may be no coincidence that by the end of the fourth century (i.e.
following the abolition of democracy) signs of abrupt economic decline had become
visible.

and the manner in which goods and services flowed from the town to the
country and vice versa are further evidence that these relationships really did
constitute a peaceful *modus vivendi*.[14] The country's contribution to town
life is illustrated by the steady supply of agricultural products that flowed
into the city, amongst which olives (according to legend, a present from
the goddess Athena to the people of Athens), wine and honey took pride of
place. Silver, one of Athens' great natural resources, came from the mines at

[14] This point is well made in Osborne 1990: 267: 'the citizen body (the *demos*) was united by its
divisions'. For the contrast between the settled condition of Attica and the unsettled nature of the
countryside in Thasos, see Osborne 1987: 79.

Laurion; building materials, especially fine marble and clay, were quarried in the mountains. The countryside also contributed wood and charcoal, used as fuel for both heating and cooking, and was itself a preserve in which game could be hunted and wild fruits and plants collected.[15] The countryside was not, however, cynically exploited, neglected or left to lag behind the town in its development. The building of an impressive series of rural sanctuaries[16] and the continual extension of agriculture into marginal areas are testament to this; both literary sources and archaeological surveys indicate that Attica teemed with villages, farmsteads, agricultural installations and sheepfolds.[17] Sophisticated defence systems were constructed to protect those who lived there (the long walls in the fifth century, a system of fortifications, garrisons and patrols in the fourth); should all else fail, the inhabitants of Attica could withdraw for protection to the Acropolis (which, with its abundant sources of fresh water, was easily defensible)[18] or to the urban area within the walls. To buy goods produced in local workshops or imported from overseas a country-dweller had only to go to the market in the *agora*, or to the Peiraeus. None of this lends much support to any contention that the city might have been parasitic upon the countryside.

During the first quarter of the fifth century the 'long walls' that embraced Athens and the Peiraeus were built (see **Fig. 2.4**). Even though these walls physically separated Attica from Athens, they seem to have done little to impair the unity between town and country. There was the occasional hint of needling (townsmen (*asteioi*) might be represented as sociable, refined and well educated, unlike countrymen (*agroikoi*), who were rough, rude and distrustful of their friends and families, or countrymen described as honest and upright despite their bluntness of speech, unlike the over-eloquent townsmen), but no very serious antagonism developed.[19] When Attica's inhabitants were forced to move inside the city walls during the Spartan invasions the sense of community must have become even stronger, while any differences blurred into insignificance. Thucydides tells us that they

---

[15] Cf. Pausanias 1.32.1: 'The Attic mountains are Pentelicus, where there are quarries, Parnes, where there is hunting of wild boars and bears, and Hymettus, which grows the most suitable pasture for bees . . .' For the interplay between town and country in general see Rich and Wallace-Hadrill 1991; for the particular case of Athens see Dover 1974: 112–14. On stone quarries, see Ampolo 1982 and Osborne 1985a: ch. 5 (with earlier literature on the subject).

[16] At Eleusis, Cape Sunion, Rhamnous, Brauron and Cape Zoster (see **Fig. 2.2a**). For the importance of extramural cults to towns in Greek city-states in general, see de Polignac 1984.

[17] Cf. Osborne 1985d; Snodgrass 1987–9; Lohmann 1992 and 1993; Hanson 1998; Foxhall 1998a.

[18] Cf. Crouch 1993: ch. 18.   [19] Ehrenberg 1951: 83–9; Dover 1974: 112–14.

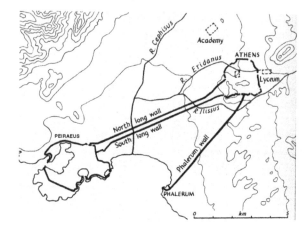

Figure 2.4 The city walls and the long walls

In 477/6, fearing a Spartan attack, the city's entire population worked together to erect a city wall. Mercilessly demolishing any private houses or public buildings that stood in their way, they threw up the wall to a defensible height in an amazingly short time. Thucydides tells us that the foundations were hastily concocted out of an assortment of ill-matched and sometimes ill-fitting pieces of stone, including fragments of sculpture and pillars taken from tombs (1.93.2). This description is borne out by a surviving fragment of the wall (lower image) and by stones from an athlete's tomb, now in the Athenian National Museum (see **Figs. 8.5** top, **8.7** bottom and **8.9** bottom), but previously built into the wall just as Thucydides describes. The long walls were built between 461 and 456 to incorporate the three natural harbours of the Peiraeus into the city's defence system. This safeguarded Athens' supply of sea-borne provisions and helped to turn her into a maritime empire. When the Peloponnesian War broke out most of Attica's population moved inside the walls and lived there intermittently until the end of the war. After the defeat of Athens in 404 the walls were pulled down to the sound of flutes (Xenophon, *Hellenica* 2.2.20–3), but they were rebuilt at the beginning of the fourth century following the re-establishment of democracy. The defeat must, however, have taught the Athenians a lesson. In the fourth century there are clear signs of a new defensive mentality that manifested itself in the creation of an elaborate system of routes, forts, watchtowers, garrisons and patrols intended to protect Athenian territory from the ravages of invasion (cf. Ober 1985; Munn 1993; Hanson 1998).

abandoned their homes 'sadly and reluctantly', leaving behind what each man regarded as his own polis.[20] They had now to prepare to change their whole 'way of life' (*diaita*, 2.16.2).

Both socially and economically, the pivotal unit of Athenian life was the propertied family.[21] Greek thinkers regarded the *oikos* (a word that can, according to its context, mean 'house', 'household', 'the property that a person owns', or 'family', either nuclear or extended)[22] and the *ousia* ('that which is one's own', 'one's substance', or 'property', usually encompassing land, houses, money and slaves) as the twin backbones of the *polis* (see **Figs. 2.5** and **5.1**). The family had ideological as well as concrete significance; each had its hearth, its religious ceremonies and its imagined connection with the ancestors, who were usually buried on the family plot.

Marriages were monogamous, property passing down from one generation to the next. The polis was most concerned that inheritance should be effected smoothly. Breaking the continuity of the family line in terms of property ownership (or, as the Athenians put it, allowing the *oikos* to become 'desolate', which would also result in the discontinuation of its cult) amounted to an outrage that only the most irresponsible of citizens would dream of inflicting upon the community.[23] Private holdings were inherited in the male line and were subdivided if the family had more than one son.[24] In the absence of male children females could inherit, but were not empowered to have legal charge of the holdings. At marriage daughters were provided with dowries in the form of money or moveable property, prosperous families vying to outdo each other in conspicuous expenditure.[25] Men married relatively late in life (probably in their late twenties), women relatively early (probably in their early teens). The demographic upshot of this was that there were a lot of widows in Athenian society.[26]

---

[20] For buildings and land occupancy, not merely in Attica but throughout Greece, see Osborne 1985d.

[21] For wider (real or fictive) kinship and cult groups in Athens (the *gene* and *phratriai*), more concerned with cultic matters than with power politics, see J. K. Davies 1981: 105–14, incorporating earlier literature on the subject.

[22] For this I am much indebted to Sallares 1991: 196–8; Cox 1998; Patterson 1998; Roy 1999.

[23] The strength of the feeling thereby generated is conveyed by (e.g.) Lysias 7.41, *On the Olive Stump*; Isaeus 2.10, *On the Estate of Menecles*; 7.30, *On the Estate of Apollodorus*; Demosthenes 43.12, *Against Macartatus*.

[24] Cf. Asheri 1963; Lane Fox 1985. For measures to counterbalance the tendency towards fragmentation, see Snodgrass 1987–9: 55.

[25] Cf. Finley 1952: 80.

[26] For the omnipresence of widows in Athenian society and the fact that they had rather greater control over their own wealth than widows in other societies, see Hunter 1989. For stepmothers, see Watson 1995: 50–91.

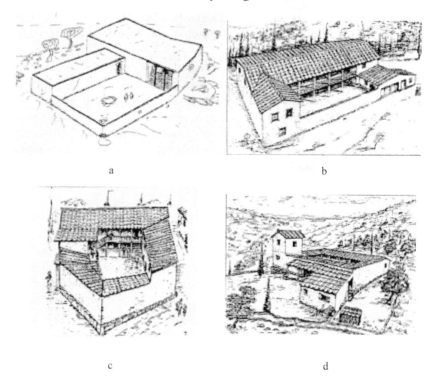

a   b

c   d

**Figure 2.5 Reconstructions of typical Attic houses: (a) a fairly modest farmhouse in
the countryside at Hagia Photini; (b) a handsome house in the countryside (the
'Dema house'); (c) a spacious late fourth-century house inside the city walls,
southwest of the Areopagus; (d) a big house near Vari (see Fig. 2.2a).**
Built out of sun-dried brick on stone or rubble foundations, houses such as these may well
have been a prominent feature of the Attic landscape under democracy. Like the farmstead
considered above (**Fig. 2.3**), they convey a picture of prosperity. This bears out literary
accounts such as that attributed to Pericles, who apparently remarked that the people of
Athens found a beauty and good taste in their houses that delighted them and drove away
their cares (Thucydides 2.38), the casual assertion of the fourth-century anonymous
Oxyrhynchus Historian that the Athenian countryside was 'the most lavishly furnished' in
Greece (12.4–5; Thucydides 2.14–16) and indeed Demosthenes' accusation that some
politicians owned houses more grandiose than many public buildings (23.207–8, *Against
Aristocrates*). Elsewhere Thucydides reports that after the Spartans devastated Attica 'the
richer classes had lost their fine estates with their rich and well equipped houses in the
country' (2.65). Houses (b) and (d) may have been two of these. On Attic houses in
general, see Jones, Sackett and Graham 1962; J. W. Graham 1974; J. E. Jones 1975;
Hoepfner and Schwander 1986: 12–19 (houses in the Peiraeus); Nevett 1999.

Under Athenian law women could not administer property unless superintended by a guardian (*kyrios*, literally 'lord', i.e. husband or male relative
of citizen status).[27] Their position in society must, however, have improved
with the legislation promoted by Pericles in the 450s. His so-called 'citizenship law', which declared all Athenians to be a sort of artificial descent
group, brought in the provision that no male Athenian should be entitled to citizenship unless not only his father but also his mother was a
citizen;[28] unless he met these criteria he counted as a 'bastard' (*nothos*).[29]
The incongruity between women's centrality in reproducing the existing
social order and their marginality in the community's economic and political life nonetheless remained striking. Restricted to the household and
largely excluded from the masculine domain, they dealt with childcare,
cleaning and washing, spinning and weaving, the storage and distribution
of goods and the supervision of slaves. If they were not particularly rich
they might also work outside the household as midwives, wet nurses, wash-
erwomen or ribbon sellers to supplement the family's income when times
were hard.[30] When they were not providing men in general with constant
emotional support (no trifling matter), the only specific medium in which
they could excel outside the household was religion. Their contribution to
private rites such as weddings and wakes and to certain public festivities and
acts of worship was indispensable.[31] In particular, the huge and magnificent
rectangular woollen robe known as the *peplos* that was displayed like a sail
on a ship's mast and drawn through the city at the Greater Panathenaea
was woven by Athenian maidens. Women were, however, excluded from
most other fields of communal activity, in particular, politics, so that their
centrality in their city's collective representations appears paradoxical. As
A. W. Gomme has put it, '. . . There is, in fact, no literature, no art of
any country, in which women are more prominent, more important, more

---

[27] For the exceptional case of the 'heiress' (*epikleros*), i.e. an orphaned daughter who was allowed to
inherit property on condition that she marry a relative, see Burford 1993: 45.
[28] *The Athenian Constitution* 26.4; Plutarch, *Pericles* 37, 2–5. Cf. Patterson 1981; Wiedemann 1983; and
especially Osborne 1997. For the origins of citizenship in earlier times, see Manville 1990.
[29] Previously only sons born outside marriage had been considered bastards. See Patterson 1990 and
Ogden 1996: 59–61, incorporating earlier literature on the subject.
[30] For the categories of Athenian women denoted in the sources as *hetairai*, *pallakai* and *pornai* (loosely
translatable as 'mistresses', 'concubines' and 'prostitutes'), see Dover 1978: 20–3; Sealey 1984; Just
1989: 52–3 and 62–6; Mossé 1991.
[31] Here I am drawing heavily on Hadas 1936; Ste. Croix 1970; Lévy 1976b; Schaps 1979; Raepsaet 1981; Arthur 1982; Humphreys 1983a; Wiedemann 1983; Just 1989; D. Cohen 1989; Pomeroy
1991; Cartledge 1993b; Demand 1994; Jameson 1997b; Osborne 1997; S. Lewis 2002; and especially
S. Blundell 1995, 1998a, 1998b. For a reflection of women's role in public ritual, see Aristophanes,
Lysistrata 641–7.

carefully studied and with more interest, than in the tragedy, sculpture, and painting of fifth-century Athens.'[32]

This brings us to perhaps the most intriguing feature of Athenian life: the exercise of state power.

ATHENIAN POLITICS AND INSTITUTIONS

In the period between 508/7 (when Cleisthenes created democracy) and 322/1 (when it was abolished by the Macedonian regent Antipater) the Athenians embarked on a constitutional experiment that had, so far as we know, never been tried before throughout the history of pre-industrial Europe.[33] Rather than concentrating power in the hands of a monarch or a small coterie of noblemen, they decided to decentralise it, widening its basis to a hitherto unprecedented extent. A correct understanding of the achievement of democracy requires recognition of two of its essential consequences: the common people were incorporated into the political community and the power of the old aristocracy diminished correspondingly. 'Our constitution is called democracy because it is governed in the interests not of a few people but of the majority', explained the idolised fifth-century democratic leader Pericles in the Funeral Oration ascribed to him by Thucydides (2.37.1). The practical implementation of this principle in the everyday life of Athens must count as a landmark in the history of the lower classes even if we allow that the relatively wealthy remained slightly over-represented among the politically active.[34]

The key terms were popular participation and collective rule. Every male Athenian citizen, irrespective of birth, occupation and, with a few exceptions, economic status, had the right to wield power as an official or Council member and actively to participate in the decision-making process at the Assembly whether or not he currently held any official position. Binding governmental decisions were reached in two essential stages: an open, coercion-free discussion, then a majority vote, taken on the egalitarian 'one man, one vote' principle. The results of such votes were often unexpected. In modern democracies the outcome of a vote can frequently be predicted given the relative numbers of party representatives present, but

---

[32] Gomme 1925: 4.

[33] For an extensive analysis of the features outlined here (and much more) see Finley 1983. Hansen 1991 is a detailed exposé of the constitution and Hansen 1987 of the Assembly. The best account of the Council of Five Hundred is Rhodes 1972. For the evolution of democracy in chronological perspective, see Forrest 1966; Ostwald 1986; Meier 1998.

[34] Cf. Osborne 1985a: 68; J. T. Roberts 1986; Eder 1997.

in Athens' direct democracy, which had no parties, voting had an essential element of unpredictability. Decisions, once taken, were put into practice in an orderly way through the agency of a large number of annually elected officials. These officials had only a small staff, in no way resembling the extensive bureaucracies of modern democracies

Two major institutions were involved in the political process. The Assembly was, in the words of a modern commentator, 'the crown of the system'.[35] It met regularly four times a lunar month, usually on the Pnyx (southwest of the Acropolis, see **Fig. 2.6**; cf. **Fig. 2.2b**), but on special occasions at the Theatre of Dionysus or in the Peiraeus. Its conventional form was that of an open-air mass meeting, most decisions being reached in a single continuous sitting. The Assembly made all policy decisions and had the power to deal with business of almost unlimited scope. It was open to all Athenians; Xenophon records the presence of 'fullers, tanners, builders, bronze-smiths, farmers, travelling merchants, and those who exchange in the *agora* and consider what they can buy for less and sell for more' (*Memorabilia* 3.7.6). Any citizen could propose a motion or an amendment.[36] The Assembly's sovereignty was one of the supreme claims of Athenian democracy, careful measures being taken to prevent any group or institution from rivalling it in power.[37] Although it was possible to appeal against an Assembly decision at the popular law courts, the conclusion, sometimes voiced by researchers, that the Assembly's sovereignty was thereby compromised seems to be largely unwarranted.[38]

The Council consisted of five hundred citizens over the age of thirty appointed annually by lot, fifty from each of the ten counties or constituencies that were styled, rather misleadingly, 'tribes' (*phylai*).[39] These men represented a cross-section of Attica's entire territory and interests, including the aforementioned demes.[40] Each 'tribe' 's contingent of fifty *prytaneis* served as the Council's executive committee for a tenth of the year, when it was also responsible for convening the Council and the Assembly. The Council of Five Hundred itself met every working day, or about 300 times per year, so that government was continuous in between the Assembly's meetings. The Council's main functions were to prepare the Assembly's

---

[35] Finley 1974: 10.
[36] For *isegoria* (the right of any citizen to address the Assembly if he wished) see Griffith 1966 and especially Ostwald 1986: 203, incorporating earlier literature on the subject.
[37] This is brought out well in Eder 1991.
[38] Cf. Ober 1989: 144–5 and Millett 2000 for refutation of Hansen 1978. See further pp. 216–21.
[39] For the tribes' eponymous heroes, see pp. 335–6 and **Figs. 2.2** and **9.13**.
[40] For demes, *trittyes* and *phylai* see Traill 1975; Siewert 1982; Whitehead 1986a.

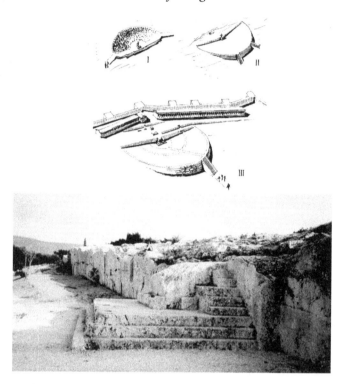

Figure 2.6 The Pnyx, supreme symbol of Athenian democracy. Above, sketches of its three phases; below, the remains of its platform (*bema*) today.

The Pnyx, a huge semicircular artificial terrace (see **Fig. 2.2b**), probably became the Assembly's meeting place after Ephialtes' reforms of 462; meetings had previously been held in the *agora*. The fact that the new site overlooked (and was not overlooked by) the site of the old aristocratic council of the Areopagus is unlikely to have been devoid of symbolic significance. Archaeological research has identified three successive phases in the Pnyx's history, each separately illustrating the great lengths to which the Athenians went to make the place suitable for mass meetings. During the second period (c. 400–345), for example, the natural slope of the hillside was reversed with the aid of a colossal retaining wall so that the people sat with their backs to the *agora*, sheltered from the wind. The auditorium's area was progressively extended (expanding to 5,550m² during its third period), giving concrete expression to the democratic creed that if sovereign bodies are sufficiently large the deficiencies of some individuals will be offset by the capacities of others (Thucydides 6.39.1, with Gomme, Andrewes and Dover 1945–81, vol. IV: *ad loco*; cf. Aristotle, *Politics* 1281b). The people attending the meetings sat on the dressed rock or on wooden benches. At the entrance arrivals were scrutinised and non-citizens excluded.

Presided over first by the *prytaneis* and then, from 400 onwards, by a board of nine 'chairmen' *(prohedroi)* selected by drawing lots, the Assembly's sessions bore the imprint of crowd behaviour: the psychology and the rules that were implicitly observed differed from those of a small group, or even those of a larger group such as a parliament today (Finley 1974: 10).

business ahead of its meetings and to supervise the city's administrative machinery, but sometimes it discharged judicial (or even executive) functions.[41] It had inherited most of the functions of the aristocratic Areopagus Council, which had originally been endowed with considerable, though largely unspecified, supervisory powers. Ephialtes' reforms of the 460s had restricted these powers considerably. From then on the Areopagus Council counted for little politically; made up of ex-archons, it retained the right of trial only in cases of homicide, wounding, arson and some religious offences.[42]

While we are discussing formal political institutions we should also mention the numerous large popular law courts,[43] which dispensed justice through the agency of more or less the same people as manned the Assembly and the Council. The locations of these courts cannot always be identified definitely with the surviving remains of buildings;[44] it would appear, however, that the bulk of them were in the *agora* itself (or in some area adjacent to it) and that trials were also sometimes held in the *agora* on sites that had not been specifically designed for that purpose. Two interconnected circumstances turned Athenian politics into a game quite unlike the one played by modern politicians: the fact that most cardinal decisions were reached at open-air mass meetings and the absence of anything resembling modern political parties. These circumstances had far-reaching consequences for the mechanisms by which leaders came to the fore and policies were made.

The prime quality required to become a leader was an ability to sway crowds. Men who lacked this ability could still influence public opinion (as Plato and Isocrates did by writing and others by other means) but were in practical terms debarred from active politics. Since democracy was direct, without parties or party machinery, anyone selected as a leader depended for the consistent execution of his programmes on the continued support of the often non-co-operative Athenian people.[45] It was, in other words, imperative that each time he appeared before a crowd he should perform in such a way as to engage its support.[46] It is true that we do sometimes

---

[41] Cf. Hornblower 1983: 116–18.
[42] The fullest account of the Areopagus Council is Wallace 1985.
[43] These are discussed at length in pp. 136–41.
[44] Cf. Hansen 1981–2; Boegehold 1995; Millett 1998.
[45] See Tacon 2001 for a demonstration that politicians at Assembly debates were not only under constant pressure to perform, but had also to contend with 'ecclesiastic *thorubos*' (interruptions, shouts, taunts and jeers from other speakers and the *demos*).
[46] According to a fragment from Eupolis' comedy *Demoi* (412), Pericles was unique amongst the popular speakers in having 'a sort of credibility on his lips' and in leaving 'a sting in his hearers' (Kassel and Austin 1983–, frg. 102).

hear of groups of relatives or friends being mobilised to assist one politician or another in informal ways. These groups, however, like the constantly changing temporary coalitions that were formed to carry through certain specific programmes, had only subsidiary roles in the political game.[47] There was no substitute for the forum of face-to-face interaction between leaders and the crowd.

Some politicians did manage consistently to hold sway over the Assembly for significant periods of time, Pericles and Demosthenes being the supreme examples.[48] There were, however, scores of less imposing figures, beginning with the so-called 'demagogues', popularly alleged to engage in politics purely to promote their own personal interests. The infamous 'sycophants' were detested by their victims; in terms of the system as a whole, however, they performed a useful function by pressuring the rich into contributing to communal causes, there being no public prosecutor.[49] Finally there were the 'temporary politicians', who might address the Assembly only once or twice in an entire lifetime. In evaluating Athens' political system it is worth bearing in mind two points whose importance will become apparent in what follows: firstly, it was largely the cumulative effect of the decisions made by these people that turned Athens into what she was, and secondly, in interactions between leaders and the masses it was customary for the leaders to appeal to national rather than factional interests.[50] The Athenians, in other words, had elevated the public good to the summit of their scale of civic values.

The way in which people elicit reactions from one another depends to a large extent on the way in which their society is structured and their accessibility to each other defined. Any complex society is made up of smaller groups and networks through which the individual's integration into that society is mediated.[51] In Athens some groupings were purely informal (for example, relatives, neighbours, occupational groups, cult associations and what we would call 'classes' or 'factions') while others were strictly formal (for example, demes, phratries, the Council and the Assembly), regulating

[47] Cf. Connor 1971, who over-emphasises the importance of such groups. For political leaders in Athens in general cf. Hansen 1991: 271: 'The political leaders in Athens were the group of Assembly speakers, generals and financial officers who did not just from time to time exercise their citizen duty to submit to election or propose decrees or laws, but took regular initiatives in the political assemblies.' The implications of the absence of parties in Athens are explored systematically in Strauss 1986: 15.

[48] On Pericles' special status and the issue of popular leadership (*tou demou prostasia*) see Thucydides 2.65, with Connor 1971; Finley 1974; see pp. 219–21.

[49] Cf. Christ 1998: 68.   [50] I am indebted for this to Finley 1974.

[51] Cf. (e.g.) J. Boissevain (1974) *Friends of Friends. Networks, Manipulators and Coalitions.* Oxford: Basil Blackwell: 30.

membership and attendance according to clearly prescribed rules. Networks were as a rule informal, consisting more often than not of one's relatives (*syngeneis, anchisteis*), friends (*philoi, hetairoi, epitedeioi, oikeioi, hetairoi*) and sometimes neighbours (*geitones, hoi plesion*). Both groups and networks were by our standards small. Small as they were, however, Athens clearly did not qualify as what would now be called a 'face-to-face' society. (This label is applied to societies that are so small-scale that each member communicates with every other member face to face and can therefore make a personal assessment of everyone else's qualities and suitability for office.)[52] Athens' sheer size and her topographic spread, together with certain casual allusions to the fact that not all of her citizens knew each other,[53] militate against any such conclusion. It is, however, reasonable to put forward the more moderate claim that many stranded relationships were prevalent in Athenian society. At this point we must make a small detour to examine this matter more closely.

The members of any closely knit, compact community may be linked together in a large or in a limited number of ways, the prime indices of interconnectedness being the number of roles they take on in interacting with others and the intensity of their interactions. A person can, for example, meet and interact with his brother not only in that capacity, but also in that of neighbour, member of the same cult association, fellow employee or member of the same political party. On the other hand, he might interact with another person who is not related to him only at his place of work and in the single capacity of fellow employee. Social scientists generally see the first type of connection as characteristic of simple, relatively isolated rural communities in which bonds between people tend to be based upon kinship. The second is seen as characteristic of large-scale, complex, industrialised societies in which relationships between people are voluntary and specialised. This distinction has an important effect upon the kind of social dynamics that each pattern engenders. In societies dominated by single-strand relationships ties tend to be impersonal, formal and contractual, with people living together, as one social scientist has put it, 'much like sardines in a can yet treating each other indifferently'.[54] In societies dominated by many stranded relationships ties tend to be intimate, friendly and confidential, with people showing much more concern for each other's well-being. People in such societies are not only more accessible to one

[52] Finley 1983: 28–9; 82–3 (cf. Homans 1951 and Laslett 1956a), criticised by Osborne 1985a: 64–6; Ober 1989: 31–3; Hunter 1994: 219 n. 4; Cartledge 1998a: 5.
[53] E.g. Thucydides 8.66.3; Lysias 1.45.
[54] E. G. Ericksen (1954) *Urban Behavior*. New York: The Macmillan Company: 3.

another, but also more open to each other's influence and pressure: interdependence in one sphere of activity can be used to enforce compliance in another.

It is very clear that many stranded relationships predominated in Athens. Even though the city had long outgrown the character of a simple, isolated rural community, it showed no signs whatsoever of developing a large-scale, impersonal social order of the type that we see as the standard of normality. With everything so close at hand and life mostly lived out of doors, it would have been difficult, indeed well-nigh impossible, to keep separate the multifarious activities that took place in the *agora* (and to a lesser extent in the Peiraeus). Private affairs mingled with public, buying and selling with administration and justice, religion with politics. Discussion of political, judicial and philosophical issues, more often than not accompanied by gossip, took place not only on the Pnyx, in the law courts and at the schools of philosophy, but also in the colonnades, perfumeries, barbers' shops and gymnasia, and on the narrow pathways through the *agora* (see **Fig. 2.7**).[55] People from very different classes and backgrounds met freely and uninhibitedly, city people associating with country folk, aristocrats with commoners, sailors with farmers, metics and visitors with citizens and slaves, so that each individual's particular characteristics were able to thrive and find expression (see **Fig. 2.8**).

This was the background against which certain ideas that were highly unconventional, not to say iconoclastic and subversive, were generated. Inequality, slavery, class privilege, all came under attack. 'Man's law of nature is equality', wrote Euripides, who elsewhere questioned the supposed sub-humanity of slaves: 'many a slave is dishonoured by nothing but the name, while his soul may be more free than that of a non-slave'.[56] Some of the Sophists had similar ideas. The deity, according to Alcidamas, had made all men free, so that no man was a slave by nature. Hippias argued that the fact that one man lived as a slave and another as a free man was merely a matter of convention; there was no natural distinction between the two.[57] Other Sophists went so far as to impugn the justice of aristocratic privilege: 'The splendour of noble birth is imaginary, and its prerogatives are based

[55] For the power of gossip in Athenian society, see Hunter 1990 and 1994: ch. 4. For organised and unofficial systems for the dissemination of news in Greek society, see S. Lewis 1996.

[56] Euripides, Fragment 831 (cf. *Ion* 854–6; fr. 511), with Garlan 1988: 124.

[57] For Alcidamas, see Aristotle, *Rhetoric* 13.1373b19, or Scholiast on Aristotle, *Rhetoric* 1.13, with Newman 1887–1902, vol. 1: 141; the view ascribed to Hippias is inferred from Aristotle, *Politics* 1253b20 (to be read with Newman 1887–1902, vol. 1: 146–58).

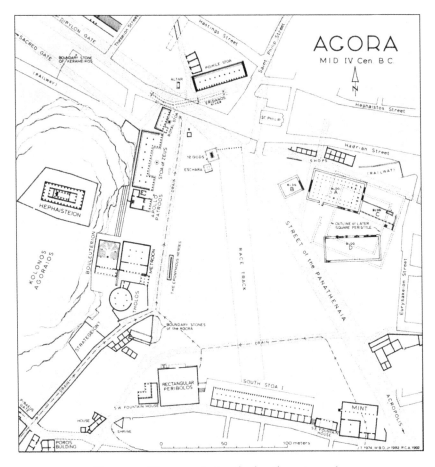

Figure 2.7 The *agora* during the fourth century: plan

During this period the spacious *agora* north-west of the Acropolis was the focus of the
city's life, a centre of seething political, commercial, cultural and intellectual activity.
Although it was sometimes decried as the home of vulgarity, idleness and gossip (Socrates
warned the jury at his trial that he would be using the manner of speech typical of the
agora, not of the law courts (Plato, *Apology* 17c)), it encouraged encounters between people
of a sort that must have exerted a profound influence on their character and thoughts.
Socrates, according to Xenophon, 'was always on public view, for early in the morning he
used to go to the promenades and training-grounds, in the forenoon he would appear in
the *agora*, and for the rest of the day he would be wherever he would meet with the most
people' (*Memorabilia* 1.1.10). Simon the shoemaker, whom Socrates used to visit, and
whose shop has now been identified on a site just outside the *agora*, noted down what he
remembered of Socrates' visits and, according to a later source, published 'dialogues' long
before Xenophon and Plato (Diogenes Laertius 2.122). Other sources of intellectual
stimulation at the *agora* included the books offered for sale, works such as those of the
philosopher Anaxagoras of Clazomenae (Plato, *Apology* 26d). The hill west of the *agora*,
the Kolonos Agoraios, was where jobbing labourers went to meet potential hirers (Fuks
1984b). On the *agora* in general, see Thompson and Wycherley 1972 and Camp 1986.

Figure 2.8 Ethnic and social types in Athens
The diversity of Attica's population is illustrated by the many ethnic origins, occupations
and social ranks expressed in portrayals of various of its members: (a) an Athenian youth,
presumably a current citizen or citizen-to-be; (b) a Scythian archer, a public slave; (c) a
groom of African origin, presumably a privately owned slave; (d) a respectable Athenian
lady, presumably of citizen status; (e) a courtesan (*hetaira*), presumably a metic or slave; (f)
a slave-girl, employed as a domestic servant. Though expressions of ethnocentric prejudice
do turn up in Athenian culture, they are a far cry from full-blown racism (Tuplin 1999).

upon a mere word.'[58] It is hard to estimate the impact of such ideas on public
opinion. We can be sure that they did not gain the upper hand in society,
but they probably had something to do with certain transformations that
slowly took place in that society. In the social sphere, a gradual fading of class
distinctions and status differences can be sensed.[59] In the intellectual sphere

[58] Aristotle, Fragment 82.1490a10 (Lycophron).
[59] This point has well been brought out by Millett 1998.

we see a progressive sharpening of the faculties of criticism and inventiveness that may or may not be reflected in the progressive refinement of the Athenians' vase-paintings. The Athenians discussed and debated everything under the sun, discarding old ideas and devising new ones, then putting them to the test. Thucydides, a participant-observer, was clearly amazed by this. In his history the Corinthians are said to have remarked that the Spartans approached new problems in the old, traditional way (it is clearly implied that they kept foreigners out lest they should contaminate the minds of Spartan youngsters), while the Athenians approached problems in a new and original way (1.71). This variety of experience made Athens by far the more 'modern' state of the two.

The direct nature of the Athenians' democracy must have stimulated their penchant for unconventional thinking still further. Since there were no periodically elected parties or representatives in the modern sense of those terms, every issue, great or small, was decided by a majority vote of the Assembly. It was as if a modern democracy were to be run by means of referenda rather than cabinet decisions. The individual citizen's weight in the decision-making process and the amount of control he had over the conditions in which he lived were immeasurably greater than those of his modern counterpart. (When an Athenian voted in favour of war with Sparta or of the Sicilian expedition, for example, he might well be voting to send himself off on campaign.)[60] Since he also devoted a correspondingly greater amount of his time and energy to running the state's affairs, it would be only a slight exaggeration to claim that every politically active Athenian would today count as a part-time politician.[61] Pericles averred that even those who were principally interested in their own affairs were extremely well informed on political matters, adding, 'This is a peculiarity of ours' (Thucydides 2.40.2).

Having sketched the essential features of Athens' political system, we may now ask what relation that system bore to the values of the people it governed. History suggests that such relations may be of three types. First, political institutions may be extensions of contemporary values. Second, they may be coloured by contemporary values, but essentially shaped by

---

[60] Cf. Meier 1990: 13; Finley 1981d: 90.

[61] Hansen 1991: 313 supplies concrete data: 'an Assembly meeting was normally attended by 6000 citizens, on a normal court day some 2000 citizens were selected by lot, and besides the 500 members of the Council there were 700 other magistrates. . . . The Assembly met thirty or forty times a year, the courts were summoned on about 200 days; the Council met on at least 250 days, and some boards of magistrates . . . were on duty every day all year round'. For the politically non-active Athenian see Carter 1986.

altogether different influences. Third, they may be largely independent of contemporary values, embodying the petrified values of a bygone age or the impositions of a ruler who acts against the will of the majority. At one time or another each of these three types of system has been seen in action. The Athenian democracy seems to have corresponded most closely to the first.

From the moment when Cleisthenes instituted the democracy a vivid interplay of values and constitutional forms began to appear at every turn. It was almost as if the people of Athens had projected their collectively agreed ideas of right and wrong into the political sphere and then consolidated them as written laws and firmly defined institutions. Take, for instance, the measures to fortify the system that were devised in the fifth century. As soon as popular democracy had been set on a firm footing the powers of the conservative Areopagus Council were curtailed, payments for holding office were introduced, enabling the poorer citizens to take part in the conduct of public affairs, and the third Solonian class, the Zeugitae, was admitted to the archonship. Or take the entire fourth century, during which democratic institutions were perfected so that all issues, large or small, were judged according to a single standard, whether or not this was beneficial to the democracy.[62] It would seem that the political organisation of democratic Athens reflected the people's collective norms almost perfectly. To contemporaries this would have come as no surprise. The people, after all, were accountable to no one, and no field of activity was exempt from their intervention. They had 'ultimate authority over all things in the polis and . . . the power to act however they [saw] fit . . .' ([Demosthenes] 59.88, *Against Neaera*).[63]

The question now arises of how these values should be interpreted. It is a well-established tenet of modern scholarship that no coherent, fully articulated theory of democracy existed in classical Athens. As M. I. Finley has put it, 'there were notions, maxims, and generalities which did not add up to a systematic theory'.[64] We may subscribe to this view, with the proviso that there must nonetheless have existed something that we could call a democratic morality or a democratic spirit: a particular package of views, values, aspirations, expectations, frustrations and fears, not always articulated, that the Athenian citizens took with them when they agitated for political change, and, even more importantly, when they went to the

[62] Rhodes 1980.   [63] See pp. 217–21 for the 'sovereignty' of the people's rule.
[64] Cf. Finley 1985a: 48. See also Connor, Hanse, Raaflaub and Strauss 1990: 33–5; Ober 1993a: 82; Farrar 1988 (for an attempt to identify Protagoras, Thucydides and Democritus as three sources of democratic theory).

Pnyx to express their wishes in the form of a vote. We may further note that the relationship between this democratic morality and political change must have been dynamic, each in turn influencing and shaping the other.[65] The end product of all this was the full-blown democracy of the fifth and fourth centuries, which could hardly have functioned so smoothly had certain rules not been scrupulously observed. Sometimes these rules were made explicit by contemporary writers; sometimes they remained implicit, but could nonetheless be inferred from the workings of the system itself. To the examination of these rules we shall now turn.

RULES AND NORMS

There were, to start with, two 'cardinal principles', which Forrest has aptly formulated thus: 'an absolute acceptance of the laws (including what we would call the constitution)' and 'the belief that everyone who was admitted to the society governed by these laws had an equal right and almost an equal duty to administer and maintain them'.[66] The centrality of these principles in the Athenian system of values is indicated by their incorporation into a civic oath of sorts that was taken by citizens in the fifth century and by young men (*epheboi*) who were about to start their military training from at least the second half of the fourth century: 'And I will obey those in authority with due regard, and the laws . . . And if anyone subverts the laws I will not permit it, as far as in me lies and along with all others . . .' (see **Fig. 9.11**).[67]

The corollary of the first principle was that anyone who broke the law, whether as a private person or in the capacity of a public official, was liable to punishment by state-empowered agents.[68] The corollary of the second was that in almost every field of public activity steps were taken to ensure equality of opportunity. It appears that these measures were enforced rigorously, despite the antagonism that they aroused and despite the occasional grumbling of the aristocrats that the wretched masses were being put on a par with the capable and the good. The Athenians insisted that their norms should be applied impartially within the citizen group, often compensating the weak, the poor and the disabled with state benefits.[69] An upshot

[65] Cf. Ostwald 1986: 129.

[66] Forrest 1966: 221, to be read with the evidence supplied by E. M. Harris 1994. For a theoretical discussion of the issue, see D. Cohen 1995b. For perceptions of the law and of Solon, the great archaic lawgiver whose legislation was said to have laid much emphasis upon *sophrosyne* (self-restraint), see Thomas 1994.

[67] *GHI* vol. ii: no. 204; Plescia 1970: ch. 2; Hansen 1991: 100; Siewert 1997; Parker 1996a: 252–3.

[68] See pp. 221–9.   [69] See pp. 412–13 for state benefits.

of this was a considerable diminution in the sort of mutually beneficial, reciprocal relationships between unequal partners that social scientists now call patronage. The idea of general equality (*isonomia*) and the practical measures that reinforced it were, as Millett has pointed out, inimical to such relations.[70]

Three technical measures were used to implement equality of rights and duties: lots, payments and rotations. The practice of drawing lots was designed to give every citizen an equal chance of holding office, irrespective not only of wealth and birth, but also of experience, military record, popularity and eloquence.[71] State pay was intended to compensate citizens for the time they devoted to political activities. To the poor it gave an opportunity to participate in government; to the wavering an incentive to attend meetings.[72] Plato regarded this scheme as setting on an equal footing 'the equal and unequal' (*Republic* 8.558c). The system of constant rotation was intended to ensure that the temporary benefits of high office were distributed evenly among the allotted office-holders. The Athenians applied these measures with such unwavering determination that the practical steps taken to ensure equality of rights and duties became safeguards against abuse and corruption. For instance, rotation of the *prytaneis* on the Council had the dual effect of impeding the use of personal connections to obtain preferential opportunities of addressing the Assembly and preventing the Council from developing any *esprit de corps* that might tempt it to compete for resources with other state organs. The allotment machine was an ingenious invention designed to randomise the selection of magistrates, jurors and courts so as to forestall corruption (see **Fig. 4.1**). Athenian political dialogue abounded in accusations of bribery,[73] and scholars have sometimes succumbed to the temptation to take these at face value. A rational examination of the system as a whole, however, affords a more balanced perspective. 'I cannot envisage', wrote Finley, 'how one proceeded, or could afford, to bribe jurors whose numbers could run to 1,000 and who were chosen by lot from a panel of 6,000 just as a trial was to begin, or citizens who attended the Assembly by the thousands.'[74] Nor was the law particularly forgiving in this respect, the punishment for bribing a juror, or accepting such a bribe, being unequivocally death.[75]

---

[70] See Stirling 1968 for the general concept of 'impartiality'; Finley 1983: 39–40 and Millett 1989 for the relative (but not total) absence of patronage in classical Athens. (Lysias 9.13, *For the Soldier*, is among the few passages that do imply the existence of patronage.)

[71] It should be noted, however, that this applied only to non-military office-holders. The military ones were elected by direct vote, when the criteria listed were very much relevant.

[72] Markle 1985; Rhodes 1992b: 81; Podes 1987.   [73] Harvey 1985; C. Taylor 2001.

[74] Finley 1983: 84.   [75] Aeschines 1.87, *Against Timarchus*. Cf. Dover 1974: 289.

This brings us to a third cardinal principle on which Forrest did not touch. Both the development and the political discourse of the Athenian democracy took place within a secularised and rational matrix of thought. I should perhaps stress this point, especially in the light of recent attempts to deny the entire ancient world any qualities that could be called 'rational'. The claim that Athens' democracy was rational does not mean that her people were never swayed by appeals to their emotions at the Assembly or in the law courts, that they were exceptionally free from passion or prejudice, or that 'irrationality' in one or other of its complex forms never crept into their considerations. Nor is anyone trying to claim that political change in Athens was entirely free from religiosity, or that the Athenian man in the street was completely and utterly emancipated from the vagaries of superstition.[76] No such claim can be made for any society that has ever existed, and it is not particularly useful to judge Athens (as is often done) by superhuman standards. In describing Athens' democracy as rational, we are asserting merely that the Athenians consciously attempted to reduce the influence of religion and irrationality in almost every field of activity and that in most cases, though not in all, they succeeded. Finley hit the nail on the head when he remarked that in Athens 'government had become generally secularised in reality though not in appearance'.[77] He illustrated this point by reference to the practice of selecting by lot. In a genuinely religious community this method of selection would be seen as leaving the decision not to chance but to a god or gods, and would be hedged about with all sorts of rituals and taboos. In Athens selection by lot had been emancipated from religion and reduced to a purely secular procedure. Had Athenian culture been nothing but a mass of seething irrationality, this could hardly have been the case.

Another glimpse of the same spirit is afforded by two incidents that took place during the Peloponnesian War, one at the beginning and the other halfway through. In communities that are swamped by weird irrational notions, major disasters such as a plague tend to trigger fixed responses. The people's representatives summon specialists. These identify the cause of the trouble, which invariably proves to be some sort of religious or moral transgression. They then perform expiation and purification rituals to appease the gods. Sequences of this sort are described repeatedly not only in the annals of the ancient Near East, but also in those of Rome.[78] If

---

[76] Wallace 1994 is an essential corrective to those modern studies that have exaggerated the importance of impiety trials and the judicial prosecution of intellectuals.

[77] Finley 1983: 94 (refers to all Greek city-states rather than just Athens) and Ostwald 1992: 349 (refers to Athens).

[78] Burkert 1996: 102.

we are to believe Thucydides, however, the Athenians did not (in public, at any rate) resort to any such measures when the plague broke out during the first years of the Peloponnesian War.[79] Nor was their response to the omens that accompanied the Sicilian expedition typically superstitious.[80] It is possible that irrational fears may to some extent have influenced the actions of the army and its leader, Nicias, a man known for the strength of his religious beliefs, when they were away from home. In 415, however, the fleet set out from Athens despite the evil omens. This fact recalls a remark made in one of Plato's dialogues by a religious expert to the effect that whenever he spoke at the Assembly about religious matters or predicted the future people laughed at him as if he were crazy (*Euthyphro* 3c). Alcibiades, finally, was recalled on grounds that were ostensibly religious but in reality political.[81]

The movement to break away from religion and tradition may well have begun with the establishment of democracy. Lévêque and Vidal-Naquet have noted that in the course of the Cleisthenic reforms at the end of the sixth century the old religious calendar was replaced with a new civic one, and that instead of the four old tribes (*phylai*) hallowed by religious belief ten new 'tribes' (more properly, constituencies) were instituted (see **Fig. 2.2a**).[82] Henceforth citizenship was to depend on membership of a deme, and fifth-century Athenians were expected to use the names of their demes rather than those of their fathers as surnames (*The Athenian Constitution* 21.5). Everything we know of traditional societies underscores the unprecedented boldness of these innovations. The Cleisthenic order, as Parker has put it, 'was rational, abstract, "geometric" and secular'.[83]

All this should come as no surprise in view of the great intellectual revolution that swept through the Greek world and reached its climax in fifth-century Athens. Philosophers, scientists and teachers from every corner of that world flocked to Athens, where their innovative ideas struck a responsive chord. The Athenians were quick to embrace these ideas, assimilating them into their own conceptions of morality and politics.[84] Above all, they believed in reason and in the capability of man; it was held that by thinking in terms of absolute and unconditional ideas man could transcend the limits of practical experience so as to achieve a fuller understanding of his environment and eventually dominate it. The spirit

---

[79] Supplications were made at sanctuaries and oracles were appealed to, but these were private measures that in any case proved futile (*anophele*: Thucydides 2.47.4).

[80] For a discussion of the mysteries and the Hermocopidae of 415, see pp. 343–7.

[81] Cf. A. Powell 1979b.   [82] Lévêque and Vidal-Naquet 1964.

[83] Parker 1996a: 117.   [84] This point is well brought out in Ostwald 1992.

reflected in the Athenian tragedies was the very spirit that fuelled democratic reform; optimistic and permeated by the conviction that prosperity and disaster were man-made and not God-given, it urged men and governments to strive to preserve the one and avoid the other.[85]

Our fourth and last cardinal principle may be observed in the city's social system rather than its political system. Athens shared her social system, inherited from the non-democratic past, with other Greek poleis. Almost two thirds of her population of about 250,000 consisted of Athenian citizen families (a figure that implies that there were between 25,000 and 45,000 adult male citizens).[86] Non-citizens existed in a state of institutionalised inequality. The power to make the law belonged exclusively to citizens, while people who were not citizens were to some extent underprivileged and exploited. Let us take a quick look at their general circumstances.

The underprivileged population was divided into two legally defined and hierarchically graded orders: resident aliens ('metics') and slaves. The metics included both freedmen and free-born non-Athenians: in Xenophon's words, 'Greeks, Lydians, Phrygians, Syrians and barbarians of all parts' (*Poroi* 2.3) who had lived in Attica for some time without becoming citizens. They enjoyed certain rights and had certain military and fiscal obligations, but were excluded from politics and land ownership, another citizen monopoly.[87] They were also stigmatised in some ways, a poll tax that they were required to pay annually marking the inferiority of their status. These disadvantages do not, however, imply that they were treated as outcasts. The poet and author Ion, the painter Zeuxis, the philosopher Aristotle and the speechwriter Lysias appear to have moved as equals in Athenian high society, which implies that the disadvantages of being a metic were largely legal rather than social.

Slaves were men, women and children who had been wrenched from their homes somewhere outside the Greek world (usually Asia Minor, Thrace or southern Russia, but sometimes Syria or Africa; see **Fig. 2.8b, c**) and

---

[85] Cf. B. M. W. Knox 1957: 107, inferring from Sophocles' *Antigone*.

[86] I adopt these figures from Garnsey 1988: 90, who allows for short-term demographic fluctuations: a total citizen family population of around 160,000 to 172,000 in 431, 84,000 or 120,000 in the fourth century; a total population of 120,000 to 150,000 in 480, around 250,000 just before the Peloponnesian War, and from 120,000 to 200,000 in the fourth century. Based on inadequate and chancy sources, quantitative data such as these are at best approximate figures.

[87] Whitehead 1977 is the standard work on metics (to be read with Whitehead 1986b). For the exclusion of metics from politics and land ownership, see Pečirca 1967 and J. K. Davies 1977–8. The numbers of metics given in the sources are notoriously unreliable. Rhodes 1992b: 83 says that about 50,000 people were members of metic families; Duncan-Jones 1980 opts for a higher figure, and Finley 1952: 77 for a lower. In this context we should also note that metic women were supervised by metic guardians.

thrust into an alien and by and large hostile world. They were bought and owned by both citizens and metics. The fact that a distinction was made between a 'homebred' (*oikogenes*) and a 'bought' (*onetos*) slave suggests that these two types may have been regarded differently, even though their legal rights were the same. Forbidden by law to possess property or contract legal relationships, slaves were thought of and treated as a kind of commodity. Aristotle called them 'property with a soul' (*Politics* 1253b32); wealthy Athenians mentioned them in the same breath with land and money, the main ingredients of wealth, and the second century AD scholar Julius Pollux says that they were sold in the *agora* at places called *kykloi* along with 'other merchandise' (*Onomasticon* 7.11). Public opinion stigmatised slaves as untrustworthy and insolent; comedy caricatured them as lazy or randy.[88] In everyday life they could be punished in various ways with the aim of, in Xenophon's words, reducing them to submission (*Memorabilia* 2.1.16–17). Their evidence was only admissible in court if it had been extracted under torture.[89] The slaves who worked in their thousands in the silver mines of Laurion were fettered and guarded in case they ran away.

There are nonetheless some signs that the condition of slaves in general was better in Athens than in other Greek states and indeed than in most of history's other major slave societies.[90] The complaint, by the anti-democratic reactionary known as the Old Oligarch, that 'the clothing of the common people there is in no way superior to that of the slaves of metics, nor is their appearance', is strikingly confirmed by a passage in the Demosthenic corpus that records a real-life mix-up between a slave and the son of a citizen (Demosthenes 47.61, *Against Euergus*).[91] The Old Oligarch further laments that the slaves and metics in Athens display 'the greatest uncontrolled wantonness; you can't hit them there, and a slave will not stand aside for you' (1.10).[92] That the Athenians were exceptional in their attitude towards slaves is to some extent confirmed by a passage from Thucydides according to which a large number of slaves from Chios who had been punished particularly severely deserted and went over to the Athenians (8.40.2), and by another from the Demosthenic corpus asserting that

---

[88] Cf. Colvin 2000.　　　[89] See pp. 301–3.

[90] I.e. Roman Italy from the third to the first century BC and Brazil, the southern states of the USA and the West Indies in the nineteenth century. Cf. K. Hopkins (1978) *Conquerors and Slaves*. Cambridge: Cambridge University Press: 101.

[91] During this period Athenian men abandoned the luxurious, elaborate garment that they had traditionally worn in favour of a simpler, poorer woollen cloak worn over a short *chiton*: Geddes 1987.

[92] Cf. pp. 113–14 for the value of the 'Old Oligarch' as a source of information about late fifth-century Athenian society.

many slaves in Athens had more freedom to speak their minds than citizens had in other cities (Demosthenes 9.3).[93] The impression is reinforced by some further pieces of information. Legislation shows that slaves in Athens (unlike those in Rome) could not with impunity be killed in the absence of any judicial sentence, or struck by persons other than their owners (perfectly permissible in some other Greek cities).[94] Some passages also suggest that a citizen could be found guilty of insulting behaviour (*hubrizein*) towards a slave.[95] Gravestones and votive tablets found in the vicinity of the silver mines indicate that slaves were allowed to establish families and participate in various slave associations. These tablets have also confirmed something that had already been inferred from literary sources, namely that slaves were allowed to keep part of their wages when their owners hired them out to work for other people.[96] Even if all this fell somewhat short of what some modern authors have termed an 'Athenian movement against slavery',[97] the disparate pieces of the jigsaw seem to point to a trend fed by two sources. One of these was the view, expressed indirectly by some of the Sophists, that slavery was not a natural phenomenon (as the traditional view expressed in Aristotle's writings would have it), but a matter of convention that ran contrary to nature.[98] The other was the democracy's uncompromising pursuit of freedom, which tended to spill over into more and more fields of activity, acting indirectly as a powerful equalizer.[99] In religion, for example, the non-Athenian members of the Athenian empire were allowed to share in the ancestral rituals of sacrifice at the Panathenaea and in the ensuing distribution of meat.[100] Plato, branding this 'drunkenness on excessive quantities of undiluted [freedom]' (*Republic* 8.562d), complained bitterly that it eroded not only the differences between citizens, metics and visiting strangers, but also those between teachers and pupils, members of the older

---

[93] For slaves in comedy, see Dover 1972: 204.

[94] Cf. Barkan 1935: 37; Morrow 1937; Dover 1974: 288; MacDowell 1978: 80–1; Wiedemann 1981: 171–2; Garlan 1988: 44.

[95] Aeschines 1.16–17, *Against Timarchus*. He hastens to add, however, that the legislator was motivated by concern not for the slaves but for the citizens: 'in a democracy that man is unfit for citizenship who outrages any person whatsoever'. Demosthenes 21.45–6, *Against Meidias*; cf. MacDowell 1978: 131.

[96] Lauffer 1979: 185–7. See Aeschines 1.54, *Against Timarchus*, for a slave (Pittalacus) who is described as wealthy.

[97] E.g. Popper 1966, vol. 1: 70.

[98] This point, long suppressed, has now been brought out in a pioneering study: Garnsey 1996.

[99] Ostwald 1986: xix; Yakobson 1998.

[100] Jameson 1997a: 178, who notes that the concept of the equal feast (*dais eïse*) 'is Homeric and may antedate the nascent egalitarianism of the early city-state, but it was no less appropriate for the fifth-century democracy when all no longer actually sat down to dine together.'

and the younger generation, masters and slaves, men and women and even masters and their domestic animals (*Republic* 8.563a–d).

I am suggesting only that the sophistic view of nature, coupled with Athens' egalitarian ethos, probably made the life of a slave less unbearable in Athens than it was anywhere else in the ancient world. This should not be taken to mean that these ideological trends mitigated the harsh realities of a slave's everyday life in every respect. Slaves continued to be exploited as Athens' most readily available, though not its largest, work-force.[101] Although most worked in mining, agriculture or domestic service, slaves could be found in any occupation, sometimes working alongside free men.[102] The records of the Erechtheum's construction, for example, show that on this site slaves and free men did the same jobs, sometimes working side by side,[103] while a passage from Thucydides, considered in conjunction with what has come to be known as 'the great triremes inscription', has revealed that 'slaves regularly formed a substantial proportion of the rowers on Athenian triremes, and their masters included fellow oarsmen'.[104] Despite sometimes working so closely together, however, the two social types were worlds apart: the slaves themselves, rather than their labour or labour power, were the commodity, and could be sold, hired out, bequeathed and generally used at will to produce wealth for someone else.[105] Demosthenes' father and Lysias' brother, for instance, both derived a substantial annual income from workshops run for them by so-called arti-san slaves 'who lived apart'(*choris oikountes*), an income that enabled both to lead a life of leisure.[106] A piece of evidence recently found in the *agora* (and subsequently published) sheds an intimate light on the life of 'chattel-slaves' of this type. It is an inscribed lead tablet, the ancient equivalent of a personal letter (see **Fig. 2.9**), in which a slave called Lesis complains to his mother that he is miserable working in the foundry to which his masters have presumably hired him out. He begs his mother, probably a freedwoman, and someone called Xenocles, perhaps her husband and him-self a freedman, to intercede with his present (and their former) masters to

---

[101] The largest force still consisted of free labourers. See Garnsey 1980.
[102] Mining: Lauffer 1979; Garlan 1988: 65–6. Agriculture: Jameson 1977–8 and 1992; de Ste Croix 1981: 505–9; Wood 1983 and 1989 (arguing that the two last named overstated the importance of 'agricultural slavery' in classical Athens); Garlan 1988: 64; Hanson 1992. Artisans: Garlan 1988: 64–5. Trade and banking: Garlan 1988: 66–7. Domestic service: Hunter 1994: 70–95. Various slave occupations mentioned in the Attic Orators: Carriere-Hergavault 1971. On 'public slaves' in general and the Scythian archers in particular, see pp. 229–31. For the image of slaves in Attic tragedy and comedy, see Vogt 1974: ch. 1.
[103] Randall 1953; Austin and Vidal-Naquet 1977: 300–7.   [104] A. J. Graham 1992 and 1998: 110.
[105] Finley 1998: 136.   [106] Perotti 1973; MacDowell 1978: 81–2.

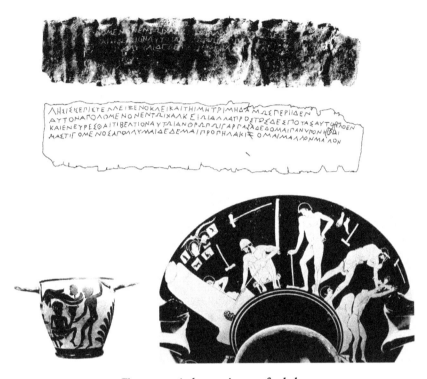

Figure 2.9 A slave crying out for help

D. R. Jordan 2000 translates the lead tablet above thus: 'Lesis is sending (a letter) to
Xenocles and to his mother by no means to overlook that he is perishing in the foundry
but to come to his masters and find something better for him. For I have been handed
over to a man thoroughly wicked; I am perishing from being whipped; I am tied up; I am
treated like dirt -more and more.' Presenting no textual or linguistic problems, the
inscription's interpretation hinges on the relationship between Lesis, his masters, the 'man'
tormenting him and Xenocles. Jordan believes that Lesis was a metic who was working in
the foundry as an apprentice. The facts that he had 'masters', that he had been 'handed
over' to another person and that he had been whipped and tied up may, however, suggest
that he was a chattel slave. Lesis appears to have hoped that his mother and Xenocles
would use their informal relationships with his present (and their former) masters to
achieve some improvement in his plight. The fact that the tablet was found in a well
suggests, as Jordan infers, that whoever was supposed to deliver it decided that it would be
easier to throw it away. The vase-painting on the right depicts a foundry such as Lesis may
have toiled in, this one specialising in bronze statues. The one on the left, from Abai in
Locris, shows a slave being whipped in a potter's workshop.

find some better arrangement for him. Lesis announces bitterly that he has been handed over to a 'thoroughly wicked' man and that he is perishing from being whipped and tied up. He concludes with the desperate cry, 'I am treated like dirt – more and more!' Circumstantial evidence suggests that Lesis' letter never reached its destination.

Figures are notoriously hard to come by, but anecdotal evidence consistently suggests that a wealthy man would have had something like fourteen to sixteen household slaves and the average peasant between two and five.[107] At times certain exceptionally opulent Athenians are said to have hired out hundreds of slaves to work in the state-owned silver mines at Laurion.[108] There are, however, serious doubts as to the validity of these last figures, and they would in any case have been exceptional: the total number of slaves owned by any one wealthy Athenian seems unlikely to have exceeded fifty. Individual slave ownership in Athens differed, in other words, from individual slave ownership either in the early Roman empire or in the southern states of the USA, where an individual might own hundreds of slaves. The total number of slaves in ancient Attica is elusive, but something between 60,000 and 100,000 would probably be a fairly good guess.[109] Whatever their exact number, it is difficult to escape the view, frequently voiced in modern times, that the existence of slaves enabled wealthy Athenians to enjoy their wealth without oppressing free citizens. In terms of the exchange relationships that we discussed earlier, masters and slaves were engaged in a lopsided variant of productive exchange:[110] both had to co-operate in order for either to obtain benefit. The benefits that accrued to each were, however, grossly disproportionate, often amounting to a life of luxury for one and bare survival for the other.

TENSIONS AND CONFLICTS

A short survey such as this cannot hope to include every minute detail of what was a highly sophisticated social edifice, incorporating a wide variety of systems and sub-systems. It can, however, draw attention to certain sources of friction that appear likely to have been capable of endangering that edifice's existence. Within the city's population, two pairs of social

---

[107] Garlan 1988: 61; Hunter 1994: 76; cf. Jameson 1977–8: 123.
[108] Athenaeus 6.264cd (more than 1,000 slaves owned by Mnason of Phokis); Xenophon, *Poroi* 4.14 and Athenaeus 6.272c, e (1,000 owned by Nicias); Xenophon, *Poroi* 4.15 (600 owned by Hipponikos, 300 by Philemonides). For the reliability of these figures see Westermann 1955: 453 and Cartledge 1985: 32–3.
[109] Cf. Finley 1998: 148, who opts for the lower figure; Rhodes 1992b: 83, who opts for the higher.
[110] See p. 34, with **Fig. 1.2**.

types were pitted against each other more or less constantly. Since Athens had no religious authority that wielded any political power, these were the only axes of conflict that could have presented a serious threat from within. Let us now consider them in terms of class, economics and ideology.

There was, in the first place, the antagonism between the collective egalitarian, non-professional civic elite at the top of the social pyramid and the large population of discontented slaves at its base. Tensions between these groups are probably under-reported in the sources, the ancient authors' own slave-owner mentality rendering them insensitive to grievances arising from exploitation. Certain subtle signs do, however, indicate the reality of these tensions. Thucydides tells us that in 413, after the Spartans had occupied and fortified Decelea in Attica, some 20,000 slaves deserted from the Athenian side.[111] Demosthenes expresses in rhetorical terms the common opinion that slaves, unlike free men, were answerable with their bodies for any offence (22.55, *Against Androtion*). Antiphon tells the story of a young slave who stabbed his master, expressing in highly emotive language the awful possibility that the slave might have exterminated the entire household had he not been scared away by his victim's cries (5.69, *On the Murder of Herodes*). Lysias, writing in the name of a well-to-do client, presents as self-evident the contention that slaves have most animosity towards their masters (7.35, *On the Olive Stump*).

The spectre that haunted slave owners was not really that of large-scale slave rebellions. These were hard to organise and, due to the notorious lack of solidarity amongst chattel-slaves, all but impossible to carry through. What the slave owners dreaded most was that their slaves would be manumitted and used by contending parties as subsidiary forces. This is precisely what happened in Corcyra in 427, during the civil war, when both the oligarchs and the democrats 'sent out to the country districts in an attempt to win the support of the slaves by offering them their freedom'. The upshot of this was that the great majority of the slaves joined the democrats (Thucydides 3.73).[112]

There was also the antagonism between rich and poor and that between the oligarchs and the democrats, the two conflicts often mingling and overlapping with each other. The economic gap between the Athenian rich and the Athenian poor looks considerable to us, but by the pan-Mediterranean standards of the time it was moderate.[113] The picture drawn

---

[111] Thucydides 7.27; cf. *Hellenica Oxyrhynchia* 12.4. See also Hanson 1992.
[112] Cf. Westermann 1955: 464.
[113] By comparison with those of wealthy Persians their fortunes were probably insignificant. Cf. Vickers 1990 and A. H. M. Jones 1957: 70.

by A. H. M. Jones nearly half a century ago can still be considered valid:
'[Athens was] a society in which, except for a small group of relatively very
rich men at the top, and a larger group of casual labourers at the bottom,
wealth was evenly distributed, and the gradation from the affluent to the
needy very gentle.'[114] A minority of 1,200 or so citizens (and their families)
could afford to lead a life of leisure.[115] The majority of citizens, however,
though not entirely penniless, had to work hard to earn their living. Here
is a point of some significance for the Athenian code of behaviour. This
relatively poor majority, the Athenian *demos*, had succeeded in forcing
political and legal equality upon the rich minority, but refrained from
pressing its success home in the economic sphere despite the fact that it
was in its power to do so[116] (the *demos* also controlled the law courts and the
repressive instruments of the state).[117] It is an inescapable conclusion that
the rich people of Athens were rich because the common people allowed
them to be.[118] The significance of this will emerge in full when this subject is
examined in a pan-Hellenic context. It will appear that what was elsewhere
the most troublesome inequality of all, that inequality that in other Greek
states gave rise to violent revolutions, was mitigated in Athens by a rational
strategy of forbearance.[119]

In the political sphere the antagonism between rich and poor took the
shape of conflict (which often assumed ideological overtones) between the
so-called oligarchs (*to beltion*, literally 'the better', *hoi gnorimoi*, the nota-
bles and *hoi chrestoi*, the respectable) and the democrats (*ho demos*, the
masses and *hoi poneroi*, the impoverished lower classes). The oligarchs,
who included some members of the 'old aristocracy' and some prosperous but non-aristocratic farmers, craftsmen and ship owners, were a small
minority amongst the city's population. They opposed democracy on the
grounds that the masses were unintelligent and unworthy of wielding such
vast power; the people who had the money were, they claimed, far better

---

[114] A. H. M. Jones 1957: 90.

[115] I accept the suggestion of J. K. Davies 1981 that those with a fortune of about one talent should be
considered as members of the leisured class. Cf. Ober 1989: 128–9 for alternative views in scholarly
literature.

[116] The principle was incorporated into legislation: the jurors who manned the law courts swore not
to allow the cancellation of private debts or the redistribution of houses belonging to Athenian
citizens; the chief magistrates swore that 'whatever anyone owns before I enter this office, he will
have and hold the same until I leave it.' Cf. Demosthenes 24.149, *Against Timocrates*, and *The
Athenian Constitution* 56.2.

[117] See Chapter 7.

[118] Cf. Finley 1981d: 92: 'Despite Pseudo-Xenophon and his co-believers, not even the Athenian demos
ever mounted an assault on the fortunes or the honours of the Athenian wealthy.'

[119] Cf. A. H. M. Jones 1957: 91–2; A. Powell 1988: 265.

qualified to rule.[120] In politics they were prepared to be radical, favouring solutions that did not entail compromise. Should the opportunity arise, they had every intention of deploying all their power, wealth and connections abroad to subvert democracy,[121] even if this could be achieved only at the cost of physically eliminating their enemies.[122] Had they succeeded in obtaining control of the state they would have made citizenship conditional upon a certain level of wealth, setting up whatever sort of regime (an oligarchy, or perhaps even a tyranny) best reflected the configuration of their ideas (it has plausibly been suggested that they might have reconstituted Athens on the model of Sparta, the supreme military state).[123] Most importantly, they would have imposed upon the community a pattern of interpersonal relationships drastically different from that worked out by the democrats.

Drawn up against the oligarchs was the ruling majority of relatively well-to-do farmers (again including some members of the old aristocracy, from amongst whom the leaders of both camps emerged).[124] This group countered the oligarchs' arguments by asserting that democracy was both intelligent and fair: intelligent because the 'many' were endowed with a natural sense of justice (Protagoras' 'divine portion') and were therefore, as a speaker in Thucydides' histories remarks, 'best at listening to the different arguments and judging between them'; fair because it gave everybody an equal share of whatever 'good things of life' the state had to offer, the sort of good things that the oligarchs wanted to keep to themselves (6.39).[125] The democrats recognised certain differences between their own and the oligarchs' intentions and outlook that related to the Athenian code of behaviour. The oligarchs wanted to rule their fellow citizens even if that meant subjecting themselves to Athens' enemies; the democrats did not object to ruling other people, but to them that meant sharing the state's

---

[120] Thucydides 6.39. For the antagonism between the democrats and oligarchs in the fourth century, see Mossé 1973: 60–7.

[121] Cf. Herman 1987 for the *xenia* networks, involving prominent Athenians, that could have been deployed as power bases to that effect.

[122] The Old Oligarch, for example, represents the struggle between the people and 'the best element' in the polis as a zero-sum game that one party must win at the expense of the other, with compromise not an option (1.8–9; cf. Nippel 1980: 36).

[123] Cf. Krentz 1982: 64 and Whitehead 1982/3, who contend plausibly that in 404 the so-called 'Thirty Tyrants' sought to set up Athens as a replica of Sparta, and D. M. Lewis 1993, who suggests that they were trying to make Athenian institutions work better. For the imitation of Spartan customs, as ridiculed in Aristophanic comedy, see David 1984. For oratorical expressions of the tension between politically equal but socio-economically unequal citizens, see Missiou 1992.

[124] Cf. *The Athenian Constitution* 28.

[125] On oligarchies in general see now Ostwald 2000b and 2000c, including earlier bibliography on the subject.

power equally with their fellow citizens (cf. Isocrates 7.68, *Areopagiticus*). The oligarchs' behaviour betrayed greed and disrespect for the law and the constitution. As soon as they became masters of the state in 411 they abolished the *graphe paranomon* procedure, a safeguard against unconstitutional legislation; in 404 they expropriated their victims' property for their own private use (Lysias 12, *Against Eratosthenes*; *The Athenian Constitution* 35.4). In similar circumstances the democrats would have acted in a diametrically opposite fashion.

At times tensions between these mutually antagonistic groups ran high, although they never broke out into an open clash of forces. Nor were they ever the immediate cause of violent revolution: the events of 411 and 404 were triggered (the former indirectly, the latter directly) by external forces. For these reasons, it would be wrong to think of these antagonisms as weak spots or built-in structural deficiencies that were constantly threatening to wreak havoc with Athenian society. According to the picture that seems to be gaining ground in modern scholarship, Athens differed from most other Greek city-states in at least three respects.

It was, in the first place, *well ordered* and *well run*. If the aim of a political system should be to translate private interests and sectarian demands into resolutions capable of binding together a community, it would appear that this one achieved its aim with masterful competence. As far as we know, all major decisions (i.e. those relating to declarations of war, peace treaties, legislation or capital punishment) were taken by the central organs of the state, all the prescribed formalities being scrupulously observed. Decisions were then transmitted to the lower levels of the executive hierarchy and implemented in full, even if they aroused opposition and proved painful to some Athenians. As examples, one might cite the policy of allowing the Spartans to devastate the fields (which they systematically did, five times) during the Peloponnesian War, or the wholesale banishment or execution of politicians who were suspected of amassing too much power, showing anti-democratic tendencies or otherwise disrespecting the system. Even the fiercest opponents of democracy had to admit that, despite some errors and setbacks, it was a highly successful system.

Athenian democracy was, in the second place, *resilient*. During the period we are talking about, Athens was on average at war for more than two years out of every three.[126] War often generated a state of extreme crisis; the social order of democratic Athens was all but shattered, with violent disruption to her social bonds, on at least five occasions. The first such crisis

---

[126] Finley 1985b: 67.

was the invasion and occupation of both the city and the surrounding countryside by Xerxes and the consequent evacuation of the population to nearby islands (480). The second was the plague that struck during the first years of the Peloponnesian War (430–427). Third was the great Sicilian naval disaster of 413, followed by the first oligarchic coup in 411. Fourth came final defeat in the Peloponnesian War, followed by the second oligarchic coup of 404. Finally, the Athenians were defeated by Philip II at Chaeronea in 338. Far from merely surviving these ordeals, however, Athens seems actually to have been reinvigorated by each new disaster (except, of course, the last). In the fifty years following the Persian invasion she completed the process of democratisation, making herself the strongest city in the Greek world. After the destruction of their great fleet in Sicily the Athenians were briefly despondent, but then decided 'that they must not give in' (Thucydides 8.1.3). After the defeat of 404 and the short-lived Spartan-sponsored oligarchy, Athens' democratic system did not, as Thucydides had predicted, collapse under the pressure of war,[127] but was speedily re-established, Athens once again becoming a major power. The restored democracy was 'also capable of continuous minor adjustments through the fourth century, demonstrating that the Athenian *demos* was consciously concerned with the continual renewal and perfection of the political system'.[128] In this respect Athens was completely unlike Sparta, whose highly sophisticated but basically precarious social edifice was devastated by a single massive defeat (at Leuctra, in 371). The simultaneous collapse of her traditional value system was sufficient demonstration that 'in the long run ancient Sparta failed, both as a power unit and as a social system'.[129]

Athenian society was, in the third place, *stable*, in that it was relatively *free from civil strife* (at least by comparison with the other Greek states, which were more often than not engulfed in *stasis*).[130] As we have seen, democratic Athens suffered only two short-lived anti-democratic coups, in 411 and 404. Neither of these owed anything to the traditional grounds for civil war in Greece (demands for the cancellation of debts and redistribution of land); one was triggered by war, the other by foreign invasion, and Athens quickly recovered from both. When in the end her system did irreversibly crumble, it was simply because she, along with the rest of Greece, had been

---

[127] Cf. Ober 1993a.
[128] Murray 1987: 333. For a critique of the once widely accepted view that Athens underwent a 'crisis' in the fourth century, see in general Eder 1995a, and in particular Eder 1995b and J. K. Davis 1995.
[129] Cartledge 1989: x.
[130] Cf. A. H .M. Jones 1957: 91–2; Lintott 1982; Fuks 1984a; Gehrke 1985.

overwhelmed by the superior Macedonian forces. Right up to 322 Athens had a well organised and vigorous social system.[131]

This conclusion may help us to adumbrate one of that series of rules that I have suggested calling a code of behaviour. 'Society . . . cannot subsist', wrote Adam Smith, 'among those who are at all times ready to hurt and injure one another . . .'[132] This has to mean that where society does subsist people are not in general prepared to hurt and injure each other, their impulse to do so having somehow been stifled. Under such conditions conflicts do not normally turn violent, and when they do they do not escalate. Escalation is avoided either because, as Gellner puts it, one group has [forcibly] secured control, or because some balancing mechanism has been developed that inhibits escalation.[133] Society has, in other words, achieved an internal balance of forces.[134]

If we except the brief oligarchic coups, it cannot be said that any party ever forcibly secured control of Athens during the period we are talking about. We must therefore conclude that the tensions that I diagnosed earlier were counterbalanced in one way or another: that they were contained, inhibited or prevented from arising by factors and processes external to the social circumstances that generated them. The conclusion that presents itself is, in other words, that Athenian democracy possessed the means of resolving its deepest structural differences.

Modern historians dealing with this subject seem to have grasped this point intuitively. Two sets of data, both pointing in the same direction, may have helped them to do so. One is the evidence that tells us how the Athenians behaved during the crises cited above. The other has to do with Athens' pre-democratic past. Plainly democracy did not spring forth overnight out of a radically non-democratic system. It was, on the contrary, the end product of a gradual and laborious process bearing the marks of many adjustments and accommodations. This process reveals a strong underlying pattern: in Athens, during the Solonian reforms, during the

---

[131] This point now seems to be gaining ground in modern research. See Herman 1994; Eder 1995b; J. K. Davies 1995; Herman 2000a.

[132] Adam Smith 1976: 124–5; cf. Coase 1976: 545.

[133] Cf. E. Gellner (1991) *Plough, Sword and Book*. London: Paladin: 178.

[134] For a similar conclusion with regard to the polis in general, see Donlan 1980: 179: '. . . the very nature of the polis had a moderating influence on social discord; the polis idea was the centripetal principle which thrust the complex of contradictory social impulses into the frame of "the common good". The nobleman may have considered himself to be above and apart from the common people, but never apart from the polis; aristocrat and non-aristocrat alike agreed that a man existed to serve the community'.

Cleisthenic reforms and even under the tyranny of the Peisistratids, violent flare-ups were consistently avoided by means of last-minute compromise.

These and certain other considerations have convinced scholars that stability was one of the keys to the Athenian democracy's success. In attempting to account for this stability they have produced various explanations that bear some relevance to our attempt to reconstruct the Athenian code of behaviour. I have selected three of these to mention here, since lack of space prevents us from considering all of the many comments that have been made on this subject.

Finley identified the key to what he called the 'pragmatic success of the Athenian democracy' as the people's 'sense of community ... fortified by the state religion, by their myths and their traditions'. 'Neither the sovereign Assembly, with its unlimited right of participation', he wrote, 'nor the popular jury-courts nor the selection of officials by lot nor ostracism could have prevented either chaos on the one hand or tyranny on the other, had there not been the self-control among enough of the citizen-body to contain its own behaviour within bounds.'[135] Josiah Ober, in an extensive and highly original study, asserted that the key to Athens' stability was to be found in what he called the 'discourse of Athenian democracy'. The process of communication between ordinary and elite citizens had, he argued, a mediating and integrative effect. It thus became 'a primary factor in the promotion and maintenance of social harmony, and it made direct democratic decision making possible'.[136] Paul Cartledge inferred from a series of papers published in 1998 with a view to re-evaluating the foundations of classical Athens' 'highly successful experiment in communal social existence' that the secret of Athens' success 'lay in its multiple forums for, and determined practice of, creative political and social adaptation. The highly pressured tensions between conflicting and often contradictory social groups, forces and ideologies were thus channelled positively – again for the most part – into progressive and above all solidary outlets, principally through the medium of civic ritual.'[137]

These contributions to our understanding of Athens' stability are important ones that I shall in due course be incorporating into my own account of the city's code of behaviour. I believe nonetheless that these authors, since they did not set out to review Athenian behaviour in the light of

---

[135] Finley 1985a: 29–30.
[136] Ober 1989: 35. Ober's 'elite' and 'mass' coincide to a large extent with the groups referred to above as rich and poor, or oligarchs and democrats. Cf. Shaw 1994.
[137] Cartledge 1998a: 12.

the established pattern of Athenian stability, did not take certain mechanisms into consideration: mechanisms that may surely be assumed to have been involved in rendering Athens stable, such as, for instance, the coercive power of the state and the ideological power of religion.[138] Let us now, with these observations in mind, set out on the search for the particular combination of rules that the Athenians designed to cope with the clash of individual wishes in the wonderfully multifarious sets of circumstances to which city life gave rise.

[138] These are analysed in Chapters 7 and 9 respectively.

CHAPTER 3

The moral image of the Athenian democracy

MORAL IDEAS AND DEMOCRACY

Having reviewed the main characteristics of the Athenian democracy and the manner in which the collective moral views of its citizens imprinted themselves upon some of its institutions, we may return to our central question, in its several aspects. Just what combination of assumptions and rules (whether explicit or implicit, written or unwritten) regulated co-operation and conflict in Athenian society? What description of that society's typical patterns of behaviour would be most faithful to the experience of the Athenian people in the course of nearly two hundred years of democratic rule? Can we somehow make explicit the code of behaviour that came into existence to reconcile an unwieldy mass of conflicting wishes of which the Athenians themselves were not always aware and that they could not always put into words?

Our question is not a new one. In principle, if not precisely in this form, it has already been asked repeatedly, in both ancient and modern times, both by scholars and by people who would not regard themselves as such. At various times and to varying extents one or another of its aspects has been emphasised. In what sort of atmosphere was democratic rule nourished and maintained? What were the average Athenian's aspirations and expectations? How should we conceive of the character and intensity of the emotions, impulses, pressures, drives and stimuli that acted upon the common people of Athens as they engaged in public life and upon men such as Socrates, Plato, Aristotle, Thucydides, Aeschylus, Sophocles, Euripides, Aristophanes, Pheidias and Praxiteles as they pursued their intellectual ends?

Expanding its focus from the individual to the community, our question has sometimes been posed in terms of polar opposites. Is the truth that city life in democratic Athens was bad-tempered, quarrelsome, intolerant, permeated by mutual suspicion, imbued with constantly smouldering hatreds and petty jealousies, and ridden with rivalries and unbridled violence? Alternatively, was it genuinely dominated by a spirit of reconciliation, tolerance, mutual trust, renunciation of revenge and avoidance of violence: in brief, by the attitudes ascribed to it in these famous words attributed to Pericles:

Tolerance is what we show in public life, and we are not suspicious about each other's daily activities. We are not angry with our neighbour if he does as he chooses, nor do we go round wearing the sort of expression that may not actually injure anybody, but causes hurt feelings. While in our private interactions we do our best to give no cause for offence, in public matters we restrain ourselves from illegal action out of reverent fear. (Thucydides 2.37.2)

Should we, in other words, think of Athenian society in terms of history's most violent societies or of its most pacific ones? Should we, coming back to the typology worked out earlier,[1] conceive of it as dominated by the spirit of the first, second or third category of moral injunction?

During the period we are examining Athenian democracy reached its zenith. Its system consisted, as we have seen, of joint rule by equals. Irrespective of birth and (with a few exceptions) of economic status, every Athenian citizen was entitled to perform administrative, political, religious and judicial functions, to cast his vote at the meetings of the sovereign Assembly and to address his fellow Athenians at these meetings whether or not he currently held any office. In terms of present-day democracies any principle of equal power and opportunities that in practice excluded a large part of the population could appear inconsequential; one might even say trivial. Looked at against the broader comparative perspective of past societies, however, the very existence of this principle cannot fail to impress. Very seldom throughout history have the free lower classes (peasants, craftsmen and shopkeepers) enjoyed the same amount of power as aristocrats and the rich. Democracy, defined as government in the interest of 'the many' (who, as Aristotle noted, coincided with 'the poor' (*Politics* 1279b4)), was until all too recently a striking rarity amongst the governmental systems of the western world.[2] Modern scholars are right to censure the Athenian democracy for leaving metics, women and slaves disenfranchised. When put in perspective, however, this criticism appears less telling. It should be remembered, for instance, that the great democracies of the nineteenth century denied women and the poor the right to vote more or less throughout that period, and that some persisted in doing so well into the twentieth century.

---

[1] See pp. 1–15.
[2] For a brief overview of ancient and modern democracies, see Dahl 1998: ch. 2.

The Athenian democracy was also remarkable for the circumstances in which it arose. Very seldom have attempts to achieve equality been successful without bloodshed or revolution,[3] and all too seldom have they resulted in the establishment of a stable, effective and relatively long-lasting political system. Apart from some fifth-century Greek cities that set themselves up as democracies in conscious emulation of the Athenians and a few others on which democracy was forcibly imposed by Athens, the search for parallels yields a very poor harvest indeed.[4]

Nor does the picture change significantly if we adopt a less stringent definition of democracy. Even if we ignore the requirement that the lower classes should be incorporated into the governmental process, democracy must surely belong to that wider category of political regimes in which the exercise of power is collective and is subordinated to explicitly formulated rules.[5] If we accept this definition we can think of a few more parallels; for example, the Greek oligarchies,[6] republican Rome and some of the cities of Renaissance Italy. We are, however, unlikely to be overwhelmed by the number of new examples springing to mind. Throughout history regimes of this sort have generally been outnumbered (and outlasted) by regimes of the monarchic type in which power is concentrated in the hands of a ruler, often one who is nothing more than a puppet manipulated by a host of scheming courtiers. The Athenian democracy stands out as highly unusual amongst the governments of the pre-industrial West. Its rarity raises the question of how, entirely against the general run of things, this one system did manage to come into existence and then survive for almost two centuries. It is my contention that we can come closest to answering this question by unravelling the specific combination of rules that the Athenians designed to administer their communal life.

There is, however, more to it than that. Most modern thinkers would probably agree with Winston Churchill's joke, 'Democracy is the worst form of government in the world – except for all the other forms.' The majority of Greek thinkers, however, were agreed that with the exception of tyranny most other forms of government really were better than democracy. Fundamentally they objected to it because they were members of the upper classes themselves and were afraid that incorporating the lower classes into the government might debase ethical standards, cause political

---

[3] This point is well brought out in Eder 1997.
[4] For democracies outside Athens, see Chapter 2, n. 6. For continuity (or lack of it) between the Athenian democracy and modern democracies, see Eder 1997.
[5] Cf. Finley 1983 and Millar 1999; 2002.
[6] For which see Chapter 2, n. 125.

institutions to degenerate, stifle intellectual activity and vulgarise cultural life. Inspired by this line of reasoning, and possibly by a modicum of personal experience, some modern scholars have followed suit. 'Is it possible', asked the great Russian-born historian M. I. Rostovtzeff in 1926, 'to extend a higher civilisation to the lower classes without debasing its standard and diluting its quality to the vanishing point?'[7]

With the benefit of subsequent research, we can aver that as far as Athens was concerned the ancient assessment of democracy was seriously at fault and the answer to Rostovtzeff's question a resounding 'yes'.[8] Far from setting Athens on the road to decline, the rule of the 'whole people' paved the way to political stability and to previously unattained levels of intellectual creativity. By a joint effort of the aristocracy and the *demos* (we may note, in passing, that Socrates was the son of an artisan, that some of the most striking masterpieces of Attic visual art were produced by metics and slaves, that the audiences who were held spellbound by the Athenian playwrights were predominantly lower-class[9] and that Aristophanes made fun of everything under the sun from a standpoint rooted in the robust common sense of the masses) the Athenians created a remarkably original culture, one that scholars today do not blush to describe as 'one of the momentous achievements of the human mind'.[10] The temporal coincidence between the apotheosis of this culture and the period of democratic rule is of central importance to the argument of this book: neither before nor after democracy did the Athenians produce anything to match what they achieved *under* it. Neither before nor after was there, in the words of an eminent anthropologist, such 'an enormous concentration of culture, energy and innovation, of production of high cultural values, and of flourishing of men of the first rank of genius . . .'[11] In other words, Athens' highest intellectual achievement and her democratic interlude coincided to such an extent that it would be illogical not to assume that they were in some way related to one another.[12]

---

[7] M. I. Rostovzeff (1926) *Social and Economic History of the Roman Empire*. Oxford: Clarendon Press: 436. At 484 Rostovtzeff asks, 'Is not every civilisation bound to decay as soon as it penetrates the mass?'

[8] Cf. A. H. M. Jones 1957: ch. 3.

[9] Raaflaub 1994: 126 puts this well: 'democracy not only "democratized" the aristocracy but "aristocratized" the demos'. For the resources and means of competition used by the aristocracy in the struggle for prestige, status and power in the archaic age and in fifth-century Athens, see Stein-Hölkeskamp 1989.

[10] Ostwald 1992: 349.

[11] A. L. Kroeber (1923) *Anthropology. Culture Patterns and Processes*. New York and London: A Harvest/HBJ Book: 135. For a demonstration that the fifth century's high literary and artistic culture continued into the fourth century, albeit in somewhat different form, see R. W. Wallace 1995.

[12] Herodotus and Thucydides certainly thought they were; cf. Strasburger 1954: 243–8.

Some contemporaries would have agreed with this view of Athenian society. In the Funeral Oration, Pericles asserted that the greatness of Athens was due not merely to her constitution (*politeia*), but also to her people's distinctive pursuits (*epitedeusis*) and way of life (*tropos*) (2.36.4). His observation may help us to bridge the gap between the 'code of behaviour' and the political and social characteristics of Athens that we discussed in chapters 1 and 2. It may also provide a clue as to how best to explore a further ramification of our central thesis. If we can succeed in revealing whatever peculiar combination of rules gave rise to the spirit and way of life celebrated by Pericles, we may find that we have hit upon a key to a better understanding of the Athenian intellectual achievement.

How, though, are we to understand the nature of that spirit and the essence of that way of life? Modern scholarship has come up with few answers that are either consistent or well argued. In the total absence of any consensus as to how this issue should be handled, Athenian morality has been subjected to a disturbingly confusing series of judgements. It may be said, anticipating a later conclusion, that these reflect modern preconceptions far better than they do any ancient state of affairs. To the examination of these assessments we shall now turn.

SOME MODERN ASSESSMENTS

Broadly speaking, three stages stand out in the history of modern perceptions of the Athenian democracy. In the eighteenth and early nineteenth centuries Athens was regarded 'as a key example of civic lawlessness, political disorder, and the absence of political security'.[13] Later in the nineteenth century this assessment underwent radical revision, the Athenians being transfigured into paragons of political and cultural excellence. Towards the turn of the century this 'optimistic' view of the Athenian democracy was gradually undermined, giving way to what was later to be called 'Greek pessimism'. With a few qualifications and some interesting exceptions, this view of ancient Athens still prevails today.

I propose now to take a closer look at these stages, although it is not my intention to produce an exhaustive survey. The point of this examination is to expose the frequently contradictory nature of history's various interpretations of the Athenian democracy. It should be noted that as far as I am aware no attempt has previously been made to reconcile

---

[13] Turner 1981: 189.

the contradictions, or to draw any conclusion from the mere fact of their existence.[14]

The more important eighteenth-century writers, among them Montesquieu and Rousseau, praised Sparta for its strong, stable political system and condemned Athens on account of the supposedly giddy and fickle spirit of its people. A typical example of this attitude is to be found in Temple Stanyan's *The Grecian History from the Origins of Greece to the End of the Peloponnesian War*, published in 1739 and translated into French by Diderot a few years afterwards. The 'Temper of the Athenians' was, according to Stanyan, 'too delicate, and capricious, to be brought to those grave and regular Austerities; and without considering the great Sway the People bore in the Execution of the Laws, the Laws themselves were more numerous and confus'd, and could not therefore be so religiously observ'd as they were at *Sparta*'.[15]

Writing in the age that spawned the French and American Revolutions, William Mitford, the author of a ten-volume *History of Greece*[16] that was the first major narrative history of Greece in English, went further. Heaping lavish praise on the Greek tyrants and on Philip II of Macedonia, he condemned Athens as corrupt and averred that her supposed political liberty existed in name alone. According to Mitford, factional rule and the tyranny of the masses had brought about a complete dissolution of her social bonds. The result was the total disintegration of any sense of a common civic interest: '[F]or maintaining civil order and holding the state together, flattery and bribes alone could persuade the multitude, and the only alternative was violence.'[17] The poor, out of sheer envy of the rich, put them on trial, extracted bribes from them, confiscated their property and filled their own pockets with jury fees. Ostracism was an instrument of 'democratic jealousy' for repressing outstandingly talented people. The so-called social compact collapsed altogether, no longer consisting 'in the security of every one against injury from others', but rather 'in the power of every one to injure others'. Unable to restrain their ambition, the people offered no protection to any group from which a more responsible leadership might emerge. Things were at such a low ebb that any attempt at reform seemed doomed to failure.

---

[14] Apart from the works cited below, I have drawn heavily upon the following general historiographical studies: Ehrenberg 1946; Loraux and Vidal-Naquet 1979; Turner 1981; Connor, Hanse, Raaflaub and Strauss 1990; J. T. Roberts 1994.
[15] 2 vols, London, 1739, vol. I: 180–1, his italics.
[16] The first volume appeared in 1784, the tenth in 1810.   [17] Vol. V: 35.

On the other side of the Atlantic, Athens was viewed with a mixture of admiration and scepticism. In his *A Defence of the Constitutions of Government of the United States of America* (published in 1787–8), John Adams suggested that America should adopt the constitutional means used by the Greek and Roman republics to preserve the freedom of their citizens within the confines of just laws and acceptable traditions. 'Every example of government', he wrote, 'which has a large mixture of democratical power exhibits something to our view that is amiable, noble, and, I had almost said, divine.' Athens, however, was apparently an exception to this rule. Her constitution was unbalanced. All her powers, legislative, judicial and executive, were concentrated in the Assembly. The Athenian state was therefore perpetually tormented by 'never-ending fluctuations in the national councils, continual factions, massacres, proscriptions, banishment and death of the best citizens'.[18] Most American intellectuals of Adams' time would have shared his view. One exception was Thomas Paine, who cherished an unreservedly enthusiastic idea of Athens. In his *Rights of Man* he wrote: '[I]n the democracy of the Athenians we see more to admire and less to condemn . . . than anything which history affords.' It was his expressed hope that what Athens was in miniature, America might be in full magnitude.[19]

In Europe Mitford's vision of Athens carried the day until the first quarter of the nineteenth century, when it came under attack from various quarters before eventually being superseded by what Victor Ehrenberg called 'the idealising view of the Greeks'.[20] The principal promoter of this view was a young city banker by the name of George Grote, described by Turner as an 'uncompromising champion of Athenian democracy'. Grote believed, in Turner's words, that the Athenians 'had mastered the art of self-government and . . . had achieved a civilisation wherein artistic excellence, positivistic thought, and individual liberty had largely, if not always perfectly, flourished'. Despite its length, Grote's account of the Athenian character and mores is worth quoting in full:[21]

The [Athenian] national temper was indulgent in a high degree to all the varieties of positive impulse. The peculiar promptings in every individual bosom were allowed to manifest themselves and bear fruit, without being suppressed by external opinion or trained into forced conformity with some assumed standard: antipathies against any of them formed no part of the habitual morality of the citizen. While much of

---

[18] *The Works of John Adams*, 1850–6. Boston, vol. IV: 488, 491–2.
[19] *Common Sense, The Rights of Man, and Other Essential Writings of Thomas Paine* (1984), with an introduction by Sidney Hook, New York: Signet Classic: 239, 242.
[20] Ehrenberg 1946.
[21] Turner 1981: 213; the quotation from Grote is from the New Edition, London, 1870, vol. V: 412–13.

the generating causes of human hatred was rendered inoperative, and while society was rendered more comfortable, more instructive, and more stimulating – all its germs of productive fruitful genius, so rare everywhere, found in such an atmosphere the maximum of encouragement. Within the limits of the law, assuredly as faithfully observed at Athens as anywhere in Greece, individual impulse, taste, and even eccentricity, were accepted with indulgence, instead of being a mark as elsewhere for the intolerance of neighbours or of the public . . . That liberty of individual action, not merely from the over-restraints of law, but from the tyranny of jealous opinion, such as Periklês depicts in Athens, belongs more naturally to a democracy, where there is no select One or Few to receive worship and set the fashion, than to any other form of government. But it is very rare even in democracies. None of the governments of modern times, democratical, aristocratical, or monarchical, presents anything like the picture of generous tolerance towards social dissent, and spontaneity of individual taste, which we read in the speech of the Athenian statesman. In all of them, the intolerance of the national opinion cuts down individual character to one out of a few set types, to which every person, or every family, is constrained to adjust itself, and beyond which all exceptions meet either with hatred or with derision. To impose upon men such restraints either of law or of opinion as are requisite for the security and comfort of society, but to encourage rather than repress the free play of individual impulse subject to those limits – is an ideal, which if it was ever approached at Athens, has certainly never been attained, and has indeed comparatively been little studied or cared for, in any modern society.

Grote's view of Athens had a considerable impact, being praised and adopted by many central figures of his age. Part of Edward A. Freeman's review of Grote's *magnum opus*, for instance, read as follows:[22]

Now a fair examination of Grecian history will assuredly lead us to the conclusion that this mob clothed with executive functions made one of the best governments which the world ever saw. It did not work impossibilities; it did not change earth into paradise nor men into angels; it did not forestall every improvement which has since appeared in the world; still less did it forestall all the improvements which we may trust are yet in store for mankind. But that government cannot be called a bad one which is better than any other government of its own time. And surely that government must be called a good one which is a marked improvement upon every government which has gone before it. The Athenian Democracy is entitled to both these kinds of praise. Dêmos was guilty of some follies and some crimes; but he was guilty of fewer follies and fewer crimes, and he did more wise and noble deeds, than any government of his own or of any earlier age.

John Stuart Mill incorporated Grote's view of the Athenians into his great essay *On Liberty.*[23]

---

[22] E. A. Freeman 1880: 149.
[23] J. S. Mill (1949) *On Liberty* (ed. R. B. McCallum). Oxford: Basil Blackwell: 55.

Notwithstanding the defects of the social system and moral ideas of antiquity, the practice of the dicastery and the ecclesia raised the intellectual standard of the average Athenian citizen far beyond anything of which there is an example in any other mass of men, ancient or modern.

The authors of these passages were principally interested in ideology and politics, often to the exclusion of social life. This gap was filled by Sir Alfred Zimmern, whose *The Greek Commonwealth* (first published in 1911) married politics, religion and economics with sociology and social psychology. Despite these methodological novelties, and despite his avowed aim of painting a portrait of 'what fifth-century Athens was really like', Zimmern, getting rather carried away, urged his readers in a footnote to conceive of Athens thus:[24]

The Athenian community during the Periclean time must be regarded as one of the most successful example of social organization known to history. Its society, that is, was so arranged ('organized' is too deliberate a word) as to make the most and the best of the human material at its disposal. Without any system of national education, in our sense of the word, it 'drew out' of its members all the power and the goodness that was in them . . . We are apt to forget that we owe the Parthenon sculptures not merely to the genius of Pheidias but also to the genius of the social system which knew how to make use of him.

Meanwhile on the continent alternative ideas of the Greek character were being formed. Friedrich Nietzsche's particular interest in the Greeks had to do with moral philosophy. Inspired by Heraclitus, the philosopher who held that 'War is the father of all things',[25] and writing in an age when the phrase '"the survival of the fittest" rolled glibly off everyone's tongue',[26] Nietzsche put forward the view that the noblest cultures were born of conflict. Not just any old conflict, of course; under Hesiod's influence, Nietzsche discriminated between good and bad ones. Bad conflicts, apparently, 'lead men against one another to a war of extermination'. Good conflicts (under which heading Nietzsche classed jealousy, spite and envy) 'rouse men to deeds, but not to deeds of war but to deeds of contest'.[27] The Greeks fitted into this scheme with gratifying neatness, the explanation of precisely how they did so being one of Nietzsche's most striking insights. The Greeks had traditionally been admired for their rational, even-tempered spirit and for their love of balanced beauty and equipoise. Nietzsche did not think that this was the whole picture. Behind the facade

[24] Zimmern 1931: 367n. 2–368n.   [25] Kirk, Raven and Schofield 1983: no. 212.
[26] R. Hofstadter (1945) *Social Darwinism in American Thought*. London: The Beacon Press: 68.
[27] Nietzsche 1971.

of temperance and moderation, he realised, lurked cruelty and savagery, wild and uncontrollable drives and overpowering irrational forces. 'The Greeks', he declared, 'the most humane men of ancient times, have a trait of cruelty, a tigerish lust to annihilate.'[28] In order to achieve anything the Athenians had first had to master these 'Dionysian' forces and redirect them into various contests and ritualistic outlets.[29] Having thus tamed the Greek character, they turned their *agon* (striving to surpass) into the main driving force behind their culture. Such was the necessary precondition of their achievement.

One of Nietzsche's older colleagues at Basel, Jakob Burckhardt, the distinguished historian of Renaissance Italy, also wrote a general study of Greek culture, one of whose openly avowed aims was to expose the idealising view of the Greeks as one of the greatest misrepresentations in the historiography of his own day.[30] Ostensibly uninfluenced by Nietzsche,[31] this work bears the marks of a tormented spirit.[32] Burckhardt's methods were, on his own admission, unconventional. He selected his evidence subjectively and arbitrarily, being 'only and exclusively' guided by whether or not it was of interest to him. He made no attempt to prevent personal bias from intruding into his judgements. A proud aristocrat and a devout individualist, Burckhardt believed that there were few higher virtues than freedom from the compulsion of state and religion, and he proceeded to judge the polis according to this standard. Identifying Sparta as the supreme example of the sort of state he most abhorred, the sort in which every last aspect of individual life was subject to official intervention, Burckhardt decided that all the other Greek states, including Athens, must have been like that as well. He thus arrived at his theory of the omnipotence of the Greek state (*Staatsallmacht*). The coercive power that it exercised, according to him, ensured that its citizens led a far less happy existence than was normally assumed.[33] Nietzsche and Burckhardt perhaps did more than anyone else

---

[28] Nietzsche 1971: 32.   [29] Cf. Hollingdale 1999.

[30] Burckhardt 1929; originally published 1898–1902, after the author's death. Sections of this work have recently been published in English; see Burckhardt 1998.

[31] Cf. Trevor-Roper 1984: 374–5: 'Between Nietzsche's *Birth of Tragedy*, which caused such a storm in the German classical establishment, and Burckhardt's *Griechische Kulturgeschichte*, which was published twenty-seven years later, in spite of all differences of form, there is much in common. Both writers sought to discover the "spirit", the psychological springs, of the Greek character. What excited Burckhardt in Nietzsche's book was the discovery – Nietzsche regarded it as his discovery – of the "Dionysian" spirit in Greek culture: the idea that the Greek achievement did not spring from a naturally balanced serenity – a view made popular by Schiller – but from a successful attempt to master and ritualize overpowering irrational impulses.'

[32] One commentator has remarked that 'to read Burckhardt is to receive the impression he is fighting to stave off a thorough-going melancholia': Hollingdale 1999: 52. Cf. E. Heller (1952) 'Burckhardt and Nietzsche', in *The Disinherited Mind*. Cambridge: Bowes and Bowes.

[33] This motif in Burckhardt's work is skilfully brought out in Nippel 1998.

to undermine 'the picture of the "gay" Greeks' and to inaugurate the trend that Ehrenberg called 'Greek pessimism'.[34]

Gustave Glotz's *La cité grecque*, first published in 1928, exemplifies what was perhaps one of the most striking variations on this trend. Drawing an excessively enthusiastic picture of Athens in the fifth century (we owe to him a now classic formulation, the 'just balance' between 'the legal power of the state and the natural right of the individual'[35]), Glotz opts for a vista of prodigious decadence, corruption and decline during the fourth. The 'just balance' having teetered off centre, excessive individualism and party loyalties now, according to him, ran riot, in complete disregard of the common interest. Glotz's indignation at the state of his own country at the time when he was writing shines through this extraordinarily value-laden characterisation of fourth-century Greek mores:[36]

The power of money was spreading and corrupting morality. Those who had just enough to live on wished to be rich; the rich wished to be still richer. It was the triumph of that insatiable passion for gain which the Greeks called πλεονεξία. There was no longer a profession which escaped the clutches of capitalism, of *chrematistike*. Agriculture was commercialized to such an extent that by the progressive eviction of small peasants and the concentration of estates in the same hands the system of large estates was recreated. Rhetoricians, advocates and artists, who had formerly reckoned it a dishonour to commercialize their talent, now felt no scruples in selling their goods as dearly as possible. Everything could be bought, everything had its price, and wealth was the measure of social values. By gain and by extravagance fortunes were made and unmade with great rapidity. Those who had money rushed into pleasure-seeking and sought every occasion for gross displays of luxury. The newly rich (νεόπλουτοι) were cocks of the walk. Men speculated and rushed after money in order to build and furnish magnificent houses, to display fine weapons, to offer to the women of their family and to courtesans jewels, priceless robes and rare perfumes, to place before eminent guests and fashionable parasites fine wines and dishes prepared by a famous chef, or to commission some popular sculptor to carve their bust.

The pessimistic view of Athenian society ushered in by these authors did not achieve popularity all at once. By the middle of the twentieth century, however, the accusations that had been levelled against Athens made up a list as long as your arm. The Athenian democracy was said to have fed parasitically on the fruits of slavery and empire. It was also corrupt, incompetent and immoral. (The same three events were usually produced

---

[34] Ehrenberg 1946.   [35] Glotz 1929: 143.
[36] Glotz 1929: 311. Though this passage is meant to refer to the whole of Greece, not just to Athens, and though Glotz remarks that 'Athens had still a certain discipline in this respect', the passage's documentation (omitted here) consists predominantly of quotations from fourth-century Athenian writers. I am grateful for this point to M. Claude Mossé.

as evidence of these qualities: the confusion surrounding the launch of the invasion of Syracuse, the execution of the victorious generals after the battle of Arginusae and Athens' failure to stave off the Macedonian conquest.) A democracy in name alone, it was really a tyranny of the masses, the trial of Socrates exemplifying the common people's irrational hatred for men of genius and the lengths to which they were prepared to go to silence the voice of reason and individual conscience.

All along, however, a few lonely dissenting views were being voiced. In the 1950s A. H. M. Jones, the author of four innovative articles about the Athenian democracy, appealed to his readers' sense of justice as follows, not without a touch of sarcasm:

My readers can judge whether the 'extreme democracy', in which the people were sovereign, and vulgar persons who worked with their hands enjoyed full political rights, including access to all offices, and owing to their greater numbers preponderated in the assembly, was indeed so pernicious a form of government as Athenian philosophers and historians represent.[37]

Jones' successor in the chair of ancient history at Cambridge, Finley, observed that it was hardly surprising that it should be easy to compile 'a catalogue of cases of repression, sycophancy, irrational behaviour, and outright brutality' in the Athenian democracy given that this had lasted for almost two hundred years. Continually accused of 'idealising Athens', he responded as follows:

In those centuries Athens was, by all pragmatic tests, much the greatest Greek state, with a powerful feeling of community, with a toughness and resilience tempered, even granted its imperial ambitions, by a humanity and sense of equity and responsibility quite extraordinary for its day (and for many another day as well). Lord Acton, paradoxically enough, was one of the few historians to have grasped the historic significance of the amnesty of 403. 'The hostile parties', he wrote, 'were reconciled, and proclaimed an amnesty, the first in history.' *The first in history*, despite all the familiar weaknesses, despite the crowd psychology, the slaves, the personal ambition of many leaders, the impatience of the majority with opposition. Nor was this the only Athenian innovation: the structure and mechanism of the democracy were all their own invention, as they groped for something without precedent, having nothing to go on but their own notion of freedom, their community solidarity, their willingness to inquire (or at least to accept the consequences of inquiry), and their widely shared political experience.[38]

---

[37] A. H. M. Jones 1957: 72.
[38] Finley 1974: 24–5, his italics. The quotation from Lord Acton is from his 'The history of freedom in antiquity' in G. Himmelfarb (ed.) (1956) *Essays on Freedom and Power*. Boston: Beacon Press: 64.

A few years after the publication of Finley's book, de Romilly remarked that during the two hundred year heyday of Athenian civilisation the ideal of gentleness (*douceur*) had surged to the fore in many guises (courteous behaviour, political tolerance, patience, forbearance, calm), marking every part of Athenian society and gaining vastly in importance by the end of the fifth century.[39]

The trend of 'Greek pessimism' to which Jones, Finley and de Romilly were reacting skimmed over the Athenian political system. Modern historians did not condemn democracy itself, continuing rather to extol its virtues. The 'pessimistic' trend did, however, begin to make its presence felt in an increasing number of works dealing with Greek morality, which, because Athens was so over-represented in the evidence, usually meant *Athenian* morality. The verdict of most modern historians who wrote about this subject was that Athenian morality was pretty much non-existent. Let us examine a few illustrations of this trend, remarking in passing that the awkward question of how so admirable a political system could have been underpinned by a moral system of such degradation appears never to have arisen.

In his highly acclaimed *The Greeks*, H. D. F. Kitto described the Greeks as vindictive, insincere and oversensitive about their standing among their peers. The Greek individual was, according to him, 'zealous, and was expected to be zealous, in claiming what was due to him. Modesty was not highly regarded, and that Virtue is its own reward is a doctrine that the Greek would think mere foolishness . . .' Musing on what Aristotle's 'man of great soul' and the average Greek might have had in common, Kitto remarked[40] that it

is his lively sense of his own worth, and his desire for 'honour', that justice should be done to him. This is which does most to explain the unashamed desire for revenge. A man owes it to himself to be revenged; to put up with an injury would imply that the other man was "better" than you are. Aristotle's character is unusual in this, that he does not bear a grudge. But why not? Not because he thinks it morally wrong, but because he judges this to be beneath him. He does not forgive: he only despises and forgets. The ordinary Greek did neither.

A leading twentieth-century British classicist, K. J. Dover, wrote the book that deservedly became the acknowledged starting point for all subsequent studies of Greek morality. In its collecting and ordering of previously unprocessed material his *Greek Popular Morality in the Time of Plato and Aristotle* would be almost impossible to surpass. A certain eccentricity in

[39] De Romilly 1979: 3.   [40] Kitto 1969: 243–7.

his method, however, attracted critical fire right from the moment of the book's publication. *Greek Popular Morality* is a work of outright subjectivity, Greek norms being avowedly seen through Dover's eyes; he himself was keen to point out that the questions he had chosen to ask about Greek morality had been prompted by his own personal experience. Classifying his Greek material under headings such as 'Human Nature', 'Heredity and Environment', 'Sex', 'Age', 'Status', 'Understanding', 'Divine Intervention' and 'Moral Responsibility', and jumbling together evidence from Athens with material from other poleis, Dover drew a pessimistic picture of Greek sentiments and emotions. Arguing that public morality was 'essentially unsystematic', he announced that he had discovered an underlying truth. This was that the moral code of the Greeks in general, and the Athenians in particular, was dominated by a non-conciliatory spirit of vengeance, a spirit that in practice manifested itself as unbridled violence. Dover's view is epitomised by the remark, 'The attempt to retaliate upon an enemy being justified ("unobjectionable", Dem. 5.15), successful retaliation was a joy, a failure a horror: a man might be respected for attempting revenge and denigrated for making no attempt.'[41]

Perhaps the most systematic attempt to penetrate the meanings of Greek value-terms, both Homeric and classical, was made by A. W. H. Adkins. In a series of books and articles, Adkins organised his material into two groups of diametrically opposed and mutually antagonistic virtues, the first group being competitive, aristocratic and egocentric, the other co-operative, lower-class and community-oriented.[42] His attitude to the so-called 'lexical method'[43] was hypercritical (he once remarked, justly in the opinion of the present author, that in English renderings of Greek value-terms we hear only 'the echoes of our voice'),[44] but he made use of it nonetheless. Doggedly disputing questions of method with Dover and with others,[45] Adkins reached a verdict on Athens' mores that was by and large pessimistic: 'In the law-courts, in internal politics and in foreign policy, competitive *arete* prevails over co-operative excellence.'[46]

Such was the legacy that was handed down to a younger generation of scholars. Many of these scholars seem consequently to have felt obliged to express some sort of dissatisfaction with Athenian morality in the course of making their own considerable contributions to the study of ancient Athens. Mary Blundell wrote an entire book-length study around a stylised

---

[41] Dover 1974: 182.   [42] Adkins 1960a, 1960b, 1963, 1969a, 1969b, 1972, 1975, 1976.
[43] See pp. 102–3.   [44] Adkins 1987: 322.
[45] Adkins 1978 (contra Dover); 1987 (contra Gagarin). For Dover's reaction see Dover 1983.
[46] Adkins 1972: 139.

saying, a proverb that she presumably regarded as having captured the essential spirit of the Greeks' mores: 'Greek popular thought is pervaded by the assumption that one should help one's friends and harm one's enemies . . . This in turn stimulated the desire to retaliate, for revenge is sweet (Aristotle, *Rhetoric* 1370b30).'[47] John Winkler asserted that 'insulting behaviour between citizens occurred aplenty, particularly in the conspicuous echelons of the ambitious and well-to-do. Inviolability of the person may have been the rule, violence was not infrequently the practice . . . Daily life in Athens for the average citizen was surely not a perpetual, near-violent squabble. But for the conspicuously wealthy . . . and for young men – i.e., for those for whom honor is a leading concern – life could certainly be lived by hair-trigger rules of contentiousness'.[48] Matthew Christ decided that 'Athenians shared with other Greeks the basic assumption that when a man suffered at the hands of another, he should pursue vengeance (*timoria*) in his own person not only to right the wrong, but also to defend his reputation.'[49] Anne Pippin Burnett, whose ideas about Athenian life are largely extrapolated from the tragedies, tells us that '[o]utside the courts, in dealing with public adversaries, it was axiomatic that "to satisfy one's heart with vengeance upon the enemy accords with the best tradition" . . . [P]rivate acts of nonbloody revenge seem to have been taken for granted. Athenians were convinced that the return of the first blow was justified . . . Everyday life was evidently rich in . . . retaliations'.[50] Nick Fisher developed a theory that Athens was constantly smouldering with some sort of low-level violence, writing, 'Much evidence confirms that a level of violence or insult could be regarded by some at least as common, be accepted fairly casually, and was not necessarily expected to produce either serious injury or major legal problems.'[51] Getting into the general mood, various other scholars added their condemnations to the list, revealing classical Athens as xenophobic, patriarchal and sexist.[52]

At this point a new formative influence appeared on the scene. In 1965 J. G. Peristiany, an anthropologist, published a collection of articles that opened up a new avenue of approach and laid the foundations of an entire anthropological sub-discipline. The central message of *Honour and Shame: The Values of Mediterranean Society*[53] was that in terms of social mores all the countries of the Mediterranean, past and present, constituted a single

---

[47] M. W. Blundell 1989: 24.   [48] Winkler 1990: 49.   [49] Christ 1998: 191.
[50] Burnett 1998: 55. Cf. Visser 1984: 194 (again extrapolated mainly from tragedy): 'Vengeance automatically followed the smirching of honor; it required equality of damage done, and "blood must have blood".'
[51] Fisher 1998: 75.   [52] E.g. Keuls 1985; Wohl 1999.   [53] Peristiany 1965.

discrete, homogenous cultural entity, marked, in particular, by a specifically Mediterranean variety of the honour-and-shame syndrome. This idea was in some ways reminiscent of Fernand Braudel's classic *The Mediterranean and the Mediterranean World in the Age of Philip II*.[54] Braudel had asserted that all Mediterranean cultures were basically very similar, being set apart from the inland areas of Europe in particular by their climate (all Mediterranean people, apparently, invariably congregating out of doors) and by having been ruled by the Romans (the Roman empire having roughly coincided with today's 'Mediterranean world'). He had not, however, included 'honour and shame' among the factors responsible for this remarkable unity. This momentous step was taken by Peristiany and his followers, who turned the idea of Mediterraneity into a sort of axiom from which to derive syllogisms ('if it is geographically Mediterranean, it will be found to have a certain specific non-continental moral code'). Apparently untroubled by local differences such as that between urban Rome and rural Sicily, Peristiany's adherents saw all Mediterranean cultures as united by 'a pervasive and relatively uniform value system based on complementary codes of honour and shame'.[55] In the introduction to a volume jointly edited by Pitt-Rivers and Peristiany (who died before it was published), the central tenet of this value system was formulated thus: 'It is in this sense that a person's honour is said to be sacred, something more precious to him than even his life, of which it was traditionally viewed as the epitome. "Rather death than dishonour" was the ideal expression of this sentiment, whether on the battlefield or in the boudoir.'[56]

Two main objections to this conception of a uniform Mediterranean code of honour were put forward. Firstly, it was very clear that certain areas outside the Mediterranean basin (northern Europe in particular) had codes of honour that were remarkably similar to the 'Mediterranean' one.[57] Secondly, the most cursory investigation sufficed to show that ideas of honour displayed considerable variation even inside the boundaries defined by 'Mediterraneity', compelling the critic to wonder whether one 'single model [were] capable of capturing local subtleties and complexities'.[58] Despite protests such as these,[59] most scholars chose not to discard the theory of a unified Mediterranean code of honour wholesale, instead retaining it in modified form. For example, a valuable collection of essays (edited by Gilmore) that set out to rethink the 'nagging questions about the alleged

---

[54] London: Fontana/Collins, 1972–3, first published in France in 1949.   [55] Gilmore 1987: 2.
[56] Peristiany and Pitt-Rivers 1992: 2.   [57] E.g. F. H. Stewart 1994: 76–7; McAleer 1994.
[58] Brandes 1987: 121.   [59] E.g. Pina-Cabral 1989; C. S. Stewart 2001.

uniformity, validity, and geographic boundedness of honor-and-shame, and of the correlative Mediterranean culture-area construct'[60] ended up identifying, 'however tentatively, a specifically Mediterranean variety of the honor-and-shame syndrome, a substratum of beliefs and attitudes that many peoples in this small, but highly diverse, part of the world share'.[61]

The idea of Mediterraneity thus gained ground rapidly, eventually finding its way into classical studies. Some scholars adopted it only superficially, without its having any very noticeable effect upon their central ideas. Others took it on board wholesale. David Cohen's *Law, Sexuality and Society*, for instance, pursues an argument whose gist is that since the non-westernised Mediterranean societies studied by anthropologists are characterised by a fanatical awareness of honour and since classical Athens was a Mediterranean society, classical Athens must have been characterised by a fanatical awareness of honour.[62] In his more recent *Law, Violence and Community in Classical Athens* Cohen goes even further. Labelling Athenian society 'agonistic' and 'feuding' (for reasons that are not explained, these terms now appear to have replaced 'Mediterranean'), he tells us that in Athens 'judges and litigants alike view[ed] the [law-]courts as a competitive arena where ongoing conflicts [were] played out, continued, and exacerbated according to the logic characteristic of *feuding societies*' (my emphases). He goes on to argue that from the time of Homer onwards Greek societies were guided by the moral principle that one ought to help one's friends, harm one's enemies and enhance one's honour by retaliating instantly to any insult. Failure to retaliate was bound to result in dishonour, and according to Cohen the idea that 'it is better to die with honor than to live ignobly in defeat' was some sort of Athenian moral imperative. This belief was, apparently, so deep-rooted that Athenian society can now only be understood in terms of the most bad-tempered, intolerant and violent societies known to history, societies such as medieval Europe, nineteenth-century Sicily, Corsica, Albania and Montenegro.[63]

Now that we have glanced at some of modern historiography's divergent and often contradictory portrayals of Athenian society, the time has come to put their cogency to the test. Two theoretical possibilities present themselves. One is that all such interpretations are equally valid. This position

---

[60] Gilmore 1987a: 1; cf. Gilmore 1990, where the same point is made more emphatically in response to Pina-Cabral 1989.

[61] Brandes 1987: 121. This view is now progressively being undermined; see Chapter 5. n. 16.

[62] D. Cohen 1991a: 36. Cf. Lendon 1997: 110: 'Sparta was an honor culture like Athens and other Mediterranean societies . . .'

[63] D. Cohen 1991b; 1995a, throughout, reviewed in Herman 1998b.

could be defended on the ground that our historians' world views were shaped by contemporary ideological debates (it is no secret that some of them, at least, used their histories as vehicles for contemporary political polemics), so that the differences between their accounts could be put down to differences between the ideological climates to which they were exposed. These divergent, contradictory portrayals of classical Athens would thus afford a neat illustration of the Crocean maxim 'all history is contemporary history'. The second theoretical possibility is that these accounts are mutually exclusive. This is the possibility that I propose now to explore. A simple exercise in logic should help to show that all these interpretations of democratic Athens cannot possibly be valid.

Our demonstration starts with the almost banal point that any worthwhile interpretation of the Athenian democracy must be based on ancient reality. It must, in other words, bear some relation to what the surviving remains suggest the people of Athens said, thought and did under democratic rule. It is their utterances, thoughts and actions, and the relations between them, that constitute the Athenians' history. Our interpretation should, however, give most weight to what the Athenians actually did, since these three constituents of the abstraction 'history' are not all of the same evidential value. The words through which ancient actors' utterances and thoughts are communicated to us are diffuse and elusive, often masking intractable hidden intentions. Such words are extremely difficult for the external observer to interpret, since fusion between the actors' moral norms and the observer's own, which will be discussed in the next section, poses a formidable obstacle to unprejudiced assessment. Actions are of a different order, having three characteristics that set them firmly apart from words and thoughts. Because it is important to counter the argument, often advanced by both laymen and professional historians, that actions (especially those of the masses) can be slippery, hazy or undetectable, and that the boundaries between these and the other two categories are so blurred as to be practically non-existent, we shall, at the risk of belabouring the obvious, now consider these characteristics in some detail.

Actions are, in the first place, *objective*, not subjective. Man being, in the words of Sir Isaiah Berlin, a 'three dimensional object',[64] his actions take place in time and space, not in anyone's imagination. An observer to whom objectivity is important should be able to describe actions accurately even if he or she has no access to the thoughts and emotions that animated them.

[64] I. Berlin (1950) 'The concept of scientific history' in *Concepts and Categories*. Oxford: Oxford University Press: 104.

Actions are, in the second place, *digital*, not analogue. They can be broken down into units that are either definitely there or definitely not there. Socrates either went out or stayed at home; Alcibiades either did or did not deliver a certain speech. If this is true of individuals, it must also be true of the communities of which they are part. Each member of the Athenian citizen body performed a particular series of actions during his lifetime. However many choices he had before acting, his subsequent actions were absolute. Much of what we call 'the history of Athens' can thus be reduced to a plurality of actions that either happened or did not.

Such pluralities of action are, in the third place, *unique* to their time and place. Each individual makes so many choices of action during his or her lifetime that the exact series of actions chosen cannot but be unique. This is exponentially more so of a community. 'The history of Athens' (and indeed the history of anywhere else) must therefore consist of a highly specific combination of actions that can have no duplicate.

What follows from this is that we are dealing with phenomena that may be described as 'natural' in the sense that they exist or existed in time and space independently of human perception. This book will seek to explore an interesting implication of this observation: that certain methods of investigation used by natural scientists to study natural phenomena may have some relevance to the study of ancient history. Whatever its further implications, this possibility underlines the necessity of approaching and reconstructing ancient actions from an entirely detached standpoint; they cannot be assimilated into our mental baggage and made over to suit our preconceptions.

The means to this end that most readily suggests itself is a refined version of the analytical tool that Herodotus called *historie*: a rational inquiry to find out something about the past that we did not already know. Our aim will be to devise a model that will help us to recapture the distinctive characteristics of those small day-to-day 'events' through which the Athenians expressed their preferences and moral choices, revealing fundamental properties rather than incidental detail.[65] The chapters that follow will be devoted to the creation of such a model.

Finally, we must explore a further implication of the conclusion that we reached above. As we have seen, many modern interpretations of democratic Athens have been mutually contradictory. It is logically impossible that any two or more of the portraits at which we have glanced should

---

[65] Cf. Finley 1985b: 60–1 for the definition of 'model' adopted here and for its relation to Weber's 'ideal type'.

correspond equally to ancient Athenian reality. The sum total of what the Athenians said, thought and did cannot, for example, have been animated both by a general desire to die with honour rather than live ignobly in defeat, as Cohen believes, and by the sublime spirit of tolerance and forgiveness championed by Grote. Athens can hardly have been both one of history's most successful examples of social organisation, as Zimmern would have it, and corrupt, incompetent, irrational and immoral, as a host of other historians would prefer. It cannot have been easy for the Athenians to express an extraordinarily humane sense of equity and responsibility (Finley) simultaneously with fierce vindictiveness, petty insincerity and over-sensitivity about their standing among their peers (Kitto and Dover). Nor can they very well have been animated by several combinations of these extreme alternatives at once. Just as no one Athenian can have taken more than one course of action at a time, the essential thrust of what the majority of Athenians said, thought and did seems likely to be susceptible of a single accurate interpretation.

The continuing and dynamic processes of scholarship are bound to produce a number of variations on this basic interpretation. The variant versions should, however, be far more recognisably related to one another than the extreme interpretations presented above. Grappling with the same problem in a totally different context, Richard Evans has chosen to illustrate it using a metaphor:

Suppose we think of historians like figurative painters sitting at various places around a mountain. They will paint in different styles, using different techniques and different materials, they will see it in a different light or from a different distance according to where they are, and they will view it from different angles. They may even disagree about some aspects of its appearance, or some of its features. But they will all be painting the same mountain. If one of them paints a fried egg, or a railway engine, we are entitled to say that she or he is wrong: whatever it is that the artist has painted, it is not the mountain. The possibilities of legitimate disagreement and variation are limited by the evidence in front of their eyes. An objective historian is simply one who works within these limits. They are limits that allow a wide latitude for differing interpretations of the same document or source, but they are limits all the same.[66]

We cannot but conclude that some of the historians responsible for the extreme appraisals of the nature of individual Athenians and of Athenian society that we have just examined have transgressed the limits of legitimate

---

[66] R. J. Evans (2001) *Lying About Hitler*. New York: Basic Books: 250.

disagreement and variation. Had they exercised their judgement more professionally, their accounts could not have been so wildly different.

THE FUSION OF MORAL NORMS

The question arises of how this distinguished gallery of scholars managed to manoeuvre itself into so impossible a position. What mental and social processes were responsible for the extraordinarily contradictory nature of these interpretations? In search of an answer, we shall turn to perhaps the most potent of the factors that tend to bias our perception of any society other than our own: the fusion of moral norms.

We are dealing with one aspect of a wider problem that has presented a challenge to historical writers ever since the time of Thucydides.[67] This problem arises from the intricate interplay between three value systems: that of the actors, that of the sources and that of the historians. The actors perform actions prompted by a motivational complex that combines their physiological makeup with the code of behaviour of the society in which they live. The sources perceive and describe these actions, but they describe them as they appear refracted through the sources' own moral norms, which may be identical to or different from those of the actors. Historians read these descriptions and try to see the actions through the sources' eyes, but for the most part fail to realise that the actions are being refracted once again, this time through their own moral norms, which are entirely different from those of either the actors or the sources. The historians' norms are thus injected into their histories of past peoples, or of contemporary but alien peoples. Given the fact that these subjects generally inhabit or inhabited entirely different worlds from the historians' own, the resulting histories are bound to be significantly distorted.[68]

The problem becomes even more acute when historians turn away from their subjects' actions to concentrate upon their value systems. Unless the historians take very firm precautionary measures, these systems will imperceptibly fuse with their own. The resulting history will be a strange hybrid in which the actions of past or alien peoples are endowed with modern and/or culturally inappropriate motivations.

---

[67] For a discussion, to which I am greatly indebted, of the more general question of how we are to understand the beliefs and actions of other people, see the articles assembled in B. R. Wilson 1970.

[68] I am excluding from consideration any conscious and deliberate attempt to tamper with the evidence in pursuit of some ulterior motive. Here we are concerned solely with those attempts to interpret other societies that have been made in good faith.

In classical studies the procedure known as the lexical approach is perhaps the most vulnerable to the process of norm fusion. This procedure rests on the assumption that it is possible to get at the moral norms of the ancient Greeks (and indeed those of any alien people) using certain key words. The scholar is first required to select ancient value terms that have no exact modern equivalents and are in a sense untranslatable; for example, *hybris* (wanton violence), *time* (honour), *aidos* (sense of shame), *dike* (justice), *timoria* (revenge), *sophrosyne* (self-control, moderation), *metriotes* (moderation, temperance), *praotes* (mildness, gentleness), *eunoia* (goodwill, favour), *epieikeia* (reasonableness, fairness), *koinonein* (to have in common with, share) and *philanthropia* (human feeling, benevolence, kind-heartedness).[69] He or she must then examine the ways in which these words are used in as many contexts as possible. Finally the inferred meaning of each term must be described in one of the modern languages now used in classical scholarship. At the end of this process it is expected not only that the 'essence' of the value terms will have been grasped, both on the 'descriptive' and on the 'evaluative' level, but also that a precise appreciation of their finest nuances will have been achieved.

Trouble arises because languages cut up the general human continuum of moral behaviour into a series of highly idiosyncratic concepts whose implications may not coincide with those of their counterparts in another language.[70] An article published in a leading journal in 1996 is a case in point.[71] The author of this article sets out to test the cogency of two rival definitions of the word *hybris* put forward by modern researchers: 'the committing of acts of intentional insult, of acts which deliberately inflict shame and dishonour on others' and 'self-indulgent enjoyment of excess energy'.

---

[69] The terms in parentheses are the most obvious dictionary translations of these value terms, some of which have been the subjects of book-length studies: North 1966 (*sophrosyne*); Fisher 1992 (*hybris*); Cairns 1993 (*aidos*). For theoretical discussions of the lexical approach, see Dover 1974: 46–73 and Adkins 1972: 1–9. I do not regard de Romilly 1979 as falling within this tradition, since although she sets out to investigate a general trend in Greek thought ('la douceur' (gentleness)) by examining a set of Greek words, expressions and phrases, she is interested in their cumulative implications rather than in their exact modern translations.

[70] Cf. Mion 1991: 48, who makes the same point while discussing the fact that Greek lacked any word for 'toleration' and quotes other authors who have taken the same view. In connection with modern anthropology, C. S. Stewart 2001 remarks 'how few Mediterranean societies actually have words for "honor" in the sense advanced by Pitt-Rivers and how infrequently equivalent terms are employed in daily life. In Greece the words *timi*, "honor", and *philótimo*, "sense of honor", are rarely heard, while in Italy the operative concept is neither shame nor honor, even though the latter would seem to be readily accessible in the Italian word *onore*. Instead, exemplary moral fibre is displayed by following "the code of silence" (*omertá*) and not disclosing details of criminal or other in-group activities to inquisitive authorities. In his early monograph describing an Andalusian village Pitt-Rivers . . . focused attention on "shame" (*vergüenza*) and made no mention of "honor".'

[71] Cairns 1996.

After discussing how this term is used in a large number of contexts, he opts for the latter definition. Without wishing to enter this debate, I would suggest that while both definitions are ostensibly Greek, in reality they are both modern in almost every respect. The meaning of 'shame and dishonour' and that of 'self-indulgent enjoyment of excess energy' are inevitably derived by reference to the scholar's own scale of values: to his or her modern English-language conceptions of shame, honour, self-indulgence, enjoyment and energy, not to those of the ancient Athenians. Assuming, now, that the basic unit of human performance is the sequence motive –> action –> consequence, it is an inescapable conclusion that although our understanding of the 'action' and the 'consequence' is appropriate to the ancient Greek reality, we have endowed the 'motive' with a content drawn from our own. This is not a very sensible way of proceeding if we wish to uncover how the motive –> action –> consequence sequence hung together in ancient Athens, or how institutional arrangements and behavioural rules arose out of the people's collective sentiments and emotions. The end product will be at best some kind of average of modern and ancient values, at worst a near-perfect reflection of modern ones. This procedure may perhaps help translators of ancient texts to refine and over-refine the descriptive meanings of certain value terms, but it can by no means help social historians to achieve a better understanding of their evaluative meanings. To anyone trying to construct a model explaining how Athenian democracy arose out of the people's values and behaviour, it is a positive hindrance.

What are we to do now, though? We seem to have gone up a cul-de-sac. Have we really ended up irredeemably imprisoned in the subjectivity trap, any attempt to retrieve the values of any society other than our own being doomed to failure? At least one trend in moral philosophy seems to take precisely that view. As early as 1759, Adam Smith wrote: 'Every faculty in one man is the measure by which he judges of the like faculty in another. I judge of your sight by my sight, of your ear by my ear, of your reason by my reason, of your resentment by my resentment, of your love by my love. I neither have, *nor can have*, any other way of judging about them'.[72]

The more simplistic modern heirs of this way of thinking seem to be those scholars who hold that the question of the morality of Athenian democracy is independent of ancient realities, depending solely upon our perceptions. This may be the right moment to insist that the fusion of moral norms is neither a philosophical necessity nor an existential inevitability. There are ways of minimising the distortions it creates. Despite his disavowal,

---

[72] Adam Smith 1976: 19, my italics.

Adam Smith did of course have at his disposal other means of judging the faculties of others than comparing them with his own. To assess how good your eyesight was, for example, he could simply have asked your optician about your lenses and visual axes. His assessment of your eyesight would then have been far more accurate than one based solely on the function of his own eyes.

In an entirely different context, an example that has become an anthropological classic illustrates even better the advantages of the approach I am advocating. In 1925 Margaret Mead returned from the Pacific island of Samoa to deliver her account of a society that by any standards appeared extraordinary.[73] Here, apparently, was a group of isolated island people basking in primeval innocence. Young men and women lived casually and easily, moving from childhood to adulthood without suffering any great adjustment trauma. Blissfully ignorant of jealousy and intrigue, they engaged in free lovemaking and had no qualms of conscience on that account. They were, moreover, entirely non-aggressive, never hating anyone enough to kill them. Mead described them as 'one of the most amiable, least contentious, and most peaceful peoples in the world'.

At first sight a mere anthropological curiosity, Mead's findings had far-reaching implications. The Samoan society that she described contrasted sharply with the entire Western world, where young people customarily underwent severe 'adolescent crises'. Apparently such crises never occurred at all in Samoa, which seemed to indicate that adolescent behaviour was a matter not of heredity or 'nature' but of 'culture'. This conclusion was taken up by both Mead and her mentor, Franz Boas, and used to score points in the great nature/nurture controversy in which they were ranged against the nature supporters. Mead's account of Samoan society appeared to constitute definite proof that nurture, not nature, was the decisive factor in moulding human behaviour. Boas' position, epitomised by his earlier comment that 'in the great mass of a healthy population, the social stimulus is infinitely more potent than the biological mechanism', seemed to have been vindicated.[74]

Mead soon became a celebrity, at first only amongst the academic community, then nationally and finally internationally. Her book became a best seller. For over fifty years it was one of the central documents of American cultural anthropology, as well as being one of the scientific books most widely read by the general public. Its influence on the millions of people throughout the world whom it led to reconsider their attitudes to sexual

[73] Mead 1928.   [74] Cf. Ridley 2003: ch. 8.

mores was immeasurable. And then, early in the 1980s, its conclusions were totally refuted.

During the 1940s and 1960s Derek Freeman spent over six years in Samoa (Mead had stayed there for only five months). What he found was that Mead had got it all completely wrong. She had been duped by her own wishful thinking and misled by her informants, two of whom even came forward to admit to Freeman that they had played a prank on Mead by hoaxing her with accounts of their supposedly flagrant promiscuity. Freeman found the Samoans to be every bit as jealous, as vicious and as duplicitous in their love affairs as their Western counterparts. In other respects they showed up even worse. Samoan society appeared to be aggressive and brutal in the extreme, a feature (or, in our terms, a sort of 'action') that Mead had somehow managed to overlook or sweep under the carpet.[75] Freeman's revelations were at first met with scepticism (and at times with hysterical opposition[76]) but then slowly gained acceptance. Today his position appears unassailable.

How could all this have happened? To answer this question we must look at Mead's and Freeman's working methods. Mead depended almost exclusively on information gathered from informants for her entire picture of Samoan society. She did not cross-check this information with any other sort of data, not even data obtained by means of personal observation. She heard what she wanted to hear. Her informants confirmed her expectations. This is how the myth of Samoa as a paradise on earth was created.

Freeman, on the other hand, made a conscious effort to minimise the intrusion of his own values and expectations into his interpretations. I shall restrict my illustration of this point to the procedure by means of which he refuted Mead's claim that the Samoans were non-aggressive.[77] As well as conducting the usual interviews, Freeman studied historical documents and investigated statistics. The records of missionaries and explorers from the 1780s to the 1960s consistently revealed the picture of an unusually bellicose people. Freeman cross-checked this information with Samoan perceptions and crime rate statistics. Amongst the comments that he gathered was a remark made by a local pastor at a public reconciliation: 'Conflict comes easily in this country of Samoa; a village that lives in peace is rarely found.' Samoa's homicide rate proved to be considerably higher than those of a wide range of other countries. Freeman drew no strict dividing line between what his informants said and what he or other people perceived the Samoans as

---

[75] D. Freeman 1983.
[76] E.g. L. D. Holmes 1987. See D. Freeman 1999: 208–9 for the reception of his book at the Eighty-Second Annual Meeting of the American Anthropological Association.
[77] D. Freeman 1983: ch. 11.

doing; he treated all the information he had as a single body. This is how he reached conclusions that were diametrically opposed to Mead's. I should perhaps point out that these conclusions have now been substantially reinforced by the total abandonment, in behavioural studies, of the culturalist position advocated by Boas. There is overwhelming evidence that human behaviour is a product of *both* nature *and* nurture.

At a higher level of theory, Freeman's methods are entirely compatible with the methods of investigation advanced by certain philosophers and psychologists. Gilbert Ryle, in particular, developed an approach that differed somewhat from that of behaviourism's founding fathers.[78] Skinner and his pupils had proposed dispensing altogether with concepts of mind and consciousness in evaluating behaviour. Ryle chose to retain these concepts, suggesting that values and moral principles could be deduced from bodily states and processes. The Oxford philosopher R. M. Hare described the essence of this method thus:

If I were to ask a person 'What are his moral principles?' the way in which we could be most sure of a true answer would be by studying what he *did*. He might, to be sure, profess in his conversation all sorts of principles, which in his actions he completely disregarded; but it would be when, knowing all the relevant facts of a situation, he was faced with choices or decisions between alternative courses of action, between alternative answers to the question 'What shall I do?' that he would reveal in what principles of conduct he really believed. The reason why actions are in a peculiar way revelatory of moral principles is that the function of moral principles is to guide conduct.[79]

Hare's description helps to underline the difference between the approach to unravelling the Athenian code of behaviour that we will be taking and the approach adopted in the works cited in the last section. The prime evidence on the basis of which we shall be attempting to reconstruct this code is what the people of Athens did throughout the period of democratic rule, rather than what they said or professed to believe. These professions are undoubtedly important, but can only be assigned any importance as evidence of a code of behaviour if backed up by actions that unambiguously demonstrate that these were indeed the principles that were embodied in the Athenians' rules and institutions.

There are signs that Thucydides, at the very beginning of historiography, was aware of the danger of value fusion and took steps to minimise its

[78] Ryle 1949.
[79] Hare 1952: 1, his italics. Note that Hare acknowledges the danger of fusion of moral norms even within the confines of a single culture.

impact on the history he was writing, even if in the end he was not entirely satisfied with the result. One such measure consisted in taking the view, which some of his contemporaries must have found unacceptable, that the story of an event was not identical with the event itself. According to this view stories are subjective and events objective. It may, however, be possible to limit the story's subjective features and reach through them into the realm of objective events so as to obtain an undistorted view of these events and their interrelationships by using the well-known Thucydidean method of 'tirelessly seeking out a vast number of witnesses from both sides, cross-questioning them closely, deciding on their veracity, piling up notes, sorting out the data, selecting and thinking and writing'.[80] Thucydides' determination to counter the danger of fusing moral norms can also be seen in the way in which he wrote contemporary history: his account begins at the beginning, with the outbreak of war (1.1), and after he was exiled from Athens in 424 he deliberately chose a new home from which he could easily observe 'what was being done on both sides' (5.26). Finally, Thucydides knew that observing behaviour was a safer route to the understanding of moral norms than analysing ideas, key words or abstract concepts. Writing about the civil war in Corcyra, he remarked, as we have seen, that value terms change their meanings in accordance with changes in the power structure (3.82). In the section of his history dealing with 'events' (*erga*) he therefore adopted the behavioural method of inferring norms from what people did when faced with choices between alternative courses of action, saving his own interpretations of abstract ideas for the section dealing with the speeches (*logoi*).

Because Thucydides consciously adopted this research policy, his account of wartime behaviour was as free as it could be from his own preconceptions and conformed as far as possible with what was actually said, thought and done during the war. It may perhaps be suggested that modern historians have created portrayals of ancient Athens that reflect their own preconceptions, biases and 'projections' more truly than they do any ancient reality because these historians did not follow Thucydides' example.

SOME CONTEMPORARY ASSESSMENTS

The many accounts that have been written of democratic Athens are by no means all modern; the Athenians' contemporaries wrote about them too. The evidence at our disposal is permeated with a general feeling that

---

[80] Finley 1972a: 11.

there was something exceptional about Athens. The starting point for these accounts was the common-sense observation that all Greeks were in many ways alike. The common bond of a shared descent, language and religion acted as a great equaliser and separated the Greeks from the non-Greeks surrounding them, whom they called 'the barbarians'.[81] Greek people were made visually conspicuous by their clothes (Sophocles, *Philoctetes* 223–4) and had established a highly visible presence along their coasts: if a person was shipwrecked and washed ashore, he could tell by the geometrical figures inscribed in the sand that he was among Greeks (Galenus, *Protreptikos* 5). The Greeks were further distinguished by their abhorrence of certain practices that other peoples endorsed. The anonymous author of the philosophical treatise known as the 'two-fold arguments' asserts that the Scythians 'think it seemly that who[ever] kills a man should scalp him and wear the scalp on his horse's bridle, and having gilded the skull [or] lined it with silver, should drink from it and make a libation to the gods. Among the Greeks, no one would be willing to enter the same house as a man who had behaved like that'.[82] Describing the Egyptians' way of life, Herodotus dwells on the ways in which their greeting rituals differ from those of the Greeks: 'unlike any of the Greeks . . . passers-by do not address each other in the street, but salute each other by making a low bow, one hand on the knee' (2.80). Most Greeks would have subscribed to Herodotus' tacit assumption: Greek salutations presupposed mutual respect and equality of status.

In other respects, however, all Greeks were by no means alike. There was, in the first place, a distinction between their two great branches, the 'soft-living' Ionians and the 'man-mastering' Dorians. Differences surfaced in the dialects spoken by these groups and in the forms of architecture and music that had developed amongst them. Other distinctions had to do with where the Greeks lived. The fact that they lived in hundreds of independent, non-contiguous city-states, often widely removed from each other, produced some strange idiosyncrasies. Each polis had an *ethos* or *nomos* (customs, usage or way of life) peculiar to itself, a constitution and a history of its own and moral aims and a manner of life that were not

---

[81] Herodotus 8.144. For Herodotus' perception of the Greek/barbarian antinomy, see Hartog 1988. Pelling 1997 argues convincingly that for Herodotus the similarities between the two peoples outweighed the differences.

[82] *Dissoi Logoi* 2.13, trans. Sprague 1968: 158. Cf. Herodotus 4.65. For Thracian graves containing the sawn-off tops of human craniums, see A. J. Graham (2002) 'The colonization of Samothrace', *Hesperia* 71.3: 231–60, at 246 (Figure 4).

normally shared by others.[83] The author of the 'two-fold arguments' again offers us some useful examples:

To the Spartans it is seemly that young girls should do athletics and go about with bare arms and no tunics, but to the Ionians this is disgraceful. And to [the former] it is seemly for their children not to learn music and letters but to the Ionians it is disgraceful not to know all these things. To the Thessalians it is seemly for a man to select horses and mules from a herd himself and train them, and also to take one of the cattle and slaughter, skin and cut it up himself, but in Sicily these tasks are disgraceful and the work of slaves. To the Macedonians it appears to be seemly for young girls, before they are married, to fall in love and to have intercourse with a man, but when a girl is married it is a disgrace. (As far as the Greeks are concerned it is disgraceful at either time.)[84]

Differences in mores found expression in the visual arts and crafts, in the shape and colour of vases, in dishes and drinks, in clothes and shoes, in religious festivals and in the architecture that the people of the various city-states produced.[85] Socially the differences manifested themselves in the 'national characteristics' stereotypically imputed to each city's most representative members. The Sybarites (whose city was obliterated just a year before the Cleisthenic reforms in Athens) were proverbially lazy, self-indulgent and devoted to sensual luxury; the Spartans were famous for their courage, toughness, austerity, secretiveness and powers of deception, and in particular for their brusque and 'laconic' speech; the Cretans were renowned liars; the semi-barbarous Aetolians were thought to speak a language that was almost unintelligible and to eat their meat raw (Thucydides 3.94); the Boeotians and the Abderites[86] (later on, at least, in the case of the latter) were known for their stupidity and the Corinthians for their wealth. Under the democratic system, the Athenians were supposed to be recognisable

---

[83] Cf. C. Morgan 1991; Nippel 1996; Asheri 1997; Lenfant 2001. See Hesk 2000: 42–3 for the observation that Demosthenes 20.13, *Against Leptines*, is 'the first extant application of the term *ethos* to the *polis* as a whole'. For humanity's inherent inclination to form groups set apart from other groups by their customs, see Erikson 1966 (who dubbed this phenomenon 'cultural pseudospeciation'). See Leviticus 18:3 for a striking Old Testament parallel: 'After the doings of the land of Egypt, wherein ye dwelt, shall ye not do; and after the doings of the land of Canaan, whither I bring you, shall ye not do: neither shall ye walk in their ordinances.'

[84] *Dissoi Logoi* 2.9–12, trans. Sprague 1968: 157–8.

[85] Insofar as pottery was concerned this was, however, more pronounced in the Archaic period than in the Classical, during which vase-painting, under the Athenian influence, underwent thorough homogenisation. Even in the Archaic period the differences were more marked between regions than between city-states. Cf. Coldstream 1983 and Snodgrass 1999.

[86] The Abderite lower classes were a by-word for stupidity, as is implied in, for example, Martialis, *Epigrammata* 10.25.4: '*Abderitanae pectora plebis*'.

by their gentleness (*praotes*), self-restraint (*sophrosyne*), fairness (*epieikeia*), generosity (*megalopsychia*), honesty and goodness.[87]

Passing fair judgement on 'national characteristics' was no simple matter; some Greeks thought it impossible. After all, every man considered his own customs to be the best, and no obvious means of refuting such contentions presented itself. The impossibility of obtaining any consensus in matters of this sort was probably the origin of the theory of epistemological relativism. According to Herodotus, a Persian king once asked some Greeks what they would take to eat the dead bodies of their fathers. They replied that they would not do it for any money. Later, in the presence of the Greeks, he asked some Indians whose custom it was to eat their parents' dead bodies what they would take to burn them. They uttered a cry of horror and forbade him to speak of such a dreadful idea (3.38). There was thus no objective standard by which to compare the relative merits of such practices. Some Greeks carried over this way of thinking onto the cities in which they lived. All the *ethe* and all the *nomoi* of the various poleis being equally 'good' (according to Plato's Protagoras), they were not amenable to comparison: 'the noble and the shameful, the just and unjust, the sacred and not, such as each polis has deemed and set up as customary for itself, these are true and valid for each, and in these matters no individual or polis is wiser than another' (Plato, *Theaetetus* 172a).

Some less sophistically minded Greeks resisted this logic, believing that the cities' *ethe* or *nomoi* could be graded according to objective standards. This created an imaginary scale on which, naturally, the Greeks appeared as superior to the barbarians.[88] Wherever this scale was applied, the Athenians consistently ranked above all the rest of the Greeks, suggesting that their image was more or less generally admired.

Many passages sing the praises of Athens, often in intensely emotional terms. These passages are so numerous and so varied that it is far more likely that they reflect the independent opinions of various individuals and groups within the Greek world than that all derive from a common source. Herodotus, for instance, lauds the Athenians' collective progress and outstanding motivation in battle, ascribing these to a sense of freedom (*isegorie*) derived by flinging off their despotic government and becoming their own masters (5.78). Following the Athenian victories of 480 and 479, Pindar eulogised Athens as a divine or semi-divine being: 'Radiant,

---

[87] *Eiothyia praotes*: *The Athenian Constitution* 22.4; *praotes*: Lysias 6.34, *Against Andocides*; *chrestoi kai philanthropoi*: Demosthenes 19.103, *On the Embassy*; *apseudes kai chreston*: Demosthenes 20.13, *Against Leptines*.

[88] For which see Cartledge 1990 and 1993a: ch. 3.

violet-crowned, famed in song, | pillar of Greece, glorious Athens, city divine.'[89] Euripides speaks of the Athenians as the sons of blessed gods 'who dwell in Athens' holy and unconquered land, | Where famous Wisdom feeds them and they pass gaily | Always through that most brilliant air . . .' (*Medea* 824–30, trans. R. Warner). Sophocles singles out Athens as a city famed for its piety, fairness and truthfulness (*Oedipus at Colonus* 1125–7). Nicias, exhorting his sailors to battle in Sicily in 413, tells them that even though they are not really Athenians they are admired throughout the Greek world merely for having learned the Athenian dialect and emulated the Athenian way of life (Thucydides 7.63.3).[90] Plato implies that the Athenians were widely regarded as wise (*sophoi*) and praises Athens as the 'City Hall of Wisdom of Hellas' (*Protagoras* 319b, 337d), recalling Thucydides' more famous reference to her as 'an education for all Hellas' (2.41.1). The author of *The Athenian Constitution* heaps praise on the Athenians' behaviour after the restoration of democracy in 404: '[They] appear to have handled their affairs, both private and public, as well and with as much statesmanship as any people ever have shown in a similar situation' (40.3). One of Isocrates' clients asserts that during the short period of oligarchic rule 'we hated each other more than we did the enemies bequeathed to us by our ancestors . . .' and 'all looked upon us as the most foolish and ill-fated of mankind', whereas under the restored democracy 'we have lived so uprightly and so like citizens of one country that it seemed as if no misfortune has ever befallen us', being now regarded 'as the happiest and wisest of the Greeks' (Isocrates 18.45–6, *Against Callimachus*). The orator Hypereides declares in a forensic speech that no people, king or nation in the world is 'more magnanimous (*megalopsychoteron*) than the people of Athens. It does not abandon to their fate those of the citizens, whether individuals or classes, who are falsely accused, but goes to their rescue . . .',[91] and in his Funeral Speech he compares Athens with the sun that 'visits the whole world' dispensing punishment to the wicked and help to the just and assuring at her own peril and expense the common safety of the Greeks (6.5).[92] Demosthenes adds that numerous incidents have demonstrated the city's character (*ethos*) to be honest (*apseudes*) and good (*chreston*).[93]

---

[89] Fragment 76 (Schroeder).
[90] Gomme, Andrewes and Dover 1945–81, vol. IV: 442, suggest that these sailors either came from subject-ally regions or were mercenaries. In either case 'many are likely to have been born at Athens and to have known no other home'.
[91] Hypereides 4.33–4, *In Defence of Euxenippus*; cf. A. H. M. Jones 1957: 60.
[92] For the Athenian character according to evidence such as this, see Raaflaub 1994.
[93] Demosthenes 20.13, *Against Leptines*.

Athens-worship even breaks through the prose of two writers who, given their personal experiences and their upper-class backgrounds, might well have been predisposed to speak ill of her: the historian Thucydides and the Old Oligarch.[94] Commanding a small squadron in 424, Thucydides failed to arrive in time to rescue the besieged city of Amphipolis. In his view this delay was due to *force majeure*. His countrymen thought otherwise, and banished Thucydides for twenty years. Bearing this episode in mind, Thucydides' readers would presumably have understood if he had every now and then allowed this grudge to poison his view of Athens. Far from running her down, however, Thucydides joined the chorus of her encomiasts. Through the mouth of Pericles, whom he unquestionably revered, he called Athens a role model for the rest of Greece. He identified two outstanding traits in her people's *ethos*: readiness to endure with resignation whatever the gods might send and courage in the face of the enemy (2.64). Elsewhere he asserted that the Athenians were also intellectually superior, writing that throughout the Peloponnesian War the disparity between their own and the Spartans' 'national character' had worked in the Athenians' favour, they being quick and full of enterprise, while the Spartans were slow and lacking in initiative (8.96). These peculiar collective features were, he believed, matched by the particular characteristics of every individual Athenian. '[Y]ou must remember that you are citizens of a great city and that you were brought up in a way of life suited to her greatness,' says Pericles (2.61.4). Elsewhere Thucydides shows us the Athenians as if from a non-Athenian point of view: 'As for their bodies', say the Corinthians' representatives in Sparta before the outbreak of war, 'they regard them as expendable for their city's sake, as though they were not their own; but each man cultivates his own intelligence, again with a view to doing something notable for his city' (1.70). Thucydides gives frequent and varied expression to the idea that life in Athens was rewarding, calling forth pleasant sentiments and emotions. In the Funeral Oration, for example, Pericles extols the annual games and sacrifices that are the Athenians' respite from toil as one of the great advantages of their way of life.

With respect to interpersonal relationships, Thucydides reiterated, as we have seen, the assertion that the Athenians were exceptionally moderate and peaceful: 'your own day-to-day interactions with each other are not all about fear and intrigue'.[95] He was careful to remind his readers that these traits were not merely abstract entities, producing in evidence an incident that had occurred during the first oligarchic revolution. After the

---

[94] Cf. Forrest 1984: 1–2.   [95] Thucydides 3.37.2; cf. 2.37.2 and pp. 19, 82, 360, 367–8 and 372–3.

Four Hundred oligarchs had seized power, a man called Chaereas arrived in Samos and gave the soldiers there (most of whom were democrats) an exaggerated account of the terrors inflicted on Athens by the oligarchs. He told the soldiers that the oligarchs had introduced flogging, restricted freedom of speech and had the soldiers' wives and children raped, and that unless the soldiers surrendered their relatives would be imprisoned and put to death. Thucydides' description of the soldiers' reaction suggests that the moderate Athenian approach and disinclination to overreact or rush into things here manifested themselves in action:

When they heard this report, the soldiers at first wanted to seize upon the main authors of the oligarchy and anyone else who had had a hand in it and stone them. Afterwards, however, listening to men of moderate views who advised them not to throw away their entire cause when enemy ships lay so close at hand drawn up for battle, they decided to let the idea drop. (8.75.1)

It has sometimes been claimed that the evidential value of such accounts is impaired by the fact that they were 'idealised'. Perhaps they were; perhaps they presented a picture of Athens that surpassed the reality. Then, however, we need some sort of explanation of why Thucydides should have painted so excessively flattering a picture of a city that had treated him so badly, unless he had some strong objective reason to do so.

The anonymous author known as Pseudo-Xenophon, whom we have already encountered under his other title of 'The Old Oligarch', may be presumed to have been very unlike Thucydides. Probably an exile from Athens and certainly a stalwart oligarch, he wrote, at some time during the Peloponnesian War, a pamphlet called *The Constitution of the Athenians* whose aim was to dissuade other Greeks from following in Athens' footsteps by setting up democracies.[96] One might think that the easiest way of pursuing this aim would have been to write a character assassination that exposed Athens' every weakness and generally dismissed her as bad news. It would seem, however, that the Old Oligarch did not regard this line of attack as advisable. Athens' image as a flourishing city must have been so widespread and so deeply entrenched in people's minds that any attempt to dismiss it out of hand would have been counterproductive. The Old Oligarch therefore resorted to different tactics, admitting some of Athens' achievements, but proceeding to censure her for various characteristics that

---

[96] For the definitive edition, see Bowersock 1966 and 1968, incorporating earlier bibliography on the subject. For the wide range of dates proposed for the pamphlet's composition (from 443 to 410), see Mattingly 1997. His own convincing suggestion, based mainly on the author's perception of the quadrennial tribute assessments as normal (3.5), is 414.

were from an aristocratic standpoint undesirable. The remarkable consequence of this procedure was that what were supposed to be examples of the city's wickedness came out as examples of great virtue from a democratic point of view. I shall briefly paraphrase a few of these impressively prejudiced descriptions, to some of which I have already referred. The real power in Athens, according to the Old Oligarch, was in the hands of a morally inferior majority (*poneroi*) rather than those of a select, morally superior minority (*chrestoi*). The slaves and metics in Athens were, regrettably, much better off than those in other cities; they wore the same sort of clothes as the Athenians and, scandalously, addressed them as equals. Worse still, one was not allowed to hit a slave whenever one felt like it (one would in any case be in some danger of accidentally hitting an Athenian citizen whom one had mistaken for a slave) and some of the slaves had a nasty habit of becoming rich and buying their own freedom. The impoverished masses of Athens forced the wealthy few to pay for their festivals, rites, sacrifices, sanctuaries and triremes. The Athenians also supported the impoverished masses of other cities, disenfranchising the morally superior minority. Finally, the Athenians celebrated twice as many festivals as any other Greek state, which, given that juries did not meet on festival days, made trying to get any public business done an uphill struggle. If Thucydides' characterisations of Athens have been called idealised, those of the Old Oligarch can probably be said to be something of an exaggeration. However exaggerated they may be, though, they seem to illustrate a trend of whose embryonic features we have independent evidence.[97]

The sceptic may argue that many of the highly flattering accounts written of Athens were no more than propaganda; that these sources deliberately exaggerated the 'seemly' and glossed over the 'unseemly' characteristics of the Athenian way of life. Other Greeks, it may be said, may well have had less flattering views of the Athenians that have been lost to us due to Athens' unfair advantage in the struggle for literary survival. Such a view, however, is not really sustainable. It is inconceivable that so many Athenian speakers, prose-writers and playwrights could have conspired to force upon their audience of both Athenians and non-Athenians an image of Athens that was seriously at odds with the general view. Nor is it likely that on this one subject alone Thucydides should have decided to betray his usual commitment to balanced evaluation by presenting us with an assessment of the Athenian character that was totally out of touch with the common perception. We are therefore led to conclude that a certain general consensus

[97] See pp. 52–72.

must have existed concerning the collective and individual character of the Athenians. The apparent nature of this consensus lends little support to the contention (already mentioned)[98] that the people of Athens, whatever their class or order, were trapped in a web of mutual distrust or even hatred. Those who *are* trapped in webs of distrust or hatred (pp. 194–6 will discuss the society of Gaul in the sixth century AD, at which time its members could well have been described thus) do not tend to leave behind glowing accounts of how much they admire themselves and their society. Most of the literature produced in Athens during this period, however, breathes an optimistic outlook, and Athens' reputation as an extraordinary city survived into later times, being reflected extensively, in particular, in Cicero's surviving correspondence. The general picture that is starting to coalesce suggests a psychology of joy, a general feeling amongst the Athenians that they were living in fortunate times.

This argument is not a straightforward one. Comparisons in well-being are notoriously difficult to make.[99] A tradition that goes back at least as far as the great Swiss historian Jakob Burckhardt holds, as we have seen, that the Greek state intervened excessively in the lives of its citizens. Any tendency to state intervention being regarded within this tradition as intrusive and unjust, the conclusion is drawn that life in the ancient poleis was miserable. This general principle is often given concrete illustration. Ostracism, for example, is said to have been grossly unjust because it implied punishment without trial, and a law going back to the time of Solon that forbade citizen-prostitutes to speak at the Assembly has been deemed unfair because it constituted state intervention in people's sex lives.[100] To see this matter aright we must distinguish between legal rights and perceptions of well-being. Greek citizens had no inalienable rights. The state, on the other hand, was omnipotent, and it was indeed possible that it might intervene in almost any sphere of a citizen's life.[101] By our standards this sort of thing looks extremely invidious. The question is not, however, how it looks to us, but how it looked to the Athenians. All the evidence at our disposal suggests that they saw things very differently. Had there indeed been a general feeling of discontent fostered by excessive state intervention, it seems unlikely that Pericles would have declared that 'each single one of

---

[98] See pp. 81–2, 100.   [99] Cf. Elster and Roemer 1991.   [100] Cf. Winkler 1990: ch. 2.
[101] This principle is expressed in rhetorical terms by Andocides: 'Alcibiades . . . instead of holding that he ought himself to conform with the laws of the state, he expects you to conform with his own way of life (*tropois*)' (4.19, *Against Alcibiades*). I am indebted to Wallace 1994 for the demonstration that 'Individual behaviour that directly harmed the polis was subject to legal control. Individual behaviour that affected only the individual was not' (at 146). See also pp. 221–9.

our citizens, in all the manifold aspects of life is able to show himself the rightful lord and owner of his own person, and do this, moreover, with exceptional grace and exceptional versatility' (2.41); key concepts such as 'to live as one likes' or 'doing what one pleases' would scarcely have been bandied about by the Athenians so frequently and with such unconcealed pride,[102] and Thucydides might have felt rather less inclined to describe Athenian life as 'free and open' and the Athenians' relationships as 'free and tolerant'. No doubt the Athenians, like everyone else, found plenty of things wrong with their social system, but the sort of state intervention that was practised in Athens was not one of them. They would, however, have regarded with the utmost revulsion at least two forms of state intervention that we view not only as perfectly fair, but as bastions of popular rights: regular taxation by a central government and compulsory education.

In the Funeral Oration Pericles urges the Athenians to become 'lovers'(*erastai*) of their city (Thucydides 2.43.1). His hyperbolic rhetoric obscures the fact that the people's enthusiasm for Athens was reinforced by material perceptions of well-being.[103] Democracy gave everybody an equal share of the 'good things of life', according to Thucydides (6.39), and numerous signs combine to indicate that the state went to great lengths to ensure a good life for its citizens. Aristeides' advice to countrymen to move to the city and seize mastery of the seas resulted, as the author of *The Athenian Constitution* put it, in 'affluence for the masses': more than twenty thousand men earned their living as a result of the tribute, the taxation and the money the empire brought in (24.3). The impression of an economic boom that we receive from the literary sources is confirmed by archaeological research, which indicates unequivocally that Attica was extremely prosperous during the fifth and fourth centuries and underwent speedy economic decline thereafter.[104] If Athens' economy was stagnant under the democracy and the life of her people miserable, how did she manage to attract to herself 'the flower of Greek intellectual life from all around the Mediterranean basin'?[105] Why did Thucydides write that the people

---

[102] Cf. Plato, *Republic* 8.557b3, and Aristotle, *Politics* 1310a29, where these are identified as democracy's essential characteristics. Cf. Wallace 1994.

[103] Cf. L. Pearson 1962: 182: 'A citizen's obligation to serve his state will be greater if the state has served him particularly well . . . Moreover, the man who refuses to serve his state is acting against his own interest.' This point is developed further in Chapter 10.

[104] Lohmann 1992, 1993 and 1995. Snodgrass 1987–9: 53 believes that this was also true of other Greek city-states: 'the centuries of the heyday of the Classical *polis* witnessed the absolute zenith, the all-time high point, in the exploitation of the Greek countryside through the whole of its long history'.

[105] Cartledge 1997: 4; cf. Field 1948 and Meiggs 1972: ch. 15, for eminent non-Athenians flocking to Athens.

of Athens 'found in their houses a beauty and good taste that delighted them and drove away their cares' (see **Fig. 2.5**)? Why were her citizens paid not only to attend the Assembly (from 403 onwards) but to go to the theatre? Why, finally, did the state pay to maintain orphans and the disabled if its attitude to its citizens was indeed one of contempt (*The Athenian Constitution* 23.3)?

In the light of all this, it is hard to avoid the conclusion that Athenian citizens must on the whole have perceived life as enjoyable and rewarding, having learnt to appreciate their city's moral and material values. This may sound a somewhat high-flown, 'soft' conclusion, but it is in fact one that is amenable to more rigorous logic. Our reward for subjecting it to this sort of logic will be the chance to illuminate another principal characteristic of the Athenian code of behaviour.

As we have already said,[106] anything done by an individual for the community of which he is a member can pay off through either or both of two channels: a direct, personal one (**P**) and a largely 'abstract' one consisting of his relationships with his community as a whole (**C**). The total reward (**R**, which can be either positive or negative) that converges in the individual is expressed by the equation $R = P + C$. The evidence presented above suggests that in Athens the value of **C**, at least, was positive. Had the individual Athenian found the communal payoffs unrewarding he would hardly have regarded his body as expendable in his city's defence, nor would it have made much sense to urge him to become the 'lover' of his city.

Despite this initially 'optimistic' conclusion, I should perhaps stress that it is not my intention to spend this book pronouncing my own encomiums upon Athens. I do not wish to rescue her reputation, or to redeem, rehabilitate or whitewash her; even less do I intend to point some moral by reference to her special code of behaviour. Nor do I propose to play down certain features of her society that from today's perspective appear unacceptable. I find nothing admirable in the Athenians' enthusiasm for war and empire (theirs lasted at least until the end of the Peloponnesian War), in their acceptance of slavery as an inevitable fact of existence, in their exclusion of women from politics, or in their practice of capital punishment and the torture of slaves. On the other hand, I would like to remind the reader that moral condemnation and historical analysis are not one and the same thing. It is easy, as Finley has put it, 'to score points over a dead society, more difficult and more rewarding to examine what they were trying to do, how they went about it, the extent to which they succeeded or failed,

---

[106] See p. 38.

and why'.[107] I shall therefore conclude this chapter by spelling out two
assumptions that will guide the analysis that follows. Firstly, it is entirely
possible for us to reconstruct the Athenian code of behaviour, if we stay as
close as we can to what the ancient Athenians actually said, thought and
did and sedulously avoid modern bias and tendentiousness. Secondly, our
picture need not be cleansed of those aspects of Athenian society that we
are inclined to view as unfair or distasteful, but should rather be a rounded
portrait in which there co-exist features of which we approve and others
of which we disapprove. Our aim in reconstructing this code of behaviour
should be neither to commend nor to condemn, but to appraise.

---

[107] Finley 1983: 84.

CHAPTER 4

Representations and distortions

THE PROBLEM OF DOCUMENTATION

The social life of the people of Athens, like that of any people who live in a compact, close-knit community, consisted of a vast number of principles of conduct and an equally vast number of interpersonal interactions. The code of behaviour of any such society consists of a relatively small number of rules that express the constant factors within these principles and inter-actions and reveal their inherent logic.[1] Principles and interactions are thus the obvious starting point for the historian who wants to discover these rules. In order to derive reliable generalisations, ideally he or she ought to internalise every principle, contemplated or declared, that ever existed and every interaction of every sort that ever took place in the community singled out for investigation. Since this would be impractical, if not impossible, I have suggested that we should confine our body of evidence to principles and actions related to circumstances involving co-operation and/or con-flict. Restricting our database in this way leaves us to investigate a rather smaller number of pronouncements and incidents recorded in Athens and the surrounding countryside between 508 and 322.

Most such words and actions have, of course, passed unrecorded into oblivion. A small number aroused sufficient contemporary interest to be incorporated into conversations and stories and thereby became part of an oral tradition. A still smaller number of pronouncements and incidents (or the stories that they inspired) were deemed sufficiently exciting to find their way into writing. The Athenians wrote voluminously, but a considerable proportion of their output has been lost to us due to a sifting process dictated by changing values and fashions through time.[2] Our chief source

---

[1] This point is dealt with in full on pp. 15–23.

[2] The progressive disappearance of Euripides' works may give us some hint of the rate at which this process has occurred. The great library established in Alexandria in the third century contained only 74 or 78 of his 90 or so plays. Today we have 18. We have less than half as many by either Aeschylus or Sophocles (Aeschylus is said to have written between 70 and 90 plays, Sophocles more than 120). Cf. R. A. Pack (1963) *The Greek and Latin Literary Texts from Greco-Roman Egypt*. Ann Arbor: University of Michigan Press, 2nd edn.

consists of scattered passages of information about co-operation and conflict in Athenian society from the relatively small amount of written material that has survived this process.

As most of this material has come down to us by virtue of its literary merits, we are dealing, essentially, with literary representations that may be either imaginative or realistic. Whatever their nature, however, they have one common trait that makes them invaluable for our purposes: they are primary sources. Transmitted directly to us from Athens as it was during the period under investigation, they have preserved the memory of at least some fragments of that Athenian society's distinct configuration of ideas and practices. This being so, they must necessarily also bear some imprints of the Athenians' ordinary day-to-day experience. Assuming that they did not would be tantamount to subscribing to the proposition that culture is an autonomous entity, entirely separate from the society that produced it. This proposition is not tenable.

The question now arises of the *precise* relation between these passages and the social organisation of Attica between 508 and 322; without knowing this we cannot accurately assess what they have to tell us about the character of Athenian society. To answer this question adequately we must make certain distinctions, starting with the literary genres to which these passages belong. For our purposes, the four main categories are drama, philosophy, history and rhetoric. Let us now take a look at one typical passage from each of these genres.

The scene in Sophocles' *Oedipus the King* known as 'the encounter at the crossroads' deals with the making of choices in circumstances of highly antagonistic conflict. The long-ago encounter is related by Oedipus to his wife (actually his mother) because he wants to reassure her that he cannot have killed his father. As he speaks, it becomes all too clear that he did in fact kill him. Refracted through the medium of fictional poetry, the story appears as follows:

When I was near the branching of the crossroads, going on foot, I was encountered by a herald and a carriage with a man in it, just as you tell me. He that led the way and the old man himself wanted to thrust me out of the road by force. I became angry and struck the coachman who was pushing me. When the old man saw this he watched his moment, and as I passed he struck me from his carriage, full on the head with his two pointed goad. But he was paid in full and presently my stick had struck him backwards from the car and he rolled out of it. And then I killed them all . . . (801–13, trans. D. Greene)

Oedipus chose to hit the coachman in response to being pushed out of the road and to kill everybody concerned (including, as it turned out, his father) in response to being hit with a goad. This is a clear example of extreme retaliation: in terms of the typology that we worked out earlier, 'a head for an eye'.[3] We have now to ask ourselves how we should see the relation between a literary incident such as this and real life. Were we to assume, as many students of literature do, that drama imitates life, or is some kind of extension of life (as Adkins would have it: 'A drama is a practical work; it involves action. People appear on the stage *and behave as they do in real life*'),[4] we might be tempted to conclude that incidents involving extreme retaliation must have been commonplace amongst Athenian citizens (the playwright's usual practice, according to this logic, having been to titillate his audience by writing about circumstances that were familiar to its members from everyday life). This might be thought to reinforce the contention that life in Athens was bad-tempered, quarrelsome, intolerant, riddled with rivalries and of course violent.[5]

The background scene at the beginning of Plato's *Republic*, our example from the philosophical genre, describes a case of co-operation. Written in lucid, realistic prose, in marked contrast to the complex abstractions to follow, it records Socrates as speaking as follows:

I went down yesterday to the Piraeus with Glaukon the son of Ariston, that I might offer up my prayers to the goddess; and also because I wanted to see in what manner they would celebrate the festival . . . When we had finished our prayers and viewed the spectacle, we turned in the direction of the city; and at that instant Polemarchos the son of Kephalos chanced to catch sight of us from a distance as we were starting on our way home, and told his servant to run and bid us wait for him. The servant took hold of me by the cloak behind, and said: Polemarchos desires you to wait. I turned round, and asked him where his master was. There he is, said the youth, coming after you, if you will only wait. Certainly we will, said Glaukon; and in a few minutes Polemarchos appeared, and with him Adeimantos, Glaukon's brother, Niceratos the son of Nicias, and several others who had been at the procession. Polemarchos said to me: I perceive, Socrates, that you and your companion are already on your way to the city. You are not far wrong, I said. But do you see, he rejoined, how many we are? Of course. And are you stronger than all these? for if not, you will have to remain where you are. May there not be the alternative, I said, that we may persuade you to let us go? But can you

---

[3] See pp. 2–7.
[4] Adkins 1960a: 127, my italics. Cf. Dover 1983: 35 for a reaction to this (to the present author's mind, an unsatisfactory one).
[5] See pp. 81–2, 100.

persuade us, if we refuse to listen to you? he said. Certainly not, replied Glaukon. Then we are not going to listen; of that you may be assured. Adeimantos adds: Has no one told you of the torch-race on horseback in honour of the goddess which will take place in the evening? With horses! I replied: That is a novelty. Will horsemen carry torches and pass them one to another during the race? Yes, said Polemarchos, and not only so, but a festival will be celebrated at night, which you certainly ought to see. Let us rise soon after supper and see this festival; there will be a gathering of young men, and we will have a good talk. Stay then, and do not be perverse. Glaukon said: I suppose, since you insist, that we must. Very good, I replied. Accordingly we went with Polemarchos to his house. (1.327a1–328b8, trans. B. Jowett)

The choice here is made when Socrates and Glaukon decide that instead of going back to Athens as planned they will do as Polemarchus wishes and stay in the Peiraeus for a party at his house. The unsophisticated reader may regard this passage as a record of a cheerful encounter in which two groups of good-tempered Athenians joke with each other and then join up to enjoy some more fun together. Influential figures have, however, announced this episode to be clear evidence of the hidden undercurrents of violence that bubbled beneath the surface of Athenian society and usually proceeded to erupt. The style and the tone in which Polemarchus' invitation is delivered, wrote John Winkler, 'shows that we are not dealing with simple hospitality, but with a mock-kidnapping'. According to Winkler, this is a case of socially repressed aggression. After the slave catches up with Socrates and makes him wait, as Winkler tells it, Polemarchus arrives and threatens him: 'Do you see how many we are?' When Socrates replies that he does, Polemarchus proceeds to another threat: 'And are you stronger than all these?' On this Socrates 'plays along with the joke, saying meekly: "May there not be the alternative, that we may persuade you to let us go?"' To this Polemarchus replies: 'But can you persuade us, if we refuse to listen to you?'

Even though Winkler concedes that Polemarchus was joking and that his threats were not 'real', his overall conclusion is that 'in a culture where issues of strength are continuously being put at stake, the threat of violence does not lie very far beneath the surface'.[6] If we accept this interpretation of Plato's passage, we can, of course, add yet another item to the list of cases whose cumulative effect is supposedly to highlight the bad-tempered and quarrelsome nature of Athenian society.

---

[6] Winkler 1990: 51–2.

Our example from history concerns the public and private behaviour of Pericles' successors, which Thucydides presents as an entire pattern rather than merely a particular series of actions:

But his successors took entirely the opposite course; driven by personal ambition and out for personal gain, they adopted policies in matters that had nothing to do with the war that damaged both themselves and their allies. Where these policies were successful they led only to individual advancement and profit; where they failed they were a serious liability to a polis at war. (2.65.7)

Here the so-called 'demagogues' are described as choosing, in situations involving both co-operation and conflict, to pursue policies that were both self-regarding in the extreme and potentially damaging to the community. The passage sheds a gloomy light upon the life of the Athenians, whom Thucydides here portrays as having been manipulated by a group of unscrupulous politicians to the latter's own advantage. Some modern scholars have interpreted the policies referred to in this passage as harbingers of forces that were gradually to gather strength, undermine the democracy and eventually bring it down. Others saw in them the seeds of a moral decadence that would, in the second half of the fourth century, culminate in the dismal state of affairs identified by Glotz and other modern scholars.[7]

Our example of the rhetorical genre is a long excerpt from the 54th Oration in the Demosthenic corpus (*Against Conon*), a forensic speech written on behalf of a man called Ariston who was suing another called Conon for assault and battery. Ariston claimed to have sustained such grievous bodily harm at Conon's hands that for a long time neither his relatives nor the attending physicians thought that he would survive (54.1). The injuries in question were sustained in the course of two series of incidents, the first of which Ariston relates as follows:

Two years ago I went out to Panacton to do my assigned garrison duty [see **Fig. 2.2a**]. This man Conon's sons pitched their tent near us, and I wish they hadn't, because that was where all their hostility and aggression towards us started. Let me tell you how it happened. All the time we were in the garrison these men used to spend the entire day from lunchtime on drinking. We, on the other hand, behaved in exactly the same way outside the city as we usually do in it. By the time everyone else was having dinner these men would already be up to some sort of drunken idiocy, starting off by hassling our body-slaves and eventually moving

---

[7] Cf., e.g., Cloché's correction of the impressionistic view that the life of even a part-time Athenian politician was rendered miserable by an endless succession of trials in which he was forced to appear as either plaintiff or defendant (Cloché 1960). See pp. 89–92, 93–7.

on to us. They used to claim that our servants had engulfed them in smoke while cooking or been rude to them or something, and would use this as an excuse to beat them up, tip their chamber-pots over them, piss on them and do every other unpleasant thing they could think of. We were indignant about all this, but began by trying to tell them we didn't like it. When they laughed in our faces and refused to stop, however, all of us (not just I) went in a body to let the general know what was going on. He told them off roundly, condemning not only their appalling behaviour towards us, but also their conduct in the camp in general. Far from stopping or feeling ashamed of themselves, however, they crashed in on us that very evening as soon as it got dark, hurling insults at us, and ending up beating me up. They made such a ferocious din round the tent that the general and the taxiarchs turned up with some of the other soldiers, which saved us from being badly hurt and indeed from doing some serious damage ourselves in return for these people's drunken provocation. Things having gone this far, it's not surprising that there should still have been very considerable ill-feeling between us even after we had returned home. I swear by the gods, though, that I had absolutely no intention of suing them or continuing to make a fuss about all this. I simply made up my mind that in future I would watch out for myself and stay well away from people like that. (Demosthenes 54.3–6, *Against Conon*)

A number of choices are made in this situation of acute conflict. Conon's sons and their friends choose to commit various acts of aggression. Ariston and his group choose to respond to these by means of remonstrations and complaints. Finally Ariston decides, after being beaten up, to avoid the aggressors and in the future to 'stay well away from people like that'. I shall analyse these choices in detail later on.[8] For now I shall simply point out that this passage is commonly adduced as glaring proof of the violent character of Athenian society. The vague but widely accepted line of thought underlying this conclusion may be spelt out as follows. This random glimpse of Athenian life shows that drunken brawls such as the one described happened all the time in Athenian society, with people beating each other up at the slightest provocation and society apparently failing miserably to prevent such incidents from occurring. This is a pattern typical of feuding societies. Democratic Athens was therefore obviously a feuding society.[9]

Having glanced at these passages and at certain of their modern interpretations, it is time for us to remind ourselves of what is at issue. We know that various incidents involving co-operation and/or conflict took place at the time and in the space that we are discussing. We also know that the stories of some of these incidents were told, retold and sometimes written down,

---

[8] See pp. 156–7, 199, 283–6.
[9] For a definition of a 'feuding society' of which proponents of this line of thinking do not always seem to be aware, see p. 160.

as a result of which we have certain information about some of them today. Serious doubt exists, however, as to whether the relation between these real-life, factual incidents and their surviving literary representations is quite as modern commentators see it, and as to whether or not the general picture of Athenian society in which their analysis has resulted is valid. This doubt is a pressing one because if Athenian society was indeed dominated by the uncompromising spirit of revenge (as we are told our passage from Sophocles suggests), if it laboured under the constant threat of violence (Plato), if it was driven recklessly downhill by self-seeking politicians (Thucydides), if it was riddled with violent feuds (Demosthenes), we are faced with the question of what to do with the unconditionally cheerful, optimistic image of life in Athens that emerges from the praises heaped upon her by a host of poets, philosophers and historians, from her widespread reputation for gentleness, self-restraint, fairness, moderation and generosity[10] and finally from the many critiques, past and present, that have acknowledged the remarkable stability and efficiency of her democracy.[11]

We could, in my view, make considerable advances towards resolving this difficulty if we faced up to the possibility that various modern commentators have simply got it wrong. Perhaps they have made incorrect assumptions and used methods of analysis unsuitable to the task of revealing the ancient experience behind the texts under analysis; perhaps they have under-estimated, or even ignored, certain distorting factors that were at work within the various literary genres. It may well be that if we adopt alternative assumptions, apply other methods of analysis and identify ways of compensating for distorting factors we will be able to perceive a very different sort of social reality behind our literary representations. It may even be that we will succeed in resolving the discrepancies pointed out above.

THE DISTORTIONS OF GENRE

It is very obvious that Sophocles' superb rhythms, Plato's velvety diction,[12] Thucydides' complex, overloaded prose and Demosthenes' flowing rhetoric differ significantly from one another. The stylistic differences that we observe follow directly from the differences between the various literary genres in which these authors found it most suitable to express their ideas.

---

[10] See pp. 109–16.   [11] See pp. 76–80.

[12] Dionysius of Halicarnassus (*On Composition*, Chapter 25) tells us that after Plato's death tablets were found among his belongings that showed that he had tried many different word orders to achieve the simple, flowing sentence with which he begins his *Republic*.

The differences between the genres in turn reflect differences in the rules, conventions and techniques adopted by each genre to achieve its desired end. Since this end was in most cases by no means the straightforward recording of factual events, passages belonging to different genres cannot all be expected to cast their light equally upon the whole of Athenian society, or to illuminate it from the same angle. This point needs to be stressed in view of the assumption, widespread in modern scholarship, that every text that has come down to us from Classical antiquity, whether tragedy or comedy, philosophy or history, poetry or rhetoric, biography or medical writing, may be placed on the same plane and assumed to possess the same evidential value.[13] In fact it is possible to grade these texts according to their genre, establishing a hierarchy according to the degree of distortion that they create.

In my view, the genre most apt to distort social reality is drama (both tragedy and comedy). In making this claim, I am not contesting the well-established view that the drama was deeply involved in Athenian social life,[14] that its cautionary moral lessons were influenced by (and in turn influenced) the particular moral dilemmas that confronted the Athenians and that the playwrights wrote into their plays elements of their own social environment. My point is that even if we allow for this wide interface between drama and reality, a considerable gap still separates one from the other. *Pace* Adkins, people on the stage do not *generally* behave as people do in real life. *Pace* Dover, they do not even *sometimes* behave as people do in real life.[15] The imaginary world of drama is governed by forces altogether different from those that govern everyday social reality. Social life is driven by the clash of individual wills in time and space, within a social system capable of imposing sanctions. The driving force of drama is the individual creative imagination. In drama the clash of individual wills takes place between

[13] In practice this often amounts to licensing the scholar to extrapolate from one genre to another, or to rely on one genre almost to the exclusion of others. At least two book-length studies may be cited that have attempted to illuminate certain aspects of Athenian (or Greek) morality using almost exclusively the evidence of drama: M. W. Blundell 1989 and B. Williams 1993; cf. L. Pearson 1962, esp. ch. 4. W. V. Harris 1997 and 2001: 173 takes me to task for excluding from earlier publications on Athenian behaviour 'everything except forensic oratory', mentioning in particular Aristotle and the theatre of Euripides, which are, I believe, irrelevant to the points that I was trying to make. The methodological issue is discussed more fully in Herman 2000a, which is also a response to W. V. Harris 1997.

[14] Cf. Vernant 1972: 24.

[15] Cf. Dover 1983: 35 (in response to Adkins 1960a): 'No one, I imagine, would contend that people on stage always and necessarily "behave as they do in real life", for they sometimes behave in a demonic way which is rare in life, and they commonly organise, intellectualise and articulate the expression of their emotions unrealistically.'

fictitious persons in fictitious circumstances.[16] Drama is thus neither the mirror-image nor an extension of social life. It interacts with social life at the most profound of levels, but ultimately the two are not the same. The theme of vengeance, in particular, illustrates the essential separation between them. Even in societies of which acts of revenge form no very significant part, revenge tragedies are often written simply because the workings of vengeance are a gripping and convenient means of carrying a plot through to its denouement. Playwrights exploit the tension between things real and imaginary that exists in the minds of the audience. Things that are impossible in real life become possible on stage, and an audience may well thrill to subliminal appeals that offstage have lost their force or been discredited. People on stage are really only behaving *as if that were how people behaved* in real life. The seductive similarity between behaviour on stage and behaviour in real life should not lure us into believing that these two sorts of behaviour are one and the same thing.

Oedipus 'at the crossroads' is far from unusual in choosing the path of tragic overkill. Greek tragedy abounds in examples of extreme vengeance. Medea responds to infidelity by murdering her young sons, her erstwhile husband's new bride and the bride's father. Displeased by failing to win Achilles' weapons, Ajax sets out to slaughter both Odysseus and those who made the decision to award the arms to him instead; this plan is frustrated only by divine intervention.[17] Extreme vengeance, whether human or divine, is a central motif of so many Greek plays (and indeed of the heroic myths that inspired them) that Said has asserted that the revenge play 'constitutes one of the essential types of tragic plot, from the *Oresteia*, in which everybody takes revenge, to the *Bacchae*, in which divine vengeance triumphs cruelly over human vengeance'.[18] This being so, the question arises of how far the principle that drama mimics life can be supposed to apply here. Does the conclusion (in my view mistaken) that the 'tragedies that Athenians attended – and which at once reflected and inculcated their values – turn on, and gloat and mull over, revenge'[19] warrant the suggestion that in everyday life the Athenians regarded the urge for revenge as

---

[16] Cf. two observations on this subject with which I find it much easier to sympathise: 'The chief obstacle to the identification of elements of popular morality in drama of any kind is the simple fact that drama consists of the utterances of fictitious persons in fictitious situations' (Dover 1974: 14). '[T]he action [of *Antigone*] takes place in an essentially fictive world in which "real-life" considerations may be set aside with comparative ease . . .' (Easterling 1997: 26).

[17] Cf. M. W. Blundell 1989: 172. A long series of further examples is paraded in Said 1984 and Burnett 1998.

[18] Said 1984: 47.   [19] Lendon 2000: 13, with the bibliography cited in his n. 38.

legitimate, admirable and enjoyable, and that their everyday life was consequently 'rich in retaliations'?[20]

Not every student of ancient Greek literature would happily embrace this conclusion. Certain plays can be regarded as firmly repudiating the fierce spirit of retaliation and revenge. Even though the *Oresteia* teems with references to vengeance (the lines, '"For word of hate let word of hate be said", crieth Justice aloud as she exacteth the debt, "and for murderous stroke let murderous stroke be paid"' (Aeschylus, *The Libation-Bearers* 309–13, trans. H. W. Smyth) have been widely quoted), it is generally agreed that its overall stance constitutes a powerful rejection of revenge. Aeschylus, as Vlastos put it, 'confronts the futility and horror of the intrafamilial blood-feud and makes the trilogy culminate in a celebration of the supersession of private vengeance by the majesty of civic law'.[21] Here the 'drama imitates life' theory appears to support the conclusion of many a student of drama that the society of fifth-century Athens witnessed a diminution in the traditional power of revenge. Which plays, we may ask, should we therefore take more faithfully to reflect the truth about democratic Athens: those akin in spirit to Aeschylus' *Libation-Bearers*, or those whose spirit more closely resembles that of Sophocles' *Ajax*?

The uncomfortable truth is that unless we are able to cross-check revenge as it appears in these plays against social attitudes to revenge (it might, for example, be useful to know how the playwrights' audiences reacted to the dilemmas with which they were presented) we have no way of knowing. A landmark article by Peter Laslett, alluringly styled 'The wrong way through the telescope', reviews the conceptual problems surrounding this issue. The English Restoration comedies written between 1660 and 1720 are notorious for their licentiousness, prompting the question of how far this 'reflected' English sexual behaviour during this period. Laslett cites a typical response to this question, based on the facile assumption that drama imitates life: 'Men abandoned themselves to the most outrageous licence. Prostitution flaunted itself without a blush, at Court, at the theatre, everywhere. Needless to say there was no longer any question of religion.'[22] The impersonal evidence of statistics, however, in the form of the very reliable 'bastardy

---

[20] Cf. Burnett 1998: 55: 'Athenians were convinced that the return of a first blow was justified . . . Anger and injury could be urged in defense of an act of violence . . . Everyday life was evidently rich in such retaliations . . .'; Lendon 2000: 13: 'Athenians no longer sought vengeance by killing: they did so in politics and intrigue and litigation. To take revenge is just and admirable . . . and enjoyable, and still felt to be the compulsory response to *hybris* in the Attic orators . . . Whatever the reason for the passing of the practice of blood vengeance from Greece, it left the ethic of vengeance intact. The ethic of vengeance was familiar, available, and indeed compelling, to politicians and statesmen, to oligarchs and citizens in democracies . . .'

[21] Vlastos 1991: 190.   [22] Laslett 1976: 335, citing Alexandre Beljame.

ratios' (recording the percentages of illegitimate children baptised in ninety-eight English parishes in every decade from the 1580s to the 1800s), has a different story to tell. 'In the ninety-eight parishes concerned', writes Laslett, 'the later seventeenth century, that is, the Puritan Interlude and the Restoration put together, represents the time when illegitimacy was at its *lowest* during the whole number of years from 1561 until 1837 . . .' He therefore concludes that 'any expectation that the licentiousness of Restoration drama, Restoration literature generally, and Restoration manners reflected a permissive attitude towards bastardy in society at large must be misplaced'. Interpreting drama as a true mirror of social structure and social change is thus, as he puts it, 'like looking the wrong way through the telescope'.[23]

We are now in a position to coin a generalisation: even though the drama interacts with real life in subtle and manifold ways, it cannot be regarded as an appropriate indicator of hard facts such as social statistics, which can more reliably be derived from other more direct sources. Such facts may then, of course, be compared with the apparent implications of contemporary drama, potentially leading to a better understanding of the social reasons for the ways in which playwrights chose to interpret their themes. Drama, however, is no substitute for sources whose connection with social reality is more direct. If Sophocles' 'Oedipus at the crossroads' scene is a dramatic device that should not be regarded as a reflection of his contemporaries' normal response to such circumstances, then it cannot tip the balance in favour of the pessimistic view of Athenian society. We cannot know just what it did reflect, or just what it meant to Sophocles' contemporaries, until we have sorted out the place of revenge in Athenian society on the basis of evidence other than high-class literature.[24]

Philosophers are real people who live in real societies during real eras, whether or not they draw most of their inspiration from books. It is important that we should remember this because so many attempts have been made to treat Plato, for instance, as a disembodied mind secluded in an ivory tower, 'the farthest removed from popular morality'.[25] This can only

[23] Laslett 1976: 336–7 and 340, my italics.
[24] See Chapters 5–7. I cannot, however, resist pointing out that W. V. Harris 2001: 172, contrary to his general acceptance of the pessimistic picture of Athenian society, and contrary to his (unspoken) assumption that drama imitates life, answers the question of 'How was this [i.e. Oedipus' overkill] seen or meant to be seen by the initial audience?' with 'Probably in a most unfavourable light . . .'
[25] Cf. Dover 1974: 2: 'My purpose in this book is to describe the morality – not the moral philosophy – of the period, roughly a century, between the birth of Plato in 428/7 and the death of Aristotle in 322. How far this morality turns out to embody principles and attitudes which resemble any Platonic or Aristotelian axioms, assumptions, hypotheses or findings is a question which I leave entirely to philosophers.'

be described as far from convincing. No philosopher, not even the most determined recluse, operates in a social vacuum. Like anyone else, the philosopher is, in Bertrand Russell's words, necessarily 'an outcome of his *milieu*, a man in whom were crystallized and concentrated thoughts and feelings which, in a vague and diffuse form, were common to the community of which he was a part'.[26] Plato's most immediate entourage may have consisted of a hard core of aristocrats, but the so-called Platonic circle was a heterogeneous bunch made up of people from various communities and from all walks of life.[27]

The factors that distort our interpretation of Plato and Aristotle do not operate equally throughout their works. In order to compensate for these factors we must first distinguish between background scenes and connecting passages of the sort that we examined earlier, which turn up every now and then in Plato's writings, and the generalised statements on morality that we find in the writings of both.

These background scenes are snapshots of Athenian life with a strong realistic thrust. Their evidential value is increased by their being incidental to Plato's central themes (they may, in other words, basically be regarded as cursory links rather than as essential parts of the message that he was trying to convey). It is hard to see any reason why Plato should have wished to use such passages to convey a distorted picture of the society of which he was a part. With this in mind, let us now return to John Winkler's interpretation of the 'visit to the Peiraeus' passage quoted earlier.[28] According to Winkler, the dialogue between Socrates and Polemarchus plays out a mimicked kidnapping, revealing sinister repressed drives and hidden undercurrents of violence. Winkler's argument is that this 'trial of strength' is typical of a society in which the threat of violence loomed constantly, so that Plato's account should be regarded as yet another pointer to the inherently dangerous and frightening nature of Athenian society.

The problem with this approach is much like the difficulty that we have already encountered in connection with interpretations of the drama: it insists that day-to-day behaviour may properly be inferred from expressed attitudes, an assertion that rests on the fallacy that a society's 'multiple psychological layers'[29] are directly expressed in that society's behaviour. These 'multiple psychological layers' (dreams, visions, obsessions, repressed drives and the psychic states that often manifest themselves in religion, art and imaginative literature) are indeed a legitimate and extremely interesting

---

[26] B. Russell (1946) *History of Western Philosophy*. London: Allen and Unwin: 5.
[27] Cf. Field 1948.   [28] See p. 122.
[29] I have borrowed this phrase from H. Perkins' review of Gay 1993, a study of the interplay between the psychological roots of violence, aggression and historical change during the Victorian period.

field of investigation.[30] They are, despite their intangibility, part of social reality, and it could reasonably be argued that they ought to be taken into consideration by anyone attempting to reconstruct a certain society's social profile. I would fully subscribe to this theory, with the proviso that in order to lead to any significant insight such 'layers' must be examined in conjunction with other evidence concerning behaviour in the society in question. If this is not done, the historian will end up investigating a dream world that exists only in his or her own fertile imagination. If we do proceed in this way we will find ourselves analysing the human drives and emotions that found expression in the law and social mores of our chosen society, were built into its institutions and consequently influenced day-to-day behaviour. Even if correct, Winkler's interpretation of the 'visit to the Peiraeus' passage does nothing to undermine the passage's common-sense interpretation (in other words, that two groups of Athenian men good-naturedly joshed each other for a few minutes before agreeing to go and have some fun together). If indeed hidden undercurrents of violence were at work during this encounter (and are such undercurrents ever wholly absent from any society?),[31] they were never allowed to break out. *This* fact may indeed be of some consequence in achieving a correct understanding of the Athenian code of behaviour.

The generalised statements about morality and behaviour that we find in the works of both Plato and Aristotle are particularly useful to us where they touch on vengeance and retaliation. The following passages from Aristotle consistently present vengeance as noble and swallowing insults as servile:

To take vengeance (*to . . . timoreisthai*) on one's enemies is nobler than to come to terms with them; for to retaliate (*to . . . antodidonai*) is just (*dikaion*), and that which is just is noble (*kalon*). (*Rhetoric* 1367a24–5, trans. J. H. Freese)

And revenge (*to timoreisthai*) is pleasant; for it is painful to be unsuccessful, and it is pleasant to succeed. Now, those who are resentful (*orgizomenoi*) are pained beyond measure when they fail to secure revenge, while the hope of it delights them. (*Rhetoric* 1370b13, trans. J. H. Freese)

And human beings also feel pain when angry, and take pleasure in revenge. But those who fight for these motives, though valiant fighters, are not courageous; for the motive of their confidence is not honour, nor is it guided by principle (*logos*), but it springs from feeling (*pathos*). (*Nicomachean Ethics* 1117a12, trans. H. Rackham)

---

[30] For a clear analysis of which see Dodds 1951.
[31] For a refined exposé of latent societal violence from an ethological perspective, see Eibl-Eibesfeldt 1979: 49ff.

... it is considered servile (*andrapododes*) to put up with an insult to oneself (*to de propelakizomenon anechesthai*) or suffer one's friends (*tous oikeious*) to be insulted. (*Nicomachean Ethics* 1126a6, trans. H. Rackham)

Statements such as these have often been adduced as evidence for the feuding spirit supposed to have pervaded Athenian society, Aristotle's phrases being taken as absolute evidence that the people of Athens were just as vindictive and just as prickly in defence of their honour as these phrases suggest. This interpretation has added considerable weight to the balance in favour of the pessimistic view of Athenian society.[32]

Is it legitimate to interpret Aristotle thus? Those who would answer this question in the affirmative are making the unspoken assumption that the typical behaviour of an entire society can be inferred from a philosophical expression of abstract principles proceeding from any one of its members. A moment's thought suffices to expose the fragility of this assumption. Firstly, it should be noted that Aristotle was writing about human nature in general, probably with the aim of refining the sophistic picture of the 'natural' man untamed by social convention. He makes no reference to the matter that most concerns us,[33] namely the manner in which the behaviour of the *conventional* Athenian man was moulded by democratic convention. Secondly, his remarks were in no way exceptional. Demosthenes too made the point that man was born with the inclination to exact revenge (54.19, *Against Conon*), yet Demosthenes, as we shall see, consistently expresses absolute opposition to the fulfilment of this impulse. Thirdly and most importantly, Aristotle's statements on insult and revenge collide head-on with the Socratic doctrine of non-retaliation expounded by Plato. The Platonic dialogues contain an entire series of injunctions forbidding us to return evil for evil, or to derive any pleasure from satisfying the low impulse to revenge:[34]

We should never do injustice (*adikein*).
... we should never reciprocate an injustice (*antadikein*).
We should never do evil (*kakourgein*).
... we should never reciprocate evil (*antikakourgein*).

To do evil to a human being (*kakos poiein*) is no different from acting unjustly (*adikein*) to him.

[32] Aristotle figures prominently in the works cited in Chapter 3, nn. 40–2 and 62–3, above. For Aristotle as the formulator of the idea of 'just vengeance', see Courtois 1984b.
[33] The section preceding the 'sweet revenge' passage deals with pleasure, desires and emotions, and contains no clue that might link it specifically with Athens (why not, indeed, with Pella, Assos or Mytilene, where the philosopher had also spent some years?).
[34] I am indebted for this point to Vlastos 1991.

Therefore, we should never return a wrong or do evil to a single human being no matter what we may have suffered at his hands. (*Crito* 48b4–49d5)

If we accept that passages of this sort must be taken as direct evidence of real-life Athenian mores, and if we concur that these two revered philosophers, long-term residents of Athens who are known to have interacted with one another, have here chosen to express diametrically opposed views on vengeance and retaliation, which of the two are we to believe?

The historical genre, to which we shall now turn, may help us to answer this question. Thucydides, Xenophon and the author of *The Athenian Constitution* (and, to a lesser extent, Herodotus and other historians whose works survive only in fragmentary form) have for our purposes a three-fold significance. Firstly, being both participants and observers, they knew exactly what it was really like to live in Athens and had an implicit understanding of the social values and behaviour of their culture. Secondly, they had chosen a genre that committed them to attempt accurate representation with a minimum of distortion. In this they were very different from the adherents of the other three genres we have considered, whose avowed aim had never been to give a balanced description of social conditions in Athens. Our historians may not always have succeeded in achieving this aim, but clearly they took it seriously. Thirdly, these historians conceived of actions and ideas as a unity in precisely the manner we have already discussed.[35] Thucydides, for instance, often supported the praises that he heaped upon Athens[36] with examples of how her society operated in practice. Here, for example, he discusses the practice of bearing arms:

These mainlanders [i.e. people regarded by Thucydides as backward: the Ozolian Locrians, the Aetolians and the Acarnanians] have retained the habit of going about armed (*to siderophoreisthai*, literally 'carrying iron'), a survival from the old days of banditry. At one time every Greek would have been armed, since homes were defenceless and communications unsafe; carrying arms was then as normal a part of everyday life for Greeks as it is for the Barbarians today. The fact that people in the parts of Greece I am talking about have kept the custom up is evidence that this way of life was once to be found everywhere. The Athenians were among the very first to give up the habit of carrying weapons (*ton te sideron katethento*) and to adopt a more laid-back and luxurious way of life. (Thucydides 1.5.3–6.3)

This crucial piece of information is entirely consistent with the idea of Athens that we derive from phrases such as 'we are not suspicious about each other's daily activities' (see p. 112, n. 95). It is, on the other hand, wholly inconsistent with the idea that she was some sort of feuding society riddled

<hr />

[35] See pp. 16 and 107.   [36] See pp. 112–14.

with rivalries and unbridled violence, since it is characteristic of the so-called feuding societies that their members view the habitual bearing of arms as normal.[37] Had the people of Athens indeed habitually gone about armed we might have been justified in contending that Athens exhibited certain features characteristic of feuding societies. The fact that they did no such thing makes it increasingly difficult to sustain any such claim. In asserting this, it may be noted, I am relying not on imaginative literature or on generalised philosophical statements, but on the results of cross-checking evidence regarding attitudes against evidence bearing directly on behaviour.

The fact that the proper aim of the historian is faithfully to represent the society that he or she is observing by no means suggests that we should blindly believe everything that historians say. When Thucydides wrote of Periclean Athens that 'in what was nominally a democracy, power was really in the hands of the first citizen' (2.65.9–10), he may well have been in error. With the benefit of hindsight it appears clear that Pericles cannot have been one of those autocrats whose power depends upon their control of some sort of party machinery, army, personal security force or secret police. Pericles might at any moment have been deposed by constitutional means. Whatever power he had depended upon his obtaining a majority vote at the Assembly; without the approval of that body his policies would have gone precisely nowhere, and unless that body had continued to re-elect him to the post of *strategos* year after year he himself would have vanished without trace.[38] The assertion that Athens became under his leadership a monopoly 'of the first citizen' must therefore be objectively incorrect.

The same is true of the passage concerning Pericles' successors that we have already mentioned.[39] Thucydides was pessimistically determined that any defeat of Athens must signal the death of democracy, and some of his descriptions were deliberately angled so as to validate this forecast. Pericles' successors thus became the principal culprits in Athens' defeat. This version of events influenced later scholarship to such an extent that 404 (or at best some year no more than a couple of decades thereafter), rather than 322, was long reckoned to have marked the end both of the Athenian democracy and of Athens' greatness.[40] It would seem, however, that Thucydides got it wrong again. With the benefit of hindsight we can aver that Athenian democracy did not by any means end with the defeat

---

[37] See pp. 209–12.   [38] Cf. Kagan 1991: 63.   [39] See p. 123.
[40] Eder 1995a, 1997 and J. K. Davies 1995 contain the evidence.

of 404 and the short-lived, Spartan-sponsored oligarchy,[41] but flourished for almost another century, despite the fact that nothing had been done to change the system since the demagogues had supposedly surrendered the actual conduct of affairs to the people (Thucydides 2.65.10). These are some of the reasons why we need to take Thucydides' interpretations with a pinch of salt, not setting too much store by his vision of the dire decadence that apparently threatened Athens. Since it would appear that Athens was not in fact run into the ground by reckless, self-seeking demagogues, accepting Thucydides' account as justification for the pessimistic view of Athenian society might not be altogether wise.

Finally, we should mention the speeches that appear in the works of all three major historians. These are of particular interest in the case of Thucydides because the speeches that have passed down to us from him shower so much praise upon Athens.[42] These speeches, which a modern expert has called 'the most striking literary feature of the greatest Greek historian',[43] have generated considerable disagreement as to whether they express the opinions of the people who are supposed to have made them or those of Thucydides himself. This controversy raged for more than a century and then fell slowly into abeyance, with scholarly opinion inclined slightly in favour of some version of the latter option.[44] The correctness or otherwise of this conclusion makes no difference to the speeches' value as evidence regarding the character of the Athenians and of the Athenian democracy. 'Both those who believe that there is some historical content in Thucydides' speeches and those who believe that he made them all up in his own head', wrote Gomme, 'are convinced that his intention in writing this is to show one aspect of the forces at work both in provoking the war and in the fighting itself . . . Thucydides was anxious to show the temper of the Athenians, Corinthians and Lacedaemonians at the time; he selects and composes (with or without authority for it) these speeches to throw some light on that temper.'[45] If Thucydides did write the speeches himself, in other words, he took great care to ensure that the 'temper' they expressed was authentic.

---

[41] Cf. Ober 1993a: esp. 97: 'After Pericles' death, the democracy existed in fact, and the flaws inherent in the democratic practice of deliberation and decision making contributed to the collapse of the Athenian δύναμις.'

[42] See pp. 112–13.   [43] Kennedy 1973: ix.

[44] Cf. Walbank 1985 and lately, W. V. Harris 2001: 178: 'Pericles' Funeral Speech . . . [was] in reality . . . an essay by Thucydides intended to reflect the great democratic leader's thinking.'

[45] Gomme, Andrewes and Dover 1945–81, vol. I: 233.

LAW COURTS AND ORATORS

Even though the speeches delivered in the Athenian law courts contain considerable distortions, I shall argue that they are the best evidence we have of how the Athenians characteristically behaved in situations of co-operation and/or conflict, the central theme of this book. I have two main reasons for asserting this. Firstly, every one of these speeches was written about an actual incident that took place in time and space, not about an imaginary event or a fictionalised or conflated version of real-life events.[46] Secondly, and more importantly, if the speeches distort the incidents they describe they do so in such a way that we can generally control and correct the distortion. We shall begin to find out how as we review the circumstances under which these speeches were written, paying particular attention to various aspects of the Athenian courts, to the relationship between speaker and audience and to the rules, procedures and standards in accordance with which the speeches had to be delivered.

To the uninitiated the courts in which these speeches were delivered may appear to have been no more than tribunals of justice, albeit supreme tribunals, against whose decisions there was no appeal. For the Athenians, however, they harboured a deeper meaning: the courts were the supreme embodiments of people power and the ultimate guardians of the constitution. They had ascended to supremacy in the fifth century, first entering the administrative sphere and gaining preponderance over the other state organs (the Assembly, the Council and the Archons). They next invaded the judicial sphere, acquiring the last say in questions of legislation and constitution. Finally they rolled on into the political sphere and secured the power to condemn politicians.[47] Add to all this the courts' predominantly lower-class composition[48] and it becomes very clear why their significance to the Athenians was so great. Aristotle remarked that Solon abolished the (oligarchic) Areopagus Council and the (aristocratic) magistracies by opening the law courts to all and giving them sovereignty in all matters.[49] The author of *The Athenian Constitution* puts it more trenchantly: 'when the people (*demos*) are masters of the vote [i.e. the votes cast to reach verdicts in the law courts] they become masters of the state (*politeia*)' (9.1).

---

[46] For the exception of the so-called 'rhetorical exercises', see n. 61 below.

[47] Cf. R. A. Knox 1985; Ostwald 2000a.

[48] For the current state of the debate as to the courts' social composition, whose general consensus has shifted from 'predominantly well-to-do' to 'predominantly lower-class', see Ober 1989: 142 and Todd 1990a. For literature regarding further characteristics of the law courts, see Ober 1989: 142, n. 98.

[49] *Politics* 1273a5; cf. Plutarch, *Solon* 18.2. See Ruschenbusch 1957; Ostwald 1986: 5–7.

The Athenian law courts appear even more extraordinary when we compare them with the various dispute-settlement agencies described by anthropologists and by historians of subsequent Western societies.[50] As far as I am aware, no remotely similar institution has ever been found. The Athenian law courts were served by 6,000 men, all over thirty years old, who were drawn yearly by lot from across almost the full spectrum of Athenian citizens. The officials who were to serve on a particular day were selected from this pool using a highly sophisticated technique (see **Fig. 4.1**). Anything from 201 to 2,501 Athenian citizens might be required to start a court session, according to the importance of the lawsuit. Socrates' trial, we are told, was conducted by a court of 501 men. On any one day there might be three, four or even five courts in session simultaneously. The Athenians' fondness for litigation, along with their attendant faculty of loquacity, was duly caricatured by Aristophanes (esp. *Wasps* 85–135).

The all-powerful holders of judicial office are customarily referred to as having served on 'juries' (Greek *dikastai*). The analogy that this implies could, however, be misleading. Unlike juries today, these were not merely groups of laymen authorised to decide issues of fact under the supervision of a judge authorised to decide issues of law. Far more powerful than that, they were in modern terms both judge *and* jury, delivering judgement on both the facts and the law. From now on I shall refer to them as dikasts, the anglicised form of their Greek title.[51]

In Athenian law an important distinction was made between 'private' (*dikai*) and 'public' (*graphai*) prosecutions. Only the victim or his immediate personal representatives (friends, kinsmen or neighbours) could bring *dikai*. *Graphai*, introduced by Solon, could be initiated either by the victim or by a third party, such a party being known in the legal language of the time as 'whoever wishes', i.e. whoever wishes to prosecute (*ho boulomenos*; *The Athenian Constitution* 9.1). One corollary of this system was that Athens had no professional state prosecutors: if no private person chose to prosecute, there was no trial. Another was that serious offences, sometimes even murders, did not necessarily go to court as *graphai*.[52] The Athenian legal system has justly been termed 'accusatorial': it took the form of a carefully monitored verbal duel (see **Fig. 4.2**, top) between the plaintiff and the defendant, enacted in front of a largely passive audience. The dikasts

[50] Cf. S. Roberts 1979; Hart 1961. For a general introduction to the Athenian legal system see Carey 1997: 1–25.
[51] Cf. Calhoun 1944: 35.
[52] See the systematic reviews of this problem in Osborne 1985c and Todd 1993: 99–112, incorporating earlier literature on the subject.

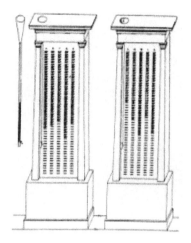

Figure 4.1 Machines for casting lots to select dikasts (*kleroteria*), reconstructed from fragment found in the *agora*; 'identification tickets' (*pinakia*) bearing the inscriptions 'Demophanes, son of Phili . . . , of [the deme of] Kephisia' and 'Euthyma[chos son of] Eryxim[achus].

Machines of this sort were used to randomise the selection of dikasts and to allocate them to the various courts in a manner that could not be predicted. According to the *Athenian Constitution* (63–4, supplemented by explanations of certain technicalities), the system worked as follows.

At each of the ten entrances to the law courts were two allotment machines and ten boxes, each representing a 'tribe'. Every box was marked with one of the first ten letters of the Greek alphabet. Each dikast lining up for service that day had with him an identification ticket, also marked with one of these ten letters. This he threw into the box marked with the same letter as the ticket (cf. Boegehold 1995: 59–61). An attendant shook the boxes and the *thesmothetes* drew one identification ticket from each box. One of the dikasts, chosen by lot, inserted the ticket drawn from each box. The same procedure was used to fill each row of slots. The dikast then threw a number of black and white bronze dice into the hollow bronze tube shown at far left (this was attached to the side of the machine), the number of white dice used equalling the number of dikasts required that day. The archon drew lots for the 'tribe' members by turning the crank at the bottom of the bronze tube on the allotment machine so that one of the dice fell out. If a white dice came out the dikasts represented by the next whole row of identification tickets were selected; if a black dice came out they were rejected. The herald then called up those who had been chosen to serve.

The next stage was the allocation of the dikasts to the various courts. The archon had beside him as many boxes as there were courts to be filled, each marked with a letter assigned by lot to a certain court. The selected dikasts drew an acorn (*balanos*), also marked with a letter, from a water-pot and showed it to the archon in charge. The archon then threw that dikast's identification ticket into the box marked with the letter on the acorn, 'so that the dikast shall go to the court to which he has been assigned by lot and not to whichever court he wishes, and no one shall be able to assemble men of his own choice in a court'. Sterling Dow, the first person to grasp the machines' true function (it had previously been thought that the term *kleroteria* referred to the rooms in which the lots were drawn), has made the point that this painstakingly detailed description affords unique insight into the Athenians' 'fair and thorough democracy, their passion for logic and for litigation, their suspicion of human nature, their fascination with luck, and their penchant for intricate machine-like institutions' (Dow 1939: 1).

Figure 4.2 Law-court equipment: water clocks (above) and voting ballots (below).
Water clocks (*clepsydra*; literally 'water-thief') such as these were one of the means by which
the Athenians measured time. A vessel with a small outflow tube near its base would be
filled with water and placed in the law court to regulate the amount of time taken by the
prosecutor and the defendant. The flow was stopped when laws were being read out or
witnesses introduced. The amount of water allowed was determined according to the
seriousness of the case (*The Athenian Constitution* 67.2). The speakers could see how much
time they had left from the curve of the water and the volume of the flow. This gave rise to
rhetorical assertions that even double the allotted amount of water would be insufficient
to recount all the acts of injustice committed by an opponent (Isocrates 18.52, *Against
Callimachus*; [Demosthenes] 53.3, *Against Nicostratus*). It is not known why the outer
wall of the vessel is marked 'Antiochidos' ('of [the tribe] Antiochis'; see caption
to **Fig. 9.13**).
By the end of the fifth century the dikasts had started voting by ballot (*psephophoria*)
according to a procedure described in detail in *The Athenian Constitution* 68.2–69.2
(previously each dikast had used a pebble to cast his vote). After the defendant and the
prosecutor had delivered their speeches, each dikast was issued with two small bronze discs
(*psephoi*). One of these was pierced, indicating a vote for the prosecution, and the other
solid, indicating a vote for the defendant. On the herald's proclamation, each dikast would
cast one of his discs into a bronze amphora, without showing the litigants which one.
When all had cast their votes, the attendants would empty the amphora onto a sort of
counting board; slotting the solid discs into the rows of holes at one end of the board and
the pierced ones into the holes at the other end. The discs were then counted and the
herald announced the result. 'Whoever receives the most votes', we read in *The Athenian
Constitution*, 'wins; if an equal number, the defendant wins.' For numerous other physical
objects used in Athenian trials, see Boegehold 1991 and 1995.

and the presiding magistrate were not allowed to address any question to either opponent, or to take any other direct part in the proceedings (though they might express their feelings informally by muttering or even roaring). Athenian trials thus did not involve the sort of crowd behaviour typical of Assembly meetings.[53]

Since it was regarded as crucial that each party should be able to present his case in as convincing a manner as possible, the litigants were allowed to call in a 'fellow speaker' (*synegoros*) to support their claims.[54] Professional speech-writers (*logographoi*) could also be employed to write a speech on behalf of the plaintiff or defendant and deliver it in court.[55] With this exception, however, no legal experts appear to have taken part in the suits.[56] The Athenians seem deliberately to have banned professionalism from their judicial system: every Athenian citizen was expected to know the law and to be able to tell right from wrong.[57] Having listened to the speeches – 'impartially', according to the oath they swore (Demosthenes 24.151, *Against Timocrates*) – the dikasts held no discussion, but proceeded straight away to the verdict, which they decided by casting a secret vote (see **Fig. 4.2**, bottom). In *graphai* they might have to vote twice, depending on the result of their first vote, which was on conviction or acquittal. If the verdict was for conviction, they voted again on the penalty. Cases involving the most serious offences (intentional killing, poisoning, intentional wounding and conspiracy to commit homicide) were tried before one of five specialised courts, among which the august court of the Areopagus took pride of place.[58] Cases involving lesser offences were brought before the regular courts of the Heliaeia.[59]

About 150 law-court speeches have survived. These are largely the work of the ten best-known Athenian speech-writers, otherwise known as 'The

---

[53] Cf. Finley 1974: 10; Bers 1985.

[54] For whose importance, long overlooked, see now Rubinstein 2000.

[55] For their fees see Dover 1968: 157–9. The speakers' often intimate knowledge of minor details of their cases suggests that Todd 1990b: 165 may be wrong to reject Dover's plausible hypothesis that the *logographos* and his client may have collaborated in composing the speech (Dover 1968: ch. 8).

[56] For the function of witnesses, who appear in Athenian lawsuits to have been overtly partisan, see Humphreys 1985.

[57] For the considerable extent of the average Athenian's legal knowledge, see E. M. Harris 1994: 135–56; 2002a.

[58] For the debate concerning the criteria for assigning homicide cases to the courts at the Areopagus and Palladion, see Thür 1991, with Wallace 1991.

[59] The five specialised courts were the Areopagus, the Palladion, the Delphinion, the Phreatto and the Prytaneion, on which see *The Athenian Constitution* 57.3–4 and Demosthenes 23.77, *Against Aristocrates*, with MacDowell 1963a: chs. 4–9 and Loomis 1972: 87. For the way in which various forms of action were matched to the offences, see Osborne 1985c. For the possibility that certain trials (particularly 'political' ones) may have exceeded the one-day time limit, see Worthington 1989.

Attic Orators': Antiphon, Andocides, Isocrates, Demosthenes, Aeschines, Lycurgus, Hypereides, Lysias, Isaeus and Dinarchus.[60] Some of the speeches cannot be attributed definitely to any particular writer. Scholars are agreed, however, that whoever wrote them must have lived in Athens under the democracy and that they are therefore not anachronistic. With the exception of seventeen meant for delivery before the Assembly or the Council, they are all forensic speeches, designed for delivery in the popular law courts of the Heliaeia or the Areopagus.[61] Two legal contests between Demosthenes and Aeschines, each consisting of both an accusation and a defence, have survived.[62] In no other case have both prosecution and defence speeches survived, so that we have usually to make do with only one side of the argument. The fact that any speeches at all have made it down to the present day can probably be put down to a general desire to emulate these paragons of Greek prose style and forensic rhetoric: the secret of how to sway mass audiences seems never to have lost its fascination for subsequent generations.[63]

Because these speeches were first written and then delivered orally (whether by the author himself or by someone else is often unclear) there may well be some discrepancy between the speeches that the dikasts heard and the versions that have survived in writing. For our purposes, however, any such differences are unimportant; for reasons that we shall shortly discover, they may even be seen as increasing the texts' evidential value.

THE EVIDENCE OF FORENSIC ORATORY

Members of the Greek leisured classes had held 'speakers of words' in high regard ever since the days of Homer (cf. *Iliad* 9.443). Being good with words was always useful in epic poetry if you needed to quarrel with another hero or win over an assembled multitude. As effective arguments, however, the speeches of epic poetry lacked the crucial ingredient of rationality ('a sustained, disciplined consideration of circumstances and their implications,

---

[60] All were Athenian citizens apart from the last three, who were metics, and all were active during the last hundred years of democracy. For the canon of the 'Ten Attic Orators', listed in [Plutarch] *Lives of the Ten Orators* 840D–E in an order other than this, see Worthington 1994b. For the extant orations in general, see Kennedy 1963: 125–263.

[61] A small minority of these are so-called 'rhetorical exercises', i.e. speeches written experimentally for study purposes that were never meant for delivery in court. Neither this nor the fact that some texts may have been revised by the speech-writer between delivery and publication makes any great difference to my argument.

[62] Demosthenes 19, *On the Embassy* (accusation), Aeschines 2, *On the Embassy* (defence); Aeschines 3, *Against Ctesiphon* (accusation), Demosthenes 18, *On the Crown* (defence).

[63] Finley 1972b.

of possible courses of action, their advantages and disadvantages'),[64] instead abounding in threats, emotional appeals, harangues and warnings. Logical argument did not become the norm until the polis emerged, with the 'iso-nomic' ('equally sharing') citizen at its centre. From then on, in order to win a public argument one needed to be able to persuade assemblies and juries of the justness of one's point of view; victory was thought to make one a worthier citizen. With her democratic process, her insistence on the rule of law and her throngs of philosophers and 'sophists' (i.e. itinerant teach-ers), Athens was perhaps the best possible hothouse for the development of oratory (the art of speaking well) and rhetoric (the theory or technique of speaking) into fine arts. Appeals to the emotions were by no means abandoned. *Pathos* (the evocation of passion by speech) was deliberately made part of the repertoire of persuasive techniques developed by the great teachers of oratory (Gorgias and Thrasymachus, for example) and the great theoreticians (men such as Aristotle and Isocrates). *Pathos* was, however, supposed to be used only in moderation. Socrates' defence speech warns that the dikasts may be more inclined to convict a person who makes his polis an object of derision by staging pathetic charades than one who keeps his composure (35b7–10). Beside the evocation of passion, appeals to reason came to take pride of place. 'They [our ancestors]', we read in the Funeral Oration attributed to Lysias, 'held that only wild animals were in the habit of controlling each other by force; men were expected to define justice according to the law, to persuade by rational means (*logo*) and to put both ideals into practice by listening to reason and abiding by the law' (Lysias 2.19, *Funeral Oration*). It would be impossible to overestimate the impor-tance of rational thought in judicial decision-making and consequently in the entire process of democratisation. The principle that, in Lloyd's words, 'in the evaluation of an argument it is the argument that counts, not the authority, status, connections or personality of its proponent'[65] must surely count as one of the cornerstones of Athenian democracy.

The Athenians' use of rational discussion in making decisions affecting the polis came close to what we would now call systems analysis. Take, for example, this excerpt from a speech by Demosthenes designed to persuade the Assembly to form an alliance with Olynthus (a city threatened by Macedonian expansionism):

For the swift and opportune movements of war he [Philip of Macedon] has an immense advantage over us in the fact that he is the sole director of his own policy, open or secret, that he unites the functions of a general, a ruler and a treasurer,

---

[64] Finley 1978a: 114. For a contrary opinion, see Schofield 1986.   [65] Lloyd 1990: 63.

and that he is always at the head of his army; but when it comes to a composition such as he would gladly make with Olynthus, the tables are turned. The eyes of the Olynthians are opened to the fact that they are now fighting not for glory, not for a strip of territory, but to avert the overthrow and enslavement of their fatherland. (Demosthenes 1.4–5, *First Olynthiac*, trans. J. H. Vince)

This argument reveals an impeccable reasoning process, essentially the one so memorably embodied in Pericles' Funeral Oration (Thucydides 2.40.2–3). It presupposes that the members of the audience will weigh every circumstance carefully and observe motivations and opportunities without prejudice, rather than acting on impulse, that they will take every relevant factor into account in making complex decisions, that they will search for the facts, rather than seizing upon whatever strikes them first or makes the most dramatic impression, and that they will try to understand the behaviour of people in an alien political system by imagining themselves in their shoes. Such are the quintessential marks of rational thinking.[66]

It is nonetheless difficult consistently to assess the speeches as a whole and the procedures of the courts in which they were delivered. Some of these speeches contain elements that by modern standards appear distinctly odd; some record procedures and behaviour of a sort unheard of in Western law courts.[67] Three partly overlapping differences in particular stand out. Unlike their modern counterparts, Athenian speakers appear to have been free to resort to personal abuse, mudslinging, vilification and innuendo. They were permitted to use not only elaborate rhetoric, but some very clever sophistry. They appear, moreover, to have been bound by no very strict standards of relevance and quality of evidence. Some scholars have contented themselves with remarking upon these differences. Others have identified them as inherent weaknesses in the Athenian system, to be added to their already lengthy lists of considerations in favour of the pessimistic view of Athenian society. We shall therefore proceed to re-examine these points, bearing in mind two questions. Firstly, do they indeed reinforce the pessimistic view of Athenian society, or do they in fact support the optimistic one? Secondly, do they in any way undermine our assertion that these speeches are the best evidence we have of the Athenian code of behaviour?

[66] Rationality is here assessed according to the sorts of procedure and consideration that precede decision-taking, rather than by a retrospective assessment of the decision's correctness or otherwise: a decision might be rational but wrong. Cf. Sutherland 1992. The use of rational rather than emotive argument in Athenian deliberative oratory (i.e. that delivered at the Assembly or before the Council) is discussed in Missiou 1992.

[67] For a good summary of these criticisms see A. Powell 1988: 299–309. For the use of speeches by playwrights, see Goldhill 1986: ch. 9.

(1) There can be no doubt that Athenian public speakers sometimes addressed each other in terms that would now be regarded as unacceptable. Strong language would be used, one litigant calling another 'son of a whore', the other countering with 'son of a slave mother'. Past misdemeanours were triumphantly produced, imputations and insinuations were flung freely about and the opponent's entire way of life was generally written off as appalling. A client of Lysias was thus permitted to express himself about the younger Alcibiades as follows:

> . . . his general conduct and the utter unworthiness as a citizen that he has dis-played from the very beginning make it everybody's duty to regard him as an enemy, whether or not they have suffered personally at his hands. His offences (*hamartemata*) are far from minor, deserve no forgiveness and suggest no glimmer of hope that he will ever improve: the way in which he has committed them and the utter wickedness that they display fill even his enemies with shame about certain events in which he takes the greatest pride. (Lysias 14.1–3, *Against Alcibiades 1*)

He later proceeded to accuse Alcibiades of sleeping with his sister and then becoming the lover of a person whom he afterwards attempted to murder (14.27–8). Demosthenes, meanwhile, was accused by an arch-rival of being a *kinaidos* (a promiscuous homosexual who allows himself to be buggered for cash) (Aeschines 2.150–1, *On the Embassy*).[68] Dover (whose collection of such passages, albeit not complete, is still the most thorough we have) has identified the three most popular grounds for accusing one's opponent of moral degradation as foreign or servile birth (with or without some attempt improperly to become an Athenian citizen), the following of some menial calling and deviant sexual behaviour.[69]

This feature of the speeches has long perturbed those commentators who would like to see in Athens a bastion of politeness and good manners. Dover himself remarked that 'accusations of this type are no longer accepted parliamentary practice, but they were at Athens';[70] another interpreter dryly notes that 'the invective is more furious than would be allowed in an English court'.[71] An earlier commentator on Demosthenes gave expression to his deep disappointment by commenting regretfully that 'there was no chivalry in Athenian political life'.[72]

Against this it may be argued that bad language and abuse are relatively rare in the forensic speeches. (A great many of Dover's examples come

---

[68] Cf. Winkler 1990: 45–70.   [69] Dover 1974: 32–3.   [70] Dover 1974: 33.
[71] J. R. King, *Demosthenes: Speech against Meidias*, xiii. I owe this reference to A. Powell 1988: 330 n. 266.
[72] J. H. Vince, in his introduction to the Loeb edition of Demosthenes, vol. 1, p. xii (first published in 1930).

from the exchange between Aeschines and Demosthenes.) The predominant tone is firm but not abusive. The oratory of the courts is also virtually free from the obscene sexual and scatological language encountered in Aristophanic comedy. It does indeed reveal some hidden undercurrents of violence, but it is hard to think of a society whose language is free of such undercurrents. We should also remember that, as has often been remarked, Athenian and modern law courts are not strictly comparable,[73] the first consisting of mass meetings headed by non-professionals, the second of small-scale meetings headed by a small and highly trained professional elite. Finally, too much fussing about chivalry and good manners (a distinctly early modern European invention, polished to perfection in the entourages of aristocrats and kings) obscures two of the Athenian system's most outstanding achievements. Firstly, whereas throughout most of human history the upper classes have kept an almost exclusive stranglehold on the twin state systems of legislation and jurisdiction, under the Athenian system the lower classes controlled both. Secondly, and consequently, whenever upper-class litigants appeared before the numerous dikasts, the quintessential representatives of the Athenian *demos*, they invariably acknowledged and reaffirmed the authority of the lower classes in running the state.[74]

On balance, then, this feature of the Athenian courts does not warrant adoption as yet another sign reinforcing the pessimistic view of Athenian society. Nor does it in any way undermine the speeches' value as evidence of the Athenian code of behaviour. Quite to the contrary, the appeals to emotion and the references to communal norms that these speeches contain make it much easier to access the innermost zone of Athenian values concerning co-operation and conflict.

(2) Another, more serious, charge levelled against the Athenian legal system is that its speakers were at liberty to use elaborate rhetoric and clever sophistry, linguistic or intellectual tricks designed, to paraphrase Gorgias of Leontini, to sway a great crowd not because they expressed the truth but because they were skilfully composed.[75] To resort to such tricks, so the argument runs, would be inconceivable in a modern court. In order to evaluate the relative merits and demerits of the two systems more precisely, let us now consider two examples.

In an essay on rhetoric spuriously attributed to Aristotle, the author considers how best to present evidence extracted under torture to a law

---

[73] Cf. A. Powell 1988: 300.
[74] I am indebted for these points to Stockton 1990: 96 and Christ 1998: ch. 3.
[75] Cf. Calhoun 1944: 36; Diels–Kranz 1964, vol. II: 290 (Gorgias): 'The word (*logos*) is a mighty power (*dynastes*) . . .; it can end fear, remove pain, bring joy, and increase pity.'

court. 'When it is in our interests to make this sort of evidence sound stronger', he writes, 'we must say that evidence obtained under torture is more trustworthy than ordinary testimony, since it is often in an ordinary witness's interests to lie, but people who are being tortured can only gain by telling the truth, since this is the fastest way of stopping the torture.' Then, without the slightest sign of compunction, he moves on to the antithetical case in which it is in the rhetor's interest to discredit such evidence: '[Y]ou must begin by asserting that slaves handed over for torture by their masters resent this furiously and are therefore ready to tell any lie about them. You should add that they are all too likely to make false confessions to the torturers in order to get their terrible experience over with as soon as possible' ([Aristotle], *Rhetoric to Alexander* 1432a).

Our second example, from a law-court speech, has to do with the relative seriousness, in the mind of the Athenian lawgiver, of the crimes of rape and seduction. In a speech written for a client whose situation seems to have been desperate, Lysias, one of the most talented composers of forensic speeches, claims that seduction is the more serious:

> ... the lawgiver, gentlemen, believed that rapists should be punished less severely than seducers, condemning the latter to death and merely doubling the damages awarded against the former. He did so on the ground that those who force themselves upon women are hated by their victims, while those who use persuasion corrupt their victims' souls, making other peoples' wives care more for them than for their own husbands, taking over the entire household and creating doubt as to whether the children are actually the husbands' or the adulterers'. (Lysias 1.32–3, *On the Murder of Eratosthenes*)

Although we cannot be sure of this, since the relevant law has not been preserved, Lysias was probably misrepresenting matters here: the Athenians probably regarded rape, not seduction, as the more serious crime.[76] We may therefore have to conclude that since the truth was not at all helpful to the client's cause (he had killed his wife's alleged lover on the grounds that the latter had seduced, not raped, his wife)[77] he or his speech-writer chose to resort to equivocation.

By clever manipulation of an impressive arsenal of techniques (exaggeration, subliminal suggestion, 'turning the weaker argument into the stronger', misquotation of the law, misrepresentation of the past) a good speaker must indeed surely have been able to induce the dikasts to vote in

---

[76] Here I am accepting the subtle arguments put forward by E. M. Harris 1990.
[77] See pp. 175–83.

his favour against their better judgement.[78] It was, after all, the Athenian orators' considerable capacity for equivocation that led the rhetoricians of later ages so eagerly to emulate their methods. Hair-splitting equivocation has, however, always been a mark of the legal profession, at all times and in all places. Whether this technique would work more effectively within the modern system (in which two professional lawyers attempt to lead by the nose a jury of twelve inexperienced people in front of a highly trained judge) or the Athenian one (in which two non-professional speakers attempted, albeit sometimes with the aid of a professional speech-writer, to lead by the nose hundreds of Athenians who, though untrained in legal matters, had highly refined discriminatory powers and an intuitive understanding of their city's best interests) is a matter for individual assessment. The claim that the legitimacy of rhetorical tricks within the Athenian judicial system reveals serious defects in that particular system and that this in turn reflects badly on Athenian society has, in other words, little substance to it.

Does the Athenian penchant for equivocation in any way undermine the speeches' value as evidence? Superficially it would seem that it does. The examples cited above do seem to support Dover's claim that Athenian popular morality was essentially unsystematic: that a speaker might at any time tap into whichever one of a range of alternative attitudes best served his purpose.[79] If this is indeed so, then any attempt to recover from this range of attitudes the combination of rules that made up the Athenian code of behaviour must become a forlorn hope.

A closer look, however, points us in quite another direction. As I have already said, the alternative attitudes that Dover was discussing were opinions, not moral norms.[80] Even though some Greeks may have thought that confessions extracted from slaves under torture were credible,[81] there were many who did not think so; even though some Athenians may have considered seduction to be a more serious crime than rape, many others may have disagreed. It was precisely this spread of opinion that opened the way to equivocation. The basic notions concerning the administration of their communal lives that the Athenians shared and that made up their code of behaviour were, however, so deeply rooted that they could not be upset by equivocation.

(3) It has further been observed that the speakers in the Athenian courts seem in practical terms to have been under no compulsion whatsoever to

---

[78] I am indebted for this and for what follows to Worthington 1994a in general and Carey 1994 in particular.
[79] See pp. 23–4. [80] See p. 24. [81] Cf. Garlan 1988: 43.

keep their speeches relevant. They seem, in fact, to have been at liberty to raise matters utterly irrelevant to the charge, to recall unrelated incidents whose sole function was to show the speaker (or his client) in a better and his opponent in a worse light (a process called *ethopoiia*, character creation), to reveal (or make up) juicy details of the past life of the defendant and his relatives, to list the accused's many services to the state as so many reasons why he should be acquitted, and to use emotional blackmail by producing weeping women and children in court. Many critics have remarked that there appears to have been nothing to stop them from deflecting attention from the legal matter at issue and concentrating it upon anything else they felt like, in flagrant disregard of the legal requirement, repeatedly referred to in the sources, that speakers should 'speak to the point' and that dikasts should cast their votes on the sole basis of 'the matters to which the prosecution pertains'. The great German sociologist Max Weber was particularly disgusted by all this, remarking that trials in fifth-century Athens were not decided 'according to formal law, but according to "material justice", in fact according to tears, flattery, demagogic invectives and jokes . . .' Beside the much stricter standards of the Roman judicial system, Athenian legal practices looked to him like 'qadi-justice'.[82]

As I have said, the view that the speakers frequently acted in disregard of the law by introducing irrelevant material into their speeches has often been registered. Recently, however, this question has been subjected to a thorough re-examination, with surprising results. In a landmark article, Peter Rhodes made a strong case for his view that given a certain feature peculiar to the Athenian legal system only a few of these speeches can technically be said to depart from the issue under the court's consideration, most keeping to the point to a far greater extent than has previously been realised. As Rhodes puts it, 'frequently the particular episode which has given rise to the formal charge is part of a larger story, a man's involvement with the oligarchy of the Thirty [Tyrants], or a family feud in which each party has a number of complaints against the other(s), and then it is clearly considered legitimate not to concentrate on the episode which has given rise to the particular charge which is being tried in this particular case but to review the whole of the larger story'.[83] There was, in other words, a substantial difference between the Athenians' conception of legal relevance and our own. If this is so, it may lead us to another important discovery about the nature of democratic justice.

If we accept Rhodes' argument, the fascinating conclusion that presents itself is that the Athenian litigants were not, as has traditionally been held, deliberately departing from the issue at hand in breach of the law, but conscientiously observing standards of relevance altogether different from ours. In other words, details of the 'larger story' that would be inadmissible in a modern court were regarded under Athenian law as legally relevant to the current case.

This conclusion could significantly reinforce the suspicion, persistently harboured by some scholars, that Athenian justice was concerned first and foremost with calculations of communal profit and loss, to which the unprejudiced examination of the facts of the case came a poor second.[84] The dikasts, in other words, did not necessarily consider discovering the absolute truth to be the principal aim of their activities.[85] In keeping with an Aristotelian definition of justice as 'that which is to the common advantage', their objective may instead have been to strike an optimal balance between individual and communal benefit, or, more specifically, to work out a viable compromise between the need to deal fairly with the accused and the city's best interests. In general it was possible to hand down decisions that were in the communal interest without violating judicial fairness (*epieikeia*), but the evidence overwhelmingly suggests that when this was not possible they did not scruple to inflict punishments that were in absolute terms unjust. This could explain how Socrates came to be convicted in the Athenian courts, and why Nicias, having failed to accomplish the task with which the community had entrusted him, pleaded that he would rather meet his death at the hands of the enemy than 'be put to death on a disgraceful charge and by an unjust verdict (*adikos*) of the Athenians' (Thucydides 7.48.4).

Whether or not the Athenian law courts were aiming for the ideal of absolute justice, they undoubtedly fell short of that ideal. The harshness of Athenian justice, though mitigated to some extent by the arbitration process that had by law to precede most civic actions,[86] was aggravated by the inadequacy of the standards that defined both relevance and the quality of evidence. It seems, for example, to have been possible to prove a case in the absence of eyewitnesses by supporting one's allegations with 'arguments from probability' (*ek tou eikotos*).

---

[84] Cf. Dover 1974: 293: 'it is tempting to believe that the Athenian jury was normally concerned less with the facts of the case than with calculation of communal profit and loss'.

[85] Cf. Meyer-Laurin 1965 for the place of *epieikeia* (fairness, justness) in Athenian law.

[86] Steinwenter 1925; Gernet 1939; Finley 1985b: 102–3; Humphreys 1983b; Hölkeskamp 1999 (for arbitration in Archaic Greece). Cf. Aristotle, *Rhetoric* 1374b20–2: 'an arbitrator looks to equity, a judge to the law, and arbitration was invented in order that equity might prevail'. For a good description of the arbitration process see Demosthenes 21.83–5, *Against Meidias*.

For our purposes, the implications of this are as follows. The law-court speeches (and, by extension, the whole body of discussion that made up the adjudication process) do not merely reveal the stories of private disputes whose participants came into collision with the law. More often than not they also lay bare contemporary perceptions of private actions, as reflected in the mirror of communal ideals. In order to comprehend the implications of this in full, let us now address the following question: Do the forensic speeches in any way reflect social reality, and if so, how?

Three basic theories have dominated this debate during the last hundred years of Classical scholarship. According to the first and oldest of these, the forensic speeches, along with every other text that has come down to us from Classical antiquity, were tantamount to Holy Writ: they could not but contain true, straightforward and undistorted descriptions of Athenian social reality. The second theory, which has only recently been elaborated, views the speeches as theatrical constructs reflecting not so much Athenian social reality as some alternative, imaginary reality.[87] According to the third theory, with which I concur, the forensic speeches do reflect Athenian social realities, in distorted form, it is true, but in a manner that makes it possible to cross-check and correct the image. Let us now look more closely at these theories and at the implications of accepting or rejecting each.

The first theory, rooted in nineteenth-century naïveté, need not detain us; it has long been discredited. Once armed with a sufficient amount of cynicism, modern commentators had no difficulty in seeing through the speeches and recognising that they consistently avoided the truth, systematically distorting, suppressing and misrepresenting the facts of the case. The second theory purported to provide an explanation of how this entire process worked. Its proponents maintained that far more than distortion, suppression and misinterpretation had taken place: the Attic Orators had in fact constructed alternative, context-dependent realities that were wholly fictional. Like actors in a dramatic performance, litigants charmed their audiences into sharing their fictional world. As one author has put

---

[87] This is something quite different from the assumption, widespread amongst modern commentators, that the speakers are often lying, the connection between what they are saying and what really happened being at best minimal, at worst non-existent. On some rare occasions, even some apparently impartial reports of 'events' turn out to be lies. For example, in a famous passage Andocides relates that a person 'arose at an early hour, mistaking the time, and started off on his walk by the light of a full moon' (Andocides 1.38–9, *On the Mysteries*). We can now be sure that he is not telling the truth: the affair that this report was supposed to expose occurred on the last night of the month, when there was no moon. The propensity of the orators to invent falsehoods has been well brought out by E. M. Harris 1995: ch. 1.

it, 'Theater-going citizens "learned" to suspend disbelief. The theatrical audience entered into a conspiracy with the playwright and actors which allowed the theatrical experience to take place. This "training" helped jurors to accept elite litigants' *fictional representations of their own circumstances* and their relationship to the Athenian masses.'[88]

While it is certainly true that the political and legal orators often behaved theatrically, it is demonstrably false that in the process they constructed a social reality that was fictional and totally out of touch with the real one.[89] The Attic orators' passing references to the size of Attic farms, for example, have now been shown to be entirely accurate.

As early as 1952 Finley concluded that landed holdings in Attica were typically small, forty-five-acre and seventy-acre holdings being larger than average. He based this conclusion on the five instances in which one of the Attic orators mentioned the size of a holding in order to make a particular point: 'in three of the instances the dimensions [being] stated by the speaker because he wishes to emphasize that these were large holdings; the last named, the 60-*plethra* farm, was specified as a sign of its small size'.[90] During the 1990s Lohmann succeeded in establishing the size of some larger than average Attic holdings by means of physical measurement: 'Of the 33 farmsteads which were discovered, 8 or 9 belonged to big farmers with properties of around 25 hectares.'[91] Twenty-five hectares equalling roughly sixty-one acres, Finley's faith in the orators was vindicated.[92] Had the writers of the Athenian forensic speeches dealt entirely in dream worlds that were totally out of touch with contemporary reality, it is improbable that any statistic derived from a combination of these speeches could have proved so reliable. We are therefore dealing not with an 'imaginary' of Athenian social or economic realities, but with at least some hard data that we may be able to uncover if we can find a suitable approach. As we shall later see, this conjecture has proved accurate wherever it has been possible to cross-check data obtained from the Attic Orators against information from other sources.

---

[88] Ober 1989: 154, my italics. It must be stressed, however, that Ober's criticism is directed against historians 'who assume that forensic rhetoric provides a straightforward description of Athenian society'.

[89] This argument has been given a hypercritical slant by I. Morris 1994a: 356, who applied the theory of fictional representations to economic matters: 'We are moving in a world of representations, the "economic imaginary" of Athens. We can identify conflicts of values and belief within these cultural systems, but it would be a grave error to suppose that we can read away these constructions to figure out how the economy "really" worked.'

[90] Finley 1952: 58. [91] Lohmann 1992: 51. [92] 1 hectare = 2.471 acres.

The third theory is derived from the approach delineated above.[93] According to this theory, most of the data contained in distorted form in the forensic speeches can be retrieved and restored to their original form, since a suitable method of identifying, cross-checking and correcting the distortions already exists. To understand this method we must view the speeches within their three-dimensional social context, paying particular attention to the ways in which the speakers chose to appeal to the dikasts' value system.

The fact that what the speakers chose to say was not entirely unrelated to what the dikasts wanted to hear has not gone unnoticed. Dover, for instance, wrote that 'the rhetorician did not teach his pupils how to override the jury's values but (like a modern barrister) how to exploit these values'. Ober suggested that 'a reasonable assumption is that the elite litigant, facing a mass jury, had a particularly pressing need to appeal to a common ideology'. Hansen remarked that 'the ideas and attitudes of the orators must reflect what the majority of their audience were only too glad to hear'. David Cohen believed that one of Demosthenes' speeches revealed 'what a mass audience expected such a feud to appear like'.[94] To put all this another way, the most sensible way forward for any speaker would clearly have been to remain in step with the dikasts' moral norms, adjusting his account to suit their tastes.

The implications of this insight have not always been followed up with due rigour. The assumption that these speeches were in some poorly defined way addressed to the modern reader, whose duty it was to deliver moral judgement upon their content, has died hard. When applied to Ariston's speech (at which we have already glanced),[95] for example, this reasoning process has led to conclusions that are highly significant to the thesis of this book. Ariston's speech has been adduced as prime evidence in support of the argument that brawls were commonplace in Athenian society, people constantly beating each other up on the slightest provocation while the rest of society stood by and did nothing to prevent it. On closer inspection, this conclusion appears devoid of any analytical validity whatsoever. Its utter futility can be exposed by following up the implications of the fact that the speakers were not, in fact, addressing themselves to the modern reader, whose relation to these speeches is that of an uninvolved bystander.

---

[93] This is, for instance, the basic assumption of Millett 1991 insofar as the forensic speeches are concerned.
[94] Dover 1983: 47; Ober 1989: 45; Hansen 1991: 25; D. Cohen 1995a: 120.   [95] See pp. 123–4.

The speakers were addressing themselves to the Athenian dikasts, and to the Athenian dikasts alone. Any moral judgement that the modern reader may choose to make is therefore utterly irrelevant. Since the key factor in all this is not our public mores, but those of the Athenians – in other words, *the manner in which the dikasts' moral world was structured* – all that should matter to the modern reader is the judgement of the dikasts. Ariston's attempt to sway them consists of portraying Conon as an aggressive attacker and himself as a moderate victim, so that he attributes a violent disposition to Conon and a non-violent one to himself. His chosen tack leaves us in no doubt that the dikasts approved of the sort of propitiatory behaviour that he attributes to himself and disapproved of the sort of violent behaviour that he attributes to Conon. Passages such as this lend absolutely no support to the 'pessimistic' interpretation of Athenian behaviour and quite a lot to the 'optimistic' one. What we learn from them is that the 'collective mind' of the dikasts, who constituted a cross section of the entire Athenian *demos*, was as much predisposed against violent behaviour as it was against feuding.[96]

Nor is this conclusion undermined by the observation that changes may have crept into these speeches when they were put into writing; any such changes could have only positive implications for our theory. If the speeches' authors (or whoever else may have decided to put the speeches into writing) did indeed decide to make changes as they wrote, they almost certainly did so in such a way as to make the arguments used sound even better, perhaps expanding them to include rebuttals of the opponent's arguments, or laying yet more emphasis upon the particular moral appeals that had secured victory in court.[97]

The inference that we derived from our examination of Ariston's speech may now be formulated as a generalised guideline. These speeches, rather than revealing what really happened, reveal what the dikasts wanted to hear. They open up our way into the dikasts' moral world, into their conceptions of good and bad, offering the best clue a historian could possibly dream of to the ideal norms of their society. In the coming chapters I propose, following this guideline, to review a selection of law-court speeches that reveal considerably more about interpersonal behaviour in democratic Athens in circumstances of co-operation and/or conflict. As my review proceeds, I

---

[96] Cf. Herman 1995, 1996a and 2000a and 2000b.

[97] For the revision of speeches and its implications for the inaccuracy of the orators with regard to historical information, as opposed to their relative accuracy concerning social or legal matters, see Worthington 1991.

shall be introducing further theoretical issues and analytical concepts into our discussion. We should, however, try never to lose sight of the fact that the passages with which we shall be dealing are not just ordinary literary passages, but unique and truthful reflections of the Athenian value system: of what the Athenian collective mind considered to be desirable patterns of conduct.

CHAPTER 5

The structure of conflicts

PROVOCATION AND REACTION

A conflict is an agonistic interaction between two or more participants animated by hostility. According to Lorenz and Tinbergen, it is one of four classes of behaviour that may be called genuinely social, the other three being the interaction of male and female for the purpose of reproduction, the actions and interactions of a male and a female in the course of bringing up their young (combined with interactions between the young and their parents and siblings) and the interactions that take place within groups, troops, bands and the like.[1] The particular sociological interest of conflict lies in the fact that it either produces or modifies communities of interest,[2] thus potentially introducing changes into the structure of the society in which it takes place. To understand precisely how (taking into account both rational and irrational, both conscious and unconscious, both impulsive and calculated behaviour) we could think of it as a game between two players in which one player's move depends on that made by the other. Both players' moves may vary in quality, intensity and motivation; they may be delayed, calculated and rational, they may be spontaneous, impulsive and irrational, or they may be somewhere in between. They may show marked variation from one culture to another and from one society to another. However great these differences may be, however, all conflicts can be broken down into four basic phases that we can use as a theoretical framework for comparative analysis.

In the first of these phases some series of circumstances brings the potential antagonists together. In the second, some event or series of events

[1] Cf. Lorenz 1965; Tinbergen 1953; Ploog 1969. This generalisation is supposed to hold good for both humans and animals. For theories of human conflict and a rough taxonomy of conflicts, see Rapoport 1974: ch. 16. The complexity of the factors involved in aggression between individuals and their essential dissimilarity to those involved in aggression between groups is well brought out by Hinde 1997.

[2] Cf. Simmel 1903–4: 490.

(although I am using morally neutral terms here, the participants usually interpret these events as deliberate and personal acts of provocation or injury) pits them against each other. In the third phase they react and/or retaliate to these events. The actions that they perform in this phase are often perceived by their opponents as provocations in themselves and thus evoke counter-reactions. The chain of provocation and reaction or reaction and counter-reaction often becomes longer and longer, involving more and more participants and various further events and circumstances. These tend, as a rule, to prolong the conflict and to expand it, so that the entire process often becomes independent of its initiating cause. In the fourth stage the conflict may reach some termination, sometimes several generations later. This stage is optional. In some societies termination is culturally unavailable, in which cases social scientists describe the conflict as 'never-ending'.[3]

Having identified our theoretical framework for the analysis of conflicts, let us see how the conflict between Ariston and Conon that we have already discussed fits into these four stages.[4]

Phase one: The circumstance that brought Ariston and Conon together was their simultaneous assignment to garrison duty. We have no indication that any state of enmity had previously existed between them.

Phase two: The event that sparked off the conflict was, if we are to believe Ariston, the abusive conduct of Conon and his drunken friends in beating Ariston's slaves and emptying chamber-pots over them. It should be noted, however, that Conon's version of events would presumably have been different: the original 'provocation', according to him, would have been the smoke with which Ariston's slaves had been choking half the camp.

Phase three: Ariston reacted by expostulating with Conon and his friends, to which Conon responded by poking fun at him. Ariston then appealed to the general, who rebuked Conon and his party. His rebuke fell somewhat short of its intended effect, since Conon and the rest next proceeded to burst in upon Ariston and beat hell out of him. To this last act of aggression

---

[3] E.g. Black-Michaud 1975.
[4] See pp. 123–4 and 153–4. In Rapoport's terms (n. 1 above), Chapters 5 and 6 deal mainly with conflicts that are endogenous, symmetric and issue oriented. *Endogenous* conflicts are those wherein 'the conflicting systems are parts of a larger system that has its own mechanisms for controlling or resolving conflict between the sub-systems'. *Symmetric* conflicts are those wherein 'the participants are roughly similar systems and perceive themselves as such'. *Issue-oriented* conflicts are 'resolved when the issue is settled; the resolution does not involve a change in the structure of either the conflicting systems or the super-systems of which they are components' (Rapoport 1974: 175–6). For structure-oriented conflicts, see Chapter 7; for exogenous conflicts, see pp. 360–73.

Ariston allegedly responded by going home. Despite harbouring feelings of anger and hatred towards Conon and his party, he chose not to sue them, deciding instead to put it all behind him. Only when they attacked him in the street, apparently inflicting such grievous injuries that neither his relatives nor the attending physicians thought he would survive (Demosthenes 54.1, *Against Conon*), did he finally make up his mind to bring an action against them.

Phase four. We have no specific information concerning the trial's outcome, though the fact that this speech has survived may suggest that Ariston won his case. Records of other cases of adjudication by the dikasts, however, entitle us to suspect that the court's decision probably put an end to this conflict, or at least prevented it from continuing to flare up again and again in a violent and unending chain reaction.

Let us now break these phases down further into their basic components. Each phase may be said to consist of a chain of simpler segments of behaviour; for example, Ariston's expostulation, or Ariston's appeal to the general. Each of these segments is initiated and controlled by a limited and highly specific set of external stimuli (the smoke, the beatings, the chamber-pots), each of our principals perceiving the stimuli proceeding from the other as intentional and personal acts of affront, insult or injury that could not be overlooked. It should, however, be noted that these stimuli vary considerably in their degree of intensity.

How did Ariston *allegedly* react to Conon's provocations, insults and injurious acts, which by modern standards too would be regarded as serious? As we have seen, Ariston's speech draws a contrast between Conon and himself, portraying Conon as actively aggressive and Ariston as passively defensive. Conon's actions are depicted as spontaneous, impulsive, irrational and excessive, while his own are purveyed to us as delayed, calculated, rational and moderate. This contrast makes Conon's actions appear all the more offensive. The effect is further enhanced by Ariston's final series of reactions. Even after being done over by Conon and his friends, he asserts, he was willing to swallow the insults and injuries inflicted on him without even considering any legal or extra-legal means of retaliation: 'I simply made up my mind that in future I would watch out for myself and stay well away from people like that' (Demosthenes 54.6, *Against Conon*). Only after he had once again been beaten up, despite this heroic act of self-restraint, did he at last decide to bring his action.

Ariston's account has certain remarkable features that may all too easily be missed or misinterpreted. Many people will be inclined to process and denature these in their minds, trivialising them by adjusting them to fit preconceived behavioural patterns derived from their own personal experience. This danger may, however, be circumvented by the making of conscious comparisons, allowing accurate assessment of the relative intensity of stimuli as they appear in descriptions of conflict proceeding from different cultures. Such comparisons may prevent the reader from falling prey to the process of fusion of moral norms to which we have already referred, enabling him or her to view these exceptional features as they really are.

At the beginning of the twentieth century Edith Durham, an early anthropological fieldworker, made an unprecedented visit to Albania. Her fragile appearance, shy manner and disarmingly unusual clothes (a 'waterproof Burberry skirt' and 'Scotch plaid golf cape') no doubt helped her to ingratiate herself with the leaders of the fierce highlanders she encountered. An incident that she witnessed at close quarters in 1909 contrasts tellingly with the Ariston–Conon encounter.

Two Albanian shepherds, one belonging to the Shoshi tribe and the other to the Ghoanni, were quarrelling in front of a fire (*phase one*) when the latter snatched a burning brand from the hearth and threw it at his opponent (*phase two, stimulus one: the provocation*). He then fled at once to avoid reprisals. The Shoshi man pursued him, crossing the border into Ghoanni territory. Failing to find either him or any of his adult kinsmen, he killed an eight-year-old boy whose only crime was to belong to the same tribe as the offender (*phase three, stimulus two: the reaction*).[5] Durham does not tell us the sequel to this deadly game, but by analogy with other such cases in Albanian society it is conceivable that it degenerated into a cross-generational, never-ending blood-feud (*phase four*).

The most striking difference between these two accounts is that the inverse relationships between intensity of stimulus and intensity of reaction that they describe are diametrical opposites. In the Albanian incident a relatively slight provocation (the ill-tempered throwing of a burning brand) is recorded as having triggered off an indiscriminate and extremely violent reprisal (killing an innocent young boy). In the Athenian incident, grave insult and serious injury (Ariston claims barely to have survived his beating) are alleged to have been answered with avoidance and self-restraint, legal action being brought only as a last resort. According to the categories that we identified earlier,[6] the Shoshi tribesman's behaviour represents over-reaction to provocation ('a head for an eye'), while Ariston's may be described as an under-reaction to provocation.

---

[5] Durham 1909: 111–12.   [6] See pp. 2–8.

The sceptic may argue that this comparison is misguided, since we are not comparing like with like. Ariston's account proceeds from an interested participant and may well therefore be subjective and skewed. Durham's account is that of a non-participant and non-aligned observer and is therefore presumably objective and impartial (or at least intended to be so). It may further be objected that the reactions described could have been one-offs that were atypical of the societies in which they occurred: in other words, that typical reactions in Athens and in Albania would not have been so dissimilar.

Further consideration suggests, however, that these objections do not invalidate our comparison. The differing responses of Ariston and the herdsman sprang from the behavioural codes of their respective societies. The Shoshi tribesman *did* what his society's code of behaviour bade him do in such circumstances: effect an overkill. Ariston *said* what his society's code of behaviour bade him say in such a position: anticipating that the dikasts' support might most readily be enlisted by casting himself in the role of a person who under-reacts to provocation and never resorts to violence (a person whom, indeed, we might now call a wimp), he proceeded to do exactly that. Having a sound grasp of the ideal norms according to which the dikasts would judge his behaviour, he calculated his presentation so as to hit precisely the right note.

It is important to make it clear that Ariston's account is by no means atypical. The forensic speeches abound in claims to have adopted similar strategies in the face of provocation. So common are these that we can identify a pattern: self-restraint and under-reaction are consistently praised and encouraged, while excessive reactions and extreme retaliations are consistently denounced as unsuitable. (I shall later argue that this corresponds to a low incidence, or even the virtual suppression, of this sort of behaviour under the democracy.) In societies of the Albanian type, by contrast, extreme retaliation is a norm that is continuously reinforced, both culturally and socially, as the preferred type of behaviour. Over-reaction is seen as a supreme duty, an axis around which one's entire social persona revolves, so that evading it entails disgrace.

AGGRESSION: INBORN AND LEARNED

We may now be in a position more precisely to define the class of society to which the Albanian tribes belong. Social scientists describe this sort of society as 'feuding'. The following dictionary entry uses war as a yardstick to identify the features that define feuding:

[F]euding is akin to warfare, but is generally distinguished from it inasmuch as the feud is a continuing state of hostilities marked by sporadic outbursts of violence. The feud is thus less generalized or less intensive than a state of war, and may be a constant state of relations between communities or between kin groups, marked, as in a blood-feud, by periodic attacks or revenge killings.[7]

This definition may help us to establish a correlation whose plausibility is increased by the results of certain research in social psychology. It has been suggested, along lines that recall the Sophistic debate about natural and conventional man,[8] that in closely knit, culturally homogeneous social systems the relationship between single, apparently isolated incidents such as our Albanian revenge killing and the general profile of the society within which they take place (in this case, marked by sporadic outbursts of violence, blood-feuds and periodic spates of revenge killings) is not fortuitous, rather displaying certain regularities that can be captured using the appropriate analytical tools. This inference rests on the premise that people's patterns of aggressive behaviour are not innate, but are communicated to them overtly, or, even more importantly, in unintentional, non-verbal ways (perhaps by a tone of voice or a gesture), during the process of socialisation.[9] Even those reactions that are called 'spontaneous' (i.e. those that are supposed naturally to spring forth from the instincts and emotions) bear the marks of cultural fashioning. If patterns of aggressive behaviour are thus learned rather than inborn, it may reasonably be claimed that conflicts at the micro level of society mirror assumptions accepted at its macro level (and vice versa).[10]

In order to achieve as accurate as possible a description of Athenian society's social profile (that is, its macro level), therefore, we shall now proceed to examine a number of Athenian conflicts in detail. Careful analysis of the details that we observe should reveal a pattern that will help us to locate

---

[7] Seymour-Smith 1986: 116. Scholarly literature consistently identifies animosity, hostility and violence as the defining features of feud. See (e.g.) L. Popisil (1968), 'Feud', in D. L. Sills (ed.), *International Encyclopedia of the Social Sciences*. The Macmillan Company and the Free Press: vol. v: 389: 'Feud has been defined . . . as "relations of mutual animosity among intimate groups in which a resort to violence is anticipated on both sides"' (citing Lasswell).

[8] See pp. 4–5.

[9] Cf. Bandura 1973, 1979. The rival, but not necessarily conflicting, theory that brain damage caused by faulty upbringing ('somatosensory deprivation') in infancy is an underlying cause of human violence does not affect my argument.

[10] This is an inference rather than a quotation from Bandura's theory of learned aggression. Not being concerned with historical societies, Bandura did not express himself in terms such as these, but the idea is implied in his writings. For the status of this theory in social psychology, see Hogg and Vaughan 1995: ch. 11.

Athenian society in its proper place on an imaginary spectrum running from feuding societies of the Albanian type to entirely pacific ones.

We shall begin with a case of Athenian intra-familial rivalry described in a speech by Isaeus, a fourth-century orator who specialised in inheritance cases. The rivalry in question had begun a long time before with a disagreement between two brothers: Euthycrates (who had a son called Astyphilus) and Thydippus (who had a son called Cleon). According to Isaeus, the brothers had quarrelled over the division of some inherited land (which should, it will be remembered, have been divided equally between them under Athenian law).[11] In the course of the quarrel Thydippus assaulted Euthycrates, injuring him so badly that he never fully recovered and eventually died from the effects of his injuries not many years later. The reported reaction of Euthycrates and his son Astyphilus to this outrage is important to our inquiry. Despite the gravity of the offence, Euthycrates is said only to have charged his relatives on his deathbed 'never to allow any of Thydippus' family to come near his tomb'.[12] Astyphilus' attitude is revealed in two passages, the first of which states that he 'had no such bitter enemy as Cleon, and hated him so much and with such good cause, that he would have been much more likely to have arranged that no one of his family should ever speak to Cleon than to have adopted his son' (9.16, *On the Estate of Astyphilus*, trans. E. S. Forster). The second passage tells us that when Astyphilus reached the age of reason, having been told in childhood that Thydippus had murdered his father, he decided that he 'would never speak to Cleon', and that he maintained 'this attitude up to his death, holding the opinion that it was impious to speak to the son of Thydippus, when the latter was charged with so grave a crime against his father' (9.20, trans. E. S. Forster). Since this speech was intended to discredit Cleon's claim on Astyphilus' estate, it was in the speaker's interest to present the relationship between the two as extremely poor. Clearly, however, he felt that he might alienate the dikasts if he attributed to Astyphilus any form of expressed resentment more radical than refusing to speak to Cleon. Cleon, meanwhile, supported his claim with the argument that his son, the homicidal Thydippus' grandson, had been adopted by Astyphilus, the son of Thydippus' victim. This implies that the dikasts (and the society of which they were part) would by no means have regarded it as ridiculous or

---

[11] For conflicts between brothers arising from the Athenian inheritance laws, see Cox 1988 and 1998: 108–14.

[12] Isaeus 9.19, *On the Estate of Astyphilus*, to be consulted with Wyse 1904: 625.

unacceptable that such an adoption should have taken place despite what had gone before.

Once again, the extraordinary features of this case may not be recognised in full until we contrast it with comparable cases from other societies. Let us now examine the course that another case of intra-familial rivalry took in a Mediterranean society exempt from state control, flouting the requirements of law and order and having no ideals to do with moderation and self-restraint: a 'feuding society' in every sense of the term.[13] This case, reported worldwide in June 1992, took place in the Lebanese village of Kalliath during the civil war in Lebanon. A nine-year old boy, Ali Chadra, shot his uncle Hussein's cow in the eye with an 0.22 rifle. On this Hussein, in a fit of rage, swore an oath to kill Ali even though he was his nephew. The village dignitaries, fearing that things could only get worse, suggested a reconciliation (*sulha*). Ali's father was all for this, offering his brother twice the value of the cow. Spurred on by his wife, however, Hussein refused to withdraw his words. The dignitaries now came up with an original solution: if Hussein felt unable to break his oath, then he should perform a mock killing of Ali in front of them and Ali's parents. Since everyone seemed agreed on this, the proposed ceremony took place, but events suddenly took a sinister turn: rather than simulating the killing, Hussein actually slaughtered Ali with a butcher's knife. On this Ali's father took a Kalashnikov automatic rifle from his car and gunned down his brother, sister-in-law and nephew, wounding nine of the dignitaries in the process. The journalist who reported the case wryly remarked that the cow, despite losing an eye, had survived.

The contrast with our Athenian incident is telling. In that case an exceedingly serious offence (a murder in the family) is said to have provoked no response more damaging than a refusal to speak to the murderer's son. The speaker's presentation of his case was no doubt intended to draw attention to a long-term attitude that was likely to help to stabilise the relationship between the two branches of the family, lessen the likelihood of blood-feud and promote communal welfare. In the Lebanese case a far lesser offence (the mutilation of a cow by a young boy, possibly even by accident) provoked a reaction whose terrible escalation culminated in a bloodbath. Hussein seems to have felt under no compulsion whatsoever to integrate into his short-term reaction any concern for the welfare of his family or his community.

---

[13] Cf. Gilsenan 1985.

This point should be stressed in view of the possible objection that Astyphilus' and Hussein's dissimilar reactions may have sprung from dissimilar psychological constitutions. The two cannot, however, have differed that radically, despite the 2,400 or so years that separated them. (Differences in personal qualities are another matter, but these also exist between members of the same society.) Aggressive behaviour in humans is the product of hundreds of thousands of years of natural selection and genetic adaptation to an environment that has now all but vanished: 'the world of the Ice Age hunter-gatherers', in the words of Edward O. Wilson. It has been very little affected by the changes that have taken place during the relatively negligible time span covered by recorded history. Psychological mechanisms may therefore be regarded as having remained constant throughout historical times,[14] which tends to reinforce the hypothesis that the difference between Astyphilus' and Hussein's reactions expressed the difference between the codes of behaviour of their respective societies. In this game, to revert to an earlier simile, the players' responses to external stimuli are not emitted directly in an unprocessed state. Such responses encode cultural messages, so that the players subconsciously enter the sorts of emotional state and perform the sorts of act that are sanctioned by their respective societies.

This point may be relevant to what we have already said about the so-called lexical method.[15] The world's many cultures have generated an astonishing variety of labels to designate various types of sentiment, emotion, mental and physical state, norm and value. Some of these terms describe features that are identical in a number of cultures. The great majority, however, do not. The Greeks may have been motivated by *hybris* and *aidos* and we may be motivated by honour and shame, but these are not necessarily the same things: key concepts such as these cannot accurately be translated from one language to another or explained in terms of each other without introducing misleading anachronisms and cultural misapprehensions. It is, of course, important to analyse them critically nonetheless. Our analysis must, however, proceed on the understanding that linguistic diversity masks basically identical psychological mechanisms. These biologically and culturally determined mechanisms, not value terms, are the prime movers of behaviour. If we wish to lay bare the rules according to which the communal

[14] Cf. E. O. Wilson 1978: 6 and 196. Certain outstandingly violent individuals have been found to have a chromosome that has been associated with their violent behaviour (Brunner, Nelen, Breakefiel, Ropers and van Oost 1993; Ridley 2003: 267–9). Many other people with this chromosome, however, show no signs whatsoever of violent behaviour, presumably due to environmental factors.

[15] See pp. 102–3.

life of any given society is administered, in other words, we must attempt to reveal the character and intensity of these mechanisms irrespective of the terms used to identify their manifestations.

THE THRESHOLD PRINCIPLE

Honour and shame are arguably amongst the most powerful incentives and disincentives affecting social behaviour. Unlike those 'basic' human drives (such as hunger, thirst and hypothermia) that express physical need, honour and shame are 'secondary' drives arising from social needs. Social psychologists ignore these concepts altogether, preferring to deal with more soothing substitutes such as 'the need to feel important', 'the achievement of meaningful goals' and 'the avoidance of embarrassment'. Historians and social scientists conceive of them as sublime, abstract notions (to be broken down into simpler categories such as reputation, prestige, physical perfection, health, moral qualities, sanctity and grace) that exist mainly in the mind, have relatively little to do with empirically observable reality and can therefore best be examined within the field of historical research known as the history of ideas. Drawing on insights developed within these disciplines, I shall now suggest a method of relating these abstract notions more closely to behaviour.[16]

People everywhere try to achieve honour and avoid shame. If they are shamed they generally seek to redress this in some way that will restore their diminished or lost honour.[17] The terms honour and shame can, however, describe emotions of differing intensity. Most researchers agree that senses of honour and shame can vary from one region to another, from one period to another and even from one social class or circle to another. Certain social types in history seem to have had far keener senses of honour than others. Homeric heroes, French noblemen (at least until the revolutionaries abolished 'feudal honour'), Italian *gentiluomini*, Prussian Junkers, Japanese samurai, Sicilian mafiosi and male Bedouins, to name but a few, are notorious for extreme sensitivity about their honour. Social types on

---

[16] I am ignoring the distinction that used frequently to be made in the social sciences between 'shame' and 'guilt' and consequently between 'shame cultures' and 'guilt cultures'; its uselessness as an analytical tool with respect to ancient Greek societies has been effectively unmasked by Lloyd-Jones 1990. Current anthropological thinking about 'honour' and 'shame' is aptly summed up by a recent encyclopaedia entry: 'Anthropologists now find that the vagueness of honor and shame and their mismatch with comparable local concepts blunt their usefulness for ethnographic research and for comparison' (C. S. Stewart 2001).

[17] For the concept of honour as 'a state of grace' or 'sacred aura surrounding each individual', see Pitt-Rivers 1968: 505.

the margins of society, on the other hand (slaves, serfs, beggars, prostitutes, court jesters and the poor in general) seem in most historical settings to have been considered wanting in honour. The question now arises of how to systematise the intuitively perceived differences between various manifestations of honour and shame. If honour and shame are nothing but abstract, sublime notions, how should we compare them across cultures?[18] How, to be more specific, should we rank a Roman senator, a mediaeval ruler and a Prussian Junker for grace, sanctity and prestige?

My own contribution to the solution of these problems may be called the 'threshold principle'. I believe that by posing two simple questions we may be able to avoid the pitfalls of the lexical method, the derivation of actions from value terms[19] and excessive idealisation. Instead of asking what the Athenians meant by, for instance, *hybris* and *aidos*, and assuming that they acted in accordance with *our* answers to these questions, we shall be asking firstly what the threshold was at which honour was deemed to have been impugned in Athenian society and secondly what kind of response that society deemed appropriate and sufficient to redress the offence. We may then be in a better position to determine how abstract ideas manifested themselves in concrete behaviour under the Athenian democracy.

The third oration in Lysias, *Against Simon*, is a good case in point. It was written in defence of an unknown Athenian who was being prosecuted by a man called Simon for wounding with intent to kill. In Athens this was a grave offence that was regarded very differently from unpremeditated wounding, the penalties for it including banishment and confiscation of property. Such cases were therefore heard before the court of the Areopagus. The strategy adopted by the defendant was to deny that his actions had been premeditated and to try to shift the blame for whatever damage he had done onto his opponent. His account of the initial phases of the conflict offers a fascinating glimpse of a homosexual affair that cut across the Athenian class structure:

Both of us, gentlemen of the Council, were drawn to Theodotus, a Plataean lad [probably a slave]. I tried to win him over by being kind to him, but this man here tried to force him to submit to his desires by behaving violently and by breaking the law . . . I think you ought to know just how much harm he has done to me personally. On one occasion when he found out that the boy was with me he came round to my house at night drunk, broke down the doors and went into the women's quarters. Inside were my sister and my nieces, who are so well brought

---

[18] Cf. F. H. Stewart 1994: 10: 'For certainly when one looks at the way the word "honor" is used, one finds it referring to things apparently quite different from each other.'

[19] See pp. 101–3.

up that they are even embarrassed to be seen by the men of their own family. His overt insolence (*hybris*) reached such a pitch that he refused to go away until passers-by and the people who had come with him, disgusted by this conduct towards fatherless young girls, made him leave. This did not cause him to feel the slightest remorse. He proceeded to find out where we were dining and to behave in a way that anyone who had not encountered his crazed behaviour (*mania*) before would have thought peculiar beyond belief. He called me outside and tried to hit me the moment I came out. When I fought back, he dodged beyond my reach and started throwing stones at me. In fact he missed me, but one of the stones hit Aristocritus, who had come along to my house with him, and cut his forehead open. I felt that I had been grossly ill-treated, gentlemen of the Council, but I was embarrassed (*aischynomenos*) . . . to find myself in this very undesirable position, so I put up with it (*eneichomen*), since I had much rather go without redress (*dike*) for these offences than have my fellow-citizens believe me to have taken leave of my senses (*anoetos*). (Lysias 3.5–9, *Against Simon*)

The pattern that this passage shares with the account of the Ariston–Conon dispute may be seen even more clearly in this case. In applying the threshold principle, we can get a very good idea of the relationship between the intensity of the stimuli and that of the reactions. We should notice particularly the contrast that the speaker draws between the macho, aggressive quality of Simon's provocations and the very different nature of his own reactions, an opposition that runs through the speech from beginning to end. To paraphrase the claims that the speaker makes in sections 5 to 14 alone: *I* tried to engage Theodotus' affections by treating him kindly; *he* tried to achieve the same end by means of violent and lawless behaviour. *He* got drunk and broke into my house at night; *he* scandalised my decent sister and nieces; *he* left only when forced to. *He* broke into the hall in which *I* was dining peacefully with friends; *he* tried to hit me; *he* threw stones at me. *I* put up with all this because my embarrassment at finding myself in this undignified position outweighed any impulse to put matters right. 'Not knowing how to deal with this man's contempt for the law', '*I* decided that it would be best to leave Athens' for a while; when *I* returned *he* and his companions attacked me, but '*I* rapidly made myself scarce; *I* was only interested in avoiding them, regarding everything that had happened to me at their hands as very bad news indeed.' Our pattern is quite clear. The speaker is deliberately casting himself in the role of what we would now call a wimp, a man who under-reacts to provocations, and Simon in that of a macho bully, a man who attacks and molests other people without provocation. He is doing so because he believes that this may induce the dikasts to vote in his favour, acquitting him of any malicious intent to wound. His parting shot would seem to give the lie to any suggestion that

Athenian society as a whole embraced the 'rather death than dishonour' principle:[20] instead of demanding satisfaction for all these far from trifling humiliations, he claims to have *put up with them*. This again can only be described as an under-reaction to provocation.

This interpretation is not the only one that has been suggested. According to another view, the defendant was already in a socially humiliating position. He had already been forced to disclose his sexual preferences, which had in itself inevitably damaged his reputation as a man of honour. He had consequently nothing left to lose by posing as a non-violent wimp. (He was, furthermore, not a young man, which gave him a convenient excuse for failing to launch a more aggressive comeback.) In other words, his decision to present himself in this role was precipitated only by his extraordinary predicament.[21] Under normal circumstances he would have kept up the image of the true Mediterranean macho man.

This hypothesis is, however, not sustainable. Acting as the defendant claims to have done might appear dishonourable in *our* eyes, but *to the Athenians* there was nothing dishonourable about it. In pursuit of this point we shall now turn to another case, that of the prolonged rivalry between the rich bully Meidias and the popular orator Demosthenes. The account that we are about to read clashes head-on with any stereotypical idea of the proper Mediterranean pattern of action. Unlike the case of the homosexual rivals, moreover, it is entirely free from ambiguity.

According to Demosthenes, the court case to which his account relates came only at the end of an extended period spent by Meidias in tormenting him with unspeakable acts of aggression, while Demosthenes tried to ignore these provocations and forbore to respond to Meidias or even to sue him (Demosthenes 21.6, *Against Meidias*). The seeds of the conflict (*echthra*) between the two had been planted much earlier. Demosthenes' father had died while his son was still a minor. Feeling his end to be near, he had placed his son in the care of three guardians who after his death betrayed his trust by robbing the boy of most of his possessions. Upon reaching maturity Demosthenes attempted to recover his patrimony by suing them. His

---

[20] See p. 97.
[21] This point is brought out more fully in Herman 2000a, which is a response to W. V. Harris 1997. Harris believes that in Herman 1994 and 1995 I have misrepresented the motives that the speaker imputes to himself in justifying his (alleged) decision not to retaliate to the insults and injuries inflicted upon him by Simon. Apparently I was quite wrong in claiming that he intended to sway the jury by passing himself off as a non-vindictive victim. In fact, *he was merely excusing himself for not having retaliated*, apologising for being such a wimp by reminding the jury of his *supposedly* advanced age. (Harris concedes, however, that although the age gap between the speaker and his 'boy' lover is mentioned, he is nowhere said to be stricken in years.)

guardians, however, countered this move by enlisting a man called Thra-sylochus to challenge the young Demosthenes to an exchange of property. Thrasylochus and his brother Meidias went to Demosthenes' house, forced its doors (allegedly) and burst in upon his family. Using foul language and abuse in the presence of Demosthenes' mother and sister, they challenged Demosthenes to take over their trierarchy (21.78–9).[22] Demosthenes' speech gives no indication of his reaction to this. He candidly admits, however, that on being threatened again he ended up paying the intruders twenty minae.

This payoff did nothing to dissipate the bad blood between them and a cycle of harassment developed. Meidias 'kept up a constant fire of insults, both trifling and serious' and found further opportunities to needle Demosthenes throughout the latter's period of liturgical service. Demosthenes, however, claims to have chosen to ignore all this because he was too mature to be influenced by personal bias. 'I am painfully aware', he says, 'that whereas I, the victim of his abusive threats and acts of aggression, was as much upset by each of these acts as I would have been by really serious offences, no one who is not personally involved in the matter can reasonably be expected to see these things as in themselves crying out for legal redress' (21.15).

For a long time Demosthenes contented himself with keeping a record of Meidias' aggressive acts. The account of these that he wrote for the dikasts is clearly intended to rub in the pattern that is becoming familiar to us: the more Meidias provoked him, the more self-restraint he exercised. Some of his account may be paraphrased as follows. In an attempt to prevent Demosthenes from winning any prizes as a liturgist in a competition that he had entered, Meidias destroyed some of the costumes and golden crowns that Demosthenes had provided for his chorus. He corrupted the performers' trainer, bribed the Archon who was to superintend the contest and incited the chorus members to gang up against Demosthenes. He also blocked up the passages in the theatre in which the chorus was to perform. Finally, on the day of the performance, his escalating acts of aggression

---

[22] Demosthenes 28.17–18, *Against Aphobos 2*. For a full account of the quarrel between Demosthenes and Meidias, see MacDowell 1990: 1–13. For the view that the speech Demosthenes 21, *Against Meidias*, was actually delivered in court (contrary to widespread scholarly opinion, according to which it was not), see E. M. Harris 1989. The challenge delivered to Demosthenes threatened him with *antidosis*, a formal judicial proceeding available to any Athenian seeking exemption from a liturgy. If he could prove that someone else was far wealthier than he, he could challenge that person either to assume the liturgy or to accept an exchange of property instead (hence the term *antidosis*, 'exchange'). If the latter refused, a formal adjudication (*diadikasia*) ensued. Cf. Finley 1952: 3; Gabrielsen 1987; Christ 1990.

reached their logical climax: under the gaze of the thousands of Greeks assembled in the theatre of Dionysus, he marched up to Demosthenes and punched him in the face (21.15–19).

This punch finally triggered some sort of response in Demosthenes. Before telling us about it, however, Demosthenes pauses to relate two incidents that have gone down in modern research as the supreme examples of Athenian violence. As Demosthenes tells it, two men called Euthynus and Euaeon were both known for having responded to a slight or imagined insult by killing someone:

> Even if you don't all know it, some of you must know what young Euthynus, who used to be big news as a wrestler, did to that all-in fighter Sophilus. Big heavy dark-haired guy; I bet some of you know the man I'm talking about. He met him in Samos at some get-together – just a private pleasure-party – and thought he was disrespecting him, so he came back at him so hard that he actually killed him. . . Everyone knows that Leodamas' brother Euaeon did for Boeotus at a public banquet and festivity just for thumping him once.[23]

Rarely can what we have called 'the fusion of moral norms' have resulted in a more lopsided view of Athenian society than has arisen here.[24] Just like the Conon passage that we discussed earlier,[25] this passage is generally analysed along the following (usually implied) lines: 'Nasty things such as this are always happening in the typical "Mediterranean" society of which democratic Athens is so obviously an example. People in societies like that are always killing each other on account of imaginary insults or tiny provocations, while society takes not a blind bit of notice.' Divorced from their rhetorical context and analysed like this, the tales of Euthynus and Euaeon do indeed shed a gloomy light on life in democratic Athens.

Let us now examine them more rationally. Demosthenes' report is not a straightforward one. This passage is a section of a long, sophisticated rhetorical piece whose grand design is to show that Meidias has been systematically breaking the rules of public behaviour, while Demosthenes has observed them religiously. Demosthenes is using these incidents to demonstrate the objective superiority of his own behaviour according to the values of his society. His point is that when Meidias punched him in the face he did *not* respond by freaking out and killing him: 'In the name of all the gods, Athenians, please consider very carefully how much more reason I had to

---

[23] Demosthenes 21.71–2, *Against Meidias*. Most of Demosthenes' commentators and translators seem to agree that the meaning of this passage is clear despite the grammatical ambiguities that it contains.

[24] For example, Fisher 1998: 73 regards these as 'examples of fierce macho violence among members of the Athenian élite'.

[25] See pp. 123–4, 153–4, 156.

lose my temper when all this was inflicted on me by Meidias than Euaeon had when he killed Boeotus' . . . 'Athenians, I believe that I was sensible, in fact positively inspired, in letting it go for the time being instead of letting myself be rushed into doing something that could never have been undone' (21.73–4).[26] In other words, instead of throwing an explosive, head-for-an-eye scene, Demosthenes held off and *sued* Meidias. He was later, if we are to believe another source, to drop the charges in return for a handsome payoff.[27]

Demosthenes was trying to get the dikasts on his side by writing what they wanted to hear. Euthynus may well have killed Sophilus in a fit of rage, as Euaeon may have killed Boeotus, and these incidents may be useful to us in reconstructing our picture of life in Athens and in Samos (where the Euthynus–Sophilus incident allegedly took place). If we want to know *how much* violence there was in Athens, however, their evidential value is nil. We have not the faintest idea of what the murder rate was like at the time; there could for all we know have been thirty, three hundred or three thousand such cases a year.[28] These incidents cast a revealing light only upon the dikasts' conceptual world.

The light that they shed on this world is, however, a remarkable one. To understand its implications in full, I propose now to examine the types of insult and provocation to which Euthynus and Euaeon are said to have over-reacted and Demosthenes to have under-reacted in the context of other societies whose 'feuding' status is undisputed.[29] As a general rule, the people who live in societies of this sort are extremely sensitive about their honour. The rules that define affront, insult and outrage (and the proper means of avenging all these) are consequently strictly prescribed. These rules are frequently enshrined in mottoes and buttressed with proverbs. Albanian men, for instance, are enjoined to believe that 'the strong man's soap is gunpowder'.[30] The North African Muslims of Kabyle react to any

---

[26] Cf. P. J. Wilson 1991 for the argument that Demosthenes' purportedly democratic rhetoric is punctuated by elitist aristocratic norms, with the corrective remarks of Ober 1994b: 102: 'Demosthenes tells his audience an interesting and complex story about honour and its relationship to *hubris*. . . By exploring the two senses of *atimia* he shows how personal honour is transubstantiated into citizen dignity in the realm of equality that characterises citizen society.'

[27] Aeschines 3.52, *Against Ctesiphon*; cf. Plutarch, *Demosthenes* 12.2, with E. M. Harris 1989 (who argues plausibly that Aeschines was lying). For the incompatibility of legal compromise and honour in feuding societies, cf. n. 57 below and Chapter 6 n. 40.

[28] For another view, based on the illusion that we do know 'whatever may have occurred in the real cases behind this rhetoric', see Fisher 2000.

[29] For a fascinating overview of the art of insulting people in Greek cultures, with updated bibliography, see Bremmer 2000.

[30] Cozzi 1910: 663–4.

perceived loss of honour by reciting stereotypical formulae: 'How can I show myself to people?' 'I can no longer open my mouth in front of others.' 'Will not the earth swallow me up?' 'My life is over!'[31] Even as late as the 1960s any Sicilian who was regarded as a substandard provider for and protector of his women was stigmatised with 'the rich vocabulary of "non-man": *una fimmina* (a woman), *un saccu vacanti* (an empty sack), or *un nuddu miscatu con nenti* (a nobody mixed with nothing)', this constituting the ultimate denial of respect.[32]

Such utterances are often accompanied by certain types of behaviour prescribed by social etiquette. There are many highly stylised ways of offering an insult, an affront or an outrage, of avenging or apologising, of offering, accepting or rejecting gifts of atonement, of duelling and of fighting. In eighteenth- and nineteenth-century Germany, for instance, where feuding took the shape of duelling, the provocations regarded as suitable grounds for a duel were systematically divided into three broad classes according to the prevailing 'thresholds of offence'. 'The first classification was the simple slight (*einfache Beleidigung*), constituted by impoliteness or inconsiderate behaviour. The second level of insult was cursing or attribution of shameful qualities, examples of which might be calling someone an *Esel* (jackass) or a *Schwachkopf* (imbecile).' The punch that Meidias inflicted on Demosthenes would have belonged to the third and gravest class of offence, 'rendered through a blow or a slap, the spectacular gauntlet-in-the-face falling under this heading . . .'[33] In nineteenth-century Corsica too public opinion was that a slap in the face constituted one of the gravest insults possible. Stephen Wilson relates the case of a Corsican called Muzzarettu who 'became a bandit in his maturity after he had killed a much younger man in 1931. This man had slapped him in the face in the course of an argument on the square of Grossa, and Muzzarettu had felt obliged "to save his honour"'.[34] Pitt-Rivers describes the 'normal' pattern of reaction to a provocation of this magnitude in early modern Europe thus: 'Even where polite society has outlawed physical violence it retains the ritual slap on the face as a challenge to settle an affair of honour, and it was commonly admitted that offences to honour could only be redeemed through blood. "La lessive de l'honneur ne se coule qu'au sang" [The laundry of honour is only bleached with blood].'[35]

In genuinely feuding societies the threshold of offence is very low and even lesser provocations such as a penetrating stare, an inadvertent gesture

---

[31] Baroja 1965: 96. [32] Schneider 1969: 148. [33] McAleer 1994: 47.
[34] S. Wilson 1988: 94, to be read with Petrusewicz 1990. [35] Pitt-Rivers 1965: 25.

or some trifling incident tend to bring about extreme responses. Stephen Wilson regards as typical the following story from Corsica: 'Conflict at Bastelica in 1852 between two branches of the Folacci developed from a quarrel between two children over a cap. Natale Folacci, the older brother of one of them, told his father: "It isn't because of the cap that I insist [on paying them back], but because they are boasting of having put me down." He therefore challenged his opponents and was killed.'[36] Honour, in genuinely feuding societies, is perceived as a condition of integrity, of not even being touched by any such affront. Campbell's classic anthropological study of the Sarakatzani, the transhumant quasi-nomadic shepherds of north-western Greece, states that this integrity 'is recognized when others take care not to give offence in these particular ways. If they do gratuitously commit an outrage against a family, they make it clear that they consider its social existence of no account. In that case, whether the violation is accidental or not, the outraged family must answer at once, and with violence, if its reputation is to survive'.[37] It may therefore be said that in genuinely feuding societies men who have been provoked, injured or otherwise dishonoured are expected at all costs to react impulsively and violently, preferably inflicting upon the offender some punishment far graver than whatever injury they have themselves sustained. According to the standards of such societies, the public nature of the punch delivered to Demosthenes and the physical affront that it entailed made it the ultimate form of insult.

The way in which Demosthenes boasts about *not* having reacted violently to Meidias' punch ('What now? I, who was so responsibly concerned to do no irreparable damage that I did not hit back – who is going to recompense me for what I have suffered? I think it should be you and the laws. You should set it up as a principle for all to follow that no victim of assault or outrage should defend himself in hot blood (*meta tes orges*). Instead the aggressors should be brought before your court, since it is you who confirm and uphold the protection that the law offers to injured parties' (21.76)) makes it clear that his position is not merely that of a man who knows that his integrity is not in question. Demosthenes is unmistakably proud (or chooses to present himself as so) of having let this series of grave insults pass without retaliating and of not having responded in kind to the punch. It is hard to avoid the conclusion that he presented his reaction in this way because this was the pattern of action that he knew would be approved of by the Athenian dikasts and sanctioned by public opinion. Sensitively

[36] S. Wilson 1988: 92.   [37] J. K. Campbell 1964: 268–9.

attuned to the dikasts' expectations, Demosthenes had only to put them into words.

Demosthenes' case is yet another indication that the Athenian democracy had a very different idea of the proper relation between the gravity of an insult or injury and the scale upon which it should be responded to from the one that we find in feuding societies. In feuding societies the slightest offence triggers off extreme and indiscriminate reprisals, whereas in Athens grave insults and serious injuries were deliberately portrayed as having been met with forbearance and self-restraint. Demosthenes behaved in a manner that a Corsican or Sarakatzani 'man of honour' would have considered dishonourable in the extreme. It is patently clear, however, that in doing so he did not merely expect *not* to run the risk of being shamed, but expected to be respected for his behaviour.[38] Demosthenes did not retaliate because, as he self-righteously explains, a man should not resort to self-help upon being provoked (*ei tis hauto beboetheken atimazomenos*); he should rather seek redress 'from the people and from the laws' (21.74–6). Yet again we see an appeal that does not merely express a defensible personal opinion, but clearly expects to invoke an accepted code of behaviour. We can only conclude that in democratic Athens exercising self-restraint in the face of adversity must have been a deeply internalised ideal that had profound effects upon the courses of action pursued by the members of that society.

It is interesting to speculate briefly about the origins of this highly unusual strategy for conducting interpersonal conflicts. Pre-Socratic philosophy contains certain hints of this way of thinking. It is, for example, reported of Thales of Miletus that when asked 'How can one live best and most righteously (*dikaiotata*)?' he answered: 'By never doing ourselves what we would rebuke another for doing' (Diogenes Laertius 1.36). Heraclitus saw eye-for-an-eye revenge killings as futile: 'They vainly purify themselves of blood-guilt by defiling themselves with blood, as though one who had stepped into mud were to wash with mud.'[39] Solon wrote, 'I want to have money, but not to get it unjustly (*adikos*); always, after injustice, comes judgement (*dike*)' (7–13). One impetus that might have given ideas of this sort a concrete foothold in Athens is described in an anecdote preserved in

---

[38] This point, which I have made in earlier publications, has sometimes been misunderstood. Fisher, for instance, ascribes to me the view that litigants were 'admitting their acceptance of continued dishonour for the sake of community peace' (Fisher 2000: 88). What I was in fact saying was that litigants were willing for the sake of communal peace to embrace certain forms of behaviour that would have been regarded as dishonourable in feuding societies, but were highly prized in Athens.

[39] Kirk, Raven and Schofield 1983: no. 241.

Plutarch's *Lives*.[40] Pericles, we are told, was greatly impressed by Anaxagoras of Clazomenae, the philosopher who set Reason (*nous*) above Chance (*tyche*) and Necessity (*ananke*) on the throne of an orderly universe. Anaxagoras was the practical philosopher under whose guidance Pericles subordinated his behaviour to the rule of reason: '. . . filling himself with this lofty and, as they call it, up-in-the-air sort of thought, derived hence not merely, as was natural, elevation of purpose and dignity of language, raised far above the base and dishonest buffooneries of mob eloquence, but, besides this, a composure of countenance, and a serenity and calmness in all his movements, which no occurrence whilst he was speaking could disturb, a sustained and even tone of voice, and various other advantages of a similar kind, which produced the greatest effect on his hearers'. Having thus absorbed the principles of rational conduct, Pericles soon underwent a test of his newly remodelled personality when he went to the *agora* to transact some urgent business and 'some vile and abandoned fellow' decided to spend the day insulting and abusing him. Pericles 'continued his business in complete silence' (*hupemeine siope*) and in the evening 'returned home composedly, the man still dogging him at the heels, and pelting him all the way with abuse and foul language; and stepping into his house, it being by this time dark, he ordered one of his servants to take a light, and to go along with the man and see him safe home'.[41]

I am not inclined to attach any more than symbolic significance to this anecdote. Plutarch, retelling it in the second century AD, may well have diluted the original with ideals drawn from the world of Roman imperial autocracy. If he did so, however, it is unlikely that he thereby distorted to any great extent the point that the anecdote was intended to make. The punchline sets a high value on a pattern of behaviour that would be exceptional in most human societies and in fact runs counter to most basic human assumptions.[42] It would, moreover, require almost superhuman determination to implement such a strategy. On the other

---

[40] This is a 'secondary' or 'derivative' source, unlike the primary ones on which I have so far relied. Most of the primary sources that Plutarch used to write his biographies of major Athenian figures have now disappeared. Since his aim was to convey moral edification by analogy rather than to represent Athenian life realistically (and since, moreover, his own life under the imperial Roman autocracy is likely considerably to have diminished his understanding of the Athenian democracy), I shall be using his anecdotes only where they betray a spirit that can also be detected in primary sources, and therefore appear likely to be authentic. For a similar approach, cf. I. Morris 1994b: 88 n. 21.

[41] Plutarch, *Life of Pericles* 5, trans. John Dryden. Cf. Vickers 1997: 113 for the comic exploitation of this incident on stage.

[42] See pp. 10–12.

hand, this anecdote embodies precisely the philosophy of action that the Athenian dikasts repeatedly approved in the law courts.

A CASE OF MARITAL INFIDELITY

A text known as Lysias 1 (*On the Murder of Eratosthenes*) is further evidence that we have discovered the principle of action underlying the logic of those surviving law-court speeches that relate to violent incidents, a principle that may therefore be assumed to have exercised a pervasive influence on Athenian life. This speech was written by a professional speechwriter, probably Lysias himself, for Euphiletus, the defendant in a case involving adultery and murder.[43] (The speech for the prosecution, which would have been delivered first, is now lost.) This case reveals an intricate interplay between the sense of honour of the individual citizen and the internal workings of the democratic polis.

Euphiletus was being prosecuted for premeditated homicide by the relatives of a man called Eratosthenes whom he had killed in front of witnesses. Euphiletus did not deny the killing, since Eratosthenes was obviously dead, but pleaded that this was a case of justifiable homicide: he had killed Eratosthenes legitimately after catching him in the act of adultery with his own wife. Since he had made this claim, the action against him would have been heard before a special court of fifty-one judges that was convened to deal with such cases.[44] If convicted, Euphiletus would have been executed and his property confiscated. We do not know the outcome of the trial, but the fact that this speech was written up and 'published' suggests that Euphiletus may have been acquitted. Perhaps this defence's watertight legal arguments, coupled with its accurately targeted appeal to the dikasts' moral norms, did the trick.

At first glance it may appear that we are looking at something utterly banal. A great many deceived husbands have killed a great many paramours in both ancient and modern societies, and nothing about Euphiletus' case immediately stands out from this pattern. Nor have modern scholars noticed anything strange about Lysias 1. This speech has customarily been used only as evidence of the procedures prescribed by Athenian legislation

---

[43] Cf. Herman 1993. For the question of authenticity, see Carey 1989: 11–12, summarising earlier literature on the subject, and 64. For the possibility that Lysias and Euphiletus collaborated in writing the speech, see Chapter 4, n. 55 this volume.

[44] Cf. *The Athenian Constitution* 57.3: 'If . . . a person admits that he has killed someone but declares that he did so within the law (for instance, when he has killed an adulterer taken in the act) . . . then the trial takes place in the Delphinion' (cf. Demosthenes 23.74, *Against Aristocrates*).

in cases of homicide and adultery, or of course as evidence for the suppos-edly 'Mediterranean' nature of Athenian society.[45] (In parenthesis, I should perhaps note that I am puzzled by the oft-repeated suggestion that there is something typically 'Mediterranean' about the killing of a lover by a jealous husband. If this is so, a recent study of domestic violence in present-day societies must surely imply that Australia has somehow floated rather a long way from its moorings.)[46]

On closer examination, however, this proves to be a highly irregular sort of speech, interspersed with remarks that appear to violate common-sense expectations. It evokes strong views and stirs up extreme emotions. Why did Euphiletus kill Eratosthenes? Ask the man or woman on the Clapham omnibus and he or she will give you the obvious answer: Euphiletus killed Eratosthenes in a blind fury to avenge his wounded honour because Eratos-thenes had slept with his wife.

Euphiletus' answer to the same question is rather different. Unconvinc-ing though this may seem, he claims to have killed Eratosthenes because the latter had violated the laws of Athens by committing adultery. In despatch-ing the culprit he was therefore merely acting as an agent of civic justice, motivated entirely by a very proper wish to uphold the law.[47]

This claim seems so extraordinary as to strain credulity. Can it be that we have misunderstood it? The speech's logical structure seems to make this impossible. Accepting, then, that Euphiletus really was claiming to have acted as an agent of civic justice, we must assume that his defence rested on the following assertions. Firstly, he had killed Eratosthenes because Eratosthenes had broken the law, not because he had upset Euphiletus by sleeping with his wife. Secondly, in killing Eratosthenes Euphiletus had been inflicting appropriate punishment rather than taking revenge. Thirdly, he had chosen this course of action in a measured and logical way rather than in a fit of rage. Finally, by controlling himself so admirably he had proved that he did not set excessive store by his manly honour. Let us see whether the speech itself bears out these inferences.

---

[45] See in particular D. Cohen 1991a, throughout.   [46] Polk 1994, esp. ch. 3.

[47] Here are the relevant passages: 'He [Eratosthenes] admitted his crime, but begged and implored me to come to some financial arrangement rather than kill him. But I replied: "It is not I who shall kill you, but the city's law, which you are flouting: you regarded it as less important than your own pleasure, and preferred committing this crime against my wife and my children to obeying the law and behaving like a decent person"' (1.25–6). Further on in the speech Euphiletus rephrases this idea: 'He [Eratosthenes] did not argue, gentlemen, but admitted his guilt, begging and pleading not to be killed, and was ready to buy me off. But I refused to fall in with this and insisted that the city's law must come first' (1.29).

Throughout the speech, Euphiletus insists that his killing of Eratosthenes was motivated only indirectly by the latter's act of adultery with *his* wife; his direct motivation was the fact that Eratosthenes had broken the laws of the polis. Euphiletus asserts that whereas Eratosthenes did indeed seduce and corrupt his wife, bring disgrace upon his children and outrage him by entering his house (1.4), none of these dire insults to his own honour was the motive for the killing. He did it purely and simply because Eratosthenes had broken the law. His act was therefore clearly one of punishment rather than revenge.[48]

In order to validate this point Euphiletus turns to various rhetorical tricks. Most significantly, he plays two codes of behaviour off against one another. Distancing himself from the code that we believe to be typical of feuding societies, the code that enjoins disproportionate *personal* retaliation, he vigorously proclaims his adherence to a code enjoining proportionate, *impersonal*, state-endorsed punishment. His purpose is to exploit the tension in the mind of the dikasts between the second code, which now dominated Athenian life, and the first, which, though now discarded, still retained a vague aura of legitimacy.

Rather than playing the betrayed husband burning with an irresistible fury to avenge his wounded pride, Euphiletus casts himself in the image of a civil agent who dispassionately insists that communal norms should be observed and violators punished. The first step in this remarkable metamorphosis is described as having taken place while Euphiletus was attempting to extract the truth from the slave-girl (1.18–20). Immediately after the disclosure of the secret love affair, Euphiletus appears as a hurt human being overwhelmed by a tide of emotion: '. . . I was at once thrown into confusion. Details came rushing back to me, and I became extremely suspicious as I recalled how I had been shut in my room, and remembered how the inner and outer doors had banged that night, which had never happened before, and how I had thought my wife was wearing make-up. All these things came back to me, and I was full of suspicion' (1.17). Almost at once, however, his tone changes to one of brusqueness. Euphiletus metamorphoses himself into a stern civic official, bent single-mindedly upon discovering the absolute truth. He induces the slave-girl to co-operate with

---

[48] The critical passages are: 'I exacted the penalty (*dike*) that you have thought it most proper to impose upon those who engage in such practices' (1.29); 'Therefore, gentlemen, the law does not merely acquit me of wrongdoing, but actively requires me to inflict this punishment' (*ten diken lambanein*, 1.34); 'I do not consider this punishment (*timoria*) to have been a private one inflicted on my own behalf, but one carried out on behalf of the whole city' (1.47).

him with a judicious combination of threats and promises, steeped in legal language.[49]

This fiction is followed up in the ensuing scene, which precedes the homicide. As soon as Euphiletus and his companions burst into the lair of forbidden passion, it turns into an impromptu court of justice. Constituting himself what we would call coroner, judge and executioner, Euphiletus makes sure that we know that his every action was properly witnessed: 'Pushing the bedroom door open, those of us who went in first saw him still lying beside my wife, and the people who followed us in saw him standing naked on the bed. I hit him and knocked him down, gentlemen, got his hands behind his back and tied them together, and asked him why he was committing the outrage of entering my house' (1.24–5).

Having pinioned Eratosthenes' arms, Euphiletus claims to have had the law read out to him and to have discussed the option of financial compensation. The gruesome details of the killing itself are glossed over: 'I exacted the penalty (*dike*) that you have thought it most proper to impose upon those who engage in such practices' (1.29). In another sublime piece of demagoguery, Euphiletus almost manages to suggest that he actually killed Eratosthenes by non-violent means.

This statement requires qualification. Euphiletus definitely knocked Eratosthenes down, pinioned his arms and then killed him. We are, however, required to believe that these actions were not ends in themselves, but means to higher ends transcending the realm of Euphiletus' personal involvement. We are not to suppose that Euphiletus might possibly have flung himself on Eratosthenes and killed him because he was in a violent rage; he was, of course, merely enforcing civic justice by means of controlled violence.

One of the overriding themes of this speech is self-restraint. Euphiletus might as well have said, 'Look, under all this pressure I never once even thought of resorting to the violent, impulsive option. I am the sort of person who can control himself and always chooses the rational path of restraint.' One odd effect of this is that acts that might have been expected to be charged with burning passion are described in his speech as having been carried out with a sort of mechanistic nonchalance. When the slave-girl informed Euphiletus that Eratosthenes was in the house, Euphiletus did

---

[49] The legal language may also have served to highlight the solemn formality of the situation: 'There must be no lies at all; tell the truth' (1.18); 'she accused (*kategorei*) him [Eratosthenes]' (1.20); 'And I expect you to show me this guilty act as they are actually committing it (*ep'autophoroi*). Words are no good to me; I want the facts of this matter to be exposed in full, if what you are telling me is right' (1.21).

not furiously rush off to confront the guilty lovers: not the slightest inkling of uncontrollable rage was stirred in him by the thought of his wife in bed with another man. Nor, apparently, did the idea of killing (or 'punishing') his unfaithful wife even cross his mind.[50] The killing of Eratosthenes was no illegitimate crime of passion, but a judicial act made up of calm, considered and legally proper moves. For example, Euphiletus' first action on learning that his wife was even then in the arms of her lover was not to charge furiously to the scene of the outrage, but to instruct the slave-girl to wait by the door and be ready to open it at the appropriate moment. He then slipped quietly out of the house and rounded up his friends, in order, of course, that everything might be appropriately witnessed (see **Fig. 5.1**). Such was his self-possession that he remembered to go and buy some torches from the nearest shop so that everybody would be able to see properly. Having caught the lovers in the act of adultery he did not, as we have seen, immediately pummel Eratosthenes to death, but held a makeshift trial. Finally he gave proper consideration to the option of financial compensation, as prescribed by the law (1.25, 29). A calm and rational spirit, we are to believe, has informed Euphiletus' every move.

Social psychologists find it useful to discriminate between affective and instrumental aggression.[51] Affective aggression is aroused by provocation, fuelled by anger and accompanied by distinctive patterns of activity in the central and autonomic nervous systems (such as heightened blood pressure and pulse rate). It is an emotional state in which the aggressor's sole aim is to inflict injury upon the provocateur. Instrumental aggression generally has no emotional symptoms. It exists where one person attacks another 'in cold blood', without feeling any malice towards him (a hired hit-man, for example). The marked difference between the two types of aggression is that the primary aim of the instrumental type is not to inflict injury upon the victim: such injury is merely a means to some other desired end.[52]

This may give us some insight into a paradoxical feature of Euphiletus' speech. In circumstances such as these we would most naturally expect to identify affective aggression (possibly even as a result of delusion, which

---

[50] According to Durham 1927: 85, even in the 1900s an Albanian husband was allowed to cut off the nose of an unfaithful wife. For the sake of contrast, we should mention that according to Aeschines Solonian legislation did not permit an adulteress to wear jewellery and fashionable clothes, or to attend the public temples, lest she should corrupt the other women with whom she mingled. 'But if she does attend, or does adorn herself, he [Solon] commands that anyone who encounters her shall tear off her garments, remove her jewellery, and beat her, without, however, killing or maiming her' (1.183, *Against Timarchus* = Ruschenbusch 1966: 115, F 115 and 116).

[51] See p. 36.   [52] Cf. Geen 1990: 5–6.

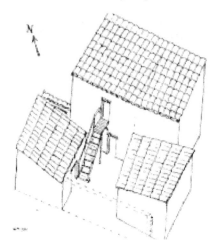

Figure 5.1 Euphiletus' *oikos* **(house and family)**
A typical Athenian house, the physical site of the *oikos*, would have had an area of about
250–350m². The ground floor was normally reserved for the male members of the family
(*andronitis*) and the upper storey for the female members (*gynaikonitis*; see S. Lewis 2002:
130–2). In the house above, reconstructed from Lysias 1 (G. Morgan 1982), the birth of a
baby had led to a reversal of this arrangement, so that Euphiletus lived above the women
(Lysias 1.9–10). A house of this type would also contain rooms for slaves and guests.
Running water was laid on. The *oikos* would often own another house on the familial plot
of land (*kleros*) outside Athens, on the *chora* (see **Figs 2.3** and **2.5a**). The personal element
of the *oikos* appears in an Athenian red-figure vase-painting (dated to
c. 430) that shows a husband, his wife and their baby, who is being handed over to a nurse
(possibly a slave-girl). The loom in the background is an eloquent symbol of one of the
household's most significant female activities (cf. Bettalli 1982).

often propels masculine violence within the context of sexual intimacy)[53] as the motive for action. Euphiletus, however, stresses the rational, instrumental character of his actions. The ultimate implication of his rhetoric, stretching logic to its utmost extent, is that Euphiletus did not really kill Eratosthenes at all: he had him executed. This act was not personal: at the time of the killing Euphiletus embodied in his person the community's right to exercise violence under certain circumstances. The community should therefore view his actions not as improper violence, but as law enforcement.[54]

In keeping with this approach, Euphiletus makes no mention of wounded masculine pride, in fact suppressing the issue of honour altogether. We are meant to believe that he was by no means a man who prized his honour above all else, that his judgement was not clouded by sexual jealousy or delusion and that he was willing to compromise. He, or Lysias on his behalf, used various tricks to construct this image.

The Euphiletus of this speech is a 'gullible, almost comic figure'.[55] In particular, he is portrayed as completely useless at keeping his wife under control, having lost the upper hand shortly after the birth of their first child. Failing to shield her from Eratosthenes' advances, he has ended up forfeiting his monopoly over her reproductive capacity.[56] Euphiletus, according to this speech, is hopelessly naïve, a trait that is revealed by juxtaposing objective and subjective realities. With the love affair in full swing and the lovers meeting regularly at his house, he persisted in believing that his wife was the finest example of chastity in the city (1.10). Even when his suspicions had finally been aroused he continued to be taken in by his wife's transparent excuses, to the point of consenting to be locked in his room (1.13). The doors banged at night as Eratosthenes paid yet another visit, but Euphiletus accepted his wife's explanations, even though she appeared to be wearing make-up when she was still supposed to be in mourning. He was, in other words, absolutely nothing like the stereotype of the possessive, domineering husband.

It is a peculiar feature of seductive rhetoric that it is capable of resonating on several levels at once, appealing both to reason and to the emotions. The issue of the compensation money (it will be remembered that Eratosthenes is supposed to have offered to pay compensation for his offences shortly before he was killed) is in one respect just another device to keep

---

[53] Cf. Polk 1994: 31.   [54] See pp. 234–7.   [55] Cf. Carey 1989: 61.
[56] For horns as a symbol of the disgrace of deceived husbands in the ancient world and in Mediterranean cultures in general (in Athens this association is conspicuously absent), see Onians 1951: 243–6; Blok 1981, respectively.

REACTION CODE	EMOTIONAL	PHYSICAL	DEGREE OF FLEXIBILITY	SELF-ESTEEM	SOCIAL	LEGAL
A	impulsive	committing individual violence	avoiding compromise at all costs	high regard for honour	revenge	murder
B	using self-restraint	activating communal violence	going to great lengths to compromise	little regard for honour	punishment	execution

Figure 5.2 The typology of Euphiletus' reaction to Eratosthenes' provocation
Throughout his speech Euphiletus plays upon the tension that would have existed in the minds of the dikasts between two codes of behaviour, A and B, of which only B was currently legitimate. A had been publicly discredited, but because of the primeval concept of fairness that it implied some were probably still inclined to allow it a certain validity.

up the fiction of legitimate execution. Exacting compensation was a standard method of dealing with adulterers in Athens; it was therefore wise of Euphiletus to point out that he had not ignored this legal option. Simultaneously, however, the reference to compensation helps to reinforce the overall point that Euphiletus is trying to hammer home, in that a man who cites civic order rather than personal honour as his motive for rejecting the money offered by his wife's seducer can hardly be accused of excessive machismo. The idea that personal honour was incompatible with litigation, with which Euphiletus clearly had no truck, was cherished by the upper classes of pre-modern Europe. As late as the sixteenth century, Michel de Montaigne wrote: 'He who appeals to the laws to get satisfaction for an offence to his honour, dishonours himself.'[57]

Had Athens been one of those societies that regard a man's honour as of paramount importance, or even one of those that accept the 'crime of passion' as a legitimate solution to disputes within the context of sexual intimacy, Euphiletus might simply have said, 'That's right, I murdered my wife's lover because he had tainted my honour,' and got away scotfree. In that case the dikasts, men in every respect like himself, would have understood such an argument. Athens was, however, no such thing, which is

[57] Cf. F. H. Stewart 1994: 80. In nineteenth-century Corsica '[t]here is no substitute for vendettas, because the Corsicans would not accept monetary compensation for stained honour' (Petrusewicz 1990: 298).

why Euphiletus adopted entirely the opposite strategy. The 'rules' by which he claimed to have played and those from which he took pains to distance himself are represented schematically in **Fig. 5.2**. Euphiletus' defence was that since he had fulfilled every last injunction of code B and avoided all those of code A the killing of Eratosthenes could only be classified as punishment rather than revenge, as an execution rather than murder. Some years ago Adkins explored the tensions between the individualistic values of the pre-polis world and the collective values whose appearance marks the emergence of the polis.[58] In *On the Murder of Eratosthenes* we see these collective values stretched to their extreme.

---

[58] Adkins 1972. Cf. Chapter 3, nn. 42, 44–6.

CHAPTER 6

Revenge and punishment

'MINDLESS' REVENGE

The arguments brought before the dikasts who heard Eratosthenes' case must have presented them with a dilemma. Should they accept the prosecution's claim that the killing of Eratosthenes was an anti-social act in breach of the law, or Euphiletus' claim that it had been done to uphold the law in the interests of society and must therefore be regarded as sanctioned by the state? If they voted in favour of the first alternative Euphiletus would be branded a criminal and punished in accordance with the law; if they voted in favour of the second he would be confirmed as a law-abiding citizen and walk free. The survival of his defence speech strongly suggests that they did the latter. This, if true, can only mean that they would have disapproved of revenge as a motive for killing Eratosthenes, but approved of the 'legitimate punishment' argument. Euphiletus' ingenious defence thus paves the way to an exploration of the Athenians' attitude towards the sort of human behaviour that goes under the name of revenge.

Vengefulness is a common human state that is expressed in the individual's outward behaviour, influences social interaction and has far-reaching implications for society as a whole. It manifests itself in different ways in different cultures. We shall begin by examining some perceptions of vengefulness in other cultures in order that we may more clearly understand the peculiar form that it took in ancient Athens.[1]

Words that have to do with vengeance seem to embrace both an emotional state and a corresponding series of acts that may result from it. Societies differ markedly in their attitudes to this state, some encouraging it and valuing highly the forms of behaviour in which it can result, while others discourage it and attempt to curtail or suppress these types of behaviour. The perceptions of vengeance found in societies of the former kind are very

---

[1] For the beginnings of a theory of societal management of feelings (including vengeful ones) see Hochschild 1979; 1983.

unlike those to which twenty-first century westerners are accustomed. In such societies the word vengeance denotes a passionate desire, a sacred duty that must be carried through at all costs, irrespective of the consequences. Acts performed in fulfilment of this duty are not only condoned, but met with enthusiastic approval, often appearing in the public conscience as a yardstick by which other acts are measured. Just as returning a favour is regarded as right, honourable and worthy of respect, it is seen as entirely the right and proper thing to exact revenge, preferably in an extreme form. Revenge has sometimes been made an official part of a state's machinery for maintaining public order: the Old Testament, for example, records a provision whereby any person found guilty of premeditated murder was to be delivered 'into the hand of the avenger of blood, that he may die' (Deuteronomy 19.11–13). In societies that have no powerful coercive apparatus, blood-feuds, vendettas and revenge killings are allowed to continue in their course unchecked. Life in such societies is continually disrupted by acts of vengeance carried out in a zealous and fatalistic spirit. The modern author and critic Milovan Djilas (who, being a Montenegrin by birth, had witnessed acts of this sort at close quarters) described this spirit with exuberant plasticity, calling vengeance 'a breath of life one shares from the cradle with one's fellow . . . the debt we paid for the love and sacrifice our forebears and fellow clansmen bore for us. It was the defence of our honour and good name, and the guarantee of our maidens. It was our pride before others; our blood was not water that anyone could spill. It was . . . the glow in our eyes, the flame in our cheeks, the pounding in our temples, the word that turned to stone in our throats on our hearing that our blood had been shed. It was the sacred task transmitted in the hour of death to those who had just been conceived in our blood. It was centuries of manly pride and heroism, survival, a mother's milk and a sister's vow, bereaved parents and children in black, joy and songs turned into silence and wailing. It was all, all. . . Vengeance is not hatred, but the wildest and sweetest kind of drunkenness, both for those who must wreak vengeance and for those who wish to be avenged'.[2]

Feelings of the sort that Djilas describes are neither repressed nor disguised in feuding societies, in which they come to the fore and are allowed to dominate social life. Metaphors having much in common with Djilas' 'sweetest kind of drunkenness' turn up in the written records of such societies with monotonous regularity. We shall now take a look at some typical

---

[2] M. Djilas (1958) *Land Without Justice*. London: A Harvest/HBJ Book: 106–7 (published some fifty years after revenge killings had been outlawed in Montenegro).

treatments of revenge, bearing in mind that neither the frequency with which such references occur nor the stylistic form in which they are cast (whether fable, myth or generalised injunction) is necessarily a straightforward indicator of the importance of vengeance in the society that produced them.[3]

As a prelude to his declaration that he could only go on living if he took vengeance on Hector, Achilles described the anger (*cholos*; literally 'gall') aroused in him by Agamemnon's violation of his honour as 'sweeter than dripping honey' (Homer, *Iliad* 18.108–9).[4] In a chain of reprisals somewhat reminiscent of the Ali Chadra incident (see p. 162), Heracles killed Hippocoön and at least ten of his sons because they had clubbed Heracles' cousin Oeonus to death for accidentally killing one of Hippocoön's dogs.[5] The pre-Socratic philosopher Anaximander extrapolated the notion of vengeance (or requital) from the human to the physical sphere: in the course of generation and destruction, according to him, everything must pay the penalty (*dike*) or exact retribution (*tisis*) for any injustice.[6] Aesop tells a moral tale about a wasp that settled on a snake's head and tormented it by stinging it continually. Mad with pain and not knowing how else to take revenge on its tormentor, the snake put its head under the wheel of a wagon, killing them both (Fable 331). Herodotus interprets the reproductory process of 'winged snakes' (locusts) as a ghastly chain of revenge killings: the female bites off the male's head during mating, but her young avenge their father's death, gnawing their way out of their mother's body while she is still alive (3.109).[7]

The literature of the Middle Ages abounds in descriptions of vengeance that are very similar in character. In sixth-century Gaul Gregory of Tours used human revenge as a metaphor for divine vengeance, describing God as keeping up feuds on behalf of his servants and exacting vengeance as though he were the head of their family or the leader of their war-band.[8] Mediaeval rulers who were keen on exacting retribution were praised, since it was regarded as dishonourable to put up with injustice or to renounce

---

[3] For a detailed analysis of this principle, see Herman 2000a.
[4] Aristotle takes this to refer to *thymos*: *Rhetoric* 1370b11 and 1378b4–5.
[5] Pausanias 3.15.3–6 relates that following this feat of vengeance Heracles founded a sanctuary of Athena and surnamed it *Axiopoinos* ('Just Requital' or 'Tit for Tat') to commemorate the justness of his revenge. Pausanias adds that the ancients called vengeance *poinai* rather than *timoria*.
[6] Kirk, Raven and Schofield 1983: no. 101.
[7] For an abundance of examples of this sort from Greek literature, see de Romilly 1971; Burnett 1998; Allen 2000. For the Herodotean concept of vengeance as a 'debt of enmity' (*proopheilomene echthre*, 5.82), see Gernet 1976b: 182; for vengeance as a sort of reciprocity, see J. Gould 1989: 82–5. On modern anecdotes concerning revenge among animals (especially monkeys), see Westermarck 1924: 37–40.
[8] J. M. Wallace-Hadrill 1962: 127.

vengeance. Marc Bloch has observed that the custom of seeking revenge obtained at every level of society.[9] To Thomas Aquinas, just wars were in general 'those which avenge(d) injustices'.[10] A thirteenth-century Austrian poet wrote that a world in which 'men no longer avenged injustice' would be one of moral chaos.[11] Dante too, in a perfectly balanced stanza, exalted revenge.[12] After him, however, a certain doubt seems to have crept in as to the wisdom of permitting avengers to deal out retribution unchecked. In Renaissance Italy the spirit of vendetta was perceived as a form of feral ferocity, the uncontrollable rage of the avenger being likened to the madness of a rabid dog.[13] Accordingly stories of exceedingly cruel revenge killings circulated, some recalling the mythical story of Atreus and the sons of Thyestes.[14] Shakespeare conveyed the same idea with a somewhat gentler metaphor: 'mad blood stirring' (*Romeo and Juliet* 3.1.4). By the eighteenth century the idea of revenge must have lost even more of its attraction; Da Ponte's libretto for Mozart's *Figaro* praises vendetta and reminds the listener that it is demeaning ever to forget an insult, but in tones that hint at playful ridicule.[15]

The concept of vengeance in so-called 'tribal' societies (some of which we have already termed 'feuding') tends to follow the same pattern, although here it is not generally represented in so stylised a manner. In such societies what we deprecatingly call 'primitive' vengeance is conceived of as the highest of duties: those who discharge this duty punctiliously are rewarded with admiration and prestige, while anyone who evades it is humiliated

---

[9] Marc Bloch (1962) *Feudal Society*, 2nd edn, London: Routledge and Kegan Paul Ltd.: 127.

[10] O. Brunner (1992) *Land and Lordship. Structures of Governance in Medieval Austria*. Philadelphia: University of Pennsylvania Press: 6–7.

[11] Seifried Helbling, cited in Brunner 1992: 20 (n. 10 above). To Albrecht I he wrote: 'My lord has suffered great injuries | He has the right to avenge himself | and destroy the houses of thieves | and conquer unrighteous people in battle.'

[12] Canzone: *Senza parlarmi*: '*Che bell'onor s'acquista in far vendetta.*'

[13] Cf. E. Muir (1993) *Mad Blood Stirring: Vendetta and Faction in Friuli during the Renaissance*. Baltimore and London: The Johns Hopkins University Press: ch. 7.

[14] Cf. this one, cited from Jacob Burckhardt (1935) *The Civilization of the Renaissance in Italy*. U.S.A.: Albert and Charles Boni: 430: 'In the district of Acquapendente three boys were watching cattle, and one of them said: "Let us find out the way how people are hanged." While one was sitting on the shoulders of the other, and the third, after fastening the rope around the neck of the first, was tying it to an oak, and the two who were free ran away and left the other hanging. Afterwards they found him dead, and buried him. On the Sunday his father came to bring him bread, and one of the two confessed what had happened, and showed him the grave. The old man then killed him with a knife, cut him up, brought away the liver, and entertained the boy's father with it at home. After dinner, he told him whose liver it was. Hereupon began a series of reciprocal murders between the two families, and within a month thirty-six persons were killed, women as well as men.'

[15] '*La vendetta, oh, la vendetta,* | *È un piacer serbatto ai saggi:* | *L' obliar l'onte, gli oltraggi* | *È bassezza, è ognor viltà*' (Act One, Scene Three).

and risks ostracism. In the old days a Montenegrin who failed to avenge a kinsman was a worthless 'nothing' with 'no place and no honour among the rest of the Montenegrins'.[16] Stephen Wilson tells us that in nineteenth-century Corsica it was considered a 'cultural imperative' never to let an insult pass without retaliating; anyone who disobeyed this imperative was called a *rimbeccu*, 'a social outcast, an object of scorn, whom anyone can insult with impunity because he lacks the courage to retaliate against such insults'.[17]

A central demand of tribal revenge is that it must be carried out at any price, no matter what the consequence may be. In extreme cases the sense of duty that motivates it commits the individual to acts whose logic is 'insane' and in which 'human sentiments and a sense of proportion are totally submerged by a strict observance of rigidly defined rules'.[18] As late as the early twentieth century, Edith Durham was able to recognise in the minds of Albanian and Montenegrin people a deep dichotomy between 'killing a man as a result of a quarrel, or when robbing him, and "taking blood". The first is murder; the second is a duty, painful, dangerous, fatal perhaps – but a duty that must be done'.[19]

The rewards for discharging this difficult duty conscientiously are often commensurately high. In traditional Bedouin society it was customary to follow a successful act of vengeance with a celebration at which the avenger would be fêted and congratulated by his admiring public.[20] In the Arab villages of the Ottoman empire the killing of an adulteress, or of a daughter suspected of having had premarital sex, was classified as 'a case of honour', not of murder. Public opinion was so much in favour of killings of this sort that 'the murderer would sprinkle his victim's blood on his clothes and parade through the streets displaying the bloody murder weapon (usually an axe or knife) to increase his honour. He was considered a "purger", one who restored honour . . . not a murderer'.[21] The Bedouins of today live in increasingly westernised societies and their vengeance killings now bring them into conflict with the laws of their nation states. When such killings are brought to court judges treat them as criminal offences,[22] but defendants often continue doggedly to insist that they have killed 'justly' in defence of their honour. They then endure with resignation whatever punishment they are sentenced to, imagining themselves the victims of

---

[16] Boehm 1984: 59, citing a text from 1860.   [17] S. Wilson 1988: 92.
[18] Black-Michaud 1975: 137.   [19] Durham 1909: 41.   [20] Kressel 1981: 143.
[21] Kressel 1981: 143.   [22] Cf. Ginat 1997.

ineluctable circumstances. Edith Durham has captured this fatalistic spirit clearly, if somewhat melodramatically: 'The unwritten law of blood is to the Albanian as is the Fury in Greek tragedy. It drives him inexorably to his doom.'[23]

The question now arises of whether interpersonal relations in Athens were dominated by a spirit of this sort or by something more like the spirit that governs interpersonal relations in modern nation states. Did the Athenians try to repress and control the spirit of vengeance, or did they embrace and nurture it? Above all, did they allow revenge freely to take its course?

As we have seen, modern researchers have generally agreed that this primitive conception of vengeance was a central driving force in the psyche of anyone in democratic Athens who felt himself to have been offended or injured.[24] The desire for revenge is supposed to have been woven into the very fabric of Athenian society, sometimes even supplementing institutional arrangements. 'When a person was killed in Athens', writes a distinguished scholar in the opening pages of a book entitled *Athenian Homicide Law*, 'the attitude of the Athenians to the event was a complex one, containing several distinguishable strands. In the first place the killed person had suffered a wrong, an injury (*adikia, adikema*), and required vengeance or retribution (*timoria*); and it was the duty of the family to obtain it for him.'[25] In support of this contention the author cites Lysias' thirteenth oration (*Against Agoratus*), written for the brother-in-law of a man called Dionysodorus who had been denounced by Agoratus and executed by the 'Thirty Tyrants' (the clique that seized power during the oligarchic coup of 404).[26] Doubtless with an eye to dramatic effect, the orator describes the actions of Dionysodorus and his fellow democrats prior to execution thus:

Now, when sentence of death, gentlemen, had been passed on them [i.e. following Agoratus' denunciation], and they had to die, each of them sent for his sister, or his mother, or his wife, or any female relative that he had, to see them in the prison (*desmoterion*), in order that they might take the last farewell of their people before they should end their days. In particular, Dionysodorus sent for my sister – she was his wife – to see him in the prison. On receiving the message she came, dressed in a black cloak ... as was natural in view of the sad fate that had befallen her husband. In the presence of my sister, Dionysodorus, after disposing of his personal property as he thought fit, referred to this man Agoratus as responsible for his death, and charged me and Dionysius his brother here, and all his friends to

---

[23] Durham 1909: 41. [24] See pp. 93–7. [25] MacDowell 1963a: 1.
[26] The trial itself took place some time after the restoration of democracy, probably in 399.

execute his vengeance (*timorein*) upon Agoratus; and he charged his wife, believing her to be with child by him, that if she should bear a son she should tell the child that Agoratus had taken his father's life, and should bid him execute his father's vengeance (*timorein*) on the man for his murder.[27]

Another modern scholar has come up with an even more striking interpretation of this passage. Not only, apparently, does it show that the Athenians regarded injuries of this sort as requiring retribution; it reveals 'the notion of vengeance as a sacred duty'. This notion is stated to be 'typical of feuding societies, where male children are raised to avenge deceased fathers and brothers',[28] reminding us of the Montenegrin mother who keeps showing a container of her dead husband's blood to her young sons to remind them of their duty to avenge his death when they are grown up.[29]

This view could hardly be more mistaken. Athenian litigants did indeed often speak of *timoria* (or *timorein*) or *diken/dikas lambanein/didonai*, words that *can* be translated as retribution or vengeance,[30] and unrestricted acts of retribution and vengeance are indeed amongst the hallmarks of feuding societies. Very often, however, as Finley has put it, 'the identity of label conceals a staggering diversity of substance'.[31] There is a very great difference between vengeance as Djilas describes it ('an overpowering and consuming fire', a 'breath of life one shares from the cradle with one's fellow clansmen', 'the wildest and sweetest kind of drunkenness') and what Athenian litigants meant when they used terms such as *timoria*. Djilas was describing private acts of vengeance arising out of passion and committed either in the absence of state authority or in defiance of it. The Athenian litigants, however, were seeking 'vengeance' for their wrongs in conformity with the laws of their state and through the medium of the dikasts, the proper agents of that state's power and authority.[32] The litigants are generally at great pains to insist that they want vengeance only in the form of state-sponsored acts

---

[27] 13.39–42, trans. W. R. M. Lamb; cf. 92 and Antiphon 1.1. Note that the child is to be enjoined to take revenge only on 'the man', not on his descendants.

[28] D. Cohen 1995a: 84. There is nothing novel about this. Cf. Glotz 1904b: 55–6: '*Les orateurs Isée et Lysias nous montrent comment on s'y prend dans les maisons athéniennes pour exciter un petit orphelin, un fils posthume, contre l'homme ou même le fils de l'homme qui lui a tué son père: toute une famille s'emploie à cette éducation dès que l'enfant a l'âge de raison*' (Isée, *Sur la succ. d'Astyph.*, 20; Lys, *C. Agor.*, 42).

[29] Cf. Boehm 1984: 63 for this Montenegrin custom and Brunner 1992: 20 (n. 10 above) for a fifteenth-century song commemorating an execution: 'Your lords know what this means | Though the child lying in the cradle | is yet unable to speak | He will have to avenge his father.'

[30] Karabélias 1991: 81–2 makes much of the identity of the words used to designate vengeance and punishment (*timoria, timoros, timorein, timoreisthai*), inferring from this that punishment in Athens was modelled on the concept of vengeance. Thereafter he concedes, however, that '*La famille étendue . . . n'exerce aucune juridiction privée . . .*'

[31] Finley 1978a: 27.   [32] See Chapter 7.

of repression and are not interested in private acts of violence. This means that what we have here has very little to do with 'primitive' vengeance and a great deal to do with what we would call punishment.[33] *Against Agoratus* makes this critical distinction in its concluding appeal to the dikasts, which clearly alludes to a Solonian principle: the opportunity (*exeinai*) for 'any who so wished' (*toi boulomenoi*) to secure punishment (*timorein hyper*) on behalf of an injured party (*ton adikoumenon*):[34]

It is the duty of you all, gentlemen, as it is of each one of us, to avenge (*timorein*) those men. For it was their dying injunction both to us and to all their friends, that we should avenge (*timorein*) them on this man Agoratus as their murderer, and do him, in a word, all the injury of which each of us is capable. Now, if they have manifestly done some good service to the city or your democracy, as you yourselves acknowledge, it must follow that you all are friends and intimates of theirs, so that they enjoined this on each of you no less than on us. Hence it would be impious as well as illegal for you to absolve this man Agoratus. And now it is for you, men of Athens, to-day . . . to punish (*timoresate*) their murderer. (Lysias 13.92–3, *Against Agoratus*, trans. W. R. M. Lamb)

Athenian litigants, then, used words such as *timoria* to designate a social process quite unlike the one denoted in feuding societies by their own words for 'vengeance'. The Athenians were referring to a process whereby person B responds to an insult or injury inflicted upon him by person A *not* by personally inflicting upon A an insult or injury equal to or greater than the one sustained[35] (see **Fig. 6.1a**), but by appealing to the appropriate part of the city's power system to inflict upon person A what we would call *punishment* (see **Fig. 6.1b**).

Any number of examples could be produced to illustrate this point. In the Demosthenic speech *Against Timocrates* the bringer of this case, Diodorus, recounts various acts of injustice that he has supposedly suffered at the hands of the defendant. As a result of these, it would appear, he came to regard Timocrates as an 'enemy with whom no personal reconciliation was possible'. He nonetheless states that he did nothing by way of revenge *until* he discovered that Timocrates had been embezzling the state's money. Only then did he decide to bring an action against Timocrates, the taking of this *legal* action in itself constituting his act of revenge: 'I proceeded against him

---

[33] The distinction was familiar to Aristotle, who wrote, 'There is a difference between revenge and punishment' (*Rhetoric* 1369b12; cf. M. W. Blundell 1989: 54). Revenge is prompted by the subjective feelings of the injured party; punishment is determined impersonally by society or its representative. 'To go to the judge is to go to justice; for the judge is supposed to be like justice incarnate' (*Nicomachean Ethics* 1132a20–2).

[34] *The Athenian Constitution* 9.1. For Solonian legislation see Glotz 1904b: ch. 9.

[35] This point is made clearly by Gehrke 1987: 129.

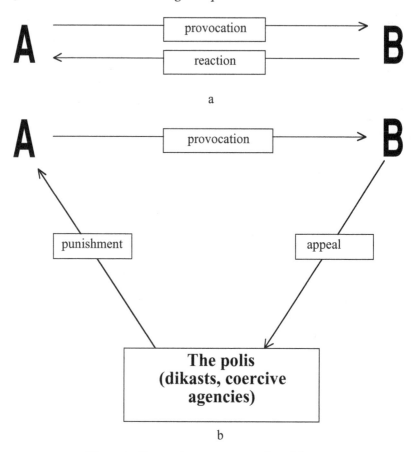

b

Figure 6.1 Provocation, vengeance and punishment
Solon instituted the law that allowed 'whomsoever wishes' (*ho boulomenos*) to take legal
action on behalf of anyone else who had been wronged in some way (in other words,
whereas previously only the victim himself or his relatives or friends had been permitted to
pursue this sort of action, anyone could now do it). Tradition has it that when asked in
which polis he thought it best to live, Solon replied: 'That polis in which people who have
suffered no injury are just as keen to punish wrongdoing as are its victims' (Plutarch, *Solon*
18). Athens' laws, officially at least, existed to help anyone who had suffered wrong
(Thucydides 2.37.3).

with Euctemon's help, thinking it a suitable opportunity to do the city a
service and to avenge my own wrongs' (Demosthenes 24.8, *Against Timocrates*). In similar vein, the speaker in the case brought against the younger
Alcibiades begins by doing everything possible to discredit Alcibiades as
a citizen, accusing him of having behaved so anti-socially that even his

enemies felt ashamed of him.[36] Only after casting these aspersions does he come to his real point and reveal that there have been differences between his own father and Alcibiades' and that Alcibiades has recently maltreated him. He claims, however, that only the combination of these circumstances has impelled him to 'try with your hand to make him pay the penalty for all that he has done' (Lysias 14.3, *Against Alcibiades*). Finally, we have the suit (*graphe*) brought by Theomnestus and Apollodorus against Neaera ([Demosthenes] 59, *Against Neaera*), supposedly to avenge two grievous wrongs (*edikemetha hypo Stephanou megala*, 59.1) suffered at the hand of Neaera's husband, Stephanus.[37] The speakers are at pains to point out that they have brought this case only as a last resort, even though apparently other people have continually exhorted them to have their opponent punished for the wrongs he has done them (*epi timorian trapesthai hon epathomen hyp'autou*, 59.12), and that any interest in private vengeance that they may feel is secondary to their deep concern for public welfare: '[People] admonished me, saying that I must be the biggest coward alive if . . . I did not take vengeance (*me lepsomai diken*) for what my sister, my father-in-law, my sister's children and my own wife had suffered, and if I did not bring before you this woman, who had so flagrantly sinned against the gods, had behaved so outrageously towards the polis, and had showed such contempt for your laws, and if I did not, by prosecuting her and convicting her of her crime by my arguments, empower you to deal with her as you thought fit' (59.12). By the speech's concluding paragraph the idea of private vengeance has vanished altogether and the dikasts are being told that it is their duty to avenge, not Theomnestus and Apollodorus, but the gods and themselves (59.126). I cannot think of a single passage in which retaliation that bypasses the law courts is presented as a realistic and acceptable alternative to legal action.

Retaliation by means of the law courts can, of course, be seen as a sort of personal vengeance, but this is true only on the level of ideas, not on that of actions. The fact that this sort of 'vengeance' was conducted officially

---

[36] Cf. p. 144.

[37] The first of these wrongs, which according to the speakers had greatly imperilled them and their entire family, had consisted of denouncing a decree that Apollodorus had passed at the Assembly as illegal (*paranomon*), taking the matter to court and demanding that the penalty should be the ruinous sum of fifteen talents. (The dikasts had subsequently reduced this to one talent.) The second wrong had consisted of indicting Apollodorus on a false charge of murder. Of this he was apparently acquitted by a large majority, since it was evident (or so the speakers claim) that Stephanus had perjured himself, having been suborned by two of Apollodorus' influential enemies to bring the charge.

via state agencies made it a social force completely unlike the 'vengeance' of feuding societies.[38]

CONTRASTING COURSES OF CONFLICT

Vengeance pursued through the Athenian law courts also differed from vengeance in feuding societies in that it had far fewer knock-on effects. In feuding societies violence invites further violence, which breeds counter-violence, and so on. This process may end up involving not only the victim and his family, but entire clans or tribes; each aggressive act demands yet more revenge, eventually giving rise to incessant wars between groups. George Simmel pointed out the significance of establishing whether or not such a conflict has any chance of ending in compromise, writing, 'In a classification of conflicts one of the most important characteristics is their intrinsic accessibility or inaccessibility to such ending.'[39] His point was that when conflicts that could never have ended in compromise end in 'victory' this victory can only be illusory and short-lived: it is inevitable that sooner or later the conflict will burst out again with fresh vigour.

One of the countless feuds that swept sixth-century Gaul is a good example of an almost interminable conflict. It was recorded by Gregory of Tours, a participant observer. I have simplified the following section of Gregory's *History of the Franks* (7.47) somewhat to make his convoluted style more accessible. Gregory's almost total indifference to his protagonists' emotional states deserves particular attention. Unlike Djilas, Gregory lived in a world in which the imperative of extreme vengeance went uncontested. He therefore felt no need to linger over its psychic roots.

Sichar, Austrogisil and their friends were giving a party (*phase one*). They were in a fairly advanced state of merriment when the local priest sent a servant to invite them to his house. One of the guests, probably a connection of Austrogisil, drew his sword and killed the servant (*phase two – the provocation*). Bound to the priest by ties of friendship (*amicitia*), Sichar engaged Austrogisil in a pitched battle, but was worsted. Leaving some money and clothing and four wounded servants at the priest's house, he bolted for his country estate. Austrogisil burst into the priest's house, killed the servants and carried off the goods. A tribunal of citizens (*iudicium civium*) found

---

[38] The differences between the two sorts of 'vengeance' are further elucidated in **Fig. 8.6**.
[39] Simmel 1955: 114.

Austrogisil guilty of homicide and theft. Arrangements were made whereby Sichar was to receive composition and forgo further vengeance.

Meanwhile, Sichar had found out that Austrogisil's kinsmen still had the stolen goods. Accompanied by a gang of armed men, he broke into the house in which they were sleeping, murdered them all (and their servants) and stole their herds and portable property. The feud now appeared to be reaching its climax and Bishop Gregory himself decided that it was time to intervene. Summoning both of the warring groups, he suggested that the party that was in the wrong should make composition. If it could not afford to pay (the composition would by now have amounted to a small fortune), the Church would do so 'rather than see any man lose his soul'.

Austrogisil's party, now represented by Chramnesind, son of a slain relative of Austrogisil, refused to accept the composition. Sichar had set out to see the king, but on the way was attacked and wounded by one of his slaves. News got about that he was dead. Chramnesind took this opportunity to get his friends and relatives together to burn down Sichar's house and those of his neighbours, carrying off all the cattle and every other movable object they could find. The count of the city then intervened to decree that Chramnesind should forfeit half the sum originally awarded him and that Sichar should pay him the other half, the money being in fact provided by the Church. At last a settlement that would put an end to the feud seemed in view.

Years later, however (*History of the Franks* 9.19), the feud flared up yet again. Sichar and Chramnesind, now bosom friends, had taken to drinking and eating together, even sleeping in the same bed. One day Sichar, who had drunk a great deal of wine, remarked jovially that Chramnesind would have been penniless had it not been for the fine composition he had received for his various slaughtered relatives. This caused Chramnesind to feel 'sick at heart', and an inner voice spoke to him, saying, 'If I don't avenge my relatives people will call me as weak as a woman, with no further right to be called a man.' Blowing the lights out, he hacked Sichar's skull in two. He then hung the body on a fence, fulfilling a feuding requirement that the outcome of vengeance should be displayed publicly. Finally he fled to King Childebert (*phase three*).

Sichar had been a protégé of Queen Brunechildis, so Chramnesind had every reason to fear the worst. Eventually, however, he succeeded in convincing everybody that he had taken Sichar's life 'for his honour' or 'of necessity' (*super se*) to avenge an affront. (This plea would have been totally inadmissible in an Athenian court of law.) This time the feud really came to an end (*phase four*).

Nothing even remotely similar could possibly have taken place in democratic Athens. Almost without exception, the Attic Orators use the word *timoria* to mean redress obtained by means of legal action against the offender. This raises once again the issue of honour and the law. To a representative of any one of a number of notoriously violent societies (for example, an Albanian shepherd, a Sicilian mafioso, a feuding Frank, Corsican or Montenegrin, or of course Sichar or Austrogisil), retaliating by suing the killer in court would have appeared a travesty of vengeance. The sort of *timoria* that MacDowell and Cohen were talking about is more like a watered-down version of this form of vengeance: 'primitive' vengeance and law courts are a contradiction in terms. 'The conflict between honour and legality', writes Pitt-Rivers, 'is a fundamental one which persists to this day. For to go to law for redress is to confess publicly that you have been wronged and the demonstration of your vulnerability places your honour in jeopardy, a jeopardy from which the "satisfaction" of legal compensation at the hands of a secular authority hardly redeems it. Moreover, it gives your offender the chance to humiliate you further by his attitude during all the delays of court procedure . . .'[40]

In Athens the word *timoria* was used to mean something more like 'punishment'. Punishment is an expression of the communal will and is applied impartially to all members of the citizen body irrespective of status, power or prestige.[41] It differs from 'tribal' vengeance in that its orientation is prospective, not retrospective: its ultimate aim is not to inflict harm in retribution for past wrongdoings, but, as Demosthenes once put it, to protect the community against future ones by means of education: 'Men of Athens, every law is established for two reasons: to deter everyone from doing anything wrong, and to punish wrongdoers to the edification of others' (25.17, *Against Aristogeiton*). Punishment also differs from tribal vengeance in that it forestalls chain reactions of the sort exhibited in Frankish Gaul.

Exactly how the Athenian state forestalled reactions of this sort will be discussed later.[42] For the moment we shall merely say that it used sophisticated structures of communal power to pose a tacit threat to anyone contemplating violent reaction. The composition of the law courts may have acted as an ancillary deterrent, the fact that anything from 201 to

---

[40] Pitt-Rivers 1965: 30; cf. Chapter 5 nn. 27 and 57.
[41] For the penal treatment meted out to metics and foreigners, see Ph. Gauthier (1972) *Symbola. Les étrangers et la justice dans les cités grecques*. Nancy: Annales de L'Est: 136–56.
[42] See pp. 203–6 and Chapter 7.

2,501 people could be required to make up a jury having perhaps been a matter not of coincidence but of design. It may have been meant to convey to the Athenian population the powerful message that anyone who attempted reprisals after being punished by the dikasts would be taking on an entire multitude. The remarkable stability of the Athenian democracy may in part be attributable to the success of the dikast system in preventing the meaning of *timoria* from regressing from 'punishment' to 'vengeance'.

The question of what course conflicts took in classical Athens should therefore be preceded by another: what course might they have taken? The Athenians seem to have known the answer to this question all too well. They must have been aware that only recently in their society had private vengeance given way to public punishment. Aeschylus' *Oresteia*, as we have seen, starts off by representing blood-feud and public punishment as interchangeable means of conflict management, but ends with a didactic celebration of 'the majesty of the civic law'.[43] Plato, like Euphiletus in Lysias 1, rejects the notion of 'mindless revenge' as a sacred duty and introduces the idea of 'rational punishment' in which the passion for revenge is curtailed and sacrificed to the higher interest of the political good (*Protagoras* 324a–b).[44]

Thucydides' description of the civil war in Corcyra identifies revenge as the principal accelerant of the strife (*stasis*; 3.81–2). Once law and order had broken down, Thucydides tells us, a torrent of ungovernable passions burst free, followed by a wave of unheard-of atrocities committed in revenge. 'There was death in every shape and form . . . [P]eople went to every extreme and beyond it. There were fathers who killed their sons; men were dragged from the temples and butchered on the very altars; some were actually walled up in the temple of Dionysus and died there' (3.81). The entire Corcyraean value system was turned upside down by the very different standards that now invaded it: suddenly revenge was all-important, oaths of reconciliation were exchanged only as a temporary measure to ward off immediate difficulties, and any opportunity of catching an enemy

---

[43] Cf. Vlastos 1991: 190.
[44] For punishment in Plato see Mackenzie 1981 and Saunders 1991: 131–2. Saunders' claim elsewhere that the central theme of Protagoras' penology (that the rational punisher looks not to the past, but to the future, in order to deter) 'collides head on with popular orthodoxy' rests on the preconceived notion that the orators claim repeatedly that punishment is inflicted for the sake of the past, so that 'to deny that punishment is or should be backward-looking would seem to them and their audiences a perversion of justice' (Saunders 1981). See, however, Demosthenes 25.17, *Against Aristogeiton* (cited above), the basic argument of Lysias 1, *On the Murder of Eratosthenes*, as seen through the eyes of the dikasts, and Diodotus' remark in Thucydides 3.45 (for which see p. 294), all of which would seem to contradict this generalisation.

off guard was immediately exploited, revenge seeming all the sweeter for having been achieved by duplicitous means.[45] The overall effect of all this was frightful: the least intelligent survived, while anyone sensible enough to hold moderate views speedily perished.

Here we may note that in his discussion of revenge Thucydides follows not the philological method of working out the meanings of key terms (which can in any case change in accordance with changes in the power relationships between the various sections of a population), but rather the behavioural method of inferring moral norms from what people do when faced with choices between alternative courses of action. Nor does he content himself with observing that the Greeks had the option of obtaining satisfaction for their wrongs by prosecuting anyone who insulted or injured them. The idea guiding Thucydides' description is that revenge must be studied both as an individual impulse that can give rise to aggressive behaviour and as a social force that must be kept under control if the delicate balance of the social order is to be preserved. Implicitly, at least, he subscribes to the view, shared by both Aristotle and Demosthenes, that the desire for revenge is innate in (we should add 'the natural') man. He also assumes, however, that in order to take on concrete form revenge must be reinforced, or, as it were, culturally amplified. This is clearly what he believes to have happened during the Corcyraean cataclysm. Alternatively, the powerful drive to revenge, so deeply rooted in human nature, can be culturally attenuated or suppressed within a society. I would suggest that the famous words on the freedom and tolerance of Athenian life that Thucydides attributed to Pericles were written in the knowledge that Athens was just such a society.[46]

We can now identify two patterns of conflict that proceed in different directions. In the first type of conflict a provocation supplied by person A triggers off in his victim, person B, a violent reaction fuelled by the spirit of 'primitive' vengeance. A (or, in the event of his demise, a friend or relative) now rounds up all his closest supporters (kin, friends, clan) and takes revenge on B. This incites B to respond in kind, and so on. Every act of violence supplies a fresh stimulus for revenge. Since there is no central authority powerful enough to intervene and no internal mechanism exists to reconcile the parties, an endless chain of violent acts, killings and counter-killings is set in motion. The seven volumes of the *Scriptores Rerum Merovingiacarum* prompted J. M. Wallace-Hadrill to comment that feuds

---

[45] See pp. 25–6.   [46] See pp. 81–2.

were like volcanoes: 'A few are in eruption, others are extinct, but most are content to rumble now and again and leave us guessing.'[47]

The outlines of a second, alternative pattern of conflict are sketched in a section of Ariston's speech with which we have not yet dealt. This account fully supports Thucydides' diagnosis of the status of revenge in Athenian public life. Having asserted that in demanding satisfaction (*dike*) for the wrongs inflicted upon him by Conon and his sons he is acting entirely according to the law (*kata tous nomous*), Ariston lays before us the rationale for the entire doctrine of self-restraint:

> Why, for my part, I am amazed if they [Conon and his sons] have discovered any excuse or pretext which will make it possible in your court for any man, if convicted of assault and battery, to escape punishment. The laws (*nomoi*) take a far different view, and have provided that even pleas of necessity shall not be pressed too far. For example . . . there are actions for evil-speaking (*kakegorias dikai*); and I am told that these are instituted for this purpose – that men may not be led on, by using abusive language back and forth, to deal blows to one another. Again, there are actions for battery (*aikeias* [*dikai*]); and these, I hear, exist for this reason – that a man, finding himself the weaker party, may not defend himself with a stone or anything of that sort, but may await legal redress. Again, there are public prosecutions for wounding (*traumatos . . . graphai*), to the end that wounds may not lead to murder. The least of these evils, namely abusive language, has, I think, been provided for to prevent the last and most grievous, that murder may not ensue, and that men be not led on step by step from vilification to blows, from blows to wounds, and from wounds to murder, but that in the laws its own penalty (*dike*) should be provided for each of these acts, and that the decision should not be left to the passion (*orge*) or the will (*bouleusis*) of the person concerned. (Demosthenes 54.17–19, *Against Conon*, trans. A. T. Murray)

In other words, laws and the penalties that they prescribe are devices deployed by civic society to keep extreme emotional outbursts in check and to forestall any escalation of trivial conflicts into violent homicidal encounters.

The argument has been put forward that litigation in Athens was some kind of continuation or extension of feuding: 'judges and litigants alike view[ed] the courts as a competitive arena where ongoing conflicts [were] played out, continued, and exacerbated according to the logic characteristic of feuding societies'.[48] Feuding, according to this theory, was built into the polis system. Failure to retaliate was regarded as dishonourable and death with honour was systematically preferred to living in ignoble defeat. For all these reasons, in the view of Cohen, Athenian society may with propriety

---

[47] J. M. Wallace-Hadrill 1962: 143.   [48] D. Cohen 1995a.

be called 'feuding'. In support of this argument he adduces a long list
of cases that supposedly illustrate the Athenian propensity to agonistic
behaviour and feuding and show that enmity, revenge, envy, insult and
honour were central to the appeals made 'to the values of the mass courts of
untrained citizen-judges'.[49] Since the Athenians' fondness for litigation was
'another form of institutionalized aggression' typical of feuding societies,
he concludes, in a 'society like classical Athens, litigation, feud, and politics
were, in a broad sense, inseparable'.[50] He is, however, unable to produce
a single example of genuine feuding in fifth- or fourth-century Athenian
society, or to refute the view that this society was very stable indeed. What
he seems to be saying is that if you scratch the surface of court rhetoric you
will find patterns of feuding behaviour underneath.[51]

The evidence that we have so far inspected, however, seems clearly to
suggest that Athenian litigants thought their mass audiences far more likely
to take their side if they distanced themselves as far as possible from any
suggestion that their actions might have been structured by the logic of
feuding. Litigation in Athens may indeed be viewed as a competitive arena,
but as one in which the competition consisted of demonstrating how little
one's own behaviour had to do with feuding; the more non-feuding characteristics a litigant managed to display, the better his chances of winning
became. When we scratch the surface of Athenian litigation, in other words,
we reveal patterns diametrically opposed to those displayed in feuding.

The evidence that has been marshalled to support the vision of Athenian society as feuding may now be seen to regroup itself around this contention. The 'feuding' argument's strongest claim seems to be that enmity,
revenge, envy, insult, honour and *hybris*, features that are indeed typical
of feuding societies, were central to the appeals made 'to the values of the
mass courts'.[52] These motifs did indeed play a central role in Athenian
litigation, with one small proviso: this central role was 'negative'. In other
words, these motifs surfaced frequently in assertions that, quite unlike
one's opponent, one definitely had *no* such motivation, motives of this

---

[49] D. Cohen 1995a: 87.   [50] D. Cohen 1995a: 101–2, 118.
[51] Three passages should give the gist of Cohen's approach: 'Eschewing, for the most part, direct
homicidal violence, the courts were a natural arena for such contests, and the rhetoric of enmity,
envy, and invective was the primary instrument with which they were waged' (82). 'This notion of
vengeance as a sacred duty enduring through time is typical of *feuding societies*, where male children
are raised to avenge deceased fathers or brothers' (84, my italics). 'In Athens, as will be further seen
in subsequent chapters, the homicidal violence of blood feud appears, for the most part, to have
been displaced into other arenas. The form which vengeance takes in *Against Agoratus* is not the
shedding of blood, but prosecution for a capital offense' (84).
[52] D. Cohen 1995a: 87.

sort being generally *out of place* in a city such as Athens. No refutation has yet been produced of the assertion that no litigant in the surviving speeches seems ever to have expected to enlist the support of the dikasts by parading himself as insulting, hubristic and possessed of an inflated sense of honour, or as prompted by envy, hatred, or even a passionate desire for revenge.[53] Instead, he would attempt to prove that his civic-minded ideals were the very antithesis of 'feuding' characteristics. Characteristics of this sort do indeed feature largely in the speeches because they were so frequently attributed to an opponent. The characteristics that the litigants ascribed to themselves were self-restraint, moderation, meekness, a deflated sense of honour, lack of any aggressive or explosive disposition and subordination to the law and to the unwritten rules of civic existence.[54] They represented themselves, in other words, as quite undismayed at the prospect of compromising the sort of principle that states that it is better to die with honour than to live ignobly in defeat.[55]

We are now in a position to summarise our findings, introducing a further qualification into our sketch of the Athenian code of behaviour. Unlike the members of genuinely feuding societies, who are generally characterised by their violent and supposedly ungovernable tempers, the people of democratic Athens seem overall to have been of an unusually mild temper. (Small wonder that they were proverbial for their gentleness, self-restraint, moderation and generosity.)[56] The threshold for taking offence was high in Athens and responses to insult or injury were low key. Victims of aggression were expected to refrain from impulsive reaction and behave rationally, subordinating any violent impulse to considerations of communal utility. These expectations were very unlike the dictates of the

---

[53] I propose not to consider the plaintiffs' claim in [Demosthenes] 59, *Against Neaera*, that they have sued the defendants partly because they wish to avenge two grievous wrongs as an instance of 'passionate desire for revenge' because its factual correlate was a judicial procedure and because this wish was allegedly tempered by concern for public welfare.

[54] This is also true of cases involving far lesser antagonisms. Consider, for instance, the following comment: 'But I, as it is, the more gentleness (*praoteron*) and consideration (*philanthropoteron*) I used in talking with the defendant, the more contempt he showed toward me (*katephronei*)' (Demosthenes 41.2, *Against Spudias*).

[55] The rest of Cohen's arguments to the effect that Athenian litigation resembled feuding are so weak as not to merit consideration. For example, the claim that 'litigation represents a public arena in which personal ambitions and competing efforts to contrive relations and rights can be expressed and legitimated' (Cohen 1995a: 21) is so general as to apply not only to Athens and the Tswana, as Cohen suggests, but also to the trial of O. J. Simpson. Nor is it possible to take seriously the suggestion that the pre-existence of a state of enmity between the litigants, or the use of the legal process as a weapon against an opponent, should be regarded as a mark of a feuding society: it is hard to envisage a legal system free of such abuses.

[56] See pp. 109–16.

'tribal' code of behaviour, which enjoins upon the provoked or injured a duty to retaliate rapidly, violently and at all costs, preferably inflicting an injury much greater than the provocation or offence that triggered off the conflict. The Athenian code of behaviour prescribed that upon being provoked, offended or injured a citizen should show respect for the communal system by exercising self-restraint, reconsidering (or re-negotiating) the case and ultimately compromising.

The upshot of all this is that we are witnessing a revolution (or shall we say a cognitive re-orientation?) in the history of moral ideas. At its heart lay not so much the renunciation of revenge as a strategy for the conduct of human affairs as an access of pride in discarding macho behaviour.[57] Self-restraint and moderation were no longer viewed as marks of cowardice, a change that we may express better using a paradox: if we define honour in terms of the 'threshold principle' that we outlined earlier, the idea that now gained ground was that honour might be acquired by acting dishonourably. In a remarkable turnaround, Athenian public opinion succeeded in turning the new sort of 'honour' into a virtue that the citizens were willing to embrace. This sea change manifests itself in Euphiletus' proud claim to have avoided any macho behaviour[58] and in the words that Thucydides puts into the mouth of Nicias, the general renowned above all for his prudence: '. . . just as in the past I have never spoken against my convictions in order to gain honour, so I shall not deny it now, but I shall tell you what I think is for the best' (6.9.2).

To re-state this point even more forcefully, I shall conclude this section with a conditional clause underscoring its logical structure. This refers to the traditional twentieth-century view of revenge in Athenian society, perhaps best exemplified by the passage from Kitto that was cited earlier:[59] 'A man owes it to himself to be revenged; to put up with an injury would imply that the other man was "better" than you are.'[60] If this theory were correct, then Athenian litigants should have attempted to win their cases by appealing to the irresistible imperative of the *point d'honneur*, or by referring to the indisputable justness of revenge. Since, however, they did no such thing, instead appealing to an unexpectedly good-natured, forgiving and

---

[57] Cf. Herman 1995, 1996a. Albeit by quite different methods, Fisher 1992 reaches conclusions not far removed from mine (which he then rejects in Fisher 1998). The people we are discussing were trying to win the sympathy of the dikasts by pretending to have exercised self-restraint. At the same time, however, they were trying to humiliate their opponents by exposing them as *hybristai* (people who, because of their inappropriately inflated senses of honour, had inflicted dishonour and shame upon others). This points once again to the conclusion that according to the moral standards of the dikasts undue concern with honour was 'bad'.

[58] See pp. 181–2.   [59] See p. 93.   [60] Kitto 1969: 243–7.

non-militant behavioural code (contrast the Kitto passage with the claim of the speaker in Lysias' *Against Simon* to have put up with a whole series of insults, molestations and injuries, preferring 'to go without satisfaction for these offences rather than be thought lacking in sense by the citizens' (3.9)), it can only be concluded that there is something very wrong with this theory. By setting behaviour in ancient Athens alongside behaviour in societies of the type in whose light she should, according to many modern scholars, be understood, I have tried in the last sections to show precisely what.

PRINCIPLES AND ACTUAL BEHAVIOUR

This interpretation of the evidence is contentious; it could (and probably will) be argued that it is entirely erroneous. It all sounds so unlikely. It runs counter to most human expectations and to primitive man's basic responses, developed by evolutionary forces to meet the challenge of extreme conditions: 'the potential to mobilize an intense fight-or-flight response, to react aggressively to challenge without undue hesitation, to be at heightened alert for danger and to produce robust stress responses that facilitate recovery from injury'.[61] Perhaps we have been misled by these masters of rhetoric. Perhaps the speakers in the forensic speeches were appealing not to real-life norms, but to idealised ones that existed only in a fantasy world, or in a purely artificial and ineffective facade of opinions that we might call 'the official version'. According to this view, the idea that retaliation was a crime and failure to retaliate a virtue would have been a complete sham, a rhetorical trick pulled by the speakers to bamboozle their audiences. Concealed behind its facade, it might be said, another code was at work, one that defined successful retaliation as a tremendous satisfaction and failure to retaliate as an intolerable act of cowardice. It might, in other words, be argued that this was a classic case of double standards: everybody paid lip-service to the 'official version', but nobody actually took a blind bit of notice of it.

Everything we know of Athenian society, however, militates against this interpretation of the evidence. Our sources reveal a multiplicity of signs that the code to which the speakers were appealing was real, influencing Athenian life more profoundly than any rival moral code. The tenets of this code were, for a start, repeatedly and confidently enunciated before the

---

[61] Cf. M. H. Teicher (2002) 'Scars that won't heal: the neurobiology of child abuse', *Scientific American*, March: 61.

law courts, arguably the most powerful institution in the entire political system. The court's approval or disapproval of this approach was, moreover, often literally a matter of life or death to the accused. In such a position no man could well afford to appeal to values that other members of his society were likely to reject out of hand as polite fantasies. Finally, such appeals were addressed to the dikasts, a fairly representative sample of the entire citizen population. If *they* had assimilated this code as a basic guide to behaviour, it is reasonable to assume that the majority of other citizens had done likewise.

The acceptance that this code of behaviour seems to have achieved in the law courts implies an attempt to reject or delegitimate the antithetical 'death before dishonour' code, particularly in cases in which this code would have demanded quick over-retaliation and 'mindless' revenge. In genuinely feuding societies it is the principles of action of this code that fuel certain violent practices and institutions such as the blood-feud, the vendetta and the duel. If we conclude that Athens had indeed rejected the 'rather death than dishonour' principle, then, the implications for our investigation of actual behaviour are considerable, since in repudiating this principle a society also rejects blood-feud and its like.

Our inquiry now reaches a critical stage. We have considered a number of accounts of behaviour in circumstances of conflict that have created a picture at odds not only with some basic postulates of twentieth-century classical scholarship, but also with the sort of behaviour that many anthropologists would expect to encounter in a pre-industrial Mediterranean society. Since our results appear so incompatible with the accepted wisdom, we should perhaps stop for a moment to contemplate the consequences of our findings and to cross-check the results of our analysis against evidence from sources other than the Attic Orators, asking ourselves how far this evidence bears out the theory that the principles professed in the Athenian law courts were also put into practice.[62] How did the Athenians really behave? To what extent were the high-flown ideals of self-restraint that were so frequently aired in the popular courts visible in their actions? If an attempt had indeed been made to delegitimate the blood-feud, the vendetta and other violence-generating institutions, had it been crowned with success?

This investigation must begin with a warning. Our access to Athenian social life through sources other than the Attic Orators is very limited indeed. Nothing even remotely similar to modern newspapers existed, no statistics were recorded and certain issues are painfully under-documented

[62] See p. 16.

(for example, domestic violence, which in Classical Athens included the maltreatment of slaves). We do, however, have at our disposal the works of a great many historians, playwrights and philosophers and a considerable number of inscriptions, public and private, all of which may help us to sketch out the social profile of Athens. Any aspect of social behaviour whose manifestation on the macro level of society can with reasonable certainty be taken to imply that highly developed codes of honour were prevalent on its micro level will, of course, be of particular interest to us. Our aim is now to find out just how violent Athenian society appeared to our other sources, and at which point along our imaginary spectrum we should therefore locate it.[63]

If we are to answer this question we have first to define violence, which is no simple matter. The question of where to draw the line between violent and non-violent behaviour has been hotly disputed.[64] In everyday conversation, even picking a pocket or hurling abuse may be classified as violent. In this case I suggest that we should define a violent act as one that deliberately inflicts bodily injury on another person either by physical force or by the administration of some harmful substance. Theft and abuse are significant acts, but it is by no means clear that in any given society their levels are directly related to levels of physical injury. On the contrary, a good case could be made for considering abuse, at least, to be a sublimation of physical violence in which verbal injury is substituted for physical damage.[65]

I also propose to exclude from our definition state-inflicted violence such as the torture and executions carried out by the Eleven in ancient Athens. In centralised political societies state-inflicted violence differs qualitatively from other forms of violence.[66] It is, in the first place, communally sanctioned and (unlike other forms of violence) deemed legitimate. It is, moreover, a mechanism that has been communally designed and systematically applied with the aim of reducing other forms of violence and thus ensuring political stability. State-inflicted violence may thus more profitably be treated as a form of moralistic and disciplinary aggression designed to enforce societal rules.

Another difficulty confronting our investigation concerns the evidence. Even in societies in which documentation is abundant and accessible, rates of violence are difficult to assess. The reasons for this are manifold and complex, but one of them is simply that many violent acts take place without leaving any trace in the records. Criminologists and historians therefore use

---

[63] See pp. 82, 160–1.   [64] Cf. Hogg and Vaughan 1995: ch. 11.
[65] See pp. 303–9.   [66] See pp. 221–8.

as an indicator that violent act whose traces are most difficult to conceal and whose documentation is consequently most reliable: murder. Homicide rates are expressed per 100,000 population per annum; it is broadly assumed that the higher the homicide rate, the more violent the society in which it occurs.[67]

Paucity of data affects homicide no more and no less than it affects anything else. The evidence of the Attic Orators and of various historians and philosophers gives us sixteen cases of confirmed or possible homicide that took place during the period between 507 and 322 in Athens, in her *chora*, Attica, or in some part of her fifth-century empire (see **Fig. 6.2**). Statistically this smattering of cases is of negligible value. We have no way of telling how many murders took place in Athens either in any single year or during the whole of the period under discussion. Murder rates thus cannot be used as evidence either that the non-retaliation rhetoric was a sham or that Athenian society was deeply violent. This is why it is unreasonable to dismiss the rhetoric of self-restraint or non-retaliation on the grounds that it was produced within the context of actual or suspected physical violence. If we conclude that, for example, Euphiletus' attempt to appear as a rational-minded civic official 'does not count' because it was made within the context of murder, we are falling victim to what statisticians call the availability error: the temptation to rely on anything that is immediately available, dramatic and evocative of strong emotions, ignoring the fact that it is a tiny part of a wider phenomenon most of which is obscured from view.[68]

There is only one type of murder for which we do have reliable figures: politically motivated assassination. If we except the assassination of Ephialtes, the entire democracy witnessed virtually no killings (or indeed woundings) of this sort. This, by any standards, is a truly remarkable record.

HOW VIOLENT WAS ATHENIAN SOCIETY?

Having expressed these reservations, we may proceed to try and evaluate the amount of violence in Athenian society.[69] Clearly there must have been plenty. Athens was no paradise on earth; nor is there much point in judging her by superhuman standards. The question here is one of degree. Every single piece of evidence at our disposal apart from the stories of violent encounters relayed to us by the Attic Orators would seem to suggest that in the period under discussion Athens was a remarkably peaceful society,

---

[67] Stone 1983.   [68] For the availability error, see Sutherland 1992: ch. 2.
[69] Cf. Herman 1994.

No.	REFERENCE	VICTIM OR INTENDED VICTIM	MEANS USED	REMARKS
1.	Antiphon 1	Philoneus	poison	speech possibly academic exercise
2.	Antiphon 1	stepmother's husband	poison	speech possibly academic exercise
3.	Antiphon 5.34, 48	slave	unknown	'execution'
4.	Antiphon 5.26	Herodes	stone	as stated by a slave
5.	Antiphon 6	Diodotus	poison	accidental killing?
6.	Antiphon 5.69	a slave's master	*machaira*	attempted murder
7.	Demosthenes 21.74	Euaeon	fists?	
8.	Demosthenes 21.107	Nicodemus	unknown	
9.	Demosthenes 22.2	Diodorus' father	unknown	insinuation of parricide
10.	Demosthenes 47.59, 67	old nurse	hands	unintentional homicide
11.	Demosthenes 59.10	Aphidnaean (slave?) woman	*autocheiria*	cf. A.R.Harrison 1971, vol. II: 40
12.	Demosthenes 58.28–9	Theocrines' brother	*biaoi thanatoi*	homicide faked
13.	Isaeus 9	Euthycrates	fists?	intra-familial killing
14.	Lysias 1	Eratosthenes	knife?	re-defined as 'execution'
15.	Isocrates 18.52	slave-woman	fists?	homicide faked
16.	Plato, *Euthyphro* 4c–d	Naxian free labourer (himself a murderer)	tied up and abandoned in ditch	death caused by negligence

Figure 6.2 Homicide in Attica, c. 507–322 BC
For a synopsis of the Athenian homicide speeches, see Carawan 1998: 390–2. The list above does not include 'political' murders.

exhibiting considerably less violence than modern research has postulated and also considerably less than an examination of other contemporary societies would suggest. We shall now consider some of the evidence that supports this contention.

To start with, random glimpses of Athenian day-to-day life tend to confirm Thucydides' observation that the people of Athens had adopted a relaxed way of living and went about unarmed.[70] In the beautiful opening scene of the *Republic* (whose evidential value is, as we have seen,[71] increased by the fact that Plato's purpose in writing it was by no means to discuss Athenian violence), Socrates and his companion are strolling near Athens without any apparent fear for their personal safety. Brigands do appear to have given the Athenian legal system some cause for concern (some of the Theseus myths may suggest that they had caused considerable trouble in the pre-democratic past), but Socrates and his friends do not seem to have regarded them as much of a threat.[72] Nor does Lysias, the metic speech-writer who kept a chest full of coins and precious objects in his house (Lysias 12.10, *Against Eratosthenes*), seem to have worried overmuch about being robbed. This seems particularly remarkable in the light of the experiences of Heinrich Schliemann, who was so appalled by the kidnapping and murder of some foreign visitors by brigands near Marathon in 1870 that he decided that the Greek countryside was simply too dangerous for him to carry out his planned excavations at Mycenae and moved on to Troy.[73]

Socrates' sense of security may have been increased by the long walls that until 404 surrounded both the city and the Peiraeus, separating this area from the rest of Attica (see **Fig. 2.4**). It may well be that the area inside the walls was safe, whereas that outside them was still infested with brigands and highwaymen, just as it had been in the old days. The sense of security of any given group of (settled) people is generally expressed in its domestic architecture, fortifications and other measures designed to deal with sudden attacks bespeaking feelings of precariousness. In the Middle Ages, for example, when chronic wars, constant attacks by dangerous rabbles and the perpetual threat of harsh and unreliable justice induced a general feeling of insecurity, a warrior's home was simultaneously his watchtower, his fortress and a base from which to launch his own attacks.[74] The same sort of architecture is found in more modern regions in which peace has never reliably been established. The Athenian *dema* house, however, expressed the atmosphere of a peaceful countryside, just as the houses inside the long walls (see **Figs. 2.5** and **5.1**) expressed that of a peaceful urban centre. 'We have many ways of winding down after hard work . . .' wrote Thucydides.

---

[70] See pp. 133–4.   [71] See pp. 121–2.
[72] The term used to designate brigands in *The Athenian Constitution* (52.1) is *lopodutai*. See D. Cohen 1983 for a demonstration that *lopodusia* signified stripping garments from a person by force or violence, a much milder form of attack than modern 'brigandry' or 'highway robbery'. For a survey of 'organised crime' in Classical Athens, which despite its title reaches conclusions similar to the one above, see Fisher 1999.
[73] See D. Traill (1995) *Schliemann of Troy*, Harmondsworth: Penguin: 80.   [74] Elias 1978b: 233.

'The good taste and elegance that we find at home are a constant delight to us, putting stress to flight' (2.38). Some of the country homes that have been reconstructed by archaeologists do, it should be said, include towers.[75] The function of these towers has never been agreed upon,[76] but for the purposes of our argument it is sufficient to note that many country houses were built without any sort of defence. This can only mean that their residents expected to live safe and peaceful lives, just as Thucydides suggests. The defences provided by the state must thus have been perceived as sufficient reassurance, again demonstrating the protective aspect of its power.

Plato's description implies that Socrates and his companion went for their stroll unarmed, which fits in with Thucydides' observation that the people of Athens were the first to give up the habit of bearing arms.[77] The forensic speeches, whose speakers all appear reluctant to admit to carrying or using any weapon, point in the same direction. Euphiletus, as we have seen, describes the lead-up to the killing of Eratosthenes in great detail, but omits any reference to the fatal weapon.[78] That he did in fact take some sort of weapon with him emerges only obliquely, from the phrase 'for how could I tell whether he too [Eratosthenes] had some weapon (*siderion*)?' (Lysias 1.42, *On the Murder of Eratosthenes*). This apparent lack of interest in deadly hardware is significant, since in societies abounding in 'flamboyant virility complexes' men tend to take great pride in their weapons and amass vast collections of firearms, daggers, knives and swords, preferably decorative and encrusted with gems.[79]

The typical Athenian litigant does not appear to have been at all interested in the impressiveness or otherwise of one's *siderion*. An anonymous defendant, charged with wounding with intent to kill, argues that not even his alleged victim has accused him of coming at him with anything like a dagger (*encheiridion*): 'he only says he was struck by a potsherd' (*ostrako*; Lysias 4.6, *On a Wound by Premeditation*). Another speaker accuses his opponent, Nicostratus, of having attacked him with his fists ([Demosthenes] 53.17, *Against Nicostratus*). The plaintiff in the Conon case does not specify any weapon at all, even though some of the violent scenes described in his speech took place while the people involved were on garrison duty.[80] Of the sixteen cases of actual, alleged or imagined homicide

---

[75] Cf. Wycherley 1978: 247.
[76] See, for instance, Lohmann 1992. In [Demosthenes] 47.56 (*Against Euergus*), female slaves (*therapainai*) are said to live in the farmhouse tower (*pyrgos*).
[77] See pp. 133–4.　　[78] See p. 178.
[79] The phrase in inverted commas is borrowed from Gilmore 1987b: 16.　　[80] See pp. 123–4, 156.

listed in **Fig. 6.2**, only five can be said with any degree of certainty to have involved weapons. (Six of the attackers definitely killed, or are said to have killed, their victims with their bare hands; in four other cases it is unknown whether or not the aggressor used any weapon.) This is in line with the conclusions that we drew from our last set of examples, particularly if we bear in mind the distinction between premeditated and unpremeditated acts of aggression (a distinction that is not made in feuding societies).

We may therefore risk the generalisation that in Athens and in its immediate surroundings people did not tend to worry overmuch about their safety and went about unarmed just as Thucydides suggests. Of course, murders and other violent acts could have been and undoubtedly were committed using only bare hands, potsherds, stones, sticks or clubs, but the habitual carrying of knives or swords would clearly have increased both the number of physical injuries incurred in unexpected violent encounters and their gravity. Comparative studies indicate a close correlation between the availability of weapons and the incidence of violence in a society. There is a striking contrast between the scarcity of weapons in hostile encounters in Athens and their omnipresence in, for example, European disagreements from the early sixteenth to the late eighteenth century.[81] Throughout this period European gentlemen in civilian dress wore weapons as a badge of status and resorted to them enthusiastically whenever their circumstances appeared to them to require it. As Lawrence Stone put it, 'tempers were short and weapons to hand'. The author of the enchanting sixteenth-century *Book of the Courtier* tells us that 'there happen oftentimes variances between one gentleman and another, whereupon ensueth a combat. And many times it shall stand him in stead to use the weapon that he hath at that instant by his side, wherefore it is safest to know how to use it . . . The fame of the gentleman that carrieth weapon, if it once be tarnished with cowardice, or any other reproach, doth evermore continue shameful in the world'.[82]

Lawrence Stone chose the following glimpse of seventeenth-century England at random to convey an impression of the level of violence in that society: 'John Aubrey, the son of a squire in Wiltshire in the seventeenth century, was nearly killed three times in his life by the thrust of a sword: once in a London street by a drunk he had never seen before; once during

[81] For the more or less constant carrying of weapons during this period, see A. V. B. Norman (1980) *The Rapier and Small Sword, 1460–1820*. London: Arno Press: 19–31.

[82] Baldasar Castiglione, *Il libro del Cortegiano*, L.xx, L.xvii, trans. Sir Thomas Hoby, 1561.

a quarrel among friends in legal chambers in the Inner Temple; and once by the Earl of Pembroke at a disorderly parliamentary election . . . '[83]

Here we see a pattern that reappears with striking regularity in feuding societies. The general resort to daggers during the civil war in Corcyra (a step implicitly condemned by Thucydides 3.70.6) plunged the city into a succession of murders and marked the final collapse of the political order. Stephen Wilson, the historian of nineteenth-century Corsica, remarks that '. . . male honour demanded that men be armed . . . The possession of firearms (which did not preclude also owning and using daggers) meant that quarrels could quickly lead to serious violence and killing'.[84] Boehm, an American anthropologist and fieldworker in Montenegro, wrote that during the 1960s Montenegrin men were fond of letting off pistols while dancing, with the result that there were generally bullet holes in the ceiling after a wedding. The birth of a son demanded exploding dynamite.[85]

Above all, the availability or non-availability of weapons affects the dynamics of crowd behaviour. If everybody is bristling with weapons, the most petty of conflicts tends to escalate rapidly. The following episode from Gregory of Tours' *History of the Franks* reveals a society in which arms were carried (and resorted to) without any inhibition whatsoever:

[A] great quarrel arose between Priscus and a certain Phatyr, one of the converted Jews, who was godson to the King in that Chilperic had sponsored him at his baptism. One Jewish Sabbath Priscus was on his way to the synagogue, with his head bound in a kerchief and carrying no weapon in his hand, for he was about to pray according to the Mosaic law. Phatyr appeared from nowhere, drew his sword, cut Priscus' throat and killed his companions. When they all lay dead, Phatyr took refuge in the church of Saint Julian, together with his servants who had been waiting in a near-by square. There they remained in sanctuary, but they heard that the King, while prepared to spare their master's life, had given orders that they themselves should be dragged out of the church and executed. One of them drew his sword. Phatyr immediately fled, but the man killed all his associates and rushed out of the church, with his weapon still in his hand. The mob fell upon him and he was cruelly done to death. Phatyr received permission to return to Guntram's kingdom, whence he had come. A few days later he was killed in his turn by some of the relations of Priscus. (6.17, trans. L. Thorpe)

Let us now compare this account with Lysias' description of a street brawl in *Against Simon* (a speech, it will be remembered, having to do with homosexual rivalry for the favours of a slave boy).[86] Having told the dikasts

---

[83] Stone 1983: 25. [84] S. Wilson 1988: 92–3. [85] Boehm 1984: 28. [86] See pp. 165–7.

that following Simon's alleged mistreatment of him he took the boy abroad in order to avoid a fight (3.32), the speaker continues,

When I thought I had left it long enough for Simon to have forgotten all about the boy and thought better of his own bad behaviour, I came back [from abroad] and went to the Peiraeus. Simon, however, found out in no time that Theodotus [the slave-boy] was back and staying with Lysimachus (who lives near the house that Simon was renting), and invited some of his friends round. While they were having a boozy lunch they left a look-out on the roof so that they could grab the boy as soon as he came out. I came back from the Peiraeus around then and dropped in on Lysimachus. After spending a little while there we [i.e. the speaker and Theodotus] left, whereupon this already drunken crew jumped us. Some of them didn't want anything to do with it, but Simon here, Theophilus, Protarchus and Autocles started dragging the boy off [i.e. towards Simon's house]. Theodotus, however, managed to wriggle out of his cloak and run away . . . All I wanted was to keep out of their way, since every time I came across them it had been a complete personal disaster, so I took myself off down another street. . . The boy then took refuge in a fuller's shop, but these men burst in *en masse* and overpowered him, while he yelled out and shouted to the bystanders to be his witnesses. A lot of people came running to express hearty disapproval of what they called outrageous behaviour. These men didn't care, and beat Molon the fuller and some others up badly for trying to protect the lad. They had got as far as Lampon's house when I, walking along on my own, ran into them. Since it would have been monstrous of me to stand by and let them maltreat a young boy in this violent and illegal way, I grabbed hold of him and demanded to know why they were doing so. They refused to answer, but let him go and started hitting me instead. There was then a fight (*mache*), council members, with the boy throwing things at them in self-defence while they threw things at us and went on beating him up drunkenly. I was defending myself. Other people on the scene had decided that we were the victims and weighed in on our side. During this brawl (*thorubos*) we all got our heads cut open. (3.10–18)

The difference between these conflicts can be summarised in two sentences. In Gaul the omnipresence of weapons and the absence of anything like self-restraint resulted in a bloodbath. In Athens the absence of any weapons more deadly than hands or stones, coupled with the active spirit of self-restraint (note how the speaker attributes all the violent behaviour to Simon and his party, while passing himself off as a passive victim who was merely defending himself and the boy), meant that a large-scale brawl ended only in a few none too serious injuries. A further crucial difference is that although the disagreement in Athens led to a court case, its physical part ended with the fight; no revenge attacks followed.

One of the spectres that haunt feuding societies is the escalation of petty conflicts into major civil wars. Aristotle included this process in his discussion of circumstances likely to give rise to revolutions (*staseis*; *Politics* 1304a15–20) and the passage from *Against Conon* cited earlier reveals that the people of Athens were well aware of the phenomenon by accurately describing the progressive escalation of conflict from abusive language through blows and wounds to murder (Demosthenes 54.19).[87] Between AD 1200 and 1500 riots sparked off by what contemporaries called *furori* and *rumori* (the excessively violent tempers of many of the citizens) were a regular occurrence in Italian cities.[88] At a lesser remove from the world of democratic Athens, Tacitus' account of a gladiatorial show in Roman Italy in AD 59 relates how an exchange of uncomplimentary chants between rival spectators from the colonies of Nuceria and Pompeii escalated into an appalling massacre. The verbal abuse led to stone-throwing, whereupon the swords (*ferrum*) started to come out. The home crowd, the Pompeiians, got the best of the bloodbath that ensued; many of the Nucerian visitors were taken home injured or mutilated, and many others never came home at all.[89]

If our analysis of Athenian ideals and the Athenian reality is correct, we must conclude that even if this sort of violence was not entirely absent from democratic Athens it was significantly less usual there. This conjecture is supported by the fact that the Athenians did not go in for keeping private armies of retainers and by a number of Thucydides' descriptions of crowd behaviour. As Hunter observes in two highly original articles, Thucydides tends to depict crowds as volatile, emotional and violent.[90] Despite this tendency to emphasise the disagreeable aspects of crowd behaviour, however, his works contain no mention of fights between Athenian mobs, or of riots or factional battles sparked off by trivial incidents. Thucydides may, of course, be offering us no more than a partial reflection of Athenian reality. His testimony nonetheless suggests that we may consider this much established: that although this sort of violence was a common pattern in Corsica and in the Italian cities, in Classical Athens it was not.

All these concrete examples allow us to observe the ideal of self-restraint as paraded in the law courts from a different angle. What the speakers are saying is that the individual should keep his own wishes in check by exercising reason, and reflect upon his actions sufficiently to curb his impulses, in

---

[87] See p. 199.   [88] Herlihy 1972: 130.
[89] Tacitus, *Annals* 14.17; see Nippel 1995: 90 for literature on the subject. For 'jealousies' springing up from trifling causes, 'as is common with the Cretans', and bringing about fateful divisions, see Polybius 4.53.
[90] Hunter 1986; 1988–9.

order to secure the long-term benefit of communal stability. This association between impulsive action and its long-term consequences often appears in moral injunctions such as 'Weigh the matter carefully while there is yet time, without anger and without prejudice (*met'orges kai diaboles*): for they are the worst of counsellors; it is impossible for an angry man (*orgizomenos anthropos*) to make a right decision, as anger destroys his one instrument of decision, his judgement (*ten gnomen*)' (Antiphon 5.71–2, *On the Murder of Herodes*, trans. K. J. Maidment). The dreadful consequences of lack of moderation were probably also imprinted on the minds of the Athenians by cautionary tales such as that of the city of Miletus, in which the rich and the poor regarded each other with intense animosity. The corrupting influence of unbridled luxury in the one case and of resentment in the other eventually left both groups completely incapable of exercising any sort of reasonable self-control (*to epieikes*). At one point the ordinary people seized power and threw the rich out of the city. They then herded together the exiles' children on the threshing-floors and used oxen to trample them to death, a horrible end. Later on, when the rich regained the upper hand, they retaliated by tarring and burning to death every one of their enemies they could get hold of, children and all (Athenaeus, *Deipnosophistae* 13.523f–524b).

The fact that the democratic Athenians were alive to the possible consequences of lack of moderation may have had something to do with the fact that their two civil wars, both of external origin, were short-lived. One of these civil wars, moreover, was the occasion for the supreme expression of the tolerance and conciliatory spirit that Thucydides regarded as one of the characteristic features of democracy:[91] following the restoration of democracy after the oligarchic coup of 404, the democrats did not seize the opportunity to repay the oligarchs' acts of injustice with extreme or even moderate vengeance, but chose instead to forgive and forget.[92]

We are now in a position to summarise our findings. The Athenian spirit of self-restraint was no orator's fantasy or 'official version'; its objective existence is confirmed by other evidence pertaining to behaviour on the macro level of Athenian society. All this evidence is consistent with the content of the law-court speeches. Had our outside evidence suggested a high incidence of violent attacks and revenge killings, or even the faintest hint of vendettas, blood-feuds or duels, we should have had to suspect that

---

[91] See p. 82.   [92] The amnesty of 403 is explored at length at pp. 396–8.

our analysis of the law-court speeches was flawed. Since it does not, we must conclude that this spirit of self-restraint was a palpable and effective influence that was actively involved in shaping communal life. It is now time to explore the general power matrix within which the individual behaviour that we have been examining took place, or, more precisely, the nature of the state power structure within which private revenge was converted into state-inflicted punishment.

CHAPTER 7

The coercive power of the state

THEORIES OF SOVEREIGNTY

In order to examine the power structure of the Athenian state in depth we shall first turn to the theory of sovereignty, which, in conjunction with its inevitable complement, the concept of state, lies at the heart of modern political thinking. Since making its first appearance in the sixteenth century this theory, formulated in various ways, has been applied to the analysis of many very different political systems, ranging from despotic governments to communities of people governed by law. According to Jean Bodin, the state is sovereign because it gives orders to all and receives orders from none.[1] Hobbes interpreted sovereignty as an agreement by which absolute power is irrevocably conferred on a ruler.[2] Thomas Paine wrote that the sovereign power of 'republics such as there are established in America' was 'a power over which there is no control, and which controls all others'.[3] William Blackstone thought it self-evident that every state should be governed by a supreme, irresistible, absolute and uncontrolled authority in which the *jura summa imperii*, or right of sovereignty, resided.[4] According to Thomas Cooley, 'sovereignty as applied to states imports the supreme, absolute, uncontrollable power by which any state is governed'.[5] More recently, Harold Laski has defined the national state as 'a society . . . which is integrated by possessing a coercive authority legally supreme over any individual or group which is part of the society' and identified this supreme coercive

---

[1] J. Bodin (1992) *On Sovereignty: Four Chapters from the Six Books of the Commonwealth* (ed. J. H. Franklin). Original edition 1576. Cambridge: Cambridge University Press.
[2] Hobbes 1983, esp. part 2.
[3] Th. Paine (1945) *The Complete Writings of Thomas Paine* (ed. P. S. Foner). New York: Citadel Press: 369.
[4] W. Blackstone (1973) *The Sovereignty of the Law. Selections from Blackstone's Commentaries on the Laws of England* (ed. G. Jones), esp. 34–7. Original edition 1865–9. London: University of Toronto Press.
[5] T. M. Cooley (1903) *A Treatise on the Constitutional Limitations which Rest upon the Legislative Powers of the States of the American Union.* 7th edn. Boston, Mass.: Little, Brown: 1.

power with sovereignty.[6] Summarising a further half-century of debate on the subject, Tilly characterised states as 'coercion-wielding organizations that are distinct from households and kinship groups and exercise clear priority in some respects over all other organizations within substantial territories'.[7] Definitions of this term may thus vary in wording and emphasis (about six basic meanings have been identified as having been attributed to it by philosophers through the ages[8]), but all of them share a single kernel. This is the idea that Crick formulated, simply and beautifully, as follows: 'in every system of government there must be some absolute power of final decision exercised by some person or body recognised both as competent to decide and as able to enforce the decision'.[9]

The term 'sovereignty' itself may be relatively new,[10] but the idea behind it is old, going back to Classical antiquity. The question of who exercised supreme power within the state engaged the attention of Greek political theorists too. It has been said that 'every book on political science, from the *Republic* of Plato and the *Politics* of Aristotle, has dealt with or touched sovereignty'[11] and it is more than probable that the authors cited above turned frequently to the Greek texts, even though none has retained the Greek terms most frequently used to express the idea (the adjective *kyrios* and the verb *kratein*, with their derivatives).[12] Plato conceived of the state as a single aggregated human personality whose fundamentally unanimous will he identified as sovereignty.[13] Aristotle echoed him, writing that a state's magistrates should be the subordinates of the properly constituted laws that should be sovereign (Plato, *Laws* 4.715d; Aristotle, *Politics* 1282b13). Elsewhere Aristotle classified states according to the quality and number of the person or persons in whom the state's supreme power (*to kyrion tes*

---

[6] Laski 1935: 21.

[7] C. Tilly (1990) *Coercion, Capital and European States, AD 990–1990*. Oxford: Basil Blackwell: 1.

[8] These are, according to Rees 1956: (1) a supreme legal authority; (2) a supreme legal authority insofar as it is also a completely moral authority; (3) a supreme coercive power exercised by a determinate body of persons possessing a monopoly of certain instruments of coercion; (4) a supreme coercive power exercised habitually and co-operatively by all, or nearly all, the members of a community; (5) the strongest political influence; (6) a permanently supreme authority, power or influence.

[9] Crick 1968: 77. The concept of the polis entertained by F. H. Hinsley ((1986) *Sovereignty*. Cambridge: Cambridge University Press) is skewed to such an extent as to pre-empt any useful analysis.

[10] It probably derives from the Vulgar Latin *superanus*, via the Old French *sovrain* and the Italian *sovran*. For the view of an alternative school that seeks to derive it from the mediaeval Latin word *supremitas*, i.e. *suprema potestas*, see W. W. Skeat (1910) *Etymological Dictionary* s.v. 'Sovereignty'. Revised edition. Oxford: The Clarendon Press.

[11] J. MacDonell (1911) 'Sovereignty', *Encyclopaedia Britannica*, 11th edn, London, vol. 25: 519–23, at 523.

[12] The Romans expressed the idea in terms derived from a different tradition of power and authority, e.g. *summa rerum potestas* and *summum imperium*.

[13] This is a concept developed by Barker 1960, esp. 201.

poleos) resided: a tyrant, a single man who was 'best of all', the 'better sort of men', the wealthy, or the people (*to plethos*) as a whole. When supreme power was vested in the people as a whole, he suggested, a constitution should be classed as democratic (*Politics* 1281a12).

Aristotle's formula was a popular one, to judge by the number of permutations of and variations upon it that appear in ancient writings. *The Athenian Constitution* described the constitution established in Athens after the return from Phyle as one in which the *demos* had made itself sovereign of everything (*hapanton gar hauton pepoieken ho demos kyrion*, 41.2). In his Funeral Oration Pericles famously declared that Athens was a democracy because it was governed in the interests not of the few, but of the majority.[14] The law-court speeches often flattered the representatives of the *demos* by asserting that they were the state's supreme authorities and had it in their power to do anything they liked (Demosthenes 59.88, *Against Neaera*). One of Aeschylus' tragedies calls the vote in Athens 'the people's ruling hand' (*demou kratousa cheir, The Suppliant Maidens*, 604). The ancient equation of democracy with popular sovereignty seems to have been accepted almost without challenge by modern researchers. In the third edition of the *Oxford Classical Dictionary*, for example, Mogens Herman Hansen writes, '*Demokratia* was what the word means, the rule (*kratos*) of the people (*demos*).'[15] This view has been shared by most modern authorities who have written on the subject.

The statement that the *demos* was sovereign in the Athenian democracy has, of course, been questioned from time to time. The occasional faint suggestion that some constituents of the Athenian state rivalled or even surpassed the *demos* in power was already to be found in Classical antiquity. The author of *The Athenian Constitution*, for instance, wrote, '[W]hen the people are masters of the vote [in the law courts] they are masters of the

---

[14] *kai to onoma dia to me es oligous all'es pleionas oikein demokratia kekletai*; Thucydides 2.37.1. Gomme remarks that *es pleionas oikein* means 'the distribution, as it were, not so much of power, as of political activity' (Gomme, Andrewes and Dover 1945–81, vol. II: 108). For the argument that Pericles was 'saying something quite different from what he seem[ed] to be saying', and that his Funeral Oration was in fact a sort of aristocratic discourse, see Loraux 1986: ch. 4 (entitled 'As for the name . . . It is called a Democracy').

[15] Hansen 1996. The same point is restated at length in Hansen 1987: 101–7. Cf. Ober 1994a: 110: 'For an ordinary Athenian, the term *demokratia* meant something like "the monopoly over legitimate public authority is held by the whole of the citizenry". For Thucydides, the same term denoted something like "the lower classes possess the raw power that gives them the means to constrain the rest of us".' For traits in the Athenian democracy, brought out more clearly by the revolutionary programmes of 411 and 404, that might be analysed in terms of the 'mixed constitution' political theory that was popular in Classical antiquity, see Nippel 1980.

state.'[16] This has sometimes been taken to imply that the popular law courts, rather than the Assembly or the entire civic population, were sovereign.[17] Aristotle's *Politics* distinguishes between democracies in which the law is sovereign (*kyrion*) and those in which the multitude (*to plethos*; that is, the *demos* with the exception of the upper classes) is sovereign and argues that the latter form of government is no democracy at all but rather a tyrannical form of monarchy,[18] a statement that has sometimes been taken to refer to the Athenian democracy.[19] Speaking of the Athenian democracy under Pericles, Thucydides remarked, as we have seen,[20] that 'in what was nominally a democracy, power was really in the hands of the first citizen' (2.65.9–10), and this statement prompted some ancient authorities and early modern theorists to wonder whether the Athenian system of government under Pericles was actually democratic at all.[21]

On the whole, however, theories such as these have failed to gain acceptance, I think with good reason. The statement that the law courts were more powerful than the Assembly or the entire civic population is problematic on at least two counts.[22] It may be true, as Hansen claims, that the law courts became supreme in matters of domestic policy and had the power to reverse decisions made by the Assembly, whereas the Assembly could not reverse decisions made by the law courts.[23] It does not, however, follow from this that the law courts were ultimately sovereign. The Assembly was the ultimate source of law and the ultimate authority in foreign affairs, the number of instances in which its final decision was reversed by the law courts being negligible by comparison with that in which it was not. It was that vast majority of its decisions that stood that turned Athens into a great city capable of repelling foreign invaders, acquiring a large empire and retaining the status of a Mediterranean power even after a major defeat.

---

[16] *The Athenian Constitution* 9.1; cf. Rhodes 1981: 162 for a list of parallels to this epigrammatic sentence.
[17] Ruschenbusch 1957; Hansen 1974; 1978; 1987: ch. 4. For a short summary of the controversy, see Todd 1993: 298–9.
[18] *Politics* 1292a4; 1292b–1293a.
[19] For seventeenth- and eighteenth-century perceptions of the Athenian democracy as a combination of tyranny and mob rule, see J. T. Roberts 1994, esp. ch. 7.
[20] See p. 134.
[21] Chief amongst these ancient authorities is Plutarch, *Pericles* 15.2–3, in which Pericles is cast in the mould of a benevolent autocrat reminiscent of Augustus in Rome. For moderns who have taken Thucydides seriously, see J. T. Roberts 1994: 153.
[22] For further arguments against this view see, for instance, Rhodes 1981: 489 ('. . . I am not persuaded that the Athenians thought of their courts as a source of authority distinct from and superior to the *demos*') and Ostwald 1986: 10 n. 29.
[23] See note 15.

The suggestion that the law courts were more powerful than the Assembly is, moreover, weakened by explicit statements to the contrary[24] and by the fact that the same people participated in both institutions: are we to imagine that they threw a party in the *Heliaeia* whenever they managed to overturn some decision of the *Ecclesia* for which they had themselves voted when assembled on the Pnyx? The dikasts in any case changed over annually and thus had no chance of developing the sort of *ésprit de corps* that would have been necessary if they were to establish themselves as a superior authority. The statement that the law courts had ultimate sovereignty thus only has any meaning at all within the narrow context of constitutional law;[25] within the wider context of the state's power structure it is not valid. That the people involved shared this view is shown by the sequel to the phrase 'the *demos* has made itself sovereign of everything', which reads, 'and controls all things by means of decrees (*psephismasin*) and law courts (*dikasteriois*), in which supreme power resides with the people' (*en hois ho demos esti ho kraton*; *The Athenian Constitution* 41.2). It is noticeable that the author did not reject the notion that the *demos* held supreme power in both the law courts *and* the state as a whole on the grounds that this would involve a logical inconsistency.[26]

Nor did the Athenian democracy fit into Aristotle's vision of democracy as mob rule. A quick glance at J. K. Davies' detailed study of the activities of the individuals who made up the Athenian 'liturgical class'[27] will suffice to confirm the already widely known fact that the wealthy classes of Athens were allowed to retain their property intact, which implies that they had *not* forfeited their share in their city's decision-making process. In Athens, in other words, the word *demos* was understood to include both the lower and the upper classes. This *demos* did indeed make the laws (a generalisation that is not refuted by the fact that sometimes they were

---

[24] E.g. Andocides 2.19, *On his Return*: 'There is no one else by whom you (the Assembly) can be accused. It is in your power, rightly, to dispose of what belongs to you – well, or, if you so wish, ill'; Demosthenes 59.88, *Against Neaera*: '[the Assembly is] absolute master of everything in the city (*kyriotatos on ton en te polei hapanton*), and able to do whatever it wishes'. For further examples see Dover 1974: 291–2.

[25] Cf. the solution offered by Dover 1974: 292: 'Sovereign power was in fact divided, according to the nature of the issues to be settled, between the citizens (over eighteen years of age) meeting as an assembly and those same citizens (excluding the under-thirties) meeting in smaller numbers as juries.'

[26] This also applies to Aristotle's theoretical works, according to which the ultimate sovereignty of the law does not rule out the exercise of limited sovereignty by various governmental bodies. The deliberative element of the state (*to bouleuomenon*), for instance, 'is sovereign (*kyrion*) on the issues of war and peace, and the making and breaking of alliances; in enacting the laws . . .' *Politics* 1298a1, trans. E. Barker.

[27] J. K. Davies 1971.

made by *nomothetai*, in other words by ordinary citizens with no special legal expertise), but it could not take arbitrary executive action to manipulate or override them at will. Once the laws were made, a whole series of safeguards came into force to protect their irrevocability; the idea that they were immutable was deeply ingrained, with more practical measures to protect them including the *graphe paranomon* procedure.[28] This casts serious doubt upon any theory that the *nomos* was infinitely malleable in the hands of the *demos*.[29] As Gregory Vlastos put it, the Athenians pursued 'the goal of political equality ... not in defiance, but in support of the rule of law'.[30]

Nor can Thucydides' maverick assessment of Pericles' position in society be given much weight. Pericles, though undoubtedly charismatic, was no autocrat, but a democratic leader who could have been deposed constitutionally at any moment and who depended on the Assembly for whatever power he had.[31] All these considerations would seem to force us back upon our initial supposition, namely that in Athens during the period under consideration the *demos* was the ultimate seat of democratic power.

Although I do not wish to contest the general validity of this contention, I should like to point out certain difficulties that emerge when we look more critically at the mechanism by which the Athenian *demos'* absolute power of final decision was translated into action. Having described these difficulties and considered their implications for our idea of the Athenian democracy, I shall try to come up with a more refined interpretation of the constitutional abstraction 'in Athens the whole people were sovereign'.

VIOLENCE: LEGITIMATE AND ILLEGITIMATE

In saying that the *demos* was sovereign our ancient authorities did not always, in my opinion, merely mean that it was the supreme legal authority (although in some contexts they did of course mean just that); they also meant that the *demos* held supreme coercive power. They were implying that the *demos* could and did force its will upon individuals or groups within the Athenian state by inflicting pain and suffering. Crito was referring to this fact when he warned Socrates that 'the populace can inflict not the least

---

[28] This point is well brought out by A. H. M. Jones 1957: 41–72.
[29] This is the main thrust of Ostwald 1986: 497, even though the time at which 'the principle of popular sovereignty' was subordinated to the 'principle of the sovereignty of the law' may have pre-dated the end of the fifth century.
[30] Vlastos 1953: 366.   [31] See n. 20 above.

of evils' (Plato, *Crito* 44d). The all-pervasive nature of this power becomes apparent when we recall that the Greeks were unfamiliar with any such concept of inalienable human rights as has evolved over the last few centuries of European history to circumscribe the arbitrary exercise of authority.[32] Within the bounds of the law, the polis had absolute power over the lives, freedom and property of its members.[33] In extreme cases (ostracism being one obvious example) it even arrogated to itself the right of inflicting what could be interpreted as a sort of pre-emptive punishment.[34] The following quotation gives some idea of the severity and ruthless efficiency with which this supreme coercive power could be wielded:

Agoratus had three brothers, gentlemen. The eldest of these was caught signalling to the enemy in Sicily; Lamachus had him executed on the plank (*apetumpanis-the*). The second abducted a slave and took him off to Corinth, then got caught again kidnapping a girl from a household there; he ended up in prison (*en to desmoterio*) and was then executed. Phaenippides here arrested the third as a foot-pad (*lopoduten*); your own court tried him, condemned him to death and deliv-ered him up for execution on the plank (*apotympanisai*). (Lysias 13.65–6, *Against Agoratus*)

Visual evidence brings our picture of the Athenian penal system to life. **Fig. 7.1** shows the remains of the building that was Athens' state prison from the middle of the fifth century onwards (the archaeologists assure us that this identification is as safe as it can be),[35] together with a plan and modern reconstruction of the building. This was the *desmoterion* in which people were imprisoned, held on remand or, like Socrates, held pending execution. **Fig. 7.2** shows some cups that were found in one of the rooms of the *desmoterion*. These are presumed once to have contained the hemlock that was given to people condemned to death.[36] **Fig. 7.3**

---

[32] See the convincing arguments in Wallace 1996 for the existence of mechanisms, largely unparalleled in modern democracies, that protected the personal freedom of the citizen against excessive state intervention (incorporating earlier literature on the subject).

[33] Cf. Dover 1974: 289: 'There does not seem to have been any limit . . . to the community's rights over the property and lives of the individuals who composed it,' and Finley 1981d: 93: 'Provided the procedures adopted were themselves lawful, there were no limits to the powers of the *polis*, other than self-imposed (and therefore changeable) limits, outside the sphere in which deep-rooted and ancient taboos remained powerful. In 411, after all, the Athenian assembly voted to abolish democracy.' For the huge amounts of private wealth confiscated after the profanation of the mysteries, see D. M. Lewis 1966.

[34] Ostracism was, of course, principally designed to remove temporarily from the political scene 'the most prominent spokesman' in favour of combative policies (Ostwald 1986: 27; Eder 1997: 118–21). For the perception of this institution as pre-emptive punishment, cf. Andocides 4.35 (*Against Alcibiades*): 'Observing that whenever members of the community are more powerful than the magistrates and the laws, it is impossible for an individual to obtain redress from them, he arranged that punishment (*timoria*) for their misdeeds should be exacted by the state (*demosian*).'

[35] Vanderpool 1980.   [36] Athens, Agora Museum P 20858.

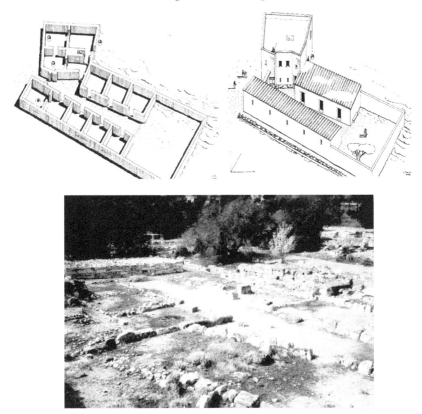

Figure 7.1 The Athenian state prison
Above, a reconstruction of the state prison (*desmoterion*), known to archaeologists as the Poros building, as it would have been in the mid fifth century, with plan; below, a photograph of its remains today. (See **Figs. 2.2b** and **2.7** for locations.) The state prison was where people awaiting trial or execution were detained. It has also convincingly been argued that others may have served sentences of imprisonment there (Allen 1997). The prison consisted of two rows of cells separated by a passage leading to a large courtyard at one end and to a semi-detached, two-storey block of rooms (probably the headquarters of the 'Eleven' executioners) at the other. One of the rooms was found to contain a large water jar and basin of the sort that Socrates may have used before he ended his life by drinking poison. The clay cups shown in **Fig. 7.2** were found in another room.

represents some familiar fifth-century *ostraka* inscribed with the names of politicians whose policies had displeased the *demos*, as a result of which they were recommended for ten years of banishment from Athens.[37] Here we have the remnants of formidable instruments. It is inconceivable that any

---

[37] On ostracism in general and on the surviving *ostraka*, see Rhodes 1994, which incorporates earlier literature on the subject.

Figure 7.2 Clay cups found in the annexe to the state prison
These fourth-century cups (*kylikes*) may once have contained the carefully measured doses
of hemlock extract that were given to people condemned to death by the law courts. On
being presented with one by the executioner, Socrates reportedly drained the cup calmly
in one breath, showing no sign of distaste. He then followed the instructions he had been
given, walking about until his legs felt heavy and then lying down on his back. Numbness
and coldness gradually spread upwards from his legs and when this reached the area of his
heart he died (Plato, *Phaedo* 117b–118b). The cup may also have contained an
antispasmodic agent to counteract the hemlock's unpleasant side-effects (vomiting and
muscular spasms), which may account for the peacefulness of Socrates' death. The
interpretation according to which this description was sanitised because the truth would
not have been sufficiently poetic (for which see Gill 1973) may have failed to take into
account the Greeks' enormous accumulation of lore regarding poisonous and medicinal
plants, now lost.

organisation that was fundamentally powerless, or that was constitutionally
endowed with power but for some reason unable to exercise it, should have
created them.

The coercive power that was concentrated in the hands of the *demos*
appears even more impressive when compared with that of the people
against whom it was wielded. Three categories of target (which overlap slightly) immediately spring to mind. The Athenian democracy used

Figure 7.3 Inscribed pieces of pottery (*ostraka*)
Ostraka such as these, some 1,200 of which were found in the *agora*, were used during the process of ostracism. Between 487 and 417, any citizen who feared that another might be planning to set up a tyranny could inscribe the latter's name on a sherd and hand it in. At least 6,000 sherds were required to make the procedure valid; if this condition was met, the man whose name appeared most frequently was required to leave the country for a period of ten years.On the sherds above the names and patronymics of four well-known politicians are clearly legible: (clockwise fom top left) Aristeides, son of Lysimachus; Cimon, son of Miltiades; Pericles, son of Xanthippus; Themistocles, son of Neocles, Phrearrhios (the name of his deme). Aristeides, who was accused of 'siding with the Medes', was ostracised in 483/2; he was formally recalled some years later and commanded a hoplite force at the battle of Salamis. Cimon, the hero of the victory over the Persians at Eurymedon (c. 466), was ostracised in 461; he was not to return until the end of the 450s. Pericles, who became the most influential politician in Athens after Cimon's ostracism, managed to escape a like fate himself; when he was charged with embezzlement he was acquitted and when he was deposed from the generalship he was re-elected. His arch-rival Thucydides, son of Melesias, was ostracised instead.Worst of all was the fate of Themistocles. Having done such exceptional service to the state that Thucydides the historian described him as one of the greatest men of his generation, he was ostracised in 472 and died in exile, having been condemned to death in his absence. Plutarch relates that Themistocles' father had tried to dissuade him from entering politics by pointing out to him the wrecked and neglected triremes on the seashore, telling him that 'the people treated their leaders in like fashion when they were past service' (*Themistocles* 2.6).

coercion against criminals and miscreants who broke the law, including anyone who dared to disobey governmental decisions (by which I mean not only the decisions of the *Ecclesia*, the *Boule* and the *Dikasteria*, but also those of the *Archontes*); it used it against popular speakers, generals and politicians, and it used it against people suspected of treason or of enmity to the constitution.[38] The second and third of these groups are particularly relevant to our purposes, since they fall neatly into a category of people described by Aristotle as 'outstandingly powerful' (*huperechein dynamei*) because of their wealth (*dia plouton*), their abundance of friends (*polyphilian*) or some other form of political strength (*politiken ischun*; *Politics* 1284a). One of the important achievements of recent scholarship has been to realise the extent to which people of this sort suffered at the hands of the Athenian *demos*; they seem virtually to have been persecuted. The following is by no means a full list of the extremely eminent Athenians of the fifth century who were fined, ostracised, exiled or executed at one time or another: Miltiades, Aristeides, Themistocles, Cimon, Thucydides son of Melesias, Pericles, Sophocles, Thucydides son of Oloros, Cleon, Nicias, Demosthenes (the general), Hyperbolus, Alcibiades, Antiphon, Peisander and Theramenes. After extensive prosopographical research into the careers of these and many other politicians, Ronald Knox wrote, 'One cannot read far in Athenian history without coming across a politician whose career is interrupted or ended by disgrace, brought on by a penalty inflicted by the law-courts or the Assembly, whether a fine, or exile, or confiscation of property, or loss of civic rights, or execution, or penalty of some other kind.'[39] We may find some reflection of the state of mind of the victims of this sort of treatment in a lamentation attributed to Demosthenes. Found guilty of taking bribes, sent to prison by the Athenian courts and regaining his liberty only by going into voluntary exile, Demosthenes, in John Dryden's translation,

did not show much fortitude in his banishment, spending his time for the most part in Aegina and Troezen, and, with tears in his eyes, looking towards the country of Attica. And there remain upon record some sayings of his, little resembling those sentiments of generosity and bravery which he used to express when he had the management of the commonwealth. For, as he was departing out of the city, it is reported, he lifted up his hands towards the Acropolis, and said: 'O Lady Minerva, how is it that thou takest delight in three such untractable beasts (*chalepotatois . . . theriois*), the owl, the snake, and the people?' (Plutarch, *Demosthenes* 26)

Since it is inconceivable that these outstandingly powerful people should without good reason have acquiesced in the ordeals inflicted on them (and

---

[38] For lists of cases in which sentence of death was carried out, see Ruschenbusch 1968; Dover 1974: 289–90; Karabélias 1991, incorporating earlier literature on the subject. I have excluded from my analysis the so-called fifth-century 'imperial jurisdiction' (for which see Meiggs 1972: ch. 12) because foreigners who were tried in Athens cannot be presumed to have had Athenian power bases of any significance by means of which to resist the legal process.

[39] R. A. Knox 1985: 134. Cf. Cartledge 2000: 22: 'They, the Athenian citizens, that is, ruled themselves, including their politicians, whereas our politicians rule for – and over – us . . .'

sometimes on their completely innocent descendants), seemingly putting up no resistance at all, all the evidence taken together would seem to confirm the view put forward above, namely that the Athenian democracy was not merely a hollow legislative, administrative or ideological shell, but a potent power structure with a finely honed capacity to enforce rules and decisions. In terms of Max Weber's definition of power (*Macht*) as the probability that one actor within a social relationship will impose his will upon another even in the teeth of the other's resistance,[40] the power wielded by the Athenian *demos* was clearly significant. It appears to have corresponded in full to Finley's definition of 'state power' as 'unique, overriding all other "powers" within the society by its acknowledged right to exercise force, even to kill, when its representatives deem such action to be necessary'.[41]

To complete our analysis, let us now turn our attention to some of the assumptions and moral judgements in which the exercise of this supreme power was steeped. These were such as in every respect to meet Weber's definition of *legitimate* violence (or, as he called it, *der gewaltsame Rechtszwang*, literally 'legal coercion by violence') as a state monopoly.[42] Democratic Athens was very different from the feuding societies analysed earlier[43] in that no one Athenian could injure another without running the risk of being sued, prosecuted and punished as guilty of an illegitimate act of violence. The Athenians as a collective, on the other hand, could freely arrest, incarcerate, banish, or if necessary even execute anyone who was found guilty of disobeying their rules, nobody being in a position to contest the validity of their decisions.

These considerations would seem to vitiate the recently advanced theory that the polis in general, and the Athenian democracy in particular, was no state at all: that it may more profitably be viewed as an example of the sort of loose, acephalous tribal organisation that anthropologists call a 'stateless state' (or 'society').[44] The crux of the reasoning process that produced this theory is, as far as I can see, as follows. Stateless societies have no clear centralised political authority and no organised form of internal coercion. The polis had no professional police force that was clearly differentiated from the rest of society, since, as we shall see, some of its coercive duties were carried out by volunteers from amongst the ordinary

---

[40] Weber 1972: 28: 'Macht bedeutet jede Chance, innerhalb einer Sozialen Beziehung den eigenen Willen auch gegen Widerstreben durchzusetzen, gleichviel worauf diese Chance beruht.'
[41] Finley 1983: 8.   [42] Weber 1972: 183.   [43] See pp. 184–203.
[44] Berent 1996; 2000. For the alternative view that the polis was indeed a state defined by her existence as an 'abstract entity', see Hansen 2002. For examples of genuinely 'stateless' states in anthropological literature, see M. Gluckman (1965) *Politics, Law and Ritual in Tribal Society*. Oxford: Basil Blackwell: ch. 3 and S. Roberts 1979: ch. 7.

population. *Ergo*, the polis was a stateless state. The fallacy here consists, in my view, in considering the *manner* in which internal coercion is organised to be the crucial test of statehood. If we now revert to the classic Weberian conception (which reigns supreme in the social sciences) according to which the crucial test for statehood is *the achievement or otherwise* within a specified territory of a monopoly of violence by the state's centralised political authority,[45] together with acceptance by the population that violence inflicted by that authority (or in its name) is legitimate and that all other forms of violence are illegitimate, we can see that Athens' claim to statehood could hardly have been more firmly established. The theory of Athens' statelessness cannot be accepted unless it can be demonstrated that Athens had no centralised political authority (in other words, it would be necessary somehow to explain away the existence of the *Ecclesia*, the *Boule* and the *Archontes* and their meticulously regulated activities, powers and interrelationships) and no coercive apparatus (which would mean coming up with some explanation other than those above of what exactly the *desmoterion*, the bottles of hemlock, the 'plank' and the *ostraka* were used for), or *at least* until examples have been produced of occasions on which Athens' coercive apparatus succumbed to or was prevailed upon by the power of some individual or group, or on which public opinion judged some act of violence inflicted in the course of a private blood feud, vendetta or duel to have been legitimate[46] or an arrest, imprisonment or execution carried out by the state's coercive apparatus to have been illegitimate.[47]

---

[45] Weber 1972: 181–7. For example, the entry under 'state' in Seymour-Smith 1986 reads as follows: 'In anthropology the state is usually seen as a stage of sociopolitical evolution characterized by the existence of a centralized government which has a monopoly on the legitimate use of force by way of conducting public affairs within a specified territory.' According to these criteria the political organisation of Athens was that of a typical state (it had a *centralised government* that had a *monopoly on the legitimate use of force* in *conducting public affairs within a specified territory*). That of, for example, the Jale people of the New Guinea Highlands (described in K. F. Koch [1974] *War and Peace in Jalemo*. New Haven: Harvard University Press) was that of a typically 'stateless state' (it lacked any centralised government with a monopoly on the legitimate use of force). Stateless societies listed in the *International Encyclopaedia of the Social Sciences* include Kung, Siriano and Murngin bands and the societies of Nuer, Turkana, the Kwakiutl, the Siane, the Ifugao, the Kalinga and the Plateau Tonga (Southall 1968).

[46] In the *Odyssey*, for instance, blood-feud is regarded as incontestably the most suitable institution for dealing with grave insults and injuries. 'If only Odysseus would come back to his own country, he and his son would soon (*aipsa*) pay these men back for their violence' (*Odyssey* 17.539–40). For the address of Antinous' father after the great slaughter amongst the suitors initiated by Odysseus, see pp. 263–3.

[47] Gregory of Tours' sixth-century Gaul, for instance, was full of 'tribunals of citizens' and other similar bodies whose judgements the feuding parties flagrantly disobeyed or tacitly ignored; cf. J. M. Wallace-Hadrill 1962: 137–40. In mediaeval Europe town governments were powerless to stop private

The theory starts to look even more shaky when we try out its central principle in other areas. The Athenian democracy, unlike its modern counterparts, raised no taxes across the population and hence was unable to maintain a standing army or extensive police force. It had no 'séparation des pouvoirs' (i.e. separation between the judiciary, the legislative and the executive)[48] and no parties in the modern sense of the term. It made almost no use of the principle of representation: its citizen members (men, women and children) made up only about a third to a half of the city's total population. Moreover, at its heart lay an extraordinary institution, the popular law courts, without parallel in any modern democracy. Despite all this, nobody has ever seriously suggested calling Athens a 'democracyless democracy'. She was a democracy because she achieved aims similar to those achieved by modern democracies, albeit by drastically different means. Unless we are prepared radically to revise our most basic rules of thought, the criterion that categorises a political system must be and will remain the attainment or otherwise of certain aims, not the manner of their attainment.

THE DEMOCRACY'S COERCIVE APPARATUS

In order to get a better view of the uses to which the Athenian state put violence, we shall now turn to the constituent elements of its coercive apparatus. To begin with, we must draw a distinction between institutions that were specifically and explicitly devoted to the exercise of coercion and institutions that were principally intended for tasks other than this but occasionally fulfilled coercive functions (see **Fig. 7.4**). Those Athenian agencies that were entirely devoted to the exercise of coercion have attracted considerable attention and their particulars are already reasonably familiar. They included ten annually elected archons, the eleven (*hendeka*) annually elected prison custodians and executioners who took their orders from the Assembly and the law courts, and three hundred public slaves, the so-called 'Scythian archers', who, equipped with whips, sticks, bows and possibly daggers, acted as attendants (*hyperetai*) to the archons and the Eleven (see **Fig. 7.5**).[49]

---

wars between families and cliques of both nobles and commoners right up until the fifteenth century: Elias 1978b: 237. Democratic Athens was very different, her records betraying no traces of any such blatant disregard of or disobedience towards the supreme state authority.

[48] Hansen 1981 points out that most modern scholars accept a basic fourfold division of the Athenian bodies of government into the *Ecclesia*, the *Boule*, the *Archai* and the *Dicasteria*, and argues, at 345, that 'a basic form of separation of powers in fourth-century democracy consists in a separation of initiative and decision'.

[49] These have recently been described in great detail by Hunter 1994 and Allen 2000.

Some 20,000 armed hoplites:
volunteers who superintended the
agencies below, acting in the name
of supra-personal norms

*Agencies specifically
and explicitly
devoted to exercising
coercion:*

*Agencies that occasionally
exercised coercion:*

- 10 archons
- The *hendeka*
- 300 Scythian
  archers

- Archons authorised to impose
  fines
- Individuals engaging in 'self-
  help'

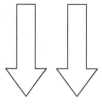

*COERCION
(LEGITIMATE VIOLENCE)*

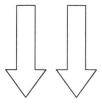

Criminals, miscreants and any one else who employed 'illegitimate' violence
and/or disobeyed governmental decisions (citizens, metics and slaves);
popular speakers, generals and politicians (citizens);
traitors and 'enemies' of the constitution (mainly citizens)

Figure 7.4 The coercive apparatus of the Athenian democracy
Designed essentially to combat Athens' enemies on land, her hoplite force came to be an
integral part of her domestic power structure. A reflection of this may be found in a
passage by Xenophon: '. . . in well-ordered cities (*poleis*) the citizens are not satisfied with
passing good laws: they go further, and choose guardians of the laws (*nomophylakes*), who
act as overseers, commending the law-abiding and punishing law-breakers' (*Oeconomicus*
9.14, trans. E. S. Marchant).

Figure 7.5 Scythian archer
The Scythian archers (*toxotai*) must have cut extraordinary figures on the streets of Athens.
They wore caps and suits embellished with ornamental patterns and were lightly armed,
but went barefoot. A popular subject amongst vase-painters, the archers are sometimes
portrayed riding horses (see **Fig. 2.8b**). This exquisite black-figure piece by Exekias,
painted in the late sixth century (i.e. before the three hundred Scythian public slaves had
become established as a regular force for the maintenance of peace and order in public
places), is famous for the flowing outlines of the figure. Public slaves of the category to
which the Scythian archers belonged (*demosioi huperetai*) were of higher status than
privately owned slaves. The archers were initially stationed on the *agora*; later they moved
to the Areopagus.

What has attracted less attention, and is consequently less familiar, is the size of this apparatus. It was, for anyone's money, very small indeed. I should perhaps illustrate this point with a comparison. During the early fourteenth century the city-state of Siena had several police forces. These were made up of hired foreigners (one for every 145 inhabitants) whose work consisted solely of enforcing curfews, patrolling the city and pursuing and seizing miscreants.[50] In Classical Athens there was one agent of coercion for every 781 inhabitants (if we estimate the population of Athens to have been 250,000, giving a ratio of 320:250,000, or 1:781) and we seldom hear of their actually engaging in any coercion.[51] The Scythian archers, in particular, figure in the sources mainly as keepers of order in public places, rather than as enforcers of the law or apprehenders of malefactors.

For all this, however, Siena was a notoriously turbulent and unstable city and Athens a remarkably peaceful and stable one,[52] a contrast that brings us back to the question of how the Athenian democracy succeeded in imposing its collective will on powerful and recalcitrant individuals and groups using only so slight a coercive apparatus. The following incident is only one of many that bring us face to face with this puzzle. In 406 BC the ten *strategoi* who had won the battle of Arginusae were tried under highly controversial circumstances.[53] Feelings ran so high, Xenophon tells us, that the Assembly even contemplated overriding the rules that governed its own procedures.[54] Despite protests, speeches, pleas and lobbying on their behalf, eight of the generals who had taken part in the battle were condemned to death and the six who were in Athens at the time were actually executed.[55] The fate of these generals is paradigmatic of that of most of the politicians, army commanders and public speakers who suffered disgrace, fines, exile or execution at the hand of the *demos* in circumstances that did not share the controversial nature of this example in that all these episodes seem to reveal a general and complete resignation to any form of state-initiated coercion.[56] How, we are impelled to ask, did the Athenians compel such important people to submit to punishment? Why did these unfortunates and their families and friends make no attempt to prevent all these executions, banishments and punishments? At a superficial glance, it looks as though it must have lain within their power to do so. They could, after all, simply have mobilised

---

[50] Cf. Bowsky 1967. [51] Cf. Herman 1994. [52] See pp. 76–8 and 214–15.
[53] Cf. Andrewes 1974; Lavelle 1988, citing earlier literature on the subject.
[54] Xenophon, *Hellenica* 1.7.12: 'The majority cried that it was monstrous that the Assembly should be prevented from acting as it wished.'
[55] Xenophon, *Hellenica* 1.7.34; cf. Diodorus Siculus 13.101–3.
[56] I am here ignoring the possibility of evading it, as when Socrates was offered the chance to escape from prison, for the simple reason that evading coercion is an act of an entirely different order from resisting it.

a group of relatives, friends and sympathisers, say fifty men per family (in the case of the wealthier citizens, we can add to this however many troops their 'foreign friends' were able to supply)[57] and overpowered the 321-strong enforcement agency. Why did they not do so?

To the best of my knowledge the first scholar to give this question serious thought was Finley. In his *Politics in the Ancient World*, Finley remarked that since the army did no large-scale policing the ancient city had 'little coercive power readily to hand'. The regime's legitimacy (that is, the citizens' acceptance as legitimate and binding of orders to go to war, pay taxes or stand trial) was therefore existential, resting on the continuity and success of its institutions and of the system as a whole.[58] This acceptance was thus determined not merely by the threat of punishment, but by 'the psychological need for identity through the feeling of continuity, and [. . .] its concomitant feeling that the basic structure of social existence and the value-system inherited from the past are fundamentally the only right ones for that society'.[59]

If this is correct, we are looking at what Max Weber called habituation (*Gewöhnung*) to traditional forms of social action. Weber considered habituation to be an extremely potent social force. 'It cannot be over-stressed', he wrote, 'that the mere habituation to a mode of action, the inclination to preserve this habituation, and, much more so, tradition, have a formidable influence in favour of a habituated legal order, even where such an order originally derives from legal enactment. This influence is more powerful than any reflection on impending means of coercion or other consequences, considering also the fact that at least some of those who act according to the "norms" are totally unaware of them.'[60]

Although I do not wish to belittle the importance of habituation as a factor in the long and successful existence of the Athenian democracy, it seems to me that a careful weighing up of the parameters will show that as an explanation for why powerful individuals so systematically failed to put up any resistance in the face of state-initiated coercion it is insufficient, especially in those cases in which it must have been evident that a miscarriage of justice was taking place.[61] To account for this generally submissive

---

[57] For foreign troops supplied within the context of *xenia*, see Herman 1987: 97–105.
[58] Finley 1983: 18, 24.   [59] Finley 1983: 24–5.
[60] The translation is from Weber 1968: 327 (= Weber 1972: 192).
[61] Of the reasons for suspecting a miscarriage of justice given by R. A. Knox 1985, the second seems to me decisive: most of the cases in which generals were fined, exiled or executed display an underlying pattern. This is the stereotypical recurrence of accusations of serious criminal activities (such as treason and taking bribes) following very similar mishaps (losing a battle, arriving too late for one or failing to prevent a revolt). The sources consistently suggest that in most cases the generals' guilt consisted in no more than bad luck, inexperience or incompetence.

attitude towards punitive and coercive acts performed in the name of the state, I believe we must take a broader view of the coercive apparatus of that state. This, as we have already mentioned, consisted not only of institutions that were specifically and explicitly devoted to coercion, but also of other individuals and bodies authorised to perform legitimate coercive functions as and when the need arose (see **Fig. 7.4**).

In modern nation-states coercion is agreed to be the exclusive preserve of armies, police forces, bodyguards and specialised secret agencies, so much so that people who perform acts of coercion on their own initiative may be said to have 'taken the law into their own hands'. These official agencies are as a rule extremely powerful; using the weaponry with which they have been provided, they can generally overpower any rival individuals or groups within their society by sheer strength of numbers. (In fact, a state is often said fully to come into existence only when its official agencies have succeeded in overpowering or eliminating such individuals or groups. Insofar as they fail in this task, their 'state''s claim to statehood is regarded as impaired.) The specifically coercive agencies of the Athenian state (the archons, the Eleven and the Scythian archers) could not possibly have overpowered every rival power within their society; there were too few of them and they had no very serious weaponry. Despite these disadvantages, however, the Athenians did somehow manage to keep their democracy stable and successful and on the two occasions on which it was overthrown (the oligarchic coups of 411 and 403) quickly brought about its reinstatement. The question that I would like to address is precisely how they did this.

It is now becoming more generally accepted that a considerable proportion of the Athenian state's coercive functions were carried out by individuals and bodies who in the normal course of events had nothing to do with coercion. This supplementary, non-professional group of people who performed coercive functions in the name of the state if the need arose is central to my argument. In everyday life their significance was especially evident in two spheres of action.

One of these spheres incorporates the phenomenon that modern literature has saddled with the unfortunate term 'self-help' (*boethein sauto*). This term is unfortunate not only because it conjures up nineteenth-century visions of honesty, virtue and self-improvement,[62] but also, and more importantly, because to the Athenians this term signified something totally different from what at least one leading modern authority has

---

[62] The finest expression of this is S. Smiles (1953) *Self-help*. London: John Murray (original edition 1859). To bypass this difficulty, Hunter 1994: 124 suggests replacing the term 'self-help' with 'private initiative'.

written on the subject: 'self-help in the technical sense of the term exists when somebody unilaterally secures or satisfies his real or pretended claim; that means that somebody takes the law into his own hands without the permission of his adversary and without the intervention of the court and proceeds against the person or the property of his adversary'.[63] Only very rarely did the term *boethein sauto*[64] signify an illicit arrogation to oneself of the use of force and concomitant usurpation of the functions of a properly constituted law enforcement authority, or 'taking the law into one's own hands'. What it normally meant was that in certain circumstances one was authorised and indeed required to take the initiative and carry out in the name of the community any one of a whole range of coercive activities on the understanding that in case of need the state's supreme power would come to one's aid and/or impart legitimacy to one's act *post factum*.[65] Here I am talking not just about the various forms of arrest and apprehension customarily discussed under the titles of *apagoge, endeixis* and *ephegesis*,[66] but about a wide gamut of coercive acts that, lacking any specific legal designation, have by and large escaped scholarly attention. These include not only such minor enforcement activities as the seizure of securities described in the Demosthenic speech *Against Euergus* (in which a man called Theophemus is said to have seized fifty of the speaker's sheep, his shepherd, one of his slave-boys and his furniture in enforced repayment of a debt (47.52)),[67] but also very much more serious ones such as the infliction of capital punishment in the name of the state. In Lysias 1, as we have seen, Euphiletus claims to have carried out not a murder but an execution, a form of violence sanctioned by the state. His defence is thus that this killing should be classed not as a private act of revenge but as a contribution to law enforcement.[68] It appears more than likely that this ingenious claim won him the case.[69] I would also assign to this category of action the amply documented licence that the state gave to all its citizens pre-emptively to kill anyone who seemed to be trying to set up a tyranny or to destabilise the rule of the *demos* in some way (see **Fig. 7.6**).[70] Coercive

---

[63] Taubenschlag 1949.

[64] Its literal meaning, 'to come to one's own aid' or 'to help oneself', is absent from the standard *Greek–English Lexicon.*

[65] This point is well brought out in Hunter 1994. The first half of Todd's definition of self-help ('taking the law [legitimately] into one's own hands') is a contradiction in terms; the second half ('the use of officially sanctioned aggression or violence . . .') does not make sufficient allowance for the prospect of state intervention (Todd 1993: 397).

[66] For which see Hansen 1976.

[67] For this and some other examples of 'self-help', see Hunter 1994: 122–4.

[68] See pp. 175–83.   [69] Herman 1993.

[70] Andocides 1.96–7, *On the Mysteries* (this refers to 410 BC, when the democracy was restored) and *SEG* XII.87 (which refers to the year 336 BC, but recapitulates large chunks of the law of 410).

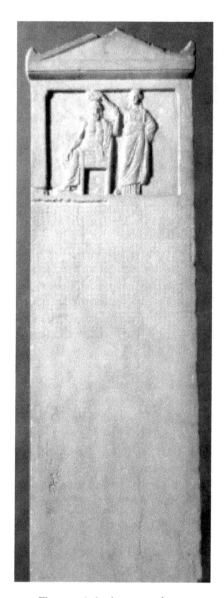

Figure 7.6 Anti-tyranny decree

Published in 337/6, this beautifully carved decree (*IG* I² 1496.131–41) calls for the pre-emptive acquittal of anyone accused of murdering a tyrant. The allegorical relief topping it expresses its message in visual form. The seated figure is Demos, representing the people of Athens; the standing, quasi-divine figure crowning him is Demokratia, a new cult figure introduced into the Athenian pantheon at the beginning of the fourth century. (The Athenian democracy, like most sophisticated power systems throughout history, sometimes forged links between its own ideals and symbols and those of traditional religion in order to reinforce its legitimacy by linking itself to the ultimate origins of existence (cf. pp. 326–47).) The message is straightforward: invested with the partly mundane, partly transcendental powers of Demokratia, Demos will succeed in thwarting Tyranny. (Cf. Meritt 1952; Parker 1996a: 228–9.)

acts of this sort were subject to three restrictions: they must be publicly seen to have been carried out, they were subject to *post factum* scrutiny by the court and they were punishable if the court found them to have involved any deviation from the letter of the law. The common denominator of all forms of self-help was therefore the expectation that in case of need some higher form of state power would intervene to assist (or to punish) the person or persons who had carried them out.

A more general form of this expectation may be seen in action in *Against Meidias*, in which Demosthenes, as we have seen, assures the dikasts that despite having been publicly punched in the face by the arch-bully Meidias he takes great pride in *not* having returned the blow. He did not return it, he claims, because he did not want to trespass upon the dikasts' proper preserve: '. . . no victim of assault or outrage should defend himself in hot blood (*meta tes orges*). Instead the aggressors should be brought before your court, since it is you who confirm and uphold the protection that the law offers to injured parties' (21.76).[71] What Demosthenes was describing, with many rhetorical flourishes, was the right of any citizen who became the victim of aggression or any other sort of injustice (or his next of kin) to mobilise the state's coercive apparatus to punish the offender. Like every other Athenian citizen, Demosthenes could lay claim to that subjective 'right' that, according to Max Weber, springs from the very structure of the state's legal order:

Sociologically, the statement that someone has a right (*Recht*) by virtue of the legal order of the state thus normally means the following: He has a chance, factually guaranteed to him by the consensually accepted interpretation of the legal norm, of invoking in favor of his ideal or material interests the aid of a 'coercive apparatus' which is in special readiness for this purpose (. . . *er hat die durch den einverständnismäßig geltenden Sinn einer Rechtsnorm faktisch garantierte Chance, für bestimmte (ideelle oder materielle) Interessen die Hilfe eines dafür bereitstehenden 'Zwangsapparates' zu erlangen*). This aid consists, at least normally, in the readiness of certain persons to come to his support in the event that they are approached in the proper way, and that it is shown that the recourse to such aid is actually guaranteed to him by a 'legal norm'.[72]

Athenian citizens were thus not merely occasional agents of state power, but also permanently entitled to expect that state power would be activated

---

[71] See p. 172. Demosthenes' point was that a person should not exercise 'self-help', i.e. carry out coercive acts in the name of the state, *when overwhelmed by emotion*. A closely related idea is expressed by the orator Lycurgus: 'A just citizen will not let private enmity (*dia tas idias echthras*) induce him to start a public prosecution against one who does the state no harm' (1.6, *Against Leocrates*).

[72] Weber 1972: 184 (= Weber 1968: 315).

on their behalf should the situation so require. The laws that dictated this had, after all, been enacted to provide (ideally, at least) 'for the assistance of persons who have suffered wrong' (Thucydides 2.37.3; cf. **Fig. 6.1**).

The second form of state-sanctioned coercion carried out by non-professional agents on behalf of the Athenian democracy was the imposition by magistrates (i.e. authorities other than the ten archons and the *hendeka*) of minor punishments, especially fines. Athens had several hundred magistrates (some of whom had slaves or other citizens working under them) who could impose fines of up to fifty drachmas. We may agree with Allen in general terms that 'the power of punishment that was diffused throughout the citizenry was by no means weak'[73] while noting in parenthesis that 'weak' is a relative term. Some Roman magistrates were allowed summarily to exercise *coercitio* against anyone who failed to obey an order in ordinary civilian life, and *coercitio* could mean a fine, the confiscation of a piece of property, imprisonment or even banishment *without any required process of law or right of appeal.*[74] Measured against *coercitio*, the punitive power of the Athenian magistrate was certainly 'weak'.

It was nonetheless another force to be reckoned with, which brings me back to the beginning of this chapter. The theory of sovereignty requires that in every system of government an absolute power of final decision should be exercised by some person or body recognised as both competent to decide and able to enforce the decision. Both ancient and modern authorities reassure us that in democratic Athens this absolute power belonged to the *demos*. This argument cannot, however, convincingly be sustained without producing concrete examples of occasions on which the entire *demos* can be seen to have come to the aid, either of an agency specifically and explicitly devoted to the exercise of coercion, or of some person or persons who had exercised legitimate coercion, because it, he or they had encountered unmanageable opposition or failed to impose its, his or their will upon some recalcitrant individual or group. I know of no such example and I doubt whether any exists. The statement that the supreme coercive power in Athens resided in the *demos* is thus true only in a vague generic sense. Had there existed no body of men powerful enough to enforce the decisions of the coercive agencies whenever they encountered opposition it would have been hard to see how this statement could be made at all. A closer scrutiny of the structure of the Athenian state suggests, however, that such

---

[73] Allen 2000: 41.   [74] Nippel 1995: 5–12.

a body did exist, and that this body consisted of the armed Athenian hoplites.

I should like to stress that this hypothesis is almost inevitable, accounting far better for the individual and collective behaviour of the democratic Athenians than can any departure from the theory of the sovereignty of the entire *demos*. It does so mainly because it takes into account a vital feature of the structure of the Athenian democracy that was by and large ignored before the publication of two late twentieth-century studies.[75] This feature is differential access to arms. What I believe these studies to have established is that ordinary people in Classical Athens went about unarmed.[76] It even appears likely that they may have been forbidden by law to own the sort of weapons that they might otherwise have used for self-defence:[77] the small arms, such as daggers, knives and swords, that were known as *sidera*. On the other hand, it is clear that some 20,000 citizens were allowed and indeed expected to own not just the sort of small arms appropriate to self-defence, but *hopla*, the far heavier weaponry and armour designed for war.[78] The so-called 'hoplite panoply', traditionally financed out of the agricultural surpluses of the land-owning citizenry, consisted of a bronze helmet, a corselet, bronze greaves, a great round shield with a double grip (*hoplon*), a single thrusting spear almost three metres long and short iron swords designed for close fighting.[79] In peacetime the citizen-soldiers known as

[75] Gröschel 1989; Herman 1994.
[76] The decisive piece of evidence is Thucydides 1.5.3–6.3 (cited in p. 133), for the importance of which see Herman 1994.
[77] The fact that no traces of any such legislation have come down to us should, in my view, rather be attributed to an accident of source survival than to there having been no such legislation. Van Wees 1998a: 368 comes to the opposite conclusion only at the price of overstating the amount and the quality of the information we do have about Athenian law and history ('it leaves one wondering why we hear of no legislation, or any kind of central initiative, against "bearing iron" in Athens, although we are rather well informed about Athenian law and history'). It would be possible to produce a very substantial list of themes no less central to Athenian life than 'bearing iron' about which we have very little information or none at all: for example, the criteria according to which people condemned to death were sent for execution by *apotympanismos* or by hemlock, the method by which the yields of individual plots of land were assessed and their owners assigned to the various property-owning classes (either Solonian or post-Solonian), or the incidence of domestic violence and the frequency with which slaves were tortured.
[78] A rough estimate of this figure will suffice for my purposes. For the numerous works on Athenian demography that suggest that there were between 18,000 and 25,000 hoplites in 431 (these estimates all being extrapolations from Thucydides 2.13) and that hoplite figures may have fluctuated considerably in later years, see Hanson 1992: 225 n. 32 and Christ 2001: 401 n. 14.
[79] Cf. Snodgrass 1967 and Anderson 1991. For 'typical' hoplite battles and the factors that contributed to victory or defeat, see Lazenby 1991; for the ideology of the hoplite battle, see Hanson 1991b; for the question of command, see Wheeler 1991; for the bearing and display of arms in Archaic Greece in general, see van Wees 1998a.

hoplites stored their equipment at home; should circumstances so demand, they were expected to use it.[80]

The hoplite force basically supplied the muscle that the Athenian state needed to secure its communal objectives on land (it also had a navy dedicated solely to the pursuit of its interests by sea). The primary purpose of this force was to protect the city of Athens and her territory, Attica: a formidable task, since it required that the hoplites match up to Athens' most probable adversaries on land in number, equipment and training. In 480 the hoplite force failed to hold off the 100,000 or so men of the Persian army, with the result that Athens was forced to evacuate her *asty*. The hoplites also failed to measure up to the invading Lacedaemonian armies during the Peloponnesian War, so that Athens had to evacuate her *chora*. In 336 they failed again, this time against the Macedonian and Thessalian forces, an event that precipitated the abolition of the Athenian democracy fourteen years later. If we exclude these fiascos, however, the Athenian hoplite force performed remarkably well throughout almost two hundred years of democracy and fully lived up to the city's expectations, winning her some of her most decisive victories: in particular, that over the non-hoplite Persian forces at the battles of Marathon (490) and Plataea (479) and that over the Spartan king Cleomenes and the Athenian Isagoras (508).[81] The Old Oligarch grumbled that the poor, or *nautikos ochlos*, who manned Athens' ships were responsible for far more of the city's strength than 'the hoplites, the high-born, and the good men' ([Xen.], *The Constitution of the Athenians* 1.2), and to some extent this was true. It was, however, true only insofar as the city's naval affairs were concerned; on land the armed hoplites enjoyed an unparalleled advantage over their opponents. Thanks to their superior weaponry and training, their fighting experience and not least their remarkable versatility and adaptability (one of the important insights of recent research is that they were not only effective in pitched battles between phalanxes, but also served as amphibious troops, besiegers, patrols and defence forces to meet the wide range of military demands that became increasingly common in Greek warfare from the fifth century on; see **Fig. 7.7**) they represented a concentration of power far more potent

---

[80] On the storage of arms at home see Snodgrass 1967: 59; Gröschel 1989; van Wees 1998a: 363–6. An important piece of primary evidence may be found in Xenophon, *Oeconomicus* 9.7.

[81] Herodotus 5.72.2. The expression that Herodotus uses to describe the besiegers who forced Cleomenes and Isagoras to leave the territory ('the rest of the Athenians who were of one mind') surely implies that these men were Athenian hoplites. For a plausible reconstruction of the sequence of events of which this episode was a part see Ober 1993b, who suggests the possibility that the besieging force was 'continually augmented as rural residents took up arms and streamed into the city' (at 224).

Figure 7.7 A Greek hoplite overpowering a non-hoplite Persian soldier
This vase-painting, which dates from after the Persian Wars, is a good visual illustration of the combat superiority of the Greek hoplite. In hand-to-hand combat his long spear and heavy shield gave him a considerable advantage over a Persian soldier such as the one depicted and over any other combatant who was not similarly equipped. The Athenian victory over the Persians at Marathon (490) and the Greek victory at Plataea (479) were both won by hoplite over non-hoplite armies. At Marathon 6,400 Persians were killed, but only 192 Athenians died. At Plataea there were only 159 casualties on the Greek side. The overall casualty rates in battles in which both armies were made up of hoplites were very different, the defeated army generally losing approximately 14 per cent of its soldiers, the victorious one 5 per cent (Krentz 1985). The superiority of the hoplites was widely acknowledged in Greece. In 427 the Messenians, who were trying to persuade the Athenian general Demosthenes to attack the Aetolians, asserted that even though the latter were 'a great warlike people' (*ethnos*) he would be able to subdue them quite easily, since they lived in un-walled villages and used only light armour (Thucydides 3.94.4; cf. Hanson 1996: 294–6).

than anything that any rival body or organisation in Attica could muster,[82] being at least potentially capable of overpowering the whole of the rest of the population (some 150,000 adults, if we include the metics and slaves, both male and female). It is true that the primary purpose of the hoplite force was

[82] For potential rivals, see pp. 253–6 below.

to repel foreign invaders rather than to repress the civic population, but it is *prima facie* unrealistic to suppose that so powerful an instrument, designed primarily to deal with manifestations of violence, albeit outside the city, would for some reason have held off from any dealings with manifestations of violence inside it. It is unrealistic not only because this was by far the most powerful concentration of forces in the whole of Attica, but also because it was the *only* readily available one. Two episodes relating to the oligarchic revolutions of 411 and 404 afford an indirect indication that the hoplite force, far from having nothing to do with internal violence, was firmly built into the city's domestic power structure.

In 411 Peisander and his allies abolished democracy in the cities of the Athenian empire and conscripted some of their hoplites 'to add to their forces'. They then put forward a programme for an apparently democratic system of government that was in fact no more than 'a piece of propaganda intended for the multitude', as they themselves intended to govern the polis (Thucydides 8.66.1; cf. *The Athenian Constitution* 29.5). Bluffing their way into a commanding position by giving the impression that they commanded many more hoplites than they actually did, they managed to terrorise the people. Thucydides describes the citizens' state of mind thus:

No one else dared to carry on speaking up against them [the conspirators] when everybody saw how many of them there were.[83] Anyone who did dare to say anything was rapidly and efficiently disposed of. No investigation of such disappearances was attempted, nor was any action taken against the most obvious suspects. The people kept their heads down, *so scared that even those who had not uttered a word on the subject felt lucky if they remained unhurt.* The city was so big that it was impossible to know very many of its inhabitants, or to be sure of the facts, so they *imagined that there were far more of the conspirators than there really were* and lost all sense of security. (Thucydides 8.66.2–3, my italics)

It should be remembered that Thucydides was writing with the benefit of hindsight. As far as the citizens knew at the time they were outnumbered, partly because many leading Athenian democrats were then away in Samos and partly because Peisander had supposedly brought so many foreign hoplites with him. This is probably why the Athenian *demos* thought it futile to mount any resistance.

In 404 the Thirty Tyrants instituted their reign of terror by means of a coercive agency that was in itself insignificant ('ten archons of the Peiraeus,

---

[83] Here I prefer Hude's reading, δεδιὼς ὁρῶν, based on MS C, to δεδιὼς καὶ ὁρῶν which occurs in the remaining MSS.

eleven guardians of the prison, and three hundred attendants armed with whips'), but became formidable when backed by what was in this case the real, rather than imagined, power of one thousand Athenians and the entire Spartan garrison (*The Athenian Constitution* 35.1; Xenophon, *Hellenica* 2.3.11–14).

In each case a relatively small and lightly armed but highly active agency was sufficient to terrorise a numerically far greater population because it was backed, or supposedly backed, by a far more substantial hoplite force whose prime function was not to police or to punish, but to back up the active agency, first psychologically, then if necessary practically. (The potency of the psychological threat posed may clearly be seen in the fact that in the case of Peisander's uprising this hoplite force was largely imaginary.) Had no such institutional interrelationship existed the Thirty would surely have had some considerable difficulty in carrying out their mass executions: ten archons, eleven prison guardians and three hundred attendants *armed with whips* can hardly be seen as a force adequate to such a purpose.

It may be no coincidence that the oligarchs' coercive apparatus was identical or very similar in structure to that previously employed by the democracy (ten archons, eleven prison guardians and three hundred Scythian archers). This may suggest that the domestic power structure of democratic Athens had a very similar formula: in other words, that the relation between her coercive agencies and her hoplite force was the same as that between the oligarchs' coercive agencies and their non-Athenian hoplites, the agencies themselves performing the actual acts of coercion, but with the implicit backing of hoplite power. The hoplites were, in other words, a deterrent, a permanent though dormant threat that would only be activated if and when the coercive agencies failed to attain some goal. If no such institutional interdependence had existed and if, in particular, the armed hoplites had not constituted the Athenian democracy's ultimate source of power, it would be very hard to account for certain incidents that took place in connection with attempts to overthrow the existing regime.

The tyrant Peisistratus is said to have deprived the *demos* of its arms in 535 by means of a trick. Having done so, he told the people that 'they should not be startled or disheartened but should go and attend to their private affairs, and that he would take care of all public affairs' (*The Athenian Constitution* 15; cf. Polyaenus 1.21.2). He thus effected a bloodless *coup d'état*, transferring supreme power from the hoplites to his own bodyguards and mercenaries without a blow being struck. It may well be that this anecdote is apocryphal and that in fact Peisistratus was never powerful enough to dare to try confiscating the hoplites' armour.[84] The fact that this account appears in a good fourth-century source (*The Athenian Constitution*), however, shows that at that time people must have thought it credible. Whether or not Peisistratus had really deprived the hoplites of their arms more than two hundred years earlier is irrelevant to my purposes; the fact that the author of *The Athenian Constitution* (and probably his readers) found this story convincing reveals his basic assumption that any successful *coup d'état* of his own time would require a pre-emptive strike at the rival hoplites' fighting potential.

In 514 Harmodius and Aristogeiton decided to overthrow the tyrants. They managed to kill Hipparchus during the Panathenaic procession, but then failed to kill his brother Hippias and seize power. Harmodius was at once cut down by the tyrants' mercenaries and Aristogeiton was arrested. At this juncture Hippias, fearing that the assassination would stir up unrest, approached those armed men in the procession who were still unaware of what had happened and, wearing an expression that gave nothing away, told them to proceed to a certain piece of ground 'without their arms' (*aneu ton hoplon*). Assuming that Hippias had something to tell them, they did as they were told. Hippias then ordered his mercenaries to remove the discarded weapons and started pulling out of line anyone of whom he felt suspicious and anyone who was found to be wearing a dagger, since traditionally a procession called only for shields and spears (Thucydides 6.58.2). On this occasion Hippias may well have prevented a *coup d'état*, at least for the time being, by depriving the hoplites of their arms. It should be noted that only after he had done so did he dare to arrest the tyrannicides' accomplices.

A very similar incident occurred during the rule of the Thirty Tyrants. Xenophon tells us that in 404 the Thirty held a review in the *agora* as a ploy to strip the Athenian hoplites of their arms. When all the hoplites were assembled, the Thirty ordered them to leave their weapons in a pile while they were off duty. To allay suspicion, they included in this order the 'Three Thousand' who were loyal to them as well as the hoplites who were 'not on the roll' (*exo tou katalogou*; in other words, those who were not loyal to them). They then ordered their Spartan troops and other citizens who were in sympathy with them to seize all the discarded arms except for those of the Three Thousand. This accomplished, they had the arms carried up to the Acropolis and lodged in the temple. Xenophon makes it clear that this was a move of profound strategic significance. 'Once this was done', he writes, 'they considered that they were now free to act exactly as they liked, and they

---

[84] Van Wees 1998a: 336 and 371 n. 15.

began to put people to death in great numbers . . .' (Xenophon, *Hellenica* 2.3.20–1). Had the armed hoplites not constituted that crucial focus of power upon which the city's constitutional form ultimately depended, this repeated insistence on stripping them of their arms would be difficult to explain.

Nor would it be easy to understand the logic behind related occurrences in cities other than Athens. During a state of *stasis* in 427 the *demos* of Mytilene decided to disobey the city's oligarchic magistrates and threatened to surrender the city to the Athenians. They made this threat immediately upon being provided with *hopla*, having previously been equipped only as light troops (Thucydides 3.27). In the same year the members of the Corcyran *demos* armed themselves (*hoplistheis*) by seizing the wealthy oligarchs' *hopla* from their houses (*ta te hopla auton ek ton oikion elabe*; Thucydides 3.75.4).[85] These were probably the weapons that they later used to club and stab to death the captured oligarchs (Thucydides 4.47).

The loyalties of the armed hoplites were thus vital determinants of a city's constitutional form. The examples cited so far suggest that bar a few exceptions the Athenian hoplites were by inclination democrats. In 411, as we have seen, the oligarch Peisander brought a large number of hoplites 'from the cities' into Athens to support him. In 404 the Thirty relied on Spartan hoplites. They appear to have done so because they were unable to win over the Athenian hoplites and saw that their only chance of overthrowing the regime lay in outnumbering or overpowering them.[86] Hence we may derive a refined version of the inference offered above: the survival of Athens' democracy required the support of the majority of its hoplites together with the constant identification of these men as democrats. Here too we may note the outlines of an emerging pattern: in order to stage a successful anti-democratic coup, it appears to have been necessary either to disarm the local hoplite force or to bring with you enough foreign hoplites to outnumber them.

That hoplites in general would probably have tended to be democrats is suggested by Aristotle's account of the relationship between military power and constitutional form. At the fall of the kings, he writes, the hoplite force had not yet become a formal part of the phalanx (*aneu syntaxeos*) and hence the cavalry was the most important military force, with the result that those who fought amongst the cavalry exercised political control. Later, however,

---

[85] See Gomme, Andrewes and Dover 1945–81, vol. II: 364. Gomme conjectures that the *demos* of Corcyra, unlike that of Mytilene, had already had *hopla* prior to seizing those of the oligarchs.
[86] Cf. the valuable observation of D. M. Lewis (1992: 384) that the sponsors of *stasis* tended in most cases to be small groups, not masses.

as the military significance of the hoplites increased, a wider spectrum of society acquired political influence, at which stage the constitutions became known as *demokratiai* (Aristotle, *Politics* 1297b16–25). We shall now examine the *demos* of democratic Athens more closely in order to test the validity of the assertion that most Athenian hoplites in particular were probably democrats.

THE HOPLITE RESERVE

A comparison of Athens with the other Greek cities shows that its *demos* was unusual in composition. It was not merely divided along economic lines into rich and poor, along class lines into citizens, metics and slaves, along ideological lines into oligarchs and democrats and along military lines into cavalrymen, hoplites and the 'naval mob'; organising the by no means inconsiderable demands that the Athenian state made upon the bodies and property of its citizens demanded a far more refined system of classification. We see something of this system in Thucydides' panoramic picture of 'the largest combined armament' (*stratopedon te megiston*), which set out for the Megarid in the summer of 431. This force included 10,000 citizen-hoplites, 3,000 metic-hoplites, 'a considerable number of light armed troops' and a fleet of 100 ships that happened to return from the Peloponnese at that point and joined the land forces. Thucydides remarks that the cavalry also participated in subsequent land invasions (2.31). Before we can tackle the question of the Athenian *demos'* political allegiances, we must first consider the interrelationship between the fighting potential of these bodies of men and the economic and social infrastructure at their disposal.

In broad outline the picture is clear enough. The chief criterion for the allocation of men to the various fighting units was wealth. In egalitarian Athens the burden of polis defence was unevenly distributed, bearing disproportionately upon the propertied sector of the population (this largely consisted of citizens, but also included some metics). The wealthy were obliged to serve as cavalrymen or as hoplites and to pay for their equipment themselves. Men from the poorer sector of the citizen-body were eligible, but not normally obliged, to serve as rowers in the fleet. We are, however, staggeringly under-informed as to how the citizens were divided up into the various property-owning classes and how the various military and economic burdens were apportioned to them.

For at least a superficial view of this complex issue we can go back to Solon, who at the beginning of the sixth century is said to have reined in the power of the traditional aristocracy of birth by instituting an agrarian timocracy.[87] The eligibility for office and the military obligations of Solon's four property-owning classes (*tele*) – the *pentakosiomedimnoi*, the *hippeis*, the *zeugitae* and the *thetes* – corresponded roughly to the value of their agricultural produce.[88] These classes survived, in name at least, into the fifth and fourth centuries, but not without undergoing significant changes in their substance. Firstly, they increasingly became dissociated from eligibility for office: in 457/6 the *zeugitae* became eligible for archonship and not many years thereafter any citizen (even a *thes*) could stand for any office.[89] Secondly, their direct connection with military service steadily dwindled. If we assume, rather simplistically, that the land-owning *pentakosiomedimnoi* and *hippeis* served in the cavalry, the land-owning *zeugitae* in the infantry as hoplites and the landless *thetes* in the navy as rowers, we have still to explain from which property class the lightly armed troops would have been recruited, how metics debarred from land ownership can have served as hoplites and in which unit a wealthy but landless citizen such as Demosthenes (some landless citizens were certainly hoplites) or a landed senior citizen would have served. Clearly some system more sophisticated than Solon's was at work, about which system we know frustratingly little. In particular, we lack precise information about the basis of the classifications it employed. The old Solonian system based on agricultural produce had plainly been discontinued, but we are left in the dark as to the system that replaced it: was it based on assessed capital, on ownership of weapons or on some combination of both?

My own guess is that the new system, introduced during the last third of the fifth century and perfected during the fourth, assessed people separately for office and for military service according to separate sets of criteria, neither of which any longer had anything to do with economic status. In politics these criteria assessed performance and nothing but performance.[90] The criteria for military service also related to performance, different units having different requirements in terms of weapons ownership, training, experience and age.[91] Unlike those used in the old Solonian system, these

---

[87] Cf. Murray 1993: 194: 'nobility of birth is discarded: wealth alone is the criterion for political power'.

[88] *The Athenian Constitution* 7.5 suggests that the *hippeis* were an exception in that their classification was based not on the amount of their produce but on their ability to keep and maintain a horse.

[89] He had, however, to claim to belong to the requisite class; cf. Rhodes 1981: 146.

[90] The Funeral Oration reads, '[W]hen it is a question of putting one person before another in positions of public responsibility, what counts is not membership of a particular class, but the actual ability which the man possesses. No one, so long as he has it in him to be of service to the state, is kept in political obscurity because of poverty' (Thucydides 2.37).

[91] For the forty-two age groups into which the hoplites were divided see Vidal-Naquet 1981a: 127 (= 1986: 86); for the conscription of hoplites by *katalogos* and age group see Christ 2001; for the relatively low price of the hoplite panoply, see Németh 1995.

sets of criteria were not *formally* interconnected; most importantly, they signalled a break with the age-old tradition according to which membership of the social elite, land ownership and service in the phalanx were strictly linked. Pre-eminence could now be achieved by scoring high in *one* of these respects alone. *Informally*, to be sure, land ownership remained the ultimate status symbol and the most promising springboard to social advancement, but it was no longer the only one. The author of *The Athenian Constitution* cites a text engraved in stone immediately after the inauguration of the Solonian reforms that commemorates the glee of a citizen called Diphilus at having managed to skip a class, presumably by acquiring and successfully cultivating a farm. Diphilus became eligible for the highest of state offices and for service in the army as a cavalryman entirely because he managed to make the leap from *thes* to *hippes* by becoming a landowner (7.4*)*. In late fifth-century Athens, by contrast, any citizen might be elected to the highest of state offices without owning a scrap of land and could serve in the cavalry or in the infantry as long as he could somehow lay his hands on a horse or a hoplite panoply, whether or not it were his own. Socrates had no property and was proverbially 'poor', but nonetheless served as a hoplite in two campaigns, probably using a panoply inherited from his father.[92]

We are thus looking at an unprecedented breakthrough in social mobility. In order fully to grasp the implications of this relaxation of time-honoured rules, we must consider it in conjunction with Athens' stupendous successes after the end of the Persian Wars. Athens' maritime empire secured for her resources so vast that at times they were equal to one and a half times her total domestic revenue. She used these resources mainly to augment her military strength, not, however, without devoting a share to improving the lot of the poorer sections of her *demos*. The author of *The Athenian Constitution* writes that more than twenty thousand men were fed 'from public funds'[93] and a decree passed in c. 445 to establish an overseas colony stipulates that the prospective colonists who were to be allocated land should be drawn from the two lowest classes, the *thetes* and the *zeugitai*.[94] A policy of helping the poorer classes seems to have been adopted deliberately, presumably with a view to enlarging the hoplite force;[95] the poor were now presented with previously unimaginable opportunities for personal enrichment. These included not only the payments for serving the state that we have already discussed, but allotments of land in territories

[92] Plutarch, *Aristeides* 1.9; Plato, *Symposium* 219e and 221a.
[93] *The Athenian Constitution* 24.3. It is clear that he has the relatively poor in mind: the moderately rich do not need to be fed.
[94] *IG* I³ 46 = *SGHI* 49.   [95] Cf. Finley 1978b: 7–8.

confiscated from rebellious allies and windfalls handed out when the booty from Athens' numerous sea and land campaigns was divided up. The poor could also now find employment in the numerous workshops that flourished in Athens and benefited indirectly from the guaranteed availability of corn.[96] The state's very active interest in augmenting (or at least not allowing to dwindle) the size of its hoplite force is illustrated by its policy of paying to provide the sons of hoplites who had been killed in action with panoplies and to equip every young hoplite who had completed his training with a shield and spear.[97]

Those who took full advantage of these emendations to the rules of social mobility could now achieve social advancement with relative ease. Hoplites of only moderate means could move up into the 'liturgical class' and aspirant *thetes* had the opportunity to break into the charmed circle of land-owning hoplites. It is clear that such opportunities were frequently seized with both hands. Dionysius of Halicarnassus cites a proposal made and rejected in 403 that would have restricted political rights to landholders. Had it been carried, this proposal would apparently have disenfranchised 5,000 citizens. This implies that at that time only 20 or 25 per cent of the citizens of Athens owned no land of any kind, or, to put it another way, that as many as three quarters of the citizens owned some workable land.[98] Hans Lohmann's extensive archaeological survey of the area near the southwestern tip of Attica (the classical deme of Atene) points in the same direction. Lohmann has inferred, mainly from the remnants of farmstead equipment and from the terraces built to prevent erosion of cultivable soil, that 'The time of greatest prosperity and the highest density of population in the area coincides with the golden age of Athens, the Classical phases of the 5th and 4th century BC. However, an abrupt change occurs as early as the end of the 4th century. The valleys become deserted and depopulated.'[99] If this observation may safely be extrapolated from Atene to the whole of Attica (as surely it may, in the absence of any indication that Atene was an unusually flourishing deme), it confirms our picture of formerly landless citizens growing rich on the profits of empire and becoming farmers. Lohmann's survey also vindicates the hunch of some scholars that under the democracy hitherto neglected areas (mostly in the hills) were brought

---

[96] Cf. Finley 1978b: 8: 'it is always the poor who are the chief victims of shortages and famine'.
[97] See Snodgrass 1967: 59 and *The Athenian Constitution* 42.4. Cf. Gomme, Andrewes and Dover 1945–81, vol. II: 404, for the arming of the *epibatae* (ten hoplites assigned to each *triere*) by the state.
[98] Dionysius of Halicarnassus, *Lysias* 52; cf. Finley 1952: 58 and 1983: 65.
[99] Lohmann 1992: 30. This point is illustrated in more detail in the monumental Lohmann 1993 and 1995.

under cultivation.[100] The abrupt agricultural decline that set in at the end
of the fourth century, coinciding with the abolition of democracy, again
points to this link.

The conclusion to be drawn from all this is that the often significant
differences that existed between the economic backgrounds of moderately
rich landowners and the landless poor were not translated into the ideological sphere. The roughly 20,000 hoplites and approximately equal number
of non-hoplites who made up the citizen body were not at war with each
other, or even rivals. As non-hoplites were presented with these unparalleled
opportunities for social advancement, they chose to identify themselves
with the hoplites. This may account for the disproportionate amount of
attention that was devoted to this group. Athenian culture was imbued
with a reverence for hoplites that verged on worship, the poor 'rowing
classes' receiving considerably less attention. The hoplites were described
as prototypes of the exemplary type of Athenian manhood, fit in body
and disciplined in spirit (Aeschines 2.150–1, *On the Embassy*; cf. the caption to **Fig. 7.8**). Aristophanes' comedies and Euripides' tragedies, to quote
Victor Hanson, 'acknowledge the great contribution of the rowing-class
of Athenian poor but somehow see in it no obstacle to their innate pride
in the achievements of their own class of hoplite farmers in both a military and agricultural sense'.[101] The battle of Marathon, fought by hoplites,
was prominently commemorated on the Stoa Poikile.[102] The hoplite helmet
became Pericles' trademark (Plutarch, *Pericles* 3.2), and the goddess Athena,
who embodied the intelligent and orderly use of force in defence of the
polis, was often depicted as wearing one. Scenes on vases and tombstones
often represent the doomed hoplite in the act of setting out for war, taking
down his shield or being brought his helmet by his wife; it is not inconceivable that in some cases the point of this was to advertise his status (see
Fig. 7.8, bottom left). The epitaph for the Athenians killed before the walls
of Potidaea (432) gives touching expression to the polis' collective sorrow
for the hoplite besiegers who 'ennobled their country giving their lives in
barter for glory'.[103] Thucydides pays tribute to the 120 Athenian hoplites
killed in a battle against the Aetolians in the same vein, describing them as
'truly the best men which the city of Athens lost in this war' (3.98.4). Somewhat earlier in history, Herodotus was probably fired by this pro-hoplite
attitude when he ascribed the collective progress of the Athenians to the
passionate motivation that they displayed while fighting in the *phalanx*

---

[100] D. M. Lewis 1973: 212.   [101] Hanson 1996.   [102] Pausanias 1.15.3.
[103] φσυχὰς δ' ἀντίρρο[πα θέντες]| ἡ[λλ]άχσαντ' ἀρετὴν καὶ πατρ[ίδ'] εὐκλ[έισαν]; *IG* I² 945.

Figure 7.8 Armed Athenian hoplites
The defence of the city appeared on the Assembly's agenda at least ten times a year. The
lion's share of this duty fell to 20,000 or so elite members of the citizen-body who had
been trained to fight in close formation as a phalanx (they were expected to provide their
own hoplite panoply). The hoplites were considered to embody an exemplary type of
personality that represented everything best in Athenian society, as Aeschines' calculated
insult to Demosthenes implies: 'I am astonished, Demosthenes, that you should dare to
criticise Philon in the presence of Athens' most reputable citizens . . . Which do you think
they are more likely to pray for: ten thousand hoplites like Philon, with bodies as well
made as his and souls as disciplined, or thirty thousand *kinaidoi* exactly like you?'
(Aeschines 2.150–1). (*Kinaidoi* were promiscuous homosexuals who took cash for sex; cf.
Winkler 1990: 45–70, with the corrective remarks of Davidson 2001.) The kind of
emotional control required to fight efficiently in the phalanx and the determination to
impress others by never showing cowardice that was expected of a hoplite (fighting in
order to display courage was thought superior to fighting courageously out of fear or
simply with the professionalism of a mercenary) were deemed to be equally appropriate to
life in a democracy (cf. Wheeler 1991).

(after flinging off their despotic government; 5.78). The hold that the hoplites had upon the minds of the Athenian citizenry must to some extent at least have reflected considerable power in society.[104]

I should perhaps say at this point that I have not manufactured this conclusion to validate the thesis of this chapter; it emerges as a necessary consequence of the evidence. Other scholars have reached it independently in the course of examining altogether different aspects of Athenian society. 'Although there was always growing tension between Athenian landed and non-landed', writes Victor Hanson in a landmark paper, 'no overt fighting broke out between hoplites and the poorer during this long process of democratization. Instead, what occurred at Athens throughout the fifth and into the fourth century BC was actually a gradual diminution of hostility between the two groups, yeomen (*zeugitai*) and landless (*thetes*).'[105] This point allows us to elaborate upon the conclusion reached at the end of the last section. The survival of Athens' democracy ultimately depended upon the support of the majority of its hoplites and/or their reliable identification as democrats. This majority support was achieved by creating an identity of interest between Athens' collective interests and the individual interests of her hoplites, and by making it increasingly easy for aspiring hoplites to join the ranks of and assimilate themselves into this group.

Returning now to the institutional aspects of Athens' domestic power structure, it remains to consider the armed hoplites' *modus operandi*. Let me repeat that we should not be tempted to regard them as some sort of ruthless secret police whose intimidating presence constantly hovered over the city. Nor do I propose to challenge Eder's open-minded response to the question of who ruled in the Athenian democracy by asserting that the hoplites did.[106] Athens was no military state and the typical Athenian was a citizen first and a soldier second. As Vidal-Naquet has put it, '[I]t was not as a warrior that the citizen governed the city, but it was as a citizen that the Athenian went to war.'[107] The armed hoplites we are discussing spent most of their time as unarmed citizens. They should therefore be seen as a remote

---

[104] Cf. Snodgrass 1967: 49: 'In all Greek art there are few subjects so popular as the hoplite, whether arming, departing to war, fighting or dying.' For the frequency with which hoplites appear in vase-paintings, see Lissarrague 2002: 113–19.

[105] Hanson 1996: 294. I shall not repeat here the further reasons adduced by Hanson for believing there to have been no such ideological split.

[106] Eder writes that 'there is no clear response to the clear question "Who Really Rules?".' After assessing the roles of the Council and the Athenian magistrates, he concludes that '[t]he role of written law must be considered crucial. Although it did not itself "rule", it played a decisive role in maintaining stability and order, especially in times of crisis' (Eder 1991: 195–6).

[107] Vidal-Naquet 1981a: 125 (=1986: 85).

and impersonal deterrent that metamorphosed into an effective practical *force* only if and when someone threatened to destabilise the democracy or obstruct the function of its coercive agencies. In this respect they fit perfectly into Laski's description of the modern state's coercive power: '. . . in the last analysis, the state is built upon the ability of its government to operate successfully its supreme coercive power. It is true (and it is, of course, important) that when the members of a state are fundamentally at one about the purposes embodied in its policy, the coercive aspect recedes into the background'.[108] In Athens, for the most part, the coercive aspect of the hoplite force remained quietly in the background of everyday life.

Very few surviving passages describe the armed hoplites in action within the domestic context. We do, however, know how they operated during one period of incipient *stasis*. The mutilation of the *hermae* and the profanation of the mysteries that coincided with the outset of the expedition against Sicily in 415 brought about near panic in Athens. Suspicion arose that a coup was being hatched to overthrow the democracy. Steps were taken to apprehend the offenders and 'self-help' procedures were invoked, ordinary citizens being mobilised to denounce others and to police the city. According to Andocides, the Council summoned the *strategoi* and bade them proclaim that citizens should proceed *under arms* (*ta hopla labontas*; 1.45, *On the Mysteries*) to three designated places. The summoning of the *strategoi* by the *Boule*, their declaration that armed citizens should assemble in significant public places (in the *agora* if they lived in the city proper, in the temple of Theseus if they lived between the long walls and in the *agora* of Hippodamus if they lived in the Peiraeus), the mustering of the cavalry at the Anaceum and the use of the Acropolis as the Council's headquarters and the *Tholos* as that of the Prytanes (Andocides 1.45, *On the Mysteries*) all suggest that these were not impromptu reactions to an unexpected crisis, but parts of an efficiently constructed contingency plan (perhaps even one that had been practised by means of routine drills) to meet a clearly foreseen state of emergency.

Andocides is a rather unreliable source, but in this case Thucydides (6.61.2) confirms his description.[109] To understand Thucydides' complex text in full we must consider the sequence of events described in the lead-up to this extract.

(1) The *demos* interpreted the Hermae affair as connected to some conspiracy (*synomosia*) aimed at establishing an oligarchy or a tyranny (60.2). (2) Many noteworthy men were imprisoned and every day surpassed the

---

[108] Laski 1935: 26.   [109] Cf. Finley 1983: 21.

last in savagery (60.2). (3) One of the prisoners came forward with information incriminating himself and others with regard to the Hermae (60.2–4).
(4) Delighted to have discovered the truth, the Athenian people brought
to trial and executed everyone whom this prisoner had implicated. They
also passed a death sentence on various people who had managed to escape
and set a price on their heads (60.4). (5) Alcibiades' enemies persuaded the
Athenians that he had committed the sacrilege against the mysteries as part
of the same plot against the democracy. The Athenians took a very serious
view of this. (6) The Athenians decided that the advance of a small force
(*stratia . . . ou polle*) of Spartans up to the Isthmus must also be part of Alcibiades' intrigues, even though that force had in fact arrived in pursuance of
an arrangement with the Boeotians.

Now comes the crucial passage: (7) The Athenians consequently believed
that if they 'had not forestalled them by arresting the people against whom
the information had been laid, the city would have been betrayed' (*ei me
ephthasan de autoi kata to menuma sullabontes tous andras, prodotenai an he
polis*; 61.2). 'They actually slept for one night under arms in the temple of
Theseus inside the city' (*kai tina mian nukta kai katedarthon en Theseio to
en polei en hoplois*; 61.3).

An alternative to the explanation propounded here would be that Thucydides believed the Athenians to have done this not because they feared an
internal revolt but because they thought that the city was in danger of being
betrayed to the foreign force that had arrived on the Isthmus. This explanation can, however, pretty much be ruled out. Thucydides is telling us that
armed men slept in the temple of Theseus so that the arrest of Alcibiades'
accomplices (and by implication the people who had previously escaped
the death sentence; see item 4 above) could be secured. If these people
were under arrest they would not be able to betray the city to the Spartans
(by, for example, smuggling them into the city or opening a secret gate).
This appears to be a perfect illustration of the pattern that we have already
derived from other sources: the hoplite army acts as a backup to the routine
coercive agency, which is thus able to overpower internal opposition despite
its own weakness. In this case the hoplites would have intervened only if the
fugitives had resisted arrest. Sleeping in the temple of Theseus was, in other
words, a palpable demonstration of the armed men's deterrent function.
Had they been called up to fight external enemies such as the Spartan and
Boeotian forces they would have assembled along or outside the city walls,
not in the temple of Theseus. The fact that they were stationed here fits in
with Andocides' passage, which leaves no doubt that these men were called
up to meet a clearly foreseen state of emergency.

In the end a violent showdown was avoided, but what we have here is sufficient to indicate that both the state representatives who were attempting to exercise their coercive powers on the fugitives and the fugitives themselves would have perceived the hoplite force as the decisive factor in this crisis.[110] This evidence shows, in other words, that everybody concerned recognised the hoplite force as Athens' ultimate defence, a signal force to be invoked whenever the city's system was under threat. By an easy extension, it also shows how both dedicated and occasional coercive agencies relied on the backing of the hoplites. Those who undertook coercive functions must have done so on the understanding that if they were unable to impose their will on some recalcitrant individual or group the hoplite force would come to their aid. This would, in most cases, have led to a state of *stasis*, which may explain the rarity of such occurrences.

Throughout Athens' stable and enduring democracy her *demos* exercised its sovereignty by means of simple authority rather than coercion on the vast majority of occasions. For almost two hundred years people were tried, executed and banished without the hoplite force having to step in. The *demos* was able to operate in this way because the majority of the population believed that the system was legitimate and that it was necessary to maintain the rule of law. In general, therefore, they followed the unwritten laws and obeyed those in power despite being under no *immediate* threat of coercion. None of this meant that the *demos* had no coercive apparatus and no superior force to fall back on. Anyone who was contemplating breaking the law or trying to undermine the people's rule already knew about that ultimate deterrent. Athenian society avoided the escalation of violence by means of an internal balance of forces in which the hoplite force was a vital ingredient. Removing it would have changed every rule of behaviour.

The hoplite force was one of the Athenian democracy's great strengths because it could so readily be called upon: in a matter of hours a group of civilians could metamorphose into a formidable fighting force. It was also, however, a weakness, one might almost say an inherent fragility. This was so because the hoplites' willingness and ability to take action at the right moment was significantly limited. In the first place, they took action primarily on their own initiative: unlike the salaried armies and police forces controlled by the governments of democratic states today, they had no 'superiors' to command them (if necessary against their will). In the second place, the rapidity with which the hoplites of Andocides' account appear to

---

[110] I am ignoring the cavalry mentioned by Andocides because in internal affairs, as in battle, their role must be regarded as having been incidental rather than decisive; cf. Hanson 1996: 290; Low 2002.

have been mobilised reflects the Athenians' abnormal living arrangements during the Peloponnesian War, when people who normally lived in the country had to move inside the city walls. Andocides tells us that the hoplites were ordered to assemble at the *agora* if they lived in the city proper, in the temple of Theseus if they lived between the Long Walls and in the *agora* of Hippodamus if they lived in the Peiraeus. Ordinarily many of them would have been dispersed throughout the Attic demes, which would have made their mobilisation a far lengthier and more cumbersome business. In the third place, the hoplites could fall victim to irrational fears and groundless suspicions, imagining themselves to be (or perhaps being in fact) outnumbered. That the majority of the hoplites were democrats was true only in theory; no hoplite could be certain of every other's political stance at any given moment. At times of crisis there could well be considerable uncertainty as to who and how many would side with whom. At one critical juncture at least (the emergency of 411) the hoplite reserve failed to act and the oligarchs took advantage of the confusion that ensued to subvert democracy.

We are now in a position to review this chapter's central argument, which begins with the identification of three constituent elements of the Athenian democracy: constitutional, punitive/coercive and military (i.e. the hoplite force). I have suggested that the reader should take a step back from the traditional view of the Athenian democracy as a two-dimensional legal/constitutional system and instead consider it as a three-dimensional structure that incorporated the three constituent elements listed above, traditionally treated independently of each other, within a single integrated power system. These elements should thus be treated as interdependent parts of a larger whole, the hoplite force representing a concentration of power far more potent than anything that any rival body or organisation in Attica could muster. This power was all the more formidable because the rest of the population was unarmed. This interpretation of the Athenian democracy is hardly improbable, but as far as I am aware it has never previously been put forward.

The question now arises of the nature of the relation between these constituent parts (as, by implication, does the further question of how the sovereignty of the Athenian democracy was maintained). I have explored this issue with reference to the *demos*' widespread and by our standards often unfair persecution of the political elite, observing that throughout the democracy extremely powerful individuals, their friends (both Athenian and foreign) and their families seem to have acquiesced in this treatment in spite of the extreme weakness, acknowledged by virtually every scholar of the period, of the formal punitive/coercive apparatus (the *hendeka*, the Scythian archers, etc.). I have suggested that an explanation for this otherwise extraordinary passivity should be sought in the implicit understanding of everybody concerned that in the last resort, if the routine punitive/coercive apparatus failed to carry through the decisions of the *Ecclesia* and the law courts, a state of *stasis* would ensue and the hoplite force would step in to restore the status quo. From the fact that this so seldom took place I have inferred that the existence of the hoplite force was an effective deterrent and one of the main sources of the Athenian democracy's now widely acknowledged stability.

Rejecting this interpretation involves accepting (1) that if anybody powerful had opposed state persecution with sufficient violence to create a state of *stasis* the superior hoplite force would have stood idly by while the law was broken and the democratic regime dissolved and (2) that condemned politicians made no attempt to resist execution out of sheer habituation or respect for the rule of law. I do not regard either of these suppositions as sustainable.

The implications of all this for our understanding of Athenian behaviour are as follows. The people of Athens did not live free of state constraints or state coercion. The understandings by which their day-to-day lives were bounded (written and unwritten laws, formal and informal relationships of mutual dependence and a strong sense of community) were backed by a power system that could in case of need be activated to deliver pain and suffering. Anything done outside the limits defined by the law (or sometimes even inside them) had consequences for the community at large, and if these were adverse the city's coercive apparatus would come into play. The coercive apparatus whose active and passive components together constituted the state's most significant concentration of power was the ultimate means by which the Athenian democracy redressed the balance of its social system in times of crisis.

CHAPTER 8

Transformations of cruelty

HEROES INTO CITIZENS

The great poets of dark-age Greece and the leading Athenian writers of the Classical age painted strikingly different pictures of their human ancestors. To Homer and Hesiod they were exemplary, larger than life size figures bearing, despite certain human frailties, a remarkable resemblance to the immortal gods. Thucydides saw his ancestors as robbers who led a quasi-barbarous existence. Their houses were insecure and communications between them were unsafe. They went about armed to the teeth and played ruthless power games, 'the strong periodically expelling the weak' (1.5.3–6.3).[1] The past envisaged by Homer and Hesiod was half imaginary and half an echo of collective memory, whereas Thucydides' version was a strictly logical extrapolation from his own observations. The wide cultural gap between his fellow-citizens and some of the more backward peoples of mainland Greece had forced on him the conclusion that his own countrymen must once have been brigands and that the high living standards and culture they now enjoyed must therefore be the result of some kind of evolutionary process. Pugnacious robbers had somehow been transformed into docile citizens.

To Thucydides' countrymen all this probably sounded unbelievable, if not shocking. The gulf that separated them from such primitive types must have appeared far too wide for Thucydides' version of the past to carry any conviction. The Athenians of their own day enjoyed a degree of safety and material well-being that had seldom been equalled. They ruled over a great empire and their state ran like clockwork in times of both peace and war. Unlike the austere Spartans, they led a relaxed and comfortable existence in solid, well-appointed, tastefully decorated houses. They could wind down from the pressures of work by attending the various games and sacrifices

[1] It is not clear how, in Thucydides' scheme, these robbers fit in with the Homeric past.

that took place throughout the year; in private they did their best not to hurt each other's feelings and in public they conscientiously obeyed the law (Thucydides 1.5.3–6.3 and 2.36–8).[2] A surviving fragment of a book now lost, *On Pleasure*, by the contemporary philosopher Heracleides of Pontus, offers us a close-up of this agreeable way of life. According to Heracleides the Athenians 'wore purple cloaks (*himatia*) and embroidered jackets (*chitones*)'.[3] They wore their hair up, fastening it with golden cicada brooches, and put on even more gold jewellery to go out (see **Fig. 8.1**). They were accompanied by slaves carrying folding chairs so that their masters could sit down in comfort wherever they went. Clearly their diet and the rest of their existence was luxurious. 'Such, then', he concludes, associating (perhaps unwittingly) this level of civilisation with military power, 'were the men who won the battle of Marathon, the only people who overcame the power of all Asia.'[4]

Were the refined, cultured and law-abiding citizens of Athens indeed descended from crude, violent, heavily armed robbers? In attempting to answer this question, we shall take the society that the Homeric poems describe as our starting point. (For the sake of convenience, I shall here-after refer to this society as 'Homeric'.) According to Thucydides' scheme of prehistory, this society represented an advance on the lawless era that preceded it. From today's perspective, however, both the age of heroes and the age of robbers may be taken to belong to the 400 or so years of 'dark ages' that followed the downfall of the Mycenaean world in c. 1200.

In the background of the *Iliad* and the *Odyssey* lurks a social world far less sophisticated than that of the Athenians. It is nonetheless a world struc-tured by morals, values and institutions. Since the middle of the twentieth century controversy has raged as to the precise nature of this world. The disagreement centres on three interconnected questions. Was this world entirely fictional, springing from the poets' creative imagination, or was it in any sense 'real', bearing at least some resemblance to an objective real-ity that once existed in time and space? If some such reality was indeed reflected in the poems, was it that of Greek society prior to 1200 or that of the radically different dark-age societies that followed? If the poems did reflect life in dark-age Greece, were they describing a single period within that wider time span during which all the aspects of society to which they refer co-existed, or were they presenting as a whole what were in fact non-coeval elements of a number of separate and disconnected periods?

---

[2] See pp. 201–3.   [3] For Athenian men's clothing in the fifth century, see Chapter 2 n. 91.
[4] Aelian, *Varia Historia* 4.22, trans. N. G. Wilson; also cited in Athenaeus 512bc.

Figure 8.1 The cult of beauty
Tombstone showing the deceased Hegeso selecting a piece of jewellery from a chest offered to her by a slave-girl. The Athenians, both men and women, set great store by their personal appearance; they rubbed their skin with oil, wore beautiful clothes and had elaborate haircuts. They fastened their hair with golden brooches and put on extra gold jewellery when they went out. The relief itself reveals how much the Athenians cared about making things beautiful. In the words of Gombrich 1966: 64, this small masterpiece 'has retained the lucidity and beauty of the arrangement, which is no longer geometrical and angular (i.e. as in Egyptian art) but free and relaxed. The way the upper half is framed by the curve of the two women's arms, the way these lines are answered in the curves of the stool, the simple method by which Hegeso's beautiful hand becomes the centre of attention, the flow of the drapery round the forms of the body – all this combines to produce that simple harmony which only came into the world with Greek art of the fifth century.'

In the 1950s Finley created a stir by putting forward the theory that the mores and institutions that appear in these poems belonged not to the social system of Mycenaean Greece, but to that of the dark ages. (The poems do refer to Mycenaean 'things' such as places and weapons, but contain very few traces of Mycenaean institutions and culture.) His arguments were initially met with scepticism, but gradually won acceptance.[5] This, however, generated a further set of problems, at the core of which lay the third question above.

The puzzle of whether Homeric society belongs to the tenth and ninth centuries or to the eighth and whether or not the apparent co-existence within it of divergent customs (for example, the bestowal of dowries *and* the payment of bride-prices) is a result of poetic conflation of practices belonging to different periods[6] is important to researchers in many fields, notably archaeology. For the purposes of this book, however, it is not significant. The reason for this is that the period between the fall of the Mycenaean world (c. 1200) and the rise of the polis (c. 750) was dominated by one, and only one, *type* of society. This type differs markedly both from the society of the preceding palace culture and from the subsequent societies of the city-state. It falls neatly, on the other hand, into the category of societies that we earlier defined as 'feuding'.[7]

During most phases of European history pro-social behaviour has been equated with virtue and anti-social behaviour with vice. In the Homeric world this equation is almost completely reversed: the virtues (*aretai*) on which the heroes pride themselves tend to be self-regarding in the extreme. Devoting all their powers to individualistic pursuits, these heroes exalt their egotistic senses of honour above everything, even 'country' and life.[8] They constantly bristle with weapons, putting on their swords as soon as they get out of bed ('even before they put on their sandals').[9] They do not discriminate between premeditated and accidental homicide, in either case taking revenge of the most extreme kind on the perpetrator. (When as a child Patroclus accidentally killed another boy, his life was spared only because he went into exile; *Iliad* 23.85–8.) Their threshold of offence is extremely low and any perceived disrespect is instantly met with disproportionate reprisals. As the following examples show, the poet seems in general wholeheartedly to approve of this self-regarding value system.

---

[5] Cf., for example, van Wees 2002.   [6] Cf. Snodgrass 1974; I. Morris 1986b.
[7] See pp. 159–60. This is merely an echo of a point that has already been made many times; cf. Hammond 1985a.
[8] Cf. Finley 1978a: 113: 'Every value, every judgement, every action, all skills and talents, have the function of either defining honour or realizing it . . . even life must surrender to honour.'
[9] Van Wees 1998a: 335.

Agamemnon manages to outrage Achilles' sense of honour simply by appropriating the captive Briseis. As their captives include thousands of other women this hardly seems like a grave insult, but Achilles is so upset that not even 'seven tripods . . . ten talents of gold, twenty glittering cauldrons, twelve prize-winning race-horses, twenty Trojan captives and seven cities' can make up to him for it. He rejects these lavish attempts at atonement and refuses to return to the battle, thus crippling the war effort and inflicting immense suffering upon the Achaeans. When Hector kills Patroclus, Achilles captures a dozen young Trojans to sacrifice by way of 'bloodprice' (*poine*) at Patroclus' funeral (*Iliad* 23.175–6). Odysseus, assisted by the eternal gods, savagely slaughters an entire army of suitors not so much to pay them back for their unconventional advances to Penelope (largely inspired by his long absence and Penelope's delaying tactics) as to punish them for damaging his immensely inflated sense of honour.[10] In terms of the provocation-reaction mechanism discussed earlier, we have here a clear pattern in which slight insults or injuries provoke disproportionately extreme responses. The poet and his audiences thus appear to have rejoiced in the 'head for an eye' strategy that the speakers in the Athenian law courts went so far out of their way to avoid.[11]

The second criterion that we may use to compare levels of aggression across cultures is the course that conflict tends to take once it has erupted. In democratic Athens, as we have seen, the norm was adjudication by one's peers. In the world of Odysseus it was blood-feud. Short of compensation and armed combat,[12] this was the only available and acceptable way of dealing with grave insults and injuries. 'If only Odysseus would come back to his own country, he and his son would soon (*aipsa*) pay these men back for their violence,' cries Penelope, and after Odysseus has duly wreaked vengeance on the suitors Antinous' father addresses their fathers and relatives thus: '. . . this is all going to go down in history as an utter humiliation unless we take revenge on these men for murdering our brothers and sons . . .' (*Odyssey* 17.539–40 and 24.433–5). As Finley observes, had the goddess Athena not intervened to break the vicious circle 'no human force in Ithaca could have prevented still more bloodshed'.[13] This was a world in which few social compromises or humanitarian ideals inhibited

---

[10] F. W. Jones 1941. [11] See pp. 164–83.

[12] Cf. *Iliad* 9.632–6: 'A man will accept a payoff even from the killer of his son or brother, allowing the guilty party to stay in the country once he has paid enough to appease the injured man's proud spirit' [the speaker is Ajax]. For feud and blood-feud in Homer see Adkins 1969b; Hammond 1985a, 1985b.

[13] Finley 1978a: 77. Cf. Svenbro 1984 for an extensive analysis of this incident.

the lust for revenge[14] and there was no peaceful outlet to channel it away. Vengeance was at the heart of the entire hierarchy of values and was treated as a categorical duty whose proper discharge would rightly result in general admiration. 'Can you really not have heard', the goddess Athena (disguised as Menthes) asks Telemachus, 'of the universal acclaim that the great Orestes won by killing that traitor Aegisthus, who murdered his father?'[15] The gods themselves were not above helping man to wreak vengeance. The seer Halitherses interprets the omen of fighting eagles sent by Zeus by announcing that Odysseus must be close at hand, 'working out the death and destruction of all these men' (*Odyssey* 2.165–6).

Some modern researchers tend nonetheless to play down the differences between Homeric and civic morality, or even ignore them, asserting that from the time of Homer onwards Greek society was governed by a single overriding system of values. According to this view, Homeric heroes and democratic citizens alike accepted as binding the premise that one ought to help one's friends, harm one's enemies and preserve one's honour in pristine condition by retaliating to the slightest insult:[16] any failure to retaliate entailed dishonour and it was clearly better to die honourably than to accept ignoble defeat.[17] The moral norms accepted as binding by the petty rulers of the Homeric world and those that guided the citizens of the city-states were, in other words, identical, or nearly so. Both social types shared the same debased set of values; both failed to attain any higher degree of humanity.[18]

---

[14] For the undeniable existence in the poems of humanitarian ideals, albeit in rudimentary form, see de Romilly 1979: 13–22 and Zanker 1994; 1998.

[15] *Odyssey* 1.298–300; cf. Finley 1978a: 76.

[16] Cf. e.g. M. W. Blundell 1989: 26: 'Greek popular thought is pervaded by the assumption that one should help one's friends and harm one's enemies. These fundamental principles surface continually from Homer onwards and survive well into the Roman period . . .'; Lendon 2000: 13 and 22, respectively: 'Whatever the reason for the passing of the practice of blood vengeance from Greece, it left the ethic of vengeance intact.' 'The citizens of Greek states envisaged their cities like Homeric heroes, ranked against each other in terms of honour.'

[17] D. Cohen 1995a, to be read with Herman 1998b. The assumption of a single ideological system is not, however, universal; cf. e.g. Donlan 1980; Karavites 1982. Cf. especially MacIntyre 1981: 127, who asserts that in Athens (as opposed to Homeric society) 'all (i.e., the Sophists, Plato, Aristotle and the tragedians) do take it for granted that the milieu in which the virtues are to be exercised and in terms of which they are to be defined is the *polis*', and Svenbro 1984: 53, according to whom in the Archaic city (again as opposed to Homeric society) 'the right to revenge . . . becomes increasingly limited' ('le droit à la vengeance se trouve . . . progressivement limité').

[18] For instance, Adkins' general thesis concerning friendship in Homer and Aristotle is that 'in essentials the conditions of life [between Homer and Aristotle] have not changed . . . that the individual paterfamilias of fourth-century Athens is still in much the same position, and has much the same values, as the head of the Homeric οἶκος' (Adkins 1963: 41).

Anyone who regards this theory as likely is, whether knowingly or unknowingly, part of a tradition in ethics known as idealism. The adherents of this influential neo-Kantian school of thought, whose tenets were formulated in the nineteenth century,[19] maintain that values are timeless, abstract entities that belong to the realm of thought. These entities are separated by an unbridgeable chasm from concrete behaviour and social structures, which belong to the realm of nature. Within this frame of reference it makes perfectly good sense to regard the Homeric and the civic moral code as one and the same thing. Since all but identical value terms and very similar moral injunctions turn up in both Homeric and post-Homeric literature, it must *by definition* be true that both Homeric heroes and Athenian citizens participated in a single ideological system and shared the same values.

One trivial objection to this mode of thinking is that it clashes with the most elementary empirical observation. Norms and values remain constant through time only so long as social structures and conditions are constant; as soon as these change, norms and values change too.[20] It is thus very difficult, if not impossible, to account for metamorphoses of this sort within the idealistic tradition. If, however, we dissociate ourselves from this tradition and instead subscribe to the 'materialistic' view of morality (according to which values, behaviour and social structure are all aspects of a single phenomenon, none existing independently of the others) it will immediately appear that the social structure of democratic Athens differed so markedly from that of Homeric society as to share no more than a handful of values with it. (It did indeed share many of its value-terms and moral precepts, but that is an altogether different matter.)

Authority in the Homeric world was concentrated in the hands of the *heroes* and was highly personalised, relating directly to the amount of physical force each hero was able to muster. Even if it was backed up by the family members and retainers on the lower levels of the social pyramid, its scope remained narrow: a hero could force individuals to comply with his will, but could not coerce the people as a whole.[21] The heroes' households (Homer's *oikoi*, the chief centres of activity and power) were either at war with each other or loosely linked by temporary alliances. No distinction being made between a hero's personal wealth and his *oikos*' treasury, or between his personal relationships and the external affairs of his *oikos*, the

[19] Albert Lange (1866) *Geschichte des Materialismus*, Leipzig: J. Baedeker (trans. into English in 1974 as *The History of Materialism*. New York: Arno Press).
[20] See pp. 25–6.   [21] Cf. Donlan 1997b: 41.

idea of community had only a shadowy existence: impersonal institutions, bureaucracies, formalised legal systems and constitutional machinery were all absent. Homeric society was undoubtedly an advance on the entirely stateless existence of primitive hunter-gatherers, nomadic pastoralists and slash-and-burn cultivators in that within it kinship was no longer the sole constituent of society's strategic links. Some quintessential attributes of statehood were, on the other hand, conspicuous by their absence: special-isation of governmental roles (beyond a bare minimum), centralisation of coercive power (or at least its location somewhere beyond the *oikos*) and above all the channelling of emotions into reasoned patterns of action.[22]

RESTRUCTURING SENTIMENTS AND EMOTIONS

Far from being subjected to rational control, Homeric emotions were allowed (and indeed encouraged) to gush forth uninhibitedly from the psyche in all their naked glory. While avenging the death of his beloved friend Patroclus, Achilles addresses the mortally wounded Hector in the following terms: 'Don't cling to my knees or speak of your parents, you cur. I only wish I had the heart (*menos*) and enough pure rage (*thymos*) to hack off your flesh and eat it raw for what you have done to me. No one is going to hang around to drive the dogs off you . . . the dogs and the birds are going to be dining in state on every last scrap of you' (*Iliad* 22.345–54).

More often than not a successful vengeance killing is followed by muti-lation of the corpse to satisfy the requirement that revenge should be exces-sive.[23] The poet and his audience, wrote Finley, 'lingered lovingly over every act of slaughter . . . a fact which cannot be hidden or argued away, twist the evidence as one may in a vain attempt to fit archaic Greek values to a more gentle code of ethics'.[24]

The transition from statelessness to statehood is a complex process entail-ing a subtle interplay between demographic and economic growth and the breakdown of deeply entrenched class systems.[25] In the case of ancient Greece the transition also involved certain unique social and technological

---

[22] I am greatly indebted for this picture to Finley 1978a.   [23] Cf. Lendon 2000: 4–6.

[24] Finley 1978a: 118; cf. Onians 1951: 3–5 and Vermeule 1979: 98–9 for further examples of excessive cruelty in Homer.

[25] Cf. Runciman 1982: 351, who in a comparative analysis of the process of state formation postulates four necessary and jointly sufficient conditions for the emergence of a state from a stateless form of social organisation: 'specialisation of governmental roles; centralisation of enforceable authority; permanence, or at least more than ephemeral stability, of structure; and emancipation from real or fictive kinship as the basis of relations between the occupants of governmental roles and those whom they govern'. All four elements were present in the fully fledged polis.

advances such as the introduction of writing and coinage and the institution of chattel-slavery and the *phalanx* (the closed formation in which
the heavily armed hoplites drew up on the battlefield).[26] Familiarity with
these developments does not, however, help us to pinpoint the cause or the
driving force behind the transition itself, which must remain an enigma for
the time being. We can, on the other hand, identify four 'lesser' transitions
without which the advance from statelessness to statehood appears virtually inconceivable. The first of these is a shift from group identities based
on kinship to group identities based on locality or territory. The second
is the stripping of the extended family of its power to avenge wrongs and
the concentration of this power in formal, centralised organs of authority.
The third is the differentiation of the public from the private sphere.[27] The
fourth is a radical restructuring of man's psychological profile.

I propose now to consider the fourth of these transitions, not least because
it has attracted considerable attention in recent years. Researchers of the
process of state formation at different periods and in various parts of the
world have observed that the transition to statehood entails profound adaptations in human emotive responses. Feelings and emotions are gradually
reined in and channelled into forms of action that take into account not
only the interests of the interacting partners (and their closest associates) but
also those of the wider group around them. Human personality is accordingly remodelled to fit the new values, a process whose traces we may
find in the language of ancient Greece. Certain words used in democratic
Athens to designate 'gentle' values, such as *praos, philanthropos* and *epieikes*,
are totally absent from Homer (or are, like *epieikes*, used in a different sense).
They abound, however, in the writings of Aeschylus, Sophocles, Euripides,
Thucydides, Xenophon, Isocrates, Demosthenes, Plato and Aristotle.[28]

The radical nature of the changes in the human psyche that these
researchers were observing impressed them profoundly. 'After the emergence of cities', wrote Robert Redfield, 'man could not be what he had
been before.' Later he wrote, 'He suddenly found himself subjected to
rules of conduct independent of his conscience, and to procedures for the
impersonal enforcement of these rules. He became a *social* being.'[29] Norbert Elias observed that during the process of state formation in the Middle
Ages the 'unimaginable emotional outbursts' in which everyone who could
afford to 'abandon[ed] himself to the extreme pleasures of ferocity, murder,

---

[26] Cf. Snodgrass 1965; Hanson 1991c; Donlan 1997b.   [27] For which see Humphreys 1977–8.
[28] De Romilly 1979: ch. 2. *Praos*: 165 times; *philanthropos*: 120 times; *epieikes*: 262 times.
[29] R. Redfield 1953; 1962: 21.

torture, destruction, and sadism' were slowly replaced by the excessively gentle, polite and refined manners of the courtier and gentleman.[30] Fernand Braudel described the impact of town life on the psyche of early modern Europeans who had previously lived in the country thus: 'Towns are like electric transformers. They increase tension, accelerate the rhythm of exchange and constantly recharge human life.'[31] Finley wrote of the evolution of Greek civic society, in the course of which the Homeric hero gradually gave way to the citizen, 'The fact is that [the] notion of social obligation is fundamentally non-heroic. It reflects the new element, the community, at the one point at which it was permitted to override everything else . . . when the community began to move from the wings to the centre of the Greek stage, the hero quickly died out, for the honour of the hero was purely individual, something he lived and fought for only for its sake and his own sake . . . The honour of the community was a totally different quality, requiring another order of skills and virtues: in fact, the community could grow only by taming the hero and blunting the free exercise of his prowess, and a domesticated hero was a contradiction in terms.'[32]

A comparison of the Homeric and democratic Athenian concepts of honour in terms of the criteria we defined earlier (the threshold at which honour was regarded as having been impugned and the type of response deemed sufficient to redress the offence)[33] appears to justify Finley's interpretation. This comparison also makes clear the magnitude of the revolution in the history of moral ideas that reached its peak in democratic Athens,[34] during the course of which men began to take pride in discarding 'macho' behaviour and the citizens turned to embrace an entirely new form of 'honour' that had nothing to do with violent retribution. The social imperative to avoid at all costs precisely those courses of action that the hero would have regarded as most honourable became part of the very structure of the democratic polis. When Nicias asserted that he had never spoken against his convictions 'to gain honour' (Thucydides 6.9.2) he was defining his own honour in terms of the honour of the whole community, as was the speaker in a Pseudo-Demosthenic speech when he claimed that the blows

---

[30] Fontaine 1978: 248; Elias 1978a.   [31] Braudel 1967: 479.
[32] Finley 1978a: 116–17. Cf. Finley 1970: 87 for an account of this process from a different perspective: 'It has already been noted that in the Dark Age the community had only a shadowy existence as a political organism. How the shadow acquired substance is a process we cannot trace, but at the heart lay *the creation of institutions which subjected even the most powerful men to formal organs and rules of authority*' (my italics).
[33] See p. 165.   [34] See pp. 202–3.

that he received while engaging in an act of self-help were struck not against him but against the Council and the entire *demos* ([Demosthenes] 47.41, *Against Euergus*). The honour of the community was indeed, as Finley says, 'a totally different quality'. What made Nicias and the speaker in *Against Euergus* so strikingly different from Achilles as human types was their will-ingness to subordinate their own self-regarding, 'natural' drives to rational considerations of communal utility.

The theoretical implications of all this may better be seen by once again taking up the issue of Mediterranean unity.[35] If the transformation from hero into citizen did indeed take place as we describe, the claim that the importance accorded to the *point d'honneur* is predicated upon geograph-ical or even climatic factors begins to appear rather more than shaky. The Homeric and democratic Athenian societies shared almost identical geo-graphical situations and climatic conditions, yet their moral systems were strikingly dissimilar. This suggests that perceptions of honour and shame are functions of political organisation and social structure rather than of geography and climate, their sway being inversely related to the potency of state power and law enforcement. I therefore suggest that we should replace the 'unity of the Mediterranean' model with a scheme taking into account the parameters I have mentioned (see **Fig. 8.2**). Considering the Mediterranean as a cultural area has its own appeal and can yield important insights. Considering it as an area within which perceptions of honour and shame are uniform,[36] however, raises insurmountable difficulties, making it impossible to account for the transition from the set of values represented by the hero to that represented by the citizen. Either another explanation must be found for this transition, or the idea of a specifically Mediterranean 'honour and shame' syndrome must be abandoned altogether.

As the human psyche gradually adapted to the requirements of civic exis-tence, honesty acquired pride of place. It was accorded no such respect in the Homeric poems, in which diametrically opposed virtues are commended. Autolycus is said to have surpassed all men in thieving and perjury, acquir-ing the famous helmet once used by Odysseus by breaking into Amyntor's house (*Iliad* 10.266). This admirable facility is in part attributed to his adroit management of his relationships with the gods: Hermes was partic-ularly gratified by Autolycus' numerous sacrifices and was always happy to help him out (*Odyssey* 19.396–8). An entire spectrum of activities involving

---

[35] See pp. 95–7.
[36] This is the view taken by Horden and Purcell 2000: ch. 12. C. S. Stewart 2001 is a salutary indication of the new tendency in anthropological studies to turn away from this paradigm.

PROVOCATION	REACTION	SENSE OF HONOUR	SOCIAL SETTING
slight	excessive, violent = REVENGE	inflated	not centralised
excessive, violent	slight + PUNISHMENT	deflated	centralised

Figure 8.2 The interrelationship of perceptions of honour and social structure
The column headed 'social setting' refers to the overall social structure within which a person is provoked, injured or attacked. 'Not centralised' means that this structure does not incorporate any mechanism or agency (outside the group formed by that person and his closest friends and relatives) that can be expected to deal capably and appropriately with the aggressor on behalf of his victim. 'Centralised' means that such an agency does exist. This model can accommodate a whole range of concrete examples drawn from a variety of societies past and present, Mediterranean and non-Mediterranean. Homeric heroes, early modern European noblemen, Lebanese *abadayat*, Sicilian *mafiosi*, Greek Sarakatsani and nineteenth-century Greek *klephths* all belong to the 'not centralised' structure. The 'centralised' structure covers people living in tightly organised social systems, whether of modern Western type (where the responsibility for punishing aggressors devolves upon special agencies such as police forces) or of ancient type (where, as in democratic Athens, responsibility devolved upon a power elite).

dishonest behaviour is evaluated positively and no bourn of acceptability divides trade from raiding trips to acquire human or other booty. A Homeric host might well casually ask respectable strangers whom he was entertaining as guests whether they were merchants or pirates (*Odyssey* 3.71; cf. *Iliad* 9.406; *Odyssey* 1.398, 14.246–300). 'Being in this line of business', writes Thucydides, 'was by no means seen as shameful, but thought to be rather dashing' (1.5.1). Oaths that were supposed to ensure that promises were kept did exist, but perjury was not regarded as any great matter. Homeric society even provided a convenient get-out by means of which obligations might be evaded: it was always possible to keep to the letter of an oath while breaking its spirit.

In fifth- and fourth-century Athens, by contrast, great store was set by the norm of honesty. Sophocles, as we have seen, singled Athens out as a city famed for its piety, fairness and truthfulness (*Oedipus at Colonus* 1125–7).

Aristeides was renowned for his justness (*dikaios*) in his relations with his fellow-citizens (Plutarch, *Aristides* 25.2). Pericles' capacity to sway the masses was put down in part to his 'known integrity' (*diaphanos adorotatos genomenos*; Thucydides 2.65.8). Incoming magistrates swore to govern justly and according to the law (see **Fig. 9.6**). According to a speech spuriously attributed to Demosthenes, holders of public office 'tend to diminish the common good (*ta koina*) if they are dishonest (*phauloi*), but do everything possible to further it if they are honest (*epieikeis*) and willing to respect the laws' ([Demosthenes] 26.2, *Against Aristogeiton* 2). Legislation was passed to enforce honest dealing in the *agora* (see **Fig. 10.3**). Dishonesty was severely censured, at least insofar as internal affairs were concerned. Deception of the people (*apate tou demou*) was considered to be one of the gravest of crimes.[37] Dicaeogenes, who was said to cheat his friends and members of his family, was portrayed by Isaeus as the stereotype of a 'bad' citizen.[38] Honesty was also supposed to be the collective virtue that guided the people in many of their enterprises. Thucydides has Pericles declare that when dealing with enemies the Athenians, unlike the Spartans, rely not so much on deception (*apatais*) as on the courage that springs from their souls (Thucydides 2.39.1). Demosthenes' speech *Against Leptines* describes how the Assembly dealt with a Spartan demand for repayment of the hundred talents borrowed from them by the Thirty Tyrants to crush democratic opposition to their rule. In a signal illustration of their general policy of under-reacting to provocation, the democratic Athenians decided to repay this debt, thereby demonstrating that they preferred honesty to material gain even in external relations and thought it important to deal fairly even with those who had done them considerable harm. These examples, as Hesk has observed, cast doubt on Dover's introspective generalisation that 'the Athenians always regarded the deception of an enemy as morally commendable'.[39]

Athenian society is frequently indicted as intolerant, bad-tempered and violent because of the moral message that appears to be contained in the injunction 'help your friends and harm your enemies' (*tous men philous eu poiein, tous d'echthrous kakos*).[40] It has often been argued or implied that

---

[37] See p. 297.
[38] Isaeus 5.39–40, *On the Estate of Dicaeogenes*. On this and on the stereotype of the 'bad' citizen, see Hunter 1994: 110.
[39] Demosthenes 20.11–13; cf. Isocrates 7, 67, *Areopagiticus*, with Hesk 2000: 41–3, esp. n. 73.
[40] Here are some further examples, supplementing the ones listed in n. 16: B. M. W. Knox 1961: 3: 'This code was already a very old one in the fifth century BC, and although more appropriate to the conditions of a heroic society, it was still recognized in democratic Athens as a valid guide to conduct'; Hester 1977: 33: To [Sophocles], '[h]elping one's friends and harming one's enemies is the

since this injunction (or at least its second half) expresses the savagery of heroic (i.e. feuding) society and since it puts in frequent appearances in both Homer and the Classical authors it must encapsulate an ethos that dominated Greek society from Homer onwards. In other words, citizens, like heroes, accepted that it was an overriding obligation to help their friends, harm their enemies and preserve their own honour by avenging every insult; citizens, like heroes, saw any failure to retaliate as dishonourable, and citizens, like heroes, deemed it better to die with honour than to live on ignobly in defeat. Both citizen and hero (or so this argument runs) participated in a single ideological system and shared the same values. Even though Plato questions the value of this injunction (the exclusive preserve, according to him, of tyrants, barbarians and despots), even though Sophocles' *Ajax* can be interpreted as a criticism of it[41] and even though to this day most people follow it while paying lip-service to higher ideals, this supposed rule of conduct has been treated as one of the most obvious pointers to Athens' execrable moral standards.

In order to examine this argument further, we shall now take a short detour into human prehistory. Every living language divides the social universe into 'us' and 'them', 'our own people' and 'the others', insiders and outsiders, friends and enemies. This dichotomy is deeply ingrained; so deeply, in fact, that it appears to represent not cultural conditioning, but some hard-wired attribute of the human mind. To the historian the most important question raised by this fact is that of which people were divided into which dichotomic categories during which period. Palaeoanthropologists are agreed that socially speaking most of the four or five million years of hominid evolution have been dominated by small kinship groups: by families, nuclear or extended, and by clans and tribes.[42] In living kinship societies, 'the conduct of individuals to one another is very largely regulated on the basis of kinship, this being brought about by the formation of fixed patterns of behaviour for each recognized kind of kinship relation'.[43] This suggests that any member of a past society of this sort would have reckoned

duty of the hero [in this case, Oedipus at Colonus], alike in life and death'; D. Cohen 1995a: 65–6: 'Since a basic moral principle of Greek societies from Homer onward is that justice requires one to help one's friends and harm one's enemies, enmity and rivalry inevitably produce mutual attempts to harm, hinder, defeat, and dishonour one's enemies'; Mitchell 1996: 11: 'The dictum "help friends and harm enemies" pervades the whole of Greek literature from Homer to Alexander, and was a basic moral principle for determining behaviour.'

[41] Plato, *Republic* 1.335e; cf. *Crito* 49b–d and B. M. W. Knox 1961.

[42] E. O. Wilson 1978: 153; 1980: 290–6. This inference was reached by backwards extrapolation from living hunter-gatherer societies.

[43] A. R. Radcliffe-Brown (1952) *Structure and Function in Primitive Society*. London: Routledge and Kegan Paul: 29.

anybody who did not count as kin and was hence excluded from the group as 'one of them', 'other', 'an outsider' or 'an enemy'. Non-kin, in other words, were tantamount to enemies; where kinship stopped enmity began, enmity that was not merely a latent sentiment, as we conceive of enmity today, but a belligerent emotion that found expression in violent action and recognised no compromise.

There were, however, forces at work that tended to blur this distinction, gradually mitigating the more extreme expressions of primordial hostility. One of these forces had to do with breeding. Man realised very early on in his prehistory that endogamy was a poor strategy for the perpetuation of the family line. It was imperative that children should be conceived with outsiders, and their conception necessitated the opening up of avenues of peaceful interaction with groups of outsiders who would normally have been regarded as hostile. Exogamy paved the way for a second avenue of peaceful interaction with the hostile 'other', modelled on marriage. This avenue was friendship, or rather what in an earlier study I have called ritualised friendship.[44] Ritualised friendship differed from what we now call friendship in three important respects: it was instituted between members of separate social units, it was forged by means of rituals and it mimicked kinship. Unlike kinship by blood, which was a 'given' relationship, ritualised friendship was (like kinship by marriage) a 'created' relationship whose creation entailed endowing non-kin with some of the attributes of 'real kinship' (see **Fig. 8.3a**). Both prehistoric marriage and prehistoric friendship being concluded with outsiders, the organisation of society left no room for the type of social relationship that we now know as 'friendship'.

Moving on now to the more familiar ground of the Homeric poems, we can see at once that the society that these poems represent consisted of more than merely kinship groups. The hero and his family were at the centre of the Homeric *oikos*, but grouped around them we find various other people to whom they were not related. Nonetheless, the twin institutions of exogamy and ritualised friendship still existed and continued to be the chief avenue for peaceful interaction with the members (and especially the rulers) of other *oikoi*. We need at this point to ask ourselves just what sort of sentiment and/or social bond the term *philia* was generally used to describe. Finley suggests that in the world of Odysseus this term 'was used in every context in which there were positive ties between people',[45] and this generalisation appears to hold good for the whole of Classical Greece. Greek *philia*, unlike modern 'friendship' (which tends to be incompatible

---

[44] Herman 1987.   [45] Finley 1978a: 126, referring to the verb *philein*.

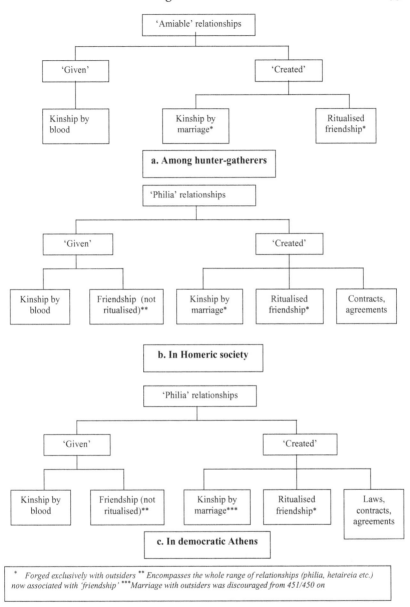

Figure 8.3 The structure of 'amiable'/*philia* relationships, representing the 'positive' alternative to relations of enmity and hostility (inspired by Pitt-Rivers 1973)

with kinship), was inclusive of kinship; the term could be used not only of a connection with someone to whom one was not related, but also of a relationship with a parent, spouse, sibling or other relative.[46] (It may be noted in passing that its scope was even wider than this: inter-state treaties were often called 'treaties of *philia*'.) Elaborating on Finley's insight, I would suggest that the reason for this was that the term *philia* expressed the conceptual alternative to the primordial hostility that prevailed between separate kinship groups in prehistoric times. It was thus the backdrop for a whole range of positive, non-hostile relationships that subsequently came into being within and between groups that were no longer dominated by the kinship principle ('normal' or 'non-ritualised' friendship, endogamy, laws, contracts and agreements). **Fig. 8.3** shows that the world of the Homeric poems (**b**) may in this respect be regarded as an intermediary stage between a kinship society (**a**) and a society such as that of democratic Athens (**c**): non-ritualised friendship, agreements and alliances already exist, albeit in poorly articulated form, but marriage alliances and pacts of ritualised friendship are still concluded exclusively with outsiders. Laws, of course, are still non-existent.

We shall now move on to examine democratic Athens against this background, taking as our starting point the primordial attributes of Greek *philia* rather than those of some imaginary ancient counterpart of modern 'friendship'. We shall, in other words, be examining the whole range of positive ties found amongst the people of Athens, both 'given' and 'created' (see **Fig. 8.3c**). Similarly, in examining enmity and hostility we shall be looking not only at instances in which our sources have thought it proper to use the word *echthra*, but at every type of negative relation in which the democratic Athenians engaged. Our central question may be formulated as follows: How did the Athenians regulate the sum total of amiable and hostile relationships within their city's bounds so as to make that sum total compatible with the democratic form of government that they designed?

We shall begin by examining two accounts of friendship gone wrong, one from dark-age Greece and the other from democratic Athens. According to a quasi-mythical story preserved in the works of later authors, a Messenian called Polychares put all his trust in his beloved *xenos* ('guest-friend', or, as I have suggested, 'ritualised friend'), a Spartan called Euaephnus. Euaephnus,

---

[46] For a systematic collection of the evidence, see Charlier and Raepsaet 1971; cf. Millett 1991: 113: '. . . we have already met *philoi* in the form of fathers, parents, brothers, comrades, benefactors, fellow-tribesmen and fellow-citizens; to which might be added, husbands and wives, fellow-voyagers (*sumplooi*), comrades-in-arms (*sustratiotai*), guest-friends (*xenoi*) and cousins . . .' For a different view, which the present writer finds unsustainable, see Konstan 1997, to be read with Herman 1998c.

however, shamelessly betrayed him, cheating him out of some valuable resources. When this perfidy was revealed Euaephnus offered to compensate Polychares, but instead of fulfilling this promise he treacherously murdered Polychares' son. On this Polychares went to complain to the kings and ephors in Lacedaemon, where he made a great nuisance of himself, loudly lamenting the loss of his son and endlessly rehearsing the wrongs that he had suffered at Euaephnus' hand. All this was in vain. Unable to obtain redress, Polychares was driven out of his mind and proceeded to murder every Lacedaemonian he could get his hands on.[47]

In this story the relationship between Polychares and Euaephnus seems to exist in almost total isolation. Things were significantly different in the Classical city, where all personal relations existed within a wider power system. This difference is evident in the following extract from the Demosthenic speech *Against Nicostratus.*

Nicostratus was a neighbour and 'intimate' of Apollodorus, who repeatedly describes him as 'a man of my own age-group' and a 'true friend'.[48] The reciprocity between the two men seems to have remained well balanced for a long time, so that the highest levels of trust and co-operation existed between them. As Apollodorus put it, 'In the end I felt so comfortable with him that I was happy to do him any favour, while he made himself extremely useful to me by keeping an eye on my business and managing it; whenever I was sent abroad on trierarch duty, or went abroad to take care of my own business interests, I used to leave him in charge of the entire farm' (53.4, *Against Nicostratus*).

The relationship took a turn for the worse when Nicostratus was taken captive while pursuing some runaway slaves. In the spirit of 'true friendship', Apollodorus put one thousand drachmae towards his ransom. When more money was needed to pay off Nicostratus' creditors, Apollodorus borrowed sixteen minae (at an exorbitant rate of interest and against a huge security) to give to Nicostratus. It was at this point, according to Apollodorus, that Nicostratus defaulted: 'But as soon as Nicostratus got his hands on the money he showed no signs of being in the least grateful to me for helping him out. Instead he instantly started working out how to rob me of my money and *become my enemy . . .*' (*eis echthran katastaie*; 53.13).

There is no need to go into the long list of hostile acts by means of which Nicostratus is alleged to have tried to defraud Apollodorus of his money.

---

[47] Pausanias 4.4.4–8; Diodorus Siculus 8.7.
[48] *Panu oikeios diekeimeta*, Demosthenes 53.4; *helikiotes*, 53.4; *alethinos philos*, 53.7, 12. A discussion of the Nicostratus incident that stresses credit relations appears in Millett 1991: 53–9.

The important point for our purposes is that Apollodorus and Nicostratus had, like Polychares and Euaephnus before them, been both 'bosom friends' and business partners. Unlike Polychares, however, Apollodorus had a centrally organised system of sanctions to appeal to when his friendship went so badly wrong. This having been both a business partnership and a friendship, he was able to call on the dikasts for justice in both the legal and the moral sphere; the dikasts had it in their power both to award compensation and to deal out punishment. It may legitimately and indeed plausibly be claimed that Athenian friendships seem to have been marked by 'an element of unpredictability and uncertainty'.[49] Unless we specify the standards according to which we intend to judge these qualities, however, the analytical value of this assertion will be negligible. Judged by the standards of dark-age Greek societies or by those of the sort of society we earlier defined as 'feuding', Athenian friendships appear remarkably predictable and certain.

Both Polychares and Apollodorus ended up 'harming their enemy'. There was, however, a considerable difference in their manner of doing so: instead of indiscriminately slaughtering a large number of people who happened to have been born in the same place as Nicostratus, Apollodorus merely sued him. The alleged identity between Homeric and Athenian value terms and moral injunctions is a red herring, a matter of form, not of substance: the stories of Polychares and Apollodorus demonstrate that a single label can mask diametrically opposed types of action. The guiding norms of Homeric society and of Athenian society differed as sharply as did the outlines of their respective social structures. We shall now examine this contention in more detail, looking first at some general and then at some more specific illustrations of my argument.

As we have seen, in 404 the oligarchs put about 1,500 Athenians to death without bothering to try them first. On their return to power in 403 the democrats chose to forgive the oligarchs and declare an amnesty. If 'helping friends and harming enemies' really was the dominant Athenian ethos, they should on regaining power surely have proceeded to settle a few scores by exterminating as many of the oligarchs as possible. Declaring an amnesty and forgiving them was all wrong.[50]

We may also note that the plaintiffs of the law-court speeches are always asking the dikasts to forgive them for suing the enemies who have allegedly

---

[49] Foxhall 1998b: 56. This sentence encompasses the essence of the article.
[50] See pp. 396–8 for a more detailed analysis of the amnesty.

done them wrong.[51] In a variation on this theme, Demosthenes accuses Aeschines of prosecuting him not because he wants to see justice done, but because he is eaten up with hatred (*echthra*) and other emotions that are out of place in a court of law (Demosthenes 18.5, 12, 16, *On the Crown*).[52] The entire principle at work here is eloquently summed up by the orator Lycurgus: 'A just citizen will not let private enmity *(dia tas idias echthras)* induce him to start a public prosecution against one who does the state (*polis*) no harm. On the contrary, it is those who break his country's laws whom he will look on as his personal enemies; crimes which affect the public will, in his eyes, offer public grounds for enmity towards the criminals' (Lycurgus 1.6, *Against Leocrates*, trans. J. O. Burtt). Had this really been a society whose dominant ethos was 'helping friends and harming enemies', no one would have tried to impress the dikasts by apologising for suing his enemy or by declaring his contempt for personal animosity.

Finally, Athenian society, like every other society, had its tensions. Many of its members felt that its power and resources were divided unfairly and feeling could run high between free men and slaves, between oligarchs and democrats and between rich and poor.[53] Athens must undoubtedly have seen her share of quarrels and enmities, both deep, structural disagreements stemming from tensions of the sort that we have mentioned and more superficial ones stemming from the clash of incompatible personalities. (Personal enmities were, in particular, frequently bound up with political differences.)[54] As we have seen, however, these tensions, quarrels and enmities did not tend to end in open confrontation, but generally came to some sort of peaceful resolution; they may have rocked the societal boat, but they did not overturn it. The explanation for this that we have already mooted is that Athens, unlike most other Greek states, had created a climate of opinion within which compromise appeared clearly preferable

---

[51] This point is brought out well in Christ 1998.

[52] It is worth quoting Goodwin's paraphrase of Demosthenes 18.12: 'The thought is as follows: – The charges include some of the gravest known to the law, which provides the severest penalties for the offences; but this suit was never brought to punish anybody for these. I will tell you what its object is (αὕτη): it is to give a personal enemy an opportunity to vent his spite and malice, while it gives the state no means of properly punishing my crimes if I am guilty' (W. W. Goodwin [1904] *Demosthenes: On the Crown*. Cambridge: Cambridge University Press: 9). Once again it is clear that the dikasts disapproved of prosecutions fuelled by personal enmity. For the observation that 'discussions on enmity in Athenian forensic speeches were to a large extent based on the normative expectation that public suits should *not* be dominated by private enmity', see Kurihara 2003: 466.

[53] See pp. 72–80.

[54] Rhodes 1996; 1998. At p. 157 of the latter work, Rhodes notes that the phenomenon whereby members of the British House of Commons may be political opponents but personal friends is hard to imagine in Athens.

to escalating conflict. Had 'helping friends and harming enemies' been her guiding spirit and had her system provided no peaceful means of resolving conflict, Athens' climate of opinion would have been one within which an escalation of conflict appeared clearly preferable to acceptance of a less than advantageous solution. If promoting conflict rather than avoiding it had been its dominant behavioural pattern, Athenian society would have fallen apart at the first onset of extreme crisis.

We shall now move on to some more specific illustrations of my argument. Had the influence of the maxim 'help friends and harm enemies' upon Athenian behaviour been anything more than negligible, it would not have made much sense for Pericles to describe the Athenians as characteristically free, open and tolerant (Thucydides 2.37.2). Gregory of Tours' thumbnail sketch of sixth-century Gaul ('Scarcely a day passed without someone being murdered, scarcely an hour without some quarrel or other, scarcely a minute without some person or other having cause for sorrow')[55] is far more convincing as a description of a society in which harming enemies was deemed so overriding an imperative as to overrule most other considerations. We have incontrovertible evidence of certain less than savoury aspects of the Athenian character: the scurrilous personal abuse that Athenian litigants habitually hurled at each other in the law courts, for example,[56] or the notorious 'curse tablets' with which they tried to hex their enemies (see **Fig. 9.7**). Crucially, however, this sort of material appears in the record side by side with far more extensive evidence that conflict was frequently resolved by the exercise of forgiveness, moderation and self-restraint. Some of this evidence has tended to be overlooked or given insufficient weight, which may have contributed something to the pessimistic view of Athenian society. Here are some examples.

The litigants of the forensic speeches often lay claim to the principle of *not* harming enemies in terms that make it clear that they expect this to be regarded as a virtue. In one of Lysias' speeches, for example, the speaker boasts that although his association with an important man called Sostratus has enabled him to advance up the social ladder he has *not* used this connection 'either to avenge [him]self on an enemy (*echthros*) or to serve a friend (*philos*)'. The fact that he expects this assertion to influence the dikasts in his favour can only mean that the received opinion of the time did not favour the settling of accounts even with enemies (Lysias 9.13, *For the Soldier*). The same was true of political rivals. Aristeides and Themistocles supported diametrically opposed policies, often attacking one

---

[55] *History of the Franks* 10.15.   [56] Cf. pp. 144–5.

another fiercely and attempting by every possible means to diminish each other's influence. We are nonetheless told that when an accusation was laid against Themistocles Aristides refused to jump on the bandwagon, turning down this golden opportunity to pay Themistocles out for his part in getting Aristides ostracised (Plutarch, *Aristides* 25.7). In the fourth century Isocrates described how the coming together of the Athenians at their great festivals reminded them of the kinship (*syngeneia*) between them and made them 'feel more kindly (*eumenesteros*) towards each other for the future'. As a result, as he put it, 'it is possible to find with us as nowhere else the most faithful friendships (*philias . . . pistotatous*) and to enjoy the most varied social intercourse' (Isocrates 4.43, 45, *Panegyricus*, trans. G. Norlin). A speech spuriously attributed to Demosthenes asserts that the Athenians shared a natural bond of mutual kindness (*philanthropia*) and lived as a corporate body in the city 'just as families live in their private homes' (*hosper hai sungeneiai tas idias oikousin oikias*). Although either of these settings may abound in divergent views, we are told, in both any form of behaviour that might stir up antagonism is stifled by the exercise of moderation (*metriotes*) and tolerance, with the result that a general spirit of concord or harmony unites the city's members (*homonoia*; [Demosthenes] 25, 87–9, *Against Aristogeiton 1*). The spirit that this passage describes is recalled by the many tombstones (see **Fig. 8.4**) that represent the binding together in *philia* of various past and present family members and friends.[57] The prevalence of similar concepts and sentiments throughout the Greek literature of this time[58] belies the conclusion that the maxim 'help friends and harm enemies' may justly be said to dominate the whole of Greek literature from Homer to Alexander. This conclusion can be supported

---

[57] Cf. Osborne 1998b: 39, who reaches a similar conclusion by examining a series of grave reliefs from an evolutionary perspective: 'In grave reliefs . . . the public world, in which the young men of sixth-century monuments display themselves, is replaced [i.e. in the fifth century] by a private world, a world dominated numerically by women, thematically by the family, and in which men appear as family members first, and as brave citizens and successful competitors in the gymnasium second. The emphasis has shifted from asserting a claim that the deceased led a glorious life, exemplary among the elite, to expressing the loss of a member of a household, of a friend or comrade. As we shift from predominantly single figures to predominantly groups, the display of competitive virtues is replaced by the assertion of collaborative virtues.' The deeply affectionate nature of parental *philia* in Athens is well brought out by Charlier and Raepsaet 1971.

[58] One of the Seven Sages, Cleoboulos of Lindos, is reported to have said that 'we should do a favour to a friend to bind him closer to us and to an enemy in order to make a friend of him' (Diogenes Laertius 1.91). A second-century law from Beroia regulating the rights and duties of a gymnasiarch reads: 'I shall exercise the duties of gymnasiarch, according to the law of gymnasiarchs, and when there is no provision in the law according to my judgement of what is just and moral, without favouring friends or harming enemies against the law . . .' (Ph. Gauthier and M. B. Hatzopoulos [1993] *La loi gymnasiarchique de Beroia*. Athens: Meletemata: Face A).

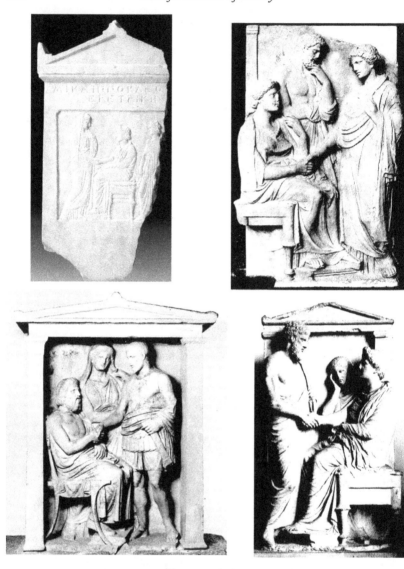

Figure 8.4 Reflections of *philia* in visual art
Attic tombstone *stelai* such as these often commemorate the intensity of the sentiments
that united relatives and friends in life and continued to bind them after one of them was
dead. One inscription praises a deceased wife for 'returning the love of her loving
husband' (*IG* II² 12067); another describes the woman it commemorates as 'one to whom
her husband felt utmost desire' (*IG* II² 10864). As works of art on public display,
monuments of this sort both reflected and fostered public attitudes. They could be
extremely expensive, 'but they were quite overshadowed by those commissioned from
Greek artists by dynasts on the fringe of the Greek world . . .' (J. K. Davies 1993: 165).

only by excluding from the evidence the many passages that attest to an entirely contrary attitude to friendship and enmity.[59] If this maxim was not the basic moral principle that directed the Athenians' behaviour, we must now ask ourselves what was. Is it possible for us to pinpoint the formula by means of which the Athenians reconciled their relationships, amiable or hostile, with the requirements of their democratic society? To answer this question we shall now examine some more aspects of the remarkable psychological metamorphosis undergone by the human psyche during the transition from the Homeric society to the civic, beginning with attitudes to cruelty.

AGONISTIC PASTIMES

If we compare the spectator sports and pastimes that were popular in Athenian society with those favoured by Homeric, Roman, mediaeval and early modern societies, we will observe some striking differences. People in the latter group of societies were particularly fond of duels, gladiatorial combats, war and circus games, tournaments and public executions, all of which offered their audiences visual satisfaction in the form of scenes of unremitting bloodshed and suffering. There is only one conclusion to be drawn from this: these audiences enjoyed cruelty enormously and liked watching people and animals in pain. Democratic Athens was another matter. Animal fights and some combat sports were popular, but any cruelty beyond this was not on offer.[60]

In most present-day Western societies cruelty to animals is rightly regarded as insufferable. There are, however, different levels of cruelty, and the Athenian attitude towards cruelty to animals must be viewed alongside the attitudes to animals displayed by other past cultures. The *Iliad* tells us that Achilles honoured the memory of his friend Patroclus by throwing onto the pyre four powerfully built horses, together with two dogs whose throats he had cut himself, and by butchering and burning twelve Trojan youths (Homer, *Iliad* 23.171–5; cf. 21.27–33). In eighteenth-century France the practice of cat burning, in which baskets full of cats were ceremonially set on fire while the crowds exulted in their pitiful cries, was popular for no other reason than that people enjoyed it. Torturing animals was

---

[59] Cf. E. M. Harris 2004a for a similar conclusion.

[60] It is necessary to emphasise this point in view of the fact that historians of sports and the arts tend to pass judgement (usually negative) on the Athenians' (or Greeks') tolerance for violence on the assumption that the Classical, Hellenistic and Roman periods comprised a single ideological system. It is generally agreed, however, that under Roman influence Greek sports and pastimes underwent considerable brutalisation. Roman gladiatorial games, for instance, were only introduced to the Greek world by Antiochus IV Epiphanes (Livy 41.20). Cf. Poliakoff 1987: 68–93.

Figure 8.5 Animal fights
Above, a fight between a cat and a dog; below, a cockfight. Both cockfighting and dicing
took place in the Athens gaming house (*kybeion*; Aeschines 1.53, *Against Timarchus*).
Animal fights were thus a part of the gambling complex. A description of a fight between
a puppy and a lion cub suggests that they may also have been used to foretell the
future (Herodotus 3.32). That many Athenians (in this case, post-Classical) were fond
of animals may be inferred from certain burial practices: during the recent construction
of the Metro, the tomb of a dog was found to contain glass offerings and the dog's
collar (Blackman 2000: 8).

generally found amusing throughout early modern Europe.[61] The Athenians were fond of animal fights, but they liked them because they enjoyed
gambling on the results rather than because it was regarded as pleasur-
able to watch animals suffering (see **Fig. 8.5**). Accordingly Theophrastus,

[61] Cf. R. Darnton (1984) *The Great Cat Massacre and Other Episodes of French Cultural History.*
Harmondsworth: Penguin.

Aristotle's pupil and successor as head of the Lyceum, condemned the killing of non-dangerous animals as unjust, arguing that animals were akin (*oikeioi*) to humans in reasoning, having developed from the same beginnings (*archai*).[62]

The Athenians' fondness for cockfights has had an unfortunate effect upon certain modern researchers, who have interpreted the aggressive fighting cock as the quintessential symbol of the Athenian male's pugnacious virility.[63] There are a number of reasons for this interpretation. In democratic Athens, for example, cocks were given garlic to eat before they were set together to fight, while men were fed onions before being sent forth to battle (Xenophon, *Symposium* 4.9). The decorative plumes that the hoplites wore on their helmets were, moreover, called *lophos*, which was also the word for a cock's comb.[64] A close reading of the sources suggests, however, that despite these and other literary parallels between the Athenian fighting man and the Athenian fighting cock, fighting cocks were not generally regarded as models of or incentives to Athenian male belligerence.

Let us now return to the Ariston–Conon encounter.[65] After recounting at considerable length the wrongs that he has allegedly suffered at the hands of Conon and his companions ('they . . . jumped me and ripped off my cloak, tripped me up and threw me in the mud, then all piled in and beat me up until I had a split lip and my eyes were swollen shut. When they had finished I was such a mess that I couldn't manage to get up or say anything'), Ariston describes his predicament as follows: 'While I was lying there I heard them saying all sorts of disgusting things. A lot of it was such foul-mouthed filth (*blasphemia*) that it wouldn't be right to repeat it in court. But I will tell you one thing that shows exactly how in your face this guy is and proves that he started the whole thing off. He started crowing like a cock that's won a fight, while his mates egged him on to flap his elbows against his sides like wings. After that I was carried home by some passers-by, without any proper clothes, since these people had gone off with my cloak' (Demosthenes 54.8–9, *Against Conon*).

This passage has frequently figured in modern research as a powerful symbol of the aggressive spirit supposed to have pervaded interpersonal relationships in Athenian society. One commentator has regarded its symbolism

---

[62] Brink 1955–6. The argument is based on a passage from Theophrastus' *Peri Eusebeias*, preserved in Porphyry's *De Abstinentia*.

[63] E.g. Hoffmann 1974; Winkler 1990: 49: 'Cock-fighting was a supremely clear representation of zero-sum competition.'

[64] Further points of resemblance are listed in Csapo 1993: 13, n. 60.

[65] See pp. 123–4, 156–9 and 213.

as so obvious as to warrant the conclusion that cockfights were actually
the theme around which Athenian social life revolved: 'The entire order of
Athenian society – men, women, children, rich and poor, free and slave – all
use the cockfight to express their relations to one another and their feelings
about those relations.'[66] 'Conon's triumphant behaviour', writes another
commentator, 'perfectly illustrates the hubris which Aristotle . . . attributes
to wealthy men anxious to demonstrate their superiority. His mimicry of
a fighting cock in a victory dance captures the agonistic element of such
hubristic behaviour: this was not just a drunken brawl, but an act deliberately designed to humiliate and subordinate.'[67] 'The role of Athenian
culture in cockfighting . . .' writes a third, 'in affording the excitements
of sport and gambling, and providing powerful, if ambivalent, images of
masculine, aggressive and phallocentric assertiveness, has been much illu-
minated recently in accounts stimulated in part by discussion of the Getty
Birds kalyx-krater, in part by Clifford Geertz's influential essay on Balinese
cockfights.'[68]

Here we should remind ourselves of the danger of fusing modern and
ancient norms.[69] Yet again a vital piece of evidence has been misunderstood
because it has been viewed as a text every part of whose content should
be understood as a direct and unambiguous revelation of the nature of the
society within which it was produced (and indeed on every part of whose
content it is appropriate to pass moral judgement without further ado).
This forensic speech is, however, a remnant of a human interaction that
took place in time and space, and it would be foolish in the extreme to
regard its content as unambiguous given that the purpose of this speech
was to manipulate the responses of the dikasts. It is vital to remember that
Ariston is addressing himself to the dikasts, not to us. It is utterly irrelevant
how *we* may choose to judge this incident morally, whether we consider it
to have been 'not just a drunken brawl, but an act deliberately designed to
humiliate and subordinate', an exhibition of phallocentrism, or any other
form of revelation that the Athenians were obsessed with fighting cocks.
All that should matter to us is how the dikasts are likely to have interpreted
this speech. Ariston obviously thought that the dikasts would be inclined to
take his side if he portrayed Conon as having attacked him in the aggressive
manner of a fighting cock and himself as a helpless victim whose aversion to
violence contrasted favourably with Conon's violent disposition. In other

---

[66] Csapo 1993: 124.   [67] D. Cohen 1995a: 125.
[68] Fisher 1998: 68–9. The relevant article by Geertz, 'Deep play: notes on the Balinese cockfight', is
reprinted in his 1973 volume *The Interpretation of Cultures*. New York: Basic Books: 412–53.
[69] See pp. 101–7.

words, he believed that they would approve of a man who presented himself as frail and un-cock-like and disapprove of Conon's cock-like display of aggressive, upper-class masculinity.[70] This court case, like every other, was indeed a contest. The contest consisted, however, of demonstrating how little one's behaviour resembled that of a fighting cock (or, by the same token, that of the Homeric hero formally taunting his opponent in battle; see **Fig. 9.8**): the less heroic or cock-like one appeared, the more likely one was to win the case.

The spectacle of the cockfight was indeed laden with symbolism. How we react to this symbolism is, however, unimportant; what we need to know is how the Athenians did. Claudius Aelianus recounts that after their victory over the Persians the Athenians passed a law requiring that the state should organise one day's cockfighting at the theatre every year. He describes their reason for doing so as follows:

While Themistocles was leading his citizen army[71] against the barbarians, he caught sight of some cocks fighting. Not content with merely watching them, he called a halt and said to his troops: 'These cocks are not fighting for their country or their ancestral gods; they are not suffering to protect their family tombs, their reputation, their freedom or their children. Each of them is fighting in order not to be beaten and in order not to let the other win.' (*Varia Historia* 2.28)

What Themistocles was telling his troops was that no citizen should go to war merely because, like a cock (or for that matter a Homeric hero), he wanted to show off how aggressive and brave he was; war was a serious business that should only be undertaken to benefit the community. Themistocles was endorsing a motivational complex that we have already encountered repeatedly, one that entailed the sort of commitment to the common good that the people of Athens expected each other to display and that therefore made for a winning argument in the Athenian law courts. Pericles refrained from punching the lout who had spent the entire day abusing

---

[70] Cockfights were especially associated with the upper classes, a link that Ariston duly exploits, identifying his opponents with aristocratic youth gangs renowned for their irresponsible behaviour: 'sons of respectable persons (*kalon k'agathon andron huieis*), who in sport (*paizontes*), after the manner of young men, have given themselves nicknames, such as Ithyphalli or Autolecythi, and that some of them are infatuated with mistresses; that his own son is one of these and has often given and received blows on account of some girl . . .' (Demosthenes 54.14, *Against Conon*). For an overview of youth violence in Athens, starting off from the premise that 'violence was embedded in Greek culture and Greek society', see van Looy 1990. For the view that Athenian culture was uncompromisingly phallocentric, see Keuls 1985.

[71] πολιτικὴν δύναμιν, as it appears in the MS, rather than the suggested emendation, πολεμικήν (i.e. military force). For πολιτικός in the sense of 'consisting of citizens' or 'consisting of one's fellow-citizens' (as opposed to 'allied' or 'mercenary' troops), which makes better sense here, cf. Xenophon, *Hellenica* 4.4.19; Aeschines 3.98 (*Against Ctesiphon*).

him because if he had hit him this bad example would have affected the entire *community* adversely. Euphiletus claims to have killed Eratosthenes not to restore his tainted honour (since such immoderate and self-seeking behaviour would have been damaging to society) but to uphold the law in the *communal* interest. Demosthenes and Ariston tell the court how meekly they have put up with endless provocations and humiliations because they expect to score points with the dikasts for sacrificing personal satisfaction (such as might be obtained by thumping one's tormentor) on the altar of the *communal* good. One of Demosthenes' clients even claims to have acted in self-defence only after taking into account the needs of the community. Apparently the need for this unimpeachably correct deed arose when a man into whose house he had gone to seize some goods as security hit him. Instead of hitting him straight back, Demosthenes' client paused to tell everybody else there that they must all bear witness to what had just happened. *Then* he hit him (Demosthenes 47.38, *Against Euergus*). This responsible and measured way of going about it quite clearly demonstrated that he had set the benefit of the entire *community* above satisfying his own impulse to throw a punch immediately. The capacity to regulate private emotions with an eye to the public good to which this speaker is rather implausibly laying claim is perhaps the most important characteristic marking off the ideal Athenian citizen from the Homeric hero.

Let us now examine this finding in the light of what social psychologists call the S–R (Stimulus–Reaction) chain (see **Fig. 8.6**). This mechanism was once thought to be almost completely automatic (as among animals it largely is). It was believed that emotional responses compelled people blindly to enact certain patterns of action on receiving certain stimuli, the quality and intensity of their reactions being rigidly predetermined by the nature of the stimuli that elicited them. This view has recently been modified: it has become clear that in humans the S–R chain is only quasi-automatic, the latency period between the stimulus and the response affording the reacting party some latitude in *choosing* a reaction appropriate to the stimulus. He or she does not, in other words, react in a set, rigidly instinctive manner, but selects from a whole range of non-instinctive reactions, integrating into his or her decision-making process considerations such as the likelihood of success and the seriousness of the consequences of any particular reaction.[72]

---

[72] For a general overview of this matter within the context of modern research into emotions, see K. R. Scherer (1996) 'Emotion', in M. Hewstone, W. Stroebe and G. M. Stephenson (eds.) *Introduction to Social Psychology. A European Perspective*. Oxford: Blackwell (2nd edn): 297–315.

THE S–R CHAIN / TYPE OF SOCIETY	A. STIMULUS (DELIVERED BY PERSON A)	B. REACTION (OF PERSON B)
A. HOMERIC, FEUDING	act of personal insult or injury	direct violent retaliation against person A (and/or his family)
B. ATHENIAN, CIVIC	anti-social, illegal act *and/or* act of personal insult or injury	abstention (in communal interest) from violent reaction, or, in last resort, bringing action against person A

Figure 8.6 The S[timulus]-R[eaction] chain in feuding societies and in democratic Athens
This table shows the divergent types of perception of and reaction to similar stimuli that may become dominant in societies of dissimilar type, demonstrating the quasi-automaticity of human emotions. As Westermarck has put it, 'Though rooted in the emotional side of our nature, our moral opinions are in a large measure amenable to reason' (Westermarck 1924, vol. I: 2–3). This view has been vindicated by modern sociobiology. '. . . [R]igidly stereotyped (i.e. genetically coded), mouse-trap-type responses', writes Barash, 'are common among nonhuman animals, especially invertebrates, fish, reptiles, and birds, but not in humans. We do not experience anything like this genetically mediated automaticity of response. We may feel vague and general inclinations to respond in certain ways, but such tendencies can be overridden consciously and modified drastically by our experience' (Barash 1977: 284).

The human capacity to control and regulate emotions should interest every historian. Because of this capacity, a human motivational complex may combine egotistic drives and desires with precepts and injunctions instilled by the community. Motivational complexes of this sort are at the root of the modern distinction between the biological and the social persona and of the Sophists' categories of natural and conventional man. To put it another way, this psychic trait bridges the gap between individual emotion at the micro level of society and the complexity on its macro level that we call 'culture' or 'civilisation'. When Pericles described the Athenians as free, open and tolerant he was referring to their collective cultural profile at the macro level. It is my suggestion that the S–R chain that corresponded to this at the micro level of individual Athenian emotion was not the one shown in row A of **Fig. 8.6**, but rather that in row B.

We may now proceed with our survey of agonistic pastimes, moving on to combat sports. Wrestling, boxing and the *pankration*, the 'heavy events'

Figure 8.7 Athenian combat sports
Boxing (*pyx*) was recognised as the most hazardous of sports in Classical times, blood
pouring from facial injuries being an expected part of the game. Unlike the Romans,
however, who wore hide gloves with metal studs (*caestus*; see above right) in order to inflict
worse injuries, Greek boxers wore light rawhide thongs intended to prevent sprained
wrists. In boxing as in wrestling (*palaisma*; see below), bouts were fought according to set
rules.

at the Panathenaea (the main Athenian festival, which also included a
wide variety of non-combat sports and athletic and artistic contests), were
the Greeks' most punishing and potentially physically damaging sports
(see **Fig. 8.7**);[73] a bout did not end until someone either gave up or was
too badly injured to carry on.[74] Even so these violent amusements pale
into insignificance beside the gladiatorial combats, tournaments, duels,

[73] See Neils 1992.   [74] Cf. Poliakoff 1987: 68–9.

war games and circus games of subsequent ages.[75] Athenian boxing was also fairly tame by comparison with some of the genuine fighting of which it may be regarded as a sublimation. In the *Odyssey*, for instance, Odysseus has Telemachus 'the wise and good' twist Melantheus' hands and feet behind his back and hang him up by a cord fastened to them 'so that he may long remain alive and suffer torments'. Their victim then has his nostrils and ears cut off, his genitals torn out for the dogs to devour raw and his hands and feet hacked about 'in a fury of rage' (22.474–6). Seen in context, the Athenian 'heavy events' look like nothing more sinister than (in Elias' words) 'a thoroughly tempered embodiment of transformed propensities to aggression and cruelty'.[76]

The Athenians had, of course, invented another agonistic spectator sport: the drama. Odysseus' world was full of competitions involving physical prowess. The world of the city-states had not abandoned physical competition, but had extended the idea of competition, in Finley's words, 'to the realm of the intellect, to feats of poetry and dramatic composition'.[77] Drama was, however, more than just a competition; it was an important part of the city's political and religious life. The spectators were not merely watching the performances passively, but participating vicariously in one of their community's central rituals. Attic drama may thus hold important clues to the levels of cruelty and violence that Athenians in general could tolerate without revulsion. I should perhaps add that my quarry here is not real-life behaviour but attitudes, which I hope to infer from the audience reactions that the authors of violent scenes seem to have expected.

It is no secret that Attic drama is dominated by violent themes and riddled with dreadful crimes. Its characters suffer acute physical pain and undergo excruciating mental torments. It would appear, however, that the spectators were not expected to enjoy watching all this suffering for its own sake, but were invited to identify and sympathise with the characters: to achieve, in Aristotle's words, 'through pity and fear a relief (*katharsis*) to these and similar emotions' (*Poetics* 5.6.4). It has often been remarked that the violent themes that are such a powerful presence in the plays are nonetheless virtually absent from the stage. Many Attic plays contain

[75] See e.g. A. Lintott (1968) *Violence in Republican Rome*. Oxford: Clarendon Press; Roland Auguet (1970) *Cruelty and Civilization: The Roman Games*. London: Routledge; K. M. Coleman (1990) 'Fatal charades: Roman executions staged as mythological enactments', *Journal of Roman Studies* 80: 44–73; Donald G. Kyle (1998) *Spectacles of Death in Ancient Rome*. London and New York: Routledge; Viljamaa, Timonen and Krötzl 1992.
[76] Elias 1978b: 240; 1986. Cf. Golden 1998; Winkler 1990: 49; Lintott 1992; Fisher 1998.
[77] Finley 1978a: 120.

violent deaths and acts of cruelty. As a rule, however, these happen off
stage, their occurrence being implied rather than enacted: cries may be
heard from the palace, a messenger may arrive with the fatal news or a
body may be carried onto the stage.[78] This tendency to keep spectacles of
violence under cover was by no means shared by late mediaeval and early
modern drama, in which the spectator could frequently look forward to
plenty of onstage perversities and sadistic tortures.[79] Literary critics have
suggested a plethora of explanations for the dearth of onstage violence in
Greek plays, most having to do with the dramaturgic difficulties created
by presenting violent deaths on stage (it is, for example, not easy to re-
use an actor in another role if he is lying on the stage pretending to be
dead).[80] Misled by the pessimistic image of Athenian society that pervades
so many publications on this subject, many modern critics have chosen
to ignore the ancient critics' explanation that spectacles of this sort were
avoided because they would have been too repulsive to the sensibilities of
the Athenian spectators.[81] It nonetheless appears crystal clear that this is
the correct explanation. Had Athenian audiences started clamouring for
horrific scenes, no doubt it could all have been managed somehow.

The Athenians evinced very similar sensibilities in other areas. The language of the courts contained a whole series of euphemisms designed to
avoid any direct mention of the painful subject of execution ('the greatest of
punishments' or 'handing over [the convicted offender] to the Eleven').[82]
Various tactful omissions are also noticeable. Although speakers generally try to turn the dikasts against their opponents by describing all their
appalling acts of violence in graphic and flamboyant detail, they skate over
their own as quickly as possible. Despite dwelling at considerable length
on his various actions in the lead-up to Eratosthenes' killing,[83] Euphiletus
somehow omits to describe the gory act itself, obviously because he is afraid
of revolting the dikasts and losing precious votes. The same reluctance to
witness bloodshed may be seen in the iconography of sacrifice, in which
the moment at which the animal's throat is actually cut is not generally

---

[78] Exceptions to this rule are Ajax committing suicide on stage in Euripides' *Ajax* and Agaue brandishing
her son's head on the end of a pole in Euripides' *Bacchae*. For cruelty and violence in Attic drama
in general, see Pathmanathan 1965; Segal 1990; 1991; T. Gould 1991; Goldhill 1991; Kaimio 1992.

[79] Cf. J. Barish (1991) 'Shakespearean violence: a preliminary survey', in *Themes in Drama* 13: 101–
21, esp. 102, which lists scenes enacted before the audience in pre- and post-Shakespearean drama
(principally the former) as including the cutting out of a son's heart and its presentation to the
grieving father, the biting out of a tongue that is then spat out onto the ground, the writhing of a
wicked person in a cauldron of boiling oil and the thrusting of a red-hot spit into the anus of a king.

[80] Cf. Kaimio 1992: 30.   [81] See the scholia to lines 346, 815a and 864 of Sophocles' *Ajax*.

[82] I am indebted for this to Todd 2000: 36–7.   [83] See p. 178.

depicted. The revelation of this pattern has forced students of religion to reconsider the entrenched notion that the Greeks viewed killing animals as murderous and that sacrifice was a violent drama designed to impress both performers and onlookers with a deep sense of awe, fear and guilt.[84] The general distaste for everything to do with blood and death may be seen in a great variety of sources. Plato demonstrates the interaction of the different parts of the psyche with an anecdote in which a man called Leontius who is walking up from the Peiraeus to the city becomes aware that there are some dead bodies lying at the place of execution. Torn between curiosity and repugnance, he covers his head and resists for some time his impulse to look. In the end, however, overwhelmed by his own longing (*epithymia*), he rushes up to the corpses and shouts at his own staring eyes, 'There, ye wretches, take your fill of the fine spectacle!' (*Republic* 4.439e–440a). Leontius' squeamish behaviour is unremarkable by our standards, but it is possible that his contemporaries the Scythians (credited with the habit of using the skulls of the people they killed as drinking bowls)[85] might not have displayed quite the same threshold of revulsion.

The democratic Athenians had no truck with quite a number of unambiguously cruel practices. Unlike some of their neighbours, they did not practise human sacrifice, and unlike the citizens of some other Greek cities, they did not go in for punishments involving maiming.[86] Unlike the Romans, they did not execute their own slaves in private. Nor did they practise decimation (killing every tenth soldier to punish a unit for insubordination or failure), Athenian military discipline in general being somewhat lax.[87] Unlike the early Greeks, most mediaeval people and certain living societies, they did not attempt to determine guilt or innocence by submitting the accused to dangerous and painful ordeals believed to be under supernatural control.[88] Most importantly, unlike most people before and many after them, they did not stage gory public executions.

[84] Peirce 1993. [85] See p. 108.

[86] Theophrastus says that human sacrifice was practised in Arcadia and in Carthage even in his own day (Obbink 1988: 277). A law in force among the Locrians embodied the principle of *lex talionis* (*to antipeponthos*) by stating that if one man put out another's eye he must be punished by having his own eye put out. Demosthenes says that this law was emended to state that if the other man had originally had only one eye the perpetrator should have both his eyes put out (24.140–1, *Against Timocrates*). Diodorus Siculus 12.17 repeats this story in connection with the legislation of Charondas. The Athenian practice that came closest to maiming was the posthumous amputation and separate burial of the hand with which a person had committed suicide (Aeschines 3.244, *Against Ctesiphon*).

[87] Pritchett 1979–84, vol. II: 243–5.

[88] Ordeal in (a) early Greece and mythology: Glotz 1904a; (b) the Middle Ages: R. Bartlett (1986) *Trial by Fire and Water*. Oxford: Clarendon Press; (c) living societies: J. M. Roberts (1965) 'Oaths, autonomic ordeals, and power', *American Anthropologist* 67 (6): 186–212.

Of the four methods of execution that have been connected with Athens (stoning, hurling the offender off a rock (*barathron*), fastening him to a plank with cramp irons and tightening them until he expired (*apotympanismos*) and poisoning by hemlock (*koneion*)) only the last two seem to have been used during the period we are discussing. The fifth- and fourth-century Athenians found stoning repulsive and discarded it as illegal; apart from two cases in the fifth century (one occasioned by the hysteria of war and the other by a religious outrage), we hear of it only in drama.[89] Criminals were executed by being hurled off rocks until the middle of the fifth century, when this practice seems to have been discontinued.[90] The two main forms of capital punishment in force in Athens during this period, *apotympanismos* and hemlock (see **Fig. 7.2**), are conspicuously bloodless,[91] breaching the central tenet of many a punitive system: that spilt blood could only be avenged with blood.[92]

The sources are notoriously ambiguous as to how the Athenians decided which of these methods to apply in each case. It has tentatively been suggested that whereas poisoning by hemlock (in Louis Gernet's words, 'an invitation to commit suicide') took place in a discreet and dignified manner inside the prison, *apotympanismos*, the nastier and certainly the more painful method of execution, was carried out in public to denote 'a more conscious, deliberate, and humiliating expulsion from the community'.[93] This interpretation is, however, vitiated by the lack of any shred of evidence for crowds gathering to watch executions in Athens. (The one case Gernet cites comes from Syracuse.) A passage in the Demosthenic corpus seems to imply that *apotympanismos* too was carried out in private: even if a prosecutor succeeds in getting a murderer convicted, says Demosthenes' client, he has no power over him because 'only the laws and the appointed officers have power over the man for punishment. The prosecutor is permitted

---

[89] Rosivach 1987a: 236. The two victims of stoning were Lycides and Alcibiades, a cousin of the famous Alcibiades. For execution by stoning (*leuein*) see also Allen 2000: 205–6; Todd 2000: 35. Allen 2000: 218–24 suggests that stoning was a method not of execution but of disposing of bodies.

[90] For the *barathron* see Todd 2000: 34, 37–8.

[91] Cf. Todd 2000: 35; Allen 2000: 213. The theory of the bloodlessness of *apotympanismos* derives some support from a seventh-century mass grave unearthed near Phaleron in 1915 (cf. Gernet 1924). The seventeen men whose skeletons were found in the grave had apparently died from thirst and exhaustion after being fastened to poles by means of iron clamps around their necks, wrists and ankles (no nails had been used). If this was a seventh-century antecedent of Classical *apotympanismos*, then *apotympanismos* was bloodless. According to Allen 2000: 213, 'The mechanism of the *apotympanismos*, which employed collars and fasten[er]s rather than nails, even seems to have been constructed with an eye to avoiding drawing blood.'

[92] Cf. M. Foucault (1975) *Discipline and Punish. The Birth of the Prison*. Harmondsworth: Penguin: 73.

[93] Gernet 1924; Todd 2000: 45.

to see him suffering the penalty awarded by law, and that is all' (23.69, *Against Aristocrates*). If *apotympanismos* had been carried out in public then clearly the prosecutor would not have needed special permission to attend; he could just have rolled up with everyone else. There is thus considerable reason to suppose that *apotympanismos* was carried out in the presence of the executioners and the successful prosecutor alone. This suggestion seems consistent with a passage in Aeschines in which the orator imagines himself in the place of the condemned killer staring for the last time into the face of the attending prosecutor: 'It is not the death that is so terrible; the really horrible thing is the insult suffered at the last moment of life. How pitiable a fate to see an enemy's face relaxing into a broad grin, and to hear with one's ears the insults of enmity' (Aeschines 2.182, *On the Embassy*, trans. C. D. Adams). This suggests that the privilege of attending the execution was a device to give the successful prosecutor what might be called cathartic drainage. (The Greeks in general conceived of anger as something that built up in the psyche like steam and must be released.)[94] Catharsis was, however, achieved by watching the execution, not by performing it; judicial killings were strictly the preserve of the public officers. This was surely the civic alternative to the Archaic scheme whereby the killer was eliminated by the victim's relatives, with or without judicial process. It cannot be claimed that either hemlock poisoning or *apotympanismos* is a particularly benign mode of execution. I regard it as noteworthy, nonetheless, that Athenian execu-tions were not gargantuan spectacles enacted in public so that all might rejoice in the triumph of retaliatory justice.

These methods of execution also appear to express a communal mind-set very unlike those of the various societies that have spent most of Western history practising painful, sanguinary and ignominious forms of execu-tion such as crucifixion, impalement, breaking on the wheel, drawing and quartering, boiling in oil, burial alive and burning at the stake, procedures largely motivated by an unconcealed desire to prolong and maximise the agony of the condemned prior to the moment of death.[95] The fact that Athens used far less prolonged forms of judicial killing and did not inflict

---

[94] For alternative concepts of anger from a psychologist's point of view, see Bandura 1973.

[95] In Western Europe startlingly cruel methods of torture and execution that bore the unmistakable marks of retaliatory justice were still in use during the period of enlightenment and secularisation. Cf. M. Bée (1983) 'Le spectacle de l'exécution dans la France d'Ancien régime'. *Annales E.S.C.* 38: 843–59; R. J. Evans (1996) *Rituals of Retribution. Capital Punishment in Germany, 1600–1987.* Harmondsworth: Penguin; P. Spierenburg (1995) 'The body and the state in early modern Europe' in N. Morris and D. J. Rothman (eds.) *The Oxford History of Prison.* Oxford: Oxford University Press: 49–77.

any form of corporeal torture prior to the execution[96] appears rather to imply a preference for minimising the victim's suffering,[97] suggesting that executions had ceased to be thought of as a form of communal vengeance on the wrongdoer and come to be seen as a rational measure designed to protect the community against any recurrence of his anti-social behaviour.[98] This conjecture is supported by the results of a debate on the purpose of capital punishment that appears to have taken place in Athens, with some maintaining that capital punishment should be retrospective in character and thus closer in spirit to vengeance and others arguing that it should be prospective in character and thus closer in spirit to deterrence. The echoes of this debate that we find in the debate on Mytilene that took place in 427 suggest that the proponents of the second view gained the upper hand. While trying to dissuade the Assembly from putting the inhabitants of Mytilene to death, Diodotus is reported to have made the following remark: 'Humanity has tried every punishment it can think of, using worse and worse ones in an attempt to abate the misery that criminals create . . . But crime for all that continues. Unless we can think up something even more frightening than death, we are going to have to admit that death is not an adequate deterrent' (Thucydides 3.45.3–4).

It was, in other words, already agreed that capital punishment should be prospective in outlook, the point of this passage being that even its utility as a deterrent was questionable. The possibility that capital punishment might represent a form of retaliatory justice does not seem even to have occurred to the speakers, which is all the more remarkable since in this particular case the punishment being debated was to be inflicted on collective enemies outside Athenian society rather than on individual criminals within it.[99]

The conjecture that the Athenians had deliberately purged their punitive system of the spirit of vengeance is strengthened by the fact that the condemned (or those who appeared likely to be condemned) were sometimes given the chance to avoid execution by going into exile. This remarkable permissiveness applied to at least three types of case. A defendant accused of voluntary homicide had the option of withdrawing into lifelong exile

---

[96] Cf. Karabélias 1991: 125, with literature cited.

[97] Cf. Barkan 1935: 4. This is true even if we agree with Todd 2000: 33 (inspired by Gill 1973) that 'Hemlock-poisoning . . . is not a particularly nice way to die.' Other ways, like crucifixion or the sword in Rome, are arguably less nice. See caption to **Fig. 7.2.**

[98] The passage that is usually cited to support the view that the penalty for homicide was meant to avenge the killing (Antiphon, *Tetralogies* 2g11) actually says nothing of the sort: 'so with this in mind come to the victim's aid (*boeteite*), punish (*timoreiste*) the murderer and cleanse (*hagneuete*) the *polis*'.

[99] In the light of this it is difficult to agree with Karabélias 1991: 81 that punishment in Classical Athens was modelled on the concept of vengeance, especially since this interpretation draws on etymology.

(*aeiphugia*) after making his first speech, in which case his property would be confiscated.[100] A defendant convicted of involuntary homicide was also given the option of exile; he was required to leave the country by a prescribed route by the end of a specified period and it was a condition of his release that he remain in exile (*pheugein*) until pardoned (*aidesetai*) by one of the deceased's relatives. In this case his property was not confiscated.[101] Finally, several passages imply that attempts to break out of prison while either awaiting execution or serving a prison sentence were generally connived at as long as the condemned person then left the country.[102]

This custom's rationale was fully articulated. In a discussion of involuntary homicide, Demosthenes asserted that, whoever ordained the option of exile, whether heroes or gods, 'did not heap further attack upon ill luck, but humanely (*anthropinos*) did as much as they fairly might to soften its evil consequences' (Demosthenes 23.70, *Against Aristocrates*). Elsewhere he added that the laws of homicide punished wilful murder with death, perpetual exile and confiscation of goods, but dealt with involuntary homicide with humanity (*philanthropia*) and forgiveness (*aidesis*; 21.43, *Against Meidias*). This coincides with two principles of the Athenian code of behaviour that we have deduced from other evidence: commitment to preventing personal conflicts from escalating into major blood-feuds and the placing of the public good above absolute justice to the individual.[103] The pardon that the relatives of an involuntary homicide's victim were expected to extend was yet another manifestation of the Solonic imperative of foregoing the private duty of revenge for the sake of the community. Had democratic Athens' punitive system really been imbued with the spirit of excessive retaliation this sort of compromise would have been unthinkable. The fact that it was not is formally reinforced by the Solonian philosophy of punishment, as reflected in a passage preserved in Plutarch: 'The laws must

---

[100] Demosthenes 23.69, *Against Aristocrates*; Antiphon 5.13, *On the Murder of Herodes*; Pollux 8.117. For modern discussions of this subject see Barkan 1935: 36; MacDowell 1963a: 113–15; Todd 1993: 273; Carawan 1998: 34–5; Allen 2000: 202.

[101] Demosthenes 23.72, *Against Aristocrates*, presumably paraphrasing lines 10–15 of what is known as Draco's law of homicide, *IG* I² 115 (to be read with Stroud 1968). For the legal aspects of *aidesis* (pardon) see Heitsch 1984; Humphreys 1991.

[102] The most famous instance of this is Crito's suggestion that Socrates should break out of prison and go to Thessaly (Plato, *Crito* 44b–c). According to Plutarch, Demosthenes, being unable to endure confinement in prison, 'ran away, through the carelessness of some of his keepers and the connivance of others' (Plutarch, *Demosthenes* 26.2). Demosthenes himself describes a hypothetical position in terms that suggest much the same attitude: 'Suppose you were told that the prison had been thrown open, and that prisoners were escaping . . . there is not a man, however apathetic, who would not help as much as possible' (24.208, *Against Timocrates*). For imprisonment, see the caption to **Fig. 7.1**.

[103] See pp. 213–15 and 149, respectively.

look to possibilities, if the maker designs to punish few in order to their amendment, and not many to no purpose' (*Solon* 21.2).

Solon is said to have repealed all Draco's laws, with the exception of those concerning homicide (*The Athenian Constitution* 7.1; Plutarch, *Solon* 17), because they were too severe and the punishments they prescribed were indiscriminate and out of proportion (death was the penalty for practically every offence, irrespective of its gravity). This raises the question of whether Solon's reforms belied the general direction in which Athens' society and culture were developing or whether they were part of an overall trend towards gentler attitudes and more refined manners within that society.

Solon famously banned loans against the security of the person (*me daneizein epi tois somasin*), thus 'liberating the people' both immediately and for the future. Thereafter large loans were normally secured against houses, land or movable property,[104] so that debt-bondage, a phenomenon that was ubiquitous in many contemporary non-Greek societies as well as in numerous Greek cities,[105] was eradicated in Athens.[106] That this was the starting point for the creation of a free Attic peasantry is one of the widely accepted tenets of modern scholarship. It has perhaps been less well appreciated how exceptional this development was. Throughout archaic societies (and not only archaic ones, as the debtors' prisons of modern times attest) the laws of debt were harsh in the extreme, particularly where the debtor and the creditor belonged to different social classes. 'It was a cruel joke', writes Finley, 'to legislate, as they did in [fifth-century] Gortyn, that if a debt-bondsman (*katakeimenos*) suffered an actionable injury and his master failed to sue on his behalf, he could do so himself provided he first paid off his debt. The whole of the Roman system of *legis actionis* was another cruel joke, in particular *sacramentum* and *manus iniectio*, to those "who lacked the backing of a mighty house". Twist and squirm as one will, the words *partis secanto* (he shall be cut into portions) cannot be expunged from the Twelve Tables, nor their ugly sound, accepted as such by all later

---

[104] Cf. Millett 1991: 48–9, 77–9.
[105] Cf. Finley 1981f. For debt-bondage outside Athens, see Lysias 12.98 (*Against Eratosthenes*); Isocrates 14.48 (*Plataicus*).
[106] Cf. Finley 1981c. There were, however, exceptions: a father could sell a daughter into slavery if he caught her having sex and a captive who was unable to pay his ransom could borrow from a citizen using his freedom as security. Non-free men who tried to take up citizenship fraudulently could also be sold as slaves by the state: *The Athenian Constitution* 42.1; cf. Glotz 1904b: 364–5. In the almost total absence of supporting evidence, I find it hard to accept the suggestion, recently put forward by E. M. Harris 2002b, that Solon abolished only the enslavement of debtors, not debt-bondage ('the status or condition arising from a pledge by a debtor of his personal services or those of a third person under his control as security for a debt' (at 417)).

Roman writers.'[107] A defaulting debtor could not become the victim of any such 'cruel joke' in Athens. He could not be enslaved, physically punished or executed, a remarkable advance even if we allow that he might in some cases risk losing the whole value of the encumbered property (rather than merely the value of the debt) in the event of default.[108]

Athenian debt law was not exceptional in its relative lenience, but a typical expression of the Athenian philosophy of punishment in terms of the proportional relation between offence and penalty. This will emerge more clearly if we consider the offences that attracted the death penalty in Athens.[109] The first and longest section of this list is made up of crimes against the state: deceiving the people (*apate tou demou*), electing an official whose name appeared on two election lists, proposing something at the Assembly that was not in the best interests of the Athenian people, receiving money or gifts from the people's opponents, bribing dikasts, making up non-existent laws to deceive the dikasts, counterfeiting coins, 'wronging the people', conducting transactions detrimental to the city's grain supply, subverting democracy (*katalysis tou demou*), committing treason, deserting and communicating with the enemy. Another group of offences has to do with the conduct of interpersonal relations: theft at the gymnasium, premeditated homicide (even if the victim were a murderer arrested in an act of self-help (*apagoge*)), serious *hybris*, planning (*bouleusis*) to commit homicide[110] and treating free men as if they were slaves. The third group contains the religious offences: destruction of the sacred olives, impiety (*asebeia*) and atheism. The list ends with two sexual offences: male prostitution and procurement.[111]

Two very important points emerge from this. The first is that the most extreme punishments Athens handed out were reserved for offences against the safety and welfare of the community. These were, in other words, by any standards serious offences to which the death penalty was not grossly disproportionate. With the possible exception of 'treating free men as if they were slaves', there is no offence on this list that could (like the

---

[107] Finley 1981f: 152–3.

[108] See E. M. Harris 1988 (against Finley 1952: 46–7, 114) for the assertion that guarantees were collateral rather than substitutive in Athens, i.e. that a defaulting debtor risked forfeiting only the value of the debt, not the entire security.

[109] Here I am confining myself to the procedure called *agon atimetos*, in which the penalty was not subject to assessment by the litigants. A convicted person could also be given the death penalty via the *agon timetos* procedure, in which the litigants proposed alternative penalties for the convicted person and the dikasts had to choose one or other proposal by voting again.

[110] Cf. MacDowell 1978: ch. 7.

[111] I am indebted for this list to Ruschenbusch 1968, who drew in turn on Lipsius 1905–14. Some of the offences that appear on this list are discussed by MacDowell 1978: ch. 11.

oft-cited crime of stealing a loaf of bread) be said to be so trifling and frivolous as to make executing the offender appear merely vengeful, vindictive or sadistic. In other words, Athens did not hand down the death penalty on the 'head for an eye' principle. Far from suggesting excessive eagerness to punish and take revenge, this list is testimony to the Athenian legislators' determination to give the citizens a good motive to shun this sort of offence.

Our second point is closely intertwined with the first. Serious *hybris*, we find, was punishable by death. As we have seen, there are a number of possible interpretations of the word *hybris*. Whatever its precise nuance of meaning, however, it was used to refer to wanton violence, pointless provocation, insults, aggression and 'the deliberate infliction of dishonour and shame upon others'.[112] If behaviour of this sort was indeed punishable by death, it becomes increasingly difficult to uphold the argument that the Athenian public conscience was suffused with the spirit of vengeance. In genuinely feuding societies whose public conscience *is* suffused with the spirit of vengeance such forms of behaviour are encouraged, not checked by the most formidable of sanctions. Everything we know of Athens suggests that even minor offences that might jeopardise public order were firmly discouraged by means of formal (though proportionately lesser) sanctions. Demosthenes remarked at one point that 'the lawgiver considered any action involving violence to be unfair to the public . . . for he believed that anyone who commits *hybris* is hurting the polis, not just the victim' (21.45, *Against Meidias*). Solon is said to have forbidden the Athenian people to speak evil (*kakos legein*) of the living at any temple, court of justice, public office or public games; anyone who did so must pay three drachmas to his victim and two to the public. Once again, the rationale behind this legislation is spelt out in full: 'A consistent inability to control one's temper is a sign of a weak nature and of ill-breeding (*to gar medamou kratein orges apaideuton kai akolaston*); controlling such a tendency is always extremely difficult, and to some impossible' (Plutarch, *Solon* 21.1).[113] The Athenian legislators drafted their laws with one overriding purpose: to make communal life possible. They achieved this by regulating certain areas of activity, repressing others and weaving together every aspect of life in Athens into a harmoniously functioning whole. 'Serious *hybris*' they

---

[112] Fisher 1992.

[113] Cf. Gagarin 1979 for the inference that the addition of *graphe hybreos* to Athens' existing penalties for *hybris* reflects a distaste for physical assault. W. V. Harris 2001: 155 notes that it is not easy to fit the Solonian policy of emotional control 'into the story that is told about Solon in every book about Athenian politics'.

chose uncompromisingly to repress, as we would expect, having observed the eagerness of Athenian litigants to distance themselves from the slightest suggestion of hubristic behaviour and to impute to their opponents a surfeit of it.[114]

One activity that the Athenians chose not to repress was the abuse of slaves. They were not alone in this respect. Throughout much of antiquity, Finley tells us, corporal punishment, whether public or private, was inflicted only on slaves, this being the cardinal feature that marked them off from free men.[115] The Athenian democracy magnified this difference, passing (during Scamandrius' archonship) a decree that protected Athenian citizens from torture during judicial investigations.[116] Free non-citizens could be tortured in extraordinary circumstances (when suspected of espionage or treason, for example),[117] but only slaves were constantly liable to physical abuse. The question, as Hunter put it, was not whether to punish them, but 'how, with what frequency and intensity, for what offenses, and in what frame of mind'.[118] Physical or mental suffering was inflicted on slaves in at least three contexts that we shall now consider, noting in passing that we do not have sufficient evidence to form any opinion of how common or how frequent such practices were.[119]

The first of these contexts included punishment, physical abuse and sexual exploitation. To get an inkling of the brutality involved in these forms of master–slave interaction we need only turn to the rhetorical question with which Xenophon's Socrates addresses the issue of how masters cope with lazy, self-indulgent slaves: 'Do they not starve them to keep their lust under control, lock up the stores to stop them from stealing, clap fetters on them so that they can't run away and beat the laziness out of them?' When Socrates asks his interlocutor, Aristippus, how *he* deals with such slaves, the latter replies: 'I make their lives a burden to them until I have forced them to start behaving like slaves (*douleuein anankaso*)' (Xenophon, *Memorabilia* 2.1.16–17). That slaves bore the brunt of their masters' bad tempers may be seen from Lesis' complaint that he has been whipped and

---

[114] See pp. 200–1. [115] Finley 1998: 161.
[116] For the evidence and the problems surrounding Scamandrius' date and identity, see A. R. W. Harrison 1971: 150 n. 6.
[117] Bushala 1968; Dover 1974: 282; Finley 1998: 161–3; Hunter 1994: 173–6.
[118] Hunter 1994: 164, to whom I am indebted for information regarding slave abuse.
[119] Cf. Finley 1998: 162, noting that some authors have gone so far as to suggest that torture was seldom actually used. Cf. Lintott 1992: 11 (with n. 10): 'References are made to the torture of slaves for judicial purposes in a quite casual way in orators and it is exploited for comic purposes by Aristophanes: does this mean that it was unimportant or so common that it hardly deserved notice?'

treated like dirt (see **Fig. 2.9**), while their 'unrestricted availability in sexual relations'[120] appears in the casual recollection of Euphiletus' wife that he had once got drunk and had a go at the servant-girl (Lysias 1.12, *On the Murder of Eratosthenes*). The most commonly used instrument of punishment was the whip, originally designed to prod cattle, but the sources also record spontaneous blows with a fist or with whatever implement happened to be to hand.[121] In extreme cases slaves could be taken to the 'mill', a house of correction in which they would be kept in chains and whipped for longer periods by professionals.[122]

The second context was that of public offences, slaves who committed offences of this sort being liable to punishment by community agents. Such judicial punishment invariably consisted of the infliction of pain and humiliation, more often than not with the 'public whip', the number of blows delivered in public being proportional to the gravity of the offence. As early as 1908 Glotz drew from the evidence available at the time the remarkable inference that the number of drachmas that a free man would be fined for a certain offence corresponded to the number of blows that a slave would receive for the same offence, and that by law neither could exceed fifty.[123] Glotz took this to be an expression of Athenian humanity, but Hunter may be closer to the truth in suggesting that 'considerations of cost or even doubts about the effectiveness of excessive punishment may underlie the frequency of fifty lashes . . .'[124] We are very poorly informed about the sorts of offence for which slaves were punished publicly, but the snippets we have (a slave who became the lover of a free boy or chased after him received fifty lashes (Aeschines 1.139, *Against Timarchus*), as did any slave who cut wood in the sacred precinct of Apollo Erithaseos (*IG* II^2 1362 = *SIG*^{3} 984)) suggest that as a rule the punishments meted out to slaves, even for trifling offences, were severe. Despite this, by comparison with the slave societies that were to follow them Greece in general and Athens in particular appear exceptionally good natured. In Greece, as de Ste. Croix has put it, 'sheer cold-blooded cruelty towards the victims of their civilisation – slaves, criminals, and conquered peoples – was on the

---

[120] Finley 1998: 164.
[121] De Ste. Croix 1981: 48: 'The Greeks on the whole showed less savagery than the Romans towards their slaves, but even in Classical Athens, where we hear most about relatively good treatment of slaves, all our literature takes the flogging of slaves for granted.'
[122] Cf. Hunter 1994: 171.
[123] Glotz 1908. I am puzzled by Hunter's lack of conviction concerning the 'universality' of this formula, in particular since Glotz's insight has been corroborated by evidence that has subsequently come to light (Hunter 1994: 155, 158).
[124] Hunter 1994: 159.

whole much less pronounced than among the Romans . . .'[125] In Athens, Hunter asserts, the '"science" of punishment' was far less developed: 'where private punishment was concerned, at least in misdemeanours of a routine nature, Athenian slavery had its own peculiar character'.[126]

Nor does the picture change significantly when we consider the last context in which slaves faced the prospect of torture. This arose when they were involved in, or witnessed, offences committed by free men. If such offences resulted in dispute, procedures could be initiated for reaching a settlement out of court. The torture of slaves in order to extract judicial information was a recognised part of these procedures. Its widely accepted (though, as we have seen, not uncontested) premise was that such evidence was *only* valid if given under torture.[127] Two circumstances suggest that the actual incidence of judicial torture may not have been that high. In the first place, although it is frequently mentioned by the orators we never hear of its actually being carried out. In the second place, the procedures involved presented the contending parties with so many obstacles as to call into question the torture's feasibility. A slave-owner could not be compelled to deliver up his slave(s) for torture; he had to do so voluntarily, and in view of a slave's relative costliness (in the fifth century prices fluctuated between 200 and 600 drachmas, the latter sum representing roughly a quarter of the value of a small city house)[128] it is questionable whether any owner would willingly have acquiesced in having his valuable property damaged. If he did so acquiesce, he had to indicate this by accepting a challenge (*proklesis*) ritually presented to him by the opponent. He had then to supply pledges and sureties, work out with the opponent the terms of the torture (its method, who was to administer it and so forth) and finally record these terms in a document that would then be sealed. On the day appointed for the torture the parties, the sureties and the witnesses would all assemble and the document would be opened and read. The torture

---

[125] De Ste. Croix 1981: 410.

[126] Hunter 1994: 170; cf. Hunter 1992: 288, where the possibility is raised that the line of demarcation between freedom and slavery was less firmly drawn in Athens than elsewhere. In eighteenth-century England, by comparison, 'Three hundred lashes, more than most men could bear, was not an uncommon punishment for the theft of a sheep, and it made no difference if the culprit was a boy of twenty or even less; he was a criminal, the curse was in the blood, and that was that.' A. Moorehead (1968) *The Fatal Impact*. Harmondsworth: Penguin: 135.

[127] See pp. 145–6.

[128] For data regarding slave prices in Athens see de Ste. Croix 1981: 585 n. 1. If the average price of a slave in fifth-century Athens was 200 drachmas, then de Ste. Croix's contention that 'the most extraordinary fact about Greek (and Roman) slaves is their cheapness' is exaggerated (de Ste. Croix 1981: 227). According to Xenophon, *Memorabilia* 2.5.2, Nicias is said to have paid a whole talent for a manager at his silver mine.

would then be carried out in public, in accordance with its terms, either by the parties themselves or by an official torturer (*basanistes*), the crowd standing by to bear witness. The favoured method of torture was whipping, always up to the limit of fifty lashes, but in some cases the wheel (*trochos*) was used.[129] Even though the torture of slaves represented, in Harrison's words, 'one of the darker rules of evidence at Athens',[130] this statement requires qualification. The torture was not an end in itself, but a means to an end, which was to elicit the 'truth'. Eliciting the truth was in turn a means to another end, which was to determine the guilt or innocence of the rivals. As a consequence of this neither whipping nor the wheel degenerated into one of those diabolical methods of execution, so common in European history, whose aim is to inflict the most protracted suffering possible until death intervenes; both methods were calculated to inflict only such pain as would elicit the 'truth', while causing as little physical damage as possible.[131]

'What was the rationale, then?' asked Finley in 1980, in a criticism of the widespread tendency merely to condemn the custom of torturing slaves as irrational and senseless rather than submit it to rigorous social analysis. 'It seems obvious to me where we must look,' he continued. 'The potential or actual employment of naked force is of course an inescapable factor in the situation, but there is more to it than that. If a slave is a property with a soul, a non-person and yet indubitably a biological human being, institutional procedures are to be expected that will degrade and undermine his humanity and so distinguish him from human beings who are not property. Corporal punishment and torture constitute one such procedure.'[132] Some twenty years earlier Finley had made the point that 'the more advanced the Greek city-state, the more it will be found to have had true slavery . . . More bluntly put, the cities in which individual freedom reached its highest expression – most obviously Athens – were cities in which chattel slavery flourished. The Greeks, it is well known, discovered both the idea of individual freedom and the institutional framework in which it could be realized . . . One aspect of Greek history, in short, is the advance, hand in hand, of freedom

---

[129] For contraptions such as the pillory (*kuphon*) and the stocks (*podokakke*), both used to facilitate flogging, see Hunter 1994: 177–81.

[130] A. R. H. Harrison 1971: 147.

[131] Cf. Lafaye 1877–1919: 897, who describes the wheel in post-Classical times as a compound torture machine: in addition to having his limbs racked, the victim tied to the wheel might be beaten with sticks, scorched with burning torches or slit open with swords. We should note in this context that in England public floggings and the pillory were only abolished in the late eighteenth century, under the impact of the moral reformation movement (G. Himmelfarb [1996] *The De-Moralization of Society. From Victorian Virtues to Modern Values*. New York: Random House: 6).

[132] Finley 1998: 163.

and slavery.'[133] Some old and some newly discovered material will enable us to see new connections between Finley's remarkable insights.

SUBSTITUTION AND SUBLIMATION

As we have seen, part of the Athenian 'civilising process' consisted in a restructuring of sentiments and emotions, in a refinement of customs and in an increasing reluctance to perform or witness acts of excessive cruelty. The entire process can be broken down into two ubiquitous, recurring and complementary phenomena that take place over a long period: substitution and sublimation. Substitution may be described as the gradual replacement of a custom or practice with a less extreme form of the same thing. Sublimation is the process whereby an instinctive, often sexual, drive is transformed into a more socially acceptable and usually more refined type of behaviour. Plato describes a form of dance that was extremely popular in Athens, the so-called Pyrrhic or war dance (*pyrrhiche*, i.e. *orchesis*), thus:

. . . it represents modes of eluding all kinds of blows and shots by swervings and duckings and side-leaps upward or crouching; and also the opposite kinds of motion, which lead to active postures of offence, when it strives to represent the movements involved in shooting with bows and darts, and blows of every description.[134]

As Plato observed, the Pyrrhic dance had evolved from actual fighting. It consisted of rhythmic motions to music that mimicked the striking of blows, the firing of arrows and the hurling of javelins in every respect except that no damage was done. In this sublimation forms of aggression were transmuted into forms of art (see **Fig. 8.8**).[135]

Transformations such as this may be found in abundance in virtually every area of Athenian history. In contests of all sorts, to begin with, 'the olive wreath and the laurel took the place of gold and copper and captive

---

[133] Finley 1981e: 114–15, his italics.

[134] *Laws* 7.815a1–3, trans. R. G. Bury; cf. Neils 1992: 94. In Sparta children and young men performed the Pyrrhic dance using fennel stalks instead of spears (Athenaeus 4.631a). Xenophon describes an assortment of other dances based on mock combat (*Anabasis* 6.1.1–13).

[135] Cf. Lawler 1964; Poursat 1968; Lonsdale 1993: 137. Darwin interpreted a corroboree that he witnessed at King George's Sound in Western Australia in February 1836 similarly: 'The dancing consisted in the whole set running either sideways or in Indian file, into an open space, and stamping the ground with great force as they marched together. Their heavy footsteps were accompanied by a kind of grunt, and, by beating their clubs and weapons, and various other gesticulations, such as extending their arms, and wriggling their bodies. It was a most rude, barbarous scene, and, to our ideas, without any sort of meaning; but we observed that the women and children watched the whole proceeding with the greatest pleasure. Perhaps these dances originally represented some scenes, such as wars and victories . . .': Charles Darwin (1989) *The Voyage of the Beagle*, Harmondsworth: Penguin: 331.

Figure 8.8 Pyrrhic dance and its unexpurgated version: warriors dancing with severed heads

The Pyrrhic dance (top), performed by naked dancers holding their round hoplite shields in front of them, was a popular feature of Athenian public life (cf. P. J. Wilson 2000: 39). Dancing around with severed heads (below), on the other hand, was not. This scene, rare in Attic vase-painting, appears on a fifth-century black-figured lekythos; the painter had thus chosen to depict either a long discontinued practice or possibly a form of that practice that was still current among non-Greeks. The Chalybians of Asia Minor, for example, 'had greaves also and helmets, and . . . a knife about as long as the Laconian dagger, with which they would slaughter whomever they might be able to vanquish; then they would cut off their heads and carry them along on their march, and they would sing and dance whenever they were likely to be seen by the enemy' (Xenophon, *Anabasis* 4.7.16). The dance that the painter depicted presumably represents some sort of midway stage in the process of substitution and sublimation by which the victor's bloody, gleefully spontaneous dance of triumph became the Pyrrhic dance, its thoroughly attenuated relic.

women as the [Homeric] victor's prize'.[136] Both combat and non-combat sports bore the traces of substitution and sublimation (see **Figs 8.7** and **8.9**): it should come as no shock to anyone that ball games of all sorts, apparently perfectly innocent leisure activities, were once played with skulls and other parts of defeated enemies' bodies. In the *Iliad* Euphorbus threatens Menelaus by telling him that he will carry back his head to his parents so that they can play with it and cheer (17.39–40).[137] Savage customs may recur in symbolic form at a later date. According to the Roman poet Juvenal, when the villain Sejanus was unmasked and Tiberius had him executed the heads of all the statues of Sejanus were removed and used to play ball games in a public bath.[138]

It has now become generally accepted that animal sacrifice, which was widely practised in historical times, was a sort of 'domesticated' version of prehistoric human sacrifice. Both the story of Isaac (Genesis 22.13) and an anthropological treatise by Theophrastus that describes animals being substituted for human victims suggest the manner in which this transformation may have taken place.[139] Athens had a scapegoat ritual that had many overtones of human sacrifice. In this ritual, according to a fragment by the third-century historian Istrus, two people selected for their ugliness would be led out by the crowd as though to execution.[140] They each wore a necklace, one of white figs, the other of black, and were presented with cakes and figs as they walked. They were then scourged and pelted out of the city with objects that could not harm them. At the end of the ritual they were supposed to be 'dead' and their 'ashes' were thrown into the sea. There is reason to believe that in the original version of this ceremony the *pharmakoi* (scapegoats) were really killed, as they were in this ceremony's aetiological myth, as they were in some other Greek cities and as they were in Rome at a later period.[141]

Occasionally we are able to observe the process of substitution and sublimation at close quarters. The children, dead of the plague, whose portraits appear on the pitcher in **Fig. 8.10** are shown wearing bone or stone

---

[136] Finley 1978a: 119–20.   [137] For further examples, see Vermeule 1979: 107.
[138] Juvenal, *Satires* 10.62.   [139] Cf. Burkert 1983a: 21; Obbink 1988: 277–8.
[140] F. Jacoby (1954) *Die Fragmente der griechischen Historiker*. Leiden: E. J. Brill: 334 F 50 (Istros). Cf. Hughes 1991: 149–54.
[141] For hints that the *pharmakoi* were originally killed, see Hughes 1991: 154–5. For a comprehensive study of scapegoat rituals, see Bremmer 1983b; for the transformations that these have undergone in various cultural settings, for 'substitute sacrifices' and for Gernet's suggestion that the Classical Athenian institution of *ostrakismos* may be viewed as a rationalised *pharmakos* ritual, see Burkert 1979b. For rites, gestures and magical practices from the 'pre-law stage' of a community's life ('prédroit') as antecedents of its law when it moves on into its 'law stage' ('droit'), see Gernet 1976b.

Figure 8.9　Athenian non-combat sports
Modern people are sometimes shocked to learn that Greek athletes exercised naked and
that they took this to be a sign of cultural advancement rather than of moral depravity.
Thucydides expresses the up-to-date Athenian attitude of his time perfectly, writing that
the Spartans 'were the first to strip in public, work out naked and rub themselves down
with olive oil after exercise. In times gone by athletes used to compete with loin-cloths
covering their genitals even at the Olympic games, and they went on doing so until quite
recently. Even today among some of the barbarians, especially in Asia, where there are
boxing and wrestling prizes to be won, the contestants wear loin-cloths. Indeed, one could
point to a number of other ancient Hellenic customs that were very similar to those of the
barbarians of today' (1.6.4–5; cf. Plato, *Republic* 5.452e). For nudity in Greek athletics and
its (homo)erotic aspects, see Golden 1998: 65–6; Miller 2000; Scanlon 2002, esp. ch. 8.

Figure 8.10 Child victim of the plague
Pitchers such as this were often placed as funeral offerings in children's tombs dating from
the last third of the fifth century (Parlama and Strampolidis 2001: no. 389). It has been
conjectured that they may reflect a high rate of child mortality due to the plague. The
pitcher above depicts what was probably the dead child's favourite game when he was alive:
throwing a ball tied to a strap for a dog to catch. Under their arms the children are wearing
prophylactic amulets known as *periamma* or *periapton* (cf. Plutarch, *Pericles* 38.2), intended
to avert pestilence and evil. While in this particular case the amulets clearly proved futile,
in one sense they did achieve their immediate purpose: they must have helped to reduce
the parents' anxiety in the face of the alarming increase in mortality rates. For attitudes to
the death of children in Classical Athens (a deeper sense of bereavement was felt than is
normally believed), see Golden 1990: 82–5. For the breed of 'Maltese' dog depicted on the
pitcher (one of some fifty breeds known in Classical antiquity) see D. Brewer, T. Clark and
A. Phillips (2001) *Dogs in Antiquity*, Warminster: Aris and Phillips: 85.

beads attached to strings round their necks and arms. Their parents probably made them wear these amulets in life to ward off sickness and general
evil. Whence could this superstitious practice have arisen? With all due
caution, we may risk the suggestion that we are looking at a sublimated
version of an exceedingly savage earlier custom that was dimly remembered
in Classical times under the name of *maschalismos*. Murderers in Archaic
times used to cut off the extremities (noses, ears and genitalia) of their
victims. They would then string them together and wear the string round
their neck and arms in the belief that what was done to the body had
the same effect on the psyche: the mutilation of the body would disable
the psyche so that it could not take revenge.[142] As this ghastly string was
transformed into the innocuous charm worn by the children, beads were
substituted for body parts and illness and general mischance for whatever
hideous vengeance might be wreaked by the malevolent spirit of the dead.[143]

At the end of the nineteenth century Sigmund Freud asserted, in a shrewd
epigram, that the man who first flung an epithet at his enemy instead
of a spear was the true founder of civilisation.[144] Freud thereby joined
forces with those thinkers who saw the origins of organised society in the
sublimation of aggression rather than its exercise.[145] Certainly in the case
of Athens he seems to have been right: the non-aggressive, highly polished,
'civilised' forms that the clash of individual wills assumed in this city in
Classical times can be seen as attenuated variants of the savage private wars
of extermination in which form clashes between individuals manifested
themselves in post-Mycenaean times. We can have no doubt that slavery
played a major role in this transformation. Slaves took the place of free men
as objects of aggression, enabling the latter to distance themselves further

---

[142] For belief in the avenging spirit of the dead, see Parker 1983: ch. 4. For the infrequency with which
the idea of psychic pollution appears in Athenian homicide law, see Arnaoutoglou 1993.

[143] The evidence on *maschalismos* is conveniently assembled in Kittredge 1885 and Rohde 1987: 582–6.
Aristophanes of Byzantium does not explain whether the murderer was supposed to put the string
round his own neck and arms or his victim's. Both authors opt for the latter possibility. Unless the
custom underwent some sort of reversal, which is by no means unlikely, **Fig. 8.10** suggests that he
put it over his own shoulder and wore it as a trophy. For more recent discussions of this custom, see
Vermeule 1979: 236, n. 30 and Garland 1985: 94; for amulets and charms in general, see Budge 1930
and D. Morris 1999. For the related French charm called 'main-de-gloire' or 'mandegloire' (hand of
glory), which was originally made from a mandrake root (the word is a corruption of 'mandragore',
mandrake) but later came to mean the hand of an executed criminal, and the protective Italian
'cornuta' (horned hand), which probably replaced the hand of an executed criminal, see D. Morris
1977: 140. For amulets in the Greco-Roman world in general, see Eckstein and Waszink 1950.

[144] Sigmund Freud (1893) 'On the psychical mechanisms of hysterical phenomena' in *Standard Edition
of the Complete Psychological Works* (translated and ed. J. Strachey et al.) 1953–1974, London: Hogarth
Press: vol. III: 36.

[145] Gay 1993: 214.

from primeval savagery and press on towards higher degrees of humanity. We have already encountered two examples of this process in action.

As we have said, the number of blows that a slave received for a public offence was equal to the number of drachmas that a free man would be fined for the same offence. It is a reasonable assumption that in the remote past a free man would also have been punished with blows. As soon as slavery became established in society, however, slaves became a substitute for free men as objects of state-inflicted violence. A similar mechanism may have been at work in the judicial torture of slaves. This practice presumably owes its origin to trial by ordeal, whose outlines are clearly recognisable in the Homeric poems. The significant difference between the two is, however, that whereas in Archaic trials by ordeal one of the disputants was submitted to torture, in the Athenian procedures designed to reach settlements out of court the slave of one of the disputants was submitted to torture. Both of these feats of substitution may have been necessary to the creation of the doctrine (which was to reach its peak in Classical times) that a citizen's body was inviolable; both illustrate Finley's conjecture that institutional procedures designed to degrade slaves tended to increase the freedom and humanity of free men. The growth of individual freedom and humanity went hand in hand with the evolution of chattel slavery.

This is not to say, however, that the humanity of the free men increased in proportion to their oppression of slaves. It would appear that the opposite was true: the evidence seems to suggest that the higher the degree of humanity attained by the Athenians the more difficult they found it to come to terms with their slaves' alleged non-humanity.[146] This peculiar feature of the Athenian code of behaviour should be stressed even though it always remained a matter of opinion, never managing to solidify into a moral norm.

---

[146] See pp. 58–9 and 67–72.

CHAPTER 9

Interactions with the divine

'[I]n the Homeric psychology', wrote Finley, 'every human action and every idea could be the direct consequence of divine intervention.'[1] Thucydides' account of the 'truest cause' of the Peloponnesian War ('the growth of Athenian power and the fear that this created in Sparta' (1.23)) is sufficient to tell us that his psychology was very different, interpreting every human action and every idea as the direct consequence of natural forces within the human soul.[2] Some fifth- and fourth-century Athenians shared Thucydides' super-rationalistic outlook, but many did not, and we can proceed no further in our analysis without examining the extent to which and the manner in which Athenian morality and behaviour were influenced by the vision of the transcendental order[3] that had taken shape in the minds of their forefathers at some time during the dark ages, probably not very long before the Homeric poems immortalised it in writing.[4]

As we have already remarked, the Athenian democracy operated within a matrix of thought that tilted towards the rational.[5] Its key institutions were built on the premise that people were driven by natural rather than supernatural forces. (Here I am including within the definition of 'natural' the irrational, repressed and hidden forces within the human soul.) Athenian law-court speakers described actions as motivated by emotions directed towards other people (fear, greed, jealousy, anger) rather than by some transcendental horror. Murder, which tends to evoke strong religious feeling in primitive societies, is presented in most of the law-court speeches

---

[1] Finley 1978a: 130, inspired by Snell 1953: ch. 2.
[2] Cf. Lloyd-Jones 1971: 137; A. Powell 1979a; B. M. W. Knox 1989: 102. For the suggestion that this difference was less extreme than Snell thought it (with particular respect to man as portrayed in Attic tragedy), see Lesky 1961. For the view that Thucydides' emancipation from the view that the world was ruled by the gods was less complete than is usually thought, see Oost 1975.
[3] This is how I propose to render the Greek term *ta theia* (literally 'things divine').
[4] Cf. Burkert 2001.   [5] See pp. 65–7.

as a secular rather than a religious threat to society.[6] Under the influence of Anaxagoras, Pericles is said to have 'risen above the sort of superstition (*deisidaimonia*) that makes people who do not understand the causes of things regard what happens in the sky above them with amazement' (Plutarch, *Pericles* 6.1). Later on, during the Sophists' heyday, some young aristocrats formed a dining club that got together to mock superstitions. The fact that some people in some spheres of life had emancipated themselves from belief in the supernatural did not, however, mean that the Athenian democracy as a whole had rejected it, or that there were no religious (and indeed pious) Athenians. Some people, as we have seen, believed in some form of divine law or justice.[7] Others may have been downright superstitious. Nicias, we are told, 'was rather over-inclined to divination and such things' (Thucydides 7.50.4) and took a lunar eclipse to be a sign from the gods that a military operation should be delayed. Theophrastus described the over-pious Athenian as a man who would not continue on his way after a cat had crossed his path until someone else went by, whereupon he would throw three stones across the street (*Characteres* 16.2). 'Hipponicus keeps an avenging spirit (*aliterion*) in his house, who upsets his table (*trapeza*)', wrote Andocides, and even though he was referring to Hipponicus' spendthrift son and the word *trapeza* was introduced for the sake of a pun on its secondary meaning (bank), the joke suggests that his audience would have been familiar with stories about ghosts, spirits and supernatural phenomena.[8]

It is difficult, if not impossible, to form any accurate estimate of the extent and the depth of the average Athenian's piety from sources such as these. Today superstitions still thrive 'even among the most logical, hard-headed, practical and unromantic of modern urbanites'; people still cross their fingers, touch wood and say 'bless you' when someone sneezes. They usually do so with a laugh, 'saying how stupid it is, but they still do them'.[9] The term *deisidaimonia*, which we translate as 'superstition', suggests a predominantly disapproving attitude towards religiosity and excessive preoccupation with the divine. It is nonetheless probably reasonable to assume that democratic Athenians were less free of the grip of religion and superstition than are modern urbanites.[10] The new democracy, it is true, assumed 'an aggressive,

---

[6] I.e. rather than as a source of spiritual pollution, cf. Parker 1983: 128.   [7] See p. 18.
[8] Andocides 1.130; cf. Dodds 1973b; 1973c: 158 n. 1; Nilsson 1940: 113–15.
[9] D. Morris 1977: 140.
[10] In antiquity the Athenians were popularly regarded as 'more devoted to things concerning the gods (*ta theia*) than other men' (Pausanias 1.24.3).

"militant" stance towards many traditional values',[11] but this stance did not amount to an outright declaration of war on religion, nor to a policy for dealing with upsurges of magic and superstition in times of crisis. Secularisation was, in other words, one of democratisation's unintended by-products, not one of its declared aims. The majority of Athenians probably occupied a position somewhere between Nicias' and Thucydides', their religious inclinations making their presence felt more forcefully in times of crisis.

The general outlook of the man in the street may perhaps be represented by Xenophon, who despite his deep-seated piety couched his sequel to Thucydides' history in the rationalistic terms preferred by the great master. Xenophon believed that the world perceived by the senses was only part of reality. Behind or beyond it there stretched, like a shadow, another world that was visible only through the eyes of faith, or through the intermediary of ecstatic seers or the performers of outlandish rituals. Belief or disbelief in this imagined world created a sharp divide in patterns of action, which we shall now briefly explore.

A group of people may light candles in order to find their way in the dark, or in order to celebrate the feast of a god or saint. In the first case their action is directed purely to the mundane order. In the second it is directed to the transcendental order, in which case it is belief in the existence of that order that renders the lighting of the candles a purposeful act rather than a totally redundant one.[12] The people of Athens performed an inestimable number of actions oriented to the transcendental order: they enacted rituals, they offered sacrifices, they celebrated festivals, they built temples. They also performed an inestimable number of actions oriented to their fellow-men: they gave gifts, they helped each other out, they engaged in hostilities. Although these two kinds of action were of entirely different orders, they nonetheless exercised certain subtle influences upon each other (see **Fig. 9.1**).

The transcendental order was the recognised dwelling-place of such products of the human imagination as dreams, fantasies, hallucinations and suppressed desires. These and some other channels of communication ensured incessant contact between the transcendental and the mundane order. Gods, just like human partners, were drawn into relationships of exchange and reciprocity with men. Like powerful human partners, they were feared and had to be appeased because they could dispense both benefit

---

[11] Parker 1996a: 123.
[12] Cf. the definition of ritual offered by Seaford 1994: xi, which I endorse: '. . . stereotypical, communicative action that relates its performer(s) in some way to superhuman powers'.

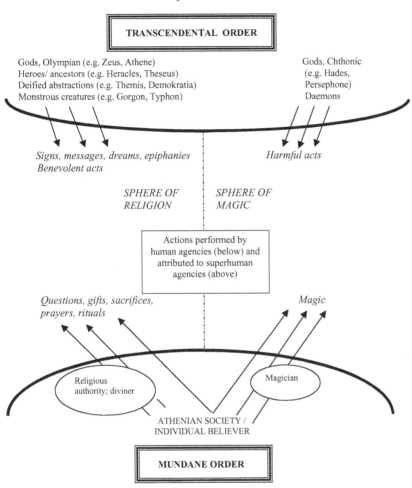

Figure 9.1 Interactions between the mundane and the transcendental
Within the mass of utterances, thoughts and actions that constituted Athenian history (see pp. 98–9), it may be possible to distinguish a category of utterance, thoughts and actions oriented to the transcendental order from a category of 'practical' utterances, thoughts and actions oriented to the mundane order. The two categories were, however, largely interdependent.

and harm.[13] Before the battle of Marathon an Athenian magistrate made a vow to Artemis that for every man that they might slay of the enemy the Athenian *demos* would sacrifice a goat to the goddess annually. In the

---

[13] This view of the connection is sometimes mirrored in iconography. Cf. Osborne 1998a: 25 '. . . the sense that human relationships must take account of divine intervention in human lives pervades . . . sixth-century and fifth-century vase painting'.

Figure 9.2 The rulers of the cosmos: Zeus, Poseidon and Hades
Herodotus believed that it had been Homer and Hesiod, four hundred years before his
time, who had first recounted the descent and birth of the Greeks' gods, given them
names, attributed special roles and abilities to each and described their outward
appearance (2.53). The vase-painting above depicts the three great gods dividing the
cosmos between them. As Homer describes it, the three brothers born to Rheia by Kronos
drew lots to decide who was to have which domain. Poseidon became lord of the grey sea,
Hades ruler of the dead who dwelt in the dark mists of the underworld and Zeus master of
the wide sky, amidst the clouds and the brilliant air. The earth and high Olympus
remained the common province of all three (*Iliad* 15.186–93).

event 6,400 Persians were killed, which was something of an embarrassment
because the Athenians could not afford to sacrifice that many goats every
year. They therefore contented themselves with a token annual sacrifice of
500 goats, asking the virgin goddess' forgiveness for this unequal quid pro
quo.[14]

The contours of the transcendental order were clearly defined. Power
over the cosmos was divided between three mighty brothers (see **Fig. 9.2**)
and most of the members of the principal categories of superhuman being
(gods, daemons and heroes) resided on Mount Olympus. From this vantage
point they kept a watchful eye on human affairs, indicating their wishes by
means of messages and signs. When they were in the mood, they granted
blessings and helped mankind to avert evil. Hades' realm harboured the
dark, malevolent gods of the earth and various evil spirits who presided
over the restless souls of the dead (see **Fig. 9.3**).[15]

Most visual representations of these beings and powers portrayed them
in human form. They were depicted as supremely beautiful human beings,

[14] This custom still existed in Xenophon's time; see *Anabasis* 3.2.11–12, with Garland 1992: 55–7.
[15] Isocrates 5.117, *To Philippus*. Cf. Dover 1974: 77.

Figure 9.3 Visions of the underworld
Some vase-paintings afford fascinating glimpses of the nature of the underworld as
conceived of by Attic artists. The upper picture shows Hermes, 'conductor of souls'
(*psychopompos*), handing over a dead woman to Charon, who ferried the shades across the
river Acheron into the underworld. Hades' domain is teeming with the 'souls (*psychai*) of
the dead', winged apparitions depicted as partly human and partly avian (their bird parts
belong to storks, or to some other member of the Ciconiidae). The lower picture shows
winged daemons pouring some sort of liquid, probably into a bottomless jar, and
Sisyphus, the trickster who once cheated death, eternally pushing his boulder up the hill
from which it would inevitably roll back down (Homer, *Odyssey* 11.593–600). For Greek
ideas of the afterlife, see now Bremmer 2002.

a   b

c   d

Figure 9.4 Divine metamorphoses
'Goddess, any mortal who meets you finds it hard to recognise you, however well he
knows you, because you can change your appearance so greatly,' says Odysseus to Athena
(Homer, *Odyssey* 13.312). Taking on other shapes and breaking the rules of physics were
habits that the Greeks commonly attributed to divine beings even in Classical times.
Image (a) shows Athena issuing from the head of Zeus, helped by Hephaestus; (b) depicts
Zeus, in the form of a swan, impregnating Leda; in (c) Zeus is giving his instructions to
Hermes, the god whose winged golden sandals carried him to and from the world of men
as fast as the wind, and in (d) Athena manifests herself to mortal beings in the form of an
owl perched above an altar.

equation of the beautiful with the divine being one of the cornerstones of
Greek art. Most divine beings were readily identifiable by some distinctive
emblem, attribute or biographical detail. The goddess Athena, for instance,
was symbolised by the screech-owl and the aegis and was known to have
sprung fully armed from the head of her father, Zeus (see **Fig. 9.4a**). Man-
made images of the gods were displayed everywhere in temples and public
places, these second-hand divine presences lending conviction to human

entreaties. Though human in appearance, the gods were in other respects superhuman. They were omniscient and immortal. Most importantly, they were indifferent to the distinction between past, present and future that holds humans in thrall. Though they did not have the sort of omnipotence attributed to the gods of the great monotheistic religions, they were considerably more potent than mere humans. Not being bound by the laws of physics, they were able to vanish into thin air, fly, pass through solid objects and metamorphose themselves into other human or animal forms (see **Fig. 9.4b–d**). Finally, they could manifest themselves to human beings, a process that greatly increased the prestige of the person concerned and generally gave rise to a mystic belief in his or her prodigious powers.[16] According to *The Athenian Constitution*, Megacles went about reinstating Peisistratus as tyrant by spreading a rumour that the goddess Athena was going to bring Peisistratus back home. He then found a suitably tall and beautiful woman, dressed her up as Athena and instructed Peisistratus to drive his divine accomplice into the city. 'Peisistratus rode on a chariot with this woman at his side. The people of the city threw themselves to the ground and greeted them with awe' (1.44) writes the author, hardly able to disguise his contempt for their gullibility. On two notable occasions epiphanies that were imagined rather than stage-managed led to the establishment of new cults. Herodotus tells the story of how the god Pan revealed himself to Pheidippides (the long-distance runner dispatched to Sparta in 490 to request military assistance) and promised to help in the ensuing crisis. After defeating the overwhelmingly superior Persian forces at Marathon (not, according to some reports, without the god's opportune help), the Athenians built a shrine to Pan under the Acropolis 'and sought to propitiate him with yearly sacrifices and a torch-race . . .' (Herodotus 6.105).[17] During the same battle, according to Plutarch, many of the Athenian soldiers saw the apparition (*phasma*) of Theseus in arms, charging against the Persians at their head (*Theseus* 35.8). This supernatural help did not go unreciprocated. In 476 the Athenians brought home from the island of Scyros what they believed to be the bones of Theseus, built a temple in his honour (Pausanias 1.17.2–6) and instituted a festival, the *Theseia*, at which young Athenian citizens marched through the city in arms.[18]

The gods communicated their wishes by means of signs that included sounds, dreams and birds. The inhabitants of the mundane order of

[16] For divine intervention in general, see Dover 1974: 133–41.
[17] Cf. Garland 1992: 47–63.   [18] Cf. Giovannini 1991.

existence[19] to whom these signs were addressed would prosper if they succeeded in interpreting them correctly (whether by themselves or by engaging the expert help of diviners (*manteis, chresmologoi*; see **Fig. 9.5**)) and do
even better if they followed their bidding, cultivating the gods' friendship
(*philia*). By showering gifts and services on the gods it was possible to forge
relations of mutual benefit (*charis*) with them. If, furthermore, one sang
their praises, avoided profanity of speech and never lied when invoking
them as witnesses (and, to elaborate on Xenophon's list, performed one's
sacrifices, prayers and rituals diligently) one would be on the right track to
peaceful coexistence with the divine, a necessary precondition for earthly
prosperity.[20] If, on the other hand, one showed no proper regard for things
divine, or transgressed certain limits predefined by the gods, one risked punishment. Not satisfied with simply impaling her defeated enemies, Queen
Pheretime of Cyrene was in the habit of first cutting off the breasts of the
women amongst them. Later on, however, she was eaten by maggots, as
'violent vengeance earns the envious retribution of the gods'.[21]

   One device that reached up into the transcendental and was said to
'hold democracy together' was the oath (Lycurgus 1.79, *Against Leocrates*).
In the Athenian democracy oaths were used in a wide range of institutional
contexts, always with an eye to ensuring honesty and fair play (see **Fig. 9.6**).
One of the functions of oaths, according to Demosthenes, was to give both
sides an impartial hearing (18.1–2, *On the Crown*). Xenophon believed, as
we have seen, that honesty in matters in which the gods were invoked as
witnesses assured one of divine grace. The spectacular rituals that more
often than not accompanied oath-taking were intended to drive home the
involvement of the divine powers. Anyone who brought an accusation of
homicide before the Areopagus had, according to Demosthenes, to

swear a solemn oath on his own life and those of his family and household. He
cannot see this as any ordinary oath, since it is one that no one takes for any other
purpose; it is sworn over the entrails of a boar, a ram and a bull slaughtered by
the appropriate officers, and at the proper time, to meet every sacred requirement.
Even then the person who has sworn this terrible oath is not believed without
question; should it be revealed that he has not told the truth, his children and his
family stand attainted by his perjury, and he gains nothing. (Demosthenes 23.67–8,
Against Aristocrates)

---

[19] Greek *t'anthropina* (literally 'human affairs').
[20] Xenophon, *Symposium* 4.47–9. For the 'God's friend' motif, see Peterson 1923. For the motif of *charis*
   in civic religion, see Parker 1997.
[21] Herodotus 4.205. For further occasions on which Herodotus is prepared to accept the anger of
   supernatural powers as an explanation (7.133–7; 137.2), see J. Gould 1989: 80–1. For his scepticism
   regarding supernatural intervention, see Garland 1992: 55.

Figure 9.5 Funerary stele of the Athenian diviner (*mantis*) Cleoboulus of Acharnae
Manteis were charismatic persons endowed with extraordinary powers and enjoying correspondingly elevated social status (Bremmer 1996). Their powers were acquired either by divine inspiration (this could be transmitted by various means, such as dreams, trances, snake bites and the separation of the soul from the body during sleep) or by learning (either from books or as an apprentice). *Manteis* knew and saw things that normal people could not. Calchas 'knew all things that were, the things to come and the things past' (Homer, *Iliad* 1.70; Hesiod, *Theogony* 38), while Teiresias was 'versed in everything, things teachable and things not to be spoken, things of the heaven and earth-creeping things' (Sophocles, *Oedipus the King* 300–3). *Manteis* could also purify anything that had been spiritually polluted and, most importantly, foretell the future. The techniques used for the latter purpose included inspection of the livers of sacrificed animals (*hepatoscopia*), augury based on the flight and cries of birds (*oionomanteia*) and interpretation of omens (cf. Halliday 1913). Often leading an itinerant life, *manteis* were usually strangers in the cities in which they practised their calling (cf. Burkert 1983b; 1985: 111–13) and thus formed no part of any religious establishment. Cleoboulus was in this respect exceptional, being an Athenian; he was in fact the uncle of Aeschines the orator (Aeschines 2.78, *On the Embassy*; cf. Daux 1958). Cleoboulus is represented symbolically on his funerary stele as an eagle holding a snake. The *manteis'* relationship with snakes derived from the ancient association of snakes with magic powers and divination. In one of Artemidorus' examples of dreams coming true, a woman is said to have dreamed that she had given birth to a snake. When he came of age, the son born to her became a *mantis* (Artemidorus, *Oneirokritica* 4.67).

Figure 9.6 The oath-stone (*lithos*)
The oath-stone stood in front of the Royal Stoa. Behind it can be seen the north wall of
the stoa and in front of it is a fourth-century terracotta drain. After undergoing a
thorough check of their qualifications to serve on the Council, all incoming magistrates
stepped onto this stone, on which the remains of the sacrificial victims lay, to swear an
oath of office. The oath consisted of a promise to govern justly according to the laws and
not to accept any presents in connection with being in office, or, if any such present were
accepted, to set up a gold statue (*The Athenian Constitution*, 55.1–5). Although the top of
the stone is level and smooth, the rest of it is unworked, its rough condition seeming to
suggest a primordiality appropriate to its sacred function.

Whatever the form that oaths and rituals took, all were designed to
achieve a single end: the spontaneous, miraculous merging of the mundane
and the divine order at precisely the moment in which an agreement or
alliance was concluded. Drawing on a much wider database, one student
of ancient treaties has described this idea thus: 'Whether the oath-taker
invokes the Almighty as witness or speaks standing on the hide of a tiger, he
brings a third partner into the agreement between himself and the opposite
party. The proper function of the oath is precisely that: to transform the
bipartite relation of the contracting parties into a triangular bond in which
the sacral force has a share.'[22]

---

[22] Bickerman 1952: 4. For the heliastic oath, see Plescia 1970: 27; A. R. W. Harrison 1971, vol. II: 48
and 150 n. 7; Todd 1993: 60. For Zeus as the protector of oaths, see Homer, *Iliad* 18.252–68, with
Lloyd-Jones 1971: 5–7 and Burkert 1985: 150–4. For a typology of oaths, see Cole 1996. On oaths in
general Hirzel 1902 is still a classic.

There were also more perilous ways of interacting with the divine. Some gods and heroes in particular, along with certain daemons and spirits of the dead, could be induced to harm the enemies of anyone who managed magically to invoke their destructive powers. The techniques used to achieve this derived from a belief in 'cosmic sympathy': since all the supernatural beings with which the transcendental order teemed and all the natural forces that governed the mundane order were interlocked, it was possible by means of certain actions to trigger a succession of other, often similar, actions whose harmful consequences would ultimately devolve upon the enemies of their initiators (see **Figs. 9.1** and **9.7**). Whether these initiators performed the appropriate actions on their own or had recourse to experts, the magic acts required fell into two main categories: rites that we would now call 'sympathetic' and others that we would call 'contagious'. Sympathetic rites were based on belief in a mystic connection (and hence in powerful reciprocal interaction) between ubiquitous earthly principles such as likeness and unlikeness, unity and opposition, activity and passivity, containing and being contained, part and whole, word and deed and signifier and signified. Contagious rites were based on the belief that natural or acquired characteristics have a material aspect and are transmissible even over a distance by means of physical contact.[23] Whether rituals were sympathetic, contagious or a combination of the two, it was believed that performing them in exactly the right manner and sequence could trigger a 'domino effect' that would eventually hit its target.

It is important to bear in mind that these magic practices represented the private, perhaps even secret, voice of the frustrated individual, not the public voice of the speaker or would-be politician. In the public sphere superhuman agencies were credited not so much with the ability to harm enemies as with the capacity to restrain behaviour.[24] This idea began with the recognition that man, unless supervised, was apt to engage in extreme and irresponsible forms of behaviour that could be detrimental not only to the people around him, but also to himself. It was the gods' role to counteract or suppress this tendency. According to Hesiod, the people of the silver race were done away with by an angry Zeus because, having alienated the Olympian gods by their disrespect, they were unable to abstain from outrage (*hybris*) and wickedness (*atasthalon*).[25] Hesiod recommended that the people of his own day should adhere to what was just (*dike*) and avoid what was violent (*bie*) because Zeus had given man a sense of justice and would confer great prosperity upon those who understood and proclaimed

---

[23] Van Gennep 1960: 4, 7. [24] I am indebted for what follows to Burkert 1985: 246–50.
[25] *Works and Days*, 134–9; cf. Dihle 1982: 20.

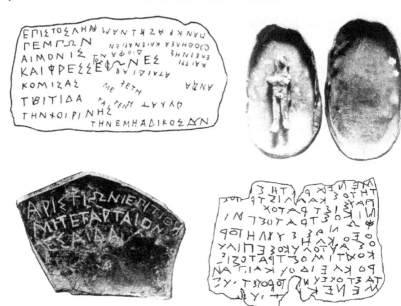

Figure 9.7 Late fifth- or early fourth-century Athenian curse tablets *(katadesmoi)* designed to harm enemies and to influence the outcome of trials

Above left: Small lead tablet whose inscription is scrambled in places, both letters and lines sometimes being in the wrong order. On side A the writer appeals to the daemons and to Persephone to injure the person and the family of a woman who has done him wrong; side B contains an appeal to Persephone, Hermes, Hades and a daemon to 'restrain' two boxers and three women, probably courtesans (Gager 1992: no. 104). Above right: Two lead plates that formed the top and bottom of a miniature sarcophagus for the lead male figurine, whose crossed arms are bound together behind its back. This figure was supposed to represent someone called Mnesimachus, as the inscriptions on its right leg and on the second plate, which contains the curse itself, indicate. The sarcophagus was discovered in a grave on the pelvis of a human skeleton. The text makes no appeal to gods or spirits, but lists the names of judicial opponents, some of whom are known from literary sources (Gager 1992: no. 41; cf. Faraone 1985 for the intrusion of this practice into tragedy). Below right: Lead curse tablet found in a well in front of the Royal Stoa. The text, written backwards, reads: 'Menecrates son of K[ra]tes, Kallistratos son of Pausistratos, Nicostratos son of Gniphon, Theocles *synegoros*, Autolykos son of Epilykos, Timostratos son of Hierokleides and all the *synegoroi* of Menekrates' (Boegehold 1995: 55–7). Below left: A piece of blackware of unknown provenance bearing the inscription: 'I lay upon Aristion a deadly *(es aida:* until his death) quartan fever' (Nilsson 1955, vol. I: 801). The common denominator of all these devices is the notion that there is a mystic tie between the thing imagined and the thing itself and that certain figurative, written or verbal representations of one's thought may have practical effects (for example, writing backwards or using words in the wrong order will confuse and disorganise the enemy and his movements will be impeded if the arms of the figurine representing him are tied). Various gods and daemons (Hermes, Hecate, Kore, Persephone and Hades were obviously thought to be particularly good at it; cf. Gager 1992: 12) could be invoked to put a curse into practice. Gager has pointed out that even if the curse tablets were not very seriously believed to be effective, merely making one may have acted as an outlet for the release of intolerable tensions (Gager 1992: 23).

its principles. If a man kept his oaths he would invest his entire house with good fortune, but if he committed perjury his descendants would perish (*Works and Days* 274–85). If men do not plan sensibly (*oikota bouleuesthai*), Herodotus tells us, 'God is not prepared (*ouk ethelei*) to support human intentions' (*anthropeiai gnomai*).[26] According to Isocrates, one of the reasons for the Athenians' greatness as a people was that they practised 'reverence (*eusebeia*) towards the gods and justice (*dikaiosyne*) towards mankind' (12.124, *Panathenaicus*). This theme recurs in fifth-century Athenian drama, but with the added element of guilt. The so-called Sisyphus fragment, from a tragedy now lost, tells us that at one time man had managed to control open acts of violence by establishing laws to contain violence and punish wrongdoers, but that secret acts of violence continued to mar men's lives. To remedy this, 'a shrewd and clever-minded man' invented the fear of the gods, which finally did the trick: 'If ever you plot some evil deed in silence, even this will not escape the gods. For they have knowledge.'[27] By the fifth century the idea that fear of the gods and fear of the law were major and complementary regulators of human behaviour had fully crystallised and people only dared to ignore either during crises (during the plague, according to Thucydides, the fear of death became so overwhelming as to brush aside both fear of the gods and fear of the man-made law; people in consequence regressed to a primeval state of violence, their behaviour recalling that of wild beasts (2.53)).

Not all Athenians believed so fervently in the transcendental order; some doubted its very existence. The seeds of the critical attitude that culminated in the dominance of certain ideas in fifth-century Athens had been planted some centuries earlier. The conditions that allowed the Athenians to exercise self-criticism, questioning the rationale of their beliefs and the morality of their actions, were created by the transition from individual self-assertion to communal interdependence. The process of examination that ensued revealed glaring discrepancies that demanded explanation. Some Greek thinkers tried to solve the problem of the transcendental by side-stepping the issue. Perturbed by the crude savagery of the battle of the gods as depicted in the *Iliad* (20.67–155), Theagenes of Rhegium (c. 525) suggested that this story was meant to be an allegory of the warring elements, Apollo, Helios and Hephaestus representing fire, Hera air, Poseidon water and

[26] Herodotus 80.60g; cf. Dihle 1982: 21.
[27] B. Snell (ed.) (1971) *Tragicorum Graecorum Fragmenta*. Göttingen: Vandenhoeck and Ruprecht, vol. 1: 180–3. Cf. Sextus Empiricus, *Against the Teachers* 1.53 for an attribution of similar views to Critias, one of the Thirty Tyrants.

Artemis the moon.[28] Others confronted the issue head-on, startling their contemporaries with provocative pronouncements. 'Homer and Hesiod', declared Xenophanes of Colophon (c. 545–478), 'have attributed to the gods everything that is a shame and reproach among men, stealing and committing adultery and deceiving each other.' 'But mortals consider that the gods are born, and that they have clothes and speech and bodies like their own.' 'The Ethiopians say that their gods are snub-nosed and black, the Thracians that they have light blue eyes and red hair.'[29]

It took an iconoclast of Xenophanes' stature to expose two features of the transcendental order that any more conventional observer would have overlooked, ignored or explained away. In the first place, this order preserved intact certain elements of the pre-polis past that in the light of the newly evolved civic norms appeared grotesque and unbecoming. This new perspective did not merely reveal the Homeric gods and goddesses as thieves, adulterers and deceivers and make some of the myths recounting their adventures look, in the words of Max Müller, 'silly, savage and senseless': it made it all too clear that the gods and goddesses were unsuited to communal life. They were short-tempered, irritable and violent, their behaviour irresistibly recalling that of the heroes of the past or the savages of the present. In the *Iliad* Apollo casts pestilence upon the entire Achaean army just because his priest, Chryses, has been disrespected. In the *Odyssey* Poseidon punishes Odysseus viciously for blinding his son Polyphemus even though Odysseus was acting in self-defence. Hera and Athena resent the fact that Paris' judgement goes in Aphrodite's favour so much that they set off the Trojan War. In terms of the provocation–reaction mechanism that we have been discussing the gods are exactly like the heroes, enacting to perfection the 'head for an eye' strategy that the speakers of the Athenian law courts clearly regarded as utterly outdated.[30]

Side by side with these Archaic embarrassments, however, there existed within the transcendental order another set of values that jarred against the current civic and democratic norms far less, or not at all. It is not hard to see why. Like the gods mocked by Xenophanes, these features were the result of a continuous 'updating' process in which whatever trends were in vogue at the time were projected onto the transcendental order. This process may be seen in action in the manner in which the democracy wove stories about Athens' mythical past and the Panhellenic gods together with

---

[28] According to the scholiast of *Iliad* 20.67 (G. Dindorf (ed.) (1901), *Homeri Ilias*, Leipzig: Teubner), 4.321.

[29] Kirk, Raven and Schofield 1983: nos. 166–8, their translations.

[30] See pp. 155–9 and 164–75.

stories about the creation and institutions of the new regime, with unusual consequences for the transcendental order. In the consciousness of fifth- and fourth-century Greeks this order became split into two blocks or layers, one dominated by the savage, cruel, rigid norms that had descended, frozen in time, from the pre-polis past, the other by the far more civilised, lenient and refined 'democratised' norms of the new age. This bipartition of the transcendental was reflected in the visual arts (cf. **Figs. 9.8** and **9.9**). Then as now, certain visual images retained their vitality by virtue of their ability to titillate latent, hidden or repressed emotions. Others remained popular because they struck a chord relevant to existing conditions or circumstances, contemporary trends and actual dilemmas.

The question now arises of whether or not any overall trend can be detected in this updating process. We need to discover whether any con- sistent pattern linked the Athenian democracy's religious innovations, its way of constructing the past and the nature and quality of the moral norms and forms of behaviour that it ascribed to its gods and heroes. We must also ask ourselves whether the norms thus expressed in symbolic, reli- gious or supernatural terms relate to antisocial and anti-communal virtues such as quarrelsomeness, intolerance, vengefulness and violence or to social and communal virtues such as reconciliation, tolerance, self-restraint and trust.

To pursue this part of our investigation we must turn to myth, which puts us in a quandary. The body of Greek divine, heroic and cosmogonic legend that goes under this name teems with inconsistencies. One principal reason for this has long been recognised: unlike the great monotheistic religions, which have organised their myths by gathering together all those that support their creed in a canon of sacred writings and getting rid of the rest, the Greeks, perhaps because their religious authorities were not as powerful,[31] left their myths in their original disorganised state. Not only did they retain their entire mythical corpus, without even expurgating the parts of it that appeared unbecoming to later tastes, but they went on adding new stories (or new versions of old ones) to it throughout Classical antiquity. As a consequence several versions of the same myth often survived, coexisting peacefully despite the often glaring contradictions between them. All this forces the historian to decide which myths to take into consideration and which to ignore, and which of two or more versions of the same myth should be preferred. It raises the question of how to use myth as historical evidence.

---

[31] Cf. Garland 1984.

Figure 9.8 Homeric duel, as represented on a sixth-century Athenian black-figure amphora
Homeric duelling scenes are formulaic. Typically, the opponents begin by exchanging verbal insults to shake each other's self-confidence. During the battle they whip up their anger to the highest possible pitch so that they can convert it into physical force at the critical moment. When the duel ends in the death of one of the combatants, the winner strips the dead body of its weapons and armour, dismembers it and uses parts of it as trophies. Duelling was not practised in Classical Athens, nor could the duelling ethic easily have been reconciled with the Athenian mode of conflict management (adjudication by peers). In other words, this image represents a behavioural pattern that for most Athenians belonged to the realm of fantasy. They clearly found it thrilling nonetheless, presumably because it evoked repressed or dormant emotions.

THE EVIDENCE OF MYTH

It is an open secret that ascribing meanings to myths is a dangerous business.[32] I should therefore point out at the outset that it is not my purpose to dig out any deep, eternal meanings supposedly revelatory of human pre-history or of human nature in general. Here, as Malinowski has put it, we are principally interested in the 'interdependence of myth with ritual and

---

[32] For an excellent discussion of this problem see Price 1999: 11–25.

Figure 9.9 Conflict and the gods
This painting depicts a violent encounter between Heracles and Kyknos. Heracles, backed by the goddess Athena, threatens to draw his sword, while Kyknos, backed by the war-god Ares, defends himself with his shield. Athena represents the intelligent and orderly use of war in defence of the polis; Ares embodies war's more destructive, though sometimes useful, side (*Iliad* 15.110–42). As the encounter is about to escalate, Zeus, father of the gods, steps in to part the combatants. It is interesting to note that Zeus alone is unarmed, imposing his will solely by force of his authority. The picture may be taken as a reflection of the view, prevalent in democratic Athens, that violent encounters must somehow be defused if they were not to drag the entire social system down into their anarchic whirlpool; a traditional mythical theme is, in other words, being used to express a contemporary moral issue.

many other forms of behaviour'.[33] In order that we may detect any patterns in this interdependence without falling prey to wishful or circular thinking, I propose to follow three rules of thumb. Firstly, we shall accept as evidence only myths, or versions of myths, that are (according to the rules of classical philology) as much as possible like the versions that were current in fifth- and fourth-century Athens. Secondly, we shall accord special importance to our interpretations of myth where we have concrete evidence that the Athenians of that time interpreted their symbolism in the same way.

[33] B. Malinowski (1926) *Myth in Primitive Psychology*. London: W. W. Norton and Co.

(The growth in popularity of the Theseus myth, for example, is confirmed by the bringing home of 'Theseus' bones' from the island of Scyros (c. 470) and by the depiction of the battle between Theseus and the Amazons in the Painted Stoa.)[34] Thirdly, we shall confine our inquiry to themes that by general scholarly consent constitute the hard core of Attic myths and cult activities (see below, nos. 1–4) and the Athenians' most important material contributions to pre-democratic polytheism (below, nos. 5–9).[35] With these principles in mind, we may now proceed to consider the chief myths of Attica in some detail.

(1) The goddess Athena wins the contest (eris) for Attica and becomes her patron goddess

The story of how Athena won the contest for Attica by gently offering the city olive trees, thereby vanquishing Poseidon, whose bid had consisted of thrusting his trident into the Acropolis in a fit of rage, was a vital part of the much valued association between the goddess and the city imprinted with her very name that was appropriately depicted on the west pediment of the Parthenon.[36] The portrayal of Athena from the supposed time of that incident onwards is therefore highly significant to our inquiry. As her association with the city of Athens made no noticeable difference to how she was portrayed in Panhellenic mythology,[37] we must regard the qualities ascribed to her as patron goddess of that city as uniquely Athenian 'projections', reflections of ideals and behavioural norms that the Athenians of the Archaic and Classical periods had adopted and therefore ascribed to their chief protective goddess. For the nature of these qualities we can hardly do better than turn to Robert Graves, whose characterisation of the goddess is of special value for our purposes because it is derived entirely from myth. I have italicised those norms that we have found to have achieved dominance and elicited social approval in an entirely mundane context in democratic Athens: 'Although a goddess of war, *she gets no pleasure from battle*, as Ares and Eris do, *but rather from settling disputes*, and *upholding the law by pacific means. She bears no arms in time of peace* and, if ever she needs any, will usually borrow a set from Zeus. Her *mercy is great*: when the judges' votes

---

[34] Cf. Garland 1992: ch. 4.
[35] Parker 1996b; cf. Parker 1990; 1996a: 228–42; Jameson 1997a: 171. I have omitted from Parker's list two myths in which no projected democratic elements are discernible: the arrival of Dionysus and Demeter in Attica and Triptolemus' mission.
[36] Her birth from the head of Zeus, symbolising her unique closeness to the father of the gods (one of her vital qualifications as a guardian goddess), was depicted on the Parthenon's east pediment: Pausanias 1.24.5. For details of the contest myth, see Parker 1990: 198–200.
[37] Parker 1996c.

are equal in a criminal trial at the Areopagus, she always gives a casting vote to liberate the accused. Yet, *once engaged in battle, she never loses the day*, even against Ares himself, being better grounded in tactics and strategy than he.'[38] The workings of the projection mechanism that we have already discussed are clearly visible in the image of the mourning Athena seen in **Fig. 9.10**. This beautiful relief from the first years of the Peloponnesian War appears to represent not so much a religious figure as a kind of corporate personality embodying the city's collective conscience.

(2) The birth of the first two kings of Attica, Cecrops and Erechtheus (or Erichthonius)

Crude pre-polis mythology is responsible for the story of Hephaestus' abortive attempt to make love to Athena; the part-man part-serpent Erichthonius was created when Athena threw Hephaestus' semen to the ground. Athena entrusted the serpent child to the care of Agraulus daughter of the mythical king Cecrops, who was himself a son of Mother Earth. The Athenians' interpretation of this myth defied the diverse origins of their population:[39] according to Lysias' high-flown rhetoric, it meant that they 'had not, like most peoples, been scraped together from all sorts of other places, nor were they the occupiers of a foreign land whose population they had ejected; they were born of the soil (*autochthones*), so that one country alone was both motherland and fatherland to them' (2.17, *Funeral Oration*).

This is a straightforward example of social manipulation whereby traditional myth was fused with civic ideology to make a point, this new interpretation of the old story clearly being designed to foster belief in the existence of a mystic bond of kinship between all Athenians.[40] It is important to our argument that the values that were deliberately enshrined in this religious image were the pro-social norms of harmony and union, rather than the anti-social norms of rivalry and separation.

(3) The daughters of Cecrops

The same is true of the intricate sequel to the story outlined in (2), which tells of the three daughters of Cecrops and Agraulus (Agraulus, Herse and

---

[38] Graves 1955, vol. 1: 96.
[39] For an effective refutation of the myths of common origin and a demonstration that the Athenians' origins were in fact diverse, see Connor 1994.
[40] Cf. Loraux 1986; Goldhill 1986: 66–7; Rosivach 1987b; Parker 1990: 193–6; 1996a: 138–9, incorporating relevant documentation and earlier literature on the subject.

Figure 9.10 The mourning Athena
'Perhaps we have another funeral monument; a monument in carven stone, of Athenians
who were slain in one of the first years of the war. A beautiful relief, found on the
Acropolis, shows the helmeted lady of the land, leaning on her spear, with downcast head,
and gazing gravely at a slab of stone. It is an attractive interpretation that she is sadly
engaged in reading the names of citizens who had recently fallen in defence of her city'
(Bury 1913: 407).

Pandrosus) and two of their grandchildren, Cephalus and Ceryx, born to Herse by the god Hermes. According to the crude version of this myth, after Hermes had turned Agraulus to stone for denying him access to Herse (he had had his way with her anyway) the remaining female members of the family could not resist inspecting the basket entrusted to Agraulus' care. Seeing in it Erichthonius, a child with a serpent's tail instead of legs, they went out of their minds and leaped off the Acropolis to their death. An alternative account of this last episode that breathes a totally different spirit has also survived. In this version Agraulus throws herself off the Acropolis not out of panic, but because an oracle has declared that the war against Eleusis will only end when an Athenian sacrifices himself for the city. There is good reason to suppose that this is a 'democratised' (probably fourth-century) version of the myth: a ritual associated with Agraulus' death survived into historical times. The ephebes of fourth-century Athens took their oath of allegiance to the state in the sanctuary of Agraulus, their patroness, apparently with the idea that her sense of self-sacrifice would thereby be passed on to them (see **Fig. 9.11**).[41] A bizarre story whose meaning is on the face of it unclear had, in other words, been refashioned and supplied with a moral message designed to promote the newly evolved ideal of patriotism.[42]

(4) The self-sacrifice of Codrus

The story of Agraulus is far surpassed in its patriotic flavour by that of Codrus. The fourth-century orator and statesman Lycurgus, who was trying to get a conviction against Leocrates, the wretched blacksmith who had allegedly fled the country after the disaster of Chaeronea, related this story to the dikasts as follows.

The Dorians invaded Attica during the reign of Codrus, supposed to have been king of Athens during the eleventh century. Reassured by the Delphic oracle that they would be successful as long as they did not kill Codrus, they entertained high hopes of taking Athens. A friendly Delphian secretly told the Athenians of this oracular statement, however, whereupon Codrus disguised himself as a humble woodcutter and slipped out of the gates. He then killed a Dorian and was duly killed by another.[43] When

---

[41] The crucial pieces of evidence are Demosthenes 19.303, *On the Embassy*, with scholia; Herodotus 8.53; Suidas and Hesychius s.v. *Agraulus*; Plutarch, *Alcibiades* 15. Cf. B. Powell 1906; Farnell 1921: 22–3. Agraulus figures sometimes in the sources as 'Aglaurus'.

[42] Cf. Parker 1990: 197.

[43] Cf. Burkert 1979c, who suggests viewing Codrus' self-sacrifice as a variation on the scapegoat theme.

Figure 9.11 The myth of Agraulus and its civic adaptations
The top picture shows the moment in which the three women peer into the chest and,
discovering the serpent-child, hurl themselves from the Acropolis. The middle picture
shows an ephebe taking the oath in the sanctuary of Agraulus (or possibly of Athena
Areia) on the solemn occasion of his being presented by the state with his shield, helmet
and spear. By this oath the young men swore, amongst other things, that they would do
their utmost to benefit the state: that they would not disgrace their arms or desert their
comrades in the line of battle, that they would strive individually and collectively to
defend their native land and hand it over to their descendants greater than it had been
when they inherited it from their ancestors, and that they would defend the constitution
and honour the city's traditional sacred institutions (cf. p. 63). The elderly man on the left
is probably a member of the Council of Five Hundred; the winged figure on the right is
the goddess Nike. The bottom picture (a woman, presumably Agraulus, offering a spear
and a shield emblazoned with a serpent to a youth seated on a rock by an olive tree)
poignantly expresses the tension between heroic self-sacrifice on behalf of the polis (the
ideal of *thanatos kalos*, 'glorious death') and the pain felt by bereaved mothers, sisters and
wives (cf. Hoffmann 1997: 71–5).

the Athenians sent a herald to ask the enemy to deliver their king for burial, the Dorians realised that they had unwittingly ruined their own chances of taking Attica. They therefore handed over the body and withdrew (*Against Leocrates* 83–6). The ancient kings of Athens, as Lycurgus put it (clearly echoing the speech in which Pericles addressed the Athenians as 'lovers of the city' (*erastai tes poleos*; Thucydides 2.43.1)), 'loved their country' (*ephiloun ten patrida*) so much that they 'preferred to die for her . . . giving their own life in exchange for the people's safety'.[44] Lycurgus was pushing the idea of patriotic self-sacrifice hard here, perhaps too hard: there is a hint in Aeschines that Leocrates may have got off, the dikasts' votes being equal (3.252, *Against Ctesiphon*). Be that as it may, the example of Codrus and indeed Lycurgus' entire speech constitutes a sermon on patriotism that suggests, in conjunction with Pericles' mode of address and some other examples that we have already considered, that patriotic sentiment was not uncommon among the Athenians. One implication of this will become apparent if we go back to Adkins' theory of conflict between competitive, aristocratic, ego-oriented ideals and co-operative, lower-class, community-oriented values.[45] The apparent prevalence of altruistic and patriotic sentiment among the Athenians runs counter to Adkins' assertion that 'in law-courts, in internal politics and in foreign policy, competitive *arete* prevails over co-operative excellence'.[46] The norms glorified by the myths that we are examining belong to the second rather than the first of Adkins' antithetical sets of values.

(5) The statues and cult of the tyrannicides

Fired by a yearning for democracy and freedom, Harmodius and Aristogeiton put an end to the tyranny by killing the ruling tyrant Hippias, son of Peisistratus. They were caught and executed, but then the *demos* rose up and took over, establishing a secure and lasting democracy. To mark this remarkable transition Harmodius and Aristogeiton were incorporated into the Athenian pantheon: they were granted statues in the *agora* (see **Fig. 9.12**), 'honours equal to those of the gods', a 'share in libations and sacrifices in every shrine' and a public funeral cult in perpetuity.[47]

---

[44] Lycurgus, *Against Leocrates* 88; cf. Hughes 1991: 74–5. For physical remains of the Codrus cult, see Wycherley 1960.
[45] See p. 94.   [46] See p. 183.
[47] Cf. Parker 1996a: 123, 136. For popular resentment of aristocratic rule and the egalitarian spirit pervading the Archaic polis, of which this version of the story might be an expression, see I. Morris 1996.

Figure 9.12 The tyrannicides

Harmodius and Aristogeiton quickly became symbols of the defeat of tyranny and the
inauguration of democracy. The strong union of weaker individual powers that brought
this about and the subsequent pouring of this power into the mould of law and communal
coercion were felt to be the supreme achievements of democracy. The tyrannicides,
according to a contemporary inscription, brought light to the Athenians, rendering their
homeland 'isonomic' (*SEG* 10.320; the last word is restored). An Athenian drinking song
preserved in a later source includes the following stanza: 'Your fame shall be throughout
the world forever, | dearest Harmodius and Aristogeiton, | because you killed the tyrant |
and made Athens a place of *isonomia*' (Athenaeus, *Deipnosophistae* 695a–b, trans. C.
Fornara [1977], *Archaic Times to the End of the Peloponnesian War*. Cambridge: Cambridge
University Press: 39).

This form of the myth does not figure anywhere in our sources, but Thucydides' attack on it is sufficient evidence that this was what the majority of Athenians believed.[48] Wielding his newly discovered tools of historical analysis, Thucydides set out to debunk one of the Athenian democracy's central myths with the information that Harmodius and Aristogeiton had in fact killed not Hippias but his younger brother Hipparchus, that they had been motivated not by their longing to establish democracy and freedom but by a petty desire for revenge stemming from a homosexual love affair and that the tyranny had not really come to an end after the murder at all, but had lasted for four more years, becoming ever more oppressive to the Athenians (6.54–9).[49] Unlike Thucydides, however, we are concerned not with the naked reality hidden behind this myth, but with the myth itself: we need to know how it figured in the city's ideological set-up and how and why it distorted whatever actually happened. To most of the Athenians, and in particular to the majority of democrats, the story and the statue of the tyrannicides stood for the transition from a form of government in which power was concentrated in the hands of one man and denied to all the rest to a form of government in which power was distributed equally amongst the people. They symbolised that memorable moment in the city's history in which the individually powerless Athenians joined forces to break the tyrant's supreme power and prevent its recurrence. This myth was a celebration of power generated by union.

This is important to our investigation because if collective power is to be effective co-operative virtues must be fostered and competitive ones repressed or substituted. This cannot be achieved unless passions are controlled and impulses reined in. The ideal of self-restraint in the conduct of interpersonal relationships is, in other words, built into the myth and the statue of the tyrannicides.

(6) The cults of the eponymous heroes

Cleisthenes' invention in 508 of ten new territorial units called 'tribes' (*phylai*) to replace the traditional four tribes is generally viewed as a

---

[48] This point is well brought out in Ober 1994a.
[49] It is not easy to understand interpretations such as that put forward by Veyne 1983: 10: 'When he [Thucydides] categorically states that the Athenians are mistaken concerning the murder of Pisistratus and gives the version he believes to be true, he restricts himself to stating it. He does not offer any hint of proof.' Thucydides' account follows the reflexive method that he developed to deal with history: he treated common beliefs (i.e. tradition) with scepticism, believed in cross-questioning as many witnesses as possible and aimed for a standard of accuracy that, as Finley put it, 'commonplace as it may seem today, was quite extraordinary in the fifth century BC' (Finley 1972a: 19).

managerial master stroke, its survival for several centuries after the end of the Athenian democracy testifying to its stupendous success.[50] Each *phyle* consisted of three, preferably not contiguous, groups of demes called 'thirdings' (*trittyes*): one group from each of the three zones (city, shore and inland) into which Attica was split (see **Fig. 2.2a**). The Cleisthenic tribe became the democracy's vital sub-unit. Aristotle writes that Cleisthenes' purpose in introducing these tribes was to 'mix everyone up in order to dissolve the previous associations (*sunetheiai*)' and thereby 'to give more people a share in public affairs (*politeia*)'.[51] Some scholars regard this explanation as inadequate,[52] but I am here concerned more with results than with motives. No group of people of anything like the same size had ever previously been reorganised in such a way. Cleisthenes' initiative redefined this group's collective identity according to an entirely new criterion. This was neither the biological principle of kinship that had held together the four previous tribes, the *gene* and phratries, nor the patron-client ties that it was presumably Cleisthenes' intention to break. Cleisthenes' artificial scheme divided all the Athenians (including many who had not previously counted as such) into ten uniform, homogeneous units held together by a kind of putative kinship that had its roots in the transcendental. Each tribe had its own tutelary hero, from whom all its members were supposed to be descended. The ten tutelary heroes (*archegetai*) had been selected by the Pythian priestess from a list of a hundred (see **Fig. 9.13**), a remarkable procedure that paralleled in the religious sphere the election of the ten archons in the democracy's secular sphere.[53] The newly enfranchised citizens were thus re-born as democrats. Their patronymics having been replaced by the names of their demes, they could ignore their former identity and mingle with the established population as equals (*The Athenian Constitution* 21.4).

Here, of course, the central point for us is that unity and equality were deliberately promoted and placed at centre stage by means of the fiction of common descent, averting the segregation and rivalry that might otherwise have arisen between people of different or 'unequal' descent.

(7) The promotion of the cult of Theseus

The ambivalence that surrounded the mythical kings recurs in the myths concerning Theseus. Theseus was famous for having brutally terminated the many brigands who infested the countryside and for having slain the

---

[50] Finley 1983: 44.   [51] *Politics* 1319b25–7; *The Athenian Constitution* 21.2.
[52] Cf. Finley 1983: 42, whose translation of Cleisthenes' alleged motives I have followed.
[53] As we have seen, Cleisthenes went even further than this, turning the inhabitants of each of the demes into each other's fellow-demesmen (*demotai*); see p. 66.

Figure 9.13 The altar of the eponymous heroes (reconstructed model)
The population of Archaic Attica was divided into four 'natural' tribes (*phylai*): Geleontes, Hopletes, Argades and Aigikoreis. Cleisthenes' scheme replaced these tribes with ten territorial units, also known as tribes, each of whose population was supposed to descend from one of ten tutelary heroes (Erechtheis, Aigeis, Pandionis, Leontis, Akamantis, Oineis, Kekropis, Hippothontis, Aiantis and Antiochis). Each *phyle* consisted of three, preferably not contiguous, 'thirdings' (*trittyes*): one thirding from each of the three zones (city, coast and inland) into which Attica was split (see **Fig. 2.2a**).

Minotaur in Cnossos. It is reasonable to suppose that this crude pre-polis motif was incorporated into Classical religion because of its ability to express, evoke and relieve the fear of unknown horrors. Theseus was, however, also honoured as a legendary king of Attica, a kind of proto-democrat who embodied qualities on which the Athenians prided themselves. As such he was believed to have achieved (this time by persuasion, not force) his greatest exploit of all, uniting the numerous small towns and hamlets of Attica in a single political unit centred on Athens (*synoecismus*). Once again, myth served as a powerful tool to express, reflect and promote the idea of pan-Attic unity, rather than separation and rivalry.

(8) The introduction of deified abstractions into the pantheon

Athenian religion, like most polytheistic religions, was not static, but in a continuous state of flux. Additions to the pantheon might be made in a variety of ways; as an alternative to 'introducing new gods'[54] or elevating

---

[54] Cf. Garland 1992.

an abstract idea to the status of divine being, an epithet characterising a
deity might be detached and invested with a newly invented divine personality. Of the deities introduced into Athenian religion during the fifth
and fourth centuries, those that have attracted particular attention include
Demokratia (see **Fig. 7.6**), *Eirene* (Peace), *Agathe Tyche* (Good Luck), *Peitho*
(Persuasion), *Ploutos* (Wealth), *Eros, Nemesis, Themis* (Established Law or
Custom), *Pheme* (Rumour, Repute or 'What People Say') and *Zeus Philios*
(Zeus of Friendship).[55] Translated into behavioural principles, these new
deities reflected and reinforced the ideas of unity, solidarity, peace, love, co-
operation, avoidance of conflict and rational thinking that we have already
identified as the main constituents of the Athenian code of behaviour. A
few examples should illustrate this point.

Eirene, though already treated as a deity in the Aristophanic comedy
of that name, was only accorded a cult after an Athenian victory over the
Spartans in 375. The sacrifices made to Peace coincided with the festival of
Synoecia, which celebrated the unification of Attica by Theseus. This has
been interpreted as meaning that the old idea of civic unity that was the
original source of Athens' power was deliberately combined with the ideal
of peace to express Athens' attitude towards the other Greek states.[56]

The deification of *Pheme* lent supernatural status to 'what people say',
in other words the power of public opinion. It is very obvious that
this is a quintessentially democratic idea, since neither tyrannies nor oligarchies tend to pay a great deal of attention to public opinion.[57] The
cult of *Nemesis*, said to be the deity most implacable (*aparaitetos*) towards
men of violence (*anthropois hybristais*), was also clearly democratic in
nature.[58]

While this last example illustrates the invocation of supernatural powers
to hold mundane violence in check, the next shows us that the Athenians
chose to celebrate and indeed deify *philia* rather than enmity. A fourth-
century dedication adorned with a relief that represents three worshippers
(a man and two women) approaching a banqueting god and goddess reveals
a remarkable feat of self-projection.[59] The relationships of love, friendship

---

[55] In what follows I have drawn heavily on Parker 1996a: 227–42.
[56] Cf. Parker 1996a: 230.   [57] Cf. Parker 1996a: 233.
[58] Pausanias 1.33.2. This should be compared with Pausanias' assessment of the cult of Mercy: 'In the
Athenian market-place among the objects not generally known is an altar to Mercy (*Eleou bomos*),
of all divinities the most useful in the life of mortals and in the vicissitudes of fortune, but honoured
by the Athenians alone among the Greeks. And they are conspicuous not only for their humanity
(*philanthropia*) but also for their devotion to religion (*theous eusebousin allon pleon*).' Pausanias 1.17.1,
trans. W. H. S. Jones.
[59] *IG* II² 4627. The inscription reads, 'Dedicated by Aristomache, Theoris and Olympiodorus to Zeus
Fulfiller, of Friendship, to the god's mother Friendship and to the god's wife Good Luck'; cf. Parker
1996a: 231, with bibliography.

and intimacy between the mother, Aristomache, her son Olympiodorus and his wife Theoris are represented as symmetrically repeating the relationships in the divine sphere between the mother Friendship, her son, Zeus of Friendship, the Fulfiller, and Zeus's wife Good Luck:

Friendship   Aristomache

| |

Agathe Tyche = *Zeus Epiteleios Philios*   Theoris = Olympiodorus

We could hardly find a better example of investing the divine with human aspirations.

(9) The construction of the Parthenon

Nowhere do the power of the people, the transcendental order and patriotic self-sacrifice mingle in more perfect harmony than in the Athenian democracy's supreme monument, the temple of Athena, built on the highest part of the Acropolis. As the Parthenon was built in the middle of the fifth century, it has been suggested that it was a thanks-offering for the successful outcome of the war with Persia. This interpretation seems too restrictive. The Parthenon may more profitably be viewed as a tribute to the collective values that had enabled the Athenians to oust the tyrants, protect Athens against foreign invaders and turn her into a great, communally governed and egalitarian city. It is generally agreed that the reliefs on the Parthenon's pediments and metopes exalt the victories that the Athenians' controlled and united power had won them over their state's real and mythical enemies, who are represented as the embodiments of lawless violence or *hybris*. The temple's friezes, otherwise known as the Elgin marbles, appear to reinforce this view. The interpretation of the central frieze has, however, generated considerable controversy. We shall now briefly consider the implications of this controversy for our investigation.

Three points should be made right at the beginning. Firstly, the Parthenon friezes belong to that genre of visual art that has a story to tell. Secondly, this was one of those stories that cannot be told by visual means alone; even though the friezes use every device known to contemporary Greek art to create the illusion of movement and change (chief amongst these devices being the creation of 'images of maximal instability'),[60] the story that they tell cannot be deduced by the uninformed observer. Thirdly, therefore, we must assume that the creators of the friezes were telling a story with which they expected the onlooker to be familiar. The problem that

[60] Cf. Gombrich 1982: 83.

confronts us is that unlike the democratic Athenians, who would have recognised the story at a glance, *we* have no idea what it was supposed to be.

At least two rival interpretations are currently in circulation, both of which duly assume that the story of the frieze was a familiar one. Boardman's theory is that the cavalcade of horsemen and chariots was a memorial to those who fought and died at Marathon, here shown participating in their last Panathenaea.[61] 192 hoplites are said to have fallen at the battle of Marathon, and according to Boardman's count there are 192 horsemen in the cavalcade. It has, however, been pointed out that the fragmentary condition of the entire frieze does not really permit so exact a count[62] and, more crucially, that this theory does not satisfactorily account for what is without doubt the frieze's central scene (see **Fig. 9.14**).

The rival theory put forward by Connelly suggests that the friezes are not just a depiction of some sort of procession, but represent the tragedy of the mythical King Erechtheus, who sacrificed one of his three daughters at the bidding of an oracle to save Athens from invasion (and so, since his daughters had vowed that if one of them should die the others would kill themselves, lost all three).[63] This interpretation is based on some fragments from a lost Euripidean tragedy quoted by the orator Lycurgus and on some newly discovered papyri from Egypt. The tragedy contained a speech by Praxithea, mother of the virgin daughters, that gives one of the most powerful expressions of all time to the patriotic idea:[64]

This is why we have children: in order to protect the altars of the gods (*theon . . . bomous*) and our parent country (*patrida*). This city has only one name, but it is made up of a great many people. How can I see all of these annihilated when instead I could give up one girl to die for all of them? . . . The devastation of one person's house matters far less and creates far less misery than the devastation of an entire city. Had I a household of sons instead of daughters, with the city under enemy fire, would I not send my sons out to fight despite my terror that they might be killed? . . . I hate women who think that their own children's lives are more important than the common good. (Euripides, fr. 10 = Lycurgus, *Against Leocrates* 100)

Both of these interpretations have their pros and cons, and the fact that neither can account satisfactorily for every detail of the frieze remains an overriding problem. Luckily the exact interpretation of the frieze is not

---

[61] Boardman 1977; 1984; 1985.   [62] Cf. (e.g.) Garland 1992: 105.   [63] Connelly 1993; 1996.

[64] Lycurgus 1.98–100, *Against Leocrates*. This speech was provoked by the unpatriotic desertion of a man called Leocrates. Lycurgus was quoting from Euripides because the playwright had, according to him, wanted to foster a love of country in the souls of the citizens. Cf. Dover 1974: 82.

Figure 9.14 The central scene of the Parthenon frieze
Since the eighteenth century this scene has been thought to represent the citizens of the
Athenian democracy participating in the annual (or quadrennial) Panathenaic procession,
an integral part of Athena's birthday festivities. The cloth that the man and the child on
the right are holding was thought to be the sacred fabric, embroidered with scenes from
the battle between the gods and the giants, that the virgin maidens of Athens wove for
Athena. The female figure in the middle was interpreted as a priestess of Athena and the
bearded figure as the *archon basileus*, or priest of Poseidon. The three girls were identified
as the *arrephoroi*, the virgin maidens who carried Athena's symbols in the procession.
Connelly has offered a far more dramatic interpretation of the frieze, suggesting that
it represents a mythological story with which it had not previously been associated. The
central scene, in her view, represents the moment just prior to the climax of a tragic act of
human sacrifice that was simultaneously an act of extreme self-sacrifice. According to
legend, King Erechtheus (whom Connelly believes to be the bearded man second from
right) was told by the oracle at Delphi that he could only save his city from foreign
invasion by sacrificing his daughter. In this scene, if Connelly is correct, he and Queen
Praxithea (in the middle) are accordingly about to kill their youngest daughter (at extreme
right). In the surviving lines of a play now lost, justification for this act is offered in terms
of fifth-century civic ideology: 'The ruin of one person's house is of less consequence and
brings less grief than that of the whole city.' Anyone viewing this scene who was familiar
with the legend would have been aware that the king was about to lose not one but all
three of his daughters, since the three had long before sworn an oath that if any of them
should die the others would not be long in following her.
It may be noted that choosing not to represent the act of sacrifice itself on the frieze
would have been in keeping with the conventions of tragedy (see pp. 289–90), which
prescribed that acts of cruelty should be implied, rather than explicit, and should take
place offstage.

vital to our investigation, since there can be no doubt that the central religious monument of the Athenian democracy was calling on the individual
Athenian to sacrifice whatever he or she held most dear for the benefit of
the community. Foreshadowing the Christian ideal of renouncing self in
the name of God, the moral climate that the Athenians created encouraged
self-abnegation in the name of the state. The Parthenon is, in other words,
a monument to community oriented, socially responsible excellence, not
to individualism or egocentric heroics.

Returning to the central theme of this section, we may assert on the
basis of the above findings that the Athenians were indeed practitioners of
what modern social psychologists would call self-projection[65] and that a
clear trend may be identified in their practice of it. Just as the Ethiopians
invested their gods with their own ideal of beauty by giving them snub
noses and black skins, while the Thracians gave theirs light blue eyes and
red hair, the Athenian democrats invested their transcendental order with
their own most highly cherished ideals.

These ideals included showing mercy to the defeated, settling disputes by
pacific means where possible, controlling violent emotions, achieving con-
certed action by repressing any tendency to act on impulse, living together
in mystic kinship (first generated in the mythical past and regenerated by
their mystic re-birth into democracy), upholding the values of democracy,
defending their country by means of controlled force, fostering sentiments
of patriotism and ultimately being willing to make the greatest of sacrifices
for their country. Attic mythology, as Parker put it, was a 'distinctively
"political mythology", through which the Athenians forged a sense of their
identity as a people'.[66] That sense of identity was made up of the ideals
that we have listed. Had the Athenians' value system encompassed quarrelsomeness, intolerance, individualistic self-assertion, selfish competitiveness,
vengefulness and unnecessary violence, it is a reasonable assumption that
these would have been the values that they projected onto their myths. As

---

[65] Cf. D. S. Holmes 1968 and especially Bandura 1973: 7: 'It has been repeatedly shown that individuals
tend to ascribe to others attributes that they themselves are known to possess. Whether the assumed
similarity represents a form of imputation or predictions about others made on the basis of one's own
response tendencies remains unclear. The empirical findings nevertheless suggest that the individuals
who are strongly disposed to behave aggressively would be most inclined to attribute hostile intent
to others and to perceive their actions as aggressive. One might also expect persons who have a low
threshold for aversive stimulation to classify a wider variety of activities as aggressive than those
whose pain tolerance is appreciably higher.' For the concept of 'religious projection' accepted by
ancient historians and for Arnaldo Momigliano's dictum that '[t]he connection between democracy
and religion in the classical world, if it does exist, is not so obvious', see Versnel 1995.

[66] Parker 1990: 187.

Clyde Kluckhohn has put it, myths are 'an easy and culturally acceptable method of projection of hostile impulses'.[67] The validity of this conclusion may be tested by examining certain symbolic aspects of one of the greatest crises ever to beset the Athenian democracy. The thoroughfares, doorways and sacred places of Athens (Thucydides 6.27.1) were crammed with representations of the god Hermes. Only the heads and erect penises of these statues were rendered naturalistically, the trunks and arms being represented by square pillars (see **Fig. 9.15a–c**). One morning in late May or early June of 415, not long before the great Sicilian expedition was launched, Athens awoke to find that the faces of nearly all of these 'Herms' had been mutilated. At about the same time rumours began to circulate that the sacred mysteries of Eleusis had been desecrated and that, even more disturbingly, the Peisistratid tyranny of about a hundred years earlier had not ended in at all the manner that had previously been supposed. Large rewards were offered for information leading to the identification of the 'hermchoppers' and immunity was guaranteed to anyone who knew about any other sacrilegious acts and was prepared to come forward with information about them (Thucydides 6.27.2). The Sicilian expedition set out nonetheless, but soon afterwards one of its generals, Alcibiades, was recalled as the prime suspect. Since there was no solid evidence against him, his recall was explained as having been occasioned by his 'unconventional and undemocratic lawlessness' (Thucydides 6.28.2). In the meantime investigations continued and some metics and personal servants came forward to testify 'that statues had been defaced even before by young men in drunken sport' (this clearly implicated the younger generation of Athens' flamboyant aristocracy)[68] and that derisive mock celebrations of the mysteries had been held in private houses (Thucydides 6.28.1). Soon a number of respectable citizens (*axiologoi anthropoi*) were in prison and what we would now call a witch-hunt began: 'every day the frenzy mounted higher and more and more people were arrested' (Thucydides 6.60.2). In the end, as we have seen, the state even mobilised its supreme coercive power.[69]

Here I am not so much concerned with the true sequence of events[70] or with the guilt or otherwise of Alcibiades or anyone else (although I think that Alcibiades was probably framed) as with two symbolic links. Modern commentators have often found the populace's response to the

[67] Kluckhohn 1942: 71.
[68] For which see now van Looy 1990; Schnapp 1997.   [69] See pp. 253–5.
[70] For which see Gomme, Andrewes and Dover 1945–81, vol. IV: 271–3.

a   b

c   d   e

Figure 9.15 Three Herms, a guardian figure from Bali and a Papuan
The first Herm's head (a), made in the late fifth century, shows obvious signs of having
been deliberately defaced, probably by 'hermchoppers'. The other head (b) was probably
carved in the early fourth century by the Athenian sculptor Alkamenes. The vase painting
(c) shows a private sacrificial festival performed in front of an ithyphallic Herm (cf. Price
1999: 35). 'People in the most varied cultures carve figures that display a threatening face
and an erect penis,' writes Eibl-Eibesfeldt 1971: 30. At bottom right we see a double
guardian figure from Bali, with erect penises (d), and a Papuan wearing a penis sheath (e).
(Cf. G. R. Scott [1966] *Phallic Worship*. London: Merchant Book Co. Ltd.; I.
Eibl-Eibesfeldt and W. Wickler [1968] 'Die ethologische Deutung einiger Wächterfiguren
aus Bali', *Zeitschrift für Tierpsychologie* 25: 719–26; P. J. Ucko [1969] 'Penis sheaths: a
comparative study', *Proceedings of the Royal Anthropological Institute*: 27–67 (with plates);
Eibl-Eibesfeldt 1971: 31; 1972: 307–11.) The homology of these figures tends to undermine
the suggestion that male Athenians exhibited exceptionally 'masculine, aggressive and
phallocentric assertiveness' (Fisher 1999: 68–9; cf. Keuls 1985, throughout): neither the
Balinese nor the Papuans are particularly famous for such qualities, though both are keen
displayers of penises.

mutilation of the Herms puzzling. 'It is not at first easy to see', wrote Thucydides' chief commentators, 'why such impieties should have been taken as evidence of a political conspiracy.'[71] This broad question can be broken down into two simpler ones: why was the mutilation of some relatively unimportant monuments not dismissed as a puerile prank rather than 'taken very seriously' and seen as part of 'a revolutionary plot to overthrow the democracy' (Thucydides 6.27.3),[72] and why did Thucydides, our chief source, think it necessary in telling this story to launch into what appears to be a digression about the tyrannicides Harmodius and Aristogeiton, thus juxtaposing two seemingly unrelated events?

The mutilation of the Herms was taken as 'evidence of a revolutionary plot to overthrow the democracy' because the god Hermes was the quintessential symbol of lower-class power. The god of boundaries (thoroughfares, crossroads, entrances and, last but not least, the boundaries that separated the gods from humans and the living from the dead; see **Figs. 9.3** and **9.4c**), Hermes was associated with prudence, cunning (*metis*) and mediation. He was the least violent and warlike of the gods, preferring persuasion to weapons and peace to war. He was also frequently represented as the patron god of orators or of lotteries, the Athenian democracy's prime guarantors of equality, making it easy to see why he became identified with the people, or rather with the united front presented by the isonomic lower-class citizens in the face of aristocratic supremacy.[73] Herodotus' comment that the Athenians (the first people to institute a democracy) were the first of the Greeks to equip their statues of Hermes with erect penises (2.51) confirms that the Athenian people must have associated the Herms with democracy and lower-class power. The erect penis, widely used in human cultures as a threat display (see **Fig. 9.15d, e**),[74] was intended as a warning to enemies of democracy that they should not test the people's patience unduly. The mutilation of the Herms was taken as a sign of an impending aristocratic attack on democracy because, as Osborne put it, 'a blow struck against the herms was a blow struck against democracy'.[75] The 'better' (or whoever was trying to frame them) had provoked the *demos* by challenging its most cherished transcendental symbols. The *demos* reacted, or in Thucydides' opinion over-reacted, by activating its coercive power.

---

[71] Gomme, Andrewes and Dover 1945–81, vol. IV: 284.
[72] It is far easier to explain why it should have been regarded as a bad omen for the expedition.
[73] Cf. Brown 1947: 101. For Hermes as the patron god of lotteries see Aristophanes, *Peace* 365, with scholia; see also Photius and Hesychius, s.v. *Hermou kleros*; Suidas, s.v. *kleros hermou*. On lotteries as a democratic institution, see Aristotle *Politics* 1294b8, *Rhetoric* 1365b32.
[74] Cf. Eibl-Eibesfeldt 1971: 30.   [75] Osborne 1985b: 67.

Thucydides thought it appropriate to discuss the tyrannicides at this point in his history because the mutilation of the Herms was accompanied by another challenge to the Athenian democracy's central foundation myth. The majority of Athenians believed, as we have seen, that Harmodius and Aristogeiton killed Hippias and put an end to the tyranny because they yearned for democracy and freedom. Now, however, an attempt was being made to undermine this belief. The rival version of this episode that had begun to circulate asserted that Harmodius and Aristogeiton had really killed Hipparchus out of petty resentment stirred up by a homosexual affair; they had not nobly sacrificed themselves to free Athens from the shackles of tyranny at all. This rumour was regarded as no less serious a symbolic affront to democratic values than the mutilation of the Herms, which is why it led to a witch-hunt. 'On hearing that the tyranny of Peisistratus and his sons had gone on getting worse and that it had not been the *demos* and Harmodius, but the Spartans, who had finally put a stop to it', wrote Thucydides, 'the *demos* became extremely anxious and started seeing causes for suspicion everywhere' (6.53.3).[76]

In the light of all this Thucydides' account of the tyrannicides takes on a new meaning, making the theory that his eagerness to correct the story was merely a matter of bookish pedantry ('the temptation to correct historical error wherever [he found] it, regardless of the relevance to [his] immediate purpose')[77] appear less likely. He clearly did regard it as intrinsically important to point out that historical inquiry had proved the traditional version of the story to be wrong and the new one to be right,[78] but this may not have been his sole motivation. Our discussion suggests that Thucydides' apparent digression was in fact intended to provide further evidence of a weak point of the Athenian democracy laid bare by the Herm episode, revealing a contradiction inherent in the ideological superstructure of any tightly knit social structure. In Athens the *demos* was sovereign, controlling both the instruments of coercion and the symbols of cohesion. This control gave it its power to call the people to collective action, uniting them into a formidable force. Now, however, one of its chief symbols of cohesion, the myth of the tyrannicides, was under attack. Thucydides was not impressed with the way in which the *demos* reacted to this attack: when told that belief

---

[76] I believe this to be the correct translation of '*epistamenos gar ho demos akoe*'. The evidence and modern bibliography concerning the 'reaction against the tyrannicides' is brought together in M. W. Taylor 1991: ch. 6.

[77] Gomme, Andrewes and Dover 1945–81, vol. IV: 329.

[78] Cf. Thucydides 6.54.1: 'I shall . . . show that the Athenians themselves are no better than other people at producing accurate information about their own tyrants and the facts of their history.'

in the myth entailed logically defective reasoning, the people did not try to come to terms with this, but clung frantically to the familiar and comforting tale of the altruistic tyrannicides. Thucydides regarded this conceptual weakness or popular anti-intellectualism, which he had also diagnosed in Cleon's inflammatory rhetoric ('[the] simpler people for the most part make better citizens than the more shrewd' (3.37.4)), as presaging Athens' defeat by the Lacedaemonians just as surely as her failure accurately to assess the difficulties surrounding the Sicilian campaign presaged the disaster that ensued.

It should by now be clear that in order to form an appropriate assessment of the patterns of ideal behaviour revealed by the Athenian democracy's transcendental beliefs we must examine the myths that were current amongst ordinary people rather than the corrected versions of the same myths proffered by a handful of intellectuals such as Thucydides. Certain statements such as '[T]he homoerotic bond [was] at the core of Athenian political freedom,' and 'The norm of adult male sexuality in Athens . . . was active, aggressive, dominant and phallic . . .'[79] must therefore appear flawed in that they have been derived directly from Thucydides' digression. Accurate inferences about the character of Athens as a whole can only be derived from precisely those popular versions of myth that Thucydides was trying to debunk. The collective memory had clearly chosen to skate over both the personal revenge motif and the homosexual love affair because they were incompatible with the democratic ethos. We must therefore infer that the evidence for Athenian phallocentrism, in the sense in which the authors above were discussing it, is non-existent. This imprecise and sensationalistic label also raises a question of method. Recourse to the concept of phallocentrism conveys an attitude of superiority to and contempt for the members of the culture being researched. This constitutes so flagrant a breach of one of the most important rules instituted by the anthropologists of the post-colonial era (namely, that the objects of anthropological research should be regarded as the researcher's equals and approached with human understanding) as to make this term's expulsion from scholarly literature desirable.

PHILANTHROPISTS, BENEFACTORS AND HEROES

As we have said, in conducting this inquiry we are regarding moral norms and actual behaviour as constituting a single inseparable whole. Having

---

[79] A. Stewart 1997: 73; Wohl 1999: 359, respectively.

outlined the norms to do with social relationships that were expressed in and reinforced by the Athenians' religion, we must now consider the extent to which they corresponded to patterns of real-life behaviour. Since these ideals related in particular to the sentiments and emotions that were expected or supposed to flow from the individual towards the community, we should focus our attention on actions that required the individual Athenian to regulate his behaviour according to the needs of the community of which he was a part. Within this category of acts an obvious target for our investigation is the sub-group of acts that we may describe as 'altruistic'. A minimalist definition of altruism would be 'self-destructive behaviour performed for the benefit of others'.[80] For the purposes of this book a more context-specific definition will be adopted. Altruistic acts will here be taken to be acts that benefit the community in general or other members of it in particular but that may be physically or economically detrimental to the person who performs them.

Central to this definition is the concept of community, which in the case of democratic Athens meant a group of people most of whom were not blood relations of the altruistic actor. As we have seen, altruism towards blood relations is a widespread, 'natural' and expected feature of human societies.[81] Altruism between people who are held together only by those 'invisible bonds of common thought' that turn a random aggregation of individuals into a community[82] cannot, however, be said to be equally widespread, the anthropological record revealing a remarkable degree of variation between societies in this respect.[83] The definition of altruism that we will be using here has two crucial advantages. The first is that it does not conceal the fact that certain communities are more successful than others in inducing their members to make sacrifices on their behalf. The second is that it does not take into account the issue of reciprocation, thus side-stepping the thorny question of what constitutes 'pure' altruism.[84] Under this definition an act may be called altruistic whether or not it is performed in the expectation of some form of reward.

---

[80] E. O. Wilson 1978: 213. Cf. Trivers 1971: 35. Most of the definitions that have been put forward are variations on this theme; cf. Barash 1977: 325: 'Behavior that reduces the Darwinian fitness of the performing individual while increasing that of the recipient'. For surveys of the extensive literature on altruism, see Krebs 1970; Monroe 1996: ch. 1.

[81] See pp. 34–5.

[82] I have borrowed this concept from P. Devlin (1965) *The Enforcement of Morals.* Oxford: Oxford University Press: 10.

[83] Cf. Montagu 1978, to be read with E. Goody 1991.

[84] On this issue see (e.g.) Davis 1992: 15.

With this definition in mind, then, let us try to find out how common altruism was in Athens. Curiously enough Thucydides, who is supposed to have inspired Hobbes' pessimistic view of human nature by his depiction of a ruthless world in which 'the strong openly assert and pitilessly exercise their right to rule of the weak',[85] took an optimistic view on this subject. The world and the war that he was describing were indeed ruled by force and violence, but this world as he portrayed it still left room for fairness and kindness.[86] Thucydides, in fact, assumes that altruism is an essential component of communal existence. Often implicitly contrasting the brutal, pre-polis past with the refined, civilised present (see, for instance, 1.5 and 1.7), he regards devotion to the community and the feelings and emotions that prompt people to prefer communal to private interests as markers of a civilised life. Any diminution in such emotions he regards as foreshadowing the breakdown of the social order. An upsurge of pre-state lawlessness and wanton violence marks their total disappearance.

Thucydides occasionally describes the operation of altruism at close quarters. Most of the people who died of the plague that struck Athens in 430 caught it, he tells us (2.51), by nursing the sick. As soon as this became known, people faced a dilemma: should they yield to their instincts and avoid the sick, or comply with social norms and visit them? Both alternatives were unattractive, the second more so than the first: in the first case they risked not being looked after if they themselves fell ill, in the second they risked contracting the disease at once. Nevertheless, writes Thucydides, some people chose to visit and nurse the sick because 'they made it a point of honour to act properly' and 'felt ashamed to think of their own safety'. To put it another way, under the constraint of social norms some people took a course of action that ran contrary to the drive for self-preservation, the feeling that one should act in the interests of society outweighing even the fear of death. The consequences of this observation are significant. One clear characteristic of the great majority of altruistic acts performed by both men and animals is that they confer great benefits upon the recipient at a relatively low cost to their performer.[87] Quite the opposite can be said of these Athenians, however: their beneficial acts conferred relatively small benefits upon the recipient at an enormously high cost to the performer.

That we have here a pattern is indicated by the recurrence of this sort of self-sacrifice in other domains. The institution of liturgies immediately springs to mind. A liturgy was 'a device whereby the non-bureaucratic state

---

[85] Lloyd-Jones 1971: 137, citing Syme 1962: 39–40.
[86] Cf. de Romilly 1974. [87] Trivers 1971: 36, 45; Irons 1979: 24.

got certain things done, not by paying for them from the treasury but by assigning to richer individuals direct responsibility for both the costs and the operation itself'.[88] The enormous sums that some of the richer Athenians donated by way of liturgies, frequently used to equip a trireme (this so-called *trierarchia* also involved taking command of the vessel) or pay for the performance of theatrical shows at the various state festivals (the so-called *choregia*), cannot fail to impress; the sacrifice involved was particularly significant during the fourth century, when the profits of empire dwindled.[89] A wealthy client of Lysias who had been charged with taking bribes listed his contributions to the state thus:

During Theopompus' archonship [411/10] I was appointed as a *choregos* with responsibility for producing tragic dramas. That cost me 3,000 drachmas initially. I laid out another 2,000 drachmas two months later, when my male chorus won a prize at the Thargelia [the festival of Apollo and Artemis]. While Glaucippus was archon [410/09] I spent 800 drachmas on a pyrrhic dance performance at the Great Panathenaea [see **Fig. 8.8**] and my male chorus of that time did very well at the Dionysia, taking part in which cost me 5,000 drachmas, if you include the dedication of the tripod. In Diocles' time [409/08] I coughed up three hundred for a cyclic chorus at the Lesser Panathenaea. While all this was going on I spent seven years serving as a trierarch, which set me back six talents. Despite all this expense and the dangers that I have faced daily while taking care of your interests abroad, I have still managed to contribute to special levies [*eisphorai*]: once 30 minae, on another occasion 4,000 drachmas... If I had chosen to do only the bare minimum that the law requires of me, I wouldn't have spent a quarter of the amounts I'm talking about. (Lysias 21.1–5, *On a Charge of Taking Bribes*)

Even though such donations were sometimes compulsory rather than voluntary, even though people sometimes avoided them[90] and even though some of them indirectly brought the liturgist tangible benefits,[91] the fact remains that the Athenian rich gave lavishly and took pride in doing so. 'No one today', wrote Finley, 'boasts in a persuasive way of the size of his income tax, and certainly not that he pays three times as much as the collector demands.'[92] Athenian liturgists did far more than merely boast of the size of their donations: they often borrowed money or mortgaged property (and sometimes lost it) as they strove to outdo each other in public outlay.[93] Theophrastus' 'boastful man' claims to have laid out more than five talents in presents to the distressed citizens during a famine (*Characters* 6.15), while

---

[88] Finley 1973: 151; cf. Lauffer 1974.
[89] On the trierarchy, see Gabrielsen 1994; on the *choregia*, see J. K. Davies 1971; P. J. Wilson 2000; on *epidoseis*, a special sort of contribution for communal purposes, see Kuenzi 1979; on *eisphorai*, see de Ste. Croix 1953; Millett 1991: 67.
[90] Christ 1990.   [91] Millett 1991: 85–7.   [92] Finley 1973: 150–1.   [93] See Millett 1991: ch. 3.

Demosthenes asserts that the Athenians are more concerned about their good reputation than about material goods (Demosthenes 20.10, *Against Leptines*). Donations were sometimes made anonymously, a procedure generally regarded as more altruistic than publicising one's generosity, which may suggest underlying selfish motives.[94] One of Lysias' clients says of his father,

> . . . he also [i.e. in addition to his numerous costly liturgies] secretly contributed to dowries for the daughters and sisters of various citizens who found themselves at a standstill, paid ransoms to secure some men's freedom from the enemy and came up with money when others were to be buried. He did all this because he believed that a good man (*aner agathos*) helps his friends out whether or not anyone else knows about it. (Lysias 19.59, *On the Property of Aristophanes*)

The cynic may argue that this man was probably just trying to build up a body of morally indebted and obedient clients.[95] In the context of our investigation, however, his underlying motives are irrelevant. This speaker decided that attributing motives of selfless generosity to his father would arouse the dikasts' admiration; in other words, he knew that this was the sort of thing they liked to hear. Whether or not his father was in fact a deeply caring public benefactor, the assertion before a court of law that he was reveals to us the Athenians' moral expectations of their citizens. From a strictly economic point of view, the wealthy Athenians' ruinous donations may conveniently be regarded as instances of 'conspicuous expenditure'. Considered as indications of the moral norms of the society within which they occurred, however, these actions clearly fall into the category that we are here describing as altruistic.

Liturgies have often been viewed as a manipulative tool used to gain the upper hand in what has been described as class struggle: the rich would give in order to appease the poor, perpetuate economic inequalities and increase their own power.[96] Since all complex social institutions function on many different levels, the liturgies may well have had such effects. They could, however, also be seen as by-products of the particular strategy of reciprocal action that the Athenians adopted in situations of conflict, generally, as we have seen, preferring long-term communal benefit to short-term personal satisfaction. More precisely, they could be viewed as a manifestation of the intense communal spirit that this strategy engendered: of the sense

---

[94] Ridley and Dawkins 1981: 19.
[95] For the 'deliberate and in large measure effective steps . . . taken to minimize the scope for patronage in Classical Athens', which were obviously not always successful, cf. Chapter 2 n. 70.
[96] De Ste. Croix 1981: 305–6.

of duty that demanded that each citizen should contribute to society in direct proportion to his bodily abilities and economic means. The same spirit animates the two slogans with which the great populist Demosthenes appealed to the people: 'pay war tax' (*eispherete*) and 'serve yourselves in the army' (*autoi strateueste*).[97]

How essential a notion this was, and how deeply entrenched within the democratic ideology, will emerge from a comparison with the sentiment that we call patriotism today. Defined as devotion to one's nation or country and concern for its defence, patriotism, in the words of a behavioural scientist, 'can involve a willingness to incur extreme costs, involving even life itself, for the sake of the in-group'.[98] Its emblematic modern expression is a saying traditionally attributed to the American hero Nathan Hale, who is said to have asserted that he only regretted that he had but one life to lose for his country. There is much evidence to suggest that the Athenians may have been motivated by similar feelings. As we have seen, the message that Athenian society constantly hammered home to its people was that the individual must make sacrifices in order that the community might thrive. We have also seen that in terms of the previous few hundred years of Greek history this was a striking novelty. The Homeric hero fought, and quite possibly died, in a self-regarding effort to assert his vast prowess and outshine all others in glory. The Athenian 'hero', by contrast, was expected to fight, and perhaps even to die, in an other-regarding effort on behalf of his community. He was expected to be driven by feelings for others that took precedence over his private feelings and emotions. Anyone who 'regards a friend as more important than his own parent country (*patras*)', says Creon in Sophocles' *Antigone* (didactically, but in a manner that allows of refutation), 'deserves no respect' (182–3). 'Happy indeed are those of us who shall win the victory and live to behold the gladdest day of all! And happy also he who is slain; for no one, however rich he may be, will gain a monument so glorious,' said Thrasyboulus, a staunch champion of democracy.[99] Demosthenes tells us that Chabrias, a general and a great patriot (*philopolis*), tried to avoid casualties among his men but never himself held back from any danger (20.82, *Against Leptines*). This sort of selfless patriotic fervour is amply documented throughout the literary

---

[97] A. H. M. Jones 1957: 23, citing Demosthenes 1.6, *First Olynthiac.*   [98] Hinde 1991a: 148.

[99] Xenophon, *Hellenica* 2.4.17, trans. C. L. Browson; cf. Plato, *Menexenus* 234c: 'Dying in battle seems to be a splendid thing in all sorts of ways. Even if a man is poor, he receives magnificent burial, and even if he is a worthless fellow, he wins praise . . .', and Nicias' boast that he is less frightened for his own safety than are most people (Thucydides 6.9.2). For further examples see Dover 1974: 161–3; Balot 2001.

Figure 9.16 The monument of Dexileos
The relief on the monument shows Dexileos striking down an enemy with a spear. The inscription underneath reads: 'Dexileos, son of Lysanias, of the deme Thorikos (see **Fig. 2.2**), born in the archonship of Teisandros (i.e. in 414–13), died [in the archonship] of Euboulides (i.e. in 394), [one] of the five cavalrymen.' The last phrase probably refers to an elite unit to which the young Dexileos was proud to belong (cf. *GHI*, vol. II: no. 105; Low 2002). The vase on the left, which shows the tyrannicides in profile (cf. **Fig. 9.12**), is said to have been found in Dexileos' grave plot.

sources. It also appears in visual form in the 'heroized' memorial (see **Fig. 9.16**) erected in the cemetery of the Ceramicus to a young cavalryman called Dexileos who fell at the battle of Corinth in 394.[100] Dexileos' grave plot contained a vase decorated with a scene that was presumably dear to his heart: it depicted the tyrannicides, regarded by the vast majority of Athenians as the arch-symbols of the democratic power in whose name Dexileos fought and died.

In a Funeral Oration preserved by Plutarch, Pericles likens those fallen in the Samian War to the gods 'for we cannot see the gods . . . but we believe them to be immortal from the honours we pay them and the blessings we receive from them, and so it is with those who have given their lives

[100] Cf. Richter 1974: 162.

for their ancestral land (*patris*)' (*Pericles* 8.6). Alcibiades, in Thucydides' history, declares himself to be a lover of his city and asserts that 'the real patriot (*philopolis*) is not the man who refuses to attack the parent country from which he has been unfairly cast out, but the man who longs for it so much that he will do anything in his power to seize back the right to live there' (6.92.4).

However one may interpret this passage (or, for that matter, the numerous passages in the Attic Orators referring to loyalty to the state and devotion to military service),[101] it is hard not to conclude that democratic Athens sparked off intense pro-communal feelings in its citizens.[102] The expectation was that the Athenians' actions should be informed by regard for others and for the community even where the ultimate sacrifice was not required: 'This polis is such that these men fought and died nobly for her rather than lose her. It is equally right that we who have survived them should, to a man, be happy to endure anything for her sake' (Thucydides 2.41.5).

The question remains, however, of the mechanisms by which these feelings were generated. Since man may be the creator of culture and society, but is also first and foremost a biological organism, we shall turn to the behavioural sciences for guidance. Patriotism, and indeed the wider class of altruistic acts to which it belongs, creates a paradox that was remarked upon by Charles Darwin. If most of the members of a group were so altruistic that they were willing to sacrifice their lives for the sake of others, he pointed out, the number of offspring carrying forward the altruistic self-sacrificing characteristic was likely gradually to diminish.[103] With the integration of the theory of genetics into Darwin's theory of natural selection during the 1930s, this paradox crystallised into a rigorously defined research project. Edward O. Wilson has restated Darwin's insight thus: '[B]ecause people governed by selfish genes must prevail over those with altruistic genes, there should be a tendency over many generations for selfish genes to increase in prevalence and for a population to become ever less capable of responding altruistically.'[104] According to Darwinian theory, altruism should disappear from the repertoire of human behaviours at some point over the evolutionary time scale unless coincidentally genes that impel certain exceptional individuals to altruistic action are repeatedly

---

[101] See Herman 1987: 156–61; see also Lysias 16.21, *In Defence of Mantitheus*; 31.7, *Against Philon*.

[102] Cf. Dover 1974: 161: '. . . the sacrifice of one's life for the community was regarded as the supreme virtue'.

[103] Charles Darwin (1980) *The Descent of Man*. Franklin Center, Pa.: Franklin Library (original publication 1871): chs. 4, 5.

[104] E. O. Wilson 1978: 153; cf. Ridley and Dawkins 1981: 20–1.

generated by random mutation. The paradox with which we are confronted consists in the fact that in defiance of this logic altruistic behaviour does persist in both men and animals.[105]

Two complementary explanations have attempted to make sense of this paradox insofar as human altruism is concerned. The first is genetic and the second cultural.[106] The genetic explanation states that the process outlined by Wilson runs its course only within the boundaries of classical evolutionary theory (according to which natural selection operates in terms of *individual* reproductive success). If, however, we broaden that theory to include *kin selection*, then the problem disappears. According to this explanation, the self-sacrifice of certain individuals over the course of man's hundreds of thousands of generations of life in kinship groups increased their siblings' chances to reproduce.[107] By producing more nephews and nieces, these siblings acted as carriers and multipliers of the genes responsible for altruistic action.[108]

Behavioural dispositions created by natural selection seem, however, inadequate to account either for those extreme manifestations of altruism in which devotion to the welfare of the 'in-group' becomes greater than the will to live or for the remarkable variation in levels of general altruism that may be observed between human societies. If altruism depended on genetic factors alone, we would expect to find it spread more evenly amongst human communities. Since it is not, a *cultural* or *societal* theory must be sought to complement the genetic explanation. Of the multiplicity of cultural factors involved in eliciting patriotic behaviour, some are regarded as more important than others. These factors seem to be related to the ability to distinguish kin from non-kin.

This ability is a necessary precondition for the altruistic provision of goods and services between kin.[109] Unless the altruist is able to make this distinction, he/she risks wasting his/her energies or even sacrificing his/her

---

[105] This point is confirmed by empirical studies. For example, researchers investigating food-sharing amongst chimpanzees put two cages, each containing a hungry chimpanzee, side by side. One of the chimpanzees was then given a small amount of food to see whether it would give any of it to its hungry companion. It did so. H. W. Nissen and M. P. Crawford (1936) 'A preliminary study of food-sharing behavior in young chimpanzees'. *Journal of Comparative Psychology* 22: 383–419; cf. Masters 1978.

[106] For a brief historical introduction to fluctuations in attitudes to altruism and helping behaviour in the behavioural sciences, see Rushton and Sorrentino 1981b.

[107] If they managed to procreate before sacrificing their lives this would, of course, also apply to their offspring.

[108] E. O. Wilson 1978: 153. Interestingly enough Thucydides, like a modern behavioural scientist, presumes the existence of altruism amongst 'backward' groups of people (1.5.1).

[109] See pp. 34–6.

life on behalf of non-kin. This may reduce his/her inclusive fitness (i.e. the positive payback that he/she receives from kin selection), eventually blocking the progress of his/her genes down the generations. In order to avoid this pitfall, the altruist must be able to recognise (not necessarily cognitively, it should be emphasised) his/her kin, using a number of cues. Three of these cues, all of which result from evolutionary processes, seem to be particularly significant in humans. These are *location, familiarity* and *similarity*.[110] The operation of all three is based on what psychologists call 'stimulus generalisation', a process in which the response to a slightly unfamiliar stimulus is determined by its similarity to a familiar one.

The cue of *location* is based on the perception of a high degree of correlation between location and kinship. People who are related to one another tend to share the same location. By a reversal of this idea, individuals who share the same location may identify each other as kin. Locality becomes, in other words, a symbol of kinship. (A modern residue of this linkage may be the evocation of profound kinship feelings by the locations of our childhood.)[111] The cue of *familiarity* causes kin to be recognised by interactions whose timing, frequency and duration are associated with interactions between blood relatives. As the demands of living, rearing and hunting generally mean that an individual associates most intimately and most frequently with blood relations, those with whom the individual associates most frequently and most intimately under such circumstances may by a similar reversal come to be considered as kin. The cue of *similarity* relies on the assumption of a correlation between the individual's genetic makeup (genotype) and its outward expression (phenotype). Blood relatives generally share, for example, the genetic traits of similar odour and colour. Since an individual's relatives tend to display traits matching those that he has identified in himself, individuals of similar odour or colour may identify each other as kin. Due to this genetically encoded imprecision all three mechanisms may become subject to exploitation: individuals mimicking location, familiarity or similarity patterns may be accepted as kin and subsequently treated as such even if they are not.

It has been hypothesised that patriotism may be elicited by cultural manipulation of these fallibility inducing cues.[112] (For the purposes of this argument, culture should be regarded as the medium through which knowledge, values and other factors that influence behaviour are

---

[110] Cf. Johnson 1986, 1989; Johnson, Ratwik and Sawyer 1987; Hinde 1991a.
[111] See Johnson 1989: 65, who offers further reasons why the association between kinship and location may have become a strong emotional force amongst early hominids.
[112] Cf. Johnson, Ratwik and Sawyer 1987: 159.

transmitted from one generation to the next by means of teaching and imitation.)[113] People genetically predisposed to altruistic action will respond to these cues more readily than others, identifying unrelated members of their communities as kin and developing a feeling that the latter's lives are inextricably interwoven with their own. Let us now see whether this theory applies to democratic Athens, and if so how.

To start with, it is essential to bear in mind the fact that the territory that the Athenians inhabited was very small, smaller by far than the territories of most of the human groups that have since aspired to statehood. This was a fixed and narrow location that could be traversed on foot in less than a day. Visual images of the city, in which the Athenians converged for political, religious and cultural purposes, and of the land, which the Athenians tilled and mined, on which they hunted, in whose defence they fought and with whose mythical history they had been made so familiar, must therefore have been deeply imprinted on every Athenian's mind. The metaphors most frequently used to describe the Athenians' relationship with their country suggest that they associated these cues with kinship. Concepts such as *patris* (fatherland), *philopolis* (one who loves his city, i.e. true patriot) and 'lovers of the city' (*erastai tes poleos*), unmistakably borrowed from the context of kinship bonding, all suggest that the Athenians' feelings towards their country were firmly interconnected with their feelings towards their families. When at the beginning of the Peloponnesian War the inhabitants of the Attic countryside were persuaded to take refuge inside the city walls they were, according to Thucydides, 'dejected and aggrieved at having to leave their homes and the temples which, inherited from their fathers (*patria*), had always been theirs . . .' (2.16.2). It cannot be doubted that this association operated at the level of full consciousness. The Athenians' ancestors, writes Isocrates, having sprung from the soil itself (*autochthones*: a reference to the story of Erechtheus), 'considered this land the nurse (*trophos*) of their very existence and cherished it as fondly as the best of children cherish their fathers and mothers' (5.124, *Panathenaicus*). Elsewhere he adds that this common origin in the very soil led them to address their city by the sort of name that they might have applied to those closest to them (*oikeiotatous*): 'at once nurse (*trophos*) and father (*patris*) and mother (*meter*)' (4.24–5, *Panegyricus*). This associative pattern is also found in other cultures. According to studies, the dynamic similarity between attachment to a country and the early attachment of

---

[113] I have borrowed this definition from Boyd and Richerson 1985: 2, whose model seeks to explain cultural evolution within a Darwinian framework.

children to their parents is a core element of patriotism: 'The patriot – that is, an individual who experiences attachment to and pride in his or her nation – is someone willing to subordinate personal interests to national interests, and is someone likely to have had a positive attachment to the father.'[114] The Athenians, as we have seen, were said to regard their bodies 'as expendable for the sake of their polis, as though they were not personal possessions, but their minds (*gnome*) as entirely their own, to be used to accomplish something remarkable on her behalf' (Thucydides 1.70.6).

The many stranded nature of Athenian society was crucial to the operation of the cue of *familiarity*.[115] The Athenians, as an expert on the social organisation of Attica has put it, 'grouped themselves into permanent or semi-permanent corporations in a number of different ways. These groups were founded on a wide variety of criteria – locality, descent, combinations of locality and descent, common occupational interests, common religious interests, mutual assistance in primarily financial matters, common military service, and so on. An individual Athenian might belong to a large number of such groups, and in these groups he would associate closely with a wide range of sorts and conditions of men. Some groups were by definition made up solely of citizens, others included metics and foreigners (or might even be dominated by them). Some included women and even slaves. Membership of these groups placed the Athenian in a wide variety of different circumstances, but in each he acted and construed his experiences and expressed his needs in basically similar ways.'[116] If it is true that the mechanism whereby kin are recognised has to do with the timing, frequency and duration of interactions, it is easy to see that this highly interactive social environment would have been conducive to the recognition of people to whom one was not related as in some sense kin.

This recognition may have been reinforced by a further piece of defective logic. The frequent and intense interactions between the members of this society, the mystic kinship that was supposed to unite them (buttressed progressively by the myth of their common birth from the soil, the unification of the country by Theseus, the artificial re-tracing of their descent back to Cleisthenes' *archegetai* and Periclean marriage law, which turned all Athenians into an artificial descent group) and the fiercely egalitarian

---

[114] Feshbach 1990: 195. Cf. also Feshbach 1995; Hinde 1991a. The usefulness of these studies is increased by the fact that their databases do not contain any material relating to ancient Athenian patriotism.
[115] See pp. 56–8.   [116] Osborne 1990: 275.

ethos of the Athenian democracy (reinforced, as we have seen, by a whole array of devices: selection by lot, the equal right to speech (*isegoria*), equal political rights (*isonomia*), equal pay for serving the community and drilling and fighting in the *phalanx*) tended to create an illusion of *similarity*. Since similarity breeds kinship, this illusion reinforced the common idea that the entire community was made up of kin, a concept that Plato borrowed when discussing *physis* and *nomos* in his *Protagoras*. Hippias speaks of the Athenians as follows: 'Gentlemen, I believe that you are all kinsmen (*syngeneis*) and friends (*oikeious*) and fellow-citizens (*politas*): by nature (*physei*), not by conventional law (*nomoi*). For like and like are kin (*syngenes*) by nature; but conventional law, the tyrant of mankind, compels us to do much that is against nature.'[117] The notion of citizenship as a species of kinship is also implied by two notable passages in Thucydides. Pericles, in the last of the speeches attributed to him, sees that the people are embittered in spirit and tries to salve their angry feelings, making them 'more gentle' (*epioteron*, 2.59.3). Thucydides uses this word again in his eighth book when he describes the creation of the Five Thousand. Following numerous interventions and discussions, he writes, the whole body of hoplites 'became gentler (*epioteron*) than before, now worrying mainly about the general state of the entire political system' (8.93.3).

The significance of this is that in both cases Thucydides described relations between citizens using a word (*epios*: gentle, kind) that was generally used to describe feelings between relatives.[118]

The Athenian's love of his city, to which he was bound by a multitude of associations[119] and by the religious and secular values that we have already discussed,[120] was thus a motivational force that gave him the moral energy he needed to perform feats of heroism. Athenian society appears to have contained far more cues to patriotic behaviour than any of the large-scale, alienated, anonymous societies examined in studies of modern patriotism, none of which societies has been characterised by limited territory, complex multivalent interactions between people (and between people and their environment) or the identification of non-kin as kin. All this suggests that modern studies of the words that the Athenians used to describe patriotic feeling have systematically under-estimated the intensity of the human emotions hidden behind these words.

---

[117] Plato, *Protagoras* 337d (my translation and italics).
[118] I am indebted for this observation to de Romilly 1974.
[119] Thucydides 2.43.1, to be read with Balot 2001.   [120] See pp. 111–15 and 326–47.

A VERY UNUSUAL EMPIRE

In 428, the fourth year of the Peloponnesian War, most of the island of Lesbos revolted against Athens. The Athenians responded by blockading Mytilene. The Spartans dispatched a relief force, but it took too long to get there: the Mytileneans ran out of food and capitulated. The local Athenian commander, Paches, seized the ringleaders of the revolt and had them taken to Athens. Here the Athenians, 'in angry mood', passed a motion, put forward by Cleon, 'to put to death not only those now in their hands but the entire adult male population of Mytilene, and to make slaves of the women and children'. By the following day, however, they were thinking rationally again. 'They began to realise that they had made an inhumane decision and that destroying an entire polis rather than just the guilty parties would be utterly unacceptable' (3.36.3–4). At the Assembly meeting convened to reconsider the issue various opinions were expressed on both sides. Cleon, whom Thucydides describes in no approving manner as 'remarkable among the Athenians for the violence of his character' and yet 'the most influential politician', spoke as follows:

It has already been borne in upon me all too many times that no democracy is up to the task of governing others, but never so forcefully as today, as I watch you all changing your minds about the Mytileneans. Just because your own day-to-day interactions with each other are not all about fear and intrigue, you assume that your allies live in the same way. You can't see that when you let them talk you into making bad decisions and when you give in to them out of sympathy (*oikto endote*) you are showing the sort of weakness that makes you vulnerable without making them feel remotely grateful to you.[121]

Cleon was warning the Athenians that the norms designed to regulate their own interpersonal relations were too open, too forgiving and too tolerant (as Thucydides puts it elsewhere; 2.37.2) to be appropriate in dealing with other states. Outside Athens norms were entirely different. Without ethics, conventions, laws or coercive measures designed to contain the raw aggression of self-assertive drives, the worst elements of human nature surfaced, impelling even the most conscientious and peace-loving of people to unscrupulous, brutal action.[122] Theophrastus tells us that Aristeides, a

---

[121] Thucydides 3.37.1–2. For the 'curious observation' that the words that Thucydides puts into Cleon's mouth sometimes echo those used by Pericles (at 2.37.2, 39.1, 7.69.2, this last being attributed to Nicias), see de Romilly 1963: 163–7.

[122] Cf. Demosthenes 15.29, *For the Liberty of the Rhodians*: 'Of private rights within a state, the laws of that state grant an equal and impartial share to all, weak and strong alike; but the international rights of the Greek states are defined by the strong for the weak' (trans. J. H. Vince). For intra- and inter-group aggression seen from an ethological perspective, see Eibl-Eibesfeldt 1979: 40–1.

man whose justness in his relations with his fellow-citizens was proverbial, found that policies in international affairs often 'required much actual
injustice' (Plutarch, *Aristides* 25.2). Thucydides relates the story of Themistocles, who used every possible form of duplicity to deceive the Spartans
about the building of the city walls and derived great personal fame by
doing so (1.90–3). Relations between states often assumed the shape of
merciless contests between naked collective interests. More often than not
these contests culminated in war,[123] and war, according to a well-known
adage, was 'a teacher of violence' (Thucydides 3.82.2). The intensity of the
destructive drives that it unleashed was exponentially magnified when the
adversary was the aggressor. In such cases a strategy of extreme retaliation
was openly adopted. 'Let us join battle with fury in our hearts,' the Spartan
general Gylippus exhorted his men in 415 before destroying the Athenian
fleet, 'let us remember that where enemies are concerned it is our absolute
right to feed our souls' hunger for revenge on the aggressor, and also that
according to the adage we are about to enjoy the highest form of pleasure
known to man: taking vengeance on an enemy' (Thucydides 7.68.1–2).

The disparity between intrastate and interstate norms introduces us to a
cluster of values and attitudes that we have so far ignored, yet that is indispensable to a fully rounded picture of Athenian morality and behaviour.
This cluster normally figures in modern studies as 'nationalism'. If patriotism entails positive feeling towards one's community, nationalism may be
said to be the assumption of and/or need for superiority and power over
other national groups.[124] The Athenians, as we have seen, scored high on
the patriotism scale. We must now ask ourselves how they scored on the
nationalism scale. To put it another way, was their general attitude towards
other states or ethnic entities more like the one that Cleon was denouncing
or the one he was defending?

Here it is essential to remember that even though certain conventions
did regulate interstate relations in peacetime, the ancient world's rules and
customs of war were uncompromisingly savage. Destroying the walls and
buildings of a defeated city, forcibly transplanting populations and even
massacring all the men of military age and enslaving the women and children were all perfectly acceptable. The Athenians, it is important to note,
never questioned these rules openly, nor did they hold back from the most
extreme punitive measures. In 427 they executed the ringleaders of the
Mytilenian revolt. When Melos surrendered to them unconditionally in

---

[123] Cf. de Ste. Croix 1972: 16, who credits Thucydides with making this distinction.
[124] Cf. Feshbach 1990: 191; 1995; Hinde 1991a: 148; 1997: 236.

416 after a prolonged siege they put all the Melian men of military age to death and sold the women and children as slaves (Thucydides 5.116). In 421 they subjugated Skione, again putting the men to death and enslaving the women and children (Thucydides 5.32). Sometimes they skipped the mass executions and simply enslaved or expelled the entire population. Early in the fifth century they captured the non-Greek city of Eion and the island of Skyrus and enslaved all their people (Thucydides 1.98). In 446 they expelled the inhabitants of the Euboean city of Histiaia and expropriated their land; Plutarch tells us that they did so because the Histiaians had put to death the crew of a captured Athenian ship.[125] In 415 they seem to have taken over the petty Sicanian seaport of Hykkara and enslaved its inhabitants just to turn a quick profit on their way to Syracuse.[126] Thucydides records that in the late 440s when the Samians capitulated after a nine-month siege the Athenians forced them to pull down their walls, give hostages, hand over their fleet and pay reparations in regular instalments.[127] This seems to have been the standard treatment meted out to any recalcitrant members of the Athenians' empire.

The emphasis here is on the 'recalcitrant'. Reluctant partners were in the minority amongst the 200 or so cities of the Athenian empire, but this minority has attracted a disproportionate amount of attention in both ancient and modern times because of the amount of turmoil it generated. The 'silent majority' of the empire's members were democratic, living at peace with the Athenians and collaborating with them willingly.[128] This brings us to a debate that raged throughout most of the twentieth century, under the title 'the nature of the Athenian empire'.[129]

In the 1970s Finley took on those scholars who were reluctant to admit that Athens' rule over most of the coastal and island communities of the Aegean basin should be described as imperialistic. 'A historian may properly call a state "imperialistic"', he wrote, 'if it exercised authority in any given

---

[125] Thucydides 1.114.3; Plutarch, *Pericles* 23.4; cf. *SGHI* no. 52.

[126] Apparently without the authorisation of the Assembly. Thucydides 6.62.2–4.

[127] Thucydides 1.117.3; cf. Diodorus 12.28.3–4; Plutarch, *Pericles* 28.1.

[128] Cf. Meiggs 1972: 208: 'One has the impression from the combined evidence of the Old Oligarch and of Thucydides that the majority of the allied cities were democratic; it is less clear what part Athens had played in bringing this about. When the League was formed in 478–477 oligarchy was the common pattern in the Peloponnesian League, in Boeotia, and in Thessaly, but among the East Greeks democracy was the prevailing form. The tyrannies of the sixth century were a symptom of Persian control.'

[129] The most important contributions to this debate are, in chronological order, Brunt 1953/4; Ste. Croix 1954/5; Bradeen 1960; de Romilly 1963; Pleket 1963; Quinn 1964; Brunt 1966; Murray 1966; Jackson 1969; Hammond 1967; Meiggs 1972 (incorporating earlier contributions to the subject); Bruell 1974; Rhodes 1992a.

period over other states (or communities of peoples), to its own purposes
and advantages, whatever they may have been, or thought to have been.'[130]
Finley was adamant that Athens met these criteria and thus belonged in
the category of great empires of the ancient world. He was right. There
is overwhelming evidence that between the 460s and 404 the Athenians
took full advantage of their naval and military superiority, using every
possible exploitative measure to squash rebellious allies or indeed anyone
who failed to produce the right amount of tribute or the right number of
ships (Thucydides 1.99). They intervened in other states' internal affairs,
they restricted their freedom of action in inter-state relations, they exacted
tribute or its equivalent in naval or military service, they confiscated land
and they performed 'other forms of economic exploitation'.[131] For all the
unattractive aspects of this *Realpolitik*, however, grouping the Athenian
empire with the great empires of the ancient world has the paradoxical
effect of highlighting some of its more positive aspects. The Athenians
undoubtedly had an empire, but an exceptional one, entirely unlike the
sort of political unit that is usually given that name.

First of all, the Athenian empire had no emperor. Its territory was ruled
over by the Athenian *demos*, creators of the earliest known democracy,
who used precisely the same institutions, decision-making processes and
concepts of right and wrong to run their empire as they did to run their
democracy. They did not, in other words, create a special non-democratic
external administrative apparatus, but extended and perhaps enlarged their
existing system, which was primarily designed to run a democratic state, not
an empire.[132] Many documents confirm that this was the case. When, for
example, the Athenians redefined their relationship with Chalcis in Euboea
after suppressing a revolt (446/5), the inscription recording the terms of the
settlement named the Athenian *demos* as a partner in the transaction, the
Council and the full panel of 6,000 dikasts taking the oath on behalf
of the city.[133] The Old Oligarch also confirms this point, from his usual
anti-democratic perspective. In oligarchic cities, he writes, agreements are
kept because those who have signed them are made responsible for abiding
by them. In democracies, however, 'it is possible to repudiate whatever
agreements the *demos* makes by laying the blame on the man who spoke

---

[130] Finley 1978b: 1.   [131] Finley 1981b: 45.

[132] For a denial of the idea that the conduct of Athenian foreign affairs was structured by pre-democratic concepts of aristocratic reciprocity, see Missiou 1998.

[133] *IG* I³ 40 = *SGHI* no. 52. For a reinterpretation of the terms imposed by the Athenians, see Ostwald 2002.

and on the man who took the vote, the others denying that they were present or approved of the agreement . . .'[134]

This sort of arrangement was conspicuously absent from any territory ruled by an emperor. Whether we consider the Achaemenid, Alexander's empire, the Hellenistic rulers' empires or the Roman empire from Augustus onwards, we see the same divide between the empire's governors (i.e. the emperor and his coterie) and the majority of the imperialistic nation. This majority, as Cartledge put it with regard to Persia, was 'subjected to the unidirectional flow of monarchical power from the top down'.[135] The decision-makers were guided by moral norms generated by life in an autocratic court, not in a wide community of equals. This difference was, as we shall see, expressed in very different concrete behaviour.

Our second difference follows on easily from the first. In empires ruled by emperors, imperial policy is dictated primarily by the interests of the emperor and his coterie. The profits of imperial rule thus tend to be channelled into the pockets of the members of that circle. Finley was the first to point out the peculiarity of the Athenian empire in this respect. Here the poorer half of the population profited directly from the empire 'to an extent unknown in the Roman empire, or in modern empires'.[136]

The third major difference emerges from a comparison of the ways in which the various empires came into existence. In empires headed by emperors incessant territorial expansionism is driven by the martial ethos of the ruling dynasty and/or a scarcity of resources (in particular agricultural produce) created by overpopulation and/or underproduction. Athens had no ruling dynasty and no shortage of resources; although her economy was flourishing, her birth rates were not so high as to arouse the appetite for conquest. Unlike the empires headed by emperors and that of republican Rome, the Athenian empire was not the outcome of a quick succession of wars and conquests, but the legacy of an alliance of Greek city-states that we now know as the 'Delian league'. This free alliance had originally been struck up to pursue the war against the Persians when their attempted invasion of Greece had been successfully repelled. Finley, no great apologist for imperialism, describes the beginnings of the Athenian empire thus: 'The Persians had twice invaded Greece unsuccessfully, and no one in 478 could have had the slightest confidence that the Great King would accept the defeats passively and would not return in a third attempt. Control of the

---

[134] [Xenophon], *The Constitution of the Athenians* 2.17. The corruption in the MS does not obscure the sentence's general meaning.

[135] Cartledge 1993a: 105.   [136] Finley 1981b: 59.

Aegean was the most obvious protective measure, and Athens successfully won the leadership of such an undertaking. . . . Within a dozen years . . . the league's formal objective was achieved. The Persian fleet of 200 triremes, most of them Phoenicians, was captured and destroyed in a great land-and-sea battle . . . Yet the "league" remained in existence without a moment's faltering and its membership grew, willingly or by compulsion as the case may have been in each instance . . .'[137] Modern critics who have interpreted Athens as aggressive, expansionist and tyrannical should bear in mind that the Achaemenid empire, which spread from the Indus to the Balkans and from central Asia to upper Egypt, surpassed the Greek world in manpower and resources (even if not in its ability to manage them effectively) even after the 460s. Consequently, the alternative to the institution in Greek cities of democracies promoted by the Athenian *demos* might well have been the setting up by the Achaemenid court of Greek tyrants at best and Persian satraps at worst. It seems important to consider the desirability of the latter option before expressing any unqualified condemnation of Athens' proceedings, remembering also that the war against Persia was a struggle by constitutional governments against despotism.

This takes us to the fourth difference, which has to do with the ideologies deployed to defend and justify imperialism and exploitation. Virtually all the empires of the ancient world justified their proceedings simply by asserting the rule of the strongest. According to this argument, the strong should not feel guilty about subjugating the weak and availing themselves of the spoils because they are acting in accordance with the rules of nature.[138] Writing about the Roman empire, Cicero unabashedly paraded this principle as a virtue, asserting that Sicily was 'the first to teach our forefathers what a fine thing it is to rule over foreign nations' (*quam praeclarum esset exteris gentibus imperare*; *II Verrines* 2.2). King Darius of Persia was fond of bombastically advertising the satisfaction he derived from subjugating, exterminating or mass-transferring anyone who refused to accept him as overlord,[139] and so were the Hellenistic rulers who fed on Macedonian and Persian traditions, although they used rather less inflated language. It has often been stated or implied that the Athenian empire was much like the other great empires in this respect, cherishing more or less the same imperialist ideologies. 'The evidence . . . suggests', writes Meiggs, 'that the Athenians, both rich and poor, thought primarily of the benefits that empire brought to them and

---

[137] Finley 1981b: 43.   [138] Frisch 1949.
[139] Cf. L. W. King and R. C. Thompson (1907) *The Sculpture and Inscriptions of Darius the Great on the Rock of Behistun in Persia*. London: British Museum.

were not ashamed to say so.'[140] No less a historian than Sir Ronald Syme claimed that Thucydides was a cruel and ruthless writer who believed that the strong had a right to rule and approved wholeheartedly of Athenian imperialism, simply because Thucydides was describing a reality in which many of the strong did openly assert and pitilessly exercise their 'right' to rule over the weak.[141]

While the 'rule of the strongest' argument is not absent from Athenian justifications of empire, it is noteworthy that where it occurs it is usually accompanied by all sorts of qualifications, afterthoughts and expressions of remorse that are not usually found in connection with the other empires of the ancient world. A good illustration of this point is the speech that an Athenian spokesman is supposed to have delivered at Sparta in 432, just before the Spartans declared war (Thucydides 1.73–8). This speech has about it a distinct air of apology. Claiming that the Athenians have done nothing extraordinary or contrary to human practice in accepting and hanging on to the empire that has fallen into their laps, the speech asserts that they had three powerful motives for doing so: honour (*time*), fear (*deos*) and self-interest (*ophelia*).[142] Of these three only the last lends unqualified support to the 'rule of the strongest' motif. The first two fit into it so uneasily as almost to do away with it altogether. The word 'honour', as we have seen, denotes an order of skills and virtues altogether different from those associated with personal honour when it is used in connection with the city.[143] The honour of the Athenians was not at all like the personal honour of the Homeric hero or the Mediterranean macho man. What the people of Athens sought to uphold was their collective reputation as a peaceful democratic community that acted rationally, a reputation that was the result of the very opposite of the glorification of personal honour: the suppression by the community of individualistic, self-assertive manifestations of physical force and courage.[144] That this was indeed what the Athenians meant when they used the term *time* in Sparta may be seen by the next item on their list: 'fear'. One would search in vain for fear

---

[140] Meiggs 1972: 404.

[141] Syme 1962: esp. 52, to be read with the criticism of Lloyd-Jones 1971: 137, to whom I am indebted for what follows.

[142] Thucydides 1.75.3, repeated in a different order in 1.76.2.

[143] See pp. 267–8. The suggestion that relations between Greek states mimicked relations between Greek individuals (e.g. Lendon 2000: 3) is not in my view borne out by the evidence. Identical vocabulary often masks a radically different social reality.

[144] For modern parallels (repudiation of aristocratic honour in favour of republican patriotism and 'national' honour) see N. Hampson (1973) 'The French Revolution and the nationalisation of honour', in M. R. D. Foot (ed.) *War and Society*. New York: Barnes and Noble: 199–212, 324–5; Blok 1981.

in the ideological baggage of the Homeric hero. To him, as Finley put it, 'every value, every judgement, every action, all skills and talents [had] the function of either defining honour or realizing it'.[145] Far from expressing overweening superiority, the speech made at Sparta employed a word that is a frank admission of human uncertainty. The Athenians had a tiger by the tail. They had acquired an empire against their will and not until their rule was thoroughly entrenched had they realised that it was no longer safe to relinquish it. What forbade them to relinquish it was fear: fear that in doing so they might imperil their entire communal existence.

Two further assertions (or perhaps excuses) made in this speech show that such is indeed its general tenor. The first refers to the familiar argument, expounded in more detail in Pericles' Funeral Oration (Thucydides 2.41.3), that a ruler with positive moral qualities is a good thing under any circumstances: while admitting that 'it has always been a rule that the weak should be subject to the strong', the speech asserts that the Athenians 'consider that we are worthy of our power'.[146] The second argues that although the strong may of course be expected to use force to control the weak, in dealing with their allies the Athenians rely on the processes of law (not merely on brute force, as do the Persians) and that this acts as a restraining force, preventing them from fully exploiting their superiority (1.77.1–4).[147]

Of itself, of course, all this rhetoric might mean precisely nothing. It is perfectly conceivable that the Athenians might have said one thing and done another, their actions belying the high-minded dislike for the 'rule of the stronger' that they professed. As it turns out, however, the qualifications, afterthoughts and expressions of remorse that we see on the level of ideas can also be seen translated into action. In 428, after deciding to put the entire adult male population of Mytilene to death, the Athenians dispatched a trireme to convey their decision to Paches. The trireme's crew, however, deliberately procrastinated because they so disliked the 'horrible business' (*epi pragma allokoton*) with which they had been charged, while the second trireme that was dispatched the next day to convey the reversal of the decision went hell for leather, its crew sleeping on a rota system and continuing to row even while they were eating. It arrived only just in time to prevent the executions (Thucydides 3.49.4). It is interesting that in recounting this episode Thucydides agreed with Cleon, whom he

[145] Finley 1978a: 113.
[146] Thucydides 2.42.3, cf. 5.49; Lysias, *Funeral Oration* 2.12, 2.14, 2.22 (in which the Athenians are praised for their willingness to lend their military power to other Greeks who have been wronged by powerful bullies); Demosthenes 60.11, *Funeral Speech*.
[147] Cf. Gomme, Andrewes and Dover 1945–81, vol. 1: 243–4.

manifestly disliked, that the Athenians were carrying over the compassion that they practised in their inter-personal relations into the international sphere.

Thucydides is not alone in presenting us with this picture of the Athenians. Herodotus tells us that when the Persians took Miletus in 494, killing most of the men and carrying everyone else off to Susa as slaves, the Athenians were filled with grief, which they demonstrated in a number of ways; most remarkably, when the famous dramatist Phrynichus staged the play 'The Fall of Miletus' the whole theatre burst into tears. 'And they fined Phrynichus a thousand drachmas', writes Herodotus, 'for bringing to mind a calamity that touched them so nearly, and forbade for ever the acting of that play' (Herodotus 6.21).[148] Taken together, the passages from Thucydides that we have examined here and the many others so meticulously analysed by Strasburger and Lloyd-Jones reveal Thucydides' moral overview of the Athenian empire. He conceived of it as a sort of human tragedy in which the Athenians began by judging events correctly, but were later betrayed by *hybris* and became unjust; finally, with the launching of the Sicilian expedition, they lost touch with reality, their faculty for rational decision-making being by now severely impaired.[149] Had Thucydides believed unconditionally in the right of the strongest to rule, or had he been a wholehearted supporter of Athenian imperialism, it is to be doubted whether his history would have revealed such an ideological schema. Had the idea that he was expressing not been discussed and commented upon in Athenian society, Xenophon could hardly have written that the Athenians, when besieged at the end of the Peloponnesian War, 'thought that they would suffer what they had *unjustly inflicted* (*edikoun*) on small cities . . .' (*Hellenica* 2.2.10, my italics).

The fifth difference emerges from the way in which the Athenians portrayed their opponents. It has been widely observed that in-groups tend to view out-groups as enemies. In the event of open conflict they may well denigrate and even demonise them, increasingly picturing them, as the conflict escalates, as dangerous, evil or even subhuman. By a process of self-indoctrination, wild fantasies are created that no longer have anything to do with the out-group's objective attributes, instead expressing the

---

[148] Cf. Karavites 1982 for further examples of preference for humanistic attitudes in the conduct of interstate relations that conflict sharply with generalisations such as 'We have seen nothing in the *arete* of the democratic Athenian assembly to suggest that its exercise encouraged co-operation with . . . any other state' (Adkins 1960a: 224) and 'coldness and emotional detachment openly characterise the Athenians in their dealings with other states' (Crane 1992: 25).

[149] Strasburger 1954; 1958; Lloyd-Jones 1971: 144.

in-group's own unconscious needs. Behavioural scientists connect this tendency with a variety of individual and collective psychological mechanisms, chief amongst which is the displacement of aggression from the in-group onto the out-group.[150]

Let us now examine some items of visual art depicting fights against real or imaginary enemies that were displayed prominently in Athens. Few of these artefacts have survived in more than fragmentary form, so we will have to rely on the judgement of contemporaries who saw them in their original form. Certain paintings by Polygnotus and Micon (particularly *Amazonomachies*, *Lapitomachies* and *Centauromachies*) and Phidias' frieze of the Throne of Zeus on the Parthenon merit special attention.[151] These were all allegorical representations of the repulse of Persia (the Amazons were represented as Persian warriors, each wearing a Phrygian cap or fox-skin toque and some sort of body-stocking), seen as the struggle of civilisation against barbarism, or of constitutional government against tyranny. What most struck ancient onlookers about these artefacts was their artistic merit (they are said to have exercised a great influence on Athenian art throughout that century and beyond), not their hideous and terrifying representation of the national enemy. Surviving fragments reveal that the Lapiths, Centaurs and Amazons were shown fighting the Athenian hoplites as equals; the manner in which they were depicted was clearly not intended to persuade the beholder that they were embodiments of evil and the Athenians shining examples of righteousness. This approach is in keeping with Herodotus' fair-minded statement that the Persians appreciated courage in battle more than anyone[152] and with the Athenians' consistent stereotypical representation of themselves as benefactors to the whole of Hellas, friends and liberators of the weak and the oppressed (both individuals and people) and champions of freedom against despotism.[153]

All this is very unlike the way in which the Romans depicted their enemies on a war memorial erected not during the period of the major conquests, when feeling was presumably running high, but during what has been called the golden age of humanity. 'The horrors which [the columns of Trajan and Marcus Aurelius] record', according to an expert on this period, 'as a matter of course, for public consumption, include scene after scene of "barbarians"

---

[150] Wahlström 1987; van der Dennen 1987; Hinde 1991a: 150; more especially Hinde 1997.
[151] For the controversy over the locations in which they were displayed see Meiggs 1972: 276.
[152] Herodotus 7.238. This concession appears all the more remarkable in the context in which it was made, Xerxes having threatened to cut off the head of the dead Leonidas and display it on a spike. Athens offered up annual sacrifices on behalf of the Amazons on the day before the Thesea.
[153] Cf. Strasburger 1958, which contains numerous further examples illustrating this point.

cringing before the emperor or his soldiers . . .' 'the repeated clearing of local villages and the massacre of the adult male population; the torching of houses . . .' '. . . the systematic execution of long lines of defenceless men . . .' 'the mass murder of unarmed prisoners . . .' 'the head-hunting done by Roman soldiers . . .' 'the abuse and killing of unarmed prisoners . . .' 'the violent seizure of women, children, infants and cattle . . .'[154]

Some literary passages support the conclusion that the Athenians' manner of picturing their enemies contained an element of rational self-criticism. It is true that the Greeks are often represented as masculine and free, unlike the effeminate, subjugated barbarians (e.g. Isocrates 5.124, *To Philip*),[155] and that there are even some manifestations (mainly in the private sphere) of what would now be called jingoism.[156] It is also true, however, that the opposition between Greeks and barbarians is not strongly articulated and, more importantly, that its legitimacy does not go unchallenged. For example, the play *Persae*, attributed to Aeschylus, displayed the national enemy in so tragic a role that some have received it with amazement. 'To write a *kommos* [dirge, lament] for a defeated enemy (especially a *kommos* for the Persian invaders to be performed in a public Athenian festival)', writes Goldhill, 'is in itself a remarkable event, and this is perhaps not sufficiently emphasised by critics.'[157] Far from accepting the traditional view that the Greeks were a superior race, another great Athenian playwright, Euripides, put on stage not only 'barbaric barbarians' and 'noble Greeks', but also 'noble barbarians' and 'barbaric Greeks'.[158] Antiphon the Sophist went so far as to claim (in his essay *On Truth*) that 'by nature we are all constituted similarly in all respects, barbarians and Greeks alike', while some Hippocratic writers, denying any innate difference between Greeks and barbarians, insisted that all human beings were of a single nature (*physis*).[159] If Pericles' citizenship law bespeaks an ethnocentric wish to emphasise the differences between Athenians and non-Athenians (both Greek and non-Greek), these pieces of evidence betoken a very different feeling.

The sixth difference between the Athenian empire and the other great empires has to do with scales of exploitation, oppression and atrocity. As Finley has pointed out, 'Athenian imperialism employed all the forms of material exploitation that were available and possible in that society.'[160] The Athenians definitely committed mass murders in Mytilene, Melos and Skione and may have committed another at Torone. These acts impair

[154] Shaw 2001: 379–80.
[155] Cf. Cartledge 1993a: 73; Nippel 2001; T. Harrison 2002, in general.
[156] Cartledge 1998b.   [157] Goldhill 2002: 60.
[158] Said 1984.   [159] Cf. Staden 1992: 580.   [160] See Chapter 3, n. 25.

their reputation as a humane people, suggesting that they had a streak of cruelty: Nietzsche's 'tigerish lust to annihilate'.[161] Their atrocities appear, however, to have been significantly fewer and less excessive than those of most of the ancient world's imperial (or merely victorious) powers. The Athenians seem to have drawn the right conclusions from their defeat in the Peloponnesian War, refraining from initiating any such action again for the next hundred years or so, during which time their city remained a great (though not imperial) power.[162]

This interpretation is supported by many of the chief authors of the period. Writing about the slaughter carried out by the Thracians at Mycalessus, Thucydides describes the Thracians as a particularly bloodthirsty people, implying that in his view the Greeks in general and the Athenians in particular were significantly less so (Thucydides 7.29).[163] The Lacedaemonians, writes Isocrates, 'put more men to death arbitrarily in three months than we brought to trial throughout our entire period of supremacy' (Isocrates 4.113, *Panegyricus*). Elsewhere Isocrates asserts that certain crimes of unparalleled wickedness and cruelty that were perpetrated routinely in other 'great' states were never committed in Athens simply because the Athenians 'were not of the same character as those who have proved themselves the most godless of men' (12.121–3, *Panathenaicus*). Returning for a moment to Trajan's column, with its matter-of-course representations of the mass murder of women, children and unarmed prisoners, Herodotus' accounts of some really spectacular Persian acts of cruelty[164] and Thucydides' comment that at the beginning of the Peloponnesian War the Lacedaemonians put to death anyone whom they captured at sea 'whether they were fighting on the side of the Athenians or not even taking part on either side' (Thucydides 2.67.4), we begin to see that even atrocities can differ in degree. The mechanisms of self-restraint that regulated internal Athenian affairs seem

---

[161] Plutarch records Duris of Samos' claim that after Samos had surrendered Pericles 'had the Samian captains and marines from each ship brought into the market-place in Miletus and crucified there, and that when they had already suffered this torture for ten days he gave orders for their heads to be beaten in with clubs and their bodies thrown on the ground unburied' (Plutarch, *Pericles* 28). Since Thucydides, Ephorus and Aristotle made no mention of these events, Plutarch concluded that Duris had invented the story, painting a horrifying picture of his country's sufferings in order to blacken Athens' name. Some modern authors who entertain a pessimistic view of Athenian society, however, believe this story to be correct (cf. Hall 1996: 88).

[162] For the (unsuccessful) attempts made to resurrect the empire during this period and their impact on the collective psyche, see Badian 1995.

[163] Cf. Cartledge 1993a: 53, who contrasts the barbarian *tharsos* (boldness) attributed by Thucydides to the Thracians with Greek *andreia* (courage).

[164] Herodotus 3.11 (punishing Phanes by cannibalising his sons); 3.14 (mass execution of Egyptian noblemen); 7.35.3 (beheading the overseers); 7.39 (cutting one of Pythius' sons in half and making the army pass between the two halves).

to some extent at least to have been used outside the state as well. Cleon seems not to have been all that far off the mark in claiming that the Athenians imagined their allies to be their fellow-citizens. He was, however, exaggerating the Athenians' naïveté; most were perfectly well aware that more hostile norms than their own tended to govern inter-city dealings and would have cast their votes accordingly.

We are, of course, in no position to quantify the extent to which such attitudes may or may not have mitigated the savagery of Athens' international encounters. Even if we grant that they did not do so at all, however, and even if, discarding all the evidence above, we insist that in the conduct of her *external* affairs Athens was no better and no worse than any other imperial power in the ancient world, we will still have an important clue to the conduct of her *internal* affairs. Thucydides, as we have seen, tended to evaluate interstate relations in terms of interpersonal morality,[165] describing Gylippus as having fired up his men to take head-for-an-eye revenge on their assailants (Thucydides 7.68). The Athenians are said to have justified killing their Spartan prisoners and throwing their bodies into a pit on the eye-for-an-eye principle, the Spartans having previously treated some Athenians in the same way (2.67.4). There is nothing unusual about any of this. What is unusual is Thucydides' suggestion, repeated at least three times in his history, that relations between states sometimes were, or could be, conducted on a principle corresponding to the third category of moral injunctions that we derived earlier: bowling the enemy over with generosity.[166]

The Spartan envoys sent to Athens in 425 to offer peace, alliance and neighbourly friendship put forward the following argument: 'We also believe that rankling mutual resentment is unlikely to find any permanent resolution where a party out for revenge is successful in dominating the hostilities and tries to tie his adversary down to some one-sided peace agreement by means of compulsory oaths. The matter is far more likely to be resolved if on finding himself in a position to do so he *instead chooses to behave more rationally and overwhelm his opponent with generosity* (arete), *putting forward peace terms that are far less stringent than his enemy expected.*'[167]

The same idea is expressed a little differently in the Funeral Oration, which asserts that the Athenians are unique in that they act on this principle

---

[165] Dover 1974: 310; Missiou 1998.   [166] See pp. 10–12.

[167] Thucydides 4.19.1–2 (my italics), to be read with MacDowell 1963b: 128. In criticising Adkins 1960a, MacDowell points out that in the sentence that follows 'to repay *arete*' (i.e. generosity) figures as the opposite of 'to fight back'.

in dealing with other states: 'When we do kindnesses to others, we are not totting up our potential profits and losses; we are acting on the moment, with the confidence that belongs to us as free men' (Thucydides 2.40.5).[168] Finally, Cleon, in the sequel to the speech that was quoted earlier in this section, seeks to prove his thesis that the Athenians are ill-adapted to the conduct of international affairs by asserting that their allies' obedience has nothing to do with any self-damaging favours that the Athenians may have done them: they are obedient not because they feel grateful, but because the Athenians are stronger than they (Thucydides 3.37.3). He is, of course, telling us that the Athenians are deluded in thinking that their strategy of generosity works, but he is also telling us that it exists.

In attributing such views on interstate affairs to his protagonists Thucydides betrays his own convictions, confirming a conclusion that we have already reached by examining sources other than his history. This conclusion is that Athenian interpersonal relations seem genuinely to have been dominated by an ideal that is conspicuous by its rarity amongst human cultures: the idea that for the sake of the public good one should give more than one has been given and hurt other people less than one has been hurt.

---

[168] Cf. Mattingly 1966: 195. Commenting on this passage, Gomme (in Gomme, Andrewes and Dover 1945–81, vol. II: 124–5) rightly pointed out the discrepancy between this ideal and Athenian behaviour abroad ('abroad, Athens could not get away with this doctrine of willing help, and at Sparta in 432, at Melos, and at Karamina a cynicism based on contemporary *sophistry* is adopted . . .'). He seems, however, to have overlooked the novelty of this passage within the history of the idea of reciprocity.

CHAPTER 10

The growth of communal feeling

PATTERNS OF ECONOMIC EXCHANGE

So far the focus of our attention has been *social exchange*. The concept of positive social exchange encompasses every form of interaction in which people exchange goods and services that they need and/or value.[1] These goods and services, whether material or immaterial (food, esteem), like or unlike (information for information, money for political support), all share one essential feature: they can only be obtained from others. The ways in which they are obtained and the patterns of interaction and dependence that they generate are amongst the most important factors determining a society's profile and quality of life. Simple societies have a uniform, homogeneous 'collective mentality': a single type of exchange dominates the circulation of most goods and services and the formation of most ties of interaction and dependence. As societies grow in complexity new types of exchange come into play, taking over the regulation of some sectors of society and creating ties of interaction and dependence that diverge from those derived directly from the central collective mentality. This sort of development can be seen in the history of the word 'gift'. In Homeric society the word *doron* was 'a cover-all for a great variety of actions and transactions'. Later on, when the polis became the focal point of all human behaviour, these actions and transactions 'became differentiated and acquired their own appellations. There were payments for services rendered, desired or anticipated; what we would call fees, rewards, prizes and sometimes bribes'.[2]

History shows that the first type of exchange to differentiate itself from social exchange was *economic exchange*. Economic exchange (explaining which has been identified as the central problem of economic inquiry)[3] is marked by three characteristics that are either absent from or present only in rudimentary form in social exchange: transactions whose primary purpose

---

[1] See pp. 31–2.   [2] Finley 1978a: 66; cf. Scheid-Tissinier 1994.   [3] Roll 1961: 371.

is to produce and distribute wealth, specialised functions and institutions for the conduct of transactions and a relative dearth of long-term relations such as kinship or friendship between the exchange partners.

Having examined Athenian behaviour from a variety of perspectives, we have good reason to suppose that one particular ideal had much to do with first converting the 'natural man' of the pre-polis world into the 'conventional man' of the polis, then converting conventional polis man into the 'isonomic man' of democracy. Central to this ideal was the cultivation of that rare human quality that Adam Smith termed 'benevolence'.[4] For his own good and for that of the community, the Athenian citizen was expected to give more than he was given, do less harm to others than they did to him, treat his fellow-citizens as if they were related to him and do everything in his power to maintain public order. We must now ask ourselves how (if at all) Athenian civic morality in general and this ideal in particular affected economic exchange.

In order to make it easier to follow the thread of my argument, I shall begin by stating my answer to this question. Economic exchange in Athens was not isolated from the constraints of morality. These constraints, however, acted upon it in a manner that has not previously been recognised: rather than impeding it, they facilitated it. The Athenians' unique code of behaviour was instrumental in establishing circumstances that boosted economic exchange and engendered popular perceptions of well-being that have rarely been surpassed in any ancient economy, or, indeed, in the annals of the entire pre-industrial west.

To refine upon this thesis we must examine a controversy that has now been raging for over a century. Two leading theories, each laying claim to exclusive validity, have attempted to explain the nature of the ancient Athenian economy.[5] In a nutshell, the 'formalists' (whose arguments overlap to some extent with those of the so-called 'modernists') assert that market exchange replaced both barter and gift-exchange as the normal way of exchanging goods and services. Emancipated from the constraints of traditional morality, the circulation of goods and services created a fully competitive, self-regulating market in which prices were determined by supply and demand. This opened up the way for the unhindered pursuit

---

[4] See pp. 10–11.
[5] I am drawing on the following theoretical works: Gernet 1933; Will 1954; H. W. Pearson 1957; Austin and Vidal-Naquet 1977; Humphreys 1978; Garnsey, Hopkins and Whittaker 1983; Vidal-Naquet 1990b; Burke 1992; I. Morris 1994a; Andreau 1995; Descat 1995; Meikle 1995; Nippel 2000; Cartledge 2002; Saller 2002.

of personal monetary gain. For these reasons, it is appropriate to use the conceptual tools of modern economics to analyse the Athenian economy.

The 'substantivists' (to some extent identified with the so-called 'primitivists') maintain that these tools are inappropriate to the study of the Athenian economy because the Athenians' economic choices were determined by something other than rational considerations of utility. According to this view, the Athenian economy was exceedingly simple (or even 'primitive') in character, retaining many features of the age-old systems of barter and gift-exchange. It was also inextricably 'embedded' in the moral and structural order of Athenian society. As a consequence, as two modern authors have put it, 'economic and non-economic functions [were] fused together in the same person without it being possible to distinguish between them'; according to another, 'economic interests were subordinated to or absorbed within politics, honor, and war'.[6] This inevitably resulted in stagnation. Finley, the chief representative of the so-called 'new orthodoxy' (the most influential modern branch of the substantivist school), believed that certain interrelated features of the Athenian economy that acted as insurmountable obstacles to economic growth persisted throughout Classical antiquity: a preponderance of agricultural produce, local self-sufficiency, limited craftsmanship, limited use of coinage and an absence of markets (in the modern sense of the term) for labour and investment.[7]

Until late on in the twentieth century the new orthodoxy appeared to be winning the day, the majority of scholars believing that its theory made most sense of the ancient evidence.[8] Over the past two decades, however, this theory has come under attack from a number of directions. Studies in areas of economic enterprise as diverse as agriculture,[9] commerce (and exchange),[10] coinage,[11] credit,[12] banking,[13] technical specialisation[14] and wages[15] have generated a spate of data and ideas demanding that we rethink some of the tenets of the new orthodoxy.[16]

These studies have identified trends within the Athenian economy that point to hitherto unsuspected levels of economic growth (and hence of sophistication and complexity). Let us now examine a few examples of this

---

[6] Austin and Vidal-Naquet 1977: 9 (paraphrasing K. Polanyi [1944] *The Great Transformation*. Boston: Rhinehart and Company: ch. 6); I. Morris 1994a: 353 (paraphrasing Weber).
[7] Finley 1973; Descat 1995: 961.   [8] Cf. Descat 1995: 962.   [9] Lohmann 1995.
[10] Bresson 2000, with review by E. M. Harris 2001.   [11] Martin 1985: ch. 9.
[12] Shipton 1997.   [13] E. E. Cohen 1992, 1993.   [14] E. M. Harris 2004b.
[15] Gabrielsen 1981; Loomis 1998.
[16] Cf. Saller 2002, who argues convincingly that modern researchers have exaggerated the polarity between the 'modernist' and 'primitivist' positions.

new research, bearing in mind that some are based on previously unavailable data.

It has been estimated, as we have seen, that as many as three-quarters of Athenian citizens owned some workable land in Attica. In itself this piece of information is ambiguous and cannot be taken to indicate any general trend within the Athenian economy. Lohmann's archaeological surveys have, however, revealed a correlation between the period of democratic rule and increased population density in the Attic *chora*. This increases the likelihood that these levels of land ownership signified economic growth, as does the fact that land ownership and agricultural produce were acknowledged means of climbing the social ladder.[17] The prospect of social advancement would have stimulated eagerness to acquire landed estates, manifesting itself in their quick turnover. Let us now examine our sources for any evidence of this.

The Attic Orators' chance mentions of land transfers suggest that land did indeed change hands frequently. A wealthy client of Lysias gives us the following history of the ownership of one piece of land (the figures in parentheses are years BC):

This piece of land (*chorion*) was Peisander's before his property was seized by the *demos* (411). They made a present of the land to Apollodorus of Megara, who then cultivated it for a while. Shortly before the [rule of the] Thirty [tyrants] (404) it was bought from him by Anticles, who let it out. I bought it from Anticles after the declaration of peace (403) . . . Five days after I took it over, in Pythodorus' archonship (404/3), I let it out to Callistratus, who cultivated it for two years . . . In the third year Demetrius here worked it for a year; in the fourth I let it out to Alcias, one of Antisthenes' freedmen, who is now dead. After that Proteas hired it for three years on the same terms . . . Since his tenancy expired, I have been cultivating it (*georgo*) myself.[18]

It would have been in this speaker's interests to exaggerate the turnover of occupants, but it seems extremely improbable that he would have dared to make up too much of his account: his manner of addressing the dikasts suggests that they were already familiar with the people involved, making it difficult to lie plausibly about names and dates.[19] It would therefore appear that this plot changed hands about four times in fifteen years and that

[17] See pp. 248–50.
[18] Lysias 7.4, 9, *On the Olive-Stump*. The speaker is trying to convince the dikasts that he is not responsible for the removal of a sacred olive and olive-stump from his plot because neither was there when he finally took physical possession of the land.
[19] It is clear that he is offering these names to refresh the dikasts' memories rather than to acquaint them with fresh details.

during that period it was hired out four or five times by two of its owners.[20] This turnover of occupants is by any standards high, suggesting that the plot was regarded as a lucrative opportunity. Both owners and lessees must have expected to turn a considerable profit by selling their produce (probably wine) on the market, the latter even after recouping their rent. Even if we accept the unlikely suggestion that the price of a plot of land was determined by something other than supply and demand, this sequence of acquisitions and the motivational complex that it suggests cannot easily be fitted into the picture of a traditional, stagnant peasant economy. It would, on the other hand, be entirely compatible with a flourishing pre-capitalist economy in which a plot of land was no longer merely a form of wealth and means of obtaining the necessities of life. When its produce enters a dynamic system of exchange the traditional, tax-free plot becomes a lever for enrichment. We should note here that Thucydides regards the selling of produce as a prime factor in the accumulation of wealth and power. According to his account, the men of earlier periods grew mainly wheat and vegetables, producing only enough for their own annual needs. As time went on, however, a surplus of wealth developed, permitting men to plant orchards (*gen phyteuontes*, normally interpreted as vines and olives) and harvest their produce (we would call this intensive farming). They were now using their land for purposes beyond the production of necessities, a result of affluence that in turn created greater affluence.[21]

At their peak, the silver mines of Laurion are estimated to have produced about 20 tonnes of silver a year.[22] The owners and lessors of property holdings in the mining areas, which were usually quite small, made substantial profits out of private exploitation of the mines, the building and running of workshops (*ergasteria*) and the hiring out of slaves.[23] Two of the richest men in fifth-century Athens are said to have derived their wealth from mining: Nicias, the general and politician, and Callias, nicknamed Lakkoploutos ('pit wealth'). The former's fortune was said to be in the region of 100 talents; the latter's family was reputed to have an annual income of about six talents from the mines alone.[24] A less well known Athenian called Epicrates was credited with having made the fabulous sum of 300

---

[20] Demetrius' relation to the speaker is obscure.

[21] Thucydides 1.1.2, with Gomme, Andrewes and Dover 1945–81, vol. 1: 92–3. Diodorus of Sicily likewise attributes the rapid growth (*tacheia auxesis*) of Sybaris in Italy to the fertility of her land (*dia ten areten tes choras*). Her inhabitants, he writes, who 'tilled an extensive and fruitful countryside' (*nemomenoi pollen kai karpophoron choran*), came to possess great riches (*megalous ektesanto ploutous*, 12.9.2). Cf. Osborne 1988.

[22] Conophagos 1980: 341–54.   [23] Cf. Osborne 1985a: ch. 6.

[24] Cf. J. K. Davies 1971: nos. 10808, 7826, respectively, with discussion of 'Lakkoploutos' at 260.

talents in three years from a private mine.[25] The silver extracted from the mines rapidly became part of a circuit of exchange whose trail it is sometimes possible to follow. Flocks of fifth- and fourth-century owl coinage travelled considerable distances east and west of Athens.[26] This suggests a corresponding flow of merchandise into the city, lending substance to Pericles' boast that she freely imported and enjoyed the luxuries 'of the whole world'.[27]

Silver coins and vessels were highly esteemed objects of value in Athenian society (see **Fig. 10.1**).[28] The metic Lysias kept more than three talents' worth of silver and four silver cups in a chest in his house, while Demosthenes senior had three talents' worth (Lysias 12.10–12, *Against Eratosthenes*; Demosthenes 27.10, *Against Aphobos* 1). The large amount of wealth in circulation suggests that a similar abundance of goods and services was on offer, which can only have been the result of specialisation amongst their providers. The departure of the Athenian fleet for Sicily in 415 affords another glimpse of the wealth of Athenian society; the splendour of this grandiose spectacle was enhanced by the libations poured onto every deck by both officers and men 'from gold and silver vessels' (*ekpomata*; Thucydides 6.32.1). The potted history of a mining property given in the 37th Oration of the Demosthenic corpus (*Against Pantaenetus*) reinforces the impression that mining generated a great deal of economic exchange. Pantaenetus had bought this property from Telemachus, who had in turn purchased it from the state. Pantaenetus had then run short of capital and borrowed money from Mnesicles and various other people. When the title of the property passed to Mnesicles, Pantaenetus sought financial assistance from two men called Nicobulus and Euergus. They agreed to buy the mine from Mnesicles and lease it to Pantaenetus on condition that they were paid interest, in the form of rent, out of the profits of the mine. Pantaenetus then failed to pay the stipulated rent. Nicobulus was away on a trip to Pontus, so Euergus took possession of the property. When Nicobulus got back some new creditors of Pantaenetus presented themselves and advanced claims against the property. Eventually a settlement was reached whereby Euergus and Nicobulus transferred ownership of the mine to these claimants in return for the sum that they had originally advanced on it. This story too is compatible with

---

[25] Hyperides 4.35, *In Defence of Euxenippus*; for Epicrates' identity and his ownership of a property reputedly worth 600 talents, see J. K. Davies 1971: no. 4908.

[26] Cf. Schönert-Geiss 1974; Kraay 1975. For the political importance of the 'owls' and their connection with democracy, see Trevett 2001.

[27] Thucydides 2.38.2; see p. 42.   [28] Cf. Vickers 1994.

Figure 10.1 Athenian silver tetradrachm, didrachm (holed) and drachm (above) and silver drinking vessel (below)

The Athenian coins that had replaced the earliest 'heraldic coins' (*Wappenmünzen*) by the end of the sixth century were being mass-produced in great quantities by the beginning of the fifth; coins were amongst the first mass-produced items in history. Most sales, loans and interest payments were calculated and transacted in terms of coinage, in ways that we would recognise today. Coins were also a means of storing wealth, both private and public. A symbol of sovereignty and independence, they were almost always made of silver. (Gold coins were issued as an emergency measure during the Peloponnesian War and bronze ones during another crisis in the fourth century.) Athenian silver coins were things of beauty. The obverse side bore the head of the goddess Athena, wearing earrings and a crested helmet adorned with olive leaves; the reverse side was occupied by her symbol, the owl, flanked by the inscription AΘE and a spray of olive leaves. It is possible that this spray represented the symbol of peace or pardon, known as *hiketeria*, that was carried ceremonially by supplicants (cf. Burkert 1979a: 43–4). Aristophanes implied that the Athenians were rather fond of their coins by jokingly describing them as 'owls of Laurion' (*glaukes . . . Laureiotikai*) that would 'build nests in purses and hatch little silver pieces' (*Birds* (produced in 414), 1106–7). A tetradrachm weighed 17.44g, a drachm 4.36g and an *obolos* (1/6 of a drachm) 0.72g. In the fourth century various very small denominations of silver coin were minted, the *hemitetartemorion* (1/48 drachm) weighing only 0.09g. An attractive theory suggests that the owls' lack of stylistic development during the fifth and fourth centuries may be related to Athens' constitutional stability throughout this period (Trevett 2001).

the picture of a prosperous economy in which *at least some* items circulated in a dynamic process of exchange. Within such an economy people would have regarded property around the mines, with their associated industries and seductive promise of a lucky strike, as a highly desirable stepping stone to paying off their debts or making a profit.

The largest private fortune of which we have solid evidence belonged, however, not to a farmer or a miner, but to a banker. Pasion, the metic who had once been a slave and was eventually made a citizen, was worth 75 to 80 talents when he died. This fabulous fortune was made up of 'a shield factory with a net annual profit of 1 talent, 50 talents invested in loans, and land to the value of 20 talents'.[29] A measure of the importance of Pasion's bank may be the survival of no fewer than nine law-court speeches touching directly or indirectly on its affairs.

As well as accepting deposits, banks offered interest-bearing loans, enabling the Athenians to acquire goods and services that they could not otherwise have afforded.[30] Lending at interest, though sometimes frowned upon, was a widespread practice in democratic Athens. Its significance as a quintessential tool of economic growth was not, as we shall see, diminished by the existence of the equally widespread practice of making 'friendly' interest-free *eranos* loans[31] and is not affected by the theory that most of the money borrowed was put to non-productive purposes. (This argument, which has recently been challenged, suggests that the ancient Athenians seldom invested borrowed money in increasing production rates, by improving workshops or extending holdings, for example, but generally put it to ostentatious, financially unproductive uses such as paying dowries and fulfilling liturgies.)[32]

Fernand Braudel asserts that the European economy functioned on two levels from the fifteenth to the eighteenth century. At the lower level, confined mainly to rural districts, relations of production and consumption were characterised by stagnation, self-sufficiency, repetitiveness, monotony and lack of innovation: 'people go on sowing wheat as they always have done, planting maize as they always have done, terracing the paddy-fields as they always have done'.[33] On the upper level, largely confined to towns and the communication routes between them, Braudel identified patterns that struck him as thoroughly modern. He discerned in them the outlines of a huge self-regulating machine, fuelled by market exchange,

[29] A. H. M. Jones 1957: 87. For an account of his wealth, see J. K. Davies 1971: no. 11762; Erxleben 1973; Trevett 1992: ch. 6.
[30] Cf. Shipton 1997; E. E. Cohen 1992: 10.　　[31] Millett 1991: ch. 6.
[32] Finley 1952: 82.　　[33] Braudel 1967, vol. 1: 28.

seeking permanently to enlarge its domain, 'drawing into its rational order more and more people, more and more kinds of traffic, local or distant, the combination of which turned the world into an economic unit'. So great an impact did this layer of exchange have on the life of people in general, so quick was it to draw into its machinery the products of the lower level, as to warrant, in his view, the designation 'capitalistic': 'Exchange invariably stimulated both supply and demand, guiding production, leading to the specialization of huge economic regions which therefore became committed to exchange, as a necessity to ensure their own survival.'[34]

I would suggest that the Athenian economy displayed a similar pattern. At its lower level we encounter the same age-old features of self-sufficiency, repetitiveness, monotony and stagnation, largely in rural areas. In the urban districts and along the routes between them we see a rapid flow of goods and services, a veritable self-regulating machine fuelled by market exchange, whose attributes are strikingly similar to those that Braudel describes. This picture of dynamic economic exchange is supported by a remark in the spurious *Oeconomica*, transmitted along with the Aristotelian corpus: 'An Athenian puts the income from his sales (*apodidomenoi gar onountai*) back to work at once, the smaller households never leaving hoarded wealth to lie idle (*thesis*)' (*Oeconomica* 1344b33–5).

'Just as Aristides says', writes the author of *The Athenian Constitution*, not without a touch of disapproval, 'they made the masses extremely comfortable. More than 20,000 men were supported by the income from taxes, the tribute and the allies. There were 6,000 dikasts, 1,600 archers and 1,200 cavalrymen, 500 councilmen, 500 dockyard guards and 50 guards at the Acropolis, about 700 officials at home and another 700 or so abroad. On top of these, when the Athenians subsequently went to war they employed 2,500 hoplites, 20 escort ships and the other ships that collected the tribute, carrying 2,000 men appointed by lot; then there were the Prytaneum, the orphans and the prison custodians. All these were supported out of public funds (*apo ton koinon*)' (24.3).

The arrangements that he describes no doubt depended largely upon 'political moneymaking'; in other words, these jobs were funded by wealth obtained from booty, indemnities and taxes rather than from any economically productive activity.[35] It would nonetheless be unwise to dismiss this process as economically insignificant. This sort of wealth was obtained by means of a formidable power structure ('the two sides were at the height of their power and preparedness'; 1.1.1) that was itself the result of economically

---

[34] Braudel 1984, vol. III: 224.   [35] Finley 1973: 55.

productive activities. As Thucydides tells us, such activities required a particular sequence of developments: an increase in commerce (*emporia*), safe land and sea communications, a surplus of agricultural products, an accumulation of capital (*periousia chrematon*; 1.1.2) and finally, as we have seen, the use of that capital to develop intensive farming. His account reads like a list of Braudel's essential requirements for a capitalist economy.

The twenty thousand public employees (to whom we may add the thousands who were paid to attend the Assembly (see **Fig. 10.2**) and many more who were paid to construct temples and public buildings or create works of art) must have had two or even three sources of income: in addition to their earnings from the state, they were making a profit out of their traditional tax-free holdings (which, as we have seen, the majority of them did not give up). We may assert without delving too deeply into Keynesian economics that a level of employment as high as this requires a commensurately high level of demand for goods and services, resulting in high profitability. The many jobs funded by the state are thus further evidence of the healthy state of the Athenian economy.

Our central question, therefore, ought not to be whether the Athenian economy was primitive or modern, whether it was embedded or disembedded (it has justly been pointed out that disembeddedness implies some sort of interaction with society's moral norms, in other words embeddedness), or even whether or not it was equipped with the conceptual and practical tools of a full-blown capitalist economy (currency, deferred payments, credit sales, double-entry bookkeeping and so forth). People have always been remarkably good at doing without tools and technical knowledge that appear indispensable once they have been invented.[36] Instead we should ask ourselves how dynamic the circulation of goods and services within the Athenian economy was and to what extent it drew Braudel's lower stratum of economic activity into its flow.

In the absence of anything resembling statistics, we cannot answer these questions with any degree of precision. It is impossible to gauge either the volume or the rate of transference of the goods and services that circulated inside Athens and those that were exchanged between Athens and the outside world. We can, however, examine the institutional foundations of Athenian exchange, or, as an economic historian has recently put it, the way in which 'commitment, trust, and the information required to

---

[36] As Millett 1990: 181 has put it, modern researchers have failed 'to appreciate that pre-capitalist economies can and do generate their own subtlety and complexity'. Millett does not, however, appear to proceed to the corollary of this, namely that the Athenian economy was flourishing.

**Figure 10.2 Lead tokens used to obtain payment for attending the Assembly (above)
and for serving as a dikast at the law courts (below)**

Instituted in about 400, payments for attending the Assembly were designed to ensure
that everyone, including lower-class citizens, could afford to be part of the democracy's
chief decision-making institution. Bronze or lead tokens of little or no intrinsic worth
(*symbola*) were issued to everyone who attended a meeting. These could later be
exchanged for the *ekklesiastikon*: the assemblyman's pay of two obols (a third of a
drachma) per session. The *symbola* were decorated with various images: a ship, a cow, a
bow, Nike, crossed torches, a dolphin, a rosette.

Payments for serving as a dikast at the law courts (*dikastikon*) were also intended to ensure
that anyone could afford to serve. On entering his court a dikast was given a token marked
with a letter of the alphabet. This designated the bench or area where he was to sit (*The
Athenian Constitution* 65.2). After he had voted he received another token bearing the
letter gamma (the third letter of the alphabet) or the sign III (i.e. 'three'). This token had
to be handed over in exchange for his fee of three obols (half a drachma) in order to ensure
that the money was paid to him and to nobody else (*The Athenian Constitution* 68.2,
69.2). Some fifty such tokens have come to light in the *agora*, most dating from the fourth
or early third century. The tokens shown here bearing the letters E[psilon] and K[appa]
probably indicated the court or seating area to which a juror had been assigned. The token
marked with the letter G[amma] is probably one of those that were handed in on receipt
of payment (cf. Boegehold 1995: 67–76, with T1–44; for a different interpretation, see
Rhodes 1981: 712, 731).

conduct exchange [were] achieved through legal institutions, private-order institutions that do not rely on the state, and hybrids of the two forms'.[37] The premise that high levels of exchange foster prosperity and low levels lead to stagnation has repeatedly been shown to be correct. The results of our investigation should therefore give us a far better idea of how fast and in what sort of volumes goods and services circulated in Athens.[38]

We need first to have some preliminary idea of the state's role in the exchange process. The Athenian state did not pursue a *laissez-faire* policy, but intervened in transactions both routinely and wherever it saw particular cause to do so. A large number of officials routinely supervised the supply of grain and water, the issue of coins and adherence to the proper weights and measures. Extraordinary intervention by the state tended to occur when the collective interest appeared to be in jeopardy, as it did during the famine of 330/29, when some of the people of Heraclea prevented a metic merchant called Heracleides from leaving for Athens with several shiploads of grain. On learning of this the Assembly dispatched an ambassador to Heraclea to order her ruler to release the ships and never again to commit any act of injustice against a merchant headed for Athens.[39] The state also attempted actively to preserve continuity between the family unit and its chief economic foundation: real estate, preferably landed. Aeschines' censure of Timarchus for irresponsibly squandering the property (*ousia*) left to him by his father (a house, landed estates, slaves and money lent out at interest) illustrates the state's determination (for reasons to do with the census and the fulfilment of liturgies (Aeschines 1.97–105, *Against Timarchus*)) that this continuity should remain intact.

All this was a far cry from a centralised, state-controlled economy. The state's interventions were sporadic and ad hoc, not manifestations of consistent, centralised, long-term economic planning. Most of the exchange process escaped state intervention altogether.[40] The state, as we have seen, levied no taxes on exchange, income or capital.[41] It did almost nothing to regulate the banks, despite the huge wealth concentrated in their hands and the power they derived from lending out money and holding deposits.[42]

---

[37] Greif 2000: 252.
[38] Finley, as Millett 1990: 168 (n. 2) has pointed out, protested against the view of the ancient economy as 'an enormous conglomeration of interdependent markets' (Roll 1961: 371), but offered no alternative explanation as to how goods might have been exchanged in 'the ancient economy'.
[39] *SIG*[3] I. 304.
[40] Cf. the more radical statement by Bresson 2000: 258 that 'the state was separate from the economy'.
[41] The sole exception was the *metoikeion*, a poll tax whereby metic men paid twelve drachmas and independent metic women six drachmas annually. Cf. Whitehead 1977: 75–7.
[42] Cf. E. E. Cohen 1992: 9.

Even the policy of enforcing honest dealing in the *agora* was not, as we shall see, the result of economic planning. The Athenian economy may most profitably be viewed as an aggregate of exchange centres provided with decentralised controls, which is just another way of saying that within it the allocation of scarce resources, products and services was determined by much the same forces as guided the negotiation of conflicting social interests.

Even though the Athenian economy was not particularly 'modern' in character, it appears to have been extremely prosperous by the standards of pre-industrial economies. A partial explanation for this apparent paradox may be found in the hidden mechanisms that compensated for what we may be tempted to regard as 'primitive' shortcomings. The potentially troubled association between masters and slaves, for example, was a lopsided variant of productive exchange (see **Fig. 1.2**) that made it necessary for both to co-operate in order for either to obtain benefits.[43] According to one interpretation, this association was so beneficial as to make growing agricultural products for sale profitable even on the smallest of plots.[44] Banks, which Demosthenes called 'business[es] yielding a hazardous revenue from money that belongs to others' (36.11, *For Phormio*), prospered by bridging the gap between people of dissimilar status (metics and citizens, for example) and controllers of dissimilar resources (such as money, merchandise and real estate). The bankers had hit upon the secret of generating wealth by sending money they did not own out into the general flow of goods and services to make more money. Their clients had such confidence in the bankers' ability to protect their deposited liquid wealth that they actually paid them interest. Even the state itself sometimes entered into relations of productive exchange with wealthy individuals. Its political intervention to force the ruler of Heraclea to release Heracleides' ships, though fundamentally motivated by the need to avert famine, also benefited Heracleides' individual commercial interests. The threat issued to Heraclea's ruler further sent out

[43] See pp. 67–72. Justification for viewing masters and slaves as engaged in some version of productive exchange in Classical times will emerge from the more general consideration that 'the need to mobilize labour-power for tasks that were beyond the capacity of the individual or the family' (Finley 1998: 136) was among the chief factors contributing to the institutionalisation of slavery in Archaic Greece. The supply of agricultural products may thus be viewed as having been secured by means of a co-operative process in which both masters and slaves benefited from their joint effort: the masters benefited by the performance of tasks that they could not have accomplished by themselves, while the slaves were fed, clothed and provided with medical care by the masters. Whether or not we approve of this sort of 'social arrangement', we must bear it in mind that for a slave the alternative was often death or forced labour.

[44] Jameson 1977–8; 1992.

the message that the Athenian state was prepared to wield its might overseas to protect anyone with whom it wanted to do business.

Most types of exchange operate, as we have seen, not in a social vacuum, but within wider systems of mutual dependence (see **Fig. 1.2**). Such systems can have about them either a feeling of stability and endurance or one of instability and precariousness. Stability and endurance generate trust. The attractive suggestion has recently been put forward that trust is not just an extremely valuable form of social capital, essential to the making of a good society, but also an 'economic' factor of paramount importance: societies in which there is a high degree of social trust are the ones most likely to generate sustainable economic growth.[45] In the light of this theory, the wide interface between the Athenian code of behaviour and the Athenian pattern of economic exchange takes on a new significance. The devices that the Athenians adopted to promote collective social interests and confer stability and continuity on their system as a whole may also have acted as catalysts to the furthering of individual economic interests.

A good case in point is the policy of enforcing honest dealing in the *agora*. Every year the state appointed by lot ten market inspectors (*agoranomoi*), five for the Peiraeus and five for the city of Athens, who were supposed 'to take responsibility for all goods that are on sale, [and] to ensure that what is sold is in good condition and genuine', and ten controllers of measures (*metronomoi*), again five for the city and five for the Peiraeus, 'who superintend all measures and weights, in order that sellers may use just ones' (*The Athenian Constitution* 51.1–2; see **Fig. 10.3**). A late lexicographer tells us that the policy was backed up by legislation; he supports this statement by quoting from Theophrastus, according to whom the *agoranomoi* were required to ensure that proper order was maintained in the *agora* and that no deceit was practised (*apseudeia*) by either seller or buyer.[46]

Since a state guarantee of fair trading is clearly a major inducement for more and more partners to enter into mutually profitable exchange, this is an excellent example of how an economy may remain 'embedded' in the moral and structural order of its society and yet generate conditions that contribute to economic efficiency. It is in the highest degree unlikely that the Athenian *agora* regulations were part of a long-term economic policy, or motivated by any clearly articulated intention to 'set the economy right':

---

[45] Fukuyama 1995.
[46] Harpokration *Lexicon of the Ten Orators*, s.v. *kata ten agoran apseudei*; cf. Millett 1990: 172–3, to whom I am indebted for this point.

Figure 10.3 Official Athenian weights and measures
The Athenian democracy was determined that dealings in the *agora* should be conducted
honestly. As Millett put it, 'There is repeated emphasis on the avoidance of deceit
(apseudeia) and, with the exception of the sale of real property and slaves, the scenario for
this bad faith is the agora' (Millett 1990: 172; cf. de Ste. Croix 1972: 399). It was the duty of
the *agoranomoi* to ensure that nothing was sold under false pretences. The official weights
and measures that they used as standards were kept in Athens and in the Peiraeus, under
the supervision of the *metronomoi*. Standard measure vessels came in either clay or bronze
and were used for both dry goods and liquids. All of them bear the inscription *demosion*
(public) or some variant of it. Above: public clay measure showing inscription and
official stamps confirming its capacity (about 1.89 litres); below, left: set of official bronze
weights weighing, respectively, 795, 190 and 126g; below, right: bronze public measure
(about 1/8 litre).

the policy of ensuring honest dealing in the *agora* was almost certainly a
more or less unselfconscious extension of the Athenian code of behaviour
into the field of economic exchange. By setting a high price on trust, the
Athenians had instinctively hit upon a device that modern theoreticians
have identified as second to none in boosting economic exchange. The same

is true of two related requirements of the Athenian code of behaviour: citizen solidarity and communal devotion.[47] Expressed in terms of reciprocity, these behavioural norms must surely have resulted in the accrual to the individual of very considerable benefits, both material and emotional (since the citizen shared the destiny and enjoyed the luxuries of a great city), through channels other than immediate 'give and take'. Jury pay, assembly pay, military pay, magisterial salaries (except in the case of the highest state officials, who were all extremely rich already), handouts to the needy and a remarkable degree of mutual support between individuals and between households were everyday facts of the democratic system.[48] We are, in other words, looking at a superabundance of generalised, delayed and indirect exchange (see **Fig. 1.2**). The significance of this fact will appear in full only if we contrast Athens with other societies in which relations of trust and any sense of citizen solidarity or communal devotion were minimal. In Homeric society, for instance, or in Gregory's Gaul, there were hardly any avenues for the provision of goods and services beyond immediate 'give and take'.[49] The economic performance of these societies was correspondingly poor.

Looked at in this oblique way, the evidence suggests that even if the Athenian economy did not consist of 'an enormous conglomeration of interdependent markets'[50] the circulation of goods and services was rapid and the involvement of Braudel's lower sector of economic activity substantial. If we concentrate our attention merely on this circulation and on the level of economic activity that it generated, the Athenian economy must surely qualify as capitalistic. If, however, this term is taken to imply a ruthlessly competitive (and thus socially disruptive) attitude in the exchanging partners, it becomes inappropriate to apply it to the Athenian economy.

The reason for this is that side by side with the competitive free market there existed a sector of the Athenian economy in which economic transactions were conducted in a friendly and uncalculating spirit. Athenian economic exchange had not, in other words, resulted in the wholesale commercialisation of reciprocal interactions. 'When we behave well towards others', as Pericles is famously supposed to have said, 'we are not totting up our potential profits and losses; we are acting on the moment, with the confidence that belongs to us as free men' (Thucydides 2.40.5; cf. pp. 372–3).

---

[47] See pp. 347–59.
[48] We are reminded that Pericles called Athens a 'salary-drawing city' (Plutarch, *Pericles* 12; cf. Ostwald 1995; Trevett 2001) and that one of the revolutionary oligarchs' first acts in 411 was to abolish state pay.
[49] This point is further elaborated upon at pp. 410–14.   [50] Cf. n. 38 above.

Pericles was referring to the Athenians as a collective, but there is good reason to suppose that he was describing an idea derived from the sphere of interpersonal relationships. Together with his description elsewhere of these relationships as free and tolerant,[51] this quotation suggests that some interactions between Athenians who were not connected by kinship or friendship no longer demanded as a precondition that strict accounts be kept of benefits received. It becomes easier to understand this if we recall that in Athens not all returns for favours were expected to come directly from the beneficiary; some came indirectly from the civic system of which all were a part.

We have already mentioned one example of how this sector operated: the *eranos* loan. This was an arrangement wherein a number of lenders collaborated to help out one needy borrower, often transferring large sums of money to him without demanding securities or charging interest.[52] We have no direct evidence of how common this practice was, but the fact that it became subject to the 'monthly suit' procedure suggests that it was by no means exceptional. The reason why these lenders should have chosen to forego the interest that filled the pockets of professional lenders is suggested by the terminology associated with the practice: this was clearly a procedure that served to express the idea of patriotic self-sacrifice (Thucydides 2.43.1–2; Lycurgus, *Against Leocrates* 143). In place of interest, *eranos* lenders received social approval. Plato's *Laws* forbids the raising of interest-bearing loans, but allows the raising of *eranos* loans. Millett has explained why: unlike interest-bearing loans, which were socially disruptive, *eranos* loans expressed and reinforced citizen solidarity.[53] They were raised among friends (*philoi*), between whom court action would have been inappropriate. The same was true of many loans that were not qualified by the term *eranos*. In ancient societies loans were generally made against securities (preferably worth more than the amount of the loan) and interest was charged on them. In Athens, however, a surprisingly high percentage of loans involved neither securities nor interest.[54] An important sector of economic exchange in Athens thus had nothing to do with the 'business is business' mentality, that supreme expression of cut-throat capitalism that

---

[51] See p. 82.
[52] Millett 1991: 153–4. See E. E. Cohen 1992: 208–10 for the demonstrably erroneous suggestion that *eranos* loans did involve the payment of interest.
[53] Millett 1991: 42. Millett argues plausibly that '[t]his is presumably the explanation behind Plato's reservation that *eranos*-contributions should not be recoverable at law'. The fact that Athens' high standards of co-operation fostered 'interpersonal risk-buffering behaviour' is well brought out by Gallant 1991: ch. 6
[54] Millett 1991: ch. 6.

sets selfish profiteering above sympathetic consideration for others. Intensive though it undoubtedly was, the Athenian economy fell far short of that fully competitive pattern of economic exchange that is the hallmark of capitalism.

THE PROBLEM OF COLLECTIVE ACTION

'Two years later', we read in *The Athenian Constitution*, 'when the mines of Maronea [Laurion] were discovered (483/2) and their exploitation left the city with a surplus of one hundred talents, some recommended that the money should be distributed to the people. Themistocles prevented this; he did not say what he thought the money ought to be used for, but recommended that one talent should be lent to each of the hundred wealthiest Athenians. If the people approved of what they spent it on, the polis would bear the expense; if not, it would recover the money from the borrowers. The terms that he suggested were accepted and he had a hundred triremes built, one by each man. This was the fleet that fought the barbarians at Salamis' (22.7).

This account reveals the operation of one of the oldest and most important ideas in the history of public finance: that individual benefits may be obtained through membership of a group (pretty much the idea that we have been calling generalised exchange). 'The political organisation (*he politike koinonia*) . . .', wrote Aristotle, 'was originally formed, and continues to be maintained, for the advantage of its members.'[55] In modern economic theory this rudimentary idea has given rise to the concept of 'the public good', which may be described in simple terms as 'the common or collective benefits provided by governments'.[56] The victory that the Athenians won at Salamis in the ships with which Themistocles' foresight had provided them, perhaps the most decisive victory in Athens' history, makes this a classic example of pursuit of the public good. From the negative advantage of freedom from slavery to the positive benefits that accrued from the vast increase of Athens' prestige in the Greek world, this collective victory conferred an entire spectrum of inestimable advantages upon every single inhabitant of Attica.

---

[55] *tou sumpherontos charin*; Aristotle, *Nicomachean Ethics* 1160a4, trans. H. Rackham. Cf. Millett 1991: 39: 'In theory, the polis was . . . a *koinonia*. The word has no exact equivalent in English, but incorporates the ideas of sharing and holding in common – a veritable "community of interests". . . . Allied to *koinonia* is the quality of *homonoia*: concord or consensus based on the common outlook of citizens about an appropriate pattern of civic behaviour . . .'

[56] Olson 1965: 14.

How, though, do the members of political organisations or of groups in general go about achieving the public good? Is there any logic in their collective action? Throughout the ages this has been regarded as a non-problem. Groups were thought to be held together by nothing but rational motives of transparent self-interest, the group's rational, self-interested members being presumed to act voluntarily in furtherance of the group's objectives because they will be better off if these are achieved. Nothing, it seemed, could be more obvious.

The first person to realise that this was not necessarily the case was Mancur Olson. In a study published in the 1960s, Olson challenged the general presumption, arguing that rational, self-interested individuals with common interests will *not* normally act so as to further those interests. What gets in the way of the pursuit of collective objectives is the problem of what Olson called 'free-riding', better known as 'freeloading'. The fact that some group members who put little effort into that pursuit (or worse still, shirk work and responsibilities entirely, putting their individual interests ahead of those of the group) nonetheless receive a share of the benefits conferred by the achievement of the collective objectives serves as a disincentive to other group members, motivating them to contribute less to the joint effort, or even start freeloading themselves. As a result collective objectives are achieved only in part, or not at all. Olson's model helps to explain how collective action by perfectly rational individuals can, under some circumstances, produce results that are entirely 'irrational' when seen from the point of view of everybody involved.

Olson allowed for exceptions, viewing freeloading as a function of group size: 'The larger a group is, the farther it will fall short of obtaining an optimal supply of any collective good, and the less likely that it will act to obtain even a minimal amount of such a good. In short, the larger the group, the less likely it will further its common interests.'[57] According to Olson three things could mitigate the problem of freeloading: small group size, coercion and the existence of 'some other special device' such as a high degree of social solidarity.

It is my contention that Athenian society fulfilled all three of these requirements and that the Athenians therefore could and did achieve collective objectives by means of the joint action of self-interested individuals, freeloading being reduced to a bare minimum. The combination of two interdependent factors, the small scale of Athens' political organisation and her special code of behaviour, created a moral climate that led individual

---

[57] Olson 1965: 36.

Athenians to identify their own well-being with that of the city to an extent that would be inconceivable in a nation state built on a larger scale. Small groups, writes Olson, 'may very well be able to provide themselves with a collective good simply because of the attraction of the collective good to the individual members'.[58] This modern idea is paralleled in the ancient sources. 'I would maintain that a polis that is succeeding as a whole confers more benefits on its private citizens than when it does well by the individual but fails as a collective body,' Thucydides has Pericles say,[59] and Athenagoras, the democratic leader of Syracuse, is said to have urged his fellow-citizens 'to work for our common goal, the good of the polis, bearing in mind that if you do so those of you who are good citizens will get not just an equal, but a more than equal share, whereas if you pursue other goals you have every chance of missing out altogether' (Thucydides 6.40.1). Predictably, this idea of the interdependence of communal and private interests was projected into the transcendental order. According to Solon, the doors of a family home (*auleioi thyrai*) are reluctant (*ouk ethelousin*) to shut out any misfortune affecting the entire community (*demosion kakon*).[60]

When the Athenians collectively resisted the temptation to distribute amongst themselves the hundred talents obtained by exploiting the mines, they were putting the city's collective interest ahead of their own private economic interests in a manner not generally associated with freeloaders. We know that they were exceptional in this respect. The populations of other cities that had made a lucky strike seldom managed to resist the temptation to get their hands on the money immediately and generally ended up paying the price.[61] The Athenians' choice is not, therefore, simply an instance of self-abnegation, of putting aside personal wishes in favour of the communal interest. This passage affords us a rare glimpse of how the strategy of foregoing private gratification for the sake of the public good was applied on the communal level, and how the rewards that accrued to the citizens (in this case, through their victory over the Persians) acted as a feedback mechanism, reinforcing the strategy.

I do not believe that anyone alive today has ever experienced anything like the feelings associated with this sort of interrelationship between personal desires and the collective interests of a sovereign political body. It is therefore impossible to offer any true modern analogy. A partial analogy does exist, however. Recent studies have identified the benefits of this rare

---

[58] Olson 1965: 36. [59] Thucydides 2.60.2; cf. Balot 2001: 512.
[60] Cited by Demosthenes 19.29–30, *On the Embassy*; cf. Dihle 1982: 20.
[61] The proceeds of the gold and silver mines on the tiny island of Siphnos, for instance, were distributed among its citizens: Herodotus 3.57; cf. Latte 1968: 296.

sort of human motivational complex within organisations that allow their employees a share in their profits and management. These studies suggest that employees who control the decisions that determine the course of their lives tend to show more self-confidence than those who do not. If they identify their own aims with those of their organisation, their level of performance is significantly higher than that of employees who abide passively by decisions taken by others.[62] This account aptly describes the spirit in which the Athenians went about securing their public good.

Another factor that has recently been identified as impeding collective action has been dubbed 'the tragedy of the commons'. A thought experiment invented by Garrett Hardin asks us to imagine a common, open to all, on which the village herdsmen pasture their animals.[63] Each is presumed to increase his gains every time he adds another animal to his herd. He can do this with impunity only up to a certain point, however, since the common cannot support an infinite number of grazing animals. Once its capacity has been exceeded any herdsman who is thinking of adding another animal to his herd must ask himself whether this will result in overall gain or overall loss for him. His gain will consist of the extra animal's yield of milk or meat, while his loss will consist of the total amount by which his herd's yield is reduced by overgrazing. As the benefit of the extra animal's yield will accrue to him alone (i.e. its positive utility will be almost $+1$), whereas the harm done by overgrazing will be shared by all the herdsmen (i.e. his share will be a fraction of -1), the rational herdsman will quickly conclude that it will pay him to add another animal to his herd, and another, then another . . . The trouble is that this also occurs to the other herdsmen, all of whom also continue to add more and more animals to their herds. Eventually the overgrazing becomes so extreme that each herdsman's returns fall below the level they were at before the common's capacity was exceeded. The sum-total of the herdsmen's individualistic, rational, self-regarding actions thus leads to a collective tragedy. Had each refrained from turning any more animals onto the common in order to avoid over-grazing, thus preferring (altruistically, according to this book's definition) the long-term communal interest above his own short-term economic interest, all of the herdsmen would have been better off and the tragedy would have been avoided.

Hardin's model was originally designed to explain problems to do with population growth, the over-exploitation of natural resources and pollution.

---

[62] Coyle-Shapiro 1999; Coyle-Shapiro, Morrow, Richardson and Dunn 2002. These organisations are not, of course, sovereign political entities.
[63] Hardin 1968.

Subsequently, however, researchers have realised that it may be applied far more widely. The tragedy of the commons is a metaphor for the risks run by any group of people whose members command resources individually and have a vested interest in communal resources, Athenian society included.

To examine the Athenians' solution to this problem, let us now go back to the category of altruistic acts that we discussed in the last chapter. This category, it will be remembered, is made up of acts that benefit the community in general or other members of it in particular, but that may be physically or economically detrimental to the person who performs them.[64] We have observed the Athenians nursing plague victims, complying with the city's code of behaviour (or, more properly, its 'unwritten laws') at considerable risk to their own lives. We have seen the vast sums that wealthy Athenians donated to the city in the form of liturgies, preferring a reputation for acting in the public interest to the furtherance of their own immediate material interests. We have seen the Athenian patriots, 'lovers of the city', giving their lives for the community, the supreme sacrifice of self-interest in order to help others. All this, taken together, suggests that the Athenians had managed to avoid the 'tragedy of the commons'; they had, so to speak, remembered to consider the over-grazing problem. In order to appreciate the significance of this, we shall go back to Olson: '. . . [D]espite the force of patriotism, the appeal of the national ideology, the bond of common culture, and the indispensability of the system of law and order, no major state in modern history has been able to support itself through voluntary dues or contributions. Philanthropic contributions are not even a significant source of revenue for most countries. Taxes, *compulsory* payments by definition, are needed. Indeed, as the old saying indicates, their necessity is as certain as death itself.'[65]

The Athenian democracy, however, *did* manage to support itself mainly on voluntary dues and contributions for almost two hundred years:[66] a fact that is also as certain as death itself.

Unlike Hardin's common, the victory at Salamis represented an indivisible public good: not a single inhabitant of Attica was excluded from the benefits that it conveyed, and none who enjoyed them did so at the expense of others. One victory, however, is only a small part of the wider public good that is national defence. National defence, in turn, is only a small part of a still wider public good, namely the social order, a concept that embraces both the security of the inhabitants (and of their property) and their perceptions of well-being. To investigate how the Athenians went

---

[64] See pp. 347–54.   [65] Olson 1965: 13 (his italics).   [66] On which point Ostwald 1995 is crucial.

about pursuing the public good at this level, we shall now turn to the amnesty of 403.[67]

An amnesty is an act of forgiveness by which political offences may pass into oblivion. As other Athenian acts that resembled amnesties were recorded at various times,[68] the amnesty of 403 was in some ways not unique. What sets it apart from these other acts is that it constituted the concluding phase of perhaps the fiercest and bloodiest internal conflict in Athenian history: the oligarchic coup of 404. The eight-month oligarchy was one of the darkest periods Athens had ever known. The Thirty began their acts of extreme cruelty and injustice immediately upon seizing power.[69] Backed by Spartan hoplites and some Athenian collaborators, they did not merely abolish the chief democratic institutions, enforcing the rules of their despotic regime with an iron fist, but illegally put to death hundreds of Athenians, drove thousands into exile and plundered wealthy foreigners to enrich themselves. Returning to the provocation-reaction pattern, their measures may uniformly be described as excessive provocation.[70]

In the autumn of 403, however, the exiled democrats regrouped in Boeotia under the leadership of Thrasyboulus and after a series of skirmishes with the oligarchs' forces marched triumphantly into Athens.[71] Democracy was restored in the same year, in the archonship of Eucleides. Thrasybulus and his liberators were honoured with crowns, a laudatory epigram likening them to the tyrannicides and the rule of the Thirty to Peisistratus' tyranny.[72] One of the first things the restored regime did was conclude a treaty of reconciliation with the oligarchs, of which the amnesty we are discussing was part.

The key expression around which the act of amnesty revolved was *me mnesikakein*. This has been translated as 'not to bear malice' or 'not to remember past wrongs'.[73] The surviving fragments of the amnesty oaths sworn by the Council members, the dikasts and the people express a spirit of conciliation and forgiveness. The Council members swore that they would 'not accept any indictment or summary process regarding actions

---

[67] This amnesty has already been referred to at pp. 92, 214 and 276.

[68] Cf. Dorjahn 1946: 1–3; Ostwald 1986: 422.

[69] Xenophon, *Hellenica* 2.3.1–2; *The Athenian Constitution* 35–6.   [70] See pp. 2–8 and 155–9.

[71] For the details of this victory as modern scholarship has perceived them see Krentz 1982; Buck 1998: 70–4. This memorable day was still being celebrated in Plutarch's time: *Moralia* 394f. For the restoration of democracy viewed as a ritual drama, see Strauss 1985.

[72] 'Upon these men the crown of valor | Was placed by Athens' ancient people; | They were the vanguard of those stalwarts | Who crushed the cruel tyrant's power | And lawless rule; nor shunned they peril. |' (Aeschines 3.190, *Against Ctesiphon*, trans. A. E. Raubitschek), quoted from a document whose considerable part has been discovered in the *agora*: Raubitschek 1941.

[73] Cf. Lévy 1976a: 214; Loening 1987: 21.

performed during this period, except in the case of exiles'. The dikasts swore that they would 'not bear malice against anyone, or allow any other person to influence their vote, but would cast their ballot according to the existing laws'. The people swore that they would bear no grudge against any citizen apart from the Thirty and the Eleven, and would extend this forbearance even to them if they submitted to an audit of the offices they had held.[74]

Regardless of their political affiliations, contemporaries acknowledged this amnesty as an act of outstanding magnanimity. Plato, an inveterate oligarch, conceded that '[i]n general those who returned to power then [after the interlude of oligarchic rule] showed the greatest fairness and moderation' (*The Seventh Letter*, 325b5). In the *Menexenus*, he also praised the kind (*asmenos*) and friendly (*oikeios*) manner in which the citizens of the Peiraeus and those of the city mixed (*synemeixan*) with each other once civil strife was at an end (243e). The author of *The Athenian Constitution* described the democrats' behaviour in highly complimentary terms: '. . . the Athenians appear both in private and public to have behaved towards the past disasters in the most completely honourable and statesmanlike manner of any people in history; for they not only blotted out recriminations with regard to the past . . .' (40.2–3, trans. H. Rackham). Isocrates contrasted the democrats' restraint (*praotes*) with the fierce and vengeful spirit of the oligarchs, interpreting the amnesty as a collective act of under-reaction to provocation (in response to the killing of some 1,500 Athenians and the exile of thousands, the victorious democrats put to death only the chief authors of their wrongs, dealing justly and indeed generously with the rest) and as a typical example of the fairness (*epieikeia*) of the people's rule (*Areopagiticus* 67–9). A client of Lysias remarked that after the restoration the Athenians, remembering that unanimity (*homonoia*) was the greatest of boons, while faction (*stasis*) was the root of all evil, 'prayed to the gods to restore the polis to unanimity rather than permit the pursuit of vengeance for what was over and done with to lead to faction in the polis . . .' (Lysias 19.17–18, *On the Property of Nicias' Brother*). Of all those who wrote in praise of the amnesty, Andocides spelt out most clearly the association of ideas that lay beneath it: 'After your return from Peiraeus you resolved to let bygones be bygones, in spite of the opportunity for revenge. You considered the safety of Athens (*sozein ten polin*) more important than your private [desire] for revenge (*tas idias timorias*) and resolved not to bear malice (*me mnesikakein*) against each other for what had

---

[74] Andocides 1.90–2, *On the Mysteries*. Cf. Plescia 1970: 27 for the frequent subsequent appeals for this oath to be remembered.

happened.'[75] Yet again a choice had been made, this time at the communal level, to maintain the social order rather than snatch at short-term
satisfaction by reacting excessively; we are reminded of the many litigants
who attempted to ingratiate themselves with the dikasts by claiming to have
abstained from violent overreaction on an individual level.[76] The democrats
who concluded the amnesty had decided that venting their anger in some
act of violent retribution would poison human relationships, doing more
harm than good to the entire social order. The *stasis* in Athens (unlike
that in Corcyra, which, like many others, deteriorated progressively into
seemingly endless savagery and bloodshed) ended right there. The amnesty
of 403 is the supreme example of the convergence on the communal level
of several interconnected imperatives of the Athenian code of behaviour
that we have already examined separately: under-reacting to provocation,
putting a stop to potentially interminable conflicts and preserving public
order.[77]

The logic of collective action and the tragedy of the commons are closely
related models that both seek to clarify the problems facing individuals
who are attempting to achieve benefits through collective action. A third
model, called the Iterated Prisoner's Dilemma (henceforth IPD), takes us
back to the initial pages of this book. This model should help us to see how
individuals can maximise the benefits accruing to them from interpersonal
interactions while at the same time promoting, or at least not harming,
the interests of the community on which their own welfare ultimately
depends.[78]

The game of Prisoner's Dilemma (hereafter PD) has received a considerable amount of attention in recent decades. With its complex ramifications
and many surprising applications, it has left an indelible imprint on a
variety of disciplines (biology, economics, political sciences, history and of
course the behavioural sciences). Many wild animals and plants, for example, are thought to be 'engaged in ceaseless games of Prisoner's Dilemma,
played out in evolutionary time'.[79] The hypothesis of the game is that two
prisoners are suspected of having collaborated in a crime. They are invited
to betray each other, neither being informed of how the other responds

---

[75] Andocides 1.81, *On the Mysteries*, trans. K. J. Maidment.   [76] See pp. 285–6.
[77] On the revolution and the amnesty in general, see Lehmann 1972; Lévy 1976a: 214–15; Ostwald
    1986: esp. 509–24; Loening 1987; Nippel 1997.
[78] For a less elaborate version of what follows, see Herman 1998a.
[79] Dawkins 1989: 203. Recent examples of the application of the IPD to animal and/or human behaviour
    include Wedekind and Milinski 2000; Mesterton-Gibbons and Adams 2002; Clutton-Brock 2002;
    Hauert, De Monte, Hoftbauer and Sigmund 2002; Stephens, McLinn and Stevens 2002; West, Pen
    and Griffin 2002; Baglione, Canestrari, Marcos and Ekman 2003; Vogel 2004.

to this invitation. The combination of moves that results determines the outcome, which is specific to the context of crime and punishment.[80] The IPD, devised by its most authoritative exponent, Robert Axelrod, is an upgraded and more general version of the PD that can be applied not merely to crime and punishment, but to a much wider range of social settings. It can have any number (or an infinite number) of rounds, in each of which the two players have to choose between 'co-operation' (refusing to speak) and 'defection' (betraying the other player). In each round they must make their moves simultaneously, neither knowing what move the other has made until the round is over.[81] As defection always returns a higher immediate payoff than co-operation, this creates a dilemma: if one player defects while the other co-operates the defecting player will do better than the co-operating player, but if both players defect both will do worse than if both had co-operated (see **Fig. 10.4**). Axelrod's purpose in developing the game was to identify the strategy that would lead to the highest possible score *in the long run*. It was his theory that where people have to interact with each other at close quarters 'what is best for each person individually leads to mutual defection, whereas everyone would have been better off with mutual cooperation'.[82]

Axelrod's search was no minor undertaking, since it is extremely difficult to predict the long-term consequences of iteration. The human mind is not good at foreseeing the cumulative effects of small, step-by-step adjustments that occur over lengthy periods, or at detecting how piecemeal changes manifest themselves in the operation of larger systems. To solve this difficulty Axelrod decided to stage a simulation. He announced a computer tournament and invited professional game theorists to send in programmes written in accordance with the rules of the IPD. A single computer was then used to set each of the fourteen entries submitted against each of the others in turn.

The outcome was surprising. The simplest programme of all those submitted, **Tit for tat**, won the tournament. Axelrod now announced a second round of the tournament, notifying all contestants of the results of the first

<hr />

[80] If either prisoner betrays the other by throwing the blame entirely upon him, while the latter remains silent, thus rendering his partner's story plausible, the betrayer gets off scot-free and the other receives a heavy jail sentence. If each prisoner betrays the other, both will be convicted of the crime; each can expect a fairly stiff sentence, but it will be reduced somewhat as a reward for giving evidence. If, finally, neither betrays the other (i.e. they 'co-operate' with each other by refusing to speak), neither can be convicted of the main offence; each is likely to receive a short sentence for a lesser offence.

[81] Axelrod 1984: 7–10.

[82] Axelrod 1984: 9, whose general thesis is outlined in Axelrod and Hamilton 1981. For the premises supporting the application of game theory to conflict analysis, see Rapoport 1974: ch. 20.

		Column player	
		Co-operate	Defect
Row player	Co-operate	**R=3, R=3** Reward for mutual co-operation	**S=0, T=5** Sucker's payoff Temptation to defect
	Defect	**T=5, S=0** Temptation to defect Sucker's payoff	**P=1, P=1** Punishment for mutual defection

NOTE: The scores for the Row player are listed first

Figure 10.4 The prisoner's dilemma
According to the choices made by each player (the 'Column' and the 'Row' player), there are four possible outcomes: (1) if both players co-operate, each gets **R**=3 points, R being the **R**eward for mutual co-operation; (2) if both players defect, each gets **P**=1 point, P being the **P**unishment for mutual defection; (3) if the Column player co-operates while the Row player defects, the Row player gets **T**=5 points, T being the Temptation to defect, and the Column player **S**=0 points, S being the Sucker's payoff; (4) if the Column player defects while the other co-operates, outcome 3 is reversed.
An intriguing feature of the IPD is that it allows the players to maximise their rewards without necessarily doing so at each other's expense: unlike chess, in which one player's gain is the other's loss (a 'zero sum game'), the Prisoner's Dilemma is a 'non zero sum game' in which the players can score at the expense of an imaginary 'banker'.

round before they submitted their entries. The second round was far more sophisticated than the first and there were many more participants. The winner, however, was again **Tit for tat**.

One intriguing feature of the IPD is that it permits an unlimited number of interactions, giving the players the chance to respond to one another's behaviour. In other words, it allows them to develop strategies in which human responses such as forgiving or avenging, trusting or mistrusting and reciprocating or placating are played out in computer language. The main features of the strategy employed by **Tit for tat** are defined by Axelrod as follows: 'avoidance of unnecessary conflict by co-operating as long as the other player does, provocability in the face of an uncalled for defection by the other, forgiveness after responding to a provocation, and clarity of behaviour so that the other player can adapt to your pattern of action'.[83] Further points of interest emerged from Axelrod's analysis of the tournament's overall results. A single property distinguished the higher-scoring from the lower-scoring entries: 'This is the property of being *nice*, which is to say never being the first to defect' . . . 'Each of the eight top-ranking entries (or rules) is nice. None of the others is.'[84] 'Of all the nice rules, the one that scored lowest was also the one that was least forgiving. This is **Friedman**, a totally unforgiving rule that employs permanent retaliation.'[85]

As we have already said, the success of any programme depended upon the responses of its adversaries, and in retrospect it was easy to find rules that would have worked better than those of **Tit for tat**. 'The existence of these rules', wrote Axelrod, 'should serve as a warning against the facile belief that an eye for an eye is necessarily the best strategy.' Of the three rules that would, if submitted, have won the tournament, I shall mention only the first. This programme 'defects only if the other player defected on the previous two moves. It is a more forgiving version of **Tit for tat** in that it does not punish isolated defections. The excellent performance of this **Tit for two tats** rule highlights the fact that a common error of the contestants was to expect that gains could be made from being relatively less forgiving than **Tit for tat**, whereas in fact there were big gains to be made from being even more forgiving. The implication of this finding is striking, since it suggests that even expert strategists do not give sufficient weight to the importance of forgiveness.'[86] More recent findings seem to confirm this conclusion, suggesting that the strategy of raising the stakes (i.e. unilaterally increasing one's investment in a relationship) yields surprisingly good results.[87]

Something of the contestants' own psychology was revealed by the games that they, as opposed to their programmes, played during the tournament. When psychologists set up games of IPD between human players, they tended to be too egoistic, too competitive, too vengeful and too suspicious of their opponents for their own good. Nearly all of the players allowed these qualities rather than 'nice' ones to come to the fore and dominate the game.[88]

Let us now examine the relevance of this conclusion to the Athenian code of behaviour. It is my contention that the strategy of reciprocal action that had gained the upper hand in Athens and regulated much of her public life

---

[83] Axelrod 1984: 20.   [84] Axelrod 1984: 33 (his italics).   [85] Axelrod 1984: 36.
[86] Axelrod 1984: 39.   [87] G. Roberts and T. N. Sherratt 1998.
[88] It is in keeping with this that when offered the options of being given £100 while their 'neighbour' gets £50 or being given £500 while their neighbour gets £1,000, most people prefer the first.

was nothing other than what Axelrod called **Tit for two tats**: the programme that resembles **Tit for tat**, but surpasses it in willingness to forgive. The ideal pattern of reciprocity in Athens appears closely to have resembled this programme, which reliably co-operates for as long as the other player does so and is forgiving in that it defects only after the other player has done so twice. In other words, the Athenians appear to have developed an ideal of reciprocal interaction that, if translated into computer language (a task by no means impossible) and entered in Axelrod's tournament, would have scored very highly indeed.

TIT FOR TWO TATS

In support of this point, I propose now briefly to review certain of our pieces of evidence that record behaviour (or claimed behaviour) resembling or approximating to the strategy of interpersonal relations that Axelrod called **Tit for two tats**.

Ariston's assertion that he responded to the many provocations and humiliations heaped on him simply by avoiding Conon and his sons, not retaliating even by means of legal action, may be viewed as an endorsement of the **Tit for two tats** strategy. Had Ariston attempted to engage the support of the dikasts by saying something such as, 'I inflicted upon them exactly the same number of / twice as many injuries as they inflicted upon me', he would have been endorsing (and implying that the dikasts would be likely to sympathise with) a **Tit for tat** or **Two tits for tat** strategy.[89]

The claim of the speaker in Lysias' third oration that he has put up with a long series of insults and injuries because he had rather 'go without redress than lose the respect of [his] fellow-citizens' is another clear endorsement of **Tit for two tats**. Had he said, 'I obtained satisfaction by insulting and injuring them as much as / more than they insulted and injured me', the reaction to which he was laying claim would again have counted as **Tit for tat** or **Two tits for tat**.[90]

Euphiletus murdered Eratosthenes on discovering that the latter was having an affair with his wife. This was a clear instance of over-reaction (**Two tits for tat**). In order to try and wriggle out of it, however, Euphiletus tells the dikasts that he killed Eratosthenes not out of lust for revenge, but out of a civic-minded desire to implement the law (something like **Half a tit for tat**). Had he sought to win over the dikasts by claiming that he had killed Eratosthenes to avenge his outraged honour, or that he had not

---

[89] See pp. 123–4 and 157.   [90] See pp. 166–7 and 203.

only done this but also injured some members of Eratosthenes' family, he would have been describing a **Tit for tat** or **Two tits for tat** pattern.[91]

Demosthenes' alleged avoidance of any sort of reaction to Meidias' lengthy persecution of him and his refusal to return in kind the punch in the face that finally caused him to sue Meidias appears to be another instance of **Tit for two tats**. Had Demosthenes punched Meidias back, or over-reacted by returning two or even three punches and perhaps harassing or harming Meidias' family instead of suing him, he would have been pursuing a strategy of **Tit for tat** or **Two tits for tat**.[92]

This is not Demosthenes' only contribution to our list. The actions of Euthynus and Euaeon, each of whom flew into a rage and killed someone in retaliation for a slight or imagined insult, were clear examples of **Two tits for tat**. Demosthenes, however, cites them as counter-examples to his own under-reaction to Meidias' punch, thereby endorsing the **Tit for two tats** strategy. Had Demosthenes cited these actions as admirable examples of the pattern he had tried to follow, he would have been endorsing **Two tits for tat**.[93]

Aristeides and Themistocles, as we have seen, promoted diametrically opposed policies and often attacked one another fiercely. Themistocles was even involved in bringing about Aristeides' ostracism. Had Aristeides seized the chance to bad-mouth Themistocles when an accusation was laid against the latter, his act would have qualified as **Tit for tat**. He chose, however, to forego this golden opportunity: **Tit for two tats**.[94]

When a 'vile and abandoned fellow' decided to spend the day abusing and insulting Pericles, the latter did not merely refrain from reacting, but even instructed a servant to see the man home. This was an instance of **No tit for two tats**. Had he returned the abuse, or had the man arrested and/or beaten up by his servant, his action would have qualified as **Tit for tat** or **Two tits for tat**.[95]

We could pile up many more examples of this sort, but there is no need to do so. To test our assumption that this pattern was deeply interwoven with the Athenian culture, let us now move on from specific examples of the **Tit for two tats** strategy to its manifestation in public acts, general pronouncements, institutional models and artistic or philosophical representations.

The amnesty of 403 and the minimal number of executions carried out by the democrats may be seen as a public endorsement of the **Tit for**

---

[91] See p. 176, with n. 47.   [92] See pp. 167–9.
[93] See pp. 169–70.   [94] See pp. 278–9.   [95] See pp. 174–5.

two tats strategy. Had the triumphant democrats decided to requite the oligarchs' killing spree with an equal or larger number of executions, or had they driven as many or even more citizens into exile, while refusing to accept reconciliation and compromise, clinging to their malice and refusing to forget their wrongs, their actions would have qualified as **Tit for tat** or **Two tits for tat.**[96]

The repayment to the Spartans of the hundred talents borrowed by the Thirty to crush the democratic opposition is another example of this sort. Had the restored democrats refused to repay money that had been borrowed in order to crush them, or had they moreover declared war on the Spartans for helping the Thirty, these actions would have been evidence of a **Tit for tat** or **Two tits for tat** strategy.[97]

The law-court speakers who asked the dikasts to forgive them for suing an enemy who had injured them did so in order to assert their preference for a **Tit for two tats** pattern. Had they claimed that their legal action was commensurate with the offence, or had they taken matters into their own hands outside the law court and injured their enemies more than their enemies had injured them, they would have been espousing a **Tit for tat** or **Two tits for tat** policy.[98]

Demosthenes' assertion that a man ought not to react violently when provoked, instead seeking redress from the people and from the city's laws, again implies approval of the **Tit for two tats** strategy. Had he said that anyone who had been provoked ought to react violently or even over-react violently, he would have been expressing his approval of the **Tit for tat** or the **Two tits for tat** strategy.[99]

At Samos in 411 the Athenian soldiers were initially inclined to react impulsively to Chaereas' exaggerated account of the oligarchs' reign of terror in Athens, but thought better of it on 'listening to men of moderate views who advised them not to throw away their entire cause': a case of **No tits for tat plus imaginary second tat**. Had they decided to pay back the oligarchs in kind or to execute a greater number than had perished under their rule, this would have been an instance of **Tit for tat** or **Two tits for tat.**[100]

The pardon (*aidesis*) that the relatives of the victim of an involuntary homicide were expected to extend to the killer in the interests of the community is another instance of **Tit for two tats**. Had there been no such

---

[96] See pp. 214, 276, 396–8.
[97] See p. 270. For the suggestion that the reconciliation agreement of 403 was in fact imbued with the spirit of vengeance, see W. V. Harris 2001: 183.
[98] See pp. 276–7.   [99] See pp. 172–3.   [100] See p. 113.

regulation, or had the regulation instructed the victim's relatives by no means to forgive the killing, we would be entitled to treat this case as **Tit for tat** or **Two tats for tit**.[101]

The portrayal of Athena as a merciful goddess who preferred to avoid battle (even though she fought fiercely once engaged), derived pleasure from settling disputes, upheld the law by pacific means and bore no arms in peacetime embodies the quintessential features of the **Tit for two tats** strategy. Had she been portrayed as vengeful, like Jehovah, the god of Israel, or bellicose, like Mars, the chief god of Rome, we would have been entitled to detect an underlying pattern of **Two tits for tat**.[102]

Aeschylus' *Oresteia* is, as we have seen, a didactic enactment of the replacement of tribal vengeance by state-inflicted punishment. This motif has overtones of **Tit for two tats**. Had the *Oresteia* glorified the majesty of tribal revenge, or had it called on Orestes to exact vengeance by means of tribal overkill rather than the law courts, Aeschylus' trilogy might have been said to endorse the **Two tits for tat** strategy.[103] The whole of Attic tragedy is in fact an endorsement of **Tit for two tats**. The crossroads scene in Sophocles' *Oedipus the King* and plays such as Sophocles' *Ajax* and Euripides' *Medea* contain ideas that may at first glance appear to suggest a **Two tits for tat** pattern. If we look more closely at these plays, however, bearing in mind that what matters is not how they appear to us, but how they would have appeared to the Athenian audience, we will find that this pattern is present only in negative form. Oedipus' overkill ('I killed them all'), for instance, was intended to arouse social disapproval. I shall leave it to the literary critics to follow up the implications of this for the play's plot, but it would seem that such apparent instances of **Two tits for tat** are in fact instances of **Tit for two tats**, a conclusion that casts doubt upon assertions such as 'Attic tragedy remembers vengeance as an honourable imperative essential to the preservation of order . . .'[104] Seen through Athenian rather than modern eyes, Attic tragedy remembers vengeance as one of the greatest of all possible evils and as a staunch enemy of the social order, by implication recommending patterns of action diametrically opposed to it.

Acts of vengeance are instances of 'negative reciprocity' that fit readily into the scheme of the IPD. Acts in which one actor spontaneously does another a good turn do not. The many acts of this sort that took place in Classical Athens can nonetheless be interpreted in terms of reciprocal

---

[101] See p. 295.   [102] See pp. 328–9.   [103] See pp. 127, 128 and 197.
[104] Burnett 1998: 6. Burnett's theory appears to imply that, for instance, the Athenian audience thought that Oedipus' overkill was 'an honourable imperative essential to the preservation of order'.

behaviour. When some Athenians chose to visit and nurse plague victims because 'they made it a point of honour to act properly' and 'felt ashamed to think of their own safety', they were performing enormous acts of self-sacrifice without being required to do so and without any expectation of reciprocation. The same was true of those Athenians who provided the daughters of the indigent with dowries, paid ransoms to deliver other Athenians from captivity, provided liturgies, or fought and died to defend Athens and her democracy. They were in fact enacting a strategy for the conduct of interpersonal relationships that can be viewed as the positive counterpart of **No tit for any number of tats**, a strategy that did not appear in the computer tournament because the game theorists thought it too unrealistic.

We may now move on to some fresh examples. The distinction that Plato draws between revenge and punishment is clear evidence of a **Tit for two tats** pattern:

No one punishes (*kolazei*) wrongdoers simply because he knows the fact and the nature of their wrongdoing, unless he is merely striking back impulsively as a wild animal does. The rational punisher is not taking revenge for what has already been done, since it cannot be undone; he is protecting the future by preventing both the wrongdoer and anyone else who sees him punished from ever doing such a thing again . . . One punishes for the sake of deterrence (*apotropes heneka*). (*Protagoras* 324a–b)

What is extraordinary about this passage is that in it the idea of punishment is purged of revenge. Plato's Protagoras is arguing that there should be no causal connection between wrongdoing and punishment. Rejecting the retrospective function of punishment (the taking of formal revenge for whatever offence has been committed), he supports only its prospective function: protecting the community against any recurrence of the crime. Wrongdoing is thus conceived of as damage done to the state, not to a particular individual. Protagoras rejects the idea of vengeance as a duty that must be carried out irrespective of the consequences in favour of that of 'rational punishment', a notion that entails sacrificing the passion for revenge to the higher interest of political stability. This is precisely the notion that is played upon by Euphiletus in Lysias 1. Plato has, in other words, elevated to the higher rank of theory the **Tit for two tats** pattern that he found encoded in popular thought.

A similar process may have been at work in Socrates' even more famous rejection of retaliation, which carries the idea of **Tit for two tats** to extremes (it might be said to propose a programme called **No tit at all for multiple**

tats). As we have already seen, he is said to have spoken as follows: 'We should never do injustice (*adikein*)'; '. . . we should never reciprocate an injustice (*antadikein*)'; 'We should never do evil (*kakourgein*)'; '. . . we should never reciprocate evil (*antikakourgein*)'; 'To do evil to a human being (*kakos poiein*) is no different from acting unjustly (*adikein*) to him'; '. . . we should never return a wrong or do evil to a single human being no matter what we may have suffered at his hands'.[105] Recognising that such an idea could not have come out of the blue, the late Gregory Vlastos looked for similar ideas in contemporary and earlier Greek literary works. I submit that the passages already quoted in this section approximate more closely to Socrates' idea than do the examples that Vlastos found. All of our quotations state or imply that one should avoid retaliation (or at least under-react to provocation) in order not to upset the delicate equilibrium of the social order. Socrates carries this idea one step further, turning it into an absolute moral imperative: one should under no circumstances whatsoever retaliate, no matter what the consequences for the community or for any other human agency or institution.

Having reviewed this evidence, we must examine the problem of whether or not it is valid to see it in terms of a computer programme and deal with certain objections that will naturally arise.

It may be objected that drawing an analogy between a computer programme and reality is simplistic, even verging on savage reductionism. A computer game of this sort is indeed not at all the same thing as reality. It is, however, an abstraction of actions that take place in reality. This means that while it faithfully reflects certain features of reality, it simplifies others or leaves them out altogether. Axelrod acknowledges these omissions: 'Examples of what is left out by this formal abstraction include the possibility of verbal communication, the direct influence of third parties, the problems of implementing a choice, and the uncertainty about what the other players actually did in the preceding move.'[106] Many further omissions could undoubtedly be added. None, however, invalidates the basic resemblance between the interaction of the Column Player and the Row Player of the IPD and that of people encapsulated within tightly knit social systems such as that of ancient Athens. The people of Athens too were engaged in an indefinite series of reciprocal actions. They too were

---

[105] See pp. 132–3. For a similar idea in the surviving fragments of Antiphon the Sophist ('it is just (*dikaion*) to do injustice (*adikein*) to no one when one is not being treated with injustice (*me adikoumenon*) oneself') see Kerferd 1955–9; Havelock 1957: 260; Morrison 1961; 1963; Moulton 1972; Saunders 1977–8.

[106] Axelrod 1984: 19.

motivated by the desire to maximise individual rewards. They too were tossed on the horns of the dilemma, 'If I co-operate, I may reap a small reward, but I also risk being cheated out of what I have; if, on the other hand, I defect, I may reap a handsome reward, but I also risk paying for my defection' (either by falling foul of the city's punitive agencies, or by suffering indirectly from the damage caused to the communal system). They too solved this dilemma by developing, over the course of an unknown number of reciprocal interactions, a strategy that they believed to be preferable to every other.

The second objection follows directly on the first. The IPD consists of an indefinite number of reciprocal interactions between *two* participants. Athenian social life involved not only interactions of this kind, but also an indefinite number of reciprocal interactions between *more than two* participants. It is perfectly conceivable that an IPD tournament in which a large number of people took part in various combinations would yield different results. This problem, which immediately caught the interest of game theorists, has now been solved: there is good evidence to suggest that the results of the IPD game are similar even when it is played out between a multiplicity of partners. In this case co-operation 'pays because it confers the image of a valuable community member to the cooperating individual'.[107]

The third objection has to do with the concept of the 'dominant strategy of personal interaction'. In order to maximise their rewards people in real societies often employ not one but several (often contradictory) strategies of interpersonal interaction according to the occasion. In most cases it is impossible to identify any of these as dominant. This may, however, not be true of Athens. Many of the most important decisions on both private and public matters in Athens were taken by plenipotentiary popular law courts made up of hundreds of citizens. These dikasts were disposed to be swayed by legally irrelevant moral appeals to an extent unparalleled in most legal systems. Their number and the manner of their appointment made it likely that any panel of dikasts would have represented a fair cross-section of Athenian society, so that it is clear that any appeal made to them must have reflected the appellant's understanding of the accepted moral code of that society. The appeals made to them reveal a consistent underlying pattern that, thanks to this unusual legal arrangement, we may safely identify as the strategy of interpersonal interaction that was regarded as most desirable in Athens.

---

[107] M. Taylor 1987: ch. 4; Nowak and Sigmund 1998.

The fourth question is about representation. Do the law-court speakers' statements stand for a single move in the IPD, a whole series of moves, or something else? To answer this question we must sharpen a distinction that we made earlier. The accounts of under-reaction listed at the beginning of this section are idealised. They do not record accomplished actions (some may have been thought of, but never put into practice; others may have been entirely fictitious), but potential ones. We are dealing, in other words, with widely approved popular ideals to which the speakers took the utmost care to make their stories correspond. The crucial point for our purposes is that in attempting to ingratiate themselves with the dikasts they chose to represent themselves as preferring **Tit for two tats** and their opponents as preferring **Tit for tat** or **Two tits for tat**. By means of an indefinite number of moves intended not only to maximise individual rewards but also to promote communal welfare (a further point of difference between the computer game and real life), the Athenians had worked out an ideal of reciprocal action against which all concrete reciprocal acts were measured. When we describe the accounts that we have examined as 'idealised', we mean that the litigants were attempting to tap into that particular ideal. Their statements therefore correspond neither to a single move in the IPD nor to a whole series of moves, but rather to Axelrod's evaluations of the programmes in terms of 'niceness', 'co-operation' and 'forgiveness'.

It may finally be objected that pronouncements of similar import appear in many other periods and places. It could be argued that if moral injunctions such as 'Turn the other cheek' and 'Love thy neighbour as thyself' were turned into computer programmes they would yield similar results. It is therefore important to point out that unless such injunctions can be identified as expressing public opinion (and thus as reflecting societal forces) they cannot legitimately be simulated by the IPD. This proposition may be illustrated by means of a counter-example.

According to Carlo Ginzburg, the seventeenth-century Italian miller Menocchio was brought to trial by the Inquisition because his views were thought to be heretical.[108] During one interrogation, the inquisitor asked Menocchio to specify 'the works of God' by means of which one went to heaven. Menocchio's reply included a long list of moral injunctions: 'love [God], adore him, sanctify him, revere and thank him; and also one should be charitable, merciful, peaceful, loving, honourable, obedient to one's superiors, pardon injuries, and keep promises; and for doing this one goes to heaven, and this is all we need to go there'. Despite its superficial

---

[108] Ginzburg 1980: 39.

resemblance to our Athenian examples, Menocchio's expressed attitude to willingness to forgive differs markedly from that of his Athenian counterparts. His 'pardoning injuries' can be presumed to have been inspired by a booklet written half a century earlier by Tullio Crispoldi, according to which 'the essence of Christianity was the "law of forgiving", the forgiving one's neighbour so as to be forgiven by God'.[109] To the Inquisition this ideal was unacceptable, as it placed one's duty to one's neighbour on a par with one's duty to God. To Menocchio's fellow-countrymen in Montereale it was probably totally unknown. In the society in which Menocchio lived the pardoning of injuries appears not to have been a dominant strategy of reciprocity; nor was it an ideal informing the actions of that society's Procrustean power agents. Menocchio was a social rebel, a non-conformist attempting heroically to derive moral support from views shared only by a minority. The litigants in the Athenian courts, however, were social conformists who were attempting to elicit support by tapping into the norms of a tribunal of justice whose outlook (and consequently verdict) was second to none in moulding societal behaviour.

It follows that we are not licensed to apply the IPD to Menocchio's utterances, or, for that matter, to any of the Christian or Jewish injunctions listed above. We are, on the other hand, fully licensed to apply it to the imperatives appealed to by the Attic Orators because these did express the predominant public opinion and reflect the societal forces that gave rise to that opinion. This offers us a rare opportunity, allowing the historian to take the unusual leap of establishing a link between the overall characteristics of Athenian society and its members' particular strategy of reciprocity. It permits him or her to bridge the gap between the short-term individual and the long-term cumulative effects of one particular strategy of interaction. It leads him or her to conclude that the Athenians had created a moral climate that motivated individual Athenians to prefer **Tit for two tats** to less forgiving strategies of interpersonal interaction.

THE ATHENIAN CODE OF BEHAVIOUR: A BALANCE-SHEET

The time has come to summarise our findings. We set out on our inquiry on the assumption that the manner in which members of a community interact when faced with choices involving co-operation and/or conflict contains the clue to unravelling that community's code of behaviour and indeed to evaluating its entire moral profile. Having reviewed a great deal of primary

[109] Ginzburg 1980: 40.

evidence and a minimal amount of secondary evidence relating to the Attic community between 508 and 322, we have identified an outstanding feature of its code of behaviour that may best be illustrated by means of comparison. In most societies, modern or ancient, it is or has been held to be self-evident that upon being provoked, offended or injured an individual (or collective) is entitled to react in accordance with the 'eye for an eye' (**Tit for tat**) or the 'head for an eye' (**Two tits for tat**) principle. The reaction of the injured party is or was, in other words, expected to be either commensurate with or in excess of the initial act of provocation, offence or injury. The Athenian ideal, however, held that upon being provoked, offended or injured a person should if possible avoid retaliation altogether and should certainly not retaliate excessively. Instead, he should exercise self-restraint, avoid violence and attempt compromise; only as a last resort should he appeal to the courts. It would thus appear that, quite unlike their Homeric forefathers, the Athenians applied themselves to the suppression of strategies of permanent retaliation with some determination. An ability to exercise the emotional control that this suppression required became the hallmark of the ideal democrat: the isonomic Athenian.

This compliance with the ideals of self-restraint and non-retaliation did not turn the Athenians into either saints or suckers. (In the language of the IPD, 'suckers' are players who allow their partners to cheat and exploit them with impunity.) The idea underlying the passages we have been examining was that immediate, heated reaction and passionate acts of revenge were dispensable as strategies of interpersonal behaviour simply because they had been rendered redundant by the community's capacity to administer punishment. The Athenians were neither saints nor suckers because the wrongs they suffered were requited by means of punishment administered by the state's coercive agencies. The strategy of self-restraint and non-retaliation that they paraded in the law courts and in public rhetoric boils down, in fact, to homage to the city's coercive power.

The city's coercive power was a central ingredient of the Athenian code of behaviour. A crucial step in the formation of the polis was the transfer of the family's unlimited and indiscriminate power to commit violent actions to carefully circumscribed, communally controlled institutions. A vital part of the development of democracy was the allocation of control of these institutions to the entire body of isonomic citizens. As a result of this, privately inflicted violence came to be defined as illegitimate and state-inflicted violence as legitimate. The Athenian state being the sum of each and every one of its citizens, the licence whereby that state inflicted violence was granted by consent of each and every citizen. We may conjecture that it was a sense of participation in communal power that allowed **Tit for two tats** slowly to emerge as the dominant strategy of interpersonal interaction, the isonomic Athenian feeling himself compensated for his decreased licence to perform acts of violence by his increased power to participate in punishment inflicted by the state.

Computerised simulations of the strategy of interpersonal relations consistently preferred by the Athenians suggest that they had hit upon a formula for exchange relationships that created an optimal balance between the maximisation of private benefits and the furtherance of the public good. The effects of this are apparent in their living standards. Aristeides' advice to his countrymen to move to the city and seize mastery of the seas resulted, as we have seen, in 'affluence for the masses'. Thucydides wrote that democracy had given everybody an equal share of the 'good things in life'.[110] There are numerous signs that the state went to great lengths to secure a good life for its citizens. The Athenians must, just as the IPD would have predicted, have found life rewarding. Their system relied upon a steady supply of state benefits to 'the many', the proceeds of empire and of the mines allowing the state to employ more than 20,000 men (both citizens and non-citizens). Magistrates, members of the Council and dikasts were all paid for their services.[111] During the fourth century citizens who attended the Assembly were also paid,[112] and even attending the theatre was subsidised.[113] The disabled (*adynatoi*), war orphans, men maimed in battle and 'those in need' received windfalls, or were sometimes even maintained out of public funds.[114] Add to this the advantages that the citizens derived from the generosity of the rich and the self-sacrifice of idealists and it will not be difficult to see why the Athenians should have 'taken good care of their democracy', as that embittered enemy of the regime, the Old Oligarch, was once constrained to admit (3.1). Anything done by an individual for the community of which he is a member can pay off through either or both of two channels, one direct and personal (**P**), the other largely 'abstract', consisting of his relationships with the community as a whole (**C**).[115] The total reward (**R**) that converges on the individual is expressed by the equation $R = P + C$. The evidence presented in this book suggests that in Athens the value of both **P** and **C** was very high indeed, fully bearing out Finley's now thirty-year-old assertion that 'Athens managed for nearly two hundred

---

[110] *The Athenian Constitution* 24.3; Thucydides 6.39.   [111] Hansen 1979; Markle 1985; Todd 1990a.
[112] Hansen 1987: 46–8; Podes 1987.   [113] Buchanan 1962.
[114] Disabled: Dillon 1995; orphans: *The Athenian Constitution* 24.3, with Stroud 1971; 'those maimed in battle': Buchanan 1962: 1–3; 'those in need': Ober 1989: 130.
[115] See p. 38.

years to be the most prosperous, most powerful, most stable, most peaceful internally, and culturally by far the richest state in all the Greek world.'[116]

That this conclusion is neither far-fetched nor utterly erroneous is shown by the vast amount of evidence suggesting that many aspects of Athenian life in general may be viewed as by-products of the **Tit for two tats** strategy as applied to the conduct of interpersonal relationships. The operation of this strategy is revealed in the generally low level of violence in Athenian society (as evidenced by the practice of going unarmed and by the absence of blood-feud, vendetta, gangs of thugs and various other violence-generating institutions), in the built-in capacity of the political and judicial systems to prevent conflicts from escalating and flaring up into civil wars and in representations of the transcendental order as governed not by strife but by conciliation. Our conclusion is reinforced by the consistency with which the proclivity to prefer **Tit for two tats** to any other strategy manifests itself in every field of activity. Had we, for instance, found that the Athenians were 'free and tolerant in their private lives' but still rejoiced in the spectacle of bloodthirsty executions, or that they perpetuated customs suffused with cruelty and bloodshed, or that they treated their slaves far worse than the other Greeks did theirs, or that they adopted merciless strategies of retaliation in their public life and in international affairs, we would have had reason to suspect that we had been misled by erroneous presumptions. Since no such dissonance appears, we appear justified in thinking that we are on the right track.

The general conclusion of this book may be contained in a single paragraph. It is a widely accepted premise that the Athenians created the first known democracy. This has been recognised as a considerable achievement. It is also a widely accepted premise that the Athenians made some strikingly original contributions to human thought. This too has been acknowledged as a significant achievement. It has, however, also been argued that the very political and cultural systems that produced these achievements were underpinned by a moral system of extremely unimpressive character, having every affinity with the moral systems of societies that we would now call 'primitive', 'Mediterranean' or 'feuding'. In this book I have attempted to show that this argument is mistaken: that, on the contrary, the moral system that supported the Athenians' political and cultural achievements

---

[116] Finley 1973: 23. For the modern connection between democracy and prosperity, cf. Dahl 1985: 45: 'A century and a half after Tocqueville's insight, we indeed do find an extraordinarily strong correlation between economic well-being and democracy. Democratic institutions exist today exclusively in countries having high per capita gross national product, with only a few somewhat precarious exceptions . . .'

displayed a remarkable level of sophistication, perhaps in objective terms surpassing the moral systems of the peoples, cities and nations that subsequently created the moral code of the west. The society of democratic Athens had, of course, a number of aspects that are now regarded as unacceptable. On the other hand, it may be doubted whether in retrospect any moral system has ever appeared immune to criticism. To the best of my knowledge, no code of behaviour other than that of the Athenians has ever turned non-retaliation into an ideal that might be seen in action in society. No other code of behaviour has ever striven consistently to apply that strategy to the conduct of public affairs. No group of philosophical thinkers apart from the Platonic school has ever formulated a universal concept of non-retaliation and turned it into a governing idea and an effective social force.[117] It is the extreme rarity of these features, however wide our comparative perspective, that forces upon us the conclusion that the code of behaviour that the Athenians devised to administer their communal life was a necessary precondition for the emergence of the two other features that make Athens appear so extraordinary: her democracy and her culture. For the Athenian miracle to unfold it was not enough that man should learn to know himself; it was necessary that he should learn to live in communities.

---

[117] Christianity, in which the concept reappears as a leading idea but not as a practical social force, drew its inspiration from Greek philosophy and late Judaism.

Bibliography

ABBREVIATIONS OF SOME PUBLICATIONS THAT APPEAR IN THE NOTES AND CAPTIONS

GHI M. N. Tod (ed.) (1946) *Greek Historical Inscriptions*, vol. I, 1946; vol. II, 1948. Oxford: Clarendon Press.

IG I³ D. M. Lewis (ed.) (1981) *Inscriptiones Graecae* I³: *Inscriptiones Atticae Euclidis Anno Anteriores*, fasc. I; fasc. 2 ed. by D. M. Lewis and L. Jeffery, 1994. Berlin.

IG II² I. Kierchner (ed.) (1913–40) *Inscriptiones Graecae* II²: *Inscriptiones Atticae Euclidis Anno Posteriores*, Berlin. 4 vols.

*OCD*³ S. Hornblower and A. Spawforth (eds.) (1996) *The Oxford Classical Dictionary*, 3rd edn. Oxford and New York: Oxford University Press.

SEG (1923–) *Supplementum Epigraphicum Graecum*. Leiden: Gieben.

SGHI R. Meiggs and D. M. Lewis (eds.) (1969) *A Selection of Greek Historical Inscriptions*. Oxford: Clarendon Press.

*SIG*⁴ W. Dittenberger (ed.) (1960) *Sylloge Inscriptionum Graecarum*, 4th edn. Hildesheim: Georg Olms.

WORKS CITED

Note: Works that are cited only once in the notes and that are not essential to the book's argument do not normally appear in the bibliography.

Adkins, A. W. H. (1960a) *Merit and Responsibility. A Study of Greek Values*. Oxford: Oxford University Press.

(1960b) '"Honour" and "punishment" in the Homeric poems', *Bulletin of the Institute of Classical Studies of the University of London* 7: 23–32.

(1963) '"Friendship" and "self-sufficiency" in Homer and Aristotle', *Classical Quarterly* 13: 30–45.

(1969a) 'ΕΥΧΟΜΑΙ, ΕΥΧΩΛΕ and ΕΥΧΟΣ in Homer', *Classical Quarterly* 19: 20–33.

(1969b) 'Threatening, abusing and feeling angry in the Homeric poems', *Journal of Hellenic Studies* 89: 7–21.

(1972) *Moral Values and Political Behaviour in Ancient Greece*. London: Chatto and Windus.

(1975) 'Merit, responsibility, and Thucydides', *Classical Quarterly* 25: 145–58.

(1976) 'Polypragmosune and "minding one's own business": a study in Greek social and political values', *Classical Philology* 71: 301–27.

(1978) 'Problems in Greek popular morality', *Classical Philology* 73: 145–58.

(1987) 'Gagarin and the "morality" of Homer', *Classical Philology* 82: 311–22.

Alexander, R. D. (1979) *Darwinism and Human Affairs*. London: Pitman Publishing Limited.

Allen, D. S. (1997) 'Imprisonment in classical Athens', *Classical Quarterly* 47: 121–35.

(2000) *The World of Prometheus. The Politics of Punishing in Democratic Athens*. Princeton, New Jersey: Princeton University Press.

Amit, M. (1961) 'Le Pirée dans l'histoire d'Athènes à l'époque classique', *Bulletin de l'association Guillaume Budé* 4: 464–74.

(1965) *Athens and the Sea*. Brussels: Latomus.

Ampolo, C. (1982) 'Le cave de pietra dell'Attica: problemi giuridici ed economici', *Opus* 1: 251–60.

Anderson, J. K. (1991) 'Hoplite weapons and offensive arms', in Hanson (1991a): 15–37.

Andreau, J. (1995) 'Vingt ans après L'Économie antique de Moses I. Finley', *Annales* 50: 947–60.

Andrewes, A. (1974) 'The Arginousai trial', *Phoenix* 28: 112–22.

Arnaoutoglou, I. (1993) 'Pollution in the Athenian homicide law', *Revue internationale des droits de l'antiquité* 40: 109–35.

Arthur, M. B. (1982) 'Women and the family in ancient Greece', *Yale Review* 71: 532–47.

Asheri, D. (1963) 'Laws of inheritance, distribution of land and political constitutions in ancient Greece', *Historia* 12: 1–21.

(1997) 'Identità greche, identità greca', in *I Greci. Stori Cultura Arte Società*. Turin: Giulio Einaudi: 5–26.

(2002) 'The prehistory of the word "democracy"', *Mediterraneo Antico* 5 (1): 1–7.

Austin, M. M. and P. Vidal-Naquet (1977) *Economic and Social History of Ancient Greece*. Translated by M. M. Austin. London: B. T. Batsford.

Axelrod, R. (1984) *The Evolution of Co-operation*. Harmondsworth: Penguin.

Axelrod, R. and W. L. Hamilton (1981) 'The evolution of cooperation', *Science* 211: 1390–6.

Badian, E. (1995) 'The ghost of empire', in Eder (1995a): 79–106.

Bagehot, W. (1872) *Physics and Politics: Thoughts on the Application of the Principles of 'Natural Selection' and 'Inheritance' to Political Society*. London: Henry S. King & Co.

Baglione, V., D. Canestrari, J. M. Marcos and J. Ekman (2003) 'Kin selection in cooperative alliances of carrion crows', *Science* 300 (5627): 1947–9.

Balot, R. (2001) 'Pericles' anatomy of democratic courage', *American Journal of Philology* 122: 505–25.

Bandura, A. (1973) *Aggression: A Social Learning Analysis*. Englewood Cliffs, N.J.: Prentice-Hall.

(1979) 'Psychological mechanisms of aggression', in von Cranach, Foppa, Lepenies and Ploog (1979): 316–56.

Barash, D. P. (1977) *Sociobiology and Behaviour*. New York: Elsevier.

Barkan, I. (1935) *Capital Punishment in Ancient Athens*. New York: Arno.

Barker, E. (1959) *The Political Thought of Plato and Aristotle*. New York: Dover Publications.

(1960) *Greek Political Theory*, 5th edn. London: Methuen.

Baroja, J. C. (1965) 'Honour and shame', in Peristiany (1965): 79–130.

Berent, M. (1996) 'An anthropological view of the polis, war and violence', *History of Political Thought* 17: 36–59.

(2000) 'Anthropology and the classics: war, violence, and the stateless *polis*', *Classical Quarterly* 50 (1): 257–89.

Bers, V. (1985) 'Dikastic *thorubos*', in Cartledge and Harvey (1985): 1–15.

Bettalli, M. (1982) 'Note sulla produzione tessile ad Atene in età classica', *Opus* 1: 261–78.

Bickerman, E. (1952) 'Hannibal's covenant', *American Journal of Philology* 73: 1–12.

Black-Michaud, J. (1975) *Feuding Societies*. Oxford: Basil Blackwell.

Blackman, D. (2000) 'Archaeological reports for 1999–2000', *Council of the Society for the Promotion of Hellenic Studies*: 7–21.

Bleicken, J. (1985) *Die athenische Demokratie*. Paderborn, Munich, Vienna, Zürich: Ferdinand Schöningh.

Blok, A. (1981) 'Rams and billy-goats: a key to the Mediterranean code of honour', *Man* 16: 427–40.

Blundell, M. W. (1989) *Helping Friends and Harming Enemies*. Cambridge: Cambridge University Press.

Blundell, S. (1995) *Women in Ancient Greece*. London: British Museum Press – Harvard University Press.

(1998a) 'Women in classical Athens', in Sparkes (1998): 232–47.

(1998b) *Women in Classical Athens*. Bristol: Bristol Classical Press.

Boardman, J. (1977) 'The Parthenon frieze – another view', in *Festschrift für Frank Brommer*, eds. U. Höckmann and A. Krug. Mainz: 39–49.

(1984) 'The Parthenon frieze', in *Parthenon – Kongreß Basel*, ed. E. Berger. Mainz: von Zabern: 210–16, 412–13.

(1985) *The Parthenon and its Sculptures*. Austin: University of Texas Press.

Boegehold, A. L. (1991) 'Three court days', in Gagarin (1991): 165–82.

(1995) *The Lawcourts at Athens*, vol. XXVIII, *The Athenian Agora*. Princeton, N.J.: American School of Classical Studies at Athens.

Boegehold, A. L. and A. C. Scafuro (eds.) (1994) *Athenian Identity and Civic Ideology*. Baltimore and London: The Johns Hopkins University Press.

Boehm, C. (1984) *Blood Revenge. The Enactment and Management of Conflict in Montenegro and Other Tribal Societies*. Philadelphia: University of Pennsylvania Press.

Bowersock, G. W. (1966) 'Pseudo-Xenophon', *Harvard Studies in Classical Philology* 71: 33–55.

(1968) 'Introduction', in *The Constitution of the Athenians by Xenophon the Orator*, ed. G. W. Bowersock. Cambridge, Mass.: Harvard University Press: 461–73.

Bowsky, W. M. (1967) 'The medieval commune and internal violence: police power and public safety in Siena, 1287–1355', *American Historical Review* 73: 1–17.

Boyd, R. and P. J. Richerson (1985) *Culture and the Evolutionary Process*. Chicago: University of Chicago Press.

Bradeen, D. W. (1960) 'The popularity of the Athenian empire', *Historia* 9: 257–69.

Brandes, S. (1987) 'Reflections on honor and shame in the Mediterranean', in Gilmore (1987): 121–34.

Braudel, F. (1967) *Civilization and Capitalism 15th–18th Century. Vol. I. The Structures of Everyday Life*. Berkeley, Los Angeles: University of California Press.

(1972) *Civilization and Capitalism 15th–18th Century. Vol. II. The Wheels of Commerce*. London, Glasgow, Sydney, Auckland, Toronto, Johannesburg: William Collins Sons & Co. Ltd.

(1984) *Civilization and Capitalism 15th–18th Century. Vol. III. The Perspective of the World*. Berkeley, Los Angeles: University of California Press.

Bremmer, J. N. (1983a) *The Early Greek Concept of the Soul*. Princeton: Princeton University Press.

(1983b) 'Scapegoat rituals in ancient Greece', *Harvard Studies in Classical Philology* 87: 299–320.

(1996) 'The status and symbolic capital of the seer', in *The Role of Religion in the Early Greek Polis*, ed. R. Hägg. Stockholm: Swedish Institute at Athens: 97–109.

(2000) 'Verbal insulting in ancient Greek culture', *Acta Antiqua Academiae Scientiarum Hungaricae* 40: 61–72.

(2002) *The Rise and Fall of the Afterlife*. London, New York: Routledge.

Bresson, A. (2000) *La cité marchande*. Bordeaux: Ausonius.

Brink, C. O. (1955–6) 'Οἰκείωσις and οἰκείοτης: Theophrastus and Zeno on nature in moral theory', *Phronesis* 1: 123–45.

Brown, N. O. (1947) *Hermes the Thief*. Great Barrington, Mass.: Lindisfarne Press.

Bruell, C. (1974) 'Thucydides' view of Athenian imperialism', *The American Political Science Review* 6 (1): 11–17.

Brunner, H. G., M. Nelen, X. O. Breakefiel, H. H. Ropers and B. A. van Oost (1993) 'Abnormal behavior associated with a point mutation in the structural gene for monoamine oxidose', *Science* 262 (October): 578–80.

Brunt, P. A. (1953/4) 'The Hellenic league against Persia', *Historia*: 135–63.

(1966) 'Athenian settlements abroad in the fifth century', in *Ancient Society and Institutions. Studies Presented to Victor Ehrenberg*. Oxford: Blackwell: 71–92.

Bryson, F. R. (1935) *The Point of Honor in Sixteenth-Century Italy: An Aspect of the Life of the Gentleman*. New York: The Institute of French Studies, Columbia University.

Buchanan, J. J. (1962) *Theorika. A Study of Monetary Distributions to the Athenian Citizenry during the Fifth and Fourth Centuries B.C.* New York: J. J. Augustin.

Buck, R. (1998) *Thrasybulus and the Athenian Democracy. The Life of an Athenian Statesman*. Stuttgart: Franz Steiner Verlag.

Bibliography 419

Budge, E. A. W. (1930) *Amulets and Superstitions*. New York: Dover.

Burckhardt, J. (1929) *Griechische Kulturgeschichte*. 3 vols. Leipzig. Original edition 1898–1902.

(1998) *The Greeks and Greek Civilization*. Translated by S. Stern. New York: St. Martin's Press. Original edition 1898–1902.

Burford, A. (1977–8) 'The family farm in Greece', *Classical Journal* 73: 162–75.

(1993) *Land and Labor in the Greek World*. Baltimore and London: The Johns Hopkins University Press.

Burke, E. M. (1992) 'The economy of Athens in the Classical era: some adjustments to the primitivist model', *Transactions and Proceedings of the American Philological Association* 122: 199–226.

Burkert, W. (1979a) *Structure and History in Greek Mythology and Ritual*. Berkeley, Los Angeles, London: University of California Press.

(1979b) 'The persistence of ritual', in Burkert (1979a): 35–58.

(1979c) 'Transformations of the scapegoat', in Burkert (1979a): 59–77.

(1983a) *Homo Necans. The Anthropology of Ancient Greek Sacrificial Ritual and Myth*. Translated by P. Bing. Berkeley, Los Angeles, London: University of California Press.

(1983b) 'Itinerant diviners and magicians: a neglected element of cultural contacts', in Hägg (1983): 115–22.

(1985) *Greek Religion*. Translated by J. Raffan. Cambridge, Mass.: Harvard University Press. Original edition 1977.

(1996) *Creation of the Sacred. Tracks of Biology in Early Religions*. Cambridge, Mass. & London: Harvard University Press.

(2001) 'The formation of Greek religion at the close of the dark ages', in *Kleine Schriften*. Göttingen: Vandenhoeck & Ruprecht. Original edition, 1992 (*Studi italiani di filologia classica* 10 (1992), 533–51: 13–29).

Burnett, A. P. (1998) *Revenge in Attic and Later Tragedy*. Berkeley, Los Angeles, London: University of California Press.

Bury, J. B. (1913) *A History of Greece*, 2nd edn. London: Macmillan.

Bushala, E. W. (1968) 'Torture of non-citizens in homicide investigations', *Greek, Roman and Byzantine Studies* 9: 61–8.

Cairns, D. L. (1993) *AIDOS. The Psychology and Ethics of Honour and Shame in Ancient Greek Literature*. Oxford: Oxford University Press.

(1996) 'Hybris, dishonour, and thinking big', *Journal of Hellenic Studies* 116: 1–32.

Calhoun, G. M. (1944) *Introduction to Greek Legal Science*. Oxford: Clarendon Press.

Camp, J. M. (1986) *The Athenian Agora. Excavations in the Heart of Classical Athens*. London: Thames and Hudson.

Campbell, D. T. (1978) 'On the genetics of altruism and the counterhedonic components in human cultures', in Wispé (1978): 38–57.

Campbell, J. K. (1964) *Honour, Family and Patronage*. Oxford: Clarendon Press.

Carawan, E. (1998) *Rhetoric and the Law of Draco*. Oxford: Clarendon Press.

Carey, C. (ed.) (1989) *Lysias. Selected Speeches, Cambridge Greek and Latin Classics.* Cambridge: Cambridge University Press.
(1994) 'Rhetorical means of persuasion', in Worthington (1994a): 26–45.
(1997) *Trials from Classical Athens.* London & New York: Routledge.
Carriere-Hergavault, M. P. (1971). 'Esclaves et affranchis chez les orateurs attiques'. Paper read at Actes du colloque 1971 sur l'esclavage, at Besançon.
Carter, L. B. (1986) *The Quiet Athenian.* Oxford: Clarendon Press.
Cartledge, P. A. (1985) 'Rebels and Sambos in classical Greece: a comparative view', in Cartledge and Harvey (1985): 16–46.
(1989) 'Foreword', in *Classical Sparta: Techniques Behind Her Success*, ed. A. Powell. London: Routledge: x–xiv.
(1990) 'Herodotos and "the other": a meditation on empire', *Echos du Monde Classique/Classical Views* 9: 27–40.
(1993a) *The Greeks. A Portrait of Self and Others.* Oxford, New York: Oxford University Press.
(1993b) 'The silent women of Thucydides: 2.45.2 re-viewed', in Rosen and Farell (1993): 125–32.
(1997) '"Deep plays": theatre as process in Greek civic life', in *The Cambridge Companion to Greek Tragedy*, ed. P. E. Easterling. Cambridge: Cambridge University Press: 3–35.
(1998a) 'Introduction: defining a kosmos', in Cartledge, Millett and von Reden (1998): 1–12.
(1998b) 'The machismo of the Athenian empire – or the reign of the phaulus?' in Foxhall and Salmon (1998): 54–67.
(2000) 'Democratic politics ancient and modern: from Cleisthenes to Mary Robinson', *Hermathena* 199: 5–29.
(2002) 'The economy (*economies*) of ancient Greece', in Scheidel and von Reden (2002): 11–32. Original edition 1998.
Cartledge, P. A. and F. D. Harvey (eds.) (1985) *Crux. Essays Presented to G.E.M. de Ste. Croix.* Exeter: Imprint Academic.
Cartledge, P. A., P. Millett and S. Todd (eds.) (1990) *Nomos. Essays in Athenian Law, Politics and Society.* Cambridge: Cambridge University Press.
Cartledge, P. A., P. Millett and S. von Reden (eds.) (1998) *Kosmos. Essays in Order, Conflict and Community in Classical Athens.* Cambridge: Cambridge University Press.
Charlier, M.-T. and G. Raepsaet (1971) 'Étude d'un comportement social: les relations entre parents et enfants dans la société athénienne à l'époque classique', *L'Antiquité classique* 40: 589–607.
Christ, M. R. (1990) 'Liturgy avoidance and *antidosis* in classical Athens', *Transaction of the American Philological Association* 120: 147–69.
(1998) *The Litigious Athenian.* Baltimore, London: The Johns Hopkins University Press.
(2001) 'Conscription of hoplites in Classical Athens', *Classical Quarterly* 51 (2): 398–422.
Cialdini, R. B. (1984) *Influence. How and Why People Agree to Things.* New York: William Morrow and Co.

(2001) 'The science of persuasion', *Scientific American* February: 62–7.

Cloché, P. (1960) 'Les hommes politiques et la justice populaire dans l'Athènes du IVe siècle', *Historia* 9: 80–95.

Clutton-Brock, T. (2002) 'Breeding together: kins selection and mutualism in cooperative vertebrates', *Science* 296 (5565): 69–72.

Coase, R. H. (1976) 'Adam Smith's view of man', *Journal of Law and Economics* 19: 529–46.

Cohen, D. (1983) *Theft in Athenian Law*. Munich.

(1989) 'Seclusion, separation, and the status of women in classical Athens', *Greece & Rome* 36 (1): 3–15.

(1991a) *Law, Sexuality and Society: The Enforcement of Morals in Classical Athens*. Cambridge: Cambridge University Press.

(1991b) 'Demosthenes' *Against Meidias* and Athenian litigation', in Gagarin (1991): 155–64.

(1995a) *Law, Violence and Community in Classical Athens*. Cambridge: Cambridge University Press.

(1995b) 'Rule of law and democratic ideology in Classical Athens', in Eder (1995a): 227–47.

Cohen, E. E. (1992) *Athenian Economy and Society. A Banking Perspective*. Princeton: Princeton University Press.

(1993) 'The Athenian economy', in Rosen and Farrell (1993): 199–206.

Coldstream, J. N. (1983) 'The meaning of the regional style in the eighth century BC', in Hägg (1983): 17–25.

Cole, S. G. (1996) 'Oath ritual and the male community at Athens', in Ober and Hedricks (1996): 227–48.

Colvin, S. (2000) 'The language of non-Athenians in Old Comedy', in Harvey and Wilkins (2000): 285–98.

Connelly, J. B. (1993) 'The Parthenon frieze and the sacrifice of the Erechteids: reinterpreting the "peplos scene"', *American Journal of Archaeology* 97: 309–10.

(1996) 'Parthenon and *parthenoi*: a mythological interpretation of the Parthenon frieze', *American Journal of Archaeology* 97 (January): 53–80.

Connor, W. R. (1971) *The New Politicians of Fifth-Century Athens*. Princeton: Princeton University Press.

(1994) 'The problem of Athenian civic identity', in Boegehold and Scafuro (1994): 34–44.

Connor, W. R., M. H. Hanse, K. A. Raaflaub and B. S. Strauss (eds.) (1990) *Aspects of Athenian Democracy, Classica et Mediaevalia. Dissertationes*. Copenhagen: Museum Tusculanum Press.

Conophagos, C. (1980) *La Laurion antique et la technique grecque de la production de l'argent*. Athens.

Courtois, G. (ed.) (1984a) *La vengeance dans la pensée occidentale*. 4 vols. Vol. IV, *La vengeance. Études d'ethnologie, d'histoire et de philosophie*. Paris: Editions Cujas.

(1984b) 'Le sens de la valeur de la vengeance, chez Aristote et Sénèque', in Courtois (1984a): 91–124.

Cox, C. A. (1988) 'Sibling relationships in Classical Athens: brother-sister ties', *Journal of Family History* 13 (4): 377–95.

(1998) *Household Interests. Property, Marriage Strategies, and Family Dynamics in Ancient Athens*. Princeton: Princeton University Press.

Coyle-Shapiro, J. A. M. (1999) 'Employee participation and assessment of an organizational change intervention', *The Journal of Applied Behavioural Science* 35 (4): 439–56.

Coyle-Shapiro, J. A. M., P. C. Morrow, R. Richardson and S. R. Dunn (2002) 'Using profit sharing to enhance employee attitudes: a longitudinal examination of the effects on trust and commitment', *Human Resource Management* 41 (4): 423–39.

Cozzi, D. E. (1910) 'La vendetta del sangue nelle montagne dell'alta Albania', *Anthropos* 5: 624–87.

Crane, G. (1992) 'Power, prestige, and the Corcyraean affair in Thucydides', *Classical Antiquity* 11: 1–27.

Crick, B. (1968) 'Sovereignty', in *The International Encyclopedia of the Social Sciences*, vol. xv. Ed. D. L. Sills. The Macmillan Company & The Free Press: 77–82.

Crouch, D. P. (1993) *Water Management In Ancient Greek Cities*. Oxford: Oxford University Press.

Csapo, E. (1993) 'Deep ambivalence: notes on a Greek cockfight', *Phoenix* 47: 1–28, 115–24.

Dahl, R. A. (1985) *A Preface to Economic Democracy*. Berkeley, Los Angeles: University of California Press.

(1998) *On Democracy*. New Haven, London: Yale University Press.

Daux, G. (1958) 'Le devin Cléoboulos', *Bulletin de Correspondance Hellénique* 82: 364–67, with Plate xxiv.

David, E. (1984) *Aristophanes and Athenian Society of the Early Fourth Century B.C.* Leiden: Brill.

Davidson, J. N. (2001) 'Dover, Foucault and Greek homosexuality: penetration and the truth of sex', *Past & Present* 170: 3–51.

Davies, J. K. (1971) *Athenian Propertied Families*. Oxford: Clarendon Press.

(1977–8) 'Athenian citizenship: the descent group and the alternatives', *Classical Journal* 73: 105–21.

(1981) *Wealth and the Power of Wealth in Classical Athens*. Salem, New Hampshire: Arno Press.

(1993) *Democracy and Classical Greece*, 2nd edn. Glasgow: Fontana. Original edition 1978.

(1995) 'The fourth century crisis: What crisis?', in Eder (1995a): 29–39 (including discussion).

Davis, J. (1992) *Exchange*. Buckingham.

Dawkins, R. (1989) *The Selfish Gene*, 2nd edn. Oxford: Oxford University Press. Original edition 1976.

de Polignac, F. (1984) *La Naissance de la cité grecque*. Paris: Editions la Découverte.

de Romilly, J. (1963) *Thucydides and Athenian Imperialism*. Translated by P. Thody. New York: Barnes & Noble.

(1971) 'La vengeance comme explication historique dans l'œuvre d'Hérodote', *Revue des Études Grecques* 84: 314–37.

(1974) 'Fairness and kindness in Thucydides', *Phoenix* 28: 95–100.

(1979) *La Douceur dans la pensée grecque, Collection d'études anciennes*. Paris: Société d'édition 'Les Belles Lettres'.

Demand, N. (1994) *Birth, Death, and Motherhood in Classical Greece*. Baltimore, London: The Johns Hopkins University Press.

Den Boer, W. (1979) *Private Morality in Greece and Rome: Some Historical Aspects*. Leiden: Brill.

Descat, R. (1995) 'L'économie antique et la cité grecque. Un modèle en question', *Annales* 50: 961–89.

Diels, H. and W. Kranz (1964) *Die Fragmente der Vorsokratiker*, 11th edn. 2 vols. Zürich.

Dihle, A. (1982) *The Theory of Will in Classical Antiquity*. Vol. XLVIII, *Sather Classical Lectures*. Berkeley, Los Angeles, London: University of California Press.

Dillon, M. (1995) 'Payments to the disabled at Athens: Social justice or fear of aristocratic patronage?', *Ancient Society* 26: 126–57.

Dodds, E. R. (1951) *The Greeks and the Irrational*. Oxford: Oxford University Press.

(1973a) *The Ancient Concept of Progress and other Essays on Greek Literature and Belief*. Oxford: Clarendon Press.

(1973b) 'The religion of the ordinary man in classical Greece', in Dodds (1973a): 140–55.

(1973c) 'Supernatural phenomena in classical antiquity', in Dodds (1973a): 156–210.

Donlan, W. (1980) *The Aristocratic Ideal in Ancient Greece*. Lawrence, Kansas: Coronado Press.

(1981–2) 'Reciprocities in Homer', *The Classical World* 75: 135–75.

(1982) 'The politics of generosity in Homer', *Helios* 9: 1–15.

(1989) 'The unequal exchange between Glaucus and Diomedes in the light of the Homeric gift-economy', *Phoenix* 43: 1–15.

(1997a) 'The Homeric economy', in *A New Companion to Homer*, eds. I. Morris and B. Powell. Leiden, New York, Cologne: Brill: 649–67.

(1997b) 'The relations of power in the pre-state and early state polities', in *The Development of the Polis in Archaic Greece*, eds. L. G. Mitchell and P. J. Rhodes. London, New York: Routledge: 39–48.

Dorjahn, A. P. (1946) *Political Forgiveness in Old Athens. The Amnesty of 403 B.C.* Evanston: Northwestern University.

Dover, K. J. (1968) *Lysias and the Corpus Lysiacum*. Berkeley, Los Angeles: The University of California Press.

(1972) *Aristophanic Comedy*. Berkeley, Los Angeles: University of California Press.

(1974) *Greek Popular Morality in the Time of Plato and Aristotle*. Oxford: Oxford University Press.

(1978) *Greek Homosexuality*. Cambridge, Mass.: Harvard University Press.

(1983) 'The portrayal of moral evaluation in Greek poetry', *Journal of Hellenic Studies* 103: 35–48.

Dow, S. (1939) 'Aristotle, the kleroteria, and the courts', *Harvard Studies in Classical Philology* 50: 1–34.

Duncan-Jones, R. P. (1980) 'Metic numbers in Periclean Athens', *Chiron* 10: 101–9.

Durham, E. (1909) *High Albania*. London: Virago.

(1927) *Some Tribal Origins, Laws and Customs of the Balkans*. London: George Allen and Unwin.

Easterling, P. E. (1997) 'Constructing the heroic', in *Greek Tragedy and the Historian*, ed. C. Pelling. Oxford: Clarendon Press: 21–37.

Eckstein, F. and J. H. Waszink (1950) 'Amulett', in *Reallexikon für Antike und Christentum*, ed. T. Klauser. Stuttgart: Hiersemann Verlag: 397–411.

Eder, W. (1991) 'Who rules? Power and participation in Athens and Rome', in *Athens and Rome, Florence and Venice. City-States in Classical Antiquity and Medieval Italy*, eds. A. Molho and K. Raaflaub. Stuttgart: Franz Steiner Verlag: 147–72.

(ed.) (1995a) *Die Athenische Demokratie im 4. Jahrhundert v. Chr.* Stuttgart: Steiner.

(1995b) 'Die Athenische Demokratie in 4. Jahrhundert v. Chr. Krise oder Vollendung?', in Eder (1995a): 11–28.

(1997) 'Aristocrats and the coming of Athenian democracy', in *Democracy 2500? Questions and Challenges*, eds. I. Morris and K. A. Raaflaub. Dubuque, Iowa: Kendall/Hunt: 105–40.

Ehrenberg, V. (1946) 'Greek civilization and Greek man', in *Aspects of the Ancient World*, ed. V. Ehrenberg. Oxford: Blackwell: 53–62.

(1951) *The People of Aristophanes*. Oxford: Oxford University Press.

(1954) 'Unwritten laws', in *Sophocles and Pericles*, ed. V. Ehrenberg. Oxford: Blackwell: 22–50.

(1960) *The Greek State*. London: Methuen.

Eibl-Eibesfeldt, I. (1971) *Love and Hate. The Natural History of Behavior Patterns*. Translated by G. Strachan. New York, Chicago, San Francisco: Holt, Rinehart and Winston.

(1972) 'Similarities and differences between cultures in expressive movements', in *Non-Verbal Communication*, ed. R. A. Hinde. Cambridge: Cambridge University Press: 297–314.

(1979) 'Ritual and ritualization from a biological perspective', in von Cranach, Foppa, Lepenies and Ploog (1979): 3–55.

Elias, N. (1978a) *The Civilizing Process*. Translated by E. Jephcott. 2 vols. New York: Blackwell. Original edition 1939.

(1978b) 'On transformations of aggressiveness', *Theory and Society* 5: 229–42.

(1986) 'An essay on sport and violence', in *Quest for Excitement. Sport and Leisure in the Civilizing Process*, eds. N. Elias and E. Dunning. Oxford: Blackwell: 150–74.

Elster, J. and J. E. Roemer (eds.) (1991) *Interpersonal Comparisons of Well-Being, Studies in Rationality and Social Change*. Cambridge: Cambridge University Press.

Erikson, E. H. (1966) 'Ontogeny of ritualization in man', in *A Discussion on Ritualization of Behaviour in Animals and Man*, ed. S. J. Huxley. Philosophical Transactions of the Royal Society, series B, 251: 337–50.

Erxleben, E. (1973) 'Das Kapital der Bank des Pasion und das Privatvermögen der Trapeziten', *Klio* 55: 117–34.

Faraone, C. A. (1985) 'Aeschylus' ὕμνος δέσμιος (*Eum.* 306) and Attic judicial curse tablets', *Journal of Hellenic Studies* 105: 150–4.

Farnell, L. R. (1921) *Greek Hero-Cults and Ideas of Immortality*. Oxford: Clarendon Press.

Farrar, C. (1988) *The Origins of Democratic Thinking*. Cambridge: Cambridge University Press.

Feshbach, S. (1990) 'Psychology, human violence, and the search for peace: issues in science and social values', *Journal of Social Issues* 46 (1): 183–98.

(1995) 'Patriotism and nationalism: two components of national identity with different implications for war and peace', in Hinde and Watson (1995): 153–64.

Field, G. C. (1948) *Plato and his Contemporaries*, 2nd edn. London: Methuen and Co., Ltd. Original edition 1930.

Finley, M. I. (1952) *Studies in Land and Credit in Ancient Athens, 500–200 B.C. The Horos-Inscriptions*. New Brunswick, N.J.: Rutgers University Press.

(ed.) (1960) *Slavery in Classical Antiquity. Views and Controversies*. Cambridge, New York: Heffer – Barnes & Noble.

(1970) *Early Greece: The Bronze and Archaic Ages*. London.

(1972a) 'Introduction', in *Thucydides, The Peloponnesian War*. Translated by Rex Warner. Harmondsworth: Penguin: 9–32.

(1972b) *Knowledge for What?*, Encyclopaedia Britannica Lecture. Edinburgh: Edinburgh University Press.

(1973) *The Ancient Economy*. London: Chatto and Windus.

(1974) 'Athenian demagogues', in *Studies in Ancient Society*, ed. M. I. Finley. London: Routledge and Kegan Paul: 1–25.

(1978a) *The World of Odysseus*, 2nd edn. Harmondsworth: Penguin. Original edition 1954.

(1978b) 'Empire in the Greco-Roman world', *Greece & Rome* 25 (1): 1–15.

(1981a) *Economy and Society in Ancient Greece, by M. I. Finley*. Edited by B. D. Shaw and R. P. Saller. Harmondsworth: Pelican.

(1981b) 'The Athenian empire: a balance sheet', in Shaw and Saller (1981): 41–61. Original edition 1978.

(1981c) 'Land, debt and the man of property in Classical Athens', in Shaw and Saller (1981): 62–76. Original edition 1953.

(1981d) 'The freedom of the citizen in the Greek world', in Shaw and Saller (1981): 77–94. Original edition 1976.

(1981e) 'Was Greek civilization based on slave labour?', in Shaw and Saller (1981): 97–115. Original edition 1959.

(1981f) 'Debt-bondage and the problem of slavery', in Shaw and Saller (1981): 150–66. Original edition 1965.

(1983) *Politics in the Ancient World*. Cambridge: Cambridge University Press.

(1985a) *Democracy Ancient and Modern*, 2nd edn. London: The Hogarth Press. Original edition 1973.

(1985b) *Ancient History. Evidence and Models*. London: Chatto & Windus.

(1998) *Ancient Slavery and Modern Ideology*. Princeton, N.J.: Markus Wiener [expanded edition, by B. D. Shaw]. Original edition 1980.

Fisher, N. R. E. (1992) *Hybris*. Warminster: Aris and Phillips.

(1998) 'Violence, masculinity and the law in classical Athens', in Foxhall and Salmon (1998): 68–97.

(1999) '"Workshops of villains". Was there much organised crime in classical Athens?', in *Organised Crime in Antiquity*, ed. K. Hopwood. London: Duckworth with the Classical Press of Wales: 53–96.

(2000) 'Hybris, revenge and stasis in the Greek city-states', in van Wees (2000): 83–123.

Fisher, N. R. E. and H. van Wees (eds.) (1998) *Archaic Greece. New Approaches and New Evidence*. London, Swansea: Duckworth and the Classical Press of Wales.

Flensted-Jensen, P., T. H. Nielsen and L. Rubinstein (eds.) (2000) *Polis & Politics. Studies in Ancient Greek History Presented to Mogens Herman Hansen on his Sixtieth Birthday*. Copenhagen: Museum of Tusculanum Press.

Fontaine, S. (1978) 'The civilizing process revisited. Interview with Norbert Elias', *Theory and Society* 5: 243–53.

Forrest, W. G. (1966) *The Emergence of Greek Democracy*. London: World University Press.

(1984) 'Herodotus and Athens', *Phoenix* 38: 1–11.

Foxhall, L. (1998a) 'The Greek countryside', in Sparkes (1998): 99–114.

(1998b) 'The politics of affection: emotional attachments in Athenian society', in Cartledge, Millett and von Reden (1998): 52–67.

Foxhall, L. and J. Salmon (eds.) (1998) *When Men were Men. Masculinity, Power and Identity in Classical Antiquity*. London, New York: Routledge.

Freeman, D. (1983) *Margaret Mead and Samoa. The Making and Unmaking of an Anthropological Myth*. Cambridge, Mass., London: Harvard University Press.

(1999) *The Fateful Hoaxing of Margaret Mead. A Historical Analysis of her Samoan Research*. Boulder, Colorado, Oxford: Westview Press.

Freeman, E. A. (1880) 'The Athenian democracy', in *Historical Essays*, by E. A. Freeman. London: Macmillan: 124–81.

Frisch, H. (1949) *Might and Right in Antiquity, I: From Homer to the Persian Wars*. Translated by C. C. Martindale. Copenhagen: Gyldenkalske Boghandel.

Fuks, A. (1984a) *Social Conflict in Ancient Greece*. Jerusalem, Leiden: The Magnes Press – Brill.

(1984b) 'KOLONOS MISTHIOS. Labour exchange in classical Athens', in Fuks (1984a): 303–6.

Fukuyama, F. (1995) *Trust: the Social Virtues and the Creation of Prosperity.* New York, London, Toronto, Sydney, Tokyo, Singapore: Hamish Hamilton.

Gabrielsen, V. (1981) *Remuneration of State Officials in Fourth Century B.C. Athens.* Odense: Odense University Press.

(1987) 'The *antidosis* procedure in classical Athens', *Classica et Mediaevalia* 38: 7–51.

(1994) *Financing the Athenian Fleet. Public Taxation and Social Relations.* Baltimore.

Gagarin, M. (1979) 'The Athenian law against hybris', in *Arktouros. Hellenic Studies presented to B. M. W. Knox*, eds. G. W. Bowersock, W. Burkert and M. C. J. Putnam. Berlin, New York: Walter de Gruyter: 229–36.

(1981) *Drakon and Early Athenian Homicide Law.* New Haven: Yale University Press.

(ed.) (1991) *Symposion 1990. Papers on Greek and Hellenistic Legal History.* Cologne, Weimar, Vienna: Böhlau.

Gager, J. G. (1992) *Curse Tablets and Binding Spells from the Ancient World.* Oxford, New York: Oxford University Press.

Gallant, T. W. (1991) *Risk and Survival in Ancient Greece.* Stanford, Calif.: Stanford University Press.

Garlan, Y. (1988) *Slavery in Ancient Greece.* Translated by J. Lloyd. Ithaca and London: Cornell University Press.

Garland, R. (1984) 'Religious authority in archaic and classical Athens', *Annual of the British School at Athens* 79: 75–123.

(1985) *The Greek Way of Death.* Ithaca, New York: Cornell University Press.

(1987) *The Piraeus.* Ithaca, New York: Cornell University Press.

(1992) *Introducing New Gods. The Politics of Athenian Religion.* Ithaca, New York: Cornell University Press.

Garnsey, P. D. A. (ed.) (1980) *Non-Slave Labour in the Greco-Roman World.* Cambridge: Proceedings of the Cambridge Philological Society.

(1988) *Famine and Food Supply in the Graeco-Roman World: Responses to Risk and Crisis.* Cambridge: Cambridge University Press.

(1992) 'Yield of the land', in Wells (1992): 147–53.

(1996) *Ideas of Slavery from Aristotle to Augustine.* Cambridge: Cambridge University Press.

Garnsey, P. D. A., K. Hopkins and C. R. Whittaker (eds.) (1983) *Trade in the Ancient Economy.* London: Chatto & Windus.

Gay, P. (1993) *The Cultivation of Hatred.* Glasgow: Fontana Press.

Geddes, A. G. (1987) 'Rags and riches: the costume of Athenian men in the fifth century', *Classical Quarterly* 37 (2): 307–31.

Geen, R. G. (1990) *Human Aggression.* Milton Keynes: Open University Press.

(1995) *Human Motivation. A Social Psychological Approach.* Pacific Grove, California: Brooks/Cole Publishing Company.

Gehrke, H.-J. (1985) *Stasis. Untersuchungen zu den inneren Kriegen in den griechischen Staaten des 5. und 4. Jahrhunderts v.Chr.* Vol. 35, *Vestigia.* Munich.

(1987) 'Die Griechen und die Rache. Ein Versuch in historischer Psychologie', *Seculum* 38: 121–49.

Gergen, K. J., M. S. Greenberg and R. H. Willis (eds.) (1980) *Social Exchange: Advances in Theory and Research.* New York: Plenum Press.

Gernet, L. (1924) 'Sur l'execution capitale', *Revue des Études Grecques* 37: 261–93.

(1933) 'Comment caractériser l'économie de la Grèce antique?' *Annales d'histoire économique et sociale* 2: 561–6.

(1939) 'L'institution des arbitres publics à Athènes', *Revue des Études Grecques* 52: 389–414.

(1976a) *Anthropologie de la Grèce antique.* Paris: Maspero.

(1976b) 'Droit et prédroit en Grèce ancienne', in Gernet (1976a): 175–260. Original edition 1951.

Gill, C. (1973) 'The death of Socrates', *Classical Quarterly* 23: 25–6.

Gill, C., N. Postlethwaite and R. Seaford (eds.) (1998) *Reciprocity in Ancient Greece.* Oxford: Clarendon Press.

Gilmore, D. D. (ed.) (1987a) *Honour and Shame and the Unity of the Mediterranean.* Washington, D.C.: American Anthropological Association.

(1987b) 'Introduction. The shame of dishonor', in Gilmore (1987a): 2–21.

(1990) 'On Mediterraneanist studies', *Current Anthropology* 31: 395–96.

Gilsenan, M. (1985) 'Law, arbitrariness and the power of the Lords of North Lebanon', *History and Anthropology* 1: 381–400.

Gilula, D. (2000) 'Hermippus and his catalogue of goods (fr. 63)', in Harvey and Wilkins (2000): 75–90.

Ginat, J. (1997) *Blood Revenge: Family Honor, Mediation and Outcasting.* Brighton: Sussex Academic Press.

Ginzburg, C. (1980) *The Cheese and the Worms. The Cosmos of a Sixteenth-Century Miller.* Translated by J. Tedeschi and A. Tedeschi. Baltimore: The Johns Hopkins University Press.

Giovannini, A. (1991) 'Symbols and rituals in classical Athens', in *Athens and Rome, Florence and Venice. City States in Classical Antiquity and Medieval Italy*, eds. A. Molho, K. Raaflaub and J. Emlen. Stuttgart: Steiner: 459–78.

Glotz, G. (1904a) *L'ordalie dans la Grèce primitive. Étude de droit et de mythologie.* Paris: Albert Fontemoing.

(1904b) *La solidarité de la famille dans le droit criminel en Grèce.* Paris: Albert Fontemoing.

(1908) 'Les esclaves et la peine du fouet en droit grec', *Comptes rendus de l'Académie des Inscriptions et Belles-Lettres*: 571–87.

(1929) *The Greek City and its Institutions.* Translated by N. Mallinson. London: Routledge & Kegan Paul.

Golden, M. (1990) *Children and Childhood in Classical Athens.* Baltimore, London: The Johns Hopkins University Press.

(1998) *Sport and Society in Ancient Greece.* Cambridge: Cambridge University Press.

Goldhill, S. (1986) *Reading Greek Tragedy.* Cambridge: Cambridge University Press.

(1991) 'Violence in Greek tragedy', *Themes in Drama* 13: 15–33.
(2002) 'Battle narrative and politics in Aeschylus' Persae', in Harrison (2002): 50–61.
Gombrich, E. H. (1966) *The Story of Art*, 11th edn. London, New York: Phaidon. Original edition 1950.
(1982) 'Ritualised gesture and expression in art', in *The Image and the Eye* ed. E. H. Gombrich. Oxford: Phaidon: 63–77.
Gomme, A. W. (1925) 'The position of women in Athens in the fifth and fourth centuries BC', *Classical Philology* 20: 1–25.
Gomme, A. W., A. Andrewes and K. J. Dover (1945–81) *A Historical Commentary on Thucydides*. 5 vols. Oxford: Clarendon Press.
Goody, E. (1991) 'The learning of prosocial behaviour in small-scale egalitarian societies: an anthropological view', in Hinde and Groebel (1991): 106–28.
Gould, J. (1989) *Herodotus*. New York: St. Martin's Press.
(1991) *Give and Take in Herodotus*. Oxford: The Fifteenth J. L. Myres Memorial Lecture.
Gould, T. (1991) 'The uses of violence in drama', *Themes in Drama* 13: 1–13.
Gouldner, A. W. (1960) 'The norm of reciprocity: a preliminary statement', *American Sociological Review* 25: 161–78.
Graham, A. J. (1992) 'Thucydides 7.13.2 and the crews of Athenian triremes', *Transactions of the Americal Philological Association* 122: 257–70.
(1998) 'Thucydides 7.13.2 and the crews of Athenian triremes: an addendum', *Transactions of the Americal Philological Association* 128: 89–114.
Graham, J. W. (1974) 'Houses of classical Athens', *Phoenix* 28: 45–54.
Graves, R. (1955) *The Greek Myths*. 2 vols. Harmondsworth: Pelican.
Greenberg, M. S. (1980) 'A theory of indebtedness', in Gergen, Greenberg and Willis (1980): 3–26.
Greif, A. (2000) 'The fundamental problem of exchange: a research agenda in historical institutional analysis', *European Review of Economic History* 4 (3): 251–84.
Griffith, G. T. (1966) 'Isegoria in the Assembly at Athens', in *Ancient Society and Institutions. Studies Presented to Victor Ehrenberg*. Oxford: Blackwell: 115–38.
Groebel, J. and R. A. Hinde (eds.) (1989) *Aggression and War. Their Biological and Social Bases*. Cambridge: Cambridge University Press.
Gröschel, S.-G. (1989) *Waffenbesitz und Waffeneinsatz bei den Griechen*. Frankfurt am Main: Peter Lang.
Hadas, M. (1936) 'Observations on Athenian women', *The Classical World* 29: 97–100.
Hägg, R. (ed.) (1983) *The Greek Renaissance of the Eighth Century B.C.. Tradition and Innovation*. Stockholm: Acta Instituti Atheniensis Regni Sueciae.
Hall, M. D. (1996) 'Even dogs have Erinyes: Sanctions in Athenian practice and thinking', in *Greek Law in its Political Setting: Justifications not Justice*, eds. L. Foxhall and A. D. E. Lewis. Oxford: Clarendon Press: 73–89.
Halliday, W. R. (1913) *Greek Divination*. London.

Hamilton, W. D. (1964) 'The genetical theory of social behaviour', *Journal of Theoretical Biology* 7: 1–52.

Hammond, N. G. L. (1967) 'The origins and the nature of the Athenian alliance of 478/7 BC', *Journal of Hellenic Studies* 87: 41–61.

(1985a) 'Arbitration in ancient Greece', *Arbitration International* 1: 188–90.

(1985b) 'The scene in Iliad 18, 497–508 and the Albanian blood-feud', *Bulletin of the American Society of Papyrologists* 22: 79–86.

Hansen, M. H. (1974) *The Sovereignty of the People's Court in Athens in the Fourth Century B.C. and The Public Action against Unconstitutional Proposals*, Odense University Classical Studies, vol. IV. Odense: Odense University Press.

(1976) *Apagoge, Endeixis and Ephegesis against Kakourgoi, Atimoi and Pheugontes: A Study in the Athenian Administration of Justice in the Fourth Century B.C.* Odense University Classical Studies, vol. VIII. Odense: Odense University Press.

(1978) '*Demos, ecclesia*, and *dicasterion* in classical Athens', *Greek, Roman and Byzantine Studies* 19: 127–46.

(1979) 'Misthos for magistrates in classical Athens', *Symbolae Osloenses* 54: 5–22.

(1981) 'Initiative and decision: the separation of powers in fourth-century Athens', *Greek, Roman and Byzantine Studies* 22: 345–70.

(1981–2) 'The Athenian Heliaia from Solon to Aristotle', *Classica & Mediaevalia* 33: 9–47.

(1986) 'The origin of the term demokratia', *Liverpool Classical Monthly* (11): 35–6.

(1987) *The Athenian Assembly in the Age of Demosthenes*. Oxford: Blackwell.

(1991) *The Athenian Democracy in the Age of Demosthenes*. Translated by J. Crook. Oxford: Oxford University Press.

(1994) 'The 2500th anniversary of Cleisthenes' reforms and the tradition of Athenian democracy', in Osborne and Hornblower (1994): 25–37.

(1996) 'Democracy, Athens', in *OCD³*: 101–7.

(2002) 'Was the polis a state or a stateless society?', in *Even More Studies in the Ancient Greek Polis*, ed. T. H. Nielsen. Stuttgart: Franz Steiner: 17–47.

Hanson, V. D. (ed.) (1991a) *Hoplites. The Classical Greek Battle Experience*. London, New York: Routledge.

(1991b) 'The ideology of hoplite battle, ancient and modern', in Hanson (1991a): 3–11.

(1991c) 'Hoplite technology in phalanx battle', in Hanson (1991a): 63–84.

(1992) 'Thucydides and the desertion of Attic slaves during the Decelean War', *Classical Antiquity* 11 (2): 210–28.

(1996) 'Hoplites into democrats: the changing ideology of Athenian infantry', in Ober and Hedrick (1996): 289–312.

(1998) *Warfare and Agriculture in Classical Greece*. Berkeley, Los Angeles, London: University of California Press.

Hardin, G. (1968) 'The tragedy of the commons', *Science* 162: 1243–8.

(1978) 'Nice guys finish last', in *Sociobiology and Human Nature*, eds. M. S. Gregory, A. Silvers and D. Sutch. San Francisco, Washington, London: Jossey-Bass: 183–94.

Hare, R. M. (1952) *The Language of Morals*. Oxford: Oxford University Press.

Harris, E. M. (1988) 'When is a sale not a sale? The riddle of Athenian terminology for real security revisited', *Classical Quarterly* 38: 351–81.

(1989) 'Demosthenes' speech Against Meidias', *Harvard Studies in Classical Philology* 92: 117–36.

(1990) 'Did the Athenians regard seduction as a worse crime than rape?', *Classical Quarterly* 40: 370–7.

(1994) 'Law and oratory', in Worthington (1994a): 130–50.

(1995) *Aeschines and Athenian Politics*. New York, Oxford: Oxford University Press.

(1999) 'The penalty for frivolous prosecutions in Athenian law', *Dike* 2: 123–42.

(2001) 'Review of Alain Bresson, La cité marchande', *Bryn Mawr Classical Review* 09.40.

(2002a) 'Pheidippides the legislator: a note on Aristophanes' *Clouds*', *Zeitschrift für Papyrologie und Epigraphik* 140: 3–5.

(2002b) 'Did Solon abolish debt-bondage?' *Classical Quarterly* 52 (2): 415–30.

(2004a) 'Feuding or the rule of law? The nature of litigation in classical Athens. An essay in legal sociology', in *Symposion. Papers on Greek and Hellenistic Legal History*, ed. M. Gagarin. (forthcoming).

(2004b) 'Workshop, marketplace and household. The nature of technical specialization in classical Athens and its influence on economy and society', in *Kerdos. Money, Labour and Land in Ancient Greece*, eds. P. A. Cartledge, L. Foxhall and E. E. Cohen. Cambridge: Cambridge University Press: 67–99.

Harris, W. V. (1997) 'Lysias III and Athenian beliefs about revenge', *Classical Quarterly* 47: 363–6.

(2001) *Restraining Rage. The Ideology of Anger Control in Classical Antiquity*. Cambridge, Mass., London: Harvard University Press.

Harrison, A. R. W. (1971) *The Law of Athens. Procedure*, vol. II. Oxford: Clarendon Press.

Harrison, T. (ed.) (2002) *Greeks and Barbarians*. New York: Routledge.

Hart, H. L. A. (1961) *The Concept of Law*. Oxford: Clarendon Press.

Hartog, F. (1988) *The Mirror of Herodotus: The Representation of the Other in the Writing of History*. Translated by J. Lloyd. Berkeley, Los Angeles, London: University of California Press. Original edition 1980.

Harvey, D. and J. Wilkins (eds.) (2000) *The Rivals of Aristophanes. Studies in Athenian Old Comedy*. London: Duckworth and the Classical Press of Wales.

Harvey, F. D. (1985) 'Dona ferentes: some aspects of bribery in Greek politics', in Cartledge and Harvey (1985): 76–117.

Hauert, C., S. De Monte, J. Hofbauer and K. Sigmund (2002) 'Vounteering as Red Queen mechanism for cooperation in public goods games', *Science* 296 (5570): 1129–32.

Havelock, E. A. (1957) *The Liberal Temper in Greek Politics*. London: Jonathan Cape.

Heitsch, E. (1984) *Aidesis im attischen Strafrecht*. Mainz: Akademie der Wissenschaften.

Herlihy, D. (1972) 'Some psychological and social roots of violence in the Tuscan cities', in *Violence and Civil Disorder in Italian Cities, 1200–1500*, ed. L. Martines. Berkeley: University of California Press: 129–54.

Herman, G. (1987) *Ritualised Friendship and the Greek City*. Cambridge: Cambridge University Press.

(1993) 'Tribal and civic codes of behaviour in Lysias 1', *Classical Quarterly* 43: 406–19.

(1994) 'How violent was Athenian society?', in Osborne and Hornblower (1994): 99–117.

(1995) 'Honour, revenge and the state in fourth-century Athens', in Eder (1995a): 43–66.

(1996a) 'Classical Athens and the values of mediterranean society', *Mediterranean Historical Review* 11: 5–36.

(1996b) 'Gift-exchange', in *OCD³*: 637.

(1996c) 'Reciprocity', in *OCD³*: 1295.

(1996d) 'Friendship, Greece', in *OCD³*: 611.

(1996e) 'Friendship, ritualised', in *OCD³*: 611.

(1998a) 'Reciprocity, altruism and the prisoner's dilemma: the special case of classical Athens', in Gill, Postlethwaite and Seaford (1998): 199–225.

(1998b) 'Review of D. Cohen, *Law, Violence and Community in Classical Athens*', *Gnomon* 70: 605–15.

(1998c) 'Review of D. Konstan, *Friendship in the Classical World*', *Journal of Roman Studies* 88: 181–2.

(2000a) 'Athenian beliefs about revenge: problems and methods', *Proceedings of the Cambridge Philological Society* 46: 7–27.

(2000b) 'La rhétorique du tribunal dans la démocratie athénienne', in *Écriture de soi et argumentation*, ed. N. Kuperty-Tsur. Caen, Tel-Aviv: Université de Caen, Université de Tel-Aviv.

Hesk, J. (2000) *Deception and Democracy in Classical Athens*. Cambridge: Cambridge University Press.

Hester, D. A. (1977) 'To help one's friends and harm one's enemies. A study in the *Oedipus at Colonus*', *Antichthon* 11: 22–41.

Hinde, R. A. (ed.) (1991a) *The Institution of War*. Basingstoke, London: Macmillan.

(1991b) 'A note on patriotism and nationalism', in Hinde (1991a): 148–54.

(1997) 'War: some psychological causes and consequences', *Interdisciplinary Science Reviews* 22 (3): 229–44.

Hinde, R. A. and J. Groebel (eds.) (1991) *Cooperation and Prosocial Behaviour*. Cambridge: Cambridge University Press.

Hinde, R. A. and H. E. Watson (eds.) (1995) *War: A Cruel Necessity? The Bases of Institutionalized Violence*. London, New York: Tauris Academic Studies.

Hirzel, R. (1900) *Agraphos Nomos*. Leipzig: Teubner.

(1902) *Der Eid*. Leipzig: Verlag von S. Hirzel. Reprinted 1979: Arno Press.

(1907–10) 'Die Talion', *Philologus Supplementband* 11: 408–82.

Hobbes, T. (1983) *Leviathan*, 9th edn. Glasgow: Collins. Original edition 1651.

Hobhouse, L. T. (1915) *Morals in Evolution.* 2 vols. London: Chapman & Hall. Original edition 1906.

Hochschild, A. R. (1979) 'Emotion work, feeling rules, and social structure', *American Journal of Sociology* 85 (3): 551–75.

(1983) *The Managed Heart: The Commercialization of Human Feeling.* Berkeley: University of California Press.

Hoepfner, W. and E.-L. Schwandner (1986) *Haus und Stadt im klassischen Griechenland. Wohnen in der klassischen Polis.* Munich: Deutscher Kunstverlag.

Hoffmann, H. (1974) 'Hahnenkampf in Athen. Zur Ikonologie einer attischen Bildformel', *Revue Archéologique*: 195–220.

(1997) *Sotades. Symbols of Immortality on Greek Vases.* Oxford: Clarendon Press.

Hogg, M. A. and G. M. Vaughan (1995) *Social Psychology*, 2nd edn. Harlow, London, New York: Prentice Hall.

Hölkeskamp, K.-J. (1998) 'Parteiungen und politische Willensbildung im demokratischen Athen: Perikles und Thukydides, Sohn des Melesias', *Historische Zeitschrift* 267: 1–27.

(1999) *Schiedsrichter, Gesetzgeber und Gesetzgebung im archaischen Griechenland*, vol. 131, *Historia-Einzelschrift.* Stuttgart: Franz Steiner.

Hollingdale, R. J. (1999) *Nietzsche. The Man and His Philosophy.* Cambridge: Cambridge University Press. Original edition 1965.

Holmes, D. S. (1968) 'Dimensions of projection', *Psychological Bulletin* 69 (4): 248–68.

Holmes, L. D. (1987) *Quest for the Real Samoa. The Mead/Freeman Controversy & Beyond.* Massachusetts: Bergin & Garvey Publishers.

Homans, G. C. (1951) *The Human Group.* London: Routledge & Kegan Paul.

(1957–8) 'Social behaviour as exchange', *American Journal of Sociology* 63: 597–606.

Horden, P. and N. Purcell (2000) *The Corrupting Sea. A Study of Mediterranean History.* Oxford: Blackwell.

Hornblower, S. (1983) *The Greek World 479–323 BC.* London, New York: Methuen.

Hughes, D. D. (1991) *Human Sacrifice in Ancient Greece.* London, New York: Routledge.

Humphreys, S. C. (1977–8) 'Public and private interests in classical Athens', *Classical Journal* 73: 97–104.

(1978) *Anthropology and the Greeks.* London: Routledge & Kegan Paul.

(1983a) *The Family, Women and Death: Comparative Studies.* London: Routledge & Kegan Paul.

(1983b) 'The evolution of social process in Attica', in *Tria Corda: Studi in onore de Arnaldo Momigliano*, ed. E. Gabba. Como: Edizioni New Press: 229–56.

(1985) 'Social relations on stage: witnesses in Classical Athens', *History & Anthropology* 21: 313–69.

(1991) 'A historical approach to Drakon's law on homicide', in Gagarin (1991): 17–45.

Hunter, V. (1986) 'Thucydides, Gorgias and mass psychology', *Hermes* 114: 412–29.

(1988–9) 'Thucydides and the sociology of the crowd', *Classical Journal* 84: 17–30.

(1989) 'The Athenian widow and her kin', *Journal of Family History* 14: 291–311.

(1990) 'Gossip and the politics of reputation in Classical Athens', *Phoenix* 44: 299–325.

(1992) 'Constructing the body of the citizen: corporal punishment in Classical Athens', *Echos du Monde Classique* 36: 271–91.

(1994) *Policing Athens. Social Control in the Attic Lawsuits, 420–320 B.C.* Princeton: Princeton University Press.

Hunter, V. and J. Edmondson (eds.) (2000) *Law and Social Status in Classical Athens.* Oxford: Oxford University Press.

Irons, W. (1979) 'Natural selection, adaptation, and human social behaviour', in *Evolutionary Biology and Human Social Behaviour*, eds. N. A. Chagnon and W. Irons. North Scituate, Massachusetts: Duxbury Press: 4–38.

Jackson, A. H. (1969) 'The original purpose of the Delian League', *Historia* 18: 12–16.

Jameson, M. (1977–8) 'Agriculture and slavery in classical Athens', *Classical Journal* 73: 122–41.

(1992) 'Agricultural labor in ancient Greece', in Wells (1992): 135–46.

(1997a) 'Religion in the Athenian democracy', in *Democracy 2500? Questions and Challenges*, eds. I. Morris and K. A. Raaflaub. Dubuque, Iowa: Kendall/Hunt: 171–95.

(1997b) 'Women and democracy in fourth-century Athens', in *Esclavage, guerre, économie en Grèce ancienne. Hommages à Yvon Garlan*, eds. P. Brulé and J. Oulhen. Rennes: Presses Universitaires de Rennes: 95–107.

Johnson, G. R. (1986) 'Kin selection, socialisation and patriotism: an integrating theory', *Politics and the Life Sciences* 4: 127–40.

(1989) 'The role of kin recognition mechanisms in patriotic socialization: further reflections', *Politics and the Life Sciences* 8: 62–9.

Johnson, R. G., S. H. Ratwik and T. J. Sawyer (1987) 'The evocative significance of kin terms in patriotic speech', in Reynolds, Falger and Vine (1987): 157–74.

Jones, A. H. M. (1957) *Athenian Democracy.* Oxford: Blackwell.

Jones, F. W. (1941) 'The formulation of the revenge motif in the *Odyssey*', *Transactions and Proceedings of the American Philological Association* 72: 195–202.

Jones, J. E. (1975) 'Town and country houses of Attica in classical times', in *Thorikos and the Laurion in Archaic and Classical Times*, ed. H. Mussche. Ghent: Belgian Archaeological Mission in Greece in collaboration with the Seminar for Greek Archaeology of the State University of Ghent.

Jones, J. E., L. H. Sackett and A. J. Graham (1962) 'The dema house in Attica', *Annual of the British School at Athens* 57: 75–114.

Jordan, B. (1975) *The Athenian Navy in the Classical Period: A Study of Athenian Naval Administration and Military Organization in the Fifth and Fourth Centuries B.C.* Vol. XIII, *University of California Publications in Classical Studies.* Berkeley: University of California Press.

Jordan, D. R. (2000) 'A personal letter found in the Athenian agora', *Hesperia* 69: 91–103.

Just, R. (1989) *Women in Athenian Law and Life*. London: Routledge.

Kagan, D. (1991) *Pericles of Athens and the Birth of Democracy*. New York, London, Toronto, Sydney, Tokyo, Singapore: Simon & Schuster.

Kaimio, M. (1992) 'Violence in Greek tragedy', in Viljamaa, Timonen and Krötzl (1992): 28–40.

Kallet-Marx, L. (1993) *Money, Expense and Naval Power in Thucydides' History*. Berkeley: University of California Press.

Kallet, L. (2001) *Money and the Corrosion of Power in Thucydides*. Berkeley, Los Angeles, London: University of California Press.

Karabélias, E. (1991) 'La peine dans Athènes classique', *Recueils de la société Jean Bodin* 55 (1): 77–132.

Karavites, P. (1982) *Capitulations and Inter-State Relations. The Reflection of Humanistic Ideals in Political Events*. Göttingen: Vanderhoeck & Ruprecht.

Kassel, R. and C. Austin. (1983–) *Poetae comici Graeci*. 8 vols. (published so far). Berlin: de Gruyter.

Kennedy, G. (1963) *The Art of Persuasion in Greece*. Princeton, N.J.: Routledge & Kegan Paul.

  (1973) 'Introduction', in *The Speeches in Thucydides*, ed. P. A. Stadter. Chapel Hill: University of North Carolina Press.

Kerferd, G. R. (1955–9) 'The moral and political doctrines of Antiphon the sophist. A reconsideration', *Proceedings of the Cambridge Philological Society* 184, n.s. 4: 26–32.

Keuls, E. C. (1985) *The Reign of the Phallus*. Berkeley, Los Angeles, London: University of California Press.

Kirk, G. S., J. E. Raven and M. Schofield (1983) *The Presocratic Philosophers*, 2nd edn. Cambridge: Cambridge University Press. Original edition 1957.

Kitto, H. D. F. (1969) *The Greeks*. Harmondsworth: Penguin.

Kittredge, G. L. (1885) 'Arm-pitting among the Greeks', *American Journal of Philology* 6: 151–69.

Kluckhohn, C. (1942) 'Myths and rituals: a general theory', *Harvard Theological Review* 35: 45–79.

Knox, B. M. W. (1957) *Oedipus at Thebes*. New York: The Norton Library.

  (1961) 'The Ajax of Sophocles', *Harvard Studies in Classical Philology* 65: 1–37.

  (1989) 'Thucydides and the Peloponnesian War: politics and power', in *Essays Ancient and Modern*, ed. B. Knox. Baltimore: The Johns Hopkins University Press: 92–109.

Knox, R. A. (1985) '"So mischievous a beaste"? The Athenian demos and its treatment of its politicians', *Greece & Rome* 32: 132–61.

Konstan, D. (1997) *Friendship in the Ancient World*. Cambridge: Cambridge University Press.

  (1998) 'Reciprocity and friendship', in Gill, Postlethwaite and Seaford (1998): 279–301.

Kraay, C. M. (1975) *Archaic and Classical Greek Coins*. London.

Krebs, D. L. (1970) 'Altruism – an examination of the concept and a review of the literature', *Psychological Bulletin* 73: 258–302.

Krentz, P. (1982) *The Thirty at Athens*. Ithaca, New York: Cornell University Press.

(1985) 'Casualties in hoplite battles', *Greek, Roman and Byzantine Studies* 26: 14–20.

Kressel, G. M. (1981) 'Sororicide/filiacide: homicide for family honour', *Current Anthropology* 22: 141–58.

Kropotkin, P. (1939) *Mutual Aid: A Factor of Evolution*. Harmondsworth: Penguin. Original edition 1902.

Kuenzi, A. (1979) *Epidosis*. New York. Original edition 1923.

Kurihara, A. (2003) 'Personal enmity as a motivation in forensic speeches', *Classical Quarterly* 53 (2): 464–77.

Labarbe, J. (1957) *La Loi Navale de Themistocle*. Vol. CXLIII, *Bibliothèque de la Faculté de Philosophie et Lettres de l'Université de Liège*. Paris: Les Belles Lettres.

Lafaye, G. (1877–1919) 'Rota (*trochos*)', in *Dictionnaire des antiquités grecques et romaines*, eds. C. Daremberg and E. Saglio. Paris: Hachette: 896–7.

Lane Fox, R. (1985) 'Aspects of inheritance in the Greek world', in Cartledge and Harvey (1985): 208–32.

Laski, H. J. (1935) *The State in Theory and Practice*. London: George Allen & Unwin Ltd.

Laslett, P. (1956a) 'The face to face society', in Laslett (1956b): 157–84.

(ed.) (1956b) *Philosophy, Politics and Society*. Oxford: Blackwell.

(1976) 'The wrong way through the telescope: a note on literary evidence in sociology and in historical sociology', *British Journal of Sociology* 27 (3): 319–42.

Latte, K. (1968) 'Kollektivbesitz und Staatsschatz in Griechenland', in *Kleine Schriften zu Religion, Recht, Literatur und Sprache der Griechen und Römer*, eds. O. Gigon, W. Buchwald and W. Kunkel. Munich: Beck: 294–312.

Lauffer, S. (1974) 'Die Liturgien in der Krisenperiode Athens', in *Hellenische Poleis*, ed. E. C. Welskopf. Berlin: Akademie-Verlag: 146–59.

(1979) *Die Bergwerkssklaven von Laureion*, 2nd edn. 2 vols. Vol. XI–XII. Mainz: Akademie der Wissenschaften und der Literatur. Abhandlungen des Geistes- und Sozialwissenschaftlischen Klasse. Original edition, 1955.

Lavelle, B. M. (1988) 'Adikia, the decree of Kannonos, and the trial of the generals', *Classica et Mediaevalia* 39: 19–41.

Lawler, L. B. (1964) *The Dance in Ancient Greece*. London: Adam & Charles Black.

Lazenby, J. (1991) 'The killing zone', in Hanson (1991a): 87–109.

Lehmann, G. A. (1972) 'Die revolutionäre Machtergreifung der "Dreißig" und die staatliche Teilung Attikas (404–401/) v. Chr', in *Antike und Univer- salgeschichte, Festschrift Hans Erich Stier*, eds. R. Stiehl and G. A. Lehmann. Münster: Verlag Aschendorff: 201–33.

Lemaire, A. (1984) 'Vengeance et justice dans l'ancien Israel', in Verdier and Poly (1984): 13–33.

Lendon, J. E. (1997) 'Spartan honor', in *Polis and Polemos. Essays on Politics, War, and History in Ancient Greece in Honor of Donald Kagan*, eds. C. D. Hamilton and P. Krentz. Claremont, California: Regina Books: 105–26.
    (2000) 'Homeric vengeance and the outbreak of Greek wars', in van Wees (2000): 1–30.
Lenfant, D. (2001) 'Mélange ethnique et emprunts culturels: leur perception et leur valeur dans l'Athènes classique', in *Origines Gentium*, eds. V. Fromentin and S. Gotteland. Bordeaux: de Boccard.
Lesky, A. (1961) 'Göttliche und menschliche Motivation im homerischen Epos', in *Sitzungsberichte der Heidelberger Akademie der Wissenschaften, Philosophisch-historische Klasse*. Heidelberg: Karl Winter Universitätsverlag: 5–52.
Lévêque, P. and P. Vidal-Naquet (1964) *Clisthène L'Athénien*. Paris: Macula.
Lévy, E. (1976a) *Athènes devant la défaite de 404. Histoire d'une crise idéologique*. Athens, Paris: École française d'Athènes.
    (1976b) 'Les femmes chez Aristophane', *Ktema* 1: 99–112.
Lewis, D. M. (1966) 'After the profanation of the mysteries', in *Ancient History and Institutions: Studies Presented to Victor Ehrenberg*. Oxford: Blackwell: 177–91.
    (1973) 'The Athenian rationes centesimarum', in *Problèmes de la terre en Grèce ancienne*, ed. M. I. Finley. Paris, La Haye: Mouton & Co.: 187–212.
    (1992) 'The Archidamian War', in Lewis, Boardman, Davies and Ostwald (1992): 370–432.
    (1993) 'Oligarchic thinking in the late fifth century', in Rosen and Farell (1993): 207–11.
Lewis, D. M., J. Boardman, J. K. Davies and M. Ostwald (eds.) (1992) *The Cambridge Ancient History*, 2nd edn. Vol. v. Cambridge: Cambridge University Press.
Lewis, S. (1996) *News and Society in the Greek Polis*. London: Duckworth.
    (2002) *The Athenian Woman: An Iconographic Handbook*. London: Routledge.
Lintott, A. (1982) *Violence, Civil Strife and Revolution in the Classical City*. London: Croom Helm.
    (1992) 'Cruelty in the political life of the ancient world', in Viljamaa, Timonen and Krötzl (1992): 9–27.
Lipsius, J. H. (1905–14) *Das attische Recht und Rechtsverfahren*. 4 vols. Leipzig.
Lissarrague, F. (2002) 'The Athenian image of the foreigner', in Harrison (2002): 101–24.
Lloyd, G. E. R. (1990) *Demystifying Mentalities*. Cambridge: Cambridge University Press.
Lloyd-Jones, H. (1971) *The Justice of Zeus*: University of California Press.
    (1990) 'Honour and shame in ancient Greek culture', in *Greek Comedy, Hellenistic Literature, Greek Religion and Miscellanea*. Oxford: Clarendon Press: 253–80.
Loening, T. C. (1987) *The Reconciliation Agreement of 403/402 B.C. in Athens*. Vol. LIII, *Hermes-Einzelschrift*. Stuttgart: Franz Steiner.

Lohmann, H. (1992) 'Agriculture and country life in classical Attica', in Wells (1992): 29–60.

(1993) *Atene. Forschungen zur Siedlungs- und Wirtschaftsstruktur des klassischen Attika*. 2 vols. Köln: Böhlau Verlag.

(1995) 'Die Chora Athens im 4. Jahrhundert v.Chr.', in Eder (1995a): 545–53.

Lonsdale, S. H. (1993) *Dance and Ritual Play in Greek Religion*. Baltimore, London: The Johns Hopkins University Press.

Loomis, W. T. (1972) 'The nature of premeditation in Athenian homicide law', *Journal of Hellenic Studies* 92: 86–95.

(1998) *Wages, Welfare Costs and Inflation in Classical Athens*. Ann Arbor: The University of Michigan Press.

Loraux, N. (1986) *The Invention of Athens: The Funeral Oration in the Classical City*. Translated by A. Sheridan. Cambridge, Mass. Original edition 1981.

Loraux, N. and P. Vidal-Naquet (1979) 'La formation de l'Athènes bourgeoise: essai d'historiographie 1750–1850', in *Classical Influences on Western Thought AD 1650–1870*, ed. R. R. Bolgar. Cambridge, London, New York, Melbourne: 169–222.

Lorenz, K. (1965) *Evolution and Modification of Behaviour*. Chicago: The University of Chicago Press.

Low, P. (2002) 'Cavalry identity and democratic ideology in early fourth-century Athens', *Proceedings of the Cambridge Philological Society* 48: 102–19.

MacDowell, D. M. (1963a) *Athenian Homicide Law in the Age of the Orators*. Manchester: Manchester University Press.

(1963b) 'APETH and generosity', *Mnemosyne* 16: 127–34.

(1978) *The Law in Classical Athens*. London: Thames and Hudson.

(ed.) (1990) *Demosthenes, Against Meidias (Oration 21)*. Oxford: Clarendon Press.

MacIntyre, A. C. (1967) *A Short History of Ethics. A History of Moral Philosophy from the Homeric Age to the Twentieth Century*. London: Routledge.

(1981) *After Virtue. A Study in Moral Theory*. London: Duckworth.

Mackenzie, M. M. (1981) *Plato on Punishment*. Berkeley, Los Angeles, London: University of California Press.

Manville, P. B. (1990) *The Origins of Citizenship in Ancient Athens*. Princeton: Princeton University Press.

Markle, M. M. (1985) 'Jury pay and assembly pay at Athens', in Cartledge and Harvey (1985): 265–97.

Martin, T. R. (1985) *Sovereignty and Coinage in Classical Greece*. Princeton, N.J.: Princeton University Press.

Masters, R. G. (1978) 'Marmots and men: animal behaviour and human altruism', in Wispé (1978): 59–77.

Mattingly, H. B. (1966) 'Periclean imperialism', in *Ancient Society and Institutions. Studies Presented to Victor Ehrenberg*. Oxford: Blackwell: 193–224.

(1997) 'The date and purpose of the Pseudo-Xenophon constitution of Athens', *Classical Quarterly* 47: 352–57.

Mauss, M. (1966) *The Gift*. Translated by I. Cunnison. London: Routledge and Kegan Paul. Original edition 1925.

McAleer, K. (1994) *Dueling: The Cult of Honor in Fin-de-Siècle Germany*. Princeton: Princeton University Press.

Mead, M. (1928) *Coming of Age in Samoa*. Harmondsworth: Penguin.

Meier, C. (1990) *The Greek Discovery of Politics*. Translated by D. McLintock. Cambridge Mass., London: Harvard University Press.

(1998) *Athens. A Portrait of the City in Its Golden Age*. New York: Holt.

Meiggs, R. (1972) *The Athenian Empire*. Oxford: Clarendon Press.

Meikle, S. (1995) 'Modernism, economics, and the ancient economy', *Proceedings of the Cambridge Philological Society* 41: 174–91.

Meritt, B. D. (1952) 'Greek inscriptions', *Hesperia* 23: 340–80.

Mesterton-Gibbons, M. and E. S. Adams (2002) 'The economics of animal cooperation', *Science* 298 (5601): 2146–7.

Meyer-Laurin, H. (1965) *Gesetz und Billigkeit im attischen Prozess*. Weimar: Hermann Böhlaus Nachfolger.

Millar, F. (1999) *The Crowd in Rome in the Late Republic*. Ann Arbor: University of Michigan Press.

(2002) *The Roman Republic in Political Thought*. Hanover, NH: University Press of New England for Brandeis University Press.

Miller, S. G. (2000) 'Naked democracy', in Flensted-Jensen, Nielsen and Rubinstein (2000): 277–96.

Millett, P. (1989) 'Patronage and its avoidance in classical Athens', in *Patronage in Ancient Society*, ed. A. Wallace-Hadrill. London: Routledge: 15–47.

(1990) 'Sale, credit and exchange in Athenian law and society', in Cartledge, Millett and Todd (1990): 167–214.

(1991) *Lending and Borrowing in Ancient Athens*. Cambridge: Cambridge University Press.

(1998) 'The rhetoric of reciprocity in classical Athens', in Gill, Postlethwaite and Seaford (1998): 227–53.

(2000) 'Mogens Hansen and the labelling of Athenian democracy', in Flensted-Jensen, Nielsen and Rubinstein (2000): 337–62.

Mion, M. R. (1991) 'Tolerance and *arete* in fifth century Athens', in *Human Virtue and Human Excellence*, eds. A. W. H. Adkins, J. K. Lowrence and C. K. Ihara. New York, San Francisco, Bern, Frankfurt am Main, Paris, London: Peter Lang: 45–72.

Missiou, A. (1992) *The Subversive Oratory of Andokides*. Cambridge: Cambridge University Press.

(1998) 'Reciprocal generosity in the foreign affairs of fifth-century Athens and Sparta', in Gill, Postlethwaite and Seaford (1998): 181–97.

Mitchell, L. G. (1996) 'New for old: friendship networks in Athenian politics 1', *Greece & Rome* 43 (1): 11–30.

(1997) *Greeks Bearing Gifts. The Public Use of Private Relationships in the Greek World, 435–323 BC*. Cambridge: Cambridge University Press.

Molm, L. D. (1997) *Coercive Power in Social Exchange, Studies in Rationality and Social Change*. Cambridge: Cambridge University Press.

Monroe, K. R. (1996) *The Heart of Altruism. Perceptions of Common Humanity.* Princeton: Princeton University Press.

Montagu, A. (ed.) (1978) *Learning Non-Aggression. The Experience of Non-Literate Societies.* Oxford: Oxford University Press.

Morgan, C. (1991) 'Ethnicity and early Greek states: historical and material perspectives', *Proceedings of the Cambridge Philological Society* 37: 131–63.

Morgan, G. (1982) 'Euphiletos' house: Lysias 1', *Transactions and Proceedings of the American Philological Association* 112: 115–23.

Morris, D. (1977) *Manwatching.* London, Glasgow, Toronto, Sydney, Auckland: Grafton Books.

(1999) *Body Guards: Protective Amulets and Charms.* Element Books.

Morris, I. (1986a) 'Gift and commodity in archaic Greece', *Man* 21: 1–17.

(1986b) 'The use and abuse of Homer', *Classical Antiquity* 5: 81–138.

(1991) 'The early polis as city and state', in Rich and Wallace-Hadrill (1991): 25–58.

(1994a) 'The Athenian economy twenty years after *The Ancient Economy*', *Classical Philology* 89: 351–66.

(1994b) 'Everyman's grave', in Boegehold and Scafuro (1994): 67–101.

(1996) 'The strong principle of equality and the archaic origins of Greek democracy', in Ober and Hedrick (1996): 19–48.

Morrison, J. S. (1961) 'Antiphon', *Proceedings of the Cambridge Philological Society* 187, n.s. 7: 49–58.

(1963) 'The truth of Antiphon', *Phronesis* 8: 35–49.

Morrison, J. S., J. F. Coates and N. B. Rankov (2000) *The Athenian Trireme. The History and Reconstruction of an Ancient Greek Warship*, 2nd edn. Cambridge: Cambridge University Press. Original edition 1986.

Morrow, G. R. (1937) 'The murder of slaves in Attic law', *Classical Philology* 32: 210–27.

Mossé, C. (1973) *Athens in Decline 404–86 B.C.* Translated by J. Stewart. London, Boston: Routledge & Kegan Paul.

(1991) 'La place de la pallake dans la famille athénienne', in Gagarin (1991): 273–9.

Moulton, C. (1972) 'Antiphon the sophist, On Truth', *Transactions and Proceedings of the American Philological Association* 103: 329–66.

Munn, M. H. (1993) *The Defense of Attica. The Dema Wall and the Boiotian War of 378–375B.C.* Berkeley, Los Angeles, Oxford: University of California Press.

Murray, O. (1966) 'Ο ΑΡΧΑΙΟΣ ΔΑΣΜΟΣ', *Historia* 15 (2): 142–56.

(1987) 'Cities of reason', *European Journal of Sociology* 28: 325–46.

(1993) *Early Greece*, 2nd edn. London: Fontana. Original edition 1978.

Murray, O. and S. Price (eds.) (1990) *The Greek City.* Oxford: Clarendon Press.

Neils, J. (ed.) (1992) *Goddess and Polis. The Panathenaic Festival in Ancient Athens.* Princeton, N.J.: Princeton University Press.

Németh, G. (1995) 'Der Preis einer Panoplie', *Acta Antiqua Academiae Scientiarum Hungaricae* 36: 5–13.

Nevett, L. C. (1999) *House and Society in the Ancient Greek World*. Cambridge: Cambridge University Press.

Newman, W. L. (1887–1902) *The Politics of Aristotle*. 4 vols. Oxford: Clarendon Press.

Nietzsche, F. (1971) *The Portable Nietzsche*. New York, London: Viking.

Nilsson, M. P. (1940) *Greek Folk Religion*. Philadelphia: University of Pennsylvania Press.

(1955) *Geschichte der griechischen Religion*. 2 vols. Munich: Beck'sche Verlags-buchhandlung.

Nippel, W. (1980) *Mischverfassungstheorie und Verfassungsrealität in Antike und früher Neuzeit*. Stuttgart: Klett-Kotta.

(1995) *Public Order in Ancient Rome*. Cambridge: Cambridge University Press.

(1996) 'La costruzione dell' "altro"', in *I Greci. Storia, Cultura, Arte, Società*, ed. Salvatore Settis. Turin: Giulio Einaudi: 165–96.

(1997) 'Bürgerkrieg und Amnestie: Athens 411–403', in *Amnestie oder Die Politik der Erinnerung in der Demokratie*, eds. G. Smith and A. Margalit. Frankfurt am Main: Suhrkamp: 103–19.

(1998) 'Von den "Altertümern" zur "Kulturgeschichte"', *Ktema* 23: 17–24.

(2000) 'Erwerbsarbeit in der Antike', in *Geschichte und Zukunft der Arbeit*, eds. J. Kocka and C. Offe. Frankfurt, New York: Campus Verlag: 54–66.

(2001) 'Die "Barbaren" aus der Sicht der Griechen', in *Fremdes in fremden Sprachen*, eds. B. Jostes and J. Trabant. Munich: Wilhelm Fink Verlag: 43–56.

North, H. (1966) *Sophrosyne: Self-Knowledge and Self-Restraint in Greek Literature*. Ithaca, New York: Cornell University Press.

Nowak, M. A. and K. Sigmund (1998) 'Evolution of indirect reciprocity by image scoring', *Nature* 393 (11 June): 573–7.

O'Neil, J. L. (1995) *The Origins and Development of Ancient Greek Democracy*. Lanham, Maryland and London: Rowman & Littlefield.

Obbink, D. (1988) 'The origin of Greek sacrifice: Theophrastus on religion and cultural history', in *Theophrastean Studies*, eds. W. W. Fortenbaugh and R. W. Sharples. New Brunswick, Oxford: Transaction Books: 272–95.

Ober, J. (1985) *Fortress Attica: Defense of the Athenian Land Frontier, 404–322 B.C.* Leiden: Brill.

(1989) *Mass and Elite in Democratic Athens*. Princeton: Princeton University Press.

(1993a) 'Thucydides' criticism of democratic knowledge', in Rosen and Farell (1993): 81–98.

(1993b) 'The Athenian revolution of 508/7 B.C.E. Violence, authority and the origins of democracy', in *Cultural Poetics in Archaic Greece*, eds. C. Dougherty and L. Kurke. Cambridge: Cambridge University Press: 215–32.

(1994a) 'Civic ideology and counterhegemonic discourse: Thucydides on the Sicilian debate', in Boegehold and Scafuro (1994): 102–26.

(1994b) 'Power and oratory in democratic Athens: Demosthenes 21, Against Meidias', in Worthington (1994a): 85–108.

Ober, J. and C. Hedrick (eds.) (1996) *Demokratia. A Conversation on Democracies, Ancient and Modern*. Princeton: Princeton University Press.

Offer, A. (1997) 'Between the gift and the market: the economy of regard', *Economic History Review* 50 (3): 450–76.

Ogden, D. (1996) *Greek Bastardy in the Classical and Hellenistic Periods*. Oxford: Clarendon Press.

Olson, M. (1965) *The Logic of Collective Action*. Cambridge, Mass.: Harvard University Press.

Onians, R. B. (1951) *The Origins of European Thought*. Cambridge: Cambridge University Press.

Oost, S. I. (1975) 'Thucydides and the irrational', *Classical Philology* 70 (3): 186–96.

Osborne, R. (1985a) *Demos: The Discovery of Classical Attika*. Cambridge: Cambridge University Press.

    (1985b) 'The erection and mutilation of the Hermai', *Proceedings of the Cambridge Philological Society* 211: 47–73.

    (1985c) 'Law in action in Classical Athens', *Journal of Hellenic Studies* 105: 40–58.

    (1985d) 'Buildings and residence on the land in Classical and Hellenistic Greece: the contribution of epigraphy', *Annual of the British School at Athens* 80: 119–28.

    (1987) *Classical Landscape With Figures. The Ancient City and Its Countryside*. London: George Philip.

    (1988) 'Social and economic implications of the leasing of land and property in Classical and Hellenistic Greece', *Chiron* 18: 279–323.

    (1990) 'The *demos* and its divisions in classical Athens', in Murray and Price (1990): 265–93.

    (1997) 'Law, the democratic citizen and the representation of women in Classical Athens', *Past & Present* 155: 3–33.

    (1998a) 'Inter-personal relations on Athenian pots: putting others in their place', in Cartledge, Millet and von Reden (1998): 13–36.

    (1998b) 'Sculpted men of Athens: masculinity and power in the field of vision', in *Thinking Men. Masculinity and its Self-Representation in the Classical Tradition*, eds. L. Foxhall and J. Salmon. London, New York: Routledge: 23–42.

Osborne, R. and S. Hornblower (eds.) (1994) *Ritual, Finance, Politics. Athenian Democratic Accounts Presented to David Lewis*. Oxford: Oxford University Press.

Ostwald, M. (1973) 'Was there a concept of agraphos nomos in classical Greece?', in *Exegesis and Argument: Studies in Greek Philosophy Presented to Gregory Vlastos*, eds. E. N. Lee, P. D. Mourelatos and R. M. Rorty. Assen: *Phronesis*, suppl. 1: 70–104.

    (1986) *From Popular Sovereignty to the Sovereignty of Law*. Berkeley, Los Angeles, London: University of California Press.

    (1992) 'Athens as a cultural centre', in Lewis, Boardman, Davies and Ostwald (1992): 306–69.

    (1995) 'Public expense: whose obligation? Athens 600–454 B.C.E.', *Proceedings of the American Philosophical Association* 139 (4): 368–79.

(2000a) 'Popular sovereignty and the problem of equality', *Scripta Classica Israelica* 19: 1–3.

(2000b) 'Oligarchy and oligarchs in ancient Greece', in Flensted-Jensen, Nielsen and Rubinstein (2000): 385–96.

(2000c) *Oligarchia: The Development of a Constitutional Form in Ancient Greece.* Stuttgart: Franz Steiner Verlag.

(2002) 'Athens and Chalkis: A study of imperial control', *Journal of Hellenic Studies* 122: 134–43.

Parker, R. (1983) *Miasma.* Oxford: Clarendon Press.

(1990) 'Myths of early Athens', in *Interpretations of Greek Mythology*, ed. J. N. Bremmer. London: Routledge: 187–214.

(1996a) *Athenian Religion: A History.* Oxford: Clarendon Press.

(1996b) 'Attic cults and myths', in *OCD³*: 212.

(1996c) 'Athena', in *OCD³*: 201–2.

(1997) 'Gods cruel and kind: tragic and civic ideology', in *Greek Tragedy and the Historian*, ed. C. Pelling. Oxford: Clarendon Press: 143–60.

Parlama, L. and N. Stampolidis (eds.) (2001) *Athens: The City beneath the City. Antiquities from the Metropolitan Railway Excavations.* New York, London: Harry N. Abrams.

Pathmanathan, R. S. (1965) 'Death in Greek tragedy', *Greece & Rome* 12: 2–14.

Patterson, C. (1981) *Pericles' Citizenship Law of 451–50 B.C.* New York: Arno Press.

(1990) 'Those Athenian bastards', *Classical Antiquity* 9: 40–73.

(1998) *The Family in Greek History.* Cambridge, Mass., London: Harvard University Press.

Pearson, H. W. (1957) 'The secular debate on economic primitivism', in *Trade and Market in the Early Empires*, eds. K. Polanyi, C. M. Arensberg and H. W. Pearson. Glencoe, Ill.: Free Press: 3–11.

Pearson, L. (1962) *Popular Ethics in Ancient Greece.* Stanford: Stanford University Press.

Pečirka, J. (1967) 'A note on Aristotle's conception of citizenship and the role of foreigners in fourth century Athens', *Eirene* 6: 23–6.

Peirce, S. (1993) 'Death, revelry and thysia', *Classical Antiquity* 12: 219–66.

Pelling, C. (1997) 'East is east and west is west – or are they? National stereotypes in Herodotus', *Histos* (*Online: http://www.dur.ac.uk/classics/histos*). 1.

Peristiany, J. G. (ed.) (1965) *Honour and Shame. The Values of Mediterranean Society.* London: Weidenfeld and Nicolson.

Peristiany, J. G. and J. Pitt-Rivers (eds.) (1992) *Honour and Grace in Anthropology.* Cambridge: Cambridge University Press.

Perotti, E. (1973) 'Contribution à l'étude d'une autre catégorie d'esclaves attiques: les andrapoda misthophorounta', in *Actes du Colloque 1973 sur l'esclavage.* Paris: Les Belles Lettres: 179–94.

Peterson, E. (1923) 'Der Gottesfreund', *Zeitschrift für Kirchengeschichte* 42: 161–202.

Petrusewicz, M. (1990) 'Corsica: old vendetta and modern state', *Journal of Interdisciplinary History* 21 (2): 295–301.

Pina-Cabral, J. de (1989) 'The Mediterranean as a category of regional comparison: a critical view', *Current Anthropology* 30 (3): 399–406.

Pitt-Rivers, J. (1965) 'Honour and social status', in Peristiany (1965): 21–77.

(1968) 'Honor', in *International Encyclopedia of the Social Sciences*, ed. D. L. Sills. U.S.A: The Macmillan Company & The Free Press: 503–11.

(1973) 'The kith and the kin', in *The Character of Kinship*, ed. J. Goody. Cambridge: Cambridge University Press: 89–105.

Pleket, H. W. (1963) 'Thasos and the popularity of the Athenian empire', *Historia* 12: 70–7.

Plescia, J. (1970) *The Oath and Perjury in Ancient Greece*. Tallahassee: Florida State University Press.

Ploog, D. (1969) 'Neurological aspects in social behaviour', in *Man and Beast: Comparative Social Behaviour*, eds. J. F. Eisenberg, S. W. Dillon and D. S. Ripley. Washington: Smithsonian Institution Press: 95–125.

Podes, S. (1987) '*Ekklesiastikon* and participation in public service in classical Athens', *American Journal of Ancient History* 12: 167–88.

Poliakoff, M. B. (1987) *Combat Sports in the Ancient World*. New Haven, London: Yale University Press.

Polk, K. (1994) *When Men Kill. Scenarios of Masculine Violence*. Cambridge: Cambridge University Press.

Pomeroy, S. (ed.) (1991) *Women's History and Ancient History*. Chapel Hill: University of North Carolina Press.

Popper, K. R. (1966) *The Open Society and Its Enemies*, 5th edn. 2 vols. London: Routledge & Kegan Paul. Original edition 1945.

Poursat, J.-C. (1968) 'Les représentations de danse armée dans la céramique attique', *Bulletin de Correspondance Hellénique* 92: 550–615.

Powell, A. (1979a) 'Thucydides and divination', *Bulletin of the Institute of Classical Studies of the University of London* 26: 45–50.

(1979b) 'Religion and the Sicilian expedition', *Historia* 28: 15–31.

(1988) *Athens and Sparta*. London: Routledge.

Powell, B. (1906) *Athenian Mythology: Erichthonius and the Three Daughters of Cecrops*. Ithaca: Cornell University Press.

Price, S. (1999) *Religions of the Ancient Greeks*. Cambridge: Cambridge University Press.

Pritchett, K. W. (1979–84) *The Greek State at War*. 4 vols. Berkeley: University of California Press.

Quinn, T. J. (1964) 'Thucydides and the unpopularity of the Athenian empire', *Historia* 13: 257–66.

Raaflaub, K. A. (1994) 'Democracy, power, and imperialism in fifth-century Athens', in *Athenian Political Thought and the Reconstruction of American Democracy*, eds. P. J. Euben, J. R. Wallach and J. Ober. Ithaca, London: Cornell University Press: 103–46.

Raepsaet, G. (1981) 'Sentiments conjugaux à Athènes aux Ve et IVe siècles avant notre ère', *L'Antiquité classique* 50: 677–84.

Randall, R. H. (1953) 'The Erechtheum workmen', *American Journal of Archaeology* 57: 199–210.

Rapoport, A. (1974) *Conflict in Man-made Environment*. Harmondsworth: Penguin.

Raubitschek, A. E. (1941) 'The heroes of Phyle', *Hesperia* 10: 284–95.

Redfield, J. (1985) 'Herodotus the tourist', *Classical Philology* 80: 97–118.

Redfield, R. (1953) *The Primitive World and its Transformations*. Harmondsworth: Penguin.

(1962) *Human Nature and the Study of Society*, ed. Margaret Park Redfield. Chicago: University of Chicago Press.

Rees, W. J. (1956) 'The theory of sovereignty restated', in Laslett (1956b): 56–82.

Reynolds, V., V. Falger and I. Vine (eds.) (1987) *The Sociobiology of Ethnocentrism*. London, Sydney: Croom Helm.

Rhodes, P. J. (1972) *The Athenian Boule*. Oxford: Oxford University Press.

(1980) 'Athenian Democracy after 403 BC', *Classical Journal* 75: 305–23.

(1981) *A Commentary on the Aristotelian 'Athenaion Politeia'*. Oxford: Oxford University Press.

(1992a) 'The Delian league to 449 BC', in Lewis, Boardman, Davies and Ostwald (1992): 34–61.

(1992b) 'The Athenian revolution', in Lewis, Boardman, Davies and Ostwald (1992): 62–95.

(1994) 'The ostracism of Hyperbolus', in Osborne and Hornblower (1994): 85–98.

(1996) 'Friends and enemies in Athenian politics, II. Personal enmity and political opposition in Athens', *Greece & Rome* 43: 21–30.

(1998) 'Enmity in fourth-century Athens', in Cartledge, Millett and von Reden (1992): 144–61.

(2004) 'Keeping to the point', in *The Law and the Courts in Ancient Greece*, eds. E. M. Harris and L. Rubinstein. London: Duckworth: 137–228.

Rhodes, P. J. and D. M. Lewis (1997) *Decrees of the Greek States*. Oxford: Clarendon Press.

Rich, J. and A. Wallace-Hadrill (eds.) (1991) *City and Country in the Ancient World*. London, New York: Routledge.

Richter, G. (1974) *A Handbook of Greek Art*, 7th edn. London: Phaidon.

Ridley, M. (1996) *The Origins of Virtue*. Harmondsworth: Penguin.

(2003) *Nature via Nurture. Genes, Experience, and What Makes Us Human*. New York: Harper Collins.

Ridley, M. and R. Dawkins. (1981) 'The natural selection of altruism', in Rushton and Sorrentino (1981a): 19–39.

Roberts, G. and T. N. Sherratt. (1998) 'Development of cooperative relationships through increasing investment', *Nature* 394 (July): 175–9.

Roberts, J. T. (1986) 'Aristocratic democracy: the perseverance of timocratic principles in Athenian government', *Athenaeum* 64: 355–69.

(1994) *Athens on Trial. The Antidemocratic Tradition in Western Thought*. Princeton, New Jersey: Princeton University Press.

Roberts, S. (1979) *Order and Dispute*. Harmondsworth: Penguin.

Robinson, E. W. (1997) *The First Democracies. Early Popular Government Outside Athens*. Vol. CVII, *Historia-Einzelschrift*. Stuttgart: Franz Steiner.

Rohde, E. (1987) *Psyche: The Cult of Souls and Belief in Immortality among the Greeks*. Translated by W. B. Hills, 8th edn. Chicago: Ares Publishers. Original edition 1893.

Roll, E. (1961) *A History of Economic Thought*. London: Faber & Faber. Original edition 1938.

Rosen, R. M. and J. Farell (eds.) (1993) *Nomodeiktes. Greek Studies in Honor of Martin Ostwald*. Ann Arbor: The University of Michigan Press.

Rosivach, V. J. (1987a) 'Execution by stoning at Athens', *Classical Antiquity* 6: 232–48.

(1987b) 'Autochthony and the Athenians', *Classical Quarterly* 37: 294–306.

Roy, J. (1999) '*Polis* and *oikos* in classical Athens', *Greece & Rome* 46 (1): 1–18.

Rubinstein, L. (2000) *Litigation and Cooperation: Supporting Speakers in the Courts of Classical Athens*. Vol. CXLVII, *Historia-Enzelschrift*. Stuttgart: Franz Steiner.

Runciman, W. G. (1982) 'Origins of states, the case of archaic Greece', *Comparative Studies in Society and History* 24: 351–77.

Ruschenbusch, E. (1957) 'ΔΙΚΑΣΤΗΡΙΟΝ ΠΑΝΤΩΝ ΚΥΡΙΟΝ', *Historia* 6: 257–74.

(1966) *ΣΟΛΩΝΟΣ ΝΟΜΟΙ. Die Fragmente des solonischen Gesetzeswerkes mit einer Text- und Überlieferungsgeschichte*. Vol. IX, *Historia-Einzelschrift*. Wiesbaden.

(1968) *Untersuchungen zur Geschichte des athenischen Strafrechts*. Edited by H. J. Wolff. Vol. IV, *Gräzistische Abhandlungen*. Cologne, Graz: Böhlau.

Rushton, J. P. and R. M. Sorrentino (eds.) (1981a) *Altruism and Helping Behaviour*. Hillsdale, New Jersey: Lawrence Erlbaum Associates.

(1981b) 'Altruism and helping behaviour: an historical perspective', in Rushton and Sorrentino (1981a): 3–16.

Ryle, G. (1949) *The Concept of Mind*. Harmondsworth: Penguin.

Sahlins, M. (1974) *Stone Age Economics*. London: Tavistock Publications.

Said, S. (1984) 'La tragédie de la vengeance', in Courtois (1984a): 47–90.

Sallares, R. (1991) *The Ecology of the Ancient Greek World*. London: Duckworth.

Saller, R. P. (2002) 'Framing the debate over growth in the ancient economy', in Scheidel and von Reden (2002): 251–69.

Sauerwein, F. (1998) 'The physical background', in Sparkes (1998): 3–20.

Saunders, T. J. (1977–8) 'Antiphon the Sophist on natural laws', *Proceedings of the Aristotelian Society* 78: 215–36.

(1981) 'Protagoras and Plato on punishment', in *The Sophists and their Legacy*, ed. G. B. Kerferd. Wiesbaden: Franz Steiner Verlag: 129–41.

(1991) *Plato's Penal Code*. Oxford: Oxford University Press.

Scanlon, T. F. (2002) *Eros and Greek Athletics*. Oxford: Oxford University Press.

Schapera, I. (1955) 'The sin of Cain', *Journal of the Royal Anthropological Institute* 85: 33–43.

Schaps, D. M. (1979) *The Economic Rights of Women in Ancient Greece*. Edinburgh: Edinburgh University Press.

Scheid-Tissinier, É. (1994) *Les usages du don chez Homère*. Nancy: Presses Universitaires de Nancy.

Scheidel, W. and S. von Reden (eds.) (2002) *The Ancient Economy*. New York: Routledge.

Schellenberg, J. A. (1982) *The Science of Conflict*. New York, Oxford: Oxford University Press.

Schnapp, A. (1997) 'Images of young people in the Greek city-state', in *A History of the Young People in the West*, eds. G. Levi and J.-C. Schmitt. Cambridge, Mass., London: Harvard University Press: 12–50.

Schneider, P. (1969) 'Honor and conflict in a Sicilian town', *Anthropological Quarterly* 42: 130–54.

Schofield, M. (1986) '*Euboulia* in the *Iliad*', *Classical Quarterly* 36: 6–31.

Schönert-Geiss, E. (1974) 'Die Geldzirkulation Attikas', *Klio* 56: 377–414.

Schuller, W. (1979) 'Zur Entstehung der griechischen Demokratie außerhalb Athens', in *Auf den Weg gebracht*, eds. H. Sund and M. Timmermann. Konstanz: Universitätsverlag Konstanz: 433–47.

Seaford, R. (1994) *Reciprocity and Ritual. Homer and Tragedy in the Developing City-State*. Oxford: Clarendon Press.

Sealey, R. (1973) 'The origins of Demokratia', *California Studies in Classical Antiquity* 6: 253–95.

(1984) 'On lawful concubinage in Athens', *Classical Antiquity* 3: 111–33.

Segal, C. (1990) 'Sacrifice and violence in the myth of Meleager and Heracles: Homer, Bacchylides, Sophocles', *Helios* 17: 7–24.

(1991) 'Violence and dramatic structure in Euripides' Hecuba', *Themes in Drama* 13: 35–46.

Seymour-Smith, C. (ed.) (1986) *Macmillan Dictionary of Anthropology*. London, Basingstoke: Macmillan.

Shaw, B. D. (1994) 'The paradoxes of people power', *Helios* 18: 194–214.

(2001) 'Rebels and outsiders', in *The Cambridge Ancient History*, 2nd edn. Vol. XI, eds. A. K. Bowman, P. Garnsey and D. Rathbone. Cambridge: Cambridge University Press: 361–403.

Shaw, B. D. and R. P. Saller (eds.) (1981) *Economy and Society in Ancient Greece, by M. I. Finley*. Harmondsworth: Penguin.

Shipton, K. M. W. (1997) 'The private banks in fourth-century BC Athens: a reappraisal', *Classical Quarterly* 47 (2): 396–422.

Siewert, P. (1977) 'The ephebic oath in fifth-century Athens', *Journal of Hellenic Studies* 97: 102–11.

(1982) *Die Trittyen Attikas und die Heeresreformen des Kleisthenes*. Munich: Vestigia.

Simmel, G. (1903–4) 'The sociology of conflict', *The American Journal of Sociology* 4: 470–525.

(1955) *Conflict. The Web of Group-Affiliations*. Translated by K. H. Wolff and R. Bendix. Glencoe, Illinois: The Free Press.

Smith, A. (1970) *The Wealth of Nations*. Harmondsworth: Penguin. Original edition 1776.

(1976) *The Theory of Moral Sentiments*. Oxford: Clarendon Press. Original edition 1759.

Snell, B. (1953) *The Discovery of the Mind in Greek Philosophy and Literature.* Translated by T. G. Rosenmeyer. 2nd edn. New York: Dover Publications, Inc. Original edition 1948.

Snodgrass, A. M. (1965) 'The hoplite reform and history', *Journal of Hellenic Studies* 85: 110–22.

(1967) *Arms and Armour of the Greeks.* Baltimore, London: The Johns Hopkins University Press.

(1974) 'A historical Homeric society?' *Journal of Hellenic Studies* 94: 114–25.

(1987–9) 'The rural landscape and its political significance', *Opus* 6–8: 53–70.

(1999) 'Centres of pottery production in ancient Greece', in *Céramique et peinture grecques. Modes d'emploi*, eds. M.-C. Villanueva Puig, F. Lissarague, P. Rouillard et al. Paris: La Documentation Française.

Southall, A. (1968) 'Stateless society', in *International Encyclopedia of the Social Sciences*, vol. xv, ed. D. L. Sills. U.S.A. The Macmillan Company & The Free Press: 157–68.

Sparkes, B. A. (ed.) (1998) *Greek Civilization. An Introduction.* Oxford: Blackwell.

Sprague, R. K. (1968) 'Dissoi logoi or dialexeis, two-fold arguments', *Mind* 77: 155–67.

Staden, H. von (1992) 'Affinities and elisions. Helen and Hellenocentrism', *Isis* 83: 578–95.

Stadter, P. A. (ed.) (1973) *The Speeches of Thucydides.* Chapel Hill: University of North Carolina Press.

Ste. Croix, G. E. M. de (1953) 'Demosthenes' TIMHMA and the Athenian eisphora in the fourth century BC', *Classica et Mediaevalia* 14: 30–70.

(1954/5) 'The character of the Athenian empire', *Historia* 3: 1–41.

(1970) 'Some observations on the property rights of Athenian women', *The Classical Review* 20: 273–8.

(1972) *The Origins of the Peloponnesian War.* London: Duckworth.

(1981) *The Class Struggle in the Ancient Greek World.* London: Duckworth.

Stein, G. J. (1987) 'The biological bases of ethnocentrism, racism and nationalism in National Socialism', in Reynolds, Falger and Vine (1987): 231–51.

Stein-Hölkeskamp, E. (1989) *Adelskultur und Polis-gesellschaft: Studien zum griechischen Adel im archaischer und klassischer Zeit.* Stuttgart: Franz Steiner Verlag.

Steinwenter, A. (1925) *Die Streitbeendigung durch Urteil, Schiedsspruch und Vergleich nach griechischem Rechte.* Vol. VIII, *Münchener Beiträge z. Papyrusforschung.* Munich: C. H. Beck'sche Verlagsbuchhandlung.

Stephens, D. W., C. M. McLinn and J. R. Stevens (2002) 'Discounting and reciprocity in an iterated Prisoner's Dilemma', *Science* 298 (5601): 2216–18.

Stewart, A. (1997) *Art, Desire and the Body in Ancient Greece.* Cambridge: Cambridge University Press.

Stewart, C. S. (2001) 'Honor and shame', in *International Encyclopedia of the Social and Behavioural Sciences*, eds. N. J. Smelser and P. B. Baltes. Amsterdam, Paris, New York: Elsevier: 6904–7.

Stewart, F. H. (1994) *Honor.* Chicago: Chicago University Press.

Stirling, P. (1968) 'Impartiality and personal morality', in *Contributions to Mediterranean Sociology*, ed. J. G. Peristiany. Paris, The Hague: Mouton: 49–64.

Stockton, D. (1990) *The Classical Athenian Democracy*. Oxford: Oxford University Press.

Stone, L. (1983) 'Interpersonal violence in English society, 1300–1980', *Past & Present* 101: 22–37.

Strasburger, H. (1954) 'Der Einzelne und die Gemeinschaft im Denken der Griechen', *Historische Zeitschrift* 177: 227–48.

(1958) 'Thukydides und die politische Selbsdarstellung der Athener', *Hermes* 86: 17–40.

Strauss, B. S. (1985) 'Ritual, social drama and politics in classical Athens', *American Journal of Ancient History* 10: 67–83.

(1986) *Athens after the Peloponnesian War*. London and Sydney: Croom Helm.

Stroud, R. S. (1968) *Drakon's Law on Homicide*. Berkeley and Los Angeles: University of California Press.

(1971) 'Theozotides and the Athenian orphans', *Hesperia* 40: 280–301.

Sutherland, S. (1992) *Irrationality*. Harmondsworth: Penguin.

Svenbro, J. (1984) 'Vengeance et société en Grèce archaïque. A propos de la fin de l'*Odyssée*', in Verdier and Poly (1984): 47–63.

Syme, R. (1962) 'Thucydides', *Proceedings of the British Academy* 48: 39–56.

Tacon, J. (2001) 'Ecclesiastic *thorubos*: interventions, interruptions, and popular involvement in the Athenian assembly', *Greece & Rome* 48 (2): 173–91.

Taubenschlag, R. (1949) 'Selfhelp in Greco-Roman Egypt', *Archives d'Histoire du Droit Oriental* 4: 79–84.

Taylor, C. (2001) 'Bribery in Athenian politics part 1: Accusations, allegations, and slander', *Greece & Rome* 48: 53–66.

Taylor, M. (1987) *The Possibility of Cooperation*. Cambridge: Cambridge University Press.

Taylor, M. W. (1991) *The Tyrant Slayers*, 2nd edn. Salem, New Hampshire: Ayer Company Publishers, Inc. Original edition 1981.

Thibaut, J. W. and H. H. Kelley (1978) *Interpersonal Relations: A Theory of Interdependence*. New York: Wiley.

Thomas, R. (1989) *Oral Tradition and Written Record in Classical Athens*. Cambridge: Cambridge University Press.

(1994) 'Law and the lawgiver in the Athenian democracy', in Osborne and Hornblower (1994): 119–33.

Thompson, H. A. and R. E. Wycherley (1972) *The Agora of Athens. The History, Shape, and Uses of the Ancient City Center*. Princeton, N.J: American School of Classical Studies in Athens.

Thür, G. (1991) 'The jurisdiction of the Areopagos in homicide cases', in Gagarin (1991): 53–72.

Tinbergen, N. (1953) *Social Behaviour in Animals*. London: Methuen.

Todd, S. (1990a) 'Lady Chatterley's lover and the Attic Orators: the social composition of the Athenian jury', *Journal of Hellenic Studies* 110: 146–73.

(1990b) 'The use and abuse of the Attic orators', *Greece & Rome* 37: 159–78.

(1993) *The Shape of Athenian Law*. Oxford: Oxford University Press.

(1998) 'The rhetoric of enmity in the Attic orators', in Cartledge, Millett and von Reden (1998): 162–9.

(2000) 'How to execute people in fourth-century Athens', in Hunter and Edmondson (2000): 31–51.

Traill, J. S. (1975) *The Political Organization of Attica. A Study of the Demes, Trittyes, and Phylai, and their Representation in the Athenian Council, Hesperia Supplement XIV*. Princeton, New Jersey: American School of Classical Studies at Athens.

Trevett, J. C. (1992) *Apollodorus the Son of Pasion*. Oxford: Oxford University Press.

(2001) 'Coinage and democracy at Athens', in *Money and Its Uses In the Ancient Greek World*, eds. A. Meadows and K. Shipton. Oxford: Oxford University Press: 23–34.

Trevor-Roper, H. (1984) 'Jacob Burckhardt', *Proceedings of the British Academy* 70: 359–78.

Trivers, R. L. (1971) 'The evolution of reciprocal altruism', *The Quarterly Review of Biology* 46: 35–57.

Tuplin, C. (1999) 'Greek racism? Observations on the character and limits of Greek ethnic prejudice', in *Ancient Greeks West & East*, ed. G. R. Tsetskhladze. Leiden, Boston, Köln: Brill: 47–75.

Turner, F. M. (1981) *The Greek Heritage in Victorian Britain*. New Haven & London: Yale University Press.

van der Dennen, J. M. G. (1987) 'Ethnocentrism and in-group/out-group differentiation. A review and interpretation of the literature', in Reynolds, Falger and Vine (1987): 1–47.

van Gennep, A. (1960) *The Rites of Passage*. Translated by M. B. Vizedom and G. L. Caffee. London: Routledge & Kegan Paul. Original edition 1909.

van Looy, H. (1990) 'Youth violence in ancient Athens: 5th and 4th century BC', in *History of Juvenile Delinquency*, eds. A. G. Hess and P. F. Clement. Aalen: Scientia Verlag: 71–125.

van Wees, H. (1998a) 'Greeks bearing arms: the state, the leisure class, and the display of weapons in archaic Greece', in Fisher and van Wees (1998): 333–78.

(1998b) 'The law of gratitude: reciprocity in anthropological theory', in Gill, Postlethwaite and Seaford (1998): 13–49.

(ed.) (2000) *War and Violence in Ancient Greece*. London: Duckworth – The Classical Press of Wales.

(2002) 'Homer and early Greece', *Colby Quarterly* 38: 94–128.

Vanderpool, E. (1980) 'The state prison of ancient Athens', in *From Athens to Gordion. The Papers for a Memorial Symposium for Rodney S. Young*, ed. K. de Vries. Philadelphia: University of Pennsylvania: 17–31.

Verdier, R. and J.-P. Poly (eds.) (1984) *Vengeance, pouvoirs et idéologies dans quelques civilisations de l'Antiquité* 4 vols. Vol. III, *La vengeance. Etudes d'ethnologie, d'histoire et de philosophie*. Paris: Editions Cujas.

Vermeule, E. (1979) *Aspects of Death in Early Greek Art and Poetry*. Berkeley, Los Angeles, London: University of California Press.

Vernant, J.-P. (1972) 'Tensions et ambiguïtés dans la tragédie grecque', in *Mythe et Tragédie en Grèce ancienne*, eds. J.-P. Vernant and P. Vidal-Naquet. Paris: Maspero: 21–40.

Versnel, H. S. (1995) 'Religion and democracy', in Eder (1995a): 367–87.

Veyne, P. (1983) *Did the Greeks Believe in their Myths?* Chicago, London: Chicago University Press.

Vickers, M. (1990) 'Golden Greece: relative values, minae, and temple inventories', *American Journal of Archaeology* 94: 613–25.

  (1994) 'Material values past and present', *European Review* 4 (2): 295–303.

  (1997) *Pericles on Stage: Political Comedy in Aristophanes' Early Plays*. Austin: University of Texas Press.

Vickers, M. and D. Gill. (1994) *Artful Crafts: Ancient Greek Silverware and Pottery*. Oxford: Clarendon Press.

Vidal-Naquet, P. (1968) 'The black hunter and the origin of the Athenian ephebeia', *Proceedings of the Cambridge Philological Society* 14: 49–64.

  (1981a) 'La tradition de l'hoplite athénien', in Vidal-Naquet (1981b): 125–49.

  (1981b) *Le chasseur noir. Formes de pensée et formes de société dans le monde grec*. Paris: François Maspero.

  (1986) *The Black Hunter. Forms of Thought and Forms of Society in the Greek World*. Translated by A. Szegedy-Maszak. Baltimore, London: The Johns Hopkins University Press.

  (1990a) *La démocratie grecque vue d'ailleurs*. Paris: Flammarion.

  (1990b) 'Économie et société dans la Grèce ancienne: l'œuvre de Moses I. Finley', in P. Vidal-Naquet (1990a): 55–94.

Viljamaa, T., A. Timonen and C. Krötzl (eds.) (1992) *Crudelitas. The Politics of Cruelty in the Ancient and Medieval World*. Krems: Jaritz, G.

Visser, M. (1984) 'Vengeance and pollution in classical Athens', *Journal of the History of Ideas*: 193–206.

Vlastos, G. (1953) 'Isonomia', *American Journal of Philology* 74 (4): 337–66.

  (1991) *Socrates. Ironist and Moral Philosopher*. Cambridge: Cambridge University Press.

Vogel, G. (2004) 'The evolution of the golden rule', *Science* 303 (5661): 1128–31.

Vogt, J. (1974) *Ancient Slavery and the Ideal of Man*. Translated by T. Wiedemann. Oxford: Blackwell. Original edition 1965.

von Cranach, M., K. Foppa, W. Lepenies and D. Ploog (eds.) (1979) *Human Ethology. Claims and Limits of a New Discipline*. Cambridge: Cambridge University Press – Editions de la Maison des Sciences de l'Homme.

von Reden, S. (1995a) *Exchange in Ancient Greece*. London: Duckworth.

  (1995b) 'The Piraeus – a world apart', *Greece & Rome* 42 (1): 24–37.

Wahlström, R. (1987) 'Enemy image as a psychological antecedent of warfare', in *Essays on Violence*, eds. J. M. Ramirez, R. A. Hinde and J. Groebel. Sevilla: Publicaciones de la Universidad de Sevilla: 47–57.

Walbank, F. W. (1985) 'Speeches in Greek historians', in *Selected Papers*. Cambridge: Cambridge University Press: 242–61.

Wallace, R. W. (1985) *The Areopagus Council, to 307 B.C.* Baltimore, London: The Johns Hopkins University Press.

(1991) 'Response to Gerhard Thür', in Gagarin (1991): 73–9.

(1994) 'Private lives and public enemies: freedom of thought and classical Athens', in Boegehold and Scafuro (1994): 127–55.

(1995) 'Speech, song and text, public and private. Evolutions in communications media and fora in fourth century Athens', in Eder (1995a): 199–226 (with discussion).

(1996) 'Law, freedom, and the concept of citizens' rights in democratic Athens', in Ober and Hedrick (1996): 105–19.

Wallace-Hadrill, J. M. (1962) 'The bloodfeud of the Franks', in *The Long-Haired Kings*, ed. J. M. Wallace-Hadrill. New York: Methuen and Co. Ltd.: 121–47.

Watson, P. A. (1995) *Ancient Stepmothers. Myth, Mysogyny and Reality*. Leiden, New York, Köln: Brill.

Weber, M. (1968) *Economy and Society*. Berkeley, Los Angeles, London: University of California Press. Original edition 1922.

(1972) *Wirtschaft und Gesellschaft*, 5th edn. Tübingen: J. C. B. Mohr (Paul Siebeck). Original edition 1922.

Wedekind, C. and M. Milinski (2000) 'Cooperation through image scoring in humans', *Science* 288 (5467).

Wells, B. (ed.) (1992) *Agriculture in Ancient Greece, Proceedings of the Seventh International Symposium at the Swedish Institute at Athens*. Stockholm: Swedish Institute at Athens.

West, S. A., I. Pen and A. S. Griffin (2002) 'Cooperation and competition between relatives', *Science* 296 (5565).

Westermann, W. L. (1955) *The Slave Systems of Greek and Roman Antiquity*. Vol. XL, *Memoirs of the American Philosophical Society*. Philadelphia: American Philosophical Society.

Westermarck, E. (1924) *The Origin and Development of the Moral Ideas*, 2nd edn. 2 vols. New York, London: Macmillan. Original edition 1906.

Wheeler, E. L. (1991) 'The general as hoplite', in Hanson (1991a): 121–70.

Whitehead, D. (1977) *The Ideology of the Athenian Metic*. Cambridge: Cambridge Philological Society.

(1982/3) 'Sparta and the thirty tyrants', *Ancient Society* 13/14: 105–30.

(1986a) *The Demes of Attica, 508/7–ca. 250 BC: A Political and Social Study*. Princeton: Princeton University Press.

(1986b) 'The ideology of the Athenian metic: some pendants and reappraisal', *Proceedings of the Cambridge Philological Society* 32: 145–58.

Wiedemann, T. (1981) *Greek and Roman Slavery*. Baltimore: The Johns Hopkins University Press.

(1983) 'Thucydides, women, and the limits of rational analysis', *Greece &Rome* 30 (2): 163–70.

Will, E. (1954) 'Trois quarts de siècle de recherches sur l'économie grecque antique', *Annales E.S.C.* 9: 7–22.

Williams, B. (1993) *Shame and Necessity*. Berkeley, Los Angeles, London: University of California Press.

Williams, G. C. (1966) *Adaptation and Natural Selection*. Princeton, N.J.: Princeton University Press.

Wilson, B. R. (ed.) (1970) *Rationality*. Oxford: Blackwell.

Wilson, E. O. (1978) *On Human Nature*. Cambridge, Mass., London: Harvard University Press.

(1980) *Sociobiology. The Abridged Edition*. Cambridge, Mass.: Harvard University Press. Original edition 1975.

Wilson, P. J. (1991) 'Demosthenes 21 (Against Meidias): democratic abuse', *Proceedings of the Cambridge Philological Society* 37: 164–95.

(2000) *The Athenian Institution of Khoregia*. Cambridge: Cambridge University Press.

Wilson, S. (1988) *Feuding, Conflict and Banditry in Nineteenth-Century Corsica*. Cambridge: Cambridge University Press.

Winkler, J. J. (1990) *The Constraints of Desire. The Anthropology of Sex and Gender in Ancient Greece*. New York, London: Routledge.

Wispé, L. (ed.) (1978) *Altruism, Sympathy, and Helping. Psychological and Sociological Principles*. New York, San Francisco, London: Academic Press.

Wohl, V. (1999) 'The eros of Alcibiades', *Classical Antiquity* 18: 349–85.

Wood, E. M. (1983) 'Agricultural slavery in classical Athens', *American Journal of Ancient History* 8 (1): 1–47.

(1989) *Peasant-Citizen and Slave: The Foundations of Athenian Democracy*. London: Verso.

Worthington, I. (1989) 'The duration of an Athenian political trial', *Journal of Hellenic Studies* 109: 204–7.

(1991) 'Greek oratory, revision of speeches and the problem of historical reliability', *Classica et Mediaevalia* 42: 55–74.

(ed.) (1994a) *Persuasion: Greek Rhetoric in Action*. London & New York: Routledge.

(1994b) 'The canon of the ten Attic orators', in Worthington (1994a): 244–63.

Wycherley, R. E. (1960) 'Neleion', *British School at Athens* 55: 60–6.

(1978) *The Stones of Athens*. Princeton, N.J.: Princeton University Press.

Wyse, W. (1904) *The Speeches of Isaeus*. Cambridge: Cambridge University Press.

Yakobson, A. (1998) 'The justification of democracy the Protagoras' simile' (in Hebrew), *Zemanin* 64: 23–32.

Zanker, G. (1994) *The Heart of Achilles. Characterization and Personal Ethics in the Illiad*. Ann Arbor, Michigan: The University of Michigan Press.

(1998) 'Beyond reciprocity: the Akhilleus-Priam scene in Iliad 24', in Gill, Postlethwaite and Seaford (1998): 73–92.

Zimbardo, P. G. (1969) 'The human choice: individuation, reason, and order versus deindividuation', in *Nebraska Symposium on Motivation*, eds. W. J. Arnold and D. Levine. Lincoln: University of Nebraska Press.

Zimmern, S. A. (1931) *The Greek Commonwealth. Politics and Economics in Fifth-Century Athens*, 5th edn. Oxford: Oxford University Press. Original edition 1911.

Index

CPSIA information can be obtained
at www.ICGtesting.com
Printed in the USA
LVHW050409081122
732583LV00004B/19

9 780521 125352